6/0

ENCYCLOPEDIA OF
EUROPEAN SOCIAL HISTORY

ENCYCLOPEDIA OF EUROPEAN SOCIAL HISTORY

FROM 1350 TO 2000

VOLUME 4

Peter N. Stearns

Editor in Chief

Charles Scribner's Sons

an imprint of the Gale Group

Detroit • New York • San Francisco • London • Boston • Woodbridge, CT

Charles Scribner's Sons
An imprint of the Gale Group
1633 Broadway
New York, New York 10019

1 3 5 7 9 11 13 15 17 19   20 18 16 14 12 10 8 6 4 2

Printed in United States of America

Library of Congress Cataloging-in-Publication Data
Encyclopedia of European social history from 1350 to 2000 / Peter N. Stearns, editor-in-chief.
    p.   cm.
    Includes bibliographical references and index.
    ISBN 0-684-80582-0 (set : alk. paper) — ISBN 0-684-80577-4 (vol. 1)—ISBN
0-684-80578-2 (vol. 2) — ISBN 0-684-80579-0 (vol. 3) — ISBN 0-684-80580-4 (vol. 4)
— ISBN 0-684-80581-2 (vol. 5) — ISBN 0-684-80645-2 (vol. 6)
    1. Europe—Social conditions—Encyclopedias.   2. Europe—Social life and
customs—Encyclopedias.   3. Social history—Encyclopedias.   I. Stearns, Peter N.
HN373 .E63 2000
306'.094'03—dc21
                                                                                    00-046376

The paper used in this publication meets the requirements of ANSI/NISO Z39.48–1992 (Permanence of Paper).

CONTENTS OF THIS VOLUME

CONTENTS OF OTHER VOLUMES

ALPHABETICAL TABLE OF CONTENTS

COMMON ABBREVIATIONS USED IN THIS WORK

A.D.	*Anno Domini,* in the year of the Lord
AESC	*Annales: Économies, Sociétés, Civilisations*
ASSR	Autonomous Soviet Socialist Republic
b.	born
B.C.	before Christ
B.C.E.	before the common era (= B.C.)
c.	*circa,* about, approximately
C.E.	common era (= A.D.)
cf.	*confer,* compare
chap.	chapter
CP	Communist Party
d.	died
diss.	dissertation
ed.	editor (pl., eds.), edition
e.g.	*exempli gratia,* for example
et al.	*et alii,* and others
etc.	*et cetera,* and so forth
EU	European Union
f.	and following (pl., ff.)
fl.	*floruit,* flourished
GDP	gross domestic product
GDR	German Democratic Republic (East Germany)
GNP	gross national product
HRE	Holy Roman Empire, Holy Roman Emperor
ibid.	*ibididem,* in the same place (as the one immediately preceding)
i.e.	*id est,* that is
IMF	International Monetary Fund
MS.	manuscript (pl. MSS.)
n.	note
n.d.	no date
no.	number (pl., nos.)
n.p.	no place
n.s.	new series
N.S.	new style, according to the Gregorian calendar
OECD	Organization for Economic Cooperation and Development
O.S.	old style, according to the Julian calendar
p.	page (pl., pp.)
pt.	part
rev.	revised
S.	*san, sanctus, santo,* male saint
ser.	series
SP	Socialist Party
SS.	saints
SSR	Soviet Socialist Republic
Sta.	*sancta, santa,* female saint
supp.	supplement
USSR	Union of Soviet Socialist Republics
vol.	volume
WTO	World Trade Organization
?	uncertain, possibly, perhaps

ENCYCLOPEDIA OF
EUROPEAN SOCIAL HISTORY

Section 14

GENDER

THE DEVELOPMENT OF GENDER HISTORY

Bonnie G. Smith

The presentation of women and femininity in history began centuries ago, most influentially with *The Book of the City of Ladies* (1405) by the French writer Christine de Pisan. Right through the early twentieth century amateur authors writing to support themselves created a rich social history of women and femininity. At that point academic scholars joined in this endeavor, producing thousands of scholarly histories. Simultaneously this branch of social history—like most other history—has been buffeted by the winds of political and cultural change, and this has resulted in an evolving set of interests, theories, and debates. Early on these debates revolved around the moral value of women and thus femininity; by the nineteenth century the rationale for writing about women often involved asserting their secular, heroic stature based on feminine contributions to the public sphere. The revitalization of social history in the academy late in the twentieth century depended on these nineteenth-century themes, especially asserting the historical value of women's active presence. Somewhat later, however, gender theory questioned whether there could legitimately be a history of women—social or otherwise.

The earliest histories of women following Pisan's work focused on women exercising moral and intellectual gifts. Women of learning, queens, and moral leaders such as Joan of Arc all served as important topics, composing a social history of the topmost layers of society. With the collapse of the Old Regime in the French Revolution, writers like Stéphanie de Genlis set about chronicling the old court ways, but in a more systematic fashion than the memoir form of the works of the comte de Saint-Simon a century earlier. Laure d'Abrantes produced much-appreciated and multivolumed histories of the salons of Paris. Women's histories of the Vendée also presented the social life of women and their families under siege, with women playing the heroic role of provisioning and maintaining the social fabric during war and genocide. The focus on moral leadership of women ultimately eventuated in the towering work of the Strickland sisters, Elizabeth and Agnes, whose mammoth histories of the

queens, princesses, and other royal women of England and Scotland focused on social habits, customs, rituals, marriages, and family life.

NINETEENTH- AND EARLY-TWENTIETH-CENTURY HISTORIES OF WOMEN

Enlightenment curiosity provoked intense travel and investigative writing that portrayed the social life of peoples past and present; the Dutch travelers Betje Wolff and Aagje Deken as well as Joanna Schopenhauer, Albertine Clément-Hémery, Ida Hahn-Hahn, and Lady Morgan were some of the most important contributors from the 1780s to 1850. These eventuated in comparative social and cultural histories such as Lydia Maria Child's *The History and Condition of Women* (1835). Social rituals such as those of guilds, festivals, religious observances and monuments, institutions for the poor and orphaned, hospitals, and charitable societies in which women played an important role filled in the picture drawn in these works. Part of the impulse to portray social life fused with concern for what was early in the nineteenth century called "the social question"—the question of the poor and their possible uprising, on which thinkers of different political views expressed opinions. Various European thinkers described the condition of the poor, and notably the condition of poor women such as seamstresses, as well as the state of the working-class home. In the 1830s, Alexandre Parent-Duchâtelet simultaneously explored the history and condition of prostitution in Paris, while early in the 1840s Bettina von Arnim produced her history and analysis of the condition of the poor in Berlin. Most of these books provided numerically informed accounts of the poor, especially poor women, and their past.

Many of these historians believed that only by studying women's activities could one achieve a clear understanding of the social fabric—an understanding that was valued very much by amateurs and their appreciative readers but very little by the newly profes-

Working Women. Workers at the Platt Bros. cotton factory in Oldham, Lancashire, c. 1870. ©HULTON GETTY/ LIAISON AGENCY

sionalizing historians of the academy from the middle of the nineteenth century on. The latter, taking their cue from Hegel, avoided private life, genealogy, and other aspects of the familial as a low kind of "memorializing" that compared ill with the high endeavor of political history. Sarah Taylor Austin, translator of Ranke, Cousin, and other historians, nonetheless maintained in her history of German social life in the eighteenth century that only by understanding the history of women could one understand the important social underpinnings of political rule. This marked an important shift in women's history, from asserting women's moral worth as an antidote to charges of innate sinfulness to affirming a secular and social contribution that women had made. Several influences fed this historiography, including burgeoning feminist and reform activism, utopian social thought, and separate-spheres ideology.

Other trends in nineteenth-century thought deepened some of these themes in the social history of women. The development of the nation-state rested in part on the provisioning of new services such as sanitation, the elimination of disease, and the prevention of epidemics. Associated with the foul and disease-bearing, prostitution became a major topic of amateur history written by such eminent doctors as Abraham Flexner. As science tried to demoralize sex, doctors and amateurs produced studies of sexual customs, most notably their evolution over time. Once it was shown that sexual customs were constantly changing, it was easier to place them under the sign of history

and science rather than religion and morality. Although a growing interest in ethnology and anthropology also fed this impulse, historians of women were among the first to write the history of the "masses" who made up the democratizing nation-state. Working with her husband, J. R. Green, Alice Stopford Green wrote history as a nationalistic study of society—a tendency in historical study which was an important component of the discovery of women by professional history later. A strong champion of women's rights, Stopford Green also wrote histories of the Irish people and their struggles for social and economic justice under English rule.

The first wave of feminism and the attendant movement of women into universities, especially in the United States and Great Britain, also kept the social history of women alive, all the while transforming it. Inspired by feminism, groups such as the Men's and Women's Club in London produced studies of prostitution, women's work, and family customs for their meetings. Lina Eckenstein, a member of that club and amateur scholar, published *Women under Monasticism,* (1896), a pioneering social history. Amateurs like Julia Cartwright and Margaret Oliphant studied women's patronage of the arts; their works also depicted a complicated social and cultural life among the upper classes, in which women's social privilege allowed them real influence in the arts. The Cambridge historian Mary Bateson studied the double monastery with similar result: within monastic society women could exert power equal to that of men despite religious denigration of women's moral capacity. The culmination of this line of argument and this tradition appeared in Eileen Power's *Medieval Nunneries* (1922), in which the social and economic organization of monastic women was vividly depicted.

Although the coeducation for which feminists fought had many inequities, those women educated by the system, like Bateson and Power, were skilled in archival and other kinds of professional research. Archives directed them not only to material for political history, but also to evidence allowing for a new social history of the lower classes and domestic life. Trained by Lilian Knowles, the pioneering economic historian at the University of London, Alice Clark in her *Working Life of Women in the Seventeenth Century* (1919) established a line of argument in the social history of European women that, like many other nineteenth-century explanatory models, remains influential to this day. For Clark, the appearance of manufacturing and protoindustry made it more and more difficult for women to earn their livelihood. Ivy Pinchbeck's *Women Workers and the Industrial Revolution* (1930) also established working women as broadly covering the field of labor, while a variety of historical and statistical studies by social scientists provided a data base for similar studies of women in almost every European country. Simultaneously women workers were writing their own social histories in such works as *Mein Arbeitstag, Mein Wochenende* (1930) and *Maternity: Letters from Working Women* (1915). Women in white-collar jobs received important treatment in Wanda Neff's *Victorian Working Women* (1929)—a study that showed the deterioration of jobs such as bank clerks, secretaries, and teachers, once women entered the profession. Like the studies of Clark and Pinchbeck, Neff's has set some of the terms for studying women in white-collar jobs and the professions.

WOMEN'S HISTORIES AFTER 1960

Even before World War II a rich social history of women in almost every class had emerged. But it was after 1960 that the field exploded with the rise of family history, quantitative demographic history, and a new history of the working class. Historians in these fields applied a somewhat different professional methodology to social history than that which had developed over the previous century. As these areas of social history emerged, they almost all took men as their important historical group and generally overlooked the possibilities for thinking of women as historical subjects. Pioneering works like E. P. Thompson's *Making of the English Working Class* (1963) described laborers who were taken as universal, though implicitly male. Even family reconstitution and population studies failed to see the gendered implications of their many and useful findings. However, that quickly changed with the new round of feminist activism that arose at almost the same time.

By the 1970s, activists were targeting the absence of women from the curriculum and research agenda of universities and schools. In part their inspiration came from major feminist writings like those of Simone de Beauvoir and Betty Friedan, whose arguments on behalf of women were grounded in detailed examination of various social categories used to group women: married women, lesbians, housewives, old women, and so on. Late in the 1960s Natalie Zemon Davis and Jill Conway, teaching a course in women's history at the University of Toronto, produced a lengthy bibliography of women's history—much of it social—that circulated in mimeographed form. Conway and Davis drew precisely on the social history—of women in the Renaissance, women in monasteries, notable women, working women, and others—that had been written during the previous

century and a half. After that, women's history and women's studies courses arose, many of them rich with the beginnings of a professionalized research agenda in the social history of European women.

Innovation was rife, with many historians expressing the belief that women's history could not be like men's history, which was mostly about high politics. Rather, as had been maintained in the mid-nineteenth century, it would take a social form. Contesting the emphasis on men in the new labor history, women's historians in the 1970s investigated the conditions under which women worked. They recognized, however, that one did not necessarily look for women workers in the same locations as male workers. For one thing, in western Europe until the end of the nineteenth century the largest category of women workers found employment as domestic helpers of various kinds. Emphasizing the experience of class, historians Cissie Fairchilds and Theresa McBride described the interactions of women servants and middle-class women in England and France and found the conditions of work in the household far more onerous than those in the factory. Isolation, scrutiny by employers, and round-the-clock responsibility prevented the development of women's labor activism. Nonetheless, both of these works pointed out, social advancement was possible in domestic labor.

Studies of factory women and artisanal women mushroomed too, though the reliance on Pinchbeck was strong because of the richness of her narrative. English historians Jill Liddington and Jill Norris explored women textile workers of the north, finding them politically astute and active. Using some autobiographies and first-person narratives as sources, Rose Glickman's *Russian Factory Women* (1984) described the divergent work experience of Russian women within the mixed agricultural and manufacturing economy of the late nineteenth century, in which women moved from one sector to the other. Many of these and similar studies were attuned to the need for working women to combine household duties with paid employment of some kind.

Women as historical agents. Already, interest in combining the social history of work with the life cycle of women had produced a different kind of history, most notably in Joan Scott and Louise Tilly's *Women, Work, and Family* (1978). Using quantitative and demographic methods, this pioneering book plotted work for pay against women's age and their fertility. It also compared the employment histories of women in different types of manufacturing towns, resulting in the idea that women were historical agents, and that they developed their family and personal "strategies" around

Women's Political Activism. *The Parliamentary Female: The Ladies of the Creation,* English drawing, nineteenth century. ©HULTON-DEUTSCH COLLECTION/CORBIS

a more varied set of factors than did men. This combination of evidence for women's agency in developing family strategies, along with a mapping of their biological life course, became influential. For example, Erna Olafson Hellerstein's early anthology of documents for the history of European women, *Victorian Women* (Stanford, Calif., 1981), used the life course rather than political events as its organizing principle.

Prostitution also came under the rubric of a life strategy. Understanding sex work as a strategy rather than a moral failing followed the line of argument explored by many nineteenth-century writers. Judith Walkowitz's depiction of the blurred boundary between working-class women and prostitution showed that casually employed women whose work had off-seasons turned to prostitution during these periods. Members of the working class saw these women as members of their own group, not as outcasts. Rather, it was the state policy of regulation that turned them into marked, disreputable members of society. Jill Harsin, in her study of the French regulatory system, found it to consist not of legislation but of police decrees from the Napoleonic period mandating regular inspections of prostitutes and their incarceration, should there be any sign of infection. Harsin's work

complemented that of Alain Corbin, whose *Filles de noce* (1978) showed the regulatory system as part of the disciplining of bodily functions in the modern period. A student of Michel Foucault, Corbin described the brothel as rationally conceived, located, designed, and managed from the nineteenth century on.

HISTORIES OF SOCIAL MOVEMENTS, NORMS, AND RESISTANCE

A history of social movements eventuated from the attention to agency and strategizing within the life course. Analyses of women as actors in the English, French, and Russian revolutions emphasized their interest in subsistence and family issues as well as their involvement for reasons that were feminist or proto-feminist. Barbara Taylor, Joan Moon, and Claire Moses explored women's activism in chartist and utopian socialist associations, while Temma Kaplan and Louise Tilly looked at housewives' and working women's involvement in protest over issues of working conditions and subsistence. Natalie Zemon Davis's work on charivari chronicled yet another kind of social activism connected to the maintenance of social norms in marriage, sexuality, and household life in the early modern period. Davis's study directed scholars' attention early on to the cultural shape and ritualistic patterns of social movements, as well as historians' focus on what seemed to be private life.

With the emphasis on rationality and agency, historians turned to the development of social norms and the inculcation of standards of femininity. Carol Dyhouse, Deborah Gorham, and Joan Burstyn studied the education of women and found that from the beginning of a young girl's life femininity was inculcated as the opposite of male privilege. Mothers, for example, forced their little girls to stay in and work while their brothers played outside. Doctors were also seen as inculcating feminine norms in their treatment of older women as unable to care for their families, themselves, or their mental health. Not only did doctors wrench health care from women, but they subjected middle-class women to all sorts of regimens to bring them into line.

Formal schooling consisted of different subject matter for girls and boys, with girls receiving a heavy dose of household arts and religion instead of the increasingly secular and liberal-arts curriculum for boys. When universities opened their doors to women, however, the innovation was often used as the occasion for curricular modernization, especially, in the case of England, the addition of modern languages, math, his-

tory, and science alongside the study of classical languages and literatures. At first social historians relied on the autobiographies of those, like Vera Brittain, who had been among the early generations of scholars. Eventually, Martha Vicinus included these women in her study of the various kinds of single women's experiences at the turn of the century, and thus helped construct the portrait of the "modern" woman. Jo Burr Margadant explored the sex-segregated postsecondary schooling of young women during the French Third Republic, and Dyhouse expanded her purview to publish *No Distinction of Sex?: Women in British Universities 1870–1939* (1995).

Studies of the development of accomplished or activist girls appeared in such works as Barbara Engel's *Mothers and Daughters: Women of the Intelligentsia in Nineteenth-Century Russia,* which discussed the inculcation both of feminine norms and adult ambition or rebellion as part of a historically-specific family process. The extraordinary array of intellectual and nihilist women emerged from a mixture of familial, emotional, and cognitive experiences that were particular to their times. Simultaneously, studies of inculcation of norms among peasant women appeared in studies of female relationships in the extended Russian and eastern European family.

The early years of second-wave feminist social history also looked at those women who did not im-

Household Arts. *School for Girls,* engraving after a drawing by H. F. B. Gravelot, eighteenth century. BIBLIOTHÈQUE NATIONALE, PARIS

7

Curricular Modernization. Science lesson at the London Grammar School for Girls, 1936.
PRIVATE COLLECTION/THE STAPLETON COLLECTION/THE BRIDGEMAN ART LIBRARY

bibe, or who resisted, feminine norms. Mary Hartman's *Victorian Murderesses* (1977) looked at the crimes, testimonies, and judicial trials of British and French women in the nineteenth century. Other works studied thievery, luddism, and rioting, often as an extension of the new social history that saw this kind of behavior as "primitive," as in the banditry and Swing rioters described by Eric Hobsbawm. This was not the conclusion of scholars like Hartman, however. Somewhat later, the violence done to women—the extreme expression of their social subordination—was described in Anna Clark's *Women's Silence, Men's Violence: Sexual Assault in England 1770–1845* (1987). Klaus Theweleit's *Male Fantasies* (1987) and Maria Tatar's *Lustmord* (1995), chronicling depictions of German men's desires to slaughter and victimize women in the most grossly violent ways, provided further context to the grimmer aspects of the social history of women in the post–World War I period.

Religion provided an intermediate place—one in which women were perhaps socialized to sex roles, but which also became a space for resistance and self-transformation. Myriad studies addressed the religious terrain, making for a rich social history both of spiritual belief and its social functioning. From the Renaissance on, much debate ensued about the social outcomes of religious fervor among nuns and intensely devout laywomen. Brenda Meehan charted the life of women religious in Russia, illuminating the social practice of widowed, married, and single women. Gillian Ahlgren demonstrated that Teresa of Avila's particular devotional writings gave women the means to bypass the worse consequences of Tridentine Catholicism and left a legacy of empowerment. Phyllis Mack's *Visionary Women* (1994), while it richly captured the specific language of women's preachings in

the seventeenth century, also showed the ways in which they moved through society. Taking up the thread from E. P. Thompson's focus on working-class men's alternative Methodism, Deborah Valenze traced the networks and the social force women developed in the late eighteenth and early nineteenth centuries through their ministries. The impact of Protestantism on women's education—particularly their instruction in reading—also engaged many social historians.

THE DEVELOPMENT OF GENDER HISTORY

By the early 1990s calls for an end to women's history and a turn to gender history caused anxiety among some practitioners. Joan Scott's "Gender: A Useful Category of Analysis" summarized the theory of gender as it had been developed by anthropologists and literary theorists. Adapting these theories for historical use, she suggested that one could not examine women's past alone, for women existed only in relationship to men. That relationship was implicated in the play of systems of power, with gender being a primary expression of power. Not everyone joined in the rush to gender history; some practitioners saw gender as yet another way of appealing to men in the profession by saying that women could not be discussed historically without them. Judith Bennett in "Feminism and History" maintained that the way to understanding power was less through analysis of gender than by dealing historically with the manifestations of patriarchy. Gisela Bock, however, argued that women's and gender history needed one another and were in fact complementary.

As it turned out, the development of gender history enhanced women's social history and shed new light on femininity. For the early modern period the histories of sexuality, women's criminality, and prostitution were all restudied. Among the prominent topics in which interpretations changed was the study of witchcraft, which also benefited from scrupulous microstudies. Although there was little debate that the majority of witches were women, the localized studies—for instance those of Wolfgang Behringer and Alison Rowland—found witches to be distributed along marital and age statuses in many cases. These works also showed that witches could be integrated into the community for long periods of time. However, the "gendered" subjectivity and narratives of witches, as explored by historians like Lyndal Roper and Dianne Purkiss, found in accuser's testimonies evidence of particularly "feminine" concerns such as those of motherhood, the body, and female duty. Women with such anxieties might project their sense of guilt onto others, who in some cases became the accused. In the case of witchcraft, oddly enough, gender turned historical analysis away from misogyny toward the conditions of femininity.

The term "femininity" gained new resonance and legitimacy as the proposal that femininity and masculinity were related added a new historical dimension to the understanding of femininity and class. For instance, *Family Fortunes* (1987) by Leonore Davidoff and Catherine Hall explored the social history of the British middle classes by looking at the mutually constructed roles of men and women in the early nineteenth century. Using this gendered perspective, Davidoff and Hall found less disparity between femininity and masculinity than earlier authors had. On working women, gender history provided insights as well. Tessie Liu's *Weaver's Knot* (1994) looked at the hero of many a labor historian—the solitary artisan of the nineteenth century—to find that his image could only be maintained if the women of artisanal families were dispatched to nearby factories to bring in additional money. Thus the image of the courageous artisan resisting proletarianization for himself depended on the proletarianization of his wives and daughters. Laura Lee Downs looked at women metallurgy workers during World War I through the prism of gender, finding that although factory owners often employed the available gender stereotypes in assigning women tasks and wages, they simultaneously noted what women could actually do. Women's work in metallurgy became a permanent feature of the industrial landscape—Downs adduced numbers—because of both factory owners' and women's experience of war.

At the close of the twentieth century historians continued their dissection of working women's experience despite the attacks on social history investigations from this perspective. For the early modern period, Heide Wunder and Christina Vanja's *Weiber, Menscher, Frauenzimmer: Frauen in der ländlichen Gesellschaft 1500–1800* (1996) explored women's work not only in vineyards and protoindustry but also in their various other occupations. Earlier conclusions about the pervasiveness of women's work in the early modern period held, but scholars gave more detailed accounts, showing, for example, that women, though often driven from certain sectors like the woolen guilds in the Netherlands, remained active as fishwives, spinners, seamstresses, and workers in the health care trades. Amy Louise Erickson, in *Women and Property in Early Modern England* (1993), showed additionally that women controlled property more extensively than hitherto thought. Finally, Natalie Zemon Davis's wide-ranging *Women on the Margins* (1995) gave a rich portrait of the work life of three very different seventeenth-century women whose labors initially complemented those of their spouses and who subsequently went off to construct a complex and intense life course combining craft with religious fervor, migration, and mental self-exploration. The life-course model for women in early modern Europe had evolved not only because of the study of gender but because of advances in the history of work and sexuality: the anthology by Judith M. Bennett and Amy M. Froide, *Singlewomen in European History 1250–1800* (1999), covered a wide variety of these new and old perspectives in social history, including demography, sexuality, and citizenship.

Cultural contextualization. Beatrice Farnsworth and Lynne Viola's 1992 anthology *Russian Peasant Women* outlined a rich history of everyday life including work, sexuality, and reproduction and set it in the context of peasant culture. This cultural contextualization of the social history of women and femininity marked a major change in the field. Similarly, Anne-Marie Sohn's massive thesis on the everyday life of French women of the lower classes analyzed their educational, social, and cultural milieu. Departing from the theories of the 1970s and 1990s that women in food movements and neighborhood activism were "prepolitical," the work of Ellen Ross showed that the neighborhood solidarity of working-class mothers laid the groundwork for shop-floor protest, an insight explored further in Anna Davin's *Growing Up Poor: Home, School, and Street in London 1870–1914* (1996). Belinda Davis's study of women food protesters in Berlin during World War I found that, far from having no political agenda or impact, these protesters challenged the government to respond to ordinary people's needs. Thus women's wartime responsibilities for food changed the nature of public discourse and, eventually, the nature of government. The 1998 anthology *Women and Socialism, Socialism and Women* (Helmut Gruber and Pamela Graves, eds.) provided a comparative look at women's connections with unions and socialist activism in the interwar years. Finally the range of women's work in the post–World War II period received comparative treatment in *Frauen arbeiten: Weibliche Erwebstätigkeit in Ost- und Westdeutschland nach 1945* (Gunilla-Friederike Budde, ed.). One study found, in the case of West Germany, strikingly different behavior on the part of working-class women who entered the work force because of the "pull" of jobs rather than the "push" of their husband's wages. The anthology additionally concluded that the largest discrepancies in worklife between East and West Germany were in the agricultural sector.

Historians also looked at the rise of service-oriented job opportunities in new ways. The connection between women's philanthropy of the nineteenth century and their work for the welfare state has long been made, but in *The Rise of Caring Power* (1999), studying philanthropy in the Netherlands, Annemieke van Drenth and Francisca de Haan concluded that women developed a system different though related to the "pastoral power" as articulated by Michel Foucault. Women's dominance of the caring professions arose from their desire to make subjects of other, poorer women and in so doing to exercise their own power. De Haan has also studied women office workers in the Netherlands, examining the battle for survival that existed in white-collar work. In studies of postindustrial work since 1945, in which women play an enormous role, Cas Wouters has described the psychological work of women flight attendants, while others have focused on the connections between service women and technology and knowledge.

Another theme of late-twentieth-century scholarship involved women's experience of consumer society. Anthologies like Victoria De Grazia's anthology *The Sex of Things* (1996) and Katherina von Ankum's *Women in the Metropolis* (1997) abandoned much of the disapproval that had earlier characterized accounts of women's consumerism. Instead, studies illustrated how consumer activity modified women's relationship to urban space, whatever the class. Arlette Farge's work on the eighteenth century showed women occupying the streets with gusto and claiming neighborhoods, doorsteps, and markets. Erika Rappaport's *Shopping for Pleasure: Women in the Making of London's West End* (2000) connected women's consumerism late in the nineteenth century with a range of social positions

they assumed—as members of an imperial power, as provisioners, and as citizens fully entitled to enter public space. Studies of women as consumers of films, as participants in beauty pageants, and in their relationship to cosmetics, clothing, household design, and architecture have all enriched historical depictions of everyday life.

Political regimes.　　The study of Nazism and fascism—as well as a new social understanding of various political regimes—benefited from the turn to gender. This construct encouraged a rethinking of the ways in which politics took the formation of masculinity and femininity as a national goal. This political mission yielded societal results under various political regimes, but they were particularly visible under Nazism and fascism. The privileging and construction of a soldierly masculinity led fascists to build a complementary, coercive femininity among Aryan women that demanded a commitment to reproduction. Building a numerous Aryan population became the mission of Aryan women, while the curtailment of reproduction was the lot of non-Aryans. These insights have led to new interpretations of the social history of the Holocaust. Aware of the gendered cast to that catastrophe, Marion Kaplan (*Between Dignity and Despair,* 1999) has been among those uncovering the conditions that made women more often its victims than men. Other studies have explored sexual relationships and judicial trials of "racial" sex offenders under Nazism.

Seeing gender and population control as major aspects of political regimes—be they international, national, regional, or local—has led scholars to compare democracies with totalitarian governments in their impact on the social lives of women and the construction of femininity. Maria Sophia Quine's *Population Politics in Twentieth-Century Europe: Fascist Dictatorships and Liberal Democracies* (1996) sees that the two types of state differed little in their desire to control domestic life, sexuality, and the relationship between generations. Studies of the policies of the Soviet state and those of Eastern Europe, from the 1920s down to the reforms of the post-Soviet nations, have uncovered a pattern of interventionist regulation of reproduction—whether allowing abortion or not, or allowing birth control or not—determining the life course of women to a far greater degree than that of men. The policies of the British welfare state, post–World-War-II France, and the new West Germany all shaped the reproductive, work, and domestic lives of women by mandating population enhancement.

As perspectives shifted to view it as not only a matter of high politics, but a more wide-ranging movement with important social components, imperialism became a full-fledged site for the study of women's social agency. European women travelers were newly evaluated as important members of imperial society and bearers of its culture as their memoirs and travel reports were republished in the 1980s and 1990s. Other studies began the process of looking at the social aspects of European imperialism in the colonies as more complex than imagined; a picture emerged in which women settlers, missionaries, and colonized peoples played major roles in shaping social and political relationships. The argument developed that women were more racist than men because, disliking the concubinage of colonized women, they ended the closeness of white men and local women that imperialism entailed. Margaret Strobel's *European Women and the Second British Empire* (1991) questioned this argument, while Helen Callaway's work on settlers in colonial Nigeria argued that women had reshaped many of the social aspects of imperialism. Sexuality as a major component of men's gendered relationship to colonized women through science, concubinage, prostitution, and rape, was investigated in a variety of works including those of Londa Schiebinger, Pamela Scully, and Luise White. Frances Gouda's *Dutch Culture Overseas: Colonial Practice in the Netherland Indies 1900–1942* (1995), her edited volume with Julia Clancy-Smith, *Domesticating the Empire: Race, Gender, and Family Life in French and Dutch Colonialism* (1998), and Kumari Jayawardena's *The White Woman's Other Burden: Western Women and South Asia during British Rule* (1995) enriched the portrait of the social functioning of women and femininity in overseas empires, while other works began showing women's use of colonial goods and their role in developing a culture of global consumerism.

Another important line of scholarship in the social history of women and femininity developed around global migration to Europe in the post–World War II period. As many women from the decolonizing world entered Europe in the 1950s and thereafter, their place in metropolitan society was shaped by the lingering values of imperialism and neocolonialism. *The Heart of the Race: Black Women's Lives in Britain* (Beverley Bryan et al., 1985) used oral testimony to compile the

experiences of moving to the metropole and working in the welfare state. The social history of women immigrants to Europe also appeared in a variety of testimonials and first-person accounts, while their central role in the post-Fordist workplace was also investigated. R. Amy Elman, ed., *Sexual Politics and the European Union* (1996) explored the social policies that affected these women's lives.

Social history of post-Soviet women also opened up in the 1990s. In the official histories of the collapse of the socialist regime, women disappeared as leaders of the social movements that had brought about Communism's collapse. Moreover, post-Soviet governments, eager to escape the appearance of hewing to socialist values, reinvigorated the ideology of separate spheres. In the midst of massive restructuring of the economy, this ideal entailed the firing of millions of women. From 70 to 80 percent of the unemployed in any job category in the 1990s and early twenty-first century were women. Some of these changes were charted in such works as Barbara Einhorn, *Cinderella Goes to Market: Citizenship, Gender, and Women's Movements in East Central Europe* (1993), Ellen E. Berry, ed. *Postcommunism and the Body Politic* (1995), and Mary Buckley, ed. *Post-Soviet Women: From the Baltic to Central Asia* (1997). Simultaneously another interesting facet of social history of women— a more complex picture of the social and cultural lives of women under Stalinism—was advanced in such works as Helena Goscilo and Beth Homgren, eds. *Russia-Women-Culture* (1996) and Rosalind Marsh, ed., *Women in Russia and Ukraine* (1996).

The social history of European women and femininity has been a fertile field of study for two centuries, with many more studies and breakthroughs still to come. More innovations should be in the offing as the historiography of gender unfolds; technology's impact on women's social history is gaining new attention; and the social history of European women since 1945 should find many new investigators. As postcolonial studies increase in importance, they, too, have been advancing social history, and they have meshed nicely with gender history to open still other paths in European history. The development of world history also holds real promise for social history's advance.

See also other articles in this section.

BIBLIOGRAPHY

Ankum, Katherina von, ed. *Women in the Metropolis: Gender and Modernity in Weimar Culture.* Berkeley, Calif., 1997.

Bennett, Judith M. "Medievalism and Feminism." *Speculum* 68 (April 1993): 309–331.

Bennett, Judith M., and Amy M. Froide, eds. *Singlewomen in the European Past, 1250–1800.* Philadelphia, 1999.

Berry, Ellen E., ed. *Postcommunism and the Body Politic.* New York, 1995.

Bryan, Beverley et al. *The Heart of the Race: Black Women's Lives in Britain.* London, 1985.

Buckley, Mary, ed. *Post-Soviet Women: From the Baltic to Central Asia.* Cambridge, U.K., 1997.

Budde, Gunilla-Friederike, ed. *Frauen arbeiten: Weibliche Erwebstätigkeit in Ost- und Westdeutschland nach 1945.* Göttingen, Germany, 1997.

Clark, Anna. *Women's Silence, Men's Violence: Sexual Assault in England 1770–1845.* London, 1987.

Davidoff, Leonore, and Catherine Hall. *Family Fortunes: Men and Women of the English Middle Class, 1780–1850.* Chicago, 1987.

Davin, Anna. *Growing Up Poor: Home, School, and Street in London 1870–1914.* London, 1996.

Davis, Natalie Zemon. *Women on the Margins: Three Seventeenth-Century Lives.* Cambridge, Mass., 1995.

De Grazia, Victoria, ed. *The Sex of Things: Gender and Consumption in Historical Perspective.* Berkeley, Calif., 1996.

Drenth, Annemieke van, and Francisca de Haan. *The Rise of Caring Power: Elizabeth Fry and Josephine Butler in Britain and the Netherlands.* Amsterdam, 1999.

Dyhouse, Carol. *No Distinction of Sex?: Women in British Universities 1870–1939.* London, 1995.

Einhorn, Barbara. *Cinderella Goes to Market: Citizenship, Gender, and Women's Movements in East Central Europe.* London, 1993.

Elman, R. Amy, ed. *Sexual Politics and the European Union: The New Feminist Challenge.* Providence, R.I., 1996.

Engel, Barbara. *Mothers and Daughters: Women of the Intelligentsia in Nineteenth-Century Russia.* Cambridge, U.K. 1983.

Erickson, Amy Louise. *Women and Property in Early Modern England.* London, 1993.

Goscilo, Helena, and Beth Homgren, eds. *Russia-Women-Culture.* Bloomington, Ind., 1996.

Gouda, Frances. *Dutch Culture Overseas: Colonial Practice in the Netherland Indies 1900–1942.* Amsterdam, 1995.

Gouda, Frances, and Julia Clancy-Smith, eds. *Domesticating the Empire: Race, Gender, and Family Life in French and Dutch Colonialism.* Charlottesville, Va., 1998.

Gruber, Helmut, and Pamela Graves, eds. *Women and Socialism, Socialism and Women: Europe between the Two World Wars.* New York, 1998.

Hartman, Mary. *Victorian Murderesses: A True History of Thirteen Respectable French and English Women Accused of Unspeakable Crimes.* New York, 1977.

Jayawardena, Kumari. *The White Woman's Other Burden: Western Women and South Asia during British Rule.* New York, 1995.

Kaplan, Marion. *Between Dignity and Despair: Jewish Life in Nazi Germany.* New York, 1999.

Liu, Tessie. *The Weaver's Knot: The Contradictions of Class Struggle and Family Solidarity in Western France, 1750–1914.* Ithaca, N.Y., 1994.

Mack, Phyllis. *Visionary Women: Ecstatic Prophecy in Seventeenth-Century England.* Berkeley, Calif., 1994.

Marsh, Rosalind, ed. *Women in Russia and Ukraine.* Cambridge, U.K., 1996.

Quine, Maria Sophia. *Population Politics in Twentieth-Century Europe: Fascist Dictatorships and Liberal Democracies.* London, 1996.

Rappaport, Erika. *Shopping for Pleasure: Women in the Making of London's West End.* Princeton, N.J., 2000.

Scott, Joan. "Gender: A Useful Category of Analysis." *American Historical Review* 91 (1986): 1053–1075.

Strobel, Margaret. *European Women and the Second British Empire.* Bloomington, Ind., 1991.

Tatar, Maria. *Lustmord: Sexual Murder in Weimar Germany.* Princeton, N.J., 1995.

Theweleit, Klaus. *Male Fantasies.* Minneapolis, Minn., 1987.

Tilly, Louise, and Joan Scott. *Women, Work, and Family.* New York, 1978.

Wunder, Heide, and Christina Vanja. *Weiber, Menscher, Frauenzimmer: Frauen in der ländlichen Gesellschaft 1500–1800.* Göttingen, Germany, 1996.

PATRIARCHY

Merry E. Wiesner-Hanks

Social historians and other scholars frequently disagree about the meaning and usefulness of the word "patriarchy." Some use it very broadly, to mean social systems in which men have more power and access to resources than women. By this definition, every culture that has left written records has been patriarchal. Others use it more narrowly, to mean social systems in which older men, particularly those who are fathers and heads of households, have authority over women, children, and men in dependent positions, such as servants, serfs, and slaves. By this definition, most Western cultures were patriarchal until the eighteenth or nineteenth century and retain vestiges of patriarchy today, such as the continued power of fathers over their children. (This narrower definition of patriarchy is sometimes termed "patriarchalism" or "paternalism.") Still others avoid using the term completely, arguing that it is too politicized and associated with feminism; they prefer terms that they see as more neutral, such as "male dominance" or "paternal power" or "inequities based on gender." Others avoid it because they feel it lacks much explanatory value; at least until the twentieth century, patriarchy was simply an aspect of human life, like breathing, and so in their opinion merits little scholarly attention.

Most historians who choose to use the word "patriarchy" emphasize that despite their ubiquity, patriarchal systems have taken widely varied forms. Male assertions of power over women, children, and dependent men have involved physical force, legal sanctions, intellectual structures, religious systems, economic privileges, social institutions, and cultural norms. Thus patriarchy does have a history, and social historians have been particularly active in investigating the changing construction of patriarchy and the responses of women and men to it. Most investigations of that history in Western cultures concentrate on three periods, which will thus be the primary topics of this article: the origins of patriarchy in antiquity, the explicit institutionalization of a father-centered patriarchy in western Europe during the fifteenth through the eighteenth centuries, and the challenges

to that patriarchy by the liberal revolutions of the late eighteenth century and radical social movements of the nineteenth century. Because patriarchal configurations of power were less explicitly a matter of concern in the Middle Ages than they were in the early modern period, most medieval historians have not felt compelled to make them a specific focus of investigation. Historians of the twentieth century tend either to use the term without explicating or defining it, or to avoid it altogether, although some investigations of authoritarian regimes that made extensive use of father imagery—such as Hitler's Germany, Mussolini's Italy, and Stalin's Soviet Union—do label these as patriarchal and explore the consequences of this ideology. Whatever century they lived in, all later supporters (and most opponents) of patriarchy hearkened back to ancient models and made references to patriarchy's origins, so it is important to understand the scholarly debate about this before looking at more recent developments.

THE ORIGINS OF PATRIARCHY

Explanations of the origins of patriarchy were first advanced in the nineteenth century, particularly by German social theorists. The scholar J. J. Bachofen asserted that human society had originally been a matriarchy in which mothers were all-powerful. The mother-child bond was the original source of culture, religion, and community, but gradually father-child links came to be regarded as more important, and superior (to Bachofen's eyes) patriarchal structures developed. Bachofen's ideas about primitive matriarchy were accepted by the socialist Friedrich Engels, who postulated a two-stage evolution from matriarchy to patriarchy. In matriarchal cultures, goods were owned in common, but with the expansion of agriculture and animal husbandry men began to claim ownership of crops, animals, and land, thus developing the notion of private property. Once men had private property, they became very concerned about passing it on to their own heirs, and attempted to control women's sexual lives to assure that offspring were legitimate. This led to the development of the nuclear family, which was followed by the development of the state, in which men's rights over women were legitimized through a variety of means, a process Engels describes as the "world historical defeat of the female sex."

The idea that human society was originally a matriarchy with female deities and female leaders continues to be accepted by some scholars and a number of popular writers, but it has been largely discredited among anthropologists and historians for lack of evidence. What has not been discredited is the notion that both property ownership and political structures were intimately related to patriarchy. The historian Gerda Lerner has tipped Engels's line of causation on its head: women, she argues, *were* the first property, exchanged for their procreative power by men with other men through marriage, prostitution, and slavery. Thus patriarchy preceded other forms of hierarchy and domination such as kin networks and social classes, and women became primarily defined by their relation to men. Like Engels, Lerner links patriarchy with economic and political change, but she also stresses the importance of nonmaterial issues such as the creation of symbols and meaning through religion and philosophy. Women were excluded from direct links to the divine in Mesopotamian religion and Judaism, and defined as categorically inferior to men in Greek philosophy. Thus both of the traditions generally regarded as the sources of Western culture—the Bible and Greek (particularly Aristotelian) thought—affirmed women's secondary position. Because other hierarchies such as those of hereditary aristocracy, class, or race privileged the women connected to powerful or wealthy men, women did not see themselves as part of a coherent group and often supported the institutions and intellectual structures that subordinated them.

Lerner's ideas have been challenged from a number of perspectives. Materialist historians have objected to her emphasis on ideas and symbols, and to the notion that gender hierarchies preceded those based on property ownership, while some classicists have argued that she misread ancient prostitution and other aspects of early cultures. Despite these objections, however, some of her—and Engels's—points are now widely accepted. Though it is unclear which came first, women's subordination emerged in the ancient Middle East at the same time as private ownership of property and plow agriculture, which significantly increased the food supply but also significantly increased the resources needed to produce that food. Men generally carried out the plowing and care for animals, which led to boys being favored over girls for the work they could do for their parents while young and the support they could provide in parents' old age. Boys became the normal inheritors of family land and of the rights to work communally held land.

The states that developed in the ancient Middle East further heightened gender distinctions. They depended on taxes and tribute as well as slave labor for their support, and so their rulers were very interested in maintaining population levels. As hereditary aristocracies developed, they became concerned with maintaining the distinction between themselves and the majority of the population, and male property owners wanted to be sure the children their wives bore were theirs. All of these concerns led to attempts to control women's reproduction through laws governing sexual relations and, more importantly, through marriage norms and practices that set up a very unequal relationship between spouses. Laws were passed mandating that women be virgins on marriage and imposing strict punishment for a married woman's adultery; sexual relations outside of marriage on the part of husbands were not considered adultery. Concern with family honor thus became linked to women's sexuality in a way that it was not for men. Men's honor revolved around their work activities and, for more prominent families, around their performance of public duties in the expanding government bureaucracies.

The states of the ancient Mediterranean built on these precedents, with the Roman Republic developing the most comprehensive notion of patriarchy in the ancient world. Roman fathers in theory held life and death power over their children, including married daughters. Such power, termed the *patria potestas,* appears to have been very rarely exercised and may actually have served to protect women from abusive husbands.

These economic and political developments were accompanied and supported by cultural norms and religious concepts that heightened gender distinctions. As agricultural communities changed the landscape through irrigation and building, they increasingly saw themselves as separate from and superior to the natural world and developed a nature-culture dichotomy. Because women were the bearers of children and because they did not own the irrigated, culturally adapted fields, they were regarded as closer to nature and therefore inferior. As more of women's labor began to take place inside the house or household complex, and as houses were increasingly regarded as owned by an individual or family, women were increasingly associated with the domestic or private realm. Men, whose work was done outside in conjunction with other men, were increasingly associated with the public realm, a realm that grew in complexity and importance as communities and then states expanded. Heavenly hierarchies came to reflect those on earth, with the gods arranged in a hierarchy dominated by a single male god, who was viewed as the primary creator of life. Both monotheistic religions that developed in the ancient world, first Judaism and then Christianity, regarded their single god as male and excluded women from official positions of authority. Christianity also adopted and adapted Roman notions of paternal power, with bishops and priests taking the title "father" and, in western Europe, ultimate authority coming to reside in a single father, the pope, whose title derived from a Latin word for father.

The development of patriarchy in the ancient world is thus a complex process, with no single cause: property ownership, the division of labor, the requirements of marriage, the growth of the bureaucratic state, cultural values, and religious ideas were all involved. Patriarchal hierarchies shaped all of these in turn, and continued to do so throughout Western history. Later Europeans referred back to the patriarchal values and institutions of the ancient world constantly, and took longer to question and challenge patriarchy than almost any other aspect of ancient culture. Indeed, the very individuals who challenged other inherited institutions and hierarchies were often the strongest supporters of patriarchy, seeing no contradiction in their refutation of traditional authorities in other aspects of life and their acceptance of those same authorities when it came to notions of gender.

PATRIARCHAL STRUCTURES IN EARLY MODERN EUROPE

Just as it had in the ancient world, the elaboration of patriarchy in early modern Europe involved economic, political, cultural, and religious issues. Economic institutions that developed in the Middle Ages, such as craft guilds, were patriarchal in both the broad and narrow sense. Women were generally excluded from formal programs of apprenticeship that led to independent mastership in a guild, although as the wife or daughter of a master a woman might work in a shop and as a master's widow might run one. Women's ability to work was thus dependent on their relationship with a man, not their own skills and training. The men involved in guilds were also arranged in a patriarchal power structure, however, with the master having authority over his apprentices and journeymen, who might be grown men. In some places journeymen objected to this situation and formed their own guilds, but these were often prohibited by state authorities, who saw them as dangerous and antithetical to the properly hierarchical arrangement of society.

Economic development in the later Middle Ages and early modern period is generally described as the rise of capitalism, which has long been recognized as offering more opportunities for men than it did for women. Because sons inherited more than daughters—a pattern established in the ancient world—women rarely controlled enough financial resources to enter occupations that required large initial capital outlay. In some areas capitalism created opportunities for wage labor, but women were regularly paid far less than men, or their pay went directly to their husbands or fathers when families rather than individuals were hired. Occupations that required advanced training were closed to women, as they could not attend universities or academies. Their domestic and family responsibilities prevented them from entering occupations that required extensive traveling, and their productive tasks within the household, even if these were for pay, such as laundering or sewing, were increasingly defined as reproductive—as housekeeping. Thus in many instances capitalism and patriarchy worked together to heighten existing gender distinctions, a process that has been analyzed in what is usually termed a "dual-systems approach."

The intertwining of capitalism and patriarchy did not have the same effects in all of Europe, however, or the same effects on all social groups. The expansion of wage labor, despite its low pay and low status, may actually have benefited some women, as it allowed them to leave the parental household and perhaps even support themselves without marrying. This possibility of greater independence was unacceptable in the minds of political authorities, who began to pass laws that attempted to force women into male-headed households. Such laws had not been necessary earlier because the opportunities for women to live alone and support themselves by their labor were much fewer. In southern Germany, unmarried women were forbidden to move into cities unless they went into domestic service in a male-headed household, and a special pejorative term, *Eigenbrötlerinnen* (women who earn their own bread), was used for women who lived on their own. These laws were often justified with explicit defenses of patriarchy, noting that if women did not live in male-headed households they would be "masterless" and "indulge in slovenly and immoral debaucheries." Such laws were largely ineffective, however, if the demand for women's wage labor was great enough, a situation that occurred especially in cloth-producing areas. In sixteenth-century Augsburg, for example, city authorities tried to force women who spun thread to live in the households of male weavers, but they refused, saying openly they were not so dumb as to work as spin-maids for the weavers when they could earn three times as much spinning on their own. Such comments incensed both the authorities and the weavers, but the demand for thread was so great that there was little they could do. Thus in this instance, the demands of patriarchy and those of capitalist development were at odds with one another, a situation that was rare, but possible.

The attempt by city governments in Germany to force everyone to live in male-headed households was only one of the many ways in which political institutions and patriarchy were linked in early modern Europe. In cities and villages, political rights—to make decisions about common concerns, to choose and hold office as a public official—were limited to men, and in some cities, such as Venice, to men who were married heads of household. Women were often considered citizens—which gave them legal advantages over noncitizens and the obligations to pay taxes—but this did not bring the rights that it did to male citizens. Though they often took oaths of allegiance on first becoming citizens, they did not participate in the annual oath swearing held in many cities and villages, in which adult male citizens swore to defend their town and support it economically. (Parts of Europe where this oath swearing was maintained and prized into the modern period were often those where patriarchy was the strongest. Switzerland, whose national mythology revolves around stories of William Tell and village democracy, was the last country to Europe to grant women the vote; they received it only in 1971, after eighty-two referenda.)

The connection between masculinity (or fatherhood) and political power was strong in early modern nation-states as well as cities and villages. The lack of male heirs in many of Europe's ruling houses led to an unusual number of female monarchs in the sixteenth century, an apparent contradiction with patriarchal ideals. This situation sparked a vigorous public debate about women's rule, with many writers arguing that women's rule was unnatural, unlawful, and contrary to Christian scriptures. The Scottish religious reformer John Knox termed rule by a woman "monstrous" and "repugnant." Defenders of female rule, who often hoped to gain favor with female monarchs through their writings, attempted to separate the private and public persons of a queen, arguing that she could be feminine in her private life—and thus subject to her husband if she was married—but still exhibit the masculine qualities regarded as necessary to a ruler in her public life.

Jean Bodin, the French jurist and political theorist, used the narrower definition of patriarchy—rule by fathers—as another reason to object to women's rule. He argued that the state was like a household, and just as in a household the husband/father has authority and power over all others, so in the state a male monarch should always rule. The English political writer Robert Filmer carried this even further in *Patriarcha,* asserting that rulers derived all legal authority from the divinely sanctioned fatherly power of Adam, just as did all fathers. Male monarchs picked up on Filmer's ideas, and used paternal imagery to justify their assertion of power over their subjects. James I of England commented in speeches to Parliament, "I am the Husband, and the whole Isle is my lawful Wife. . . . By the law of nature the king becomes a natural father to all his lieges at his coronation. . . . A King is trewly *Parens patriae,* the politique father of his people." Though such language was usually used to justify royal absolutism, it was also used by those who opposed certain royal actions; they stressed, in these cases, that the king was *not* acting as a beneficent and loving father would and thus merited criticism.

This link between royal and paternal authority could also work in the opposite direction to enhance the power of male heads of household. Just as subjects were deemed to have no or only a very limited right of rebellion against their ruler (James asserted that it was "monstrous and unnatural for sons to rise up"), so women and children were not to dispute the authority of the husband/father because both kings and fathers were held to have received their authority from God. The household was not viewed as private but as the smallest political unit and so as part of the public realm. Jean Bodin put it succinctly: "So we will leave moral discourse to the philosophers and theologians, and we will take up what is relative to political life, and speak of the husband's power over the wife, which is the source and origin of every human society."

Concerns about the patriarchal state and household led not only to theoretical treatises and royal speeches but also to new laws. Rulers intent on increasing and centralizing their own authority supported legal and institutional changes that enhanced the power of men over the women and children in their own families, in what the historian Sarah Hanley has termed the "family/state compact." In France, for example, a series of laws were enacted between 1556 and 1789 that increased both male and state control of marriage. These were proposed and supported by state officials because they increased their personal authority within their own families and simultaneously increased the authority of the state vis-à-vis the Cath-

The Father-King. *The Triumph of James, the King of Peace,* an engraving by Willem van de Passe, portrays the English monarch as the father of both his country and his progeny. The engraving dates from before James I's death in 1625. Charles, prince of Wales (later Charles I), stands at the left, his hand on the open Bible. On the right is James's daughter Elizabeth with her husband, Frederick V, elector of the Palatinate, and their large brood of children. James's two deceased daughters sit at his feet like angels. REPRODUCED BY COURTESY OF THE TRUSTEES OF THE BRITISH MUSEUM

olic Church, which had required at least the nominal consent of both parties for a valid marriage. Children who disagreed with their father's decisions on marriage or other matters could be imprisoned by a *lettre de cachet,* a warrant of arrest signed by the king of France and closed with a seal *(cachet),* ordering their imprisonment without trial until further notice. *Lettres de cachet* were also used occasionally by husbands seeking to control wives who were disobedient or whom they regarded as harming family reputation and honor.

Religious institutions occasionally worked against patriarchy, as in the requirement of spousal consent in marriage, but more often worked to reinforce it. During the fifteenth century, humanists and religious reformers increasingly emphasized that God had set up marriage and families as the best way to provide spiritual and moral discipline. In sermons, homilies, and catechisms, they stressed the role that godly men were to play in leading these families and the corresponding duties of pious and obedient women and

children. Such paternalistic households fit well with those envisioned as ideal by the craft guilds and became an essential part of Protestant moral ideology after the Protestant Reformation of the sixteenth century. Because Protestants—beginning with Martin Luther—put such an emphasis on marriage as the proper life for all people and patriarchal households as the cornerstone of society, the Protestant Reformation used to be viewed as the originator of these ideas. It is now recognized that such ideas were quite common already in the fifteenth century and that they were based on still earlier social and economic changes that had made the marital pair the basic production and consumption unit in Europe. Thus Protestant ideas about the family did not create the patriarchal bourgeois family but resulted from it, a causal line that can help explain why the ideal family in Catholic writings was exactly the same as that in Protestant: a pious, responsible, forceful husband and father, who lovingly but firmly governed his pious, deferential, and obedient wife and children.

19

Though the patriarchal family did not originate with the Reformation, certain aspects of Protestantism worked to strengthen patriarchy at both the household and state level. Protestantism, and in England, Puritanism, granted male heads of household a larger religious and supervisory role than they had under Catholicism, in which the priest could serve as an alternate source of authority for a wife or child, who could thus use one patriarchal structure to limit the power of another. (Wives in Protestant areas could turn to their pastor or city authorities if their husband was abusing his authority or acting irresponsibly, but authorities usually intervened only if the husband's actions were causing financial ruin for the family.) The fact that Protestant clergy were themselves generally married heads of household also meant that ideas about clerical authority reinforced notions of paternal and husbandly authority; priests were now husbands, and husbands priests. Most Protestant writers also gave mothers a role in the religious and moral life of the household, but this was always secondary to that of fathers and derivative from paternal authority. At the state level, the ruler was now in charge of the church, thus not only—as patriarchal theory had it— deriving his power from God but having direct power over God's deputies on earth. This situation made opponents of female rule in Protestant areas even more adamant in their opposition, although astute female rulers were careful not to highlight the issue. Elizabeth I, for example, commented that she had the "heart and stomach of a king," but chose the rather neutral title "governor" rather than the more clearly dominant "head" to describe her position vis-à-vis the Church of England.

This brief sketch of various issues has indicated that a range of relationships of governance in Europe from the fifteenth through the eighteenth centuries were clearly patriarchal: husbands and wives, fathers and children, masters and servants, pastors and parishioners, rulers and subjects, and (in some instances) employers and workers. The multifaceted nature of early modern patriarchy served to make it appear an inevitable part of life, as both God-given and natural. Thus those who were regarded as opposing or subverting patriarchy were described and sometimes treated very harshly. Female rulers were largely protected from the effects of such attitudes by their position, but women accused of witchcraft, scolding, or infanticide were not. The very ubiquitousness of patriarchy could also create conflicts, however, as cities and pastors defended wives against their husbands, or states ordered fathers to send their children to school, or guild masters "adopted" young women as their "daughters" to gain more workers and contravene laws

that forbade female labor. Patriarchal systems could thus work at cross-purposes to one another and be manipulated in ways that served individual and group interests.

CHALLENGES TO PATRIARCHY

The contradictions within and conflicts between patriarchal structures were joined in the early modern period—or even earlier—by intentional challenges to patriarchy. Very soon after craft guilds were formed, for example, journeymen in many parts of Europe formed their own guilds and objected to the power of masters (and masters' wives, who usually decided what they would be fed) over them. These journeymen's guilds were often banned by city and state governments, but they continued as clandestine or quasi-clandestine groups and maintained their power by refusing to work in shops that did not follow their rules. Such guilds—termed *compagnonnages* in France—were egalitarian in their relationships within the group, with members calling each other "brother" and electing their leaders, but they were also hostile to women's labor and often to women in general. Thus they opposed patriarchy among men but supported it in relation to women.

This same pattern can be found among English men who overthrew the monarchy and supported a parliamentary form of government in the seventeenth-century Civil War. Even the most radical groups in the Civil War never suggested that ending the power of the monarch over his subjects should be matched by ending the power of husbands over their wives. The former was unjust and against God's will, while the latter was "natural," as the words of the radical Parliamentarian Henry Parker make clear: "The wife is inferior in nature, and was created for the assistance of man, and servants are hired for their Lord's mere attendance; but it is otherwise in the State between man and man, for that civil difference . . . is for . . . the good of all, not that servility and drudgery may be imposed upon all for the pompe of one." Despite Parker's sentiments (which were shared by most of his colleagues), groups of women did petition Parliament several times. A few of these petitions were received respectfully, but most were not, and the women were called "bawds and whores" whose husbands should give them more to do at home. Such treatment led many women who reflected on women's condition to remain loyal to the monarchy and occasionally to point out the irony of Parliament's position. The writer Mary Astell, for example, commented: "If all men are born free, how is it that all women are born slaves? . . ." Why does Parliament "not cry up Liberty to poor female slaves?"

By extending political power to a somewhat larger group of men, parliamentary governments in the early modern period in fact heightened the gendered nature of patriarchy and the importance of sex as a determinant of political power and rights. Once the decision of an all-male representative body became the most important factor in determining who would rule, women even lost the uncontrollable power over political succession they had through bearing the next monarch. (The fact that parliamentary power over the choice of a monarch freed men from being dependent on women's biology was not lost on early modern advocates of republican governments or limited monarchy.)

During the seventeenth century, some thinkers began to question the basis of patriarchy in the same way they questioned other traditional institutions. In his *On the Equality of the Two Sexes* (1673), François Poulain de la Barre argued that men and women have equal capacity for reason and that differences between the two are a matter of inherited prejudices. His ideas were adopted by several of the leading figures in the Enlightenment, who argued that gender hierarchies were no more rational or tolerable than aristocratic hierarchies. The marquis de Condorcet, for example, commented, "Why should individuals subject to pregnancies and to brief periods of indisposition not be able to exercise rights that no one ever thought of denying to people who suffer from gout every winter or who easily catch cold?" For a brief period during the early years of the French Revolution, *lettres de cachet* were abolished, the property rights of women and children were improved, and women were granted the right of divorce; these measures gave women more civil rights in economic and marital concerns than anywhere else in Europe.

For most of the revolutionaries, however, the possibility of getting pregnant created a type of distinction unlike any other when it came to civic political rights. Whereas wealth, family background, social class, and status of birth were distinctions they increasingly took to be meaningless in terms of the limits of citizenship—the 1791 Constitution limited voting rights to those men who had some property, but by 1793 all men over twenty-one could vote—sex remained, in their eyes, an unbridgable chasm. Pierre-Gaspard Chaumette, a Parisian official, commented in 1793, "Since when is it permitted to give up one's sex? Since when is it decent to see women abandoning the pious cares of their households, the cribs of their children, to come to public places, to harangues in the galleries, at the bar of the Senate? Is

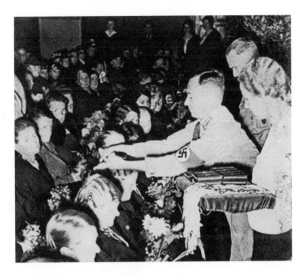

Rewarding German Women. A Nazi official bestows the Mother's Cross, 1939. AKG LONDON

it to men that nature has confided domestic cares? Has she given us breasts to feed our children?" In the eyes of most revolutionaries, patriarchal relationships of authority and governance among men were socially constructed and thus alterable, but those involving men and women were established by nature and were thus unchangeable.

Many women in Paris and other cities in France paid no attention to such ideas and actively opposed all forms of patriarchy. Poor women marched from Paris to the king's palace at Versailles demanding that the king sign a new constitution; they signed petitions and formed clubs calling for further political changes and, along with men, carried weapons in armed protest marches through the streets of Paris. Throughout all of these activities, they identified themselves as citizens—*citoyennes* in the feminine in French—and as patriots. The writer Olympe de Gouges drafted a *Declaration of the Rights of Woman and the Citizen* as a counterpart to the earlier *Declaration of the Rights of Man and the Citizen,* proclaiming "Woman, awake! The tocsin of reason is making itself heard the world over. Assert your rights. . . . This sex, too weak and too long oppressed, is ready to throw off the yoke of a shameful slavery."

Such actions and words did not lead to greater gender egalitarianism. Six months after they formed, women's political clubs were banned as threats to "public order," and none of the various constitutions drafted during the Revolution allowed women to vote. The conservative backlash after the Revolution led to greater restrictions on women's civil rights regarding economic and family issues as well as their civic po-

The Paternal Great Leader. "Beloved Stalin—Happiness of the People," poster by
V. Koretsky. The poster was included in the All-Union 1949 Art Exhibit in Moscow.
SOVFOTO

litical rights. In Napoleon's Civil Code of 1804—
which became the basis of many law codes in Europe
with the Napoleonic conquests—adult unmarried
women were relatively free to engage in business and
legal affairs, but married women were to be totally
subservient to their husbands. As Article 213 of the
Code puts it, "A husband owes protection to his wife,
a wife obedience to her husband." Napoleon himself
suggested that this article ought to be read aloud at
weddings, for in a century when women "forgot the
sense of their inferiority it was important to remind
them frankly of the submission they owe to the man
who is to become the arbiter of their fate."

Napoleon's opinion on other matters was firmly
rejected throughout Europe in the nineteenth century,
but his opinions about the centrality of patriarchy
were accepted by men of widely varying political per-
suasions. The word "male" was included in laws regarding political rights, thus barring women at the
same time that such laws removed property requirements for male voters. Though some socialist thinkers
took Engels's attacks on patriarchy seriously, others
did not. The socialist leader Pierre-Joseph Proudhon,
angered in 1848 that socialist women were endorsing
political candidates, wrote

> The role of women is not the exterior life, the life of
> activity and agitation, but the intimate life, that of sen-
> timent and of the tranquility of the domestic hearth.
> Socialism did not come only to restore work, but also
> to rehabilitate the household, sanctuary of the family,

> symbol of matrimonial union. . . . We invite our sisters
> to think about what we have said and to penetrate to
> this truth, that purity and morality gain more in the
> patriarchal celebrations of the family than in the noisy
> manifestation of politics.

The labor organizations that developed in the nineteenth century often used similar language, arguing
not for women's right to work but in favor of a "family
wage" high enough to allow married male workers to
support their families so that their wives could concentrate on domestic tasks. Such wages were only an
ideal, and industrial workplaces often replicated the
patriarchy of the household in their organization.
Male overseers replaced parents as supervisors of production and often claimed the right to control the
activities of workers while off the job, ostensibly to
guard their morals and honor. In many industries,
young unmarried women and children predominated
among the workers, with hierarchies based on age reinforcing those based on gender.

Along with the affirmation, reinvigoration, and
creation of patriarchal structures based on gender, the
nineteenth century also saw the beginning of social
movements to overthrow these structures. Women's
exclusion from formal political rights sparked an international movement for women's rights, which gradually succeeded in lessening husbands' controls over
their wives' property and persons and, in the twentieth century, obtained voting rights for women in Europe. Social reformers increasingly called on the state

to intervene or at least get out of the way when fathers or husbands were abusive or unsupportive; divorce laws were slowly liberalized and programs of foster care for children established. Women workers sometimes organized their own unions or otherwise pressured the labor and socialist movements to address their concerns, recognizing that higher wages for women were a more secure avenue to economic independence than was a family wage for men. Governments eventually yielded to pressure by reformers and banned child labor in factories and mines; they were less willing or able to prohibit children working directly for their parents on farms and in the household, though mandatory public schooling acted to lessen this.

This slow dismantling of patriarchal structures was too fast for many people in Europe, and twentieth-century authoritarian regimes in Europe played on people's fears about social change to gain support for their own dictatorial powers. Using explicitly patriarchal imagery, Hitler, Mussolini, Stalin, and Franco portrayed themselves as loving fathers to their countries, who would reward their good children and discipline those who disobeyed. They praised women for their roles as wives and mothers—particularly as mothers, for they were extremely concerned with maintaining or increasing population—and promised a return to the traditional values of the past. Such rhetoric was successful in gaining them mass support and allowing the construction of states dependent on the will of one man to a level unimaginable to early modern patriarchs such as James I. This very concentration of patriarchy was a force for its continued erosion, however, for the totalitarian regimes continued to limit the power of fathers, employers, religious leaders, and other lesser patriarchs, just as the social reformers whose policies they attacked had recommended. Thus all patriarchal structures other than the state continued to lose authority, a pattern that persisted after the totalitarian leaders died.

Some social historians have seen this pattern persisting in Europe at least until the 1980s, for they view the state welfare programs which developed in most countries of Europe after World War II as state paternalism or patriarchy. Immediately after the war, such programs also promoted patriarchal relations within the family because they were geared toward a male breadwinner–female homemaker model. These programs became more egalitarian in the 1970s under pressure from feminist groups and some political parties, however, and their curtailment because of political changes and economic dislocations in the 1980s has, in fact, increased gender disparities as women decrease their hours of paid work and time for activities beyond the household in order to care for family members. The fact that women remain responsible for a disproportionate share of all domestic tasks provides evidence for analysts who point to the continued power of patriarchy to structure people's lives. They point out, as well, that nationalistic and ethnic-separatist leaders often promote a patriarchal family ideal no different from that advocated by Robert Filmer over three centuries ago. Thus, though the official legal and political privileging of certain types of men over women and other types of men has largely ended in Europe, patriarchy continues to shape relationships, cultural values, and institutions in significant ways. These differ in different parts of Europe, however, and it is difficult to say whether increasing contacts among people within Europe and beyond its borders will serve to shorten or lengthen patriarchy's endurance.

See also **Capitalism and Commercialization** *(volume 2);* **Gender and Popular Protest** *(volume 3);* **The Household; Inheritance; Courtship, Marriage, and Divorce; The Family and the State** *(in this volume); and other articles in this section.*

BIBLIOGRAPHY

Amussen, Susan Dwyer. *An Ordered Society: Gender and Class in Early Modern England.* London, 1988.

Bachofen, Johann J. *Myth, Religion, and Mother Right: Selected Writings of J. J. Bachofen.* Translated by Ralph Mannheim. Princeton, N.J., 1967. Contains long selections from Bachofen's 1861 work on primitive matriarchy.

Bast, Robert. *Honor Your Fathers: Catechisms and the Emergence of Patriarchal Ideology in Germany, 1400–1600.* Leiden, Netherlands, 1997.

Bennett, Judith M. "Feminism and History." *Gender and History* 1, no. 3 (1989): 251–272. Stresses the importance of explicitly studying patriarchy as a historical phenomenon.

Engels, Frederick. *The Origin of the Family, Private Property, and the State.* New York, 1972.

Fauré, Christine. *Democracy without Women: Feminism and the Rise of Liberalism in France.* Translated by Claudia Gorbman and John Berks. Bloomington, Ind., 1991.

Filmer, Robert. *Patriarcha and Other Writings.* Edited by Johann P. Sommerville. Cambridge, U.K., 1991.

Fraisse, Genevieve. *Reason's Muse: Sexual Difference and the Birth of Democracy.* Translated by Jane Marie Todd. Chicago, 1994.

Hanley, Sarah. "Engendering the State: Family Formation and State Building in Early Modern France." *French Historical Studies* 16 (spring 1989): 4–27.

Hardwick, Julie. *The Practice of Patriarchy: Gender and the Politics of Household Authority in Early Modern France.* University Park, Pa., 1998.

Harrington, Joel. *Reordering Marriage and Society in Reformation Germany.* Cambridge, U.K., 1995.

Howell, Martha. *Women, Production, and Patriarchy in Late Medieval Europe.* Chicago, 1986.

Hunt, Lynn. *The Family Romance of the French Revolution.* Berkeley, Calif., 1992.

Landes, Joan B. *Women and the Public Sphere in the Age of the French Revolution.* Ithaca, N.Y., 1988.

Lerner, Gerda. *The Creation of Patriarchy.* New York, 1986.

Merrick, Jeffrey. "Fathers and Kings: Patriarchalism and Absolutism in Eighteenth-Century French Politics." *Studies on Voltaire and the Eighteenth Century* 308 (1993): 281–303.

Miller, Pavla. *Transformations of Patriarchy in the West, 1500–1900.* Bloomington, Ind., 1998.

Murray, Mary. *The Law of the Father?: Patriarchy in the Transition from Feudalism to Capitalism.* London, 1995.

Pateman, Carol. *The Sexual Contract.* Stanford, Calif., 1988.

Roper, Lyndal. *The Holy Household: Women and Morals in Reformation Augsburg.* Oxford, 1989.

Schochet, Gordon J. *Patriarchalism in Political Thought: The Authoritarian Family and Political Speculation and Attitudes, Especially in Seventeenth-Century England.* Oxford, 1975.

Smith, Hilda L., ed. *Women Writers and the Early Modern British Political Tradition.* Cambridge, U.K., 1998.

Sommerville, Margaret R. *Sex and Subjection: Attitudes to Women in Early-Modern Society.* London, 1995.

Walby, Sylvia. *Theorizing Patriarchy.* Oxford, 1990. Focuses on the contemporary West, especially Britain, with some historical examples.

WOMEN AND FEMININITY

Bonnie Smith

The social experience of European women over the past five hundred years has consisted of productive activity in agriculture, manufacturing and industry, and domestic work. Simultaneously, reproduction and sexuality have also shaped women's lives, complicating their work as producers. Although conditions increasingly differed from eastern to western Europe, growing most divergent in the nineteenth century as industrialization and urbanization accelerated to the west, the intersection of reproduction and production remained a constant determinant of social experience. Cultural values and political systems as expressed in legal codes and religious belief constructed community practices that also influenced social experience. Finally, the march of history included the development of colonization and imperialism, the quickening pace of globalization, and the rise of consumer culture—all affecting the lives of ordinary women in Europe. These developments often helped produce social differences of ethnicity, race, and class, which also served as determinants of women's lives and of their social practices of solidarity and institution-building.

THE RELIGIOUS AND LEGAL BACKGROUND

Western religious belief and legal systems spelled out many of the social and cultural practices that communities and individuals followed. Although elements of Judeo-Christian doctrine proclaimed the dignity of women and femininity, religious leaders generally emphasized male superiority. As inheritors of Eve's sinfulness, women were pronounced disobedient, lustful, and physically foul. Institutionally they had no right to preach or to hold priestly or rabbinical office. The coming of Protestantism in the sixteenth century, while stressing the direct accessibility of God to all souls, nonetheless underscored women's wifely and maternal roles and simultaneously closed down religious orders that had heretofore offered women a realm for their exercise of spiritual and social power.

Religious institutions deemed that women's bodily functions needed special purification and monitoring. Thus, both Christians and Jews set rules for sexual relations, menstruation, childbirth and post-parturition, most of them based on ideas of women's unique filthiness. From these ideas developed the social practices of femininity, many of which remained in effect through the twentieth century.

From 1500 on law codes increasingly privileged men by giving them the bulk of inheritance (especially in land) and by stripping women of all possessions and property upon marriage, transferring ownership (though sometimes just the administration of property) to the husband. Although in some regions married businesswomen had the right to conduct business as if unmarried, in most places there was a law of coverture that merged a wife's interests and property in her husband's. This was part of a general Western trend that systematically impoverished women from young adulthood through old age by transferring wealth to men. By the onset of industrialization early in the nineteenth century modern legal codes were mandating the confiscation of married women's property and extending it to include all wages and other earnings of women. The system was reinforced by laws forbidding women to bring lawsuits, to serve as witnesses in law courts, to exercise full guardianship of their children, or to hold business licenses in their own name. Late in the century reformers, mostly in western Europe, tried to alleviate some of the worst abuses of this legal reallocation of women's wealth in a series of married women's property acts that allowed women ownership of their wages and personal property.

PATTERNS OF ECONOMIC ACTIVITY

Over the past five hundred years women's economic activity has changed dramatically, from a situation in which approximately 90 percent of women were peasants in a predominantly agrarian economy to the beginning of the twenty-first century when the majority

The Dignity of Woman. The good wife performs the spiritual and corporal works of mercy. Her eyes discern the honest from the false, her ears are opened by the word of God, her lips are locked against speaking harmful words. In her right hand she holds the mirror of Christ and in her left a tankard representing service of others. The turtledove on her breast represents her faithfulness to her husband, the snakes around her waist protection from scandal, and her horse's hooves steadfastness. "Any woman who has such traits / Will maintain her honor undiminished / And surely earn from God above / An eternal kingdom in heaven." Woodcut by Anton Woensam, c. 1525. GRAPHISCHE SAMMLUNG ALBERTINA, VIENNA

held service-sector jobs in an advanced industrial and information society. Several factors remained relatively constant, however: Women received lower remuneration whether in food or wages, while their entry into virtually any job category lowered the status and pay for that work; they often had the greatest responsibility for household work and childcare while working for pay; their economic activity generally took place in the context of a gendered division of tasks, although the assignment of any particular job to one sex or the other might vary from country to country or region to region; and finally, many experienced sexual harassment on the job.

In the relatively self-sufficient peasant societies of early modern Europe women tended to household chores like cooking and cared for vegetable gardens, barnyard animals, and dairying. Around towns they sold eggs, cheese, and other produce. Women who were serfs (unfree laborers) owed household and field work to the aristocracy of their locale. At harvest women joined men in cutting, bundling, and gleaning grain. In winter spinning, weaving, and sewing garments replaced outdoor activity.

Townswomen in the early modern period grew more numerous as commercialization, urbanization, and state-formation progressed. Within towns their work included selling in markets (in some cities three-quarters of all market people were women), domestic service, and artisanal activity of many kinds. For the most part guilds banned women from becoming master artisans, but in some crafts such as printing and carpentry, they could take over their husband's business when widowed. Because household and artisanal work was little mechanized, urban homes demanded much arduous labor such as gathering water and fuel. Thus, in early modern France one urban person in twelve was a servant and two-thirds of them were women, as was also the case in early modern Florence. Service likewise provided important employment for young rural women, who constituted two-thirds of farm servants assisting hard-pressed farm families. There was movement back and forth between urban and rural work well into the twentieth century as factory workers returned to their families for the all-important harvest or as underemployed craft workers headed to the countryside in the summer to work in the fields. At the bottom of urban society were slave women, brought by traders to the ports of Spain and other countries where they served as domestics, spinners, and prostitutes. Rural families as well might sell young daughters into prostitution in the early modern period.

Improvements in agriculture, the rise of landlessness (for example with the enclosure system instituted in seventeenth- and eighteenth-century England), urbanization, and the development of widespread trade in goods and agricultural products gradually increased demand for many items, notably textiles. Merchants in towns distributed raw materials for spinning to underemployed women in the countryside. From that time on productive work for pay at home accompanied the rise of manufacturing in a system called protoindustrialization. As domestic industry or outwork became a staple of advanced economies, women at home did an array of tasks from knitting stockings, making straw hats, and polishing buttons to late-twentieth-century outwork involving the production of leather goods and computer data entry. The most emblematic out- or pieceworker was the seamstress, especially prominent from the early nineteenth century on when the need for military uniforms in the Napoleonic wars led to the breakdown of clothing production into its component parts—collars, sleeves, buttonholes, etc.—which were then apportioned to individual outworkers. Because these workers were isolated at home, they were often exploited, with low rates per piece, long working hours in the event of high demand, and seasonal unemployment of up to six months per year. Outwork nonetheless allowed women to coordinate work for pay with childcare and permitted employers to profit from an elastic workforce while minimizing their investment in buildings and equipment.

From the mid-eighteenth century on the new factory system employed women workers. The mule jenny and water frame made practical the mechanization of spinning powered by a central source of energy—a cluster of innovations that brought entire families as well as individuals into the industrial workforce. Where industry hired families, a sexual division of labor held, in which women carded fiber and sometimes tended machines, while men repaired and also ran machines. Young single women worked in factories, their lower wages making them an attractive labor pool for what in its early days was an experimental and risky form of production. Sometimes these workers were housed and boarded (as in the traditional system of domestic service) and factory work could be seasonal, allowing women to return to rural areas for harvests. This was usual in pre–World War I Russia, for example. Unlike piecework, domestic service, or agricultural employment, factory work ran by the clock, paid regular wages, and followed a discipline partly shaped by the needs of the machine. Nonetheless, several traditional conditions remained: a sexual division of labor, lower wages for whatever work women did, and on-the-job sexual harassment. Paying higher wages than domestic service or the nascent service sector, factory work appealed to many women.

Overall, however, industrialization tended to reduce women's opportunities for formal work; this was the case for over a century. The displacement of rural production hit women harder than men. Even in the cities, domestic service outpaced factory work as a source of jobs for women. Developments like laws restricting women's (but not men's) hours of work further reduced demand for women. Most middle-class women did not work formally at all, while many working-class women labored only until marriage. There was some variation—larger numbers of women retained formal employment in France, for example, than in Britain—but the overall pattern was clear. Only in Russia did industrialization coexist with high levels of employment for women, both before and after the Revolution of 1917.

The service sector started to grow in the mid-nineteenth century, becoming the largest employer of women in the last third of the twentieth century. Consisting of retailing, office work, healthcare, librarianship, and other non-blue-collar work, the new sector reflected the growing complexities of management, the rising knowledge-based component of the industrial order, and the need to realize the economy's potential for consumerism. These jobs were said to appeal to women's desire for clean work, and many (such as secretary, bank clerk, and librarian) had been formerly held by men. As women took the rapidly expanding jobs, the positions lost status, pay declined, and the various categories of service work became female ghettos lacking any opportunity for advancement. Simultaneously, professionalization occurred in medicine, university teaching, and the law, and this entailed rigorous training from which women were generally excluded, and licensing, which also tended to disfavor women. These high-paying male service jobs or professions had their low-paying female counterparts—for example, male university professor and female primary school teacher or male physician and female nurse. Service jobs tended to go to young attractive women who lost their posts as they aged or married. Most service positions demanded literacy and numeracy, more accessible with the spread of secondary and university education late in the nineteenth century. The growth of the service sector was accompanied by the elimination of women from the top levels of business management. If some women had run extensive mercantile and industrial firms before the middle of the nineteenth century, thereafter men generally were able to keep women out of executive positions (and in secretarial or clerical ones) even until the early twenty-first century. Nonetheless, a few

women gained wealth or distinction as writers, artists, musicians, poets, editors, and performers. Travel to the colonies and other distant places also brought renown, as athletic feats, wartime heroism, or flights into space did later.

During World Wars I and II some posts opened in the higher paying manufacturing jobs (notably munitions) and in government bureaucracies, expanded at the time to militarize economies. The socialist revolution in Russia in 1917 and eventually the Soviet Union announced an expanded work role for women, especially in the drive to industrialize the USSR after 1928. Although much was made of Soviet women as tractor drivers and factory workers, the same segmentation of the workforce existed as in the rest of Europe. Only the jobs assigned women differed: they served as doctors and sanitation workers, for example, both of these low status, badly paid, and onerous work. After 1945 the Soviet bloc had approximately 90 percent female employment, and the percentage of women in the paid workforce generally expanded across Europe in the twentieth century. There were notable exceptions: Hitler and Mussolini professed to want women out of the workforce, but their policies actually resulted in driving them from good jobs in the professions and civil service to menial and low-paid work such as domestic service. After World War II West Germany prided itself that its women still not hold important jobs in industry and commerce. Mediterranean countries such as Spain also had a lower percentage of employed women, as did the Netherlands, which noticeably kept women from prestigious work like university professorships. By the late twentieth century part-time work was 80 to 90 percent female. As the welfare state contracted to reduce benefits from the 1980s on and as the lower echelons of the entire workforce faced competition because of globalization, more of the European workforce was said to be feminized—that is characterized by lower benefits and pay and a lack of security. Outwork in the growing information technology sector, also lacking benefits, employed an increasing number of women at home.

After the mid-twentieth century the arrival of large numbers of people from the former colonies changed the composition and nature of the female workforce. Since the sixteenth century women had served colonizing societies as slave and forced laborers who performed domestic, agricultural, and sex work for their imperial rulers. Some had come to Europe long before the late twentieth century as servants, free artisans, performers, military aides, students, and travelers. With post–World War II decolonization, immigration swelled, and while not all immigrant women

Agricultural War Workers. A group of women march to the fields in the Klishevo Collective Farm, near Moscow, during World War II. SOVFOTO/EASTFOTO

worked, many did. Most found that however skilled and well-educated they were, they could obtain only menial jobs, among them domestic service or low-level jobs such as janitors, nurses' aides, and sweatshop workers. Second- and third-generation women migrants were often similarly thwarted in finding decent employment, but many worked to ensure that anti-discriminatory legislation (some of it in the form of European Union regulations) helped to provide some kind of employment assistance, especially in reaching higher level service-sector jobs. Nonetheless cultural discrimination and the growing success of racist political leaders beginning in the 1980s often meant harassment at work.

SEXUALITY AND REPRODUCTION

The coordination of productive work with the reproductive, domestic, and sexual conduct of society shaped women's lives. Because of the pronounced, though varying, sexual division of labor in the context of a subsistence economy in the early modern period, the majority of the population lived in families and mar-

ried, with marriage and reproduction coordinated to family and societal needs. Arranged marriages occurred as late as the early twentieth century made by parents determined to create agricultural, commercial, or political alliances, usually with economic and lineage interests foremost. In England and northwest and central Europe, women married relatively later than elsewhere with their age at marriage somewhere in their mid-twenties in the late seventeenth and early eighteenth centuries. In these areas married couples generally lived by themselves or in a household with parents, while in eastern and southeastern Europe family members congregated in large multigenerational families. Women in these households lived in a hierarchical organization of female kin, dominated by the senior woman, although ultimate power lay in the hands of the patriarch. By contrast, married women and their daughters in northwestern Europe enjoyed greater autonomy and opportunity to be enterprising. By the late nineteenth century, urbanization, changes in agriculture, and the development of consumer society allowed more people to live outside marital and extended family relations. These conditions also loosened the grip of the family on marital, sexual, and reproductive behavior. By the late twentieth century even a family of two parents and their children was no longer the norm, as there were more single-parent families, the vast majority headed by women.

From the sixteenth to the twenty-first century several distinct reproductive trends were evident. The span of fertile years increased dramatically because of two phenomena: the falling age of menarche (the onset of menstruation) from fifteen to eighteen years of age in the sixteenth century to thirteen or younger in the twenty-first century and the delay in menopause from around forty to fifty or a bit later. The biological expansion of fertility resulted from improved diet and health. To limit fertility in the early modern period in order to coordinate family size with available resources, late marriage was a common practice. In addition women used a variety of potions and cervical blocks to prevent conception; they also practiced abortion and infanticide when unwanted conception did occur. Nursing children also inhibited conception, as did the social custom of sexual abstinence after childbirth and during nursing. Coitus interruptus was also known. After the mid-nineteenth century condoms (made more practical by the vulcanization of rubber in the 1840s) and the diaphragm (invented and perfected in the second half of the century) contributed to the decline in fertility. The spread of literacy expanded knowledge of other birth control practices, notably the withdrawal method, while scientific understanding of the ovulatory cycle in women allowed for more effective practice of the rhythm method. Abortion nonetheless remained common. In the twentieth century surgical sterilization, the birth control pill, IUD, and morning-after pill became available to European women. In the Soviet bloc, where especially from 1945 to 1989 other forms of birth control were less available than in western Europe, abortion was a major form of birth control. The average woman in the sixteenth century might have raised only two or three children to adulthood because of late age at marriage, a limited number of fertile years, higher infant and child mortality rates, and certain birth control customs. In the twenty-first century women raised even fewer children almost exclusively because of mechanical and chemical forms of family limitation.

In the early modern period reproduction constituted an essential component of femininity, defining what it was to be a woman and encouraging women to try to adopt the social roles of such cultural icons as Mary and Old Testament heroines. Reproduction was also a major anchor of female solidarity, bringing women together around childbirth. Child-

Caryatid. The woman upholds the family, while her husband reads the sports pages and children play. Cartoon commemorating International Women's Day from the Soviet magazine *Krokodil*, March 1984. FROM *KROKODIL MAGAZINE*

birth was attended by a midwife and occurred in the individual's living quarters with the women of the family or neighborhood playing a major role in the delivery. The midwife and other women were the main repositories of reproductive knowledge. Over the centuries the decline in fertility attenuated the equation of femininity with reproduction not only in the case of individual women but in terms of social knowledge, as professional medicine gradually brought pregnancy, childbirth, and childcare within its social orbit. Late in the nineteenth century 90 percent of births occurred at home; by the twenty-first century more than 90 percent occurred in hospitals and were attended by doctors. Knowledge and practices of childbirth were not necessarily better when controlled by women: midwives could deform or even kill infants in the birthing process, while they also were known to leave mothers permanently injured. Mothers themselves had many practices, such as a fear of cleanliness, considered wholly unwise today. These aspects of femininity and ties of group solidarity around reproduction deteriorated with urbanization, the rise of literacy and spread of public education, and the triumph of birth control. Childcare centers complemented public schools in diminishing the childrearing component of women's lives, while modern medicine and birth control lessened the bodily damage and pain associated with reproduction and femininity. One ingredient of reproductive femininity—breast-feeding—ran a more erratic course as it went in and out of fashion over the entire five-hundred-year period, with aristocratic and urban working women often putting their children out to wet nurses until the late nineteenth century. An ideological push for breast-feeding in the eighteenth century and scientific understandings of breast-feeding's health benefits in the second half of the twentieth were two elements that brought new, if not enduring, appeal to the practice.

Sexuality first shaped femininity in the religious production of feminine typologies—as either the sinful, voracious, or seductive biblical antiheroines or the biblical models of chaste virgins or reproductive exemplars. Because a subsistence economy demanded reproduction to be well coordinated with productivity, sexuality was sufficiently constrained to ensure replacement of the population within a well-regulated marital system. The legal translation of this exigency was to make women's sexual fidelity an important social norm with deviation punishable by death or imprisonment to the late nineteenth century. Sexual excess was a prerogative only of the nobility in this subsistence society, and noblewomen as well as men could exercise this prerogative. Sexual behaviors and norms were monitored by various community groups to deter premarital sex, sodomy, bestiality, old coupling with the young, and other practices that upset the reproductive system. Often non-heterosexual behavior was ignored so long as the individual functioned within the reproductive, heterosexual system—that is, so long as she married and had children.

With urbanization and the development of an economic surplus, illegitimacy became more common, constituting more than half of all births in late eighteenth and early nineteenth century in many European cities and becoming a widely accepted social practice by the twenty-first century. The breakdown of the heterosexuality-reproduction-marriage triad within the context of urbanization allowed for the public emergence of homosexual couples—for example, Lady Eleanor Butler and Sarah Ponsonby, known as the ladies of Llangollen, in the late eighteenth century. There are many indications of a variety of sexual practices and behaviors for the early modern period, and great discussion over whether those engaged in non-heterosexual behavior had a homosexual or lesbian identity. With the birth control revolution of the late nineteenth century, and the drop in European fertility by half, a group of "new women" emerged who often worked in the service sector, remained single, and set up domestic partnerships with other women. Sexual boundaries were permeable at this time, allowing movement between all-female and heterosexual relationships—the English writers Radclyffe Hall and Mary Renault described this fluidity along with its attendant heartbreak in their novels. Lesbians who lived their sexual identity shaped urban neighborhoods, organizing networks of sociability from at least the mid-nineteenth century. In addition, transvestism has long been an important sociosexual practice, sometimes providing access to male privilege and to partnerships outside social norms (though some maintained that these partnerships with their stereotypically heterosexual appearances were very much within those norms). Some observers believe that despite a greater variety of sexual identification, by the twentieth century there was actually less fluidity. Others disagree, citing the substantial majority of the population living in heterosexual marriages in the early modern period.

WOMEN'S SOCIABILITY AND SOLIDARITY

Patterns of sociability operated within a matrix of economic/class and reproductive/sexual concerns. Agricultural women in the early modern period came together around childbirth and childcare but simultaneously worked together in such activities as quilting or nightly spinning sessions during which social information was transmitted in the form of gossip, news, or storytelling. Marriages were also arranged, courtships begun, and transactions negotiated, as men and boys sometimes stood on the fringes of the nightly session. These also allowed sharing and thus saving light and heat. Because private interior space was limited and possessed few utilities, in villages and cities early modern sociability took place in the streets. Women gathered at water fountains, markets, and laundering spots such as riverbanks. By the beginning of the twentieth century solidarity continued to germinate in urban neighborhoods where women shared information on school policies, welfare programs, markets, and local affairs. Working women's solidarity matured in guilds, church organizations, mutual welfare clubs, and by the late nineteenth century in unions. A variety of unions existed including church-sponsored organizations and those attached to political organizations such as the Social Democratic and Labor parties. Mutual welfare groups and the earlier guilds had often tended to workers in sickness or provided death benefits. Unions sometimes played this role, but they also helped women organize around issues of pay and working conditions. The period before World War I saw strike activity, some organized by unions, among women workers: the work stoppages by London match-girls in the 1880s, or the Italian agricultural workers in the 1890s, or the protests by anarchist women in Barcelona early in the twentieth century. As the service sector grew, women telegraph operators and teachers also unionized, gaining some gender equity in pay after World War II.

Working women could not always afford the dues for union membership because their wages were lower than men's; nor could they take time from the double burden of home and factory work to attend union functions. So neighborhood bounds often brought activism in times of economic crisis, with working women joining women at home (whether working for pay in the outwork sector or not) in protest. In the eighteenth-century periods of scarcity working-class women launched food riots; market women marched on Versailles during the early months of the French Revolution and captured the royal family; in German cities in 1847 townswomen stormed bakeries and markets to protest the high cost of food; the protests of women everywhere during World War I kept the home front periodically in turmoil, ultimately playing a role in the Russian Revolution of 1917; under the Nazis women staged protests against scarcities, connecting one another through handwritten bulletins full of survival tips. On the whole, however, women's roles in the leading forms of protest declined in the nineteenth century. Men substantially dominated unions and strikes and led in protest voting. The rise of feminism in the late nineteenth century, though more vigorous in places like Britain and Scandinavia than elsewhere in Europe, responded to this context.

Aristocratic and upper-class women's solidarity revolved around different forms of social life. A small group of women participated in the social transformation of early modern European court life during which the certain refinements and rituals of etiquette replaced the crude and violent military style of royalty and the aristocracy. Early modern courts set patterns for behavior, including the establishment of rank and hierarchy, arrangement of marriages, maintenance of kin alliances, and institution of codes for dress and etiquette. As courts came to concentrate on state-building through political and economic mechanisms instead of through military control, women advanced cultural unification with their patronage of the arts and humanistic learning and participated in some of the religious struggles of the sixteenth and seventeenth centuries in which the social power of the state had a large stake. Using kin connections, notable aristo-

cratic women like the Guise in France advanced the careers of chosen men in their families. Noblewomen outside the courts often lived on isolated estates in early modern Europe, sometimes taking responsibility for the well-being of their families through farm management while their husbands attended to their military, court, and other political activities. They would often have responsibility for the village dwellers' health, for supporting religious institutions, and for educating children. Unlike court women their opportunities for intraclass solidarity would be few. As urbanization and state-building occurred, the nobility came to inhabit towns and cities, though not necessarily central courts, participating more actively in intellectual and social life. Holding entertainments and intellectual discussions in their homes, wealthy women (both aristocratic and upper-class) shifted social and cultural power away from the court center when they ran their salons. Such salons continued to have social, cultural, and political force until World War I, but never so much as during the late seventeenth- and eighteenth-century Enlightenment.

In the next centuries, middle- and upper-class women performed works of philanthropy, easing some of the real suffering caused by agricultural change, industrialization, and urbanization. They directed their work toward poor families, particularly in commercial and industrial centers, and made charitable work part of a feminine identity. Based on a new ideology of separate spheres, middle-and upper-class women spent most of their time in the home nurturing and providing a comforting atmosphere, while men forged the new capitalist order or engaged in politics and professional life outside the home. Some critics see the middle-class woman as primarily engaged in fostering adherence to new social rules for cleanliness, propriety, and consumption. The "angel in the house," however, quickly took her nurturing mission to the outside world as a distributor of charitable relief, womanly wisdom, or religious salvation. Although Judeo-Christianity had long mandated concern for the poor, the nineteenth and twentieth centuries witnessed the development of male and female benevolent organizations, sometimes tied to religion but also increasingly secular in focus. Women's organizations set up daycare centers and schools for poor children, distributed aid to poor mothers, helped wayward girls and orphans, and helped prostitutes, women inmates, and released female criminals.

These philanthropic organizations often had moral and religious foundations, but by the middle of the nineteenth century women reformers imbibed the secular message of the burgeoning social sciences. The sociological formulations of Auguste Comte, notably expressed in his ideas about "positivism," maintained that one could determine the laws by which society functions and then set policy to ameliorate social conditions. Positivism and other social science teachings led women to found schools of domestic science to teach poor women the "laws" of housekeeping, to do statistical surveys of various kinds of women's work, and to study the working-class household and at the same time try to make it better regulated and more cost-efficient. As factory legislation came to determine the conditions under which women worked, some women reformers started working for the government as inspectors of conditions in the workplace. And, as governments late in the century started national programs to improve the health of the working class, women reformers also moved from private philanthropy to government jobs. Increasingly women's role in this developing "welfare state" replaced their involvement in personal charity, although never entirely.

Education for these social roles occurred in a variety of places, in the early modern period especially in churches, in the public observance of rituals, and in the everyday productive and familial life of the household. Women taught their daughters the practical skills of a subsistence, agrarian society, while boys usually worked with their fathers. Both sexes learned family norms through observation coupled with additional religious lessons. With the growing importance of scientific, humanistic, social scientific, and technical knowledge, children came to learn not only these topics but sex and civic roles in school. Girls' education often lagged behind boys', but in many European countries, governments eager to inculcate civic and scientific values sponsored mandatory public education—often secular. The gap in home education and literacy closed in the nineteenth century, though school curricula did urge domestic duties and loyalties on women. Although wealthy women tutored at home could be intellectually accomplished, it was not until women were admitted to universities in the second half of the nineteenth century that higher education became readily available. By the late twentieth century the single-sex institutions of secondary and higher education had given way to predominantly coeducational high schools and universities. This expansion of education lay behind the emergence of the New Women who entered the service economy and eventually the professions. However, the media, including print media, radio, film, and television, also produced models of normative feminine roles that women could absorb or resist. By the late twentieth century both the media and the pervasive educational system were as influential as the family in the inculcation of feminine norms. Under fascism, Nazism, and commu-

nism an array of social clubs for children and youth also inculcated correct gender norms as part of political education.

Despite this array of institutions for instilling the rules of femininity, women's behaviors were often deviant or seen as such by communities, churches, and governments. In the early modern period some of the primary deviants were those practicing or said to practice witchcraft. Witches were those who by virtue of a sinful agreement with the Devil committed personal and social harm. Amid periodic outbursts of witchcraft hysteria, women were executed as witches out of proportion to their numbers, although some historians studying local outbreaks of witchcraft hysteria maintain that men and women were accused equally. Urbanization brought more secular crimes such as theft to the fore, much of it committed by poor women stealing anything from firewood to small items from the families for whom they worked. With the rise of department stores, kleptomania was a form of deviance attributed to women. Also in the nineteenth century some of the most spectacular crimes were those of women murderesses, whose acts were interpreted as stemming from a special female pathology originating in the reproductive organs. However, because the crimes of many murderesses involved close relatives, some historians interpret them as rooted in libidinal states—partly love stories—and in gender roles.

At the opposite extreme of femininity and women's sociability were those women who formed religious communities, whether conventual or informal, under Orthodox or Roman Catholic supervision. Many of these women come from wealthy or noble families. In the late medieval period, as abbesses or leaders of religious communities women held social and even political power. Women religious served social functions by engaging in health care, educational, or economic activities, or by providing spiritual services such as prayer. Some especially talented women religious, Teresa of Ávila for example, wrote meditations on spiritual life and on the social roles of women, often questioning the denigration of their sex. Protestantism saw women's social role to be within the nuclear family rather than in all-female congregations. Socializing children, including teaching reading and religion, became a fundamental part of these women's identity. Almost from the beginning, however, Protestantism's emphasis on the direct relationship of the individual soul with God inspired many women to preach and prophesy even to the point of social and political persecution. Although Jewish women did not undertake this kind of preaching, they were responsible for much of the sociability and ritual in their religion. From this

Woman Religious. A nun leads a group of girls in Barcelona, 1951. BERT HARDY/©HULTON-DEUTSCH COLLECTION/CORBIS

number of men, and spontaneous religious observances, such as pilgrimages and special devotions to new holy women, increased. Although this has led historians to judge that a "feminization of religion" occurred in the modern period, others note that religion remained a prime example of the gender hierarchy at work in social institutions; church hierarchies remained totally male until the late-twentieth century. Nonetheless, religious organizations provided a forum in which women could resist such norms, and in the twentieth century religion became a rallying point for resistance to Soviet rule, in the 1980s and 1990s drawing crowds of hundreds of thousands testifying to religious belief; many of these were women. Finally with the migration of women from foreign colonies, the social practice of religion such as wearing special clothing became a particular bone of contention. For secular leaders, headscarves and other apparel breached the secular social solidarity on which national unity depended.

The social experience of women in Europe over the past five centuries has revolved around certain constants: a gender division of labor; a primacy accorded women's reproductive activities; the development of social activism and solidarity; a constant practice of varying forms of resistance to norms, whether criminality or innovative styles of living or heterodox sexualities. Simultaneously individual aspects of these social practices have been immensely varied, often differing not only from country to country but from locality to locality. Changes occurred frequently, but the nineteenth century stands out as a period of particular change and tension. Restrictions on political rights tightened and work roles become increasingly circumscribed for women; at the same time more women had access to education, and birthrates declined. An ideology stressing women's domestic virtue served as an attempt to bring coherence to these contradictory elements. The expansion of political and legal rights and the opening-up of new work roles in the twentieth century relieved some of the tensions. A certain homogenization between men and women has occurred with the development of effective media for the transmission of social norms. Despite the rise of media and mandatory education, there has been a seemingly more rapid change in norms of femininity over the past century and even, some imagine, the development of a genderless society in the Western world and a turn to the disembodied sociability of the Internet in the communications revolution.

time to the twenty-first century, however, they experienced incredible persecution at the hands of Christians, peaking with the Nazi genocide but not ending even with the collapse of the Soviet Union, whose anti-Semitic policies continued in the successor and former client states. Historians judge that especially in the Holocaust more women than men experienced what has been called the "social death" inflicted on Jews under Hitler because they did not migrate, staying to care for aged parents, for example. And they were sent in larger numbers than men to the death camps and died there in larger numbers.

From the eighteenth century European society underwent secularization, during which a noticeable dimorphism occurred in religious practice. Women's participation in religion dramatically outstripped that of men, which is not to say that men stopped being religious. Whether in Protestant or Catholic countries men's social participation in religion diminished while that of women became strong. As examples the number of women in religious orders far surpassed the

See also **The Population of Europe: Early Modern Demographic Patterns** *(volume 2);* **New Social Movements** *(volume 3);* **History of the Family** *(volume 4); and other articles in this section.*

BIBLIOGRAPHY

Anderson, Bonnie, and Judith Zinsser. *A History of Their Own: Women in Europe from Prehistory to the Present.* 2 vols. Rev. ed. New York, 2000.

Bennett, Judith M., and Amy M. Froide, eds. *Single Women in the European past, 1250–1800.* Philadelphia, 1998.

Boxer, Marilyn, Jean H. Quataert, and Barbara Franzoi Bari. *Connecting Spheres: European Women in a Globalizing World, 1500 to the present.* New York, 2000.

Bridenthal, Renate, and Claudia Koonz, eds. *Becoming Visible: Women in European History.* 3d ed. Boston, 1998.

Clements, Barbara, Barbara Alpern Engel, and Christine D. Worobec, eds. *Russia's Women: Accommodation, Resistance, Transformation.* Berkeley, Calif., 1991.

De Grazia, Victoria. *How Fascism Ruled Women: Italy, 1922–1945.* Berkeley, Calif., 1992.

Duby, Georges, and Michelle Perrot, eds. *A History of Women in the West.* 5 vols. Cambridge, Mass., 1992–1998.

Einhorn, Barbara. *Cinderella Goes to Market: Citizenship, Gender, and Women's Movements in East Central Europe.* London and New York, 1993.

Engel, Barbara, and Anastasia Posadskaya-Vanderbeck, eds. *A Revolution of Their Own: Voices of Women in Soviet History.* Translated by Sona Hoisington. Boulder, Colo., 1998.

Frevert, Ute. *Women in German History: From Bourgeois Emancipation to Sexual Liberation.* Translated by Stuart McKinnon-Evans with Terry Bond and Barbara Nordern. New York, 1989. Translation of *Frauen-Geschichte zwischen bürgerlicher Verbesserung und neuer Weiblichkeit.*

Hanawalt, Barbara, ed. *Women and Work in Preindustrial Europe.* Bloomington, Ind., 1986.

Kent, Susan. *Gender and Power in Britain, 1640–1990.* London, 1999.

Lewis, Jane, ed. *Women and Social Policies in Europe: Work, Family and the State.* Aldershot, U.K., 1993.

Muir, Edward, and Guido Ruggiero, eds. *Sex and Gender in Historical Perspective.* Translated by Margaret A. Gallucci with Mary M. Gallucci and Carole Gallucci. Baltimore, 1990.

Smith, Bonnie G. *Changing Lives: Women in European History since 1700.* Lexington, Mass., 1989.

Strobel, Margaret, and Nupur Chaudhuri, eds. *Western Women and Imperialism: Complicity and Resistance.* Bloomington, Ind., 1992.

Trumbach, Randolph. *Sex and the Gender Revolution.* Chicago, 1998.

Wiesner, Merry E. *Women and Gender in Early Modern Europe.* Cambridge, U.K., and New York, 1993.

Wikander, Ulla, Alice Kessler-Harris, and Jane Lewis. *Protecting Women: Labor Legislation in Europe, the United States, and Australia, 1880–1920.* Urbana, Ill., 1995.

MEN AND MASCULINITY

Peter N. Stearns

The rise of women's history was predicated in part on the claim that most prior history, including social history, had focused on the doings of men. This was of course true. But the success of women's history and the insights it produced have increasingly made it clear that historical attention to men as a gender can be rewarding as well. Indeed, some probing of the nature of masculine standards and behaviors is essential for women's history, lest men become mere stock figures in a story of oppression or glorious liberation.

Men's history has not, to be sure, generated a vast literature as yet, and work on developments in the United States exceeds that devoted to European history. The subject of boyhood, for example, a crucial component of men's history, has yet to find elaborate European treatment. Fatherhood also needs more explicit treatment. Some findings are available, however. In certain cases they derive from more familiar segments of social history. Thus working-class behavior has been partially reinterpreted in light of gender issues, and what by contemporary standards is the highly sexist orientation of many workers has gained attention. Divisions among peasants have gender implications. The split among eighteenth-century Danish peasants, between land-buying peasants and those content to work less hard and drink more involves predominantly male behavior. Histories of crime, punishment, and disease cast light on male behavior and expectations applied to men over the course of recent centuries. The list of connections here is long, and it gains further detail from the discoveries of women's history. Studies of the sixteenth- and seventeenth-century witchcraft craze bear on masculinity, for instance. The disproportionate attacks on women as witches, usually (in Europe, as contrasted with New England) by predominantly male accusers, raise obvious questions about the relationship between this phenomenon and larger confusions in male perceptions of women.

Particular focus, in this still-young field, goes to the issues generated for masculinity by the industrial revolution. While "crisis of masculinity," as a concept, risks being overused (there are two candidate periods in the nineteenth century itself), male standards were called into serious question by industrialization, and a host of compensatory behaviors and rhetoric resulted.

PATTERNS IN EARLY MODERN EUROPE

Early modern Europe was clearly a male-dominated society—what some historians call patriarchal. Most men had clear and fairly traditional ways to find and demonstrate identity. Peasants became fully men when they acquired land of their own and were able to marry, artisans when they had mastered a craft and could set up shop (and, again, marry and sire children). Attitudes toward women could be correspondingly dismissive. A substantial division of labor was assumed. A French peasant proverb argued, "It is the husband who carries the stones, but the wife who makes the house." But lest this seem too benign, another proverb held that "It is easier to replace a wife than a cow." On the death of a spouse, as in most patriarchal societies, widows were hedged with restrictions, lest the property generated by their late husbands be jeopardized, while widowers often remarried quickly. Male superiority extended to emotions. Men could try to argue away bad behavior on grounds of anger, which was too powerful an emotion for women to claim; jealousy, an emotion stemming from a weaker bargaining position, was their best bet.

For the early modern centuries, beyond highlighting dominant patriarchy, three historical issues surface. First is the question of variety. Not all men were the same. In Catholic countries, a few men singled themselves out by holy celibacy, an interesting complication of standard male demonstrations. Homosexuals were officially reproved—Christian culture had become unusually vigorously opposed to homosexuality since the Middle Ages. But some homosexual communities existed in the larger cities like London and Paris. Policing of their activities existed, for example in eighteenth-century Paris, but was not con-

Honor. Men in a tavern have hung their weapons behind them. Fresco in the Catello d'Issogne, Val d'Aosta, Italy. Castello d'Issogne, Italy/Scala/Art Resource, NY

sistently harsh or effective. The extent to which homosexual options or fears figured into the lives of most men is simply not clear.

Variations in social class are more obvious. Aristocrats could indulge a code of male-based honor that was not available for most other men. Maneuvering to protect one's honor, and to extend honor-based controls over wives and daughters, was a vital part of aristocratic masculinity, showing up for example in duels and vendettas. In the Mediterranean, these standards of combative honor extended more widely, affecting even the peasantry and leading among other things to high rates of murder based on revenge. But in other parts of Europe, the distinctions ran strong. Differences between property-owning men and the growing number of landless formed another important distinction. If establishing oneself as peasant owner or artisan master was masculinity's badge, what about the rural laborers and permanent journeymen—many of whom could never marry and, judging by characteristic illegitimacy rates, did not usually sire children?

The second issue bears some relation to the first, and it involves the question of change. For example, the rise of wage laborers, without access to property, from the seventeenth century onward seems to have altered male (and female) sexual and marriage patterns. While a large percentage of men still never married, new marriage forms did allow some family formation and sexual expression for some members of this growing class. Another sign of change resulting from economic shifts involves the clear effort by male journeymen to exclude and vilify women as economic competitors in the crafts. Not only were guilds increasingly closed to women, but journeymen's rituals often gained a distinctly misogynist cast. Men were

reacting to economic threats to established masculine status.

Other kinds of change loom large. The Protestant Reformation, initially itself reflective in part of Martin Luther's relations with his own father, increased the importance both of the family (since celibacy was no longer a special virtue) and of the father within the family. Protestant men often claimed special responsibility for the moral upbringing of children, taking the lead for example in family Bible reading. Stricter paternal discipline may have been part of this picture, particularly between fathers and sons. In terms of images, Protestantism reduced Catholic emphasis on a suffering Christ and on Mary as intermediator, heightening the focus on a stern, paternal God. At the same time, Protestant writings by the seventeenth century urged affection between husband and wife, which may have softened this domestic aspect of patriarchalism in some cases.

A few historians have speculated about another, possibly related, kind of change in male behavior by the seventeenth century. The intensity of male friendships may have declined. As in other societies, traditional European society often featured dramatic instances of tight emotional bonds between two men, as comrades in arms or even fellow workers. Stories about this bond, which was often stronger than that between men and women, and the devotion and sacrifice it could inspire, were readily available. As the European economy became more commercial, however, men increasingly saw themselves as competitors, which limited this kind of boundless affection. The result was a pronounced shift in male relationships, which among other things helped turn men toward the family as their primary source of emotional fulfillment.

The third aspect of early modern history that wins attention involves comparative issues. Was the European version of patriarchal status for men at all distinctive, compared to other patriarchal societies? Christianity imposed some complexities, compared say to Hindu or Confucian (but not Buddhist or Islamic) traditions. Christian theology emphasized women as a prime source of evil, but also insisted that women, like men, had souls and could be saved. The distinctive European-style family that emerged by the early modern centuries has implications as well. Characteristically late marriage tended to emphasize the nuclear family unit. In this situation, husbands and wives may have had to cooperate in work more fully than was true in societies where larger extended families held sway. Despite all the talk of division of labor and female inferiority, then, in practice men and women may have interacted with greater equality and informality (beneath the aristocratic class) than was normally the case. At the same time, the late marriage age gave fathers greater power over sons, who could not normally assume full manhood, demonstrated by marriage, without winning property from their fathers through gift or inheritance. Tensions between adult sons and fathers ran high as a result, at an extreme leading to violence, more normally generating elaborate legal arrangements that would protect aging fathers against economic retaliation by their more vigorous sons once the older men lost the ability to administer their property outright. Exploration of European masculinity in comparative context is at its infancy, but some possibilities are intriguing.

THE IMPACT OF INDUSTRIALIZATION

A number of changes came together for men, particularly in western Europe, during the late eighteenth and early nineteenth centuries. They had diverse implications, some pointing to new opportunities, others dramatically challenging established status. The net result was a significant shift in male self-definitions as well as new relationships between men and women.

Dramatic population growth drove increasing numbers of men from any prospect of property ownership. The growth of landless laborers and the flocking of men to cities, looking for wage work, were the manifest signs of this new pressure. Even when men successfully won a livelihood, the impact on their self-esteem could be considerable. During this period, to put the point simply, many men could not replicate their fathers' version of masculine success, either as peasants or as artisans. One interesting result was an increasing "masculinization" of popular protest. Riots over food shortages, which once linked women and men in joint action, saw men taking increasing roles. This presaged nineteenth-century protest patterns, in which male predominance (as political rioters, union members, and strikers) was increasingly assumed. Another result was a reduction in the authority fathers

Combative Honor. *Brawling Cardplayers in a Tavern,* painting by Adriaen Brouwer (1605 or 1606–1638). Bayer. Staatsmaldesammlungen, Munich

had over sons. When there was not enough property to offer as inheritance, sons found the need to listen to their fathers' instructions dramatically reduced—antagonizing the old man made little difference to one's economic prospects.

Enlightenment ideas, pushing toward new kinds of political participation, offered new opportunities for some men. Except for the pioneer feminist writers like Mary Wollstonecraft, when Enlightenment writers spoke of the need to defend freedoms or gain political voice, they assumed they were talking about men. From the French revolution onward to 1900, new political rights and experiences were almost exclusively male.

Then came industrialization. Gradually, urban men were pushed into new roles as factory owners or as businessmen or professionals in an industrial context. The most striking general result, bearing on a variety of social groups, was a reduction of the opportunities men had to interact with children. Work was now located outside the household. Men might compensate to a degree by bringing their sons or nephews into their office or factory, but this did nothing to remedy the lack of time available to spend with infants. Furthermore, the burdens of factory work for young children, or the needs of education for middle-class children, quickly reduced the opportunities for fathers and sons to work together. Some historians have argued that, as a result, father-child relationships dramatically deteriorated. At the very least, they changed.

Women came to be seen as the primary caretakers for children. European culture began an apotheosis of motherhood, to some extent from necessity. Fatherhood was redefined, reducing its qualities of moral mentorship and increasingly emphasizing breadwinning. The good working-class father was the one who consistently supported his wife and children. Whether he spent much time with them or how he related to them emotionally faded in significance. For their part, many men abandoned claims of particular competence, at least with young children. By the end of the nineteenth century many French men claimed to find it perfectly natural that most primary school teachers were now women, for they had qualities that men lacked.

Working-class masculinity was shaped by the nature of work, even apart from the shifts in family life. Many aspects of factory labor were degrading by the customary standards of masculinity. There was no chance, for most, to rise to ownership. Workers would spend their lives not just working for others, but taking detailed instructions from supervisors. Deskilling was another important feature of factory life for many. While some workers could take pride in their ability

to direct machines, most found the loss of personally identifiable skills disconcerting—particularly if they came from an artisanal background. In some industries, like textiles, the lack of clear differentiation between skills for male and for female workers drove home the point that manhood was under attack.

In this context, working-class men developed a partially new and highly gendered culture that provided compensatory identity and pride. Considerable leisure focused on the tavern, where men could join with other men—women were often excluded outright. Tavern culture encouraged demonstrations of male prowess in drinking and, often relatedly, in fighting. This was a tough culture. As Clancy Segal, a British miner, put it in a 1960 autobiography: "The collier regards himself as A Man, in every department of his life. The slightest traces of femininity, of softness . . . of sexual ambiguity, are ruthlessly rooted out, or suppressed." Learning to be this kind of man was a vital part of growing up male, a target heightened in fact by the absence of fathers from their sons' daily lives.

Part of working-class male culture spilled over into relationships with women. Marriage became more important than ever, if only because the family made new sense in terms of division of labor, with men working, and women providing supplemental income but also taking care of consumer and household chores. But many working-class men (though surely not all) were abusive of women. Violence within the family may have increased as men came home exhausted, sometimes drunk. While rates of beatings may have declined by the later nineteenth century, perhaps because women were forced into greater docility, occasional wife murders remained a problem. In 1850, the typical working-class murder resulted from a barroom brawl, but by 1900, with men spending more time at home, the victim was most often a wife.

Demonstrations of sexual prowess could be part of this new culture. Women who worked in factories, often in partial undress, were often sexual targets. Sexual taunting was part of the factory scene, and though impossible to prove precisely, rape probably increased as well, if only because more young men and women were operating without close parental or community supervision. The vaunted sexual revolution of the late eighteenth century, among working people of both countryside and city, showed particularly in the increased rate of illegitimate births. Historians have debated the gender context for this development. Without question, some individual women found the new freedom to engage in premarital intercourse exhilarating. But it is likely that more of them found it something of a necessity, as a means of trying to win a man, while men found the opportunity to dally with possibly several women an exciting opportunity to demonstrate masculine prowess—as one German worker, Moritz Bromme, put it, "to become a Don Juan." Many men waited until a girlfriend became pregnant before committing further, and some never committed at all.

Male workers also strove to limit economic competition from women, a counterpart to their new economic vulnerability and their desire to prove themselves as distinctive breadwinners. Efforts to limit women's hours of work flowed from a sincere desire to make sure the home could be cared for, but also from a hope that, with limited hours, women would become less desirable as employment targets. Long union struggles over wages frequently invoked the concept of a "family wage," itself based on the assumption that men should be paid enough to care for the whole family, while the levels of women's wages mattered little if at all. This was the context in which most early unions and many strikes became exclusively masculine affairs, with women urged to cheer on their husbands and sons. Correspondingly, working-class protest often indulged in the language of masculinity, with strikers insisting to employers that they were acting against conditions "contrary to our manhood."

Masculinity in the growing middle classes had its own challenges. Here there was property ownership or possession of professional skill, so the problems of demonstrating masculinity were less severe. But successful middle-class masculinity did depend on considerable periods of schooling, which was not clearly a masculine pastime, and then on often-sedentary work that did not automatically reinforce one's sense of being a man. One reaction was rhetorical: discussions of business life often evoked images of hunting or war. Men were engaged in a survival of the fittest, in which every masculine strength must be mobilized against the possibility of weakness or failure. Another reaction was exclusionary. Women were removed from most business offices. Industrialists themselves noted that, early in the nineteenth century, their wives often did their accounts and helped supervised sales, as had been traditional in business life. But with success this pattern abruptly ended, save in the small shops. Respectable women were pulled out of work, increasingly confined to domestic duties. The masculinity of office work itself was suitably reinforced.

Here too there could be sexual expression. Middle-class men married late, so that they could establish the economic base for the family. Once married, they increasingly faced the need to limit the number of children born and this often had to be accomplished through sexual restraint. Middle-class culture urged men to exercise self-control. Growing concern

about masturbation enforced a discipline on boys. But sexual interests emerged nonetheless. Young men often patronized the growing number of urban prostitutes, and later in the century formed an audience for pornography as well. Sexual coercion of female servants or factory employees was not uncommon. While not applicable to all middle-class men, a sexual double standard undoubtedly developed, with women held to much stricter norms of respectability than were men.

Middle-class men also sought recreational outlets that could demonstrate masculinity. Some adopted aristocratic codes of honor. It was noteworthy that in several European countries, rates of dueling exploded in the later nineteenth century among student populations, which were becoming increasingly middle-class.

Growing interest in sports formed another key middle-class outlet, quickly shared by working-class men. Sports provided an ideal way to train boys to be men in a setting in which actual educational and work skills were not highly gendered. Sports also formed another way to link middle-class attainments with interests of the aristocracy, in contexts such as the great British public schools. The growth of soccer (football) and other sports, initially as opportunities for participation but soon as occasions for vicarious indulgence as spectators, owed much to the needs of middle-class masculinity.

Attitudes toward women reflected gender needs. Middle-class men might concede women's greater morality (though this was truer in Protestant than in Catholic cultures) as a recognition of some of the ambiguities of their own public lives, but they often also stressed women's frailty. The Hamburg businessman whose wife frequently fainted in public was not entirely displeased, for it confirmed his superior strength and authority. Arguments about women's irrationality went far back in western history, but they were trotted out more vigorously in a period in which dependence on education for economic success was growing.

NEW CRISES

Basic patterns of industrial masculinity were clearly established in western Europe by the later nineteenth century. Some have persisted into our own time. Some additional perturbations affected the turn of the century period, introducing a few new factors, while relaxing some earlier pressures. The results point in several directions and invite further analysis.

The rise of feminism reflected some of the earlier constraints on gender relationships, but they provoked additional change. Some men supported feminism, but others found it a new source of threat.

Working-Class Protest. The London dockworkers' Great Procession, 1889. JAVER KLUGMAN COLLECTION/MAC DONALD PHOTO LIBRARY

Feminism combined with women's advances in education—which had occurred despite male asides about emotionalism and irrationality—and their halting entry into the professions. For the working class, technological advances allowed women new opportunities in fields such as machine building and printing. In offices, white-blouse workers made interaction with women on the job, if mainly with women as inferiors, a standard part of middle-class work life. For some men, all this added up to an undesirable challenge, which must be bitterly opposed.

All social classes were now involved in new levels of birth control. Some men doubtless welcomed this as a relief to their obligations as breadwinners. Others, however, were frustrated by the new limitation on their ability to demonstrate procreative prowess. Groups of workers particularly associated with masculine imagery, like coal miners, were as a result slower to cut birth rates than the class average. Individual middle-class men were also disoriented by the new limitations of paternity.

Within the middle class, the rise of management employment and the decline of individual entrepreneurship could pose a new challenge to male identity. More middle-class people now worked for others, lifelong, than ever before.

Signs of stress surfaced in several areas. Growing male (including boy) interest in military toys and activities may have reflected new needs for male self-expression. Movements like scouting surged as a means to give boys a chance to develop masculine achievement in a world increasingly described by school and female schoolteachers. Slightly later, fascist organizations expressed masculine aggressiveness quite explicitly. Nazi arguments about restoring women to traditional roles and costumes were matched by the jackbooted masculinity of the Party faithful.

New concerns about homosexuality surfaced (and were also mirrored in the Nazi movement). Homosexuality was now scientifically labeled and regarded as a disorder. European and American psychologists highlighted homosexuality as a serious issue, and it became a growing concern for parents and boys alike. To be sure, opportunities for heterosexual expression gradually increased, among other things with the growing availability of birth control devices, but the new anxiety about homosexuality maintained some sense of constraint in this aspect of male life.

In the United States, the turn of the century decades also featured a growing, if halting, interest in new family roles. Time spent at work was declining. While male leisure life remained active, and partly separate from family concerns, many men were spending more time around the home. A downside to this was the increase in certain forms of domestic violence, both in Europe and the United States. But new attention to fathering possibilities was possible as well. In the United States, fathers began to grope for new roles, ultimately emerging with a strong emphasis on being pals with children. This seems not to have been the case in Europe, where the paternal disciplinary role remained stronger, and the friendly sharing of leisure pastimes did not so quickly develop. But how fathers defined their time with children remains unclear in the European case. One interesting straw in the wind: men began to report greater pleasure in daughters than in sons, possibly because girls seemed more emotionally rewarding.

TWENTIETH-CENTURY DEVELOPMENTS

The focus on the fundamental reshufflings of nineteenth-century masculinity has overshadowed historically informed evaluations of change and continuity in the twentieth century. Obviously, one key development has involved modification, if not elimination, of some characteristic industrial reactions. Masculinity no longer depends on keeping wives in the home, away from significant work opportunities. Male differentiation and superiority at work and in work rewards remain, but with much narrower margins. Correspondingly, the breadwinner justification for masculinity has been modified, which may mean that men need to seek other family roles. Within the home, also, gender differentiations have become less sharp. Many couples share consumer interests, home repair projects, and family vacations. Low birth rates and widespread use of artificial birth control devices condition male-female sexual relations, more in Europe than in the United States.

Several studies—dealing for example with Germany and with Holland—suggest a shift in men's parental style, dating from the late 1950s, toward a modification of traditional disciplinary authority and a more emotionally relaxed approach to children. This corresponds to the chronology of women's reentry into the labor force. It may correspond also with new concerns about men's health, associating with growing realization of the disproportionate male liability to coronary disease and stroke (this is a connection that has been suggested for the United States).

The rise of white-collar work and the growing public interactions between men and women, from school to office to leisure site, have produced complex codes of behavior for many men. Manners became more informal, for example in male-female interactions, but this was not the same as complete permissiveness. Men now had to learn more subtle forms of self-control, appropriate to particular situations. A Dutch sociologist studied the rise and nuance of social kissing as one instance of this new pattern. It became appropriate for middle-class men to greet certain women with a kiss, in contrast to the greater restraint and formality of nineteenth-century patterns. But the kiss should also be carefully asexual, demonstrating clear self-control. Knowing the right rules, now that they are less codified, becomes an important part of growing up male from the mid-twentieth century onward.

At the same time, important continuities persisted. They included a tremendous identification with sports and significant divisions in the identity and leisure cultures of middle- and working-class males. Emphasis on women as responsible for beauty continued an older theme as well, though with new particulars as a result of changes in costume and desired body shape. Even amid freer sexual behaviors, men were only half as likely as women, in countries like France, to seek emotional commitment as part of sexual contact; remnants of a double standard reaction thus persist as well. Contemporary masculinity is composed of this complex interplay between recent change and patterns inherited from past adjustments.

See also other articles in this section.

BIBLIOGRAPHY

Brandes, Stanley H. *Metaphors of Masculinity: Sex and Status in Andalusian Folklore.* Philadelphia, 1980.

Humphries, Stephen. *Hooligans or Rebels?: An Oral History of Working-Class Childhood and Youth, 1889–1939.* Oxford, 1981.

Leites, Edmund. *The Puritan Conscience and Modern Sexuality.* New Haven, Conn., 1986.

Mangan, J. A., and James Walvin. *Manliness and Morality: Middle-Class Masculinity in Britain and America, 1800–1940.* New York, 1987.

Merrick, Jeffrey. *Homosexuality in Modern France.* New York, 1996.

Nye, Robert A. *Masculinity and Male Codes of Honor in Modern France.* Berkeley: Calif., 1998.

Ozment, Steven E. *When Fathers Ruled: Family Life in Reformation Europe.* Cambridge, Mass., 1983

Stearns, Peter N. *Be a Man!: Males in Modern Society.* 2d ed. New York, 1990.

FEMINISMS

Laura E. Nym Mayhall

Feminism is frequently defined as the collective organization of women on behalf of women. In this respect, feminism serves as a subject of social history. But European feminism, properly understood, engages with intellectual, political, and cultural history as well, for feminism historically has been both political ideology and social movement. The development of feminism coincided with and was part of the global expansion of Europe, the emergence of political liberalism, and the growth of capitalism from the fifteenth century. Feminism, like other systematic critiques and ideologies such as liberalism, has become part of the common discourse of many cultures in the West, but its legacy and inheritance are often confused with contemporary meanings.

While the term "feminism" did not enter usage in Europe until the 1880s, the concept remains useful as a way of thinking about women's power and political authority since the Renaissance. The historians Tjitske Akkerman and Siep Stuurman have identified three criteria for feminist activity: a critique of misogyny and male superiority, a challenge to the putative naturalness of women's oppression, and an awareness of gender solidarity and the desire to speak on behalf of women. Drawing upon these guidelines, we can speak of feminist traditions, or feminisms, but must be careful to define those traditions historically, within the context of their time and with reference to other contemporary ideologies and developments.

We have only to look to the ancient Greeks for evidence of a long history of skirmishing between the sexes. Aristophanes's *Lysistrata,* after all, makes high comedy of this antagonism, positing a scenario where women uphold their respect for life by withholding sex from their men at war. Yet we would be mistaken to see in such gender solidarity the seeds of a feminist consciousness. The texts of the ancients are useful, however, for establishing the extents and limits of the feminist impulse as forged within the European tradition. Through the adoption by early Christians of selected elements of Greek and Roman culture, and the rediscovery of ancient texts by humanists in the

Renaissance, Europeans inherited certain ways of thinking about relations between the sexes, which rooted male superiority in mythology, science, and the law. Only after women had attained levels of education sufficient to leave traces upon the historical record, however, did they register objections to this sexual hierarchy and their subordinate status within it. Modern feminism, therefore, can be traced to the Renaissance, when a few highly educated women protested the deprecation of their sex.

RENAISSANCE FEMINISM, 1400–1688

Renaissance feminism produced a set of cultural discourses, participated in by men and women, about women's power and authority. A long tradition of discussion of women's inferiority existed within classical and Christian texts. The Greek philosopher Aristotle argued for a duality of human nature, positing the intrinsic superiority of the active masculine principle over the passive feminine. The inferiority of women relative to men underlay medieval theology, philosophy, and medicine. Between the fifteenth and eighteenth centuries, however, developments in Europe created conditions within which a number of increasingly educated and articulate women would challenge these cultural assertions of women's inferiority. The Renaissance's celebration of human potential, and the Protestant Reformation's elevation of individual spirituality, gave rise to a feminist consciousness. The development of an urban, educated elite created a constituency for the dissemination of these new ideas.

From the fifteenth through the eighteenth centuries, in what became known as the *querelles des femmes* (disputes about women), the educated daughters of humanists, businessmen, and clergy wrote to counter arguments for female inferiority and subordination to men. Christine de Pisan's *Livre de la cité des dames* (Book of the city of ladies; 1405) marks the first significant contribution of a woman to this debate. While historians disagree about the precise ori-

Christine de Pisan. Christine de Pisan at her desk. From
Harleian MS. 4431 fol. 4., c. 1410–1415. BRITISH LIBRARY,
LONDON/THE BRIDGEMAN ART LIBRARY

gins of feminism in the early modern period, the aesthetic beauty and analytic rigor of Pizan's text make it an important point of departure for discussions of European feminism. Pisan (c. 1364–1430) argued that the education and training of women, not their natures, made them inferior to men. She argued for women's inborn equality with men, based on women's virtue, a point she illustrated with reference to prominent women from the Bible, fables, and history. Women's subordination, she asserted, resulted not from women's natural inferiority but from men's envy of women's virtue. Only cultural customs and practices perpetuated women's position relative to men's.

A number of European women elaborated upon these arguments, including the French writer Marie de Gournay (1566–1645), the Venetian poet Lucrezia Marinella (1571–1653), and the British playwright Aphra Behn (1640–1689). These early feminists wrote in a variety of genres, each contradicting notions of women's inferiority inherited from classical authors and Christian texts and arguing that women were fully human, not restricted by their natures or biology. This early feminist movement was largely literary and phil-

osophical and did not involve ordinary women in large numbers. However, as historians have shown, an impressive number of feminist texts were produced between 1400 and 1688, with a predominance of texts by Italian authors in the fifteenth century, and from Britain, France, and the German-speaking lands in the sixteenth century. Thus, for over two hundred years, Renaissance feminism generated vibrant debate about the status of women relative to men.

ENLIGHTENMENT FEMINISM, 1689–1789

New ways of discussing the power and authority of women emerged during the Enlightenment movement that swept all of Europe in the late seventeenth century. Discussion of "women's nature" took place within the context of a rationalist, scientific discourse; changing conceptions of political obligation; and the worldwide imperial expansion of Europe. Enlightenment feminism represented a veritable explosion of feminist discourse and a shift in argumentation from early critiques of misogyny to specific proposals for freeing women from men's control. Women participated in Enlightenment feminist discourse in greater numbers as well, as hostesses for intellectual exchange in salons and as authors and readers. The period witnessed dramatic increases in literacy among European women (from 14 to 27 percent in some regions), in the publication of books, periodicals, and tracts by women authors, and in private book ownership.

Revolutions in science and politics and the global expansion of Europe challenged hierarchical assumptions about women's natural inferiority. Applying the French philosopher René Descartes's critique of ordinary experience to social life, the Frenchman François Poulain de la Barre argued in the 1670s for a distinction between the sexed body and the unsexed mind. John Locke's contract theory, which replaced divine authority with that of natural rights, not only limited the power of monarchs, it also established the marital relationship as a voluntary agreement entered into by consenting partners. The expansion of Europe into Africa, the Indian subcontinent, and the New World led to comparative analyses of women across cultures and set enlightened Europe on a mission to civilize the rest of the world. An emerging feminism was part of the gospel.

Enlightenment feminists critiqued three aspects of women's subordination, proposing alternatives to existing structures. All three expanded the scope of the Enlightenment's challenge to tradition and to institutions of church and state. First, men and women examined the idea that husbands possessed natural authority over their wives. The English writer Mary Astell, the French jurist Montesquieu, and the French novelists Marie-Jeanne Riccoboni and Jeanne-Marie le Prince de Beaumont argued that male dominion in marriage violated natural law and human equality. Second, debate about women's education emerged in response to the French philosophe Jean-Jacques Rousseau's didactic novels of the 1760s, *Émile* and *Julie,* in which Rousseau proposed that the ideal education for women prepared them to serve men. Feminist writers such as Charlotte Nordenflycht in Sweden, Mary Astell in England, and Josefa Amar y Borbón in Spain asserted women's intellectual capacity and their unique moral and maternal qualifications for educating citizens. Third, the controversy over women's political authority gave rise to a quantity of prescriptive literature, in every European context, advising women to be virtuous and obedient, and a less prolific but influential set of texts asserting women's capacity for public office, military service, and voting.

Enlightenment feminism bequeathed a complex legacy to subsequent generations. Largely a cultural and political discourse engaging elite women, it nevertheless gave women access to universal notions of justice, equality, and freedom, while simultaneously emphasizing women's difference from men. Never a large-scale social movement, Enlightenment feminism created a discourse among educated men and women that celebrated women's sexual difference while rejecting traditional notions of sexual hierarchy.

THE FRENCH REVOLUTION, 1789–1815

The French Revolution marks a turning point in the modern history of European feminism. The Revolution's political theory engaged directly with the power and authority of women, and for the first time, a wide cultural discourse about women's citizenship emerged in France in which women played a large role. The French Revolution was only part of a wave of democratic revolutions of the late eighteenth century, in the Americas and Europe, in which bourgeois men articulated political grievances that were then extended by some women and men on behalf of women. Nevertheless, the French Revolution left an ambiguous legacy for feminism. The Revolution never fulfilled its promise, for women or men, but women's experience of participation in politics, and the set of rich and controversial texts inherited by the next century, circulated feminist ideas across Europe and indeed around the world.

Between 1789 and 1792 in France, changes in the legal status of women and their practice of active citizenship opened new possibilities for women in political life. The Revolution introduced legislation endowing women with legal rights unprecedented in Europe, including the right to own property and sign contracts in their own names. Divorce was also legalized for the first time. The expansion of women's civil identities granted them the standing, in name if not in fact, of citizenship. Women then claimed the rights of citizenship through membership in women's revolutionary clubs, formed in Paris as part of the wider club movement of the Revolution, but which eventually emphasized women's emancipation more specifically. In 1791 women addressed the National Assembly on behalf of women's rights as citizens, and in 1792 some women went so far as to claim the natural right of organizing themselves within armed units of the National Guard. On the streets, before the legislature, and in their own organizations, women challenged the Revolution's designation of women as passive—i.e., nonvoting—citizens and claimed for themselves the perquisites of active citizenship. Encouraged by revolutionary leaders in Paris, for a time women's participation in the momentous events of the Revolution promised them a new status as social and political actors.

The French Revolution was not only a social movement, however; it was also a literary and cultural movement. The Revolution inspired a flood of writing across Europe, in every genre, much of which addressed the relationship of women to civil society. Three texts in particular defined the juridical, political, and social aspects of women's condition into the next century. The marquis de Condorcet argued on strictly legal grounds for the inclusion of women in the political process in *On the Admission of Women to the Rights of the City* (1790). In *The Declaration of the Rights of Woman and the Female Citizen* (1791), the French playwright and monarchist Olympe de Gouges revised the revolutionary manifesto of September 1791 to include women, thereby revealing the implicit exclusion of women from the ostensibly universal language of the early Revolution. The English author Mary Wollstonecraft argued, in her *Vindication of the Rights of Woman* (1792), for the inclusion of women's virtues into social life. All of these texts exemplify the complex legacy of the French Revolution for feminism as women sought to force ostensibly universal definitions of citizenship to include the particularity of women's sexual difference. These texts and others also made analogies between sex and other forms of difference, including race, to demonstrate the reality of the embodiment of rights rather than their purely abstract expression.

Feminist success during the Revolution in appropriating masculine standards and active citizenship

47

was short-lived, however. The fall of the monarchy in August 1792 and the triumph of the radical Jacobins in May 1793 led to the suppression of women's political clubs and social organizations later that year. By 1804, consolidation of French law under the Napoleonic Code legislated women's subordination, revoking civil rights gained earlier. Nonetheless, the French Revolution, by making the status of women a central component of democratic revolutions, by briefly changing women's status before the law, and by allowing women to act as citizens, left a record against which feminist activity would be measured into the next century.

UTOPIAN FEMINISM, 1815–1850

Utopian feminism developed from within three different social movements of early-nineteenth-century Europe: socialism, evangelical revivals, and democratic and nationalist movements. These strands of utopian feminism grew out of male radical movements, and all appropriated language and imagery from these movements on behalf of women's emancipation. The term "utopian" was one used by Karl Marx and Friedrich Engels in *The Communist Manifesto* (1848) to contrast their own scientific, materialist understanding of socialism with earlier European movements for social justice. "Utopian" in this context thus refers to a range of early-nineteenth-century movements working toward the radical transformation of society. Utopian feminism marked a movement away from the French Revolution's emphasis upon individual and civil rights, to imagining new forms of social organization, of work and family life, of production and reproduction.

Utopian socialist movements in England and France connected women's oppression to economic and political concerns. Groups of men and women following charismatic leaders devoted themselves to the creation of new social orders based on cooperation, love, and peace. In the 1820s and 1830s, groups of Saint-Simonians, Fourierists, and Owenites grew and thrived in England, France, Egypt, and the Americas, with flowerings in Spain and Italy in the 1840s. Women working within these movements theorized connections between women's sexual subordination and the social and economic oppression of class. They drew analogies between bourgeois marriage, prostitution, and slavery, and they implemented innovative cooperative measures for child care and domestic labor.

Utopian socialist feminists focused upon women's difference from men and upon the social and economic consequences of women's sexual subordi-

nation. Irish Owenists William Thompson and Anna Doyle Wheeler addressed women's sexual repression in relationship to their lack of political representation. In an 1825 manifesto entitled *Appeal of One Half the Human Race, Women, against the Pretensions of the Other Half, Men, to Retain Them in Political and Thence in Civil and Domestic Slavery,* they argued against the notion that women's interests were subsumed under their husbands', countering that women should have equality of political representation. Thompson and Wheeler argued as well for the collectivization and mechanization of labor to aid women in child care and, ultimately, for the abolition of the wage relation through the eradication of private capital.

Evangelical revivals in Europe, both Protestant and Catholic, produced other groupings of utopian feminists. Religious dissenters formed breakaway groups in which men and women developed social and political critiques of women's roles in modern society. These included the Radical Utilitarians in London, Quaker prayer meetings in the United States and Britain, charity organizations in Holland and Switzerland, and Free Protestants and German Catholics in the German-speaking lands. Members of these groups considered new modes of social organization, giving women leadership roles in their communities. Women sat on councils, edited journals, circulated petitions, and worked for adult education. Radical Utilitarians in Britain went so far as to argue for the inclusion of female suffrage on the Chartist platform of demands in the 1840s. Involvement of these evangelical organizations in the international antislavery movement imbued their rhetoric with a vocabulary with which they could discuss domestic relationships; analogies between women's condition and that of chattel slaves frequently characterized their critique of women's position in society. Feminists in subsequent organizations would claim the movement of women on behalf of the abolition of slavery as an important precursor to later feminist activity.

A final grouping of utopian feminists grew out of the democratic and nationalist movements flourishing during the 1848 revolutions in Europe. Working- and middle-class women in the German-speaking lands, in Poland, Italy, and Czechoslovakia, formed political clubs and mobilized around a variety of issues, including the abolition of serfdom and the future emancipation of their nation-states. Women also played a central role in the radical democratic Chartist movement in England. While much of this feminist activity was stimulated by concern for the deplorable social conditions arising out of early industrialization, its focus was upon democratic issues and bridging social distance between women of the middle and working classes. The failure of the 1848 revolutions to effect real, democratic change signaled the collapse of these feminists' attempts at social and political transformation.

LIBERAL FEMINISM, 1850–1890

By 1850, what contemporaries called "the woman question" had entered mainstream political debate and shaped a range of social and political questions. From the growing political assertiveness of the middle class and the end of cross-class political coalitions after the revolutions of 1848 emerged a feminist movement at midcentury with largely liberal, evangelical Protestant, middle-class proponents and goals. The mid-nineteenth-century movement was the first mass organization of feminism as a social movement, mobilizing thousands of women across Europe in a number of different causes. These middle-class women organized on behalf of women's rights, attacked the subordinate legal status of women, and challenged women's exclusion from higher education and professional employment. They mounted moral reform campaigns against prostitution and felt empowered to speak for other women, exploiting growing European empires abroad for professional development in fields like teaching and medicine.

Liberal feminists across Europe engaged in a variety of efforts at expanding the civil status of women. Reform of the divorce laws and of laws regarding married women's property and custody of children figured prominently in the midcentury movement. Feminists viewed education as a central component of elevating women's status and made the secondary education of girls, and then the university education of young women, a priority of their activism. Educational reform and a demographic situation of "surplus" women at midcentury led to widening expectations of and demands for women's professional opportunities. The period between 1850 and 1920 witnessed a flowering of suffrage campaigns, beginning in Norway in the 1830s, France in the 1840s, and Britain and Sweden in the 1850s. By the turn of the century, European women participated actively in political life at the local level and pressed for inclusion at the national level.

Feminists mobilized also in the realm of social reform, with women's philanthropic work bridging the gap between feminism and bourgeois society. The diagnosis of prostitution as a social problem in the 1860s and 1870s prompted liberal evangelical Protestants in England and Switzerland, and Catholics and freethinkers in Paris, to form the International Abolitionist Federation in Geneva in 1877 for the eradication of prostitution. Feminists mounted numerous social purity campaigns across Europe, urging an end to the sexual victimization of women and the adoption of a universal and strict moral code among men and women.

Feminists combined these political and moral imperatives in campaigns that simultaneously expanded the roles of middle-class European women in colonial contexts and engaged them as imperial actors. Arguing for the right and obligation of women's participation in the imperial nation, feminists in Germany, Britain, and France sought positions as doctors and teachers in Europe's Asian and African colonies. British feminists based arguments for women's suffrage on the assertion of white women's responsibilities to their less advantaged sisters and brothers of color.

The textual production of liberal feminism exceeded the output of earlier periods. The feminist press, important throughout the nineteenth century for circulating ideas and creating community, flourished in Switzerland, Italy, France, and Britain from the 1860s. Important feminist theorists of this period included the English philosopher John Stuart Mill, whose *Subjection of Women* (1869) analyzed the marital relationship as potentially analogous to both slavery and tyranny and urged the enfranchisement of women as remedy. The French dramatist Ernest Legouvé argued in *Histoire morale des femmes* (The moral history of women; 1849) for the protection of separate but equal spheres in family and social life and for reforms in education and the law on the grounds of women's maternal function.

"NEW WOMEN," 1890–1918

By the late nineteenth century, the expanding political activism of working- and middle-class women, an increase in the number of women who never married, and a marked decline in the European birthrate fostered cultural anxiety about women's changing roles. New conceptions of women emerged, along with bolder feminist critiques of marriage and women's role within the family. Feminists organized nationally and internationally on behalf of women's political rights in suffrage movements across Europe and the white settler colonies, in defense of women's economic opportunities in socialist organizations, and in support of their sisters at home and abroad. Some national variations continued in the strengths and arguments of feminist movements, for example between countries of Protestant and those of Catholic traditions.

The "New Woman" figured largely as a literary type in the fiction of the 1890s and served as a vehicle

Suffrage Militancy. Emmeline Pankhurst (1858–1928) addresses a crowd in Trafalgar Square, London, 13 October 1908. MUSEUM OF LONDON

for discussing changing expectations about women. At the heart of the "New Woman" controversy raged a debate about marriage, begun in 1879 with *A Doll's House,* the Swedish playwright Henrik Ibsen's shocking portrayal of the spiritual and moral vacuum at the heart of bourgeois marriage. Ibsen's critique was reiterated by the English suffragist Cicely Hamilton, whose 1909 *Marriage as a Trade* argued that marriage differed from prostitution only in the social approval attached to its status. Concern about the fate of bourgeois marriage was linked to anxieties about the falling birthrate. Since the Franco-Prussian conflict of 1871, European nations had understood military preparedness as a function of the available conscripts. Contemporaries pointed to declining birthrates among bourgeois families, falling most precipitously in France, from twenty-six per thousand in 1870 to twelve per thousand in 1918. Feminists joined the state in proposing maternal endowment as a way to solve the population problem. Feminists in Britain, France, and Italy walked a difficult line as they sought to improve conditions for mothers, protect children, attain state recognition for female work and values, and challenge the exclusive power of fathers over women and children.

While discussion of issues like sexuality and reproduction became more pointed in the feminist and mainstream press, women's political activism itself took more extreme forms. Suffrage militancy, most pronounced in Great Britain but emulated around the world, included violence against property and various forms of passive resistance, such as resistance to registration by the census and to payment of taxes. Inspired by August Bebel's best-selling text, *Die Frau und der Sozialismus* (Woman and socialism; 1879), which argued that women's oppression, like class oppression, was rooted in historical circumstance and hence could be overcome, working- and lower-middle-class feminists in Britain, France, Germany, Italy, and Russia mobilized in ever larger numbers in socialist organizations. And middle-class women throughout Europe discovered new opportunities to act on behalf of the public good through the philanthropic work they pursued in secular and religious organizations. Women's work on behalf of other women and children gave them valuable managerial experience and created ambiguous zones between home and public life, zones later filled by the activities of welfare states.

The late nineteenth century produced unprecedented international feminist cooperation. The formation of transnational feminist organizations was spurred by the continuing expansion of Europe into Africa and the Indian subcontinent and by the desire of European women to speak for women of color. European feminists, however, cast their efforts in universalist language as the creation of a global sisterhood.

To name but the largest of these organizations, feminists organized to gain women's rights around the world in the International Council of Women (1888) and the International Woman Suffrage Alliance (1904), and in opposition to war in the Women's International League for Peace and Freedom (1915). Many of these organizations expanded beyond their original mandates in the years following World War I, gradually becoming more inclusive and less hierarchical.

FEMINISM IN THE TWENTIETH CENTURY, 1918–1968

In the years following World Wars I and II, feminism in Europe was framed within the context of maternity as women struggled to reconcile their roles as wives and mothers with a desire for political and economic independence. Women negotiated the meanings of motherhood against a backdrop of tremendous loss and anxiety—about the continuation of democracy after World War I, and the future of Europe after World War II. The loss of life experienced by European nations during the World War I gave impetus to postwar concern about the birthrate, while the emerging disciplines of psychology and sexology encouraged the development of heterosexual companionate marriage. Feminists continued their campaigns to expand the democratic franchise to include women. Historians have seen this period as one of relative decline for feminist activity, but the quantity of research demonstrates the extent to which feminist organizations and institutions were maintained and developed.

In the period between the wars, feminists across Europe argued that women's economic dependence upon men contributed to women's lack of employment opportunities and the devaluation in status of women's unwaged labor in the home. Campaigns for both equal employment opportunities and family endowment benefits for mothers and children emerged from this analysis. Much feminist activity of the interwar years was devoted to fighting new restrictions on married women's work and to expanding the range of possibilities for women's professional development. A major shift in marital relations became apparent with the success of Marie Stopes's 1918 best-seller, *Married Love: A New Contribution to the Solution of Sex Difficulties,* which sold 200,000 copies in its first two weeks, and a million by 1939. Stopes set as a goal the births of only happy, healthy, and desired children. She viewed birth control as a means to improve maternal health and advocated contraceptive use only for married women. Stopes opened numerous birth control clinics in Britain. Similar work was done in France

Simone de Beauvoir. Photograph by Henri Cartier-Bresson, 1944. ©HENRI CARTIER-BRESSON/MAGNUM PHOTOS

after World War II by the Association Maternité Heureuse (Happy motherhood association), which led the fight to reform a 1920 law banning contraception. Feminists in these years approached the question of contraception as a women's health issue rather than a question of rights. Companionate marriage, mutually pleasurable sexual relations, and controlled fertility, while becoming part of feminist thinking for the first time, were not beliefs widely held by feminists, and would not become so until the years following World War II.

The most influential feminist text published during these years was Simone de Beauvoir's *Le deuxième sexe* (*The Second Sex*; 1949). Beauvoir took on women's oppression within the private sphere, critiquing the limitations of marriage, the family, and housework in women's lives. The influence of *The Second Sex,* however, was felt only in the generation of women coming of age during the next phase of feminism, the women's liberation movement. Far more characteristic of the period was *Women's Two Roles*

(1956), an attempt by Alva Myrdal and Viola Klein to reconcile women's waged work and familial responsibilities.

THE WOMEN'S LIBERATION MOVEMENT AND AFTER, 1968–1980

The resurgence of feminist activity around the world in the late 1960s is frequently referred to as "second wave feminism," implicitly connecting late-twentieth-century feminism with earlier campaigns for women's political rights, most notably for the suffrage. The women's liberation movement, however, grew from the specific historical circumstances of Europe after World War II. Stagnation of male wages and European commitment to fair competition for men and women in the workforce made waged labor for women increasingly desirable and, indeed, in many cases imperative. The development of a contraceptive pill gave women control over their fertility and meant that for the first time in human history, women could decide to have sexual relations without unwanted pregnancies. The women's liberation movement was part of a number of protest movements known as the "New Left," which emerged in the period of affluence characteristic of European nations after 1960. Women active in organizations of students, trade unionists, and antiwar activists experienced great frustration with men's inability to recognize women's sexual oppression as an issue.

The women's liberation movement utilized consciousness-raising as a means of educating women about the political dimensions of their own experiences. "The personal is political," the movement's slogan, exemplified feminists' attempt to raise awareness of the political significance of issues traditionally deemed outside of politics, such as sexuality and reproduction. Feminists fought for access to contraception and abortion, against the sexual victimization of women, and for an end to discrimination against lesbians in the arenas of employment, health care, and child custody. Ecofeminism explicitly linked women's condition to that of the earth, with large numbers of women belonging to and supporting the Green Party in Germany and protesting the United States' cruise missile installation at Greenham Common in England.

By 1980, feminism had entered mainstream European culture and had become a familiar concept in most countries. In the 1980s more than half a million women in West Germany, France, and Italy marched in favor of abortion rights. The United Nations declared the years from 1975 to 1985 the decade of women, sponsoring conferences in Mexico City, Copenhagen, and Nairobi, where the public visibility of women's issues and networks of activists brought women's condition before the world. And in Germany by the end of the decade, abortion rights became a significant issue in negotiations over national unification.

This phase of feminist activity implemented forms of protest used by other New Left movements, including spontaneous demonstrations. More organized campaigns, such as the "Reclaim the Night" marches in England and West Germany in 1977 and Italy in 1978, drew attention to the effect of violence against women upon their personal freedom. Feminists also engaged in acts of civil disobedience, as in the 1972 open letter to the French press signed by three hundred women, attesting to their procurement of illegal abortions. The women's liberation movement largely sought change peacefully, with notable exceptions like the Italian group Rivolta Femminile, which argued that feminism and pacifism were not synonymous. Like other feminist movements before it, the women's liberation movement produced its own journals, magazines, books, and celebrities. And like earlier movements, this phase of feminism generated not only critiques of women's oppression but also alternative ways of analyzing the world. The creation of entirely new fields of inquiry, like women's studies in the university curriculum, is perhaps its most lasting legacy.

The women's liberation movement generated a number of texts analyzing the sexual and psychological dimensions of women's oppression and emancipation. Kate Millett's *Sexual Politics* (1970) explored male supremacy in European and American literature. In *Woman's Estate* (1971), Juliet Mitchell continued the tradition of linking women's subordination to other forms of oppression, such as class. Feminists also grappled with the oppression of race, particularly within feminism itself. The 1981 essay by the black British feminist Hazel Carby, "White Woman Listen! Black Feminism and the Boundaries of Sisterhood," challenged the implicit whiteness of feminist theory. French and Italian feminists, in particular, celebrated women's sexual difference in texts such as *Ce sexe qui n'en est pas un* (This sex which is not one; 1977), by the French philosopher and linguist Luce Irigaray.

POSTFEMINISM?

Opponents and proponents of contemporary feminism alike frequently characterize the 1980s and 1990s as postfeminist. With the institutionalization of women's studies in universities, attainment of voting rights for European women, reform of divorce and marriage laws, and the integration of feminist activists into mainstream politics, many people believe that feminism has reached the end of its trajectory as a protest movement. Yet many men and women claiming to be feminists would see in the term "post-feminism" a less sanguine assessment of feminism's accomplishments. Many feminists profess disillusionment with the gains women have made, pointing to the double burden of waged and household labor borne by most women of the working and middle classes. Women's roles in families, they argue, remain largely unchanged, with few men willingly accepting equal domestic responsibilities. Feminists also claim dissatisfaction with women's gains in the political sphere, pointing to the relatively small number of female representatives in the political process at both local and national levels in every European country. Finally, tensions exist between feminists in first- and third-world countries over cultural practices such as clitoridectomy and veiling, leading to a disavowal by many of the notion of a global sisterhood, for European feminists a unifying conceit since the mid-nineteenth century.

Yet perhaps the measure of feminism's accomplishments should be the extent to which it has become part of common public discourse. While many women claim not to be feminists, they simultaneously assert their right to the independence, equal rights, and sexual pleasure feminists have claimed for themselves over preceding generations. If the history of feminism can instruct us as to its future, then we can predict that a tension will remain always within feminism between women's sexual difference and their desire for equality, and feminism will reinvent itself continually in relationship to contemporary ideologies, current issues, and national concerns.

See also **The Family and the State; Sexual "Revolutions"** *(in this volume); and other articles in this section.*

BIBLIOGRAPHY

Primary Works

Bell, Susan Groag, and Karen M. Offen, eds. *Women, the Family, and Freedom: The Debate in Documents.* 2 vols. Stanford, Calif., 1983.

Bono, Paola, and Sandra Kemp, eds. *Italian Feminist Thought: A Reader.* Oxford, 1991.

Gordon, Felicia, and Máire Cross. *Early French Feminisms, 1830–1940: A Passion for Liberty.* Brookfield, Vt., and Cheltenham, U.K., 1996.

Waelti-Walters, Jennifer, and Steven C. Hause, eds. *Feminisms of the Belle Epoque: A Historical and Literary Anthology.* Lincoln, Nebr., 1994.

Secondary Works

Akkerman, Tjitske, and Siep Stuurman, eds. *Perspectives on Feminist Political Thought in European History: From the Middle Ages to the Present.* London, 1998.

Bridenthal, Renate, Susan Mosher Stuard, and Merry E. Weisner, eds. *Becoming Visible: Women in European History.* 3d ed. New York, 1998.

Caine, Barbara. *English Feminism, 1780–1980.* Oxford, 1997.

Daley, Caroline, and Melanie Nolan, eds. *Suffrage and Beyond: International Feminist Perspectives.* New York, 1994.

Duby, Georges and Michelle Perrot, eds. *A History of Women in the West.* Vol. 4, *Emerging Feminism from Revolution to World War.* Edited by Genevieve Fraisse and Michelle Perrot. Vol. 5, *Toward a Cultural Identity in the Twentieth Century.* Edited by François Thébaud. Cambridge, Mass., 1992–1994.

Frevert, Ute. *Women in German History: From Bourgeois Emancipation to Sexual Liberation.* Translated by Stuart McKinnon-Evans. Oxford, 1989.

Herzog, Deborah. *Intimacy and Exclusion: Religious Politics in Pre-Revolutionary Baden.* Princeton, N.J., 1996.

Jordan, Constance. *Renaissance Feminism: Literary Texts and Political Models.* Ithaca, N.Y., and London, 1990.

Kaplan, Gisela. *Contemporary Western European Feminism.* New York, 1992.

Koven, Seth, and Sonya Michel, eds. *Mothers of a New World: Maternalist Politics and the Origins of Welfare States.* New York, 1993.

Mohanty, Chandra Talpade, Anna Russo, and Lourdes Torres, eds. *Third World Women and the Politics of Feminism.* Bloomington, Ind., 1991.

Moses, Clare Goldberg. *French Feminism in the Nineteenth Century.* Albany, N.Y., 1984.

Offen, Karen. *European Feminisms, 1700–1950: A Political History.* Stanford, Calif., 1999.

Rendall, Jane. *The Origins of Modern Feminism: Women in Britain, France, and the United States, 1780–1860.* London, 1984.

Riley, Denise. *Am I That Name? Feminism and the Category of "Women" in History.* Basingstoke, U.K., 1987.

Rupp, Leila J. *Worlds of Women: The Making of an International Women's Movement.* Princeton, N.J., 1997.

Scott, Joan Wallach. *Only Paradoxes to Offer: French Feminists and the Rights of Man.* Cambridge, Mass., 1996.

Sinha, Mrinalini, Donna J. Guy, and Angela Woollacott, eds. *Gender and History* 10, no. 3 (1998). Special issue: "Feminisms and Internationalism."

Taylor, Barbara. *Eve and the New Jerusalem: Socialism and Feminism in the Nineteenth Century.* New York, 1983.

GENDER AND WORK

Merry E. Wiesner-Hanks

All cultures from prehistoric times to the present have drawn distinctions between men's work and women's work. In some societies these distinctions are so strong that individuals who are morphologically male but who do tasks normally assigned to females are regarded as members of a third gender. The link between gender and work has not been this strong in European culture, but economic institutions, technological developments, cultural norms, religious and intellectual currents, and popular beliefs have all played a part in shaping clear distinctions between men's and women's work. These distinctions have, in turn, determined how tasks would be valued, with tasks normally done by men valued more highly than those done by women, even if they took the same amount of time, skill, and effort. In fact, the very definition of "work" has often been gender-biased, with men's tasks defined as "work" while women's have been defined as "assisting," "helping out," or "housework." Some tasks done by women, such as the care and nurturing of family members, have generally not been regarded as "work" at all.

In the same way that gender history in general grew out of women's history, the study of gender and work developed primarily out of studies on women's work. Economic and labor historians whose primary focus was work were often more attentive to class differences than to those of gender; their focus was the male work experience, but its gendered nature was not analyzed or explored. This is beginning to change, but there are still many more studies that focus explicitly on women's work than on men's work defined as such. Historians themselves have thus contributed to the notion that men's work is simply "work," whereas women's is "women's work," but this is slowly changing as more scholars recognize and highlight the gendered nature of their subjects.

Gender hierarchies in the division of labor have survived massive economic changes in Europe over the last five hundred years, with new occupations valued—and paid—according to whether they were done primarily by men or women. This resiliency has led social historians into several different lines of investigation. One of these has been to search for the reasons why women's labor has been undervalued, a question historians began investigating as early as the 1920s. A second line of inquiry, which began in the 1970s, explores how economic changes, such as the development of commercial capitalism, industrial production, or the global labor market, were experienced differently by men and women. A third and more recent line of inquiry reverses the second, and investigates how gender hierarchies (or sometimes more pointedly stated, how patriarchy) shaped economic developments. In all of these areas, historians are increasingly cognizant not only of work itself but also of the meaning of work for individuals and for society at large. Thus they use as their sources economic data such as employment statistics, census records, business reports, union records, and account books, and also more subjective records such as letters, diaries, newspaper editorials, advertisements, and personal memoirs.

Of these three lines of inquiry, the second has received the most attention, with many studies tracing how men's and women's work changed as the result of new production methods, labor structures, kinds of technology, or market organization. Many of these studies focus on a single village, city, or region, and it is clear that any generalizations across all of Europe must be made very carefully. Innovations were often made in one area decades or even centuries after they were made in another, during which time other things that shaped gender structures, such as religious ideas, public schooling, political structures, or the availability of contraceptives, had also changed. The impact of a similar change in work patterns might therefore be very different in one region from another, depending on when it was introduced. Local studies have made clear that along with this chronological difference, other axes of difference such as social class, race, marital status, and age must be taken into account when exploring changes and continuities in the gender division of labor or the meaning of work.

EARLY MODERN EUROPE (1450–1750)

The period from the fifteenth through the eighteenth century in Europe is often described economically as "the rise of capitalism," during which larger and more complex forms of economic organization developed in some parts of Europe, leading them to become economically dominant. These new forms changed the relationship between gender and work somewhat, but capitalism did not generally alter the existing form of economic organization, which was based on the household.

The household economy and wage labor in rural areas.

During the Middle Ages, the household became the basic unit of production in most parts of Europe, a process some social historians label the "familialization of labor." The central work unit was the marital couple, joined by their children when they became old enough to work. Though in some parts of southern and eastern Europe extended families lived together, in central and northern Europe couples generally set up independent households upon marrying, making the production unit also a residential unit.

Until at least the eighteenth century, and even later in many parts of Europe, the vast majority of people lived in the countryside, producing agricultural products for their own use or that of their landlords, or for local and international markets. Serf households on the vast estates of eastern Europe produced almost completely for an export market. Agricultural tasks were highly, but not completely, gender specific, though exactly which tasks were regarded as female and which as male varied widely throughout Europe. These gender divisions were partly the result of physical differences, with men generally doing tasks that required a great deal of upper-body strength, such as cutting grain with a scythe; they were partly the result of women's greater responsibility for child care, so that women stayed closer to the house and carried out tasks that could be more easily interrupted for nursing or tending children; and they were partly the result of cultural beliefs, so that women in parts of Norway, for example, sowed all grain because people felt this would ensure a bigger harvest. Whatever their source, gender divisions meant that the proper functioning of a rural household required at least one adult male and one adult female. Remarriage after the death of a spouse was very fast, and few people remained permanently unmarried, although widows faced far more barriers than widowers. These households sometimes hired young people as live-in servants or occasional laborers during harvest, and by the early seventeenth century some rural households lived by their labor alone.

Technological changes and new types of crops introduced during the early modern period altered the tasks that people did, but did not end the gender division of labor or the basic household unit of production. During the seventeenth century, for example, turnips and other root crops were increasingly grown in many parts of Europe and then fed to animals in stalls. Both tasks were very labor-intensive and generally done by women, who had traditionally taken care of the animals housed with the family. Women also tended and harvested crops that provided raw materials for manufactured products, such as flax, hemp, silk, and plants for dye. As animal products and these more specialized crops became more significant parts of the rural economy in some areas of Europe, agricultural labor became feminized. This increased the demand for female wage laborers in the countryside, although most women (and men) continued to work as part of a household economy and did not receive separate wages for their work.

In some rural areas, commodities other than agricultural ones were a significant part of the economy, and their extraction or production shaped the gender division of labor. In Portugal, Norway, and Galicia (the northwest part of Spain), adult men were away fishing during the summer months, leaving women and children responsible for all crop and stock raising. Visitors from other parts of Europe often commented that women in these areas were more independent and forceful than was appropriate, that they boasted how little they needed men to survive. Men from these areas sometimes agreed with their critical visitors, but sometimes praised the strength and self-reliance of their women. Strength was also an important quality for women who lived in mining areas, where they carried ore, wood, and salt; sorted and washed ore; and prepared charcoal briquets for use in smelting. Most of the work underground was carried out by adult men in the preindustrial period, though the mining companies that hired them assumed they would be assisted by their families. Men were paid per basket for ore, but it was expected that this ore would be broken apart and washed, jobs that their wives, sisters, and children did, though they did not receive separate wages for their work.

Mining provides one example of how the familial organization of production carried over into the world of wage labor in rural areas, and in some parts of Europe cloth production followed a similar path. Beginning in the fifteenth century, urban investors hired rural households or individuals to produce wool, linen, and later cotton thread or cloth (or cloth that was a mixture of these), paying the household or individual only for the labor and retaining

Gender Divisions in Agricultural Tasks. *The Courtyard of the Farm,* painting by Jan Siberechts (1627–1723). Among other tasks, women carry fodder to the animals and tend vegetables. The woman in the center right is delousing a child. IRPA, BRUSSELS

ownership of the raw materials and in some cases the tools and machinery used. Historians use several different terms to describe this development—domestic or cottage industry, the "putting-out" system, or protoindustrialization—and stress that it continued as a significant form of economic organization in more isolated rural areas such as Switzerland or Slovakia well into the nineteenth century or even the twentieth. In parts of Europe where whole households were hired, protoindustrialization strengthened the familial organization of production but broke down gender divisions, as men, women, and children who were old enough all worked at the same tasks. In other parts of Europe, individuals were hired separately during slack times in the agricultural cycle; because such periods often differed for men and women, this hiring was gender specific, and wages were paid directly to the individual rather than to the family as a whole. Thus in these areas the familial organization of production was disrupted, but gender divisions were maintained.

Individual wages did not mean equal wages; women's wages for agricultural or manufacturing tasks were generally about one-half to two-thirds those of men for the same or similar tasks. Women's wages appear to have been determined more by custom than the market, for they fluctuated much less than men's both over the life cycle and with shifts in the economy. Even during periods of rising wages, women's wages rose more slowly. Married women's wages were also

less than those of widows for the same task, a wage structure based on the idea that married women needed less because they had a husband to support them, not on an evaluation of the quality of their work. The difference between male and female wages meant that in areas where wage labor was available for both sexes, men generally worked for wages while women concentrated on subsistence farming and maintaining the household.

Historians disagree about the effects of wage labor and protoindustrialization on gender structures. Some analysts find that as more young people, especially women, received wages, they gained power within the family and were more able to make independent decisions about such issues as their marital partner or place of residence. A few even see wage labor as the reason European illegitimacy rates rose in the eighteenth century as young women felt more free to search for sexual satisfaction and love. Others note that women often turned over their wages to male family members, or had no right to them at all, as was the case for married women in some parts of Europe, whose wages legally belonged to their husbands; thus a woman's income was rarely her own to spend as she pleased. There has been much less discussion of the effects of gender structures on protoindustrialization, but some studies are emerging which suggest that investors often chose areas in which there was significant female seasonal unemployment when they were developing cotton or linen production.

Households, guilds, and capitalism in urban areas. The familialization of labor was not simply a rural phenomenon in medieval Europe, but also occurred in urban areas. Most goods were produced in household workshops, with all stages of production, from the purchase of raw materials and tools to selling the finished product, carried out by members of the household, and the goods produced traded either within that particular city or regionally. Urban households often included individuals who were not family members—servants, apprentices, journeymen—but at their core in most parts of Europe was a single marital couple and its children.

During the thirteenth and fourteenth centuries, urban producers of certain products began to form craft guilds in many cities to organize and regulate production. There were a few all-female guilds in cities such as Cologne, Paris, and Rouen, with highly specialized economies, but in general the guilds were male organizations and followed the male life cycle. One became an apprentice at puberty, became a journeyman four to ten years later, traveled around learning from a number of masters, then settled down, married, opened one's own shop, and worked at the same craft full-time until one died or got too old to work any longer. This process presupposed that one would be free to travel (something that was more difficult for women than men), that on marriage one would acquire a wife as an assistant, and that pregnancy, childbirth, or child rearing would never interfere with one's labor. Transitions between these stages were marked by ceremonies, and master craftsmen were formally inscribed in guild registers and took part in governing the guild. By the late fifteenth century, journeymen in some parts of Europe began to define their interests as distinct from and often antithetical to those of the masters, and to form their own guilds; these, too, had elaborate rituals reinforcing group identity and loyalty.

Women fit into guilds much more informally. Masters' wives, daughters, and domestic servants worked in guild shops or sold the goods produced in them, and masters' widows ran them briefly after their husbands' deaths, but women's ability to work was never officially recognized and usually depended not on their own training but on their relationship with a guild master. Even this informal participation was challenged in the early modern period, and the only women allowed to continue working were those who could convince political authorities that they would otherwise need public welfare. Both craft and journeymen's guilds supported prohibitions on female labor, as maintaining an all-male shop became a matter of honor and status as well as a way to limit com-petition for jobs. Women were also excluded from certain occupations because they were barred from attending universities or professional academies. Occupations seeking to improve their status regularly banned women as a mark of growing professionalism. The decline of women in the crafts was a major development on the eve of industrialization.

The masculine nature of high-status work played an important role in determining class distinctions. Whereas in the Middle Ages middle-class women worked alongside their husbands, by the seventeenth century changing notions of bourgeois respectability meant that such women concentrated on domestic tasks, on purchasing and caring for the increased number of consumer goods that were a mark of class status. Shopping and housework could be very labor-intensive and physically demanding, but they were not defined as "work." Increasingly anything a woman did within her home, including work for which she was paid or which supported the family, such as taking in boarders or doing laundry, was regarded as reproductive rather than productive, as housekeeping or helping out rather than work. No matter how much of her day she spent on tasks to support the household, a bourgeois woman did not "work."

The gendered meaning of work affected not only middle-class urban residents but lower-class ones as well. Domestic industry—particularly in cloth production—expanded in many cities as well as the countryside in the early modern period, with households and individuals hired to do one specific stage of production. Those stages regarded as "women's work," such as spinning and carding, were paid less than those regarded as "men's work," such as weaving. Spinners' wages were kept low by employers seeking to reduce the costs of their products and by the number of women seeking employment in spinning as other occupations were closed to them. Employers and government officials seeking to increase production and exports also justified low wages by asserting that spinning was simply a substitute for poor relief or a stopgap employment until women found a man to support them. They also argued that keeping wages low would prevent unmarried spinners from being able to live on their own, and would force them to live in proper, male-headed households where their activities could be more easily controlled.

As the growth of domestic industry created more opportunities for wage labor, and economic changes such as enclosure (the fencing of land previously available for common use) drove more people to migrate in search of work, political authorities became increasingly concerned with what they termed "masterless persons," those without a fixed place of residence and under no one's control. They regarded the household as the smallest unit of social control, and aimed to have everyone under the authority of a responsible household head, preferably male. These efforts were sometimes directed specifically against women, for whom wandering was a mark of sexual looseness rather than an occupational stage as it was for journeymen. In Germany and France, laws were passed that forbade unmarried women to move into cities, required widows to move in with one of their male children, and obliged unmarried women to move in with a male relative or employer; in England city officials could force any unmarried woman between the ages of twelve and forty to become a servant. Such laws, combined with the fact that men had a broader range of occupations open to them, led to a gradual feminization of domestic service. In the seventeenth century, about 60 percent of the servants identified in some urban censuses were female; by the nineteenth century, 90 percent of the domestic servants in England were female.

Along with production and domestic service, early modern cities offered a range of other occupations for men and women, most of which had their own gender hierarchies. Health care was undertaken by male physicians, barber-surgeons, and apothecaries, along with female midwives, hospital workers, and informally trained medical practitioners. Urban commercial life comprised long-distance merchants who brought in luxuries such as spices and precious metals or necessities such as grain from far away; regional merchants who handled commodities such as wool and cloth; local wholesale traders; and market vendors who sold food, alcoholic beverages, clothing, and household items. The top of this range was almost all male, for women controlled less wealth and were barred by social constraints or law from traveling or conducting business independently. Women did invest in commercial ventures and later in joint-stock companies, however, and they predominated at the bottom of the range as local retail vendors. Although economic historians discussing the rise of capitalism and the market economy in this period have primarily focused on male capitalist investors, bankers, and wholesale merchants, female retail traders, pawnbrokers, and moneylenders shared their capitalist values. Such women developed a strong work identity, and often played a significant role in urban disturbances, from bread riots to the French Revolution.

For the very poorest city dwellers, gender was a less significant shaper of occupational life than was poverty. Some historians ruefully term this an "equality of misery," and note that it was true for very poor rural residents as well. People with no property, skills,

WOMEN AND SPINNING

No occupation has been gendered female in Europe as clearly as spinning. When English peasants in the fourteenth century wished to describe the lack of social classes at the beginning of human history, they sang: "When Adam delved and Eve span, who was then the gentleman?" Women of all social classes were expected to spin, from those in city jails or municipal brothels (between customers) to the highly educated elite. King James I of England's reaction to a young woman presented at court who could speak and write Greek, Hebrew, and Latin was "But can she spin?" The female branch of a family was often termed the "distaff" side, after the staff used to hold flax or wool in spinning before the invention of the spinning wheel, and commentators wishing to describe the ultimate breakdown in the expected gender division of labor in areas of protoindustrialization noted that men were spinning.

Spinning was the bottleneck in cloth production, for preindustrial techniques of production necessitated at least twenty carders and spinners per weaver, so authorities developed a number of schemes to encourage more spinning. They attached spinning rooms to orphanages, awarded prizes to women who spun the most, made loans easier for those who agreed to spin, set up spinning schools for poor children. They did not use what would probably have been the most effective method—paying higher wages—as they worried this would promote greater independence in young women and allow them to live on their own rather than in a male-headed household. Declining opportunities for women in other occupations did lead more of them into spinning, however, and by the seventeenth century unmarried women in England all came to be called "spinsters." The equivalent male term, "bachelor," did not come from the world of work, but from feudalism: a "knight bachelor" was a member of the lowest order of knights, who served a higher noble.

or family connections did any type of small job they could; hired by the day or the job, they put together an "economy of makeshifts," in which survival was very dependent on the price of bread. They traveled to rural areas during harvest time, repaired city walls and fortifications, and carried messages and packages from place to place. Women (and in some cities, men) might combine such work with occasional prostitution, and a few of these made selling sex a full-time occupation. Until the sixteenth century, most cities had an official municipal brothel in which prostitution was fully legitimate; these were closed in some cities of Europe with the moral fervor of the Protestant and Catholic Reformations, though in others prostitution was simply regulated rather than criminalized.

MODERN EUROPE (1750–2000)

Historians have traditionally regarded the development of industrial capitalism in Europe as one of the world's most significant events, one of the very few economic developments to warrant the term "revolution." The impact of industrialism on men and women was not uniform, however, but varied, particularly for women, according to such factors as age and marital status. Developments of the twentieth century, such as the growth of information technology and policies of state welfare, were similarly complex in their effects.

Change and continuity in the industrial economy. The earliest studies of women's work saw the growth of industrial capitalism as a dramatic break, transforming the household organization of production, in which the home and workplace were united, into a factory organization, in which they were separate. This narrative was modified somewhat during the 1990s, as historians paid more attention both to earlier changes, such as agricultural wage labor and domestic production, and to continuities in industrial economies, such as women's continued responsibility for housework, which has given them a "second shift" of work until today in most of Europe.

Some of the gendered processes first identified by historians of industrialism are now recognized as having occurred earlier as well. Historians of the industrial period have pointed to the de-skilling of certain occupations, in which jobs that had traditionally been done by men were made more monotonous with the addition of machinery and so were redefined and given to women, with a dramatic drop in status and pay; secretarial work, weaving, and shoemaking are prominent examples of this. They have noted that notions of "skilled" and "unskilled" work are often, in fact, gender divisions, with women excluded from certain jobs, such as glass cutting, because they were judged clumsy or "unskilled," yet those same women made lace, a job that required an even higher level of dexterity and con-

centration than glass cutting. This link between gender and "skill" had actually begun in the preindustrial period, though in these cases the addition of machinery often made jobs "male" instead of "female." Both brewing and stocking knitting, for example, were transformed into male-dominated occupations in some parts of Europe. When knitting frames and new brewing methods were introduced, men began to argue that they were so complicated women could never use them; in reality they made brewing and knitting faster and increased the opportunities for profit. Women were limited to small-scale brewing and knitting primarily for their own family's use.

Links between gender and "skill" have continued in the postindustrial economy. Using a typewriter was gendered female in the early twentieth century, but working with computers has been gendered male and accompanied by an increase in pay and status. This regendering of work on a keyboard has been accomplished by associating computers with mathematics and machinery, fields viewed as masculine, which girls have been discouraged from studying. Advertisements in computer magazines often portray women at the keyboard only if they are emphasizing how easy a computer system is to use.

There are thus significant continuities from the preindustrial to the industrial (and postindustrial) period in the links between gender and work, but industrialism also brought change. Factories brought new forms of work discipline in which overseers replaced parents as supervisors of production, machines concentrated in large numbers determined the pace of work, production was split into many small stages, and work was not easily combined with domestic or agricultural tasks. All of these changes made it difficult for adult women to combine factory work with their family responsibilities, so that factory work was the province of men, younger unmarried women, and children. Existing wage scales and notions of the value of women's work as compared to men's meant that young women were often the first to be hired as factories opened, particularly in cloth production, because they could be hired more cheaply. Tasks that were regarded as more highly skilled or supervisory were reserved for men. Certain industries that developed slightly later, such as steel, also came to be regarded as "men's work," so that the industrial labor market was segmented by gender both within factories and across industries.

Though the work women did in factories was often very similar to that done in household workshops, it was also more visible, and became a topic of public discussion in the nineteenth century. Politicians and social commentators debated the propriety

Gendered Female Work. An office worker types with the aid of a Dictaphone, London, 1930s. POPPERFOTO/ ARCHIVE PHOTOS

of young women working alongside or being supervised by men who were not their relatives, a debate fueled by instances of rape and sexual exploitation in the factories. Intermixing of the sexes at the workplace was described as leading to "immorality," hasty marriages, and increased illegitimacy, and female factory workers were often charged with having dubious sexual morals. Such fears led to further segmentation of the labor market by gender, as women—or their families—chose sex-segregated workplaces, which were viewed as more "respectable." Concerns about morality shaped the work opportunities even for those needing public support. City and parish authorities often set up small endowments for poor children to learn a trade; while boys were apprenticed widely, girls were increasingly limited to such things as the making of hats or mantuas (ladies' loose robes, usually worn over other clothing), trades generally regarded as "genteel."

Sex-segregated workplaces could only go so far in controlling morality, however, and an even better solution, in the minds of many commentators, was for women to avoid paid employment entirely. Middle-class authors, male and female, extolled the virtues of women remaining home to care for their husbands and children, arguing that motherhood and not wage labor was women's "natural" calling and a full-time occupation. Economic as well as moral concerns played a role in these debates, for male workers also opposed women in the factories because their lower wages drove all wages down. The labor organizations that developed in the nineteenth century often argued in favor of a "family wage," that is, wages high enough to allow married male workers to support their families so that their wives could concentrate on domestic tasks and not work outside the home. Laws were passed, as in England in 1847, limiting the hours of work for women in the factories, but not those of men, a differentiation that would limit women's desirability as workers.

Both full-time motherhood and a "family wage" were only an ideal, of course, because in actuality most working-class families survived only by the labor of both spouses and the older children. Older daughters—and less often, sons—often gave part of their wages to their parents even when they lived apart from them, and married women took in boarders or did laundry and piecework at home in order to make ends meet. However, these domestic activities rarely showed up in the new statistical measures such as gross national product, which governments devised in the nineteenth century, because they were defined as "housekeeping" and thus not really work. According to the German industrial code of 1869, women who spun, washed, ironed, or knitted in their own homes were not considered workers (and thus not eligible for pensions), even though they worked for wages, while male shoemakers and tailors who worked in their own homes were. The invention of the sewing machine in the late nineteenth century probably increased the number of women and children who supported their families with such home work, though statistics are hard to obtain, as such work was not counted as a full-time occupation even if it was undertaken ten hours a day, as it often was.

The labor organizations that developed in Europe during the nineteenth century varied in their gender politics. In Great Britain, labor unions organized primarily along craft lines and, like the earlier craft guilds, often opposed women's labor as dishonoring or cheapening their craft. Many British unions specifically limited membership to men, which led to the formation of a few all-women's unions. On the Continent, labor unions generally organized along industrial lines and had closer connections with socialist and other left-wing political parties. This made them slightly more open to including women members, particularly as some socialist parties, such as those in Germany, began to advocate greater political and legal rights for women. Still, socialist party policies were often ambivalent, supporting women's right to work while recruiting women as wives and mothers, not workers, into the parties. In general, however, women made up a much smaller share of union membership than they did of the work force, though they often participated with men in strikes, demonstrations, and protests for better conditions, even if they were not members.

Industrialization was an uneven process; many areas remained primarily agricultural until well into the twentieth century, with mechanized farming methods adopted only slowly. Particularly after the advent of large-scale steel production, the opportunities for men in industry pulled male workers out of agriculture. Women made up a larger percentage of the agricultural work force of both France and Germany in 1910 than they had fifty years earlier. As they had in the preindustrial period, both men and women in rural areas often engaged in domestic production alongside farming, processing raw materials such as flax for linen or finishing goods such as cloth, which had been made in a factory.

Notions of propriety and appropriate gender roles shaped the work lives of middle-class Europeans perhaps even more than working-class ones. Universities were open only to male students until the last half of the nineteenth century (or later in some countries), when pressure from social reformers led to the slow admission of a few female students; thus women could not enter occupations that required university training, including medicine and law. Positions within growing government bureaucracies were similarly limited to men, though middle-class women did involve themselves on a volunteer basis with causes of social reform such as child labor laws or the improvement of conditions in hospitals. Such activities were acceptable because they were seen as an extension of women's caring activities in the home, though they also led women to call for better access to professional training and ultimately led to paid labor in occupations such as social work and teaching. The expansion of primary and secondary schools in the late nineteenth and early twentieth centuries created new jobs for women; judgments about the relative value of female and male labor shaped wages in teaching, making young women the cheapest option. In teaching as well as factory work, supervisory positions were reserved for men, a situation that continues in many parts of Europe today.

At the same time that teaching expanded, changes in communications technology and the distribution of goods also created new types of jobs for women as secretaries, postal clerks, telegraph and telephone operators, and department store clerks. Because such occupations required serving customers or assisting supervisors, they came to be viewed as especially appropriate for young women, who were hired for their appearance and pleasing demeanor as well as their abilities. In some areas women who held these positions were fired if they married or planned to marry—men in similar positions were not—or if they became too old. Open discrimination by age or marital status continued in some "female" service occupations until the 1970s, with flight attendants being the best-known example.

War and state welfare in the twentieth century.

The links between gender and work in the twentieth century were shaped to a greater extent than earlier by military developments and state policies. The advent of "total war" introduced the phenomenon of full economic mobilization in the two world wars. The state's role in economic organization grew dramatically in the twentieth century, partly as a result of total warfare and partly in response to economic crises like the Great Depression. During World War I, government propaganda campaigns combined with improved wages encouraged women to enter the paid labor force to replace men who were fighting. The granting of female suffrage in many countries right after the war was in part thanks for women's work as nurses and munitions workers. Though the demobilization of men once the war was over led to women being fired or encouraged to quit, the enormous losses among soldiers in the war also made it impossible to return completely to prewar patterns. The lack of men in some countries, especially Germany, meant that more women would remain single and thus in the labor force their whole lives. Throughout Europe, between one-fourth and one-third of the total paid labor force was female after the war.

Trends in work patterns during the 1920s and 1930s continued those that had begun in the nineteenth century, with a few new twists. Both men and women left agriculture for industry, though women fled farms faster than men, as they could earn relatively more in the city. (Female agricultural laborers earned about 50 percent of the male wage in the interwar period, while female industrial workers earned 60 to 70 percent of the male wage; rural workers were rarely covered by policies such as maternity leave, which were guaranteed to women in industry in many European countries by the 1920s.) As industries changed, the gender segmentation within them did as well. Growing chemical and electrical industries often produced standardized parts on assembly lines, with female workers supervised by male foremen. Many of the women in these industries came from declining textile and clothing factories, but there was often a perception that women were "taking men's jobs." This sentiment was heightened during the Great Depression of the late 1920s and 1930s, and women who married routinely lost their jobs. Vast numbers of men also became unemployed during the period, of course, though it is difficult to make comparisons based on gender because women's work had often not been measured in the first place, and married women were excluded from unemployment benefits in many countries, so they never applied and thus were not counted among the unemployed. Labor organizations contin-

A Telephone Exchange. Telephone operators, Paris. Illustration in *Le Petit Journal,* April 1904. MUSÉE DE LA POSTE, PARIS

ued to be ambivalent toward women, at times encouraging their inclusion or separate women's unions, but more often opposing women's work and trivializing women's issues. Women were harder to organize than men, as their wages were often too low to pay union dues, their family responsibilities prevented their attending union meetings, and they had been socialized to view their work as temporary and not to challenge male authorities.

In many countries of Europe, the 1920s and 1930s saw the development of authoritarian dictatorships, which transformed ideas about women's "natural" role as wives and mothers into government policies promoting maternity and reproduction. In the Soviet Union, this exaltation of motherhood was accompanied by measures that encouraged women's labor, as married women—except for the wives of high-level Communist Party and business leaders—were also expected to engage in productive work outside the home. Women's literacy rose from 43 to 82 percent between 1926 and 1939, and women formed a significant share of the technical, scientific, and industrial labor force. In Fascist Italy, working women were denounced as taking jobs away from men, and work was celebrated in vigorous propaganda campaigns as inherently masculine. Despite this rhetoric, women continued to make up an increasing part of the paid labor force in industry and government bureaucracy. Only in Nazi Germany was mobilization for war accomplished without increasing women's participation in the labor force, a situation made possible only by the Nazi regime's drafting of nearly 8 million forced and slave laborers—most of them male—from occupied countries.

World War II brought a feminization of the industrial and agricultural labor force in England and France similar to that of World War I, and in all of Europe there were attempts after the war to return to what was perceived as "normalcy," with male breadwinners responsible for supporting women and children. These attempts no longer included outright bans on women's work, however, and they were less successful in Europe than in the United States. Women's labor force participation rose during the 1950s and 1960s, though educational and training programs leading to higher-paying jobs were often still limited to men. Gradually during the 1970s through the 1990s access to education and jobs previously limited to men was opened to women, though most employed women continued to be concentrated in lower-paying service jobs such as office work, child care, hairdressing, and cleaning (dubbed the "pink collar ghetto"), so that women's average full-time earnings remained about two-thirds those of men. (Sweden was the most egalitarian country in Europe, with female wages about 90 percent of male in 1985.)

Relying on statistics about the paid labor force for understanding gender divisions of labor in the twentieth century is misleading for a number of reasons, however. Women often predominated in the

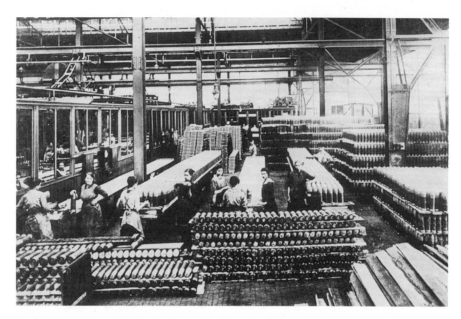

War Work. *Munitionettes,* women munitions workers, in France during World War I.
©L'ILLUSTRATION/CORBIS SYGMA

"underground" or "gray market" economy in many areas, selling commodities and services—including prostitution—on a small scale as they had for centuries. Most of these transactions were intentionally unrecorded to avoid taxes and do not form part of official statistical measures, but are the only way people survived. Such work "off the books" was an important part of many European economies; estimates from Italy judge that the unrecorded exchange of goods and services probably equaled that of the official economy after World War II.

Evaluating the gender division of labor must also take unpaid work within the household into account. Even in areas in which women made up more than half of the full-time labor force outside the household, such as the Soviet Union, women continued to do almost all of the household tasks. In the Soviet Union and communist Eastern Europe, shortages in foodstuffs and household goods such as soap meant that women had to spend hours each day (after their paid workday was done) standing in lines; because of this "second shift," women were not free to attend Communist Party meetings or do extra work on the job in order to be promoted. This situation did not change when communism ended in Eastern Europe in 1989, though more women had time to spend in lines because they were more likely than men to be unemployed, a result of economic restructuring and of the resurgence of a domestic ideology encouraging women to leave the workforce. The time needed to obtain basic consumer goods was much shorter in

Western Europe so that the second shift was less onerous, but it was no less gender specific; even in relatively egalitarian Sweden, women who worked full-time spent at least twice as long on household tasks as men, and even longer if there were children in the house. (See figure 1.) This situation led some feminists in the 1970s to advocate "wages for housework," while others opposed this idea as reinforcing an unfair gender division of labor.

During the 1950s through the 1980s, most of the countries of Europe promoted social programs in which the burdens of poverty, unemployment, sickness, old age, and child rearing would be shared by the state. Such state welfare programs were initially geared toward a male breadwinner and female homemaker model, with women in some countries receiving family allowances if they had children and unemployment compensation and other benefits limited to full-time (and thus more likely male) workers. Under pressure from feminist groups and some political parties, these policies became more egalitarian in the 1970s, with benefits extended to part-time workers and paid parental leave or shortened hours available for both fathers and mothers. Such policies have not changed the actual work situation in most parts of Europe, however; men in the 1990s continued to be much less likely to take parental leave or a shortened workweek than women, and women far less likely than men to be found among labor or business leaders.

Economic dislocations and the rise of neoconservative political leadership in the 1980s led to cutbacks in social provisions and healthcare in many countries, in what has been described as an "assault on the welfare state." This trend has pushed much responsibility for care back onto the family, or, more accurately, onto the women in families, which further increases the likelihood that women work part- rather than full-time. Statistics bear this out: according to a study by Eurostat, women made up 41.4 percent of the paid labor force in the twelve countries of the European Union in 1995, but they made up 80 percent of the part-time labor force. Employers often favor part-time or temporary workers, as it allows them to be more flexible and pay little or no health insurance or other benefits. Many of these employees work from their own homes rather than in factories, as computer and communications technology allows a very decentralized workforce. Like the domestic production of much earlier centuries, such work is often paid by the piece rather than the hour, which allows for greater flexibility but also greater exploitation, as there is no limitation of the workday. Because it can be combined with minding children and cooking, home production is often favored by women; such work includes data processing and other forms of computerized office work, but also more traditional jobs such as making gloves or shoes, for the sewing machine continues to be an effective tool of decentralization.

At the beginning of the twenty-first century, the relationship between gender and work in Europe is far more affected by developments and events outside of Europe than ever before, as Europe becomes simply one player in a global economy. Workers from outside Europe, particularly from former colonial possessions, bring their own cultural values about proper gender relations with them when they migrate in, altering what is viewed as appropriate work for men or women. Companies from outside Europe, especially from Japan, structure the workforces in their Euro-

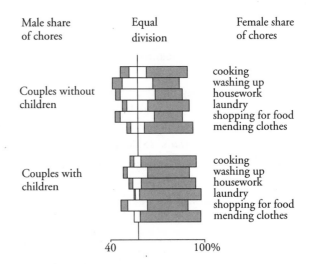

Figure 1. Division of tasks in homes where the wives are in full-time employment in Sweden, 1990. From David Gaunt and Louis Nyström, "The Scandinavian Model," in André Burguière et al., eds., *A History of the Family*, vol. 2, *The Impact of Modernity* (Cambridge, Mass.: Harvard University Press, 1996), p. 482.

pean factories along gender and ethnic lines, with European women clustered at the lowest levels, European men in the middle, and Japanese men at the top. European companies choose to build factories and invest outside of Europe, where labor costs are much less, supporting what are often extremely exploitative situations involving the work of women and children. It is difficult to predict where these trends will lead, and also too early to discern what the effects of the movement within Europe toward economic and political unity will be. It is clear, however, that gender will continue to structure work in Europe, and that changing work patterns will also alter gender roles.

See also **Gender Theory** *(volume 1);* **Capitalism and Commercialization; Proto-industrialization; The Industrial Revolutions; The Welfare State** *(volume 2);* **Servants; Prostitution** *(volume 3);* **Preindustrial Manufacturing; Factory Work; Middle-Class Work** *(in this volume); and other articles in this section.*

BIBLIOGRAPHY

Alsop, Rachel A. *Reversal of Fortunes?: Women, Work, and Change in Eastern Germany.* Oxford, 1998.

Bennett, Judith. *Ale, Beer, and Brewsters in England: Women's Work in a Changing World, 1300–1600.* New York, 1996.

Bennett, Judith M., and Amy M. Froide, eds. *Singlewomen in the European Past.* Philadelphia, 1999.

Bourke, Joanna. *Husbandry to Housewifery: Women, Economic Change, and Housework in Ireland, 1890–1914.* Oxford, 1993.

Bradley, Harriet. *Men's Work, Women's Work.* Minneapolis, Minn., and Cambridge, U.K., 1989.

Canning, Kathleen. *Languages of Labor and Gender: Female Factory Work in Germany, 1850–1914.* Ithaca, N.Y., 1996.

Charles, Lindsey, and Lorna Duffin, eds. *Women and Work in Pre-Industrial England.* London, 1985.

Clark, Alice. *Working Life of Women in the Seventeenth Century.* 1919. Reprint, London, 1992.

Coffin, Judith G. *The Politics of Women's Work: The Paris Garment Trades, 1750–1915.* Princeton, N.J., 1996.

Einhorn, Barbara, and Eileen Janes Yeo, eds. *Women and Market Societies.* Aldershot, U.K., 1995.

Engle, Barbara Alpern. *Between the Fields and the City: Women, Work, and Family in Russia, 1861–1914.* Cambridge, U.K., 1994.

Eurostat. *Women and Men in the European Union: A Statistical Portrait.* Luxembourg, 1995.

Frader, Laura L., and Sonya O. Rose. *Gender and Class in Modern Europe.* Ithaca, N.Y., 1996.

Goldberg, P. J. P. *Women, Work, and Life Cycle in a Medieval Economy: Women in York and Yorkshire c. 1300–1520.* Oxford, 1992.

Hafter, Daryl M., ed. *European Women and Preindustrial Craft.* Bloomington, Ind., 1995.

Hanawalt, Barbara A., ed. *Women and Work in Preindustrial Europe.* Bloomington, Ind., 1986.

Herlihy, David. *Opera Muliebria: Women and Work in Medieval Europe.* New York, 1990.

Hilden, Patricia. *Women, Work, and Politics: Belgium 1830–1914.* Oxford, 1993.

Hill, Bridget. *Women, Work, and Sexual Politics in Eighteenth-Century England.* Oxford, 1989.

Howell, Martha C. *Women, Production, and Patriarchy in Late Medieval Cities.* Chicago, 1986.

Hudson, Pat, and W. R. Lee, eds. *Women's Work and the Family Economy in Historical Perspective.* Manchester, U.K., 1990.

Jenson, Jane, Elisabeth Hagen, and Ceallaigh Reddy, eds. *The Feminization of the Labour Force.* Cambridge, U.K., 1988.

Lewis, Jane. *Women in Britain since 1945: Women, Work, and the State in the Postwar Years.* Oxford, 1992.

Liu, Tessie P. *The Weaver's Knot: The Contradictions of Class Struggle and Family Solidarity in Western France, 1750–1914.* Ithaca, N.Y., 1994.

Phizacklea, Annie, and Carol Wolkowitz. *Homeworking Women: Gender, Racism, and Class at Work.* London, 1995.

Probert, Belinda, and Bruce W. Wilson, eds. *Pink Collar Blues: Work, Gender, and Technology.* Melbourne, 1993.

Sainsbury, Diane, ed. *Gendering Welfare States.* London, 1994.

Sharpe, Pamela. *Adapting to Capitalism: Working Women in the English Economy, 1700–1850.* New York, 1996.

Tilly, Louise A., and Joan W. Scott. *Women, Work, and Family.* 2d ed. New York, 1987.

Valenze, Deborah. *The First Industrial Woman.* New York, 1995.

Wiesner, Merry E. *Working Women in Renaissance Germany.* New Brunswick, N.J., 1986.

GENDER AND EDUCATION

Linda L. Clark

Gender, like social class, economic realities, religious background, and national origins, long affected Europeans' access to education and the content of instruction, formal and informal. Indeed, widely accepted notions about differences between men's and women's psychological and physical characteristics and about the relationship of gender differences to appropriate social roles, for which education prepared the young, predated the Renaissance and Reformation. As one English author observed in 1913, "our educational institutions and practices descend from Greece." Aristotle, like many later theorists, defined the family as the basic unit of society and assigned leadership of the family and civic society to men, grounding the separation of gender roles and women's formal exclusion from public life in notions about men's intellectual, moral, and physical superiority. Xenophon's pronouncements on women's household roles were also still disseminated by some late nineteenth-century educators. Judeo-Christian biblical texts likewise provided rationales for female subordination to men, dating from Eve's punishment for leading Adam to sin. Although Christianity offered messages about the spiritual equality of the sexes, as well as of the rich and poor, the apostle Paul enjoined women to remain silent in the public space of the church. Biblical and Aristotelian gender polarities, combined in Thomas Aquinas's *Summa theologica* (1266), continued to figure in the pedagogical recommendations of Renaissance humanists in Italy and northern Europe.

EDUCATION, GENDER, AND SOCIAL STATUS IN EARLY MODERN EUROPE

The best-known Renaissance writings on the value of a classical education addressed male social and political elites, and typically treated female education as a secondary concern. Nonetheless, Plato's call for educating both men and women of the elite "guardian" class, the imagined leaders of his ideal Republic, sup-

plied one precedent for advice dispensed by Baldassare Castiglione and Thomas More, among others. Already in 1405 Christine de Pisan, daughter of an Italian doctor employed by the French court, had regretted women's inferior education in her *Book of the City of Ladies*. Perhaps the first woman in European history to earn a living solely from her pen, she turned to writing once widowed with three children, and she recognized literacy's potential value for women in similar financial straits. Castiglione's *Book of the Courtier* (1528), a widely translated guide to comportment in a court, recommended that women receive much of the same instruction in letters and arts as men but also assumed different uses for this learning, men's knowledge serving to impress princely employers while women's learning enhanced the ability to orchestrate social gatherings. A badge of social distinction, instruction in Latin and Greek long remained central to the education of upper-class European men and, eventually, of the middle classes, who aspired to emulate aristocrats' tastes and later to supplant their political dominance. Long before nineteenth- and twentieth-century debates about whether a classical education was suitable preparation for men's careers in commerce and industry, secular and religious spokesmen questioned whether such learning was necessary or even morally appropriate for women.

Furthermore, well into the twentieth century many Europeans assumed that a rigorous academic education did not suit children of the lower or popular classes, either because it lacked practical value for their work lives (which often began as early as age seven or eight) or because it could expose them to ideas possibly threatening to the established social order. The intertwined variables of class and gender, as well as political, religious, economic, and demographic realities, thus influenced both elite and popular education from the sixteenth to the twentieth centuries. For both sexes, access to education was determined by the goals of religious institutions and governments, as well as by the growth of commercial and industrial economies wherein literacy in the vernacular proved more

Instruction for Women. Women learning arithmetic, from *Arithmetic,* Flemish tapestry, c. 1520. MUSÉE DE CLUNY, PARIS/ LAURIE PLATT WINFREY, INC.

useful than it was in traditional agrarian societies. Not surprisingly, both men and women in urban areas often attained much higher literacy rates than their rural counterparts, long before most European states made primary education compulsory during the later nine-

teenth century, Prussia having led the way a century earlier.

Although families' demand for schooling often preceded laws mandating it, some states approached mass or universal literacy sooner than others. Protestant emphasis on Bible reading to deepen piety also furthered literacy for both sexes, and Counter-Reformation competition between Catholics and Protestants spurred popular literacy in some French regions. The Catholic schools of Christian doctrine in sixteenth-century Italian cities likewise taught reading and writing as an aid to learning the fundamentals of faith: boys and girls were instructed in separate churches on Sundays by lay and religious men and women. However, in other areas where religious rivalry was lacking, as in Spain, Counter-Reformation bans of the 1550s on printing, selling, or owning vernacular editions of the Bible reinforced negative attitudes toward reading printed matter, and religious culture remained oral, visual, and social. Moralists long worried that literacy would expose the "weaker sex" to ideas encouraging immoral acts, such as writing love letters.

The dovetailing of political and religious goals could produce the most dramatic literacy statistics for both women and men. Against a backdrop of Protestant Pietism, the Prussian king Frederick William I made primary education compulsory in 1717, as did Frederick the Great, whose 1763 decree envisioned eliminating school fees for the poor. Despite uneven compliance, especially in rural areas, by 1800 perhaps three-fourths of Prussian men and half the women were literate, as compared to 68 percent of men and 43 percent of women in Protestant England. In France on the eve of the Revolution of 1789, women were also noticeably less literate than men (27 percent, as compared to 47 percent), and revolutionary leaders soon announced the goal of universal primary education for both sexes, considering that it would prepare men to exercise their new rights as citizens and enable women to transmit the values of the new political culture to their children. During the Revolution, however, other concerns took priority, and the educational goal was not attained.

Before the nineteenth-century expansion of public primary schooling, privileged girls and young women often received instruction from private tutors and governesses, while boys and young men of comparable background increasingly progressed from private lessons to schools. On the Continent, Jesuit schools for boys were the most numerous category of advanced primary and secondary schools in many Catholic countries, and they specialized in training future social and political elites. Less privileged girls learned much of a practical nature from their mothers or other female relatives, and some briefly attended day schools. Parisian records for elementary schools (*petites écoles*) in the 1620s indicate the existence of at least 42 teachers, 20 of them priests and 20 women

(5 of them married). In Catholic lands, nuns from orders like the Ursulines and Sisters of Charity also ran boarding or day schools for girls. Although these schools served a range of social groups, individual institutions often appealed to a particular class or segregated pupils according to social origins. Separation of the sexes was the norm in elite education and in many larger or city schools for the humbler classes, but by 1632 the Czech exile Jan Amos Comenius had provided a rationale for coeducation.

Apart from national and regional studies, historians have examined particular schools, such as Saint-Cyr, opened in 1686 and inspired by François de Fénelon's and Mme de Maintenon's interest in not only preparing French upper-class girls to manage complex households but also diverting them from the worldly salon society of Louis XIV's reign. Maintenon thus wanted to exclude history and geography from the Saint-Cyr curriculum, which became the model for Russia's Smolny Institute for Noble Girls, founded in St. Petersburg in 1764, three decades after the launching of a school to prepare young noblemen to become army officers. Instruction in religion, good manners and morals, foreign languages, music, and dancing marked the Smolny curriculum, which was soon copied in a parallel school for nonnoble girls, who would not, however, study architecture and genealogy. After an inspection in 1783 reported that most Smolny teaching was in French, Russian received greater emphasis, and lessons on child rearing were prescribed. Austria created a school for army officers' daughters in 1775 and another for civil servants' daughters in 1786, both institutions preparing their charges to become governesses if they should need to work.

A more varied clientele benefited from girls' schooling in late eighteenth-century Paris. There were places for about one out of every five Parisian girls in schools mostly subsidized by the Catholic Church, and nearly 90 percent of seats in day schools were occupied by daughters of artisans and merchants, noble girls being somewhat more likely to attend boarding schools. Empress Catherine the Great's 1786 education statute furthered her emphasis on westernization of Russia's elites, envisioning an urban network of secondary and coeducational primary schools that would be free and open to all the nonserf classes but not addressing rural education. In 1800 Russian boys in school outnumbered girls by a ratio of ten to one, and, as in other countries where public schooling was free before it was compulsory, aristocratic and middle-class youngsters often benefited more than poorer groups. At the same time, nobles reluctant to have their children mix with other social classes in

Saint-Cyr. Engraving of the women's school founded by Madame de Maintenon in 1686. From *Histoire de la Maison Royale de Saint-Cyr* by Théophile Levallée, 1856. ©FOTOMAS INDEX (U.K.)

public schools also resorted to private boarding schools.

The first French public postprimary schools for girls were the Legion of Honor institutions founded in 1807 by Napoleon and intended largely for the daughters of army officers. Initially headed by Mme Jeanne Campan (formerly in the employ of the deposed Bourbon dynasty), Legion of Honor schooling was the task of three institutions, stratified along lines of social class. The curriculum did not match the academic rigor of the *lycées,* the elite public secondary schools for males also created by Napoleon, and so it did not prepare girls for study in universities or the newer *grandes écoles* for training engineers and scholars. Nonetheless, many Legion of Honor girls needed to work and often became teachers, thus countering Napoleon's much quoted assumptions about women's domestic destiny and intellectual inferiority.

Such assumptions had also been central to Jean-Jacques Rousseau's famed pedagogical treatise *Emile* (1762), which enjoined mothers to provide children with emotional nurturing and to breast-feed infants instead of hiring wet nurses. Interpreted today as indicating the development during the Enlightenment of a new and more positive phase in the history of childhood, *Emile* was also a critique of aristocratic and bourgeois women's participation in eighteenth-century salons. Many women readers thought that Rousseau's emphasis on the contribution of mothering to children's development enhanced appreciation of feminine roles, but Catherine the Great preferred

Fénelon's educational treatise. Certainly Catherine's public role was not one that most French revolutionary leaders found suitable for women, for they denounced the meddling in Old Regime affairs by Queen Marie-Antoinette and aristocratic women and in 1793 formally closed women revolutionaries' political clubs.

PRIMARY SCHOOLING IN THE NINETEENTH AND EARLY TWENTIETH CENTURIES

During the nineteenth century primary schooling expanded considerably. There was demand from families alert to its possible economic value for both girls and boys, and governments wanted a training ground for an informed and law-abiding citizenry. At the same time, the Catholic Church, alarmed that anticlerical men increasingly avoided churchgoing in such countries as France and Italy, advocated religious schooling and the presence of religious orders in public as well as private school classrooms, hoping that nuns' education of girls would maintain the church's influence in family life. Jewish communities had traditionally attached more importance to men's than to women's education, but as legal restrictions on Jewish minorities were removed, rabbis worried about Judaism's survival in societies where assimilation was possible and so also emphasized women's role in preserving Jewish identity. Where political and religious considerations had limited impact on educational policy or parental choices and where economic development was slow, as in Spain, the push for primary education lagged behind other parts of Europe and was tied particularly to demand in growing urban areas. In 1860, 65 percent of Spanish men and 86 percent of women were illiterate, and in 1900 that was still true for 56 percent of men and nearly 72 percent of women.

England allowed local school districts to make primary education compulsory in 1870 but did not guarantee free schooling until 1891, whereas both free and compulsory schooling figured in the French primary education laws of 1881–1882, sponsored by the new, democratic Third Republic (1870–1940) and education minister Jules Ferry. By the time of the Ferry Laws, the great majority of French school-age children of both sexes already received some primary schooling, but the improved training of teachers and curricular reform enhanced the quality of much instruction. Before the political drive for universal education, 30 percent of English bridegrooms and 45 percent of brides in 1850 could not sign the marriage register, as was also true in 1854 for 31 percent of French grooms and 46 percent of brides. By 1900 only 5 to 6 percent of French spouses could not sign, and in England in 1913, that was true for only 1 percent of either sex. When German unification was completed in 1871, the kingdom of Prussia was close to achieving universal literacy (90 percent of men, 85 percent of women), although Catholics' illiteracy rates were twice as high as Protestants' rates. Italy lagged in comparison. Piedmont's Casati Law of 1859, extended to the rest of the newly unified Italy in 1861, formally organized public education and created normal schools for women, and the 1877 Coppino Law made three years of schooling compulsory for both sexes. Yet many communities did not adequately fund free schooling, and some families were resistant. In 1861, 78 percent of Italians were illiterate, and nearly half remained so in 1901, when regional rates varied from a low in Piedmont in the industrializing north—14 percent of males, 21 percent of females—to a high in remote Sicily, with 65 percent of males and 77 percent of females.

French and Italian educational reform also had a pronounced anticlerical dimension, partly linked to the governments' concern about the influence of Catholic education on women's beliefs and political leanings. In France anticlericalism reflected the continuing combat between republicans and Catholic monarchists. Accordingly, republicans secularized the public school curriculum and replaced religious teachers with lay men and women. The latter change had greater impact on girls' schools because lay male

teachers had long been more numerous in boys' schools than teaching brothers, whereas the number of nuns teaching in public schools had risen under the terms of the Falloux Law of 1850. In the new Italian state, unified between 1860 and 1870, anticlerical education policies were a response to the antagonism of Pope Pius IX and his successors, who opposed the demise of the independent Papal States. Count Camillo di Cavour, prime minister of Piedmont and architect of Italian unification, had ended religious orders' role in public schools, and 1877 legislation removed religion lessons, not returned to the state curriculum until the Fascist era. In Spain, however, the brief moment of liberal distancing from the church, due to the Carlist rebellion against Queen Isabella II, was soon replaced by an accommodation epitomized by the 1857 Moyano Law, which mandated religious lessons in public schools, allowed clerical inspection, and was not altered until the Second Republic (1931–1939) imposed the secularizing policies that the Franco dictatorship subsequently discarded.

In imperial Russia, gender differences in schooling and literacy also long complemented rural/urban differences and were influenced by the Orthodox Church as well. In 1897, 64 percent of urban males and 70 percent of females aged nine and older were literate, as compared to 35 percent of males and only 13 percent of females in rural areas. Peasants themselves evidently initiated the first major push for expanding rural primary education, immediately after the 1861 emancipation of serfs. During the 1890s, when social turmoil accompanied protracted famine, local government councils and the Orthodox Church assumed more control over schools, as did the central government after the 1905 revolution. Although perhaps half of all school-age children received some education by 1914, gender and geographical differences persisted: 75 percent of urban boys and 59 percent of girls attended school, but the respective rural figures were 58 percent and 24 percent. These lags have been attributed not only to a large rural population's failure to see economic value in literacy, especially for girls, but also to Russian Orthodoxy's fear that knowledge of Western science and languages would divert people from religion.

The expansion of schooling, public and private, enlarged the market for textbooks and other curricular materials, and much school literature contained messages that reinforced both social class distinctions and gender norms. In the wake of the French Revolution, anxious European elites had expressed new interest in the need to educate mothers, the first educators of young children and thus the first purveyors of social values. Like conservative elites, liberals and progressives endorsed tailoring educational content to gender, for women were formally excluded from the political rights for male citizens introduced by the Revolution of 1789 and later nineteenth-century European revolutions or voting reforms.

French primary school textbooks for both sexes emphasized the virtues of hard work and respect for authority and also discouraged expectations of upward social mobility. Third Republic textbooks for girls' schools maintained the emphasis on women's domestic and maternal roles familiar in the texts of the July Monarchy (1830–1848) and Second Empire (1852–1870). Typical female role models were nurturing and gentle but also watchful of the behavior of their children and husbands. Good housekeeping was presented as a way to divert men from cafés and cabarets, and some textbooks presumed that a loving and dutiful wife could dissuade a working-class husband from participating in disruptive strikes. One 1892 textbook was relatively unusual because its central woman character not only survived but also prospered in the world of work, rising from humble seamstress to successful proprietor of a Paris dressmaking establishment. Lest that example inspire unrealistic ambitions, a preface by a former education minister cautioned readers that the odds were a hundred to one that they would remain workers.

An 1878 Spanish textbook authored by an archbishop's sister depicted Queen Isabella I as not only pious and intelligent but also dedicated to sewing shirts for her husband, King Ferdinand. Comparable differences in gender attributes and roles appeared in pedagogical materials used by the states in imperial Germany, although there the greater prevalence of co-education also minimized the insertion of specifically feminine images. Nonetheless, the curriculum in the last two grades of Berlin's elementary schools for girls devoted four hours less per week to math and science than did the boys' curriculum, so that girls could devote four hours to sewing and needlework.

Unlike the United States, where coeducation in schools largely taught by women was the prevailing model by the mid-nineteenth century, many European countries still favored separate boys' and girls' schools, provided that economic resources were available. If public finances were limited, as in many rural areas, the maintenance of boys' schools or small one-room coeducational schools took priority. The anticlerical Third Republic followed Catholic tradition by mandating separate primary schools for boys and girls in communes with a population of at least five hundred, but in Protestant Prussia, imperial Germany's largest state, two-thirds of all elementary school classes—particularly in rural areas—were mixed in 1906. Coeducation was also typical in another schooling option that emerged during the first half of the century: the infant or nursery school, first created in cities and towns where many mothers worked outside the home. While boys' schools had male teachers, women teachers were usually, but not necessarily, preferred for girls' schools and nursery schools, and their growing numbers reflected expanded opportunities for attending secondary schools or normal schools.

In contrast to the United States, in many European countries young men's and women's path to the normal schools that trained primary teachers took them first from a primary school to a higher primary school, rather than to an academic secondary school, which catered to a more socially elite clientele and was, in many instances, long a masculine preserve. Indeed, well into the twentieth century, the divide between primary and secondary schooling in Europe was often not only one of age brackets but also of social class, and the attachment of fee-paying elementary classes to some public secondary schools enabled pupils to avoid mingling with children of the popular classes.

SECONDARY SCHOOLING AND ISSUES OF ACCESS AND GENDER

Secondary schools were not only more elite but also more often single-sex than were primary schools, in both Catholic and Protestant countries, and girls' access to secondary schooling lagged because of belief that their domestic destiny did not require extensive academic training. What the English termed an "accomplishments" curriculum (literature, foreign languages, the arts, and needlework) prevailed in many countries' private and boarding schools for teenage girls until parental demand and public policy effected a change. Indeed, the English government's delayed response to such demand, orchestrated by the National Union for Improving the Education of Women, prompted the foundation in 1872 of the Girls' Public Day School Company, whose shareholders supported the mission of forming "character by moral and religious training" and "fitting girls for the practical business and duties of life." Even after England's Education Act of 1902 promoted publicly funded secondary schools, girls' schools could, for pupils over fifteen years of age, substitute a combination of domestic subjects for part or all of the curriculum in science and mathematics. For boys, secondary schooling, particularly in England's elite private "public" schools like Eton and Harrow, remained a mark of social distinction even when they did not continue studies at a university. In 1891, only 2.7 percent of German boys aged ten to fourteen were enrolled in secondary schools, and the comparable figures for France, Spain, and Italy were, respectively, 2.56 percent, 2 percent, and 1 percent.

France launched public secondary schools for girls in 1880, anticlerical republicans presenting their purpose not as professional preparation but rather as additional education for middle-class daughters, who would become republican wives and mothers. Accordingly, the curriculum of the new girls' *lycées* and *collèges* was two years shorter than that for boys' schools, and until the 1920s it did not include Latin and Greek or advanced courses in mathematics, sciences, and philosophy, all necessary to pass the examination for the secondary degree (*baccalauréat*) required for formal admission to universities. Young women thus needed private tutoring to prepare for that degree hurdle, first negotiated by a woman in 1861, and eventually some Catholic girls' schools tried to compete with public schools by offering baccalaureate subjects. The Italian government, however, began allowing girls to attend boys' secondary schools during the 1870s, for the priority in public funding was remedying deficiencies in primary education. Nonetheless, Italian upper-class families continued to send daughters to Catholic boarding schools or convent-like secular boarding schools, which were typically finishing schools not emphasizing preparation for work. Spain's official enrollment of female secondary school students occurred after 1900, and in 1923 they were still only 12 percent of secondary students.

In the Austrian half of Austria-Hungary, the first school preparing young women for university admission was one opened in Prague for Czech speakers by a women's organization. Like France, Austria did not have girls' public secondary schools with a classical curriculum leading to the diploma (*Matura*) required for university entry, but after Prussia introduced official regulations for higher girls' schools in 1894, Austria followed in 1900 with a six-year program, two years shorter than that for males. Prussia's important curricular revisions of 1908 still differentiated between girls' and boys' secondary schooling but also enabled some girls' public schools to prepare pupils for the degree (*Abitur*) needed for university admission. No state-run school in pre-1914 Austria did the same, and in 1910 the government actually halted some provincial towns' practice of admitting girls to boys' secondary schools for such preparation. Belgium similarly excluded ambitious young women from male secondary schools until the 1920s and had only one publicly funded course (created in 1907) to pre-

pare them for universities. Most Russian girls' secondary schools also lacked a curriculum equivalent to that for boys until one was mandated in 1916.

Coeducation in secondary schools was most common in Scandinavian countries but did not affect the Swedish state grammar schools. It also became somewhat more prevalent in England after the 1902 Education Act enabled local education authorities to open a number of new secondary schools and upgrade others, some becoming coeducational in the process. The English Headmistresses' Association was not enthusiastic about coeducation, however, and neither were German women teachers, who had a vested professional interest in opposing it because teaching jobs for women were not plentiful in Germany.

TEACHERS

National variations in women's place in teaching corps during the later nineteenth century were noteworthy. Under the French Second Empire, nuns outnumbered lay women as teachers in girls' schools and nursery schools, and the anticlerical Third Republic retained the Catholic penchant for sex-segregated schools. Lay women, however, became the favored teachers for the Republic's girls' schools, and for the first time the national government and departmental administrations provided adequate funding to open new normal schools to train lay women teachers; the state also assumed responsibility for paying teachers' base salary in 1889. Against the backdrop of extended conflict between state and church, the Republic emphasized the maternal nature of lay women teachers, as compared to nuns, and unlike most other nations, did not expect women to leave teaching if they married or became mothers. Although French women teachers, like most of their counterparts elsewhere, received less pay than men at some levels of the official scale before World War I, the number of women applicants exceeded the availability of posts in most locales by 1900, and many women secondary school graduates also obtained primary teaching credentials to secure employment.

Whereas women were half of France's lay primary teachers by 1906 and more than 60 percent of Italian primary teachers, the same was not the case in imperial Germany (1871–1918), where educational policy remained the preserve of its individual states, independent before national unification. Women were still only 18 percent of German elementary teachers in 1906 because opportunities for women were retarded by older educational traditions, notably Protestant pastors' role and state bureaucracies' long ex-

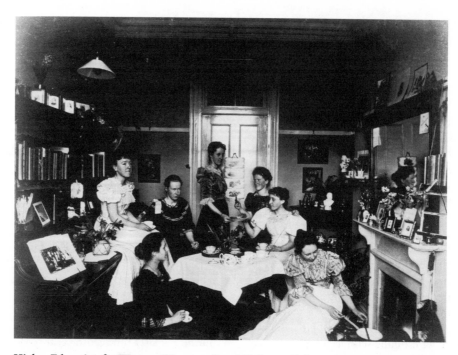

Higher Education for Women. Women at Royal Holloway College, University of London, c. 1895. ©HULTON GETTY/LIAISON AGENCY

perience with certifying male teachers and school inspectors. Authorities thus preferred hiring men, particularly for the many rural coeducational primary schools, and women more typically taught in sex-segregated schools in cities. In Russia, Orthodox priests and seminarians had long dominated primary teaching, but in 1871 a shortage of male applicants for teacher-training institutes led the government to admit women. By 1911 most primary teachers in Russian cities were women and, despite prolonged rural resistance, they were also a majority in the countryside. Both Germany and Austria lagged in training and allowing women to teach math, sciences, and classical languages at the secondary level. Austrian women could not teach academic subjects in middle and upper grades of girls' secondary schools until after 1900, a possibility acquired by Russian women in 1903.

In England, as in the United States, the teaching force was overwhelmingly feminized by 1900, for reasons more economic and cultural than political or religious. Women teachers would accept lower pay than men, for whom better-paid employment was more plentiful, and teaching, particularly in primary schools, had become stereotyped as a "woman's profession." In 1900, nearly 75 percent of American, 73 percent of British, 66 percent of Swedish, and 68 percent of Italian teachers were women, many of them single.

UNIVERSITIES AND ACCESS TO PROFESSIONS

Academic secondary schools gave access to European universities, the training ground since the Middle Ages for prestigious professions and long closed to women. The history of women's presence in universities often displays a lag between their informal and formal admission and also between their formal enrollment and the possibility of utilizing a degree to enter a profession. Whereas special colleges for women were attached to some English universities, continental countries—with the exception of Russia—typically rejected separate women's institutions at this level and did not open existing universities to women until dates much later than the founding of the first English and American women's colleges. At first, some of the latter were, in fact, more like high schools than real universities. Queen's College and Bedford College in London, established in 1848 and 1849, admitted younger teenagers, and only in 1878 did the University of London open its degrees to women. A half century elapsed between the founding of Girton College for women in 1869 and Cambridge's awarding of degrees to women, although in the interim women were admitted to the examinations of both Oxford and Cambridge Universities.

Swiss universities were in the vanguard of continental institutions offering admission and degrees to foreign women from countries where universities excluded them, such as Russia, Austria, and Germany. The University of Zurich admitted women as degree candidates in 1867, and a Russian woman was the first degree recipient. Subsequently the tsarist regime concluded that political radicalism was fueled by exposure to freer circulation of ideas in other countries and in 1873 ordered Russian women studying in Switzerland to return home. At the same time, however, Russia opened special higher courses and advanced medical training for women. Thereby Russian women had more access to advanced education than other European counterparts of the 1870s, but a backlash occurred during the reign of Tsar Alexander III, who attributed his father's assassination in 1881 to liberal policies. By 1886 all women's higher courses except those in St. Petersburg were closed, not to be reopened or newly launched until the reign of Nicholas II (1894–1917), who endorsed the St. Petersburg Medical Institute for Women in 1895 and allowed new courses in the capital and Moscow in 1900 and in nine other towns after the 1905 revolution. Although Russian women were allowed to audit courses at the regular universities for several years after the 1905 revolution (until 1908), they could not matriculate at these before 1914.

Social custom and administrative rulings delayed the enrollment of women students in France and Italy. The first French university degree awarded to a woman was conferred in 1868, but until 1913 more foreign than French women were enrolled in France's universities. Italian women began to receive advanced degrees after universities were opened to them in 1876, and in Denmark the first women obtained degrees during the 1880s. After a woman received a medical degree from a Spanish university in 1881, an 1882 decree barred women's access, and subsequent decrees limited their status to auditors until full official access was granted in 1910. In England, Scotland, and Wales the timetable for awarding degrees to women varied by university, with the newer public or "red brick" universities acting well before Oxford and Cambridge, which did not grant women degrees until 1920 and 1921. Indeed, Cambridge delayed women's voting membership in the university until 1948.

The first Austrian women university graduates were also schooled in Switzerland, and, as in Russia, the desire of some women to utilize Swiss diplomas in their native country created pressure for opening universities to women. In 1890 Emperor Francis Jo-

No Higher Education for Women! Undergraduate men at Cambridge University protest the presence of women students, 1897. ©HULTON GETTY/LIAISON AGENCY

seph allowed a Swiss-educated ophthalmologist to open a clinic with her husband, and in 1896 Austrian-born women with foreign medical degrees were allowed to practice in the empire if they first passed the requisite Austrian university examinations. By 1897 a campaign launched by Czech feminists to open Austrian universities to women had resulted in access to faculties of philosophy, and although medicine also opened in 1900, law faculties remained inaccessible until 1918. Germany lagged behind Austria in letting women matriculate in universities, but in 1900 Baden became the first German state to admit women, and in 1908 the doors of the University of Berlin fully opened, with all German universities accessible by 1909. In sum, on the eve of World War I, women were 6 percent of university students in Germany and Italy, 3 percent in Belgium, 10 percent in France, and over 16 percent in England. The comparable Russian figure is 27 percent, but women were restricted to special higher courses.

Once graduated from universities, women faced both formal and attitudinal obstacles to entering the more prestigious professions. Access to medical practice preceded access to legal practice, partly because of some countries' receptivity to the argument that women were the appropriate doctors for women patients and infants. Nonetheless, women medical school graduates often encountered problems with securing hospital internships, and many accepted posts on state payrolls because establishing successful private practices was difficult. Russia's special medical training for women resulted in more registered women doctors than in more politically and socially progressive countries: 698 in Russia by 1888, as compared to 258 in England by 1900, 107 in Germany by 1907, and 95 in France by 1913. A 1900 law made France the first major European country to admit women with law degrees to the bar, a right already accorded in Sweden in 1897 and approved in Norway and Geneva, Switzerland, in 1904 but not provided in Germany, England, Austria, Italy, Belgium, Portugal, and Romania until after World War I. Yet as of 1914, only eleven French women had been admitted to the bar, and another nineteen held probationary status. Russia's first women law graduates could not practice until after the 1917 revolution. There would be similar lags in women's admission to the most prestigious civil service ranks or university professoriates. Russian-born Sofia Kovalevskaia obtained a chair in mathematics in Stockholm in 1883, and Polish-born Marie Curie was the first woman to do so in France (largely because of prior collaboration with her husband Pierre, with whom she won the Nobel Prize for physics in 1903).

FROM WORLD WAR I TO WORLD WAR II

World War I proved to be a watershed in women's rights and education in more than one respect. Women's new professional opportunities in law and the civil service paralleled the postwar granting of suffrage in England, Germany's Weimar Republic (1919–1933), and Czechoslovakia, among other countries, but a gap remained between educational opportunity and political rights for French and Italian women, not enfranchised until after World War II.

The Bolshevik (Communist) takeover of the 1917 Russian Revolution ushered in new promises of both class and gender equality, as the prewar socialist Second International had demanded. The first Soviet census in 1920 rated 44 percent of the population as literate (58 percent of men, 32 percent of women), and twenty years later Stalin's regime could boast of an 87 percent rate (94 percent of men, 82 percent of women). Communists ordered the merger of women's higher courses with local universities in 1919, but politicization for a time reduced women's representation among students. Women were 38 percent of university students in 1923–1924 but 28 percent by 1928, for many students of bourgeois origins were removed and only 15 percent of students enrolled in Communist groups were women.

After World War I, other more economically backward areas of eastern and southern Europe also began filling gaps in primary education. Poland, independent for the first time since 1795, made schooling compulsory in 1919, but nearly a quarter of the population remained illiterate in 1931. Whereas the more industrialized Czech state already boasted of nearly universal literacy in 1921, Hungary lagged behind western Europe until the 1930s, and more than half of all girls and women were illiterate in Romania and Yugoslavia in 1931 and 43 percent in Bulgaria in 1934. Thus much of eastern Europe did not achieve either universal literacy or the closing of the gender gap in literacy until after World War II, under newly implanted Communist regimes. Spain also lagged, even though increased public funding, coupled with greater demand for schooling, reduced illiteracy between 1920 and 1940 from 35 to 17 percent for men and from 50 to 28 percent for women. The attempt to secularize Spanish public schools by the ill-fated Second Republic incurred the wrath of traditionalists, who launched the protracted Civil War (1936–1939) that toppled the Republic. Francisco Franco's authoritarian regime, in keeping with the 1929 papal condemnation of coeducation as harmful to Christian learning, then abolished coeducation, which had been favored by the Republic.

Access to secondary schooling that was the equivalent of the best schooling for young men of the middle and upper classes also remained an issue for advocates of equal opportunities for women and poorer children of both sexes. Czechoslovakia in 1922 promised young women equal access to secondary schools, and France in 1924 finally responded to long-standing demands by feminists and middle-class parents and allowed girls' secondary schools to offer the option of an academic curriculum matching that for boys. Subsequently, French public secondary schooling became free. Throughout the interwar period, French advocates of a single schooling system (*école unique*) for all children also tried, but with minimal success, to break down the structural obstacles facing bright children who wanted to advance from the primary to the secondary school system. Achievement of that goal would not occur until after World War II and, for most schoolchildren, not until the Fifth Republic (1958–).

The woman university student also became a more frequent sight after World War I than before, although professional advances remained limited. Women were a quarter of all university students in France, England, and Czechoslovakia by 1928, but only 5 percent in Spain. In medicine there were, by 1929, at least 2,231 women doctors in Germany, 860 in Poland, 519 in France, 450 in Yugoslavia, 411 in Austria, about 350 in Italy and the Netherlands, 256 in Latvia, 198 in Bulgaria, 109 in Norway, about 100 in Sweden, and 85 in Lithuania. France, which had pioneered in admitting women to legal practice, then had only 96 women lawyers, as compared to 15 practicing in Fascist Italy, 65 in the Netherlands, 180 in England, and 251 in late Weimar Germany. Many other women recipients of law degrees had opted for newly opened professional posts in the civil and social services. Farther east, Hungary and Bulgaria still denied women the right to practice law in 1930.

During the Great Depression of the 1930s the woman professional often encountered antagonism in more than one setting. Blamed in some democracies for taking jobs away from men, she also faced the hostile propaganda of Fascist regimes, which accused her of not fulfilling her maternal obligation to produce children who could serve their nation at home or at war. In 1928 Mussolini's Fascist state banned the future appointment of women as directors of middle schools, having already excluded them from new appointments to prestigious university and secondary posts. Nonetheless, women remained about 70 percent of all Italian teachers, and their place among secondary school students actually increased from 19 to 26 percent between 1927 and 1938 and among uni-

Adult Education. Literacy class in the Soviet Union, 1930s. SOVFOTO

versity students from 13 to 15 percent. Hitler's regime imposed a 10 percent quota on German women university students in 1933 and, in 1934, also required six months of obligatory labor service before university entrance. Although that quota was not always rigorously enforced, and numbers of male university students also dropped sharply because of new employment possibilities or other Nazi service obligations, women's place among students declined from 18.5 percent in 1932 to 14.2 in early 1939, their number falling from 18,813 to 6,342.

SINCE 1945

After World War II, the gender gap in literacy in the more economically backward parts of Europe was largely closed, and, as before the war, women in western and central Europe increasingly moved from the classroom to jobs in offices and services in the tertiary sector of the economy rather than the industrial sector. Under Franco's dictatorship (1939–1975), Spanish illiteracy rates fell from 17 percent for males in 1940 to 5 percent in 1970, and for females, from 28 percent to 12.5 percent, although the 9 percent female illiteracy recorded in the 1981 post-Franco census was still more than double that for men. In the Soviet Union, by comparison, the 23 percent rural female illiteracy rate of 1939 had been virtually eliminated by 1959, even though the dismantling of coeducation in favor of single-sex schools during World War II had delayed educational advances for some young women.

Another educational reform affecting boys and girls in many countries was the new emphasis on a common middle school experience, promoted by the French Fifth Republic during the 1960s and provided for in Italy by a 1962 measure. From middle schools larger numbers of young women and men advanced to secondary schools and universities. In Italy in 1961, 19 percent of all adolescents attended secondary schools, and by 1974, 35 percent. Young French women received half of all academic high school diplomas by the 1960s, and increasingly they attended coeducational rather than single-sex schools, which ceased to be the norm by the 1970s. In Spain, however, the secondary diploma (*bachillerato*) remained an elite, male degree until after 1960, for the Franco regime's new secondary schools for girls only partially met needs and required pupils to take courses in domestic arts. Spanish university regulations in effect until 1970 also continued gender distinctions: male students did mandatory military service, and women did a six-month social service program, consisting of lessons on political values and home economics and then work in an office, nursery, or shelter.

During the later 1960s women university students in France, Italy, and West Germany joined male students in various protests directed not only against inadequate educational facilities but also toward larger social issues, and, as in the United States, displays of male chauvinism by radical spokesmen helped spur a revival of feminism. New attention to the gender bias in educational institutions and curricular materials was prompted by the renewed feminist awareness of how assumptions about gender traits and roles limited opportunities for women in the workplace and other aspects of public life.

By the mid-1980s women were more than half of the students in Polish, Hungarian, Norwegian, Portuguese, and French universities, and more than 40 percent in most other countries. At both the secondary school and university levels, the latest gender gap was less often a matter of smaller enrollments and more often one measured by the differences between women's and men's choices for academic and professional specialization. In France and elsewhere, choices made at the secondary school level typically limited options for higher education. Thus in 1983 French women obtained four-fifths of all secondary school baccalaureates in the humanities but only one-third

of those in the natural sciences and mathematics; in turn, women comprised only 10 percent of students at France's elite engineering school, the École Polytechnique (finally opened to women in 1972), and only 15 percent at the prestigious National School of Administration. Similarly, at universities in Great Britain in 1988 women were 77 percent of education students and 71 percent of language and literature students but only 11 percent in engineering and 26 percent in the physical sciences. Women's underrepresentation in engineering and the sciences limited their access to many of the higher-paying jobs offered by those specializations.

Farther down the educational ladder, gender differences in options selected in technical high schools left many young women vulnerable to unemployment or underemployment. At the end of the 1980s many European professional women continued to work in education, where they numbered about two-thirds of those so employed, even as more opportunities gradually opened to them in other fields. Women were more likely to work and to have fewer children during the 1980s than during the 1950s but, as in the United States, they often earned less than men and were less likely to attain the highest posts.

Despite the dropping of most formal barriers to gender equality in the laws, education, and workplaces of the fifteen states of the European Union of the 1990s, there was thus still concern about cultural and societal factors retarding women's educational achievement in certain fields, just as attention was also focused on factors retarding educational progress by working-class children, more likely to be made to repeat grades than middle-class offspring. The French sociologist Pierre Bourdieu and his disciples made trenchant critiques of the role played by elite institutions in perpetuating male social and economic elites and their "cultural capital." Other commentators, however, doubt that schools in democratic capitalist societies function merely to perpetuate elites, suggesting that for girls and women, as for the sons of workers, education also remains a key to achieving both intellectual growth and the possibility of professional and social advancement.

See also **Gender Theory** *(volume 1);* **Students** *(volume 3);* **Child Rearing and Childhood; Youth and Adolescence** *(volume 4);* **Schools and Schooling; Higher Education** *(volume 5); and other articles in this section.*

BIBLIOGRAPHY

Albisetti, James C. "The Feminization of Teaching in the Nineteenth Century: A Comparative Perspective." *History of Education* 22 (1993): 253–263.

Albisetti, James C. *Schooling German Girls and Women: Secondary and Higher Education in the Nineteenth Century.* Princeton, N.J., 1988.

Boyd, Carolyn P. *Historia Patria: Politics, History, and National Identity in Spain, 1875–1975.* Princeton, N.J., 1997.

Charrier, Edmée. *L'évolution intellectuelle féminine.* Paris, 1931.

Clark, Linda L. *Schooling the Daughters of Marianne: Textbooks and the Socialization of Girls in Modern French Primary Schools.* Albany, N.Y., 1984.

Copelman, Dina. *London's Women Teachers: Gender, Class, and Feminism, 1870–1930.* New York, 1996.

A Cyclopedia of Education. Edited by Paul Monroe. 5 vols. New York, 1911–1913.

De Grazia, Victoria. *How Fascism Ruled Women.* Berkeley, Calif., 1992.

Dyhouse, Carol. *No Distinction of Sex? Women in British Universities, 1870–1939.* London, 1995.

Gemie, Sharif. *Women and Schooling in France, 1815–1914.* Keele, U.K., 1995.

Gold, Carol. *Educating Middle Class Daughters: Private Girls Schools in Copenhagen, 1790–1820.* Copenhagen, 1996.

Gorham, Deborah. *The Victorian Girl and the Feminine Ideal.* Bloomington, Ind., 1983.

Graff, Harvey J. *The Legacies of Literacy: Continuities and Contradictions in Western Culture and Society.* Bloomington, Ind., 1987.

Grendler, Paul F. *Schooling in Renaissance Italy: Literacy and Learning, 1300–1600.* Baltimore, 1989.

Grew, Raymond, and Patrick Harrigan. *School, State, and Society: The Growth of Elementary Schooling in Nineteenth-Century France, A Quantitative Analysis.* Ann Arbor, Mich., 1991.

Johanson, Christine. *Women's Struggle for Higher Education in Russia, 1855–1900.* Kingston, Ontario, 1987.

Kennedy, Katharine D. "Domesticity in the Volksschule: Textbooks and Lessons for Girls, 1890–1914." *Internationale Schulbuchforschung* 13 (1991): 5–21.

Lougee, Carolyn C. *Le Paradis des femmes: Women, Salons, and Social Stratification in Seventeenth-Century France.* Princeton, N.J., 1976.

Madariaga, Isabel de. "The Foundation of the Russian Education System by Catherine II." *Slavonic and East European Review* 57 (July 1979): 369–395.

Margadant, Jo Burr. *Madame le Professeur: Women Educators in the Third Republic.* Princeton, N.J., 1990.

Mayeur, Françoise. *L'enseignement secondaire des jeunes filles sous la Troisieme République.* Paris, 1977.

Meyers, Peter V. "From Conflict to Cooperation: Men and Women Teachers of the Belle Epoque." In *The Making of Frenchmen: Current Directions in the History of Education in France, 1679–1979.* Edited by Donald N. Baker and Patrick J. Harrigan. Waterloo, Ontario, 1980. Pages 493–505.

Morcillo Gómez, Aurora. "Shaping True Catholic Womanhood: Francoist Educational Discourse on Women." In *Constructing Spanish Womanhood: Female Identity in Modern Spain.* Edited by Victoria Lorée Enders and Pamela Beth Radcliff. Albany, N.Y., 1998. Pages 51–69.

Oram, Alison. *Women Teachers and Feminist Politics, 1900–1939.* Manchester, U.K., 1996.

Pauwels, Jacques R. *Women, Nazis, and Universities: Female University Students in the Third Reich, 1933–1945.* Westport, Conn., 1984.

Petschauer, Peter. *The Education of Women in Eighteenth-Century Germany: New Directions from the German Female Perspective.* Lewiston, N.Y., 1989.

Purvis, June. "Towards a History of Women's Education in Nineteenth-Century Britain: A Sociological Analysis." *Westminster Studies in Education* 4 (1981): 45–79.

Quartararo, Anne T. *Women Teachers and Popular Education in Nineteenth-Century France: Social Values and Corporate Identity at the Normal School Institution.* Newark, Del., 1995.

Ruane, Christine. *Gender, Class, and the Professionalization of Russian City Teachers, 1860–1914.* Pittsburgh, Pa., 1994.

Snyder, Paula. *The European Women's Almanac.* New York, 1992.

Sonnet, Martine. *L'éducation des filles au temps des lumières.* Paris, 1987.

Stock, Phyllis. *Better than Rubies: A History of Women's Education.* New York, 1978.

Turin, Yvonne. *L'éducation et l'école en Espagne de 1874 à 1902.* Paris, 1959.

Wolchik, Sharon L., and Alfred G. Meyer, eds. *Women, State, and Party in Eastern Europe.* Durham, N.C., 1985.

Section 15

THE FAMILY AND AGE GROUPS

HISTORY OF THE FAMILY

David Levine

In the world we have lost, the prevaling model of family relations was derived from the Fourth Commandment injunction to honor fathers and mothers. Premodern families were supposed to be organized hierarchically along the age axis and organized patriarchally along the gender axis. This discursive conceit was deeply embedded in everyday life; alternatives to patriarchy were dishonorable because they were essentially unthinkable. Familial pluralism could only be the product of uncontrollable demography abetted by the rigidity of social hierarchies. By way of contrast, in the world we are making, familial pluralism would appear to be the product of centrifugal forces of individualism. In the age of late modernity, the family is castigated as being both repressive and antisocial. The disintegration of a uniform model of family relations is not just the result of novel discursive strategies; indeed, one analyst has estimated that there are as many as two hundred different "family" arrangements recognized by contemporary Americans and Europeans. Within these fields of forces, social experience is now widely variable. It was not always so.

Family history is complicated not only by changes over time, which have been a primary focus of research, but also by class and regional variations. This essay deals extensively with social class, including characteristic divisions between upper-class and mass patterns. Regional factors must also be kept in mind. The bulk of the work on family history concentrates on western and central Europe; southern and particularly eastern Europe have been less well served. In eastern Europe there has been more emphasis, historically, on extended family relationships as opposed to the nuclear links emphasized in the "European-style family" that emerged in the early modern period. By the late nineteenth century, however, industrialization brought eastern European, and even Russian, patterns closer to those of western and central Europe.

THE EMERGENCE OF FAMILY HISTORY

Historians have studied the family as both structure and process. Its patterns have been analyzed in terms of demographic characteristics of both individuals and the married couple, residential arrangements in the household, and kinship relations reaching beyond the walls of the primary residence. The family's changing configuration over time—its process—has been examined in relation to both the centripetal pull of collective strategies and the centrifugal force exerted by individual interests, principally those of gender and age. In addition, the family has been studied as a prescriptive image which was regulated by the exercise of power that was generated for sustaining religious and political order. Finally, it has been recognized that for most of the past millennium individual identities were created within the orbit of family life.

The explosion of social-historical writing that has occurred in the last four decades of the twentieth century has been keyed by the desire to rescue the common people of the past from the massive condescension of posterity. In urging historians to adopt this stance, E. P. Thompson was surfing the crest of a long wave. Thompson was not alone; indeed, he was part of an insurgent movement that had the common intention of writing history from the bottom up as opposed to the traditional, top-down practice of focusing on elites, governments, diplomacy, and wars as if that were all that mattered in history. The historical project was refocused and its main concern was the mundane vie quotidienne. The everyday life of anonymous people in the past became a significant concern of scholarly study.

Two key texts highlighted this first phase of family history: Philippe Ariès's *Centuries of Childhood* and Peter Laslett's *The World We Have Lost*. These two pioneers had, to quote Marc Bloch, followed "the smell of burning flesh" into the archives. Their path, however, was hardly direct—Ariès was a director of the Institute of Tropical Plants while Laslett was a political scientist who had published the definitive edition of John Locke's *Two Treatises on Government.* Ironically, it was in doing this editorial work that Laslett was made familiar with Locke's opponent, Robert Filmer, who was a hard-line defender of the Stuart monarchy. Filmer's arguments in favor of the divine right of Stuart kings was based on his explication of the Fourth Commandment injunction to honor fathers (and kings, too). Wanting to know more about Filmer's ideas and their relationship to the social milieu of seventeenth-century England led Laslett to do his initital research on household structure.

If imitation is the sincerest form of flattery, then Ariès and Laslett are to be lionized. Their books were, at one and the same time, a demonstration of what was possible and an invitation to learn more. Laslett, in particular, devoted himself to spreading the gospel of family history by inaugurating the Cambridge Group for the History of Population and Social Structure, by organizing international conferences, and by continuing to publish extremely influential journal articles as well as several collections of scholarly essays. Laslett's contribution was enormous although his primary concerns with residential organization—Did people in the past live in nucleur or complex households? What was the incidence of coresidence and kinship ties? What was the relationship between illegitimacy and marriage?—hardly kept pace with the expanding frontiers of this new universe of studies which he had helped to reveal.

If Ariès and Laslett were the originators of the new field of family history, they were prolific progenitors. The most significant monograph on the subject published in the 1970s was Edward Shorter's *The Making of the Modern Family.* This book was not without its critics but *The Making of the Modern Family* was successful because Shorter had not only provided a coherent overview of the subject but had also done so by connecting the material and emotional aspects of the subject. Shorter's claims were overblown—it is not a simple matter, as he asserts, to move from high infant mortality rates to maternal indifference and neglect—but he pinpointed key connections. If later analysts would dispute his claims of maternal neglect and challenge his anachronistic quest for romantic love, he forced them to counter his claims. The subject was enlivened by Shorter's incursion even though the framework he set forth was never a dominant paradigm.

Shorter's writing on the organization of family life was written in the grammar of the borrowed language of the sentimental family which reached its apotheosis in the immediate postwar world. His historical vision reflected that time-honored disguise, bereft of a foundation in the exigencies of daily life. It is not too much to say that if this image of the sentimental family was first repeated tragically in the 1950s, then Shorter repeated it farcically. In particular, Shorter politicized the subject because he enraged feminist historians, provoking them to reply with analyses of their own. After the publication of *The Making of the Modern Family,* the easy verities of patriarchalism would never again be acceptable.

In response to the groundbreaking impact of Ariès's, Laslett's, and Shorter's monographs, a number of scholars began to do primary research that scholarly journals were eager to publish. These studies illuminated new and unexpected aspects of the history of the family. Many of these articles occupied a kind of scholarly no-man's-land between the recognized, disciplinary frontiers of the academy. If journals devoted to demographic studies and economic history were the most welcoming, the older mainstream publications were decidedly uninterested in this new venture. In the late 1960s and early 1970s, supply met demand in a virtuous circle of growth and expansion as new journals appeared that positively welcomed material on the history of the family.

In North America, the *Journal of Social History* and *The Journal of Interdisciplinary History* both began their lives in the wake of—and in response to—Thompson's injunction to rescue the common people from "the massive condescension of posterity." Studying history from the bottom up meant that questions of social reproduction had become problematic, which, in turn, meant that issues of biological reproduction followed suit. The turn to social history was thus complemented by a rising interest in population, demography, residential arrangements, and kinship organization. In France, the journal *Annales de démographie historique* began publication and although its primary concern was with historical demography, articles appeared there which were tangentially concerned with the history of the family.

Family history was on the academic map. During the 1970s, the field became closely studied and universities began to advertise for—and appoint—"historians of the family"; the Newberry Library in Chicago began its summer seminars on new research methods that enabled traditionally trained historians to borrow social scientific methods to analyze routinely generated data banks in their quest to study family history. In mid-decade, the Social Science History Association was launched; one of its primary aims was to draw together scholars from diverse academic pigeonholes who shared an interest in the history of the family.

A landmark was reached in 1976 when the *Journal of Family History* first appeared. However, that event did not significantly alter the characteristic borderline status of historical family studies despite the unflagging energy and boosterism of Tamara Hareven, the *Journal's* first editor. In the late 1970s and into the 1980s, another crop of new journals began publication that were also well disposed to printing articles on the history of the family: *Social History, Histoire Sociale/Social History, Social Science History, Continuity and Change*. In addition, articles on the history of the family also appeared in journals primarily devoted to agricultural history, educational history, feminist history and gender studies, labor history, modern history, and medical history. Furthermore, a complete bibliography would be studded with references to works published in journals concerned with demography and population studies, economic history, geography, marriage and the family, medieval and renaissance studies, peasant studies, and urban studies. And academic journals tied to national constituencies (*American Historical Review, Canadian Historical Review, English Historical Review,* and so on), devoted to particular national histories (such as *Archive for Reformation History, French Historical Studies, Journal of Central European History, William and Mary Quarterly*), or devoted to particular time periods (such as *The Sixteenth Century Journal* or *Victorian Studies*), all welcomed contributions that were concerned with the family's history insofar as it could be connected with their primary area of interest. True to its frontier position between established academic disciplines, the history of the family would continue to be a house of many mansions. It is quite simply impossible to do justice to the extraordinary variety of topics that assembled under the rooftree of family history.

Interest in the field mushroomed in these decades and monographic studies exploded. A tiny proportion—like Shorter—were devoted to providing an updated overview of the subject, but far and away the majority were concerned with a particular take on the larger image. Like a CAT scan, whose imaging system recursively slices through a body to analyze its inner structures, this spate of studies gave shape to the historical subject of the family once they were viewed together. Furthermore, it became quite common for historians studying local social systems to devote a chapter or two to issues that are relevant to the study of family history. Similarly, biographers' concerns with prominent individuals now had a new relevance as these studies provided further insight into the family dynamics of famous people's lives. Historians of widely different interests contributed to the subject's growth by showing how it bordered on aspects of bio-

logical, cultural, material, political, psychological, and social experience.

By 1980 a plethora of articles and monographs that touched on the history of the family had been published. The first generation had not only discovered a field of study but had also created paradigms that have been essential to its definition. Several aspects of this pioneering effort are worthy of comment:

1. The history of the family was a recentered field of study that shifted emphasis from large-scale events and processes to the reproduction of primary social units.
2. The issue of reproduction had become problematic in its own right as demographic studies made it evident that the modernization boilerplate associated with the Princeton Fertility Project did not do justice to the intricacies of premodern family systems.
3. Alongside this demographic complexity, historians uncovered an assortment of residential arrangements.
4. Within the household, family systems seemed to be connected to wealth-holding in the sense that the families of the propertyless were less coherent because the younger generation was freed from its constraints—but at the cost of having to find a haven in a heartless world.
5. The Old Testament ideology of patriarchalism sounded like a backbeat driver to the rhythms of family life but its orchestration was attuned to a combination of factors—age, sex, wealth, residence, and occupation were recombined to create a medley of family systems.
6. New ideologies of sexuality led to novel forms of gendering in the Victorian age which Lawrence Stone, in *The Family, Sex and Marriage in England* had suggested was a cyclical reassertion of early modern patriarchy but which other analysts, following Thomas Laqueur's argument in *Making Sex* and Michel Foucault's claims in *The History of Sexuality*, located in the power-knowledge techniques of medicalization and state-formation initiatives.

After two decades of exciting study, the family now had its history (Hareven, 1991; Herlihy, 1983; Lynch, 1994; Stone, 1981; and Tilly, 1987). Yet if the overall shape of this field was decidedly different from the "before/after" models first suggested by theories of modernization, and if the beauty of science lies in the details, then the historical contours of the family's history remain to be discussed. So, in the remaining sections of this essay, the history of the family will be reanalyzed in very broad chronological terms; first, the ancient and medieval period with special attention being paid to the impact of Christianity and the shift from slavery to serfdom; second, the early modern period with regard to residential organization, the biological aspects of reproduction, and the issue of family strategies; and, third, the modern period with particular heed being paid to the interventionist role of state-formation initiatives.

THE EMERGENCE OF THE
EUROPEAN FAMILY

Starting with a contrast between the ways that the ancients defined individuals, David Herlihy draws our attention to the enormous implications of the transition away from antiquity. Herlihy's reorientation makes it evident that the modernization of the family was not only the product of a long evolution but also built upon very deep foundations. This meant that much of what the modernizers took for granted was problematic in the sense that it, too, needed to be explained. Christianity had made the correspondence between social harmony and sexual order problematic by radically restructuring the meaning of sexual heat; in its campaigns against infanticide, it diminished the powers of fathers; in its reorganization of religious life, it altered dramatically what it was to be male and female; in its advocacy of virginity, it proclaimed the possibility of a relationship to society and the body that most ancient doctors would have found injurious to the health. Nonetheless, in contrast to the ancient models of self-representation, Christians believed in the equality of all sinners and the necessity of conjugality for those who could not devote themselves to a monastic existence. The emergence of the family as a moral unit was linked to the Christian concern with *ordo caritatis* (ordered love). The love of God and salvation of one's soul outstripped all other forms of love; it was followed by the elevation of conjugal relationships.

In combination with the demise of slavery, this Christian model of marriage created a social mutation of the most profound importance. It was an explosive mixture that radically transformed the way in which the educated classes represented social reality. Herlihy's writings alert us to the fact that medieval surveyors made the humble peasant hearth and farm the standard units by which the entire community was measured. Ancient censuses had not used the household in counting subjects or in assessing their wealth but by the eighth and ninth centuries the family farm, called variously *mansus, focus, familia, casata, casa mas-*

saricia (in Italy), *hufe* (in Germany), *hide* (in England), had become the basic component of manorial and fiscal assessment. Vast differences in wealth and power did not break the bonds of comparability. This uniformity indicated the emergence of a single ethic of marriage from which there could be no variant standards of behavior—or morality—within the Christian community.

Christianity proved to be a particularly felicitous partner in legitimating this state of affairs. Jack Goody argued that the fourth-century emergence of new family forms was the direct result of the transition from sect to church that was paralleled by the enactment of ecclesiastical bans on incest. In so doing the church reconfigured "strategies of heirship," and in particular the control over close marriages, those between consanguineous, affinal, and spiritual kin. These novel restrictions on the ancient practices of endogamy, adoption, and concubinage made it more difficult for the propertied classes in the Roman Empire to transfer property within the family over generations because it closed the option of creating tight, endogamous knots of restricted elementary families within which wealth could be secured in the face of demographic uncertainties.

In effect, the new institutional church thrust itself into the process of inheritance by making it both possible and attractive for the dying to divert wealth from family and kin to its coffers. Not surprisingly this created tensions between the interests of the senior generation using its earthly possessions to secure heavenly benefits and those of the junior generation more concerned with the production of material goods. Goody suggested that it was not accidental that the church appears to have condemned the very practices that would have deprived it of property. A great buildup in church wealth rapidly ensued so that by the seventh century about one-third of the productive land in France, for example, was in ecclesiastical hands. Thus it had become possible for the church to accumulate wealth—to create an endowment of property for itself—and to establish places of worship as well as fund its charitable, ecclesiastical, and residential activities.

Given the importance of Goody's controversial argument it is hardly surprising that much debate followed its publication. In essence, there have been three thrusts to this criticism: the first point has been that Goody has oversimplified the organization of family life in the pre-Christian Mediterranean by overemphasizing the importance of endogamy and paternal power; the second criticism has been that he has confused motivation for creating new rules regarding both spirituality and sexuality with the implementation of these rules that were created for their own reasons; and the third line of dissent has suggested that Goody's argument makes the mistake of fusing the church's ability to legislate in matters of family formation with its ability to enforce these laws.

Quite obviously, Goody has drawn our attention to an extremely complex historical development, although for our present purposes it is probably worthwhile to worry less about the veracity of Goody's account than to agree with his emphasis on the end product's distinctive character. Indeed, for Goody—as for others who have been interested in the history of the family—the subject has encouraged a form of regressive history in which the familiar, known systems of human reproduction are set in contrast with the unknown and unfamiliar family formations of earlier ages.

In addition to the maintenance of a stable domestic government among his dependent population, "the lord's interest in the supply of demesne labour induced him to interfere in the personal affairs of his servile dependents, extending regulation beyond the immediate tenant to include the peasant family as well." (Middleton, p. 110). It is not clear, however, to what extent this "interference" was conducted on a daily basis as opposed to the more generalized maintenance of frontiers and boundaries within the social formation. There is, for instance, no evidence that lords played an active role in pairing up peasants and acting as marriage brokers. In considering this question it is perhaps useful to remember that while the slave had been treated like an ox in the stable, who was always under his master's orders, the villein, even if he was a serf, was a worker who came on certain days and who left as soon as the job was finished.

Even before the Carolingians reorganized the governance of western society, other forces were changing its basic productive relations. The creation of peasant tenements was the result of a far-reaching innovation, a new method of utilizing dependent labor. From the end of the sixth century, great landowners married off some of their slaves, settling them on a manse. In the Carolingian period the peasant tenement (*manse*) seems to have had three different meanings: often, it was an enclosure on which the house was built; sometimes, it was the whole farmstead including its landed properties; and, it was also used in a generic form to denote a measurement of land. But this physical connotation was only one side of the coin; the other side was the fact that the manse was a kind of tenure, heritable in the family of the man who had cleared and worked that property. When the word first appeared around 650 it already had a strong seigneurial stamp as we learn about manses from the ac-counts of lords and kings who have adopted the single-family farm as the basic unit on which rents and dues were imposed. Peasant families cultivated the manse's appurtenant lands in order to feed their own families. This devolution of responsibility reduced the master's staff-maintenance costs while generating enthusiasm for work on the part of the servile task force. Slave couples were now entrusted with seeing to their childrens' upbringing themselves until they became of working age. This transformation of slaves and freemen into serfs and villeins forms the baseline from which subsequent developments materialized.

This process of settlement was not a complete novelty however; rather, Herlihy connects the manse with the ancient squatters' sovereignty and argues that there was an element of continuity in the customs governing colonization in western Europe. The work of settlement, it would seem, had to be organized in relation to the supply of willing workers at a time when capital, markets, and transport were defective. Peasant pioneers survived largely by foraging in the wilderness over those critical years until the land should fructify; willing, not driven like the slave to the sloppy performance of his *sordidum servitium,* and able through spontaneous effort to sustain the hard labors that colonization required.

The manse thus arose out of settlement, it was permanently in the possession of the man who worked it, it was heritable in his family although burdened with service to the owner of the land, and it was roughly equal in size. It meant a heritable tenement that was the colonizers' analogue to the landowners' property rights. The seventh-century peasantry were not taxed on their land per se, but rather they continued to fulfill personal tax obligations by cultivating the soil. The peasants' *retrait lignager*—the right to inheritance of villein holdings for customary tenants' families—was a crucial counterweight to the arbitrary power of seigneurs. In a sense this was a quid pro quo—it gave the lord a solid core of reliable tenants who had some interest in the vitality of the manor while it gave the peasant patriarchs the semblance of control over their property thereby entrenching their power within the manse. And, of course, the peasant patriarch was given control over the women and children under his cottage's roof.

If the peasantry—90 percent of the population—were defined by their relationship to the primary means of production (the soil), the thin upper crust was defined by its relationship to power. And the primary indicator of a family's power was its hold over land. In making this argument, Herlihy draws our attention to Georges Duby's landmark studies of family formation in France around the year 1000. By then Christianity had radically broken away from its Judaic and pagan inheritance in separating descent from reproduction. Christianity was from its beginnings a religion of revelation which believers joined by being reborn in Christ's grace. For Christians, therefore, expectations of salvation were not linked with lineage nor were the achievements of ancestors passed on to descendants. For this reason—because charisma was not transmitted through priestly dynasties—Christians were not enjoined to maintain the patriliny as a religious task nor were they expected to continue the cult of the dead through physical or fictitious descendants. Formal marriage rules were an indicator of deeper, more important changes in the way in which the world was understood. This changed around the year 1000.

The key aspect of knightly survival was a new form of inheritance which limited descent to the eldest male heir. Patrimonies were thereby maintained intact rather than being divided and subdivided as had been the case before the year 1000. The conjugal family was only a single cell of a larger organism, the lineage. The shift from clan to lineage—from extended to dynastic family—was a relatively gradual process. The Norman Conquest of England in 1066 captures this transition in a snapshot. It must be seen as involving not simply the replacement of one aristocracy by another but also the replacement of one set of family relationships by another, a change not merely in personnel, not merely in all those external relations of the aristocracy, but a change in internal organization, in familial structure, in assumptions about property. Before the Normans, English surnames were neither hereditary nor toponymic; after the Battle of Hastings it became possible to identify individual families—their history and their fortunes—by their property.

The whirlwind of military energy that flung the Normans across the length and breadth of Europe in a few generations satisfied the ambitions of brothers and younger sons through the establishment of colonial lineages in their vanquished territories. Behind the fictions of lineal descent, most members of this new upper strata were "men raised from the dust" whose primary characteristics had been their loyalty to the Crown and their luck in staying onside through all the twists and turns of civil war, attempted parricide, and fratricide. Those who were disobedient lost everything—at the time of Magna Carta, only four of the twenty-one family heads among the Twenty-Five Barons could trace their lineage back to the Conquest, 150 years earlier. And, of course, many lines simply did not reproduce themselves in the male line. Indeed, only one family lineage that was prominent in pre-Conquest Normandy was still influential in early thirteenth-century England.

Clerical intervention followed a few decades after the secular ruling class had radically shifted its marriage strategies through the exercise of strict control of the lineal patriarch over his sons and daughters. Their new system of primogeniture effectively reduced the possibility of dividing the patrimony and thereby played a crucial role in the invention of family traditions. At the same time, however, the Gregorian church's fear of incest was based on the view that consanguineous marriages occurred among kin related to the seventh degree. This was an awkward and essentially unenforceable rule: who was not someone else's sixth cousin among the aristocracy? Jean-Louis Flandrin has computed that someone who followed these rules would have had at least 2,731 cousins of his/her own generation with whom marriage would have been forbidden. It was therefore expedient for noble husbands to discover they were living in sin and to demand a divorce or annulment; the historical record is full of such discoveries which usually occurred—fortuitously, no doubt—when the marriage was without children or when political realities swiftly changed in an unexpected fashion. In 1215, at the Fourth Lateran Council, the ruling on incest was amended so that marriages outside the fourth degree of kin were ruled nonconsanguineous. By bringing canon law into line with social reality there was a much greater chance that marriage could be made indissoluble; at the very least, a spurious divorce would be more difficult to obtain for the rich and powerful.

The insistence on clerical celibacy prevented the creation of a hereditary caste of priestly scholars. In each generation, the clergy was sustained by the donation of oblates to holy orders. This had two very significant implications: first, literacy was not confined to a self-perpetuating caste but was widely dispersed among the children of the whole population from whom the clergy was recruited; and, second, it brought the clerical aristocracy and the secular aristocracy to a common ground. Great lords frequently donated one of their sons to the church; such endowments were inspired partly by piety and partly as form of familial insurance. By the end of the twelfth century there was a shared bond of common interest between landlords, who sought an orderly system of inheritance, and the clerics who were trying to enforce Christian monogamy. Aristocrats were prepared for most purposes to be subject to clerical control—"not only in fits of penitence, but actually when making marriage treaties affecting their inheritances and standing in the world. This was largely because legitimate monogamy had come to be the heart of the system of inheritance, as it was to be the heart of the Church's idea of marriage as an institution." (Brooke, p. 154)

While much attention inevitably devolves upon the marital alliances and strategies of the upper class, it would seem that the post-Gregorian church's new marriage policies had a significant resonance for the lower orders. In establishing the centrality of consent in the making of a Christian marriage, the canon law of marriage made the marital union easy to create, endowed it with serious consequences, and made divorce difficult. This was exactly the opposite of the situation prevailing in both Roman and barbarian law. The Christian desire to evangelize the servile population and draw it into the cultural domain of the church was founded on a remarkably democratic principle: all men and women—no matter whether free or servile—were considered to be morally responsible agents whose sins were an abomination in the sight of God. Is it merely coincidental that the creation of a radically new system of marriage was installed at exactly the same time that the last vestiges of slavery were disappearing from northern Europe? The post-Gregorian church's marriage policies were deliberately fashioned to help the lower orders avoid the sins of concupiscence and adultery, at the cost of abridging the rights of feudal lords to control the intimate lives of their dependent, servile population.

NEW TRENDS IN THE EARLY MODERN PERIOD

The advent of the printing press is indirectly responsible for shifting our frame of reference in studying the early modern history of the family. Moveable-type presses made it possible to create printed records that, when production was routinized, provided new sources for studying the subject. Ironically, this impact was indirect as most of the parish registers and census-type enumerations were handwritten, but these were produced in response to a massive ratcheting up of the administrative technologies of early modern state-formation.

Renaissance states began to make it a requirement that the state's church record all baptisms (births), burials (deaths), and marriages that were celebrated in each parish. The primary reason for doing this was that it was in keeping with the Renaissance state's novel desire to intensify its surveillance over the subject population. These parish registers supplied the raw material that enabled the study of historical demography to enjoy enormous growth in the 1970s and early 1980s. The two most crucial questions that the demographers addressed related to age at first mar-

riage for women and levels of mortality. In the nature of things, family reconstitution studies also provided information about fertility rates—both illegitimate and marital—and birth control.

The most significant finding to emerge from the first generation of primary research into parish registers was that early modern women married about a decade after puberty, in their mid-twenties. Wealth played a small role in marital strategies—it was usual for propertied young women to be married at an early age, whereas if they had no property they were more likely to be on their own and marry at a later age—but both rich and poor belonged to a common culture of family values. To marry, a couple need some level of capital and this meant that a period of enforced saving usually acted to extend the courtship as money had to be set aside to outfit a home, albeit in a minimal fashion. Propertyless women, therefore, usually married at a later age, which often meant that they were also marrying away from the close scrutiny of their natal families. For them, the peer group played a crucial role in courtship rituals, the marriage ceremony, and the wedding celebrations. The emergence of a distinctive "European-style family" sums up some of the special features of marriage ages and rates in the majority of the population.

Arranged marriages were hardly unknown but they were much more likely to occur when significant dynastic or property considerations gave the older generation reasons to intervene in the decision-making process. In fact, for those youths who were wealthy enough to attract this kind of close concern from their elders it was often the case that the Christian right to marital choice was narrowed to a kind of veto power over the alternatives offered to them by concerned parents and/or guardians. The key point is that very few marriages took place between partners who had not met before they knelt together in front of the altar.

For many, this late age at first marriage meant that a significant amount of time was spent outside the parents' residence; service was a common experience among the lower classes as children and their labor were shifted upward from the propertyless to the propertied. An ancillary implication of this demographic system was that it gave enormous rationale in support of the patriarchal homilies drawn from the Fourth Commandment to honor fathers and mothers by extending its meaning to fictive parents. In early modern England, France, and, especially, Germany, there was an extensive literature that commented upon patriarchalism and the housefather's relationship to state-formation: as Filmer knew in his bones, the king was the father of his people in the same way that the head of the household was the father-figure of both

Seventeenth-Century Family. *Family Group in a Landscape,* painting (c. 1647–1650) by Frans Hals (between 1581 and 1585–1666). NATIONAL GALLERY, LONDON/THE BRIDGEMAN ART LIBRARY

the natural and fictive children who lived in his cottage. This patriarchal definition of identities was one of the primary reasons why the man who assumed the identity of Martin Guerre was executed as a traitor— Arnaud de Tilh had called into question the God-given order of society. Therefore, a traitor's death was not only logical but also just in the legal mind-set of the sixteenth century.

Mortality was high in the parish register populations but it has been found to be the product of three factors: epidemic disease, which was a constant threat; residential location—cities and even densely packed villages were hospitable environments for microorganisms that attacked defenseless babies without mercy; and maternal nursing practices. Women who breast-fed their children had much, much lower levels of infant mortality than those who began feeding them on solids almost immediately after birth. Childbirth and childrearing were the primary experiences of most adult women for most of their adult lives. Nursing had a significant bearing on family life not only because it kept children alive longer but also because it was correlated with longer birth intervals. Families in which the mother nursed for as long as thirty months usually had fewer births and more survivors.

In contrast to the silent treatment given to nursing practices, illegitimacy, which was most decidedly a minority experience, has been the subject of a large number of articles. In part, this is a reflection of the impact of Shorter's arguments—and the desire to re-

fute them. In addition, the subject has been easier to study as there were discrete legal prohibitions and sanctions levied against single mothers. To be sure, toward the end of the early modern age—after 1750—rates of illegitimacy skyrocketed, but it is important to keep in mind that during the 1500 to 1750 period the ratio of illegitmate to legitimate births hovered around 1 percent.

Fertility statistics have also been gleaned from family reconstitution studies. The most significant finding has been a negative one—with a few exceptions, most couples practiced unregulated intercourse. For demographers, this state of affairs suggested that their fertility was "natural" but, of course, matters are not as simple as that. Indeed, there was nothing natural about "natural fertility" since optimal levels were only about one-third the level that could be achieved by fertility maximizers. Rather, natural fertility was the product of a variety of cultural and biological adjustments as couples sought to optimize their family size—not maximize it.

Unfortunately, however, we know almost nothing about sexual habits or the intimacies of married life. Lawrence Stone tried to get at these secrets but he was stymied by the fact that all but a few upper-class, diary-keeping males say anything about their conquests. Few commented on their day-to-day activity in the marital bed. No women spoke of these matters, even to their own locked diaries. What went on in the peasants' cottages—or in the fields surrounding them, for that matter—is a matter of surmise; guesswork, really. Shorter, for example, postulated that plebeian sexuality was Hobbesian—nasty, brutish, and short—rather than playful, but his examples are drawn from middle-class, urban missionaries who saw only darkness and ignorance among the peasantry. By and large, therefore, the early modern marital bed is a terra incognita of historical analysis.

After Thomas Robert Malthus had published his *Essay on the Principle of Population* in 1798 it became something of a bourgeois parlor game to suggest that the lower orders were oversexed and underresponsible but, in point of fact, not much is to be learned about plebeian sexuality from this nineteenth-century, blame-the-victim discourse. The new rhetoric of sexuality that emerged with the medicalization of social relations suggested that respectable women were passionless but that lower-class women tended to be more "masculine" and, therefore, more at the mercy of their passions. In the 1867 *Report on the Employment of Children, Young Persons and Women in Agriculture,* for example, it was claimed that "Not only does it [i.e., agricultural labor] almost unsex a woman in dress, gait, manners, character, making her rough coarse, clumsy and masculine; but it generates a further very pregnant mischief by infitting or indisposing her for a woman's proper duties at home." At the heart

of the writers' concerns is a worry that the supposed "natural" character of rural, proletarian women was threatened by "masculine" work. Such women would not only be "unsexed" but also socially deranged since they would be indisposed to "a woman's proper duties at home."

This notion of "a woman's proper duties at home" had a different meaning from what earlier generations understood to be the proper ordering of a family and household. By the high Victorian period, the privatized family had been by and large divorced from production, becoming instead the matrix for biological and social reproduction, consumption, and sentimentality. In order to understand what earlier generations had experienced as family life it is necessary to look at the literature concerning "family strategies" that enjoyed a substantial vogue from the early 1970s through the late 1980s. The concept's popularity really took off in response to Shorter's many articles that preceded the appearance of *The Making of the Modern Family* in 1975. Louise Tilly and Joan Scott wrote two articles (one of which was coauthored with Miriam Cohen) and a book (*Women, Work, and Family*) that were directly aimed at countering Shorter's assertions of female passivity and economic marginality. Their work enjoyed enormous celebrity because

Nineteenth-Century Family. *The Bellelli Family,* painting (c. 1858–1860) by Edgar Degas (1834–1917). Musée d'Orsay, Paris/Lauros-Giraudon/Art Resource, NY

it not only provided a credible reply to Shorter but also showed a way forward to women's historians (and I use the term "women's historians" advisedly because in the 1970s the concepts of "feminist history" and/or "gender history" were not yet widely current).

The Tilly-Scott argument began with the proposition that Shorter's vision of the pre- and early industrial family was anachronistic because he neglected the ways that subsistence imperatives overlapped into the private sphere. Beginning from the basic fact that more than half the European population was either completely landless or else living on a marginal piece of property, Tilly and Scott were able to show that much of Shorter's discussion of courtship strategies was beside the point as more than half the population did not engage in marital alliances. Next, by looking into the basic ways the majority's catch-as-catch-can family economy functioned to piece together a subsistence income—Olwen Hufton had called this "an economy of makeshifts"—Tilly and Scott demonstrated that plebeian women held up more than half their family's economy through their involvement in marketing, gardening, petty farming, fowl-keeping, looking after the family pig, and various forms of protoindustrial production. By looking at what plebeian women did—as opposed to what middle-class, urban, male social commentators said about them—Tilly and Scott presented a vastly different reconstruction of the historical experience of plebeian family life.

The Tilly-Scott emphasis on protoindustrialization neatly dovetailed with one of the other preeminent concerns of family historians of the late 1970s and 1980s. Beginning with Franklin Mendels's 1972 article, the study of industrialization before the classic industrial revolution became a hot topic. In part, this newfound interest could be linked with a pervasive unease at the earlier explanations of "the take-off into self-sustained growth" that had been popularized by cold warriors like W. W. Rostow and, in part, comparative studies among the English, continential European, and Third World experiences of industrialization were making it evident that the prehistory of the classic industrial revolution was a subject of extraordinary importance. Industrialization did not just happen in the weeks after Richard Arkwright set up the first spinning mills, based on ideas purloined from the rural spinners who had sat in his barber's chair in Lancashire in the 1760s.

To rephrase Rostow's image: reaching a threshold of economic preparation along the runway now seemed to be more significant that the actual takeoff. This lead-up took on even more significance as Raphael Samuel made it clear that during the classic industrial revolution much of the actual production was still based on subdivided handicrafts; for almost two generations, steam power had been limited in its application to production routines in machine spinning. Outside the textile industry, steam power was even less significant for even longer. Curiously, however, while the subdivision of labor was fully appreciated there has been little study of the ways in which skill was transmitted; labor historians prize skill (as did the laborers they study) yet they have been reluctant to explore how it was reproduced. Educational historians, who should be concerned with skills-learning, are abysmally silent about it.

The protoindustrial family economy captured social historians' imaginations for a variety of reasons: first, it conferred agency on the lower classes in keeping with the Thompsonian injunction to rescue them from the massive condescencion of posterity; second, it recentered the practice of social history away from great men and great events and toward the strategies of reproduction which the popular classes employed in their everyday life; third, it gave a logic to the study of demographic trends and family formation systems as well as connecting the study of domestic organization to a narrative structure; fourth, it made sense in terms of the reevaluation of industrialization that was current among economic historians; and, fifth, it provided historians with a way of demonstrating that family history could not simply be read off a sociological template, such as that provided by modernization theories. The past needed to be studied on its own terms.

Beginning with the point that proletarianization was the dominant process in the majority of plebeian families well before tie industrial revolution, social historians of the family discovered a new kind of past. The exigencies of work and material life assumed a primordial importance. Instead of the well-housed, well-fed patriarchal family of the peasantry—the English yeomen, the German *bauern*, or the French *laboureurs*—social historians introduced us to masterless men, independent women, and cultures of misrule in which youths of both sexes (though predominantly males) turned the social world upside down, mocking their elders and their elders' conventions. In particular, charivaris were occasions for mocking "inappropriate" marriages and publicly shaming those housefathers who were less than masterful. In place of residential stability, social historians discovered a lost world of footlooseness, wandering, and mobility. Oddly, however, studies of marital breakdown and desertion have never been pursued in a systematic manner.

For most members of the lower classes, the long years of service between puberty and marriage was a

Subsistence Income. *The Gleaners,* painting (1857) by Jean-François Millet (1814–1875). Musée du Louvre, Paris/Alinari/ Art Resource, NY

life-cycle phase when fathers and mothers were fictive, not genuine parents. Rather than a Bible-reading patriarch sternly disciplining his household, the plebeian family seemed to be a more contingent arrangement. Kinship, too, seems to have been looser among the propertyless than among their betters, whether in the middling sort or the upper classes. Furthermore, it seemed that the protoindustrial family had its own peculiar demographic dynamic: freed from the constraints of property transmission, men and women were able to contract marriage at an earlier age. The first family reconstitution studies of Belgium and the English Midlands pointed toward a protoindustrial family that was reproducing itself vigorously while streams of migrants from rural regions supplemented their rising numbers. In rural industrial regions, the countryside thickened as workers' cottages were built, quite literally overnight.

The key to protoindustrial demography was thought to have been a falling age at first marriage for women, which meant that generations followed one another more closely while families were reproducing for a longer period of time. In addition, there are hints in the data that illegitimacy rates were higher, more protoindustrial brides were pregnant at marriage, and levels of marital fertility stayed up rather than slumping as women got older. What seemed strikingly evident from simulation exercises was that massive shifts in annual rates of growth would have resulted from relatively small declines in the age at first marriage for women. David Levine's original study of Shepshed was designed to capture one such community. While it would be a mistake to generalize as if all Europe was Shepshed, it is a far graver mistake to miss the point that even if only a fraction of the original proletarians living in Europe in 1750 fully and completely took on these new characteristics—or if all took on some of these behavioral changes to only some degree—then we can explain the observed growth within the parameters of the model propounded by Hans Medick, Jürgen Schlümbohm, and Peter Kriedte's "theory of protoindustrialization."

Changes in the early modern period, particularly by the eighteenth century, also involved shifts in emotional definitions. Without arguing that premodern families were devoid of emotion, it does seem that emotional expectations for parent-child as well as spousal relationships began to increase by the seventeenth century. Protestantism played a role, as did the commercialization of the economy, which prompted more attention to emotional support within the family. Love was redefined and gained a greater role, for example in choices of marriage partners, while anger within the household was newly criticized. How much these changes entered daily relationships, and what the pattern was among various social classes, continue to be debated. But the emotional emphasis would continue into the modern period, particularly as some of the economic and production functions of the family declined when work moved outside the home.

THE NINETEENTH CENTURY AND INDUSTRIALIZATION

When the debates surrounding the prolific power of protoindustrialists peaked in the early-middle 1980s, they were superseded by new concerns about the ways in which gender was organized. In part, this new concern derived from the increasing pressure of feminist historians to distance themselves from the now-older issues of women's history; and, in part, it gained inspiration from the writings of Michel Foucault whose influence was at its height at this time. Foucault's writings provided a fertile ground for exploring issues of identity formation, which began to take the place of materialist concerns with family strategies and socioeconomic change as the driving force of historical analysis. The key text in this historiographical shift, *Family Fortunes,* was written by Leonore Davidoff and Catherine Hall, who set out to explore how two sets of English middle-class women's lives were organized by changing images of gender. While they paid close attention to the material forces that influenced the lives of the female Cadburys of Birmingham and the Taylors of Essex, the most exciting parts of their argument derived from Davidoff and Hall's close attention to the ways these women fashioned and represented themselves in accommodating the exigencies of social change. As they write,

> The concept of purity had taken on a special resonance for women partly because of fears associated with the polluting powers of sexuality. One of the distinguishing characteristics of the middle class was their concern with decorum in bodily functions and cleanliness of person. Thus, maintaining purity and cleanliness was both a religious goal and a practical task for women. (Davidoff and Hall, p. 90)

This point is tremendously important in the Victorian emphasis on women's roles as mothers—as opposed to the early modern concern with women as wives. Such women were enjoined to make their homes a safe haven in a heartless world. And, as Davidoff and Hall write, it was a task that was taken on with a religious fervor. It should be added that emphasis on this new orientation in middle-class women's self-definition was accompanied by a missionary desire to implant these behaviors on those below them in the social structure whose family lives were thought to be backward, crude, and primitive.

This argument is superbly demonstrated by the historical anthropologists Orvar Löfgren and Jonas Frykman, whose work compares and contrasts family life among the peasantry, the proletariat, and the middle classes in Oscarian Sweden. The confidence of the bourgeoisie in labeling other behaviors as backward, crude, and primitive provided an enormous impetus to social reform. Lower-class families were to be the object of surveillance and those whose behavior was not in conformity with the new standards were to be the object of state-sanctioned policing. At the heart of this vision, then, is the arrogation of truth by the instrumentality of social reason which takes place alongside the marginalization of those who do not—or will not—conform. Exercising control through the discipline of the body, the mind, and the soul is one of the key themes in modern history. The internalization of discipline was part of a long and arduous process of education which was an extremely protracted issue in the making of modern societies.

In the course of the early modern period, this technology of the self was severed from both religion and its patrician class origins; self-examination became popularized as the real way of life, not just a formalized set of ritual observances in the charge of specialists. The modern state has bureaucratized self-policing by incorporating it into the daily life of its citizens—from cradle to grave—and by cloaking it in the positivistic mantle of medical science. The regulatory thrust of this command structure was built upon deep foundations; in this regard, nineteenth-century state-formation was modern in that it was able to avail itself of new institutions, new techniques, and new technologies while deploying these strategies against a fundamentally new class.

The family axis in this way became both more narrowly construed and more attentively policed. It became the site for sentiment-building in some of the trends at the end of the early modern period. In it, the most rigorous techniques of repressive discipline, as Michel Foucault writes, "were formed, and, more particularly, applied first, with the greatest intensity, in the economically privileged and politically dominant classes." He further states that "what was formed was a political ordering of life, not through an enslavement of others, but through an affirmation of self" so that "it has to be seen as the self-affirmation of one class rather than the enslavement of another: a defense, a protection, a strengthening, and an exaltation that were eventually extended to others—at the cost of different transformations—as a means of social control and political subjugation." (Foucault, p. 120)

Resistance to this disciplinary project was based on something more than an irrational adherence to tradition. Family formation strategies were not reflex actions; they represented something deeper that adapted to changing pressures by assimilating what was needed and rejecting the rest. In an age of revolution, the pressures to adapt became more intense and the resistance to change more complex. In the course of adapting themselves to change, both discursive and behavioral practices were being beaten on the anvil of plebeian resistance with the hammer of bourgeois prescription and so came to develop a shape of their own.

In place of the independent paternal authority that characterized the early modern family—and provided the organizing metaphor for its political theory—the modern state apparatus permeated domestic space. Coincident with the fertility decline, a new disciplinary complex congealed; orchestrated by the state, the helping professions coordinated the application of power and knowledge in the daily lives of the citizenry. Teachers, social workers, psychologists, and the whole battery of social welfare agencies were created from a patchwork of voluntary institutions that had previously been called upon to aid the sick and infirm.

Under the mantle of professionalization, the job of interpretation devolved into the province of a new technology of the self staffed by "the directors of conscience, moralists and pedagogues." Foucault writes, "the discovery of the Oedipus complex was contemporaneous with the juridical organization of loss of parental authority." (Foucault, pp. 128, 130). This reconstituted family became not just the locus of what Foucault calls "bio-power" (and which might be termed "human capital formation" to conform to Anglo-American understanding) but also, and inevitably, the apparatus through which the practical regimen of reproduction was carried out. The reproduction of "bio-power" was thus both the means and the end of the revolution in the family. Foucault's insistence on the nature of power relations in the politics

of family formation provides an important dimension to the processes of social change within which the decline of fertility, class formation, compulsory schooling, social welfare, and democratization occurred. The hallmark of this new knowledge-politics was the state's enhanced powers of surveillance—to police, supervise, discipline, punish, and reward. The growth of a state apparatus concerned with human capital speaks very much to this point. Indeed, it provides the glue that joins together the public and the private, the social and the individual.

The fundamental sites of this new disciplinary program were the public school and the private family. The proletarian family was revolutionized in the course of the transition from early modern to modern times, when the proletariat became the overwhelming majority in the European population. The working-class household became the site of social and biological reproduction, not production, and in the process it came to be judged by the quantity and the quality of its product—human capital. We can see the pre-history of this transformation in the debates on police and charity initiated by the early modern political arithmeticians and political economists, but it was not until two centuries later that the institutional instruments were put in place to realize this Malthusian positivity, the modern family.

Faced with recalcitrance and outright resistance from plebeians, social disciplinarians sought recourse to the courts and argued that it was both a social and an individual good to break up immoral family units. When a child's "home environment" is deemed "unsatisfactory" a huge caseload of bureaucratic paper is developed by a team of "experts" (in the helping professions) while the threat of constant intrusion into a "problem family" remains as long as their file is "active." This was the field of moral force within which the massive expansion of compulsory schooling orbited.

Many of the social functions of the working-class family—education, health, and welfare—were superseded by the aggressively intrusive actions of the modern state while its productive functions were redefined by industrial capitalism. The restructuring of the social relations of production—as a result of the exclusionary tactics of trade unionization and a renewed patriarchy which privileged adult males—was intimately connected with the implosion of the working-class family as women and children were removed from the world of work. The restriction of working-class fertility was another tactic by which the labor supply was controlled when the cost of its reproduction began to soar and even teenaged children were removed from productive, waged-work and kept in school by the rules and regulations of the state. It was only in these radically transformed circumstances—not just in response to the prescriptions urged upon them by respectable moralizers—that the working-class family reorganized itself. But it would be misleading to suggest that it was able either to resist or to ignore the prescriptive demands of the moralizing modernizers. We can see the impact of this intrusion most clearly in the changing life cycles and gender roles of its members.

In contrast to the corporate life cycle of its predecessors, the urban proletariat was decidedly modern in that its children stayed at home until marriage. Marriage was itself predicated on the ideal of the male breadwinner and the domestication of the wife/mother. The commodification of labor-power, and the concomitant devaluation of skill, compressed the life cycle of the proletariat. Instead of a two-phase transition from childhood to youth and then from youth to adulthood—the first marked by leaving home and the second by marriage—which characterized the corporate life cycle (as well as its rural equivalent of service), the proletarian life cycle was marked by a single transition in which leaving home and marriage were squeezed together.

The huddling of working-class families was necessitated by the disintegration of older modes of production and compounded by the massive increase in the supply of labor as a result of the demographic revolution. On one hand, adult male workers lost control of the labor process while on the other they lost control over their patriarchal family capital. In these circumstances, by the end of the nineteenth century, it was possible for only a tiny minority of labor aristocrats to approximate the male breadwinner ideal urged upon them by the dictates of proletarian claims of respectability in concert with the bourgeois chorus of Malthusian moralizing.

The transformation of demographic behavior was strongly influenced by the way in which those who had been marginalized made their own history. It was their proactivity—expressed in demographic terms by their recourse to fertility control (for their own reasons it must be added) and expressed in social terms by their rising expectations for inclusion in both civil and consumer society—that acted as the sorcerer's apprentice, transforming the task facing our historical Sisyphus. This task was further complicated because the relative openness of the marketplace was challenged by a mean-spirited class-consciousness sparked by the Malthusian project of blaming the poor for their poverty. Yet the openness of the marketplace survived; so, too, did the responsiveness of the political system. Marginalization intensified the contradictions which could promise inclusion but was predicated on the exploitation of one half of society for the liberation of the other half. Consumer culture is now within the reach of everyone and in the grasp of most. The remarkable modernization of the working-class family was not a matter of bourgeoisification so much as a convergence around a certain normative standard that was acknowledged by all even though it was interpreted in quite distinctive ways according to one's class, ethnicity, gender, and age.

The power of disciplinarians was neither absolute nor uncontested; rather, their aims (discursive and practical) were hammered out against the anvil of working-class resistance. The blows that the working class absorbed were directed in an attempt to refashion its identity. To a large extent, this refashioning has occurred; but, equally, this new identity is not exactly what those who wielded the hammer of social change had in mind. But, then, they didn't have computerized, automated production routines in mind either; nor did they envisage the insistent demand for equality—social and political, personal and private—which has distinguished twentieth-century social politics.

This brings me to conclude with a question: Is the "modern age" over? If so, then, when did it end and what is replacing it? If we connect the modern age with a prescriptive vision of family discipline, then we are now living in an age of "late modernity." The prescriptive center no longer holds. The loss of that prescriptive unanimity is a matter of fact. Those who mourn that loss cannot forget the sentimental family; they seem to believe that it was a natural form of social organization and not one constructed in the transition from early modern to modern times. The cost exacted by modern memory is that those who cannot forget the family often mistake its appearance and in so doing betray a fundamental misunderstanding of the contingency of the world we have made. The splintering of prescriptive unanimity has led to the emergence of familial pluralism. More particularly, I would suggest that if the early modern world was characterized by "government of families," the modern world by "government through the family," then the world of late modernity will be characterized by "government without the family."

Along with increasing diversity of family types in the twentieth century has come a redefinition of many family functions. Except for a brief post–World War II baby boom, numbers of children per family continued to decline, and in general childrearing declined as a family function. The entry of married women into the labor force from the 1950s onward changed their bargaining power within marriage. Many families increasingly served as recreational and consumer units, and many people found they could do without the family altogether for these purposes. Rising divorce rates and, particularly in areas such as Scandinavia, increasing numbers of unions without marriage, signaled this redefinition of functions.

See also other articles in this section.

BIBLIOGRAPHY

Books

Ariès, Philippe. *Centuries of Childhood.* Translated by Robert Baldick. New York, 1962. Translation of *Enfant et la vie familiale sous l'Ancien Régime.*

Bernardes, Jan. "Do We Really Know What 'The Family' Is?" In *Family and Economy in Modern Society.* Edited by Paul Close and Rosemary Collins. London, 1985. Pages 192–195.

Brooke, Christopher. *The Medieval Idea of Marriage.* Oxford and New York, 1989.

Davidoff, Leonore, and Catherine Hall. *Family Fortunes: Men and Women of the English Middle Class, 1780–1850.* London and Chicago, 1987.

Davis, Natalie Zemon. *The Return of Martin Guerre.* Cambridge, Mass., 1983.

Donzelot, Jacques. *The Policing of Families.* Translated by Robert Hurley. New York, 1979.

Duby, Georges. *The Early Growth of the European Economy: Warriors and Peasants from the Seventh to the Twelfth Century.* Ithaca, N.Y., 1978.

Duby, Georges. *The Knight, the Lady, and the Priest: The Making of Modern Marriage in Medieval France.* Translated by Barbara Bray. New York, 1983. Translation of *Chevalier, la femme et le prêtre.*

Flandrin, Jean-Louis. *Families in Former Times: Kinship, Household, and Sexuality.* Translated by Richard Southern. Cambridge, U.K., 1979.

Foucault, Michel. *The History of Sexuality.* Volume 1: *An Introduction.* Translated by Robert Hurley. New York, 1980.

Goody, Jack. *The Development of the Family and Marriage in Europe.* Cambridge, U.K., 1983.

Laqueur, Thomas. *Making Sex: Body and Gender from the Greeks to Freud.* Cambridge, Mass., 1990.

Laslett, Peter. *The World We Have Lost.* London and New York, 1965.

Levine, David. *Family Formation in an Age of Nascent Capitalism.* New York, 1977.

Löfgren, Orvar, and Jonas Frykman. *Culture Builders: A Historical Anthropology of Middle-Class Life.* Translated by Alan Crozler. New Brunswick, N.J., 1987. Translation of *Kultiverade människan.*

Medick, Hans, Jürgen Schlümbohm, and Peter Kriedte. *Industrialization before Industrialization: Rural Industry in the Genesis of Capitalism.* Translated Beate Schempp. Cambridge, U.K., 1981. Translation of *Industrialisierung von der Industrialisierung.*

Shorter, Edward. *The Making of the Modern Family.* New York, 1975.

Tilly, Louise, and Joan Scott. *Women, Work, and Family.* New York, 1978.

Articles

Hareven, Tamara. "The History of the Family and the Complexity of Social Change." *American Historical Review* 96 (1991): 95–124.

Herlihy, David. "The Carolingian *Mansus.*" *Economic History Review,* 2d ser. 13 (1960): 79–89.

Herlihy, David. "Family." *American Historical Review* 96 (1991): 1–16.

Herlihy, David. "The Making of the Medieval Family: Symmetry, Structure and Sentiment." *Journal of Family History* 8 (1983): 116–130.

Holt, J. C. "Feudal Society and the Family in Early Medieval England: I. The Revolution of 1066." *Transactions of the Royal Historical Society,* 5th ser. 32 (1982): 193–212.

Lynch, Katherine. "The Family and the History of Public Life." *Journal of Interdisciplinary History* 24 (1994): 665–684.

Mendels, Franklin. "Proto-Industrialization: The First Phase of Industrialization." *Journal of Economic History* 32 (1972): 241–261.

Middleton, Chris. "Peasants, Patriarchy and the Feudal Mode of Production in England. A Marxist Appraisal: I. Property and Patriarchal Relations within the Peasantry." *Sociological Review* 29 (1981): 105–135.

Middleton, Chris. "Peasants, Patriarchy and the Feudal Mode of Production in England. II: Feudal Lords and the Subordination of Peasant Women." *Sociological Review* 29 (1981): 137–154.

Scott, Joan, and Louise Tilly. "Women's Work and the Family in Nineteenth-Century Europe." *Comparative Studies in Society and History* 17 (1975): 36–64.

Scott, Joan, Louise Tilly, and Miriam Cohen. "Women's Work and European Fertility Patterns." *Journal of Interdisciplinary History* 6 (1976): 447–476.

Sheehan, M. M. "Theory and Practice: Marriage of the Unfree and the Poor in Medieval Society." *Mediaeval Studies* 50 (1988): 457–487.

Stone, Lawrence. "Family History in the 1980s." *Journal of Interdisciplinary History* 12 (1981): 51–87.

Tilly, Louise. "Women's History and Family History: Fruitful Collaboration or Missed Connection?" *Journal of Family History* 12 (1987): 303–315.

KINSHIP

Andrejs Plakans

When used by historians, the term "kinship" and its variants ("kinship ties," "kin networks") commonly point to a domain of social connections individuals had by virtue of birth and marriage. In everyday life these ties generated kinship roles (father, mother, son, daughter, brother, sister, uncle, cousin, etc.) which, if and when enacted, entailed certain rights, responsibilities, and behaviors. The enactment of these roles left various kinds of evidence in the historical record. In earlier research, scholars often drew a line between "family" (parents and children) and "kin" (other relatives), but because of the influence of anthropology on social history, this practice has now faded. Historical researchers usually include within kinship investigations not only family but also types of "fictive" kinship, such as godparenthood. In the study of historical kinship in Europe, most of the questions raised initially about the continent are still very much open: Which persons in a pool of potential kin were socially recognized as such, and how did these practices differ among traditional European societies? What rights and obligations did various kinship statuses entail? Were there "systems" of kinship, and how binding were the "rules" of such systems? Did enactment of kinship roles over time produce a collective "tilt," so that a past society can be characterized as, for example, "patrilineal" or "bilateral"? And how did the kinship domain interact with other social domains such as marital practices, property relationships, friendship circles, and the legal order?

The expectation among historians of Europe that kin ties had significance in historical explanation of both individual and collective behavior is of long standing. With some exceptions, however, prior to the 1960s and 1970s research tended to follow a biographical model, focusing on concrete historical individuals and their kin involvements when the narrative required. Sometimes this thrust was enlarged, as when in prosopographical research (collective biography) a collection of individuals of the same kind were investigated. But in the 1960s the confluence of new research directions changed this approach and produced, within the context of a "new social history," what might be called a new kinship history as well. The research mode identified with the French journal *Annales* called for an exploration of social (and other) "structures of long duration" (*la longue durée*); and in England the Cambridge Group for the History of Population and Social Structure initiated major quantitative projects in what were termed historical sociology and historical demography. A greater openness among historians toward the methods and subject matter of such social sciences as sociology and anthropology (particularly the latter, as far as kinship was concerned) complemented these philosophical and methodological changes. As a result, among historians studying Europe both European and non-European, much more attention than ever before came to be paid to the social relationships that connected people by birth and marriage.

This new "agenda" remained highly decentralized, of course, with some researchers seeking to identify kinship structures that persisted over long periods of time, others investigating the "kinship content" of such microstructures as the household, and still others exploring how long-term changes in fertility, mortality, and migration affected the number and types of kin available in particular historical situations. Much of this work was conducted within other specialties of the new social history, such as family history, the history of women, and the history of children. The new kinship history shared the new social history's interest in nonelites ("history from the bottom up"), though a number of prominent researchers continued their work on nobilities. Historians who did not find these new directions compelling continued to work in the older but still very vibrant biographical mode. One might also observe that these new directions were as fruitful to the study of kinship patterns in the medieval period of European history as in the period after the Renaissance.

In the post-1970s decades, researchers of historical kinship have continued to work largely along the lines established in the founding period, while absorbing yet newer emphases. Among the latter have been the stress on such variables as class, ethnicity, and sex—since kin ties may have been understood and experienced differently by the rich and the poor, men and women, German and Swede—and the injunctions stemming from postmodernism, which underline that all social relationships and accompanying vocabularies must be examined within the context of the deployment of power. There has also been a general deemphasis on the search for "kinship rules" and a new stress on the instrumental nature of kinship ties—on the notion, in other words, that such ties can be bent or ignored or treated playfully when situations warrant. With respect to research tools, historical kinship study has benefited from computers, which are of immense assistance not only in compiling and managing databases but also in producing data configurations with lightning speed. Because historical kinship research normally begins with the scrutiny of complex networks of linked individuals, rapid mechanical reconstruction of such configurations has saved countless research hours.

Though four decades of development seem a long time, the operations of kinship in most of the societies of historic Europe still have not received systematic description. Most of the newer research has been conducted in the history of western and northern Europe (England, France, the Scandinavian countries), with central Europe (the German lands, the Habsburg monarchy) next in line. The Balkan Peninsula has long held a special place in European kinship research because of the work of anthropologists on its complex patrilineal household formations (the *zadruga*); similar work in other areas of eastern Europe did not begin until the 1990s. (Here, the Marxist-Leninist paradigm that controlled historical research for many decades pictured kinship largely as a feudal matter, that was being left behind by a society evolving toward socialist modernity.) Nonetheless, in spite of the unevenness of research, the study of kinship has become an inextricable part of European social history.

THE QUESTION OF EVIDENCE

In moving from the study of concrete historical personages and their kin to an examination of kinship as a structuring principle of communities and entire societies, historians turned their attention to new ways of merging primary sources. Those that had been used earlier—such documents as wills and testaments, autobiographical accounts, marriage contracts, retirement contracts, letters, and land and court records—

had to be supplemented in order for coverage to include not only the classes of people who used such instruments but the common people as well. The new sources included household lists and registers of birth, death, and marriage. Listings frequently contained a profusion of kin terms, while vital registers, if integrated through nominal linkage, by definition could yield examinable networks of related people.

In the analysis of these newer sources, historians were at a disadvantage when compared to anthropologists, who had studied kinship in living communities for about a century. First, anthropologists could question the people whose relations they studied and obtain from them the meaning of kin terms and information about rights and obligations kin statuses entailed. Also, true to the imperatives of their discipline, anthropologists had elaborated a vast body of theory about kinship phenomena, so that results of fresh studies could be, in a sense, fitted into and made sense of by reference to an existing corpus of propositions about how kinship worked. Historians, by contrast, had no such theories about the past, though they were aware of the quasi-historical theories put forth by nineteenth-century sociologists about long-term changes in kinship relations on the European continent—that with increased migration kin networks had become diluted, that kinship had become a spent force with the onset of modernity, that the typical kin cluster of the modern world had become the two-generational nuclear family. These ideas, as it turned out, were, at best, hypotheses to be tested continually; certainly, given their generality they could not help in organizing the close-to-the-ground information to which historians now turned their attention.

The problems of dealing with the new evidence were numerous. To begin with, the most useful sources for kinship research about common people—household listings that used relational terminology, vital registers that listed kin-connected persons over time and in separate volumes—not only did not state the names of all possible kin roles a given configuration could yield, but they also rarely supplied evidence about how kin behaved toward each other. For example, a configuration of terms such as "husband, wife, son, daughter"—all that was usually needed for an enumerator to produce a household list—stated only four role labels but implied at least as many others—father, mother, brother, sister. In evidence culled from vital registration lists, the problem of implicit roles became even more serious because careful linkage of, for example, a series of father-son dyads could implicitly yield such role labels as grandfather, grandson, uncle, nephew, and so on, even though the terms for these roles would not actually appear in the source itself. Moreover, these sources yielded static relationships rather than direct evidence about behavior, leaving it to the historian to impute social significance to an uncovered relationship. In other words, when it came to kinship, even the smallest data set required much inferential thinking, as well as necessitating the linking of these genealogical constructs to sources that would yield evidence about transactions among the named persons.

Continued research at the level of individual persons also raised the question of the representativeness of the communities being researched, in two senses. First, there was the question of how many examples of an enacted kin relationship were needed before the relationship could be judged to be a significant one for the community in question. Second, the question arose of what kind of hierarchies of kin relationships existed, so that certain of them could be judged to be more important than others. Clues to the questions that needed asking could be obtained from anthropological research on kinship, but historians could not—as anthropologists could—ask the people being studied for their views on the matter. Beyond that, it was not at all clear what kinds of kin relations had to be identified as socially significant before an entire community could be described as having an operative kinship rule, or how much variation could be permitted without losing the ability to characterize a region as one that had, say, patrilocal postmarital residence (i.e., newly married couples coming to live in the husband's father's household).

To avoid the problems of imperfect historical sources, some researchers, aided by the computer, made use of the technique of microsimulation. In this the starting point was either a real or an imagined population, the development of which over time was simulated rather than followed in the historical record. The technique required the stipulation of rates of birth, death, marriage, and migration, as well as the stipulation of the mean ages at which these events were likely to have taken place. The exercise was useful for answering such questions as, for example, how many different kin of certain types could a person have in a given demographic regime. Moreover, by comparing real-world findings with simulated results, it was possible to gauge whether a particular community was "normal" or somehow extraordinary. The technique did not call for the substitution of simulated populations for real ones, but it did improve the chances of evaluating the findings about real populations.

A final problem pertained to the evidence that presumably was needed for documenting kinship change over long periods of time—a goal of prime importance to historians. Several choices presented themselves. One could study kinship cross-sectionally at several points in time in many communities and infer long-term change from the nature of the structures present at these points. One could also follow the kinship domain in a single community for as long as the sources permitted, thus obtaining a more reliable record of changes but sacrificing geographical coverage. Beyond that, one also had to choose among the configurations that best manifested long-term kinship change—the lineage, the coresident kin group, the shifting meaning of a particular dyadic relationship—and make the case that these and not others were the best indicators of kinship change in the long term. Alternately, one could invest all research effort in analyzing a community at a single point in the past, in the hope that others would complement the effort by studying similar communities in later and earlier time periods. None of these alternatives has shown itself as being easy, nor as the clear path to unchallengeable characterizations of long-term kinship change.

KIN TIES WITHIN AND OUTSIDE THE HOUSEHOLD

The origins of the new direction in kinship research during the 1960s and 1970s are to be found in the work of, and the research engendered by, the Cambridge Group for the History of Population and Social Structure. In some respects, its innovations were inadvertent, because the group's concerns were focused not on kinship per se but on the comparative long-term history of the domestic group (or family household). In the course of laying out an agenda, researchers found the need to create a system of classification that counted, among other things, the kin of the household head—relatives who were not the spouse and offspring of the head (coresident kin). Though in household listings from northeastern Europe (including Great Britain) the proportion of coresident kin turned out to be comparatively low, in listings from other European sites (particularly eastern Europe), the proportion was much higher. This information provided an important clue to how domestic groups differed across the European continent. In some places, kin-linked groups dispersed, while in others there was a pronounced tendency for kin groups to stay close together—even coreside—as long as the resources of the holding supported them. These differing characteristics were judged to be important because they provided a clue to how groups perpetuated their structures over generations. It was hypothesized that children growing up in groups of certain structures—ranking from simple to complex—were likely to internalize the values of such groups and to recreate the same structures over the course of many generations.

Moreover, anthropological theory suggested that the "coresident kin" were an important clue to general kinship principles active in the community under study. Where no coresident kin were present in the household, the practices of the community endorsed "neolocal postmarital residence" (i.e., newly married couples set up households separate from their parents). By contrast, the presence in the household of married sons and married brothers of the household head suggested patrilocal postmarital residence principles at work. In the developmental cycle of the household, sons upon marriage remained living with the parental couple, but married daughters went to live with the parents of their husbands. Somewhat later in the cycle, after the parental couple had died, a listing of the group would show a structure consisting of married brothers. Moreover, the types of kin who coresided indicated other kin preferences in the community. Coresiding married sons and married brothers (as contrasted with coresiding married daughters and married sisters) suggested that the community, and perhaps the region, valued patrilineality (i.e., males in the father's line staying together as long as possible). The presence of only one married son could be considered a clue to the active use of the stem-family principle, which means that a designated male heir stays with the parents while others disperse. The presence of sons-in-law suggested that in times of crises (no sons, death of designated heir, underage sons), the family could violate postmarital patrilocality and allow a married daughter and her husband to coreside with the current head. In areas where there were no coresident kin or the proportions were very low, the question of how domestic groups worked to perpetuate themselves would have to be sought in other evidence, but where coresident kin did exist, they were an important interpretive resource. In their work anthropologists readily moved from findings about the characteristics of domestic groups to statements about general kinship principles underlying group structures, and researchers following the Cambridge Group's approach tended to adopt this strategy as well.

In order to provide a framework for ongoing research, in 1983 Peter Laslett proposed a four-part regionalization of the European continent in light of the evidence that had been uncovered to date about historical domestic group structures. This scheme, consisting of thirty-three criteria, suggested that "tendencies in domestic group organization" in Europe demonstrated the existence of four broad zones—west, west-central, Mediterranean, and east. With respect to kinship within the household, the proposal suggested that the proportion of coresident kin in the domestic groups of the western zone had tended to be very low, in the west-central zone low as well, and in the Mediterranean and eastern zones high. Married brothers in the western zone had been virtually absent from the historical record of households, while in the west-central zone their proportions had been low, and in the Mediterranean and the eastern very high. Subsequent research on household kinship has not overturned this schema, even while scholars dealing with particular communities have found the formulation problematic, especially as far as the eastern and Mediterranean zones are concerned.

Prolonged comparative research on kin within the household necessarily led to questions about kin who were not in coresidence with each other—a line of inquiry that has yet to run its full course. The main questions were whether dispersed kin maintain relations with each other so that they could be conceptualized as a corporate group; if so, what structures these groups had; and what difference the existence of such groups made for the individuals and families composing the group. The main obstacle to systematic research about non-coresident kin was always the nature of the primary sources, all of which—especially household lists and vital registers—required time-consuming and expensive linkage projects before such broader questions could be addressed. The yield of positive links from such linking projects tended to be socially skewed (the propertied and titled classes having much better documentation than the common people) and problematic (names did not match, and in many parts of Europe population turnover was much more rapid than had been believed). Turnover led to the dispersion of sibling groups, sometimes far beyond the borders of the community and thus beyond the reach of reconstruction. There was no warrant for believing that such far-flung ties were always and everywhere broken permanently, because they could always be reactivated. But it did mean that whereas kin configurations within the domestic group could be described comparatively precisely, those that involved different residences and different communities continued to lead a shadowy existence as far as empirical research was concerned. In principle, through the adept use of precise genealogical information it was possible to reconstruct—at least for the higher social orders—all manner of wide-reaching kin networks, but the act of reconstruction was not in and of itself evidence that the network members used their ties or even recognized them. It remains to be seen what use, if any, was made of such ties, whether some were activated more than others, and whether distance tended to equalize all such kin relationships.

Work on these and related questions produced research strategies to overcome the obvious difficulties. One such strategy has been to choose a defining framework and to define kin ties outside the frame as irrelevant. This strategy is an expanded variant of the study of household kinship, where the household boundary provides the frame. A larger frame can be provided by the community—village, serf estate, neighborhood of a city—and the kin ties deemed important are those which play out within the history of the unit. This choice is analogous to traditional anthropological field research, in which the small community was the focus. Another strategy focuses on a particular time-based kinship formation—a lineage, for example, and most commonly a patrilineage—and uses only its members (individual and families) as objects of study. This strategy can produce results at a point in past time when the relationships of all living lineage members are scrutinized, as well as over time, if the lineage is successful in persisting and has an existence over many generations. If a particular community's past is well documented, it is of course possible to study lineage formation and lineage extinction within a community over a long period of time. A third strategy has been to explicate the kinship ties of a single historical person within and outside that person's place of residence, starting with the information in an exceptionally informative historical document such as a diary. Identifying the composition of personal kin networks has been a normal part of the anthropologists' arsenal of weapons in kinship study, but, in the historical context, this strategy leaves unanswered the question of the representativeness of the individual and the community in which the individual resides.

A fourth strategy for examining kin activity outside the household is to focus on social processes that are not by definition a result of kinship activity but do involve kin. Thus, for example, studies of migration have revealed that kin of migrants could be helpful in the move by providing temporary homes at the point of arrival or a set of temporary residences during the move itself. In such studies, it is not kinship itself that is of interest but the uses to which kin ties can be put. Similarly, the workings of inheritance systems have yielded valuable information about kinship ties. Another example is recruitment to political office in premodern governments, since in these nepotism played a substantial role. In these studies, of course, there is no need to identify all existing kin ties, since the only directly relevant ones are those which the evidence marks as having been used. Yet without in-

formation on the ties not used, the researcher remains in the dark about why these ties and not others were activated, since the "population at risk" from which the used ties were drawn remains unknown.

During the last three decades of the twentieth century, investigations of kinship outside the household moved forward at a slower pace than studies of household kinship. Moreover, the same geographical skewing exists in both subfields, with one notable exception. Generally, we know far more about kinship outside the household in western Europe than in central or eastern Europe. The exception is, again, the Balkan Peninsula, which has fascinated anthropologists for several generations. The kin-focused studies of the English nobility have few parallels—in studies of, for instance, the Russian nobility—and, at a different end of the social spectrum, studies of kinship in the villages of eastern Europe remain sparse in comparison with the numerous village studies in France. In the 1980s, German and Italian scholarship began to turn to questions about social microstructures and kinship as well, but in all cases many of the questions this research direction raised at the outset remain only partially answered.

KINSHIP STRUCTURES, KINSHIP RULES, AND HISTORICAL SHIFTS

Implicit in kinship research efforts has been the assumption that kin ties bind persons to certain behaviors. If generalized throughout a community, region, and society, and if demonstrated to be operative over long periods of time, such constraints could then be thought of as examples of "structures of long duration," predisposing (or binding) people to act in certain ways, even if only half-consciously. Dedicated empiricists among kinship researchers would have liked to wait for sufficient micro-level research before drawing such macro-level conclusions, but, generally speaking, work has proceeded in a somewhat less ordered fashion. Findings about the operation of kinship in everyday life have confirmed, rather than uncovered, the long-held view that traditional European society placed greater emphasis on relatives on the father's than on the mother's side (patrifocal rather than matrifocal), that Europeans who found lineage reckoning of use tended to favor patrilines rather than matrilines, that in postmarital residence decisions it was the groom's father's household that was favored, and that in many inheritance settlements it was sons rather than daughters who benefited the most. In such matters, kinship research about Europe has brought no surprises. To the extent that kinship ties manifested themselves as long-term practices or structures, these favored males while not always totally disadvantaging females. What kinship research has accomplished, however, is to demonstrate how everyday life, when it involved kinship ties, did not necessarily treat structures as sacrosanct, as a set of hard and fast rules. Thus Laslett's concept of "tendencies" in domestic group characteristics is useful in an even larger sense. Even though research on kinship has repeatedly demonstrated that custom and tradition favored males, it has also demonstrated just as convincingly Europeans' readiness not to disfavor females. This emerges when the starting point of research is shifted from "structures" and "rules" to individual-centered networks and to events in the individual life course.

Existing research has shown that such a shift is not simply a matter of changing research strategies but the logical next step in how historical kinship needs to be studied. It is entirely possible to view a "kinship system" from different positions, with structural features being one position and individual kinship another. The principles demonstrably operating in these different realms may seem to be incongruous, but that is evidence that a kinship system may itself contain seemingly incongruous elements. Empirical research on kinship in the European past has demonstrated quite convincingly that great care must be exercised before assuming that there was one European system or that, within it, we can easily delineate cultural areas in which determinative subsystems with certain characteristics operated over time.

Within the general context of male-favoring kinship structures, it has become obvious that when necessary individuals used kin connections on both the father's and mother's side: ego-based kinship, to use the anthropological term, was bilateral. Assistance, favors, support, and other help of various kinds for a person in trouble could just as easily flow from one's matrilineal as patrilineal relatives. At times, this was dictated by necessity, when demographic cataclysms had reduced the number of patrilineal kin; but even when both sides were thriving numerically, Europeans could count on help on both sides when they needed it.

Certain practices that seemed to favor females over males were profoundly disturbing when brought into play. An example is the in-marrying son-in-law, a kin type that appears in those traditional societies where coresidence of married couples was common. Ordinarily, household succession concerned sons, but when a couple had had only daughters or when sons had died, there was little hesitancy to incorporate into the domestic group a son-in-law as a potential heir. In communities where this was common, the practice was frequently surrounded by loss of face for the parental couple and the son-in-law. In these situations, however, it is clear that it was the survival of the family's base—the farm or holding—that was of principal importance, even though survival was accomplished through a break in the patriline.

A much more direct threat to the perpetuation of kinship structures and rules was the growing significance of the nuclear family unit, a slow process starting perhaps in the seventeenth but definitely present by the eighteenth century. In this shift, wider kin ties were not necessarily severed but were deemphasized. Thus the husband-wife and parent-child ties became more important than the ties between the same husband and his father and other patrilineal relatives. Emphasis shifted from a kind of equality among one's own children and the children of one's siblings and became focused on one's own children. In this situation the wife ceased to think of herself as still attached, even after marriage, to her father's line, and increasingly began to think of herself as the spouse of her husband, irrevocably removed from the father's kin network.

It is very probable that this shift, operating from the eighteenth century onward, gradually equalized kin ties to persons outside the conjugal family unit. Specific kin ties to particular individuals lost whatever force they had had before, and all kin beyond the conjugal family became more or less interchangeable. Such a shift did not invent a new feature of European kinship but simply enhanced the importance of existing bilaterality. In some societies, especially in western and northern Europe, where domestic groups were always small and did not often include coresident married relatives, this shift—judging by the fuzziness of kinship terminology—was already under way before the eighteenth century. Elsewhere, where coresidential kinship was more complex, the specificities of individual links were maintained for a longer time. Demographic trends clearly accentuated the equalization of kin relationships. In the nineteenth century, as levels of intracontinental migration increased dramatically, and as out-migration to North American and other continents increased as well, kin ties were severed and the specificities of relationships lost. Reforms in the law came increasingly to enshrine equal inheritance among offspring, so that it became increasingly difficult to favor sons over daughters.

Several features of these long-term shifts appear to stand out. First, it has not been demonstrated unequivocally that, with the so-called "triumph" of the modern nuclear family, kin ties beyond the family have been permanently abrogated. Repeatedly, research has shown that kin remained an important point of reference, and kin networks could be mobilized to fulfill various kinds of support functions. Kinship obligations to specific persons might no longer be felt as mandatory, but kin continue to be recognized as a group distinct from friends and strangers. This has been particularly evident in European societies in which the twentieth century has brought long periods of social stress. Documentation of familial behavior during the two world wars, for example, shows repeated instances of the use of kin networks for survival, and the collapse of communist regimes and the transformation of state systems in Eastern Europe in the 1989–1991 period has demonstrated again the importance of kin networks for all manner of assistance. Stories associated with continuing insurgencies in the post-1991 Balkan area (e.g., Kosovo) document Kosovo Albanians mobilizing transcontinental networks of relatives to assist in the battle for "national independence." Though there is considerable evidence about the equalization and democratization of kin connections, there is little that suggests that kin have been made equal to friends.

Second, kinship theorists have at times made reference to "modern" European kinship, which carried the implications that "modernity" was a permanently achieved state and that the interchangeability of kin ties had permanently superseded all other kin characteristics. With increasing doubts about the permanence of the "modern," however, it is fair to say that there is no historical warrant for assuming that the present state will last forever. The appropriate assessment would be that the present is a phase—neither higher nor lower—of the continually unfolding social history of the European continent, and that the current configurations do not provide any usable clues to what the characteristics of future phases will be.

Third, some features of "modern" European family life may make kin reckoning more difficult and dethrone lineage reckoning entirely. The high proportion of marriages that end in divorce, the equalization of state benefits to married and unmarried cohabiting couples, the diminishing fertility rate, and the growing popularity of no-child or single-child families all disrupt lineage formation and lineage calculation. The proportion of Europeans involved in such phenomena appears to be growing. If such trends continue, the identification of lineages will clearly become virtually impossible, and perhaps irrelevant.

See also **The European Marriage Pattern** *(volume 2) and other articles in this section.*

BIBLIOGRAPHY

Anderson, Michael. *Family Structure in Nineteenth Century Lancashire*. Cambridge, U.K., 1971.

Brandes, Stanley H. *Migration, Kinship, and Community: Tradition and Transition in a Spanish Village*. New York, 1975.

Cressy, David. *Coming Over: Migration and Communication between England and New England in the Seventeenth Century*. Cambridge, U.K., 1987.

Flandrin, Jean Louis. *Families in Former Times: Kinship, Household, and Sexuality*. Cambridge, U.K., 1979

Fortes, Meyer. *Kinship and the Social Order: The Legacy of Lewis Henry Morgan*. Chicago, 1970.

Goody, Jack, Joan Thirsk, and E. P. Thompson. *Family and Inheritance: Rural Society in Western Europe, 1200–1800*. Cambridge, U.K., 1976.

Halpern, Joel M., and Barbara Kerewsky Halpern. *A Serbian Village in Historical Perspective*. New York, 1972.

Imhof, Arthur E. *Lost Worlds: How Our European Ancestors Coped with Everyday Life and Why Life Is So Hard Today*. Translated by Thomas Robisheaux. Charlottesville, Va., 1996.

Kertzer, David I. *Family Life in Central Italy, 1880–1910: Sharecropping, Wage Labor, and Coresidence*. New Brunswick, N.J., 1984.

Langham, Ian. *The Building of British Social Anthropology: W. H. R. Rivers and His Cambridge Disciples in the Development of Kinship Studies, 1898–1931.* Dordrecht, Holland, 1981.

Lynch, Joseph H. *Godparents and Kinship in Early Medieval Europe.* Princeton, N.J., 1986.

Macfarlane, Alan. *The Family Life of Ralph Josselin, a Seventeenth-Century Clergyman: An Essay in Historical Anthropology.* Cambridge, U.K., 1970.

Maynes, Mary Jo, et al., eds. *Gender, Kinship, Power: a Comparative and Interdisciplinary History.* New York, N.Y., 1996.

Murray, Alexander C. *Germanic Kinship Structure: Studies in Law and Society in Antiquity and in the Early Middle Ages.* Toronto, 1983.

Plakans, Andrejs. *Kinship in the Past: An Anthropology of European Family Life, 1500–1900.* Oxford, 1984.

Sabean, David Warren. *Kinship in Neckarhausen, 1700–1870.* Cambridge, U.K., 1998.

Segalen, Martine. *Fifteen Generations of Bretons: Kinship and Society in Lower Brittany, 1720–1980.* Translated by J. A. Underwood. Cambridge, U.K., 1991.

Segalen, Martine, and Marianne Gullestad, eds. *Family and Kinship in Europe.* London, 1997.

Smith, Richard M., ed. *Land, Kinship, and Life-Cycle.* Cambridge, U.K., 1984.

Strathern, Marilyn. *Kinship at the Core: An Anthropology of Elmdon, a Village in North-West Essex in the Nineteen-Sixties.* Cambridge, U.K., 1981.

Wall, Richard, Jean Robin, and Peter Laslett, eds. *Family Forms in Historic Europe.* Cambridge, U.K., 1983.

Wolfram, Sybil. *In-laws and Outlaws: Kinship and Marriage in England.* London, 1987.

THE HOUSEHOLD

Richard Wall

This essay assesses the multifaceted character of the household as a residential and social unit. Later sections of the essay consider the role of economic, demographic, and social factors in shaping household forms, and discuss the strengths and weaknesses of the various attempts that have been made to map the variation in household patterns across Europe.

The household is usually defined as a residence unit. The members of a household include all persons, whether or not they are related to each other, who share a clearly defined living space or dwelling. The household is in this way clearly distinguished from the family, whose members are related to each other, however distantly, but do not necessarily coreside. Households can also have other attributes. Members of the household (or some of them) may pool their incomes, eat communally at least once a day, and earn their livelihood from working together to exploit assets rented, leased, or owned by the household, such as a farm or workshop. Other ties may develop from this level of cooperation: a sense of mutual dependence among the members of the household, respect for the authority of the household head, and a desire to preserve the privacy of the physical space occupied by the household. The household may also undertake the socialization of the young and afford shelter to members of the local community (primarily relatives but in some cases also nonrelatives such as foster children and the childless elderly) unable to provide for themselves from their own resources. Vestiges of the religious and judicial functions of the household lingered from medieval times.

CONCEPTUALIZATIONS OF THE HOUSEHOLD

The multifaceted character of the household has been a major source of its appeal to economists, sociologists, and social geographers as well as historians. The household has attracted attention both as the unit which ensures the reproduction of the labor force and the unit through which capitalist economies pressurize individuals as workers. The household has also been viewed as the locus of many of the relationships between men and women, where much work, domestic labor, and child care is undertaken. Different theorists have stressed some functions of the household at the expense of others. For Michel Verdon it is the criteria of residence; for Kathie Friedman it is its role as an income-pooling unit. This leads the latter to redefine the household to include persons who live elsewhere who contribute to its economic well-being, thereby identifying as the significant unit in societies not those persons who live together but the wider group of persons who share (some) of their income. As Diana Wong has pointed out, such an approach assumes that this support network provided generalized support according to need rather than, as was usually the case, limited assistance in exceptional circumstances. Inequalities in access to the resources of the household on the part of husband and wife, parents and children, master and servant, are also ignored.

Nevertheless, many households are not autonomous economic and social units. For example, Martine Segalen has documented for the west of Brittany in the nineteenth century the extent to which networks of neighbors as well as kin, smallholders as well as farmers, cooperated in a range of labor-intensive tasks such as ploughing, harvesting, and threshing. Such networks also channeled information, offering the individual material, social, cultural, and political privileges and introductions to a potential spouse. Euthymios Papataxiarchis has argued that on the Greek island of Lesbos in the nineteenth century, mutual aid, care of children, and even significant interpersonal relationships extended beyond the household. Women's ties were with their families of origin, while the men had their (exclusively male) social groups. Variation can be expected in the strength of the social ties which united members of different households according to area of residence, time, the nature of the particular household economy, and the social standing of the household, but too little research has been completed to provide a wide-ranging comparative perspective.

The situation is considerably better as regards the economic ties between households. Analysis of the time budgets collected by Frédéric Le Play and his followers indicate that in Europe in the middle and later nineteenth century more than half of young couples working as peasants, artisans, tenant farmers, and laborers had received substantial financial support from their parents or parents-in-law either at the time of their marriage or later. In most cases, and in particular in western and northern Europe, this support was received without the necessity to coreside. Parental support was forthcoming less frequently in England, the Low Countries, Spain, Germany, Switzerland, and Paris than in other parts of Europe. Underlying these variations were differences in the nature of the household economy. Couples who were peasants or smallholders were much more likely to receive financial support from their parents than were couples who were factory workers or laborers. Other than parents, more distant relatives, employers and landlords, and other nonrelatives also made significant contributions to the standard of living of persons resident in other households.

In practice it is no easy matter when working with historical documents to identify an unambiguous, let alone a consistent, definition of the household. The lists of inhabitants which furnish the information on family and household patterns in England prior to the official censuses of the nineteenth century almost without exception fail to provide any definition of how individuals were set out in groups, whether separated by lines, spaces, or numbered consecutively. The most detailed of these lists have been identified as listing households on the basis of the information provided on the members of these groups: spouse, sons and daughters, other relatives, and servants were all described in relation to the person listed first in the group. This also has the advantage of providing a measure of consistency with the definition proposed in the British Census of 1851, where the household (referred to as the family) was defined as follows: "The first, most intimate, and perhaps most important community, is the family, not considered as the children of one parent, but as persons under one head; who is the occupier of the house, the householder, master, husband or father; while the other members of the family are, the wife, children, servants, relatives, visitors, and persons constantly or accidentally in the house" (quoted in Wall, 1972, p. 160). Even so, total consistency is not assured, as the British censuses of the nineteenth century were conducted on a de jure basis, recording all persons resident in a household on a given night, whereas the precensus lists of inhabitants registered only the de facto population, the habitual residents of the household.

One of the severest problems encountered by historians seeking a coherent definition of the household is occasioned by the presence of lodgers and other nonrelatives who rented their accommodation from the principal household but budgeted separately. Some relatives and even adult children may occasionally have been in the same situation. On a definition of the household which focuses on income pooling, they should logically be considered as constituting separate households. Conversely, on a definition of the household based on common residence they should be counted as members of the same household unless known to be occupying separate living space. Most nationwide surveys of living arrangements in present-day Europe attempt to give equal weight to the common dwelling and common housekeeping in their definitions of the household, as recommended by the United Nations.

EUROPEAN FAMILY AND HOUSEHOLD SYSTEMS

If the way households function and even the way a household is defined are embedded in a particular culture as well as in a particular economic system, considerable care is required in comparing the structure of households across both time and space. Some scholars have argued that all comparative work is flawed, as it simplifies and distorts social realities by using the criteria of areal coverage and prevalence in conjunction with the selection of supposedly objective standards or norms to determine the significance of a social structure. Classifications of household types, David Sabean has declared, are useless unless they take into account power relationships within and beyond the household and the networks which linked household with household, family with family, and individual with individual—an approach that can only be achieved through the study of a particular locality. The contrary view is that each local or regional study needs a wider comparative survey to place it in context. This is the approach adopted here. The loss of precision and context that this entails is admitted, as is the fact that similarity in household structure of populations from different time periods or regions is not to be taken as evidence that social relations invested in that structure were necessarily identical.

There have been a number of attempts to map the variation in household forms across Europe. In a two-stage process, first the distinguishing features of the household system are arbitrarily determined and then, second, the regional prevalence is measured. For John Hajnal, building on his earlier work on European marriage patterns, the key aspects of the household system of northwest Europe in the seventeenth and eighteenth centuries were a late age at first marriage by men and women (over twenty-six for men and over twenty-three for women), the immediate assumption by the newly married couple of the headship of a household, whether newly formed or a continuation of the parental household (in which case the parents would retire), and the circulation of young people between households as life-cycle servants prior to marriage. Northwest Europe as defined by Hajnal encompassed Scandinavia (including Iceland but excluding Finland), the British Isles, the Low Countries, the German-speaking area, and northern France.

Hajnal's rule about headship runs counter to Peter Laslett's earlier (and later) conceptualizations of the west European family system, which envisaged the formation of an independent household on marriage as one of its key characteristics. In his 1983 paper "Family and Household as Work Group and Kin Group: Areas of Traditional Europe Compared," Laslett also argued that it was possible, using a broader set of criteria as the defining characteristics of each family and household system, to identify four, rather than two, distinct family and household systems that were dominant in, if not entirely exclusive to, particular areas of Europe: northwest, west and central, Mediterranean, and east. These criteria included, in addition to household formation rules, procreational and demographic characteristics and the types of kin present in the household, as well as aspects of the role of the household in the area of work and welfare. The effect, possibly unintentional, was to anchor each household system more firmly within a particular economy and broader social structure, the latter reflecting in particular the extent and nature of community and state support for disadvantaged groups within the population.

According to Laslett, the family and household system of northwest Europe was distinguished not only by the formation of new households at the time of marriage, a late age at first marriage, and the predominance of simple-family households (households consisting of couples with or without unmarried offspring or lone parents and unmarried offspring) but by the rarity with which households functioned as work groups and the presence of households which received a large part of their income in the form of transfer payments from the community. By contrast, the family and household system of central Europe contained a large proportion of stem-family households (where a married son, on his marriage or later, continued the parental household by succeeding his father as the household head), and many households were work groups. In other respects, Laslett argued that the household systems of central and western Europe were similar. The household systems of Mediterranean and eastern Europe shared with central Europe the association between the household and the work group but departed from its other features through higher proportions of complex households (particularly in eastern Europe), early ages at first marriage (for both sexes in eastern Europe; for men only in Mediterranean Europe), and absence of the link between marriage and the formation of a new household.

Hajnal's and Laslett's delineations of European family and household systems have now been challenged from a number of quarters. One concern has been the fluidity of the boundaries between the various regions. Boundaries between "systems" might also shift over time. During the course of the eighteenth and nineteenth centuries the household system of Hungary evolved from the simple-family household system as in northwest Europe toward more complex structures in the face of land scarcity in one part of the country and labor scarcity in another. In the latter part of the nineteenth century, as the economy of Corsica deteriorated, extended- and multiple-family households came to predominate in place of less complex households. Other societies moved in the reverse direction. For example, in the southwest of Finland simple-family households increased at the expense of complex households during the late eighteenth and nineteenth centuries in response to legal reforms which permitted the division of farms and the formation of households by the landless. After 1850 the trend toward more simple household forms was reinforced by innovations in methods of fishing which reduced the amount of capital and labor required. Simple-family households also replaced complex-family households for reasons still uncertain in some parts of Sweden during the eighteenth century. Instances in which, in different parts of Europe between 1750 and 1950, there were fewer complex households than fifty years earlier were almost matched by instances when there were more complex households later on. In some populations (Hruni, Iceland, and Cuenca, Spain) a trend toward more complex households is even evident after 1900, although increasing complexity of household structures was most in evidence in the nineteenth century.

A second challenge to both Hajnal's and Laslett's conceptualization of marriage and family patterns has involved a search for inconsistencies within the defining characteristics of a particular family system: for example, signs of the presence of a late age

Extended Household. *Living Off the Fat of the Land, a Country Feast,* painting by Thomas Unwins (1782–1857). DREWEATT NEATE FINE ART AUCTIONEERS, NEWBURY, BERKSHIRE, U.K./THE BRIDGEMAN ART LIBRARY

at first marriage in conjunction with low proportions remaining unmarried and a high proportion of complex households, or, alternatively, of an early age at first marriage coexisting with a preponderance of simple-family households. Such evidence has been duly produced, particularly from Italy, making it difficult to maintain that there was just one Mediterranean family pattern. It is clear that the variability is too great to be accommodated within one household system, even with a generous allowance for the fluidity of boundaries between systems and the presence of marriage and household patterns incompatible with the characteristics of the household system of which they were supposedly part, as argued by Laslett.

An even more fundamental attack on the premises of the conceptualization of the northwest European household system has been mounted by Daniel Scott Smith. According to Smith, two of its key characteristics, a late age at first marriage and a high rate of permanent celibacy, were not intrinsic elements of the family system but the product of external constraints. Whenever there was an open frontier, as in North America, age at marriage and the proportions of never married fell below the levels associated with a northwest European household pattern, leaving only the establishment of a new household on marriage as the defining characteristic of the system. Yet it is possible to show that even this principle might be violated at times, such as when economic circumstances, in

the form of a shortage of housing at a suitable price or the need for young married women to seek employment outside the home, enforced the coresidence of relatives outside the immediate nuclear family of parents and unmarried children. Smith also envisages, as does Michel Verdon, a universal preference for small and simple households. Households, they argue, would always adopt this form but for the existence of a variety of constraints which prevent such preferences being implemented.

Demographic, economic and social change, particularly in the twentieth century, has had a profound effect on household forms. One such change was the fall in fertility which substantially reduced the size of the average household during the first half of the twentieth century. Rising living standards, in conjunction with an increased preference for residential independence on the part of both the elderly and their adult children, has also reduced the frequency of multigenerational households since the end of World War II. For the same reason, boarders and lodgers, so common in households in western Europe in the nineteenth century, all but disappeared during the twentieth century. Instead of living with relatives or non-relatives, many more persons at the beginning of the twenty-first century lived on their own, in a one-person household. Some changes, of course, occurred earlier, such as the decline in demand for male farm servants throughout much of England in the late eighteenth century. However, the reduction in demand for female domestic servants, and the willingness of young women to undertake such work, can be dated, at least for England, to the first half of the twentieth century.

THE GEOGRAPHY OF EUROPEAN HOUSEHOLD FORMS

Tables 1 through 3 provide a more detailed perspective on family and household patterns in the European past by setting out the variation in the proportions of extended- and multiple-family households and in membership of the household defined by relationship to the household head. Table 1 measures the variation in the proportions of extended and multiple households in the middle of the nineteenth century, when data are most plentiful. Extended-family households include both a family group (couple with or without unmarried offspring or lone parent with unmarried offspring) and other relatives such as a parent, sibling, or grandchild. If these relatives themselves constitute a family group (couple or parent and child), then the household is classified as multiple. In mid-nineteenth-century England, as table 1 indicates, there were almost five times as many extended-family households as multiple ones (the average frequency [median] for the eleven populations is 14 percent against 3 percent). Just under one in six households were complex: i.e., either extended or multiple. The range in values was also considerable: 1 to 7 percent for multiple family households, 11 to 16 percent for extended households, and 12 to 21 percent for complex households. This, then, is the English experience behind Laslett's suggestion that northwestern Europe in the past had very low proportions of multiple-family households. There is, therefore, some justification for the claim of "very low" proportions of multiple-family households, given a maximum 7 percent of households of the multiple type in mid-nineteenth-century England. However, the fact that up to a fifth of households in some English populations in the middle of the nineteenth century were complex must raise doubts about the claim that the proportions of complex households were "very low."

Nor are these patterns particularly distinctive. Multiple-family households were equally rare in some French populations: as, for example, in Montplaisant, although located in the south of the country, as well as in a number of populations in northern France. There were also Spanish, Italian, Swedish, and Icelandic populations with as few multiple-family households, and even some populations from southwest Finland with no more multiple-family households than in the English populations with the highest frequency of multiple-family households of the eleven English populations. On the other hand, there were other French, Spanish, Italian, Icelandic, Swedish, and Finnish populations with proportions of multiple-family households far in excess of the experience of any of the English populations. What is therefore most distinctive about the English experience is its uniformity, relative to the variation in household forms occurring in other parts of Europe.

The division of Europe into distinct familial regions as proposed by Laslett—northwest, central and middle, Mediterranean, and east—also looks problematic. Most distinctive, and with very high proportions of multiple and complex households, are the populations of eastern Europe. Yet even in this instance, multiple-family households occur almost as frequently in some of the northern Italian populations (and in higher proportions than on the Linden Estate in Kurland, Lithuania), and proportions of complex households present were as frequent in western districts of Finland. Mediterranean populations look particularly diverse, as others have noted. In the middle of the nineteenth century, there were fewer extended-family households in southern Italian populations than in England (although probably more multiple-family households), whereas in northern Italy the proportions of multiple-family households were close to those of eastern Europe. Household patterns in the Nordic countries were also extremely variable, with several populations from Iceland and Sweden not conforming to the tenets of the northwest European household system, although placed by Hajnal within the ambit of this system for the seventeenth and eighteenth centuries. Unfortunately, we cannot proceed further with delineation of the sphere of influence of west (or northwest) European family patterns, as the selection criteria used to produce table 1 resulted in the inclusion of only one population from Germany and one from Switzerland, and none at all from Ireland, the Netherlands, Belgium, and Denmark. Other studies indicate, however, that rural households in England contained as many relatives as did households in Denmark and Flanders and more relatives than households in the Netherlands. We may reasonably infer, therefore, similar proportions of complex households in Denmark, Flanders, and England (lower in the case of the Netherlands). By the same token, households in nineteenth-century Ireland were considerably more complex.

Rural households. Table 2 sets out the membership of the household in a number of rural populations enumerated at a variety of dates between the late sixteenth and early nineteenth centuries, with mem-

TABLE 1
VARIATION IN EUROPEAN HOUSEHOLD FORMS IN THE MID-NINETEENTH CENTURY

Region and Country	Locality	District	Date	Percentage of All Households			
				Extended	Multiple	Complex[1]	N
			Western Europe				
England	Binfield	Berks	1851	13	3	16	190
	West Wycombe	Buckingham	1851	12	2	14	413
	Littleover	Derby	1851	15	7	21	121
	Mickleover	Derby	1851	16	7	23	154
	Corfe Castle	Dorset	1851	12	2	14	407
	Puddletown	Dorset	1851	11	1	12	264
	Ardleigh	Essex	1851	15	2	16	371
	Forthampton	Gloucester	1851	14	3	17	95
	Barkway & Reed	Hertford	1851	14	6	20	326
	Bampton[2]	Westmorland	1851	16	4	20	491
France	Saint-Jean Trolimon	Brittany	1851	12	8	20	197
	Montplaisant	Perigord Nord	1836	14	1	15	81
	Vescovato[3]	Corsica	1846	2	1	7	310
	Loreto[3]	Corsica	1846	17	2	23	201
	Porri[3]	Corsica	1846	5	3	24	78
	Esparros	Pyrenees	1846	23	14	37	
Germany	Belm[4]	Osnabrück	1858	–	–	36	527
Switzerland	Törbel	Valais	1850	18	8	26	98
			Nordic Countries				
Iceland	Hruni[5]	Arnesyssla	1845	–	–	34	38
	Gardan[5]	Gullbringusyssla	1845	–	–	9	140
Sweden	Hållnäs	Uppland	1851	21	18	38	393
	Tynderö	Västernorrland	1860	12	3	15	232
	Hasslö	Blekinge	1850	2	1	3	115
	Dala[6]	Västergötland	1850	–	–	11	287

bership of the household expressed in terms of the number of persons present of each type: heads of household (married and nonmarried), offspring, relatives, servants, and, finally, any other persons not known to be related to the head of the household. The number of persons of all types found within the household varies considerably, and the variation would no doubt be greater if it had been possible to include more populations from southern and central, let alone from eastern, Europe. In the case of servants, for example, in the selected rural populations the range is from 118 per hundred households in Iceland in 1703 to fewer than 20 per hundred households in the

countryside around Gouda in the Netherlands in 1622, in certain Swiss communities between the mid-seventeenth and early eighteenth centuries, and in the Spanish province of Cuenca in the eighteenth century. For offspring, the range is from 279 per hundred households in Egislau in Switzerland, in the area around Gouda, and in West Flanders in 1814, to 157 per hundred households in Cuenca in 1724.

Gauging the significance of the variation is more difficult but can be considered from the following points of view. In the first place there is the question of the smoothness of the distributions when the populations are placed in rank order from those with most

Region and Country	Locality	District	Date	Percentage of All Households			N
				Extended	Multiple	Complex[1]	
Finland	Finström	Åland	1840	18	15	34	65
	Korpo + Houtskär	Finland Proper	1859	16	7	23	728
	Kumlinge + Brändö	Åland	1859	26	24	50	290
	Replot	Osthrobothnia	1860	31	20	51	75
	Lavansaari	Province of Viborg	1860	33	14	47	93

Southern Europe

Region and Country	Locality	District	Date	Extended	Multiple	Complex[1]	N
Portugal	Lanheses	Minho	1850	12	14	27	210
Spain	Echelar	Basque	1842	–	–	28	332
	Cuenca	Castile	1860	4	1	5	3231
	La Ñora	Murcia	1850	8	2	10	357
Italy	Alagna	Piedmonte	1848	16	12	28	188
	Rongio	Piedmonte	1843	12	24	36	–
	San Bononio	Piedmonte	1840	18	17	35	–
	Oseacco	Friuli	1844	17	30	47	–
	Gniva	Friuli	1844	15	21	35	–
	S. Giovanni al Natisone[7]	Friuli	1850	15	29	44	242
	Corniglio	Emilia	1850	21	13	33	141
	Parma	Emilia	1851	9	5	14	1523
	Lucera Cattedrale	Capitanata	1838	14	9	24	1751
	Molfetta	Bari	1839	9	2	11	1896
	Turi	Bari	1855	10	6	16	1106
	Procida	Campana	1856	4	4	8	2585

Central and Eastern Europe

Region and Country	Locality	District	Date	Extended	Multiple	Complex[1]	N
Estonia	Sangaste	Southern Estonia	1850	17	31	48	451
	Türi	Northern Estonia	1850	23	33	56	388
	Anesküla	Saaremaa	1850	19	47	66	165
Lithuania	Linden	Kurland	1858	24	24	48	92
Croatia	Cernik	Slavonia	1854	11	34	45	194
Bulgaria	Seldzhikovo	Southern	1838	20	50	70	44
Russia	Mishino	Raizan	1850	7	66	73	166

1. Extended and multiple family households except where stated.
2. Localities of Bampton, Barton, Hackthorpe, Kings Meaburn, Lowther, Morland, Newby, and Great Strickland.
3. Category of complex households includes no family households of coresident unmarried siblings. Households with siblings and no other relatives are excluded from the categories of extended- and multiple-family households.
4. Percentage of households with relatives.
5. Percentage of households with relatives.
6. With Dolegano and Bolzano.
7. With Borgrunda and Högstena.
Source: Wall, 1997, p. 281.

offspring, kin, or servants to those with least. Three populations, for instance, stand out as having an above average number of servants (Iceland, Denmark, and West Flanders). Then follow a number of populations with more moderate numbers of servants (Norway, west Nord Brabant, and England) and finally three populations with very few servants (the Swiss com-

munities, Cuenca, and three of the rural areas in the Netherlands). In a similar vein, populations can be identified where very few households were headed by nonmarried persons (Denmark, West Flanders, and the Swiss communities) or contained a large number of unrelated persons (Iceland and to a lesser extent Norway). On the other hand, there are very few occasions

TABLE 2
PERSONS PER HOUSEHOLD BY RELATIONSHIP TO HOUSEHOLD HEAD, EUROPEAN RURAL POPULATIONS

Country	Area	Dates	Household Heads		Offspring	Relatives
			Married Couples	Others		
Belgium	West Flanders	1814	167	16	272	20
Denmark	Rural sample	1787	177	12	194	24
	Rural sample	1801	175	12	191	26
England	5 settlements	1599–1749	134	33	189	19
	18 settlements	1750–1821	150	25	209	22
Iceland	–	1703	139	31	191	38
Netherlands	Rijnland	1622	177		252	6
	Krimpenerwaard	1622	178		272	9
	Noorderkwartier	1622–1795	155		176	5
	West-Nord Brabant	1775	142	28	230	10
Norway	Rural districts	1801	175	12	217	34
Spain	Cuenca	1699–1794	142	31	157	
Switzerland	Egislau	1647–1671	166	17	279	13
	Flaach	1671–1736	157	19	234	12
	Volcken	1671–1736	165	17	237	20

Source: Wall, 1995, p. 31.

when any one population is sufficiently distinctive as regards a particular component of the household—for example, the number of its offspring, relatives, or servants—to stand apart from all other populations. Of the various populations examined so far, the most distinctive in view of the large number of servants and other unrelated persons is Iceland, but even Iceland may come to look less distinctive as investigations of other European populations are completed.

Indeed, already the differences between Iceland and the rest of Europe look quite modest when set alongside the structure of the household in some non-European populations—that of India, for example, where there were 122 relatives per hundred households in 1951, and the Russian serfs of the nineteenth century, with their 520 relatives per hundred households. Nevertheless, it is obvious that there has been considerable variation in household structure even within the confines of northern and central Europe. For example, the Danish, Norwegian, and West Flemish populations had many married household heads and many offspring and servants, the number of off-

spring being boosted in West Flanders by the frequency with which both widowers and widows remarried. The populations of rural Holland stand out on account of the relative rarity of kin and servants in the household. The distinctiveness of Iceland, on the other hand, as has already been mentioned, was due to the large number of servants and other unrelated persons attached to its households. Finally, a fourth household pattern may exist, exemplified by the relative frequency with which nonmarried persons headed households. This pattern is found in England, west Nord Brabant, and Cuenca. Iceland, it will be noticed, also had many nonmarried heads of household.

Urban households. A place may also have to be reserved for a European urban household. Table 3, using the same classification scheme as table 2, shows that, in general, urban households were less likely than rural households to be headed by a married couple and that they contained fewer offspring but more relatives and many more unrelated persons, many of whom

Servants	Other Unrelated	All	Total Households
84	26	585	656
99	16	521	1,283
81	12	497	1,483
51	9	435	481
51	24	481	1,900
118	99	616	8,177
26	7	468	2,578
19	6	484	2,073
24	13	373	3,269
70	10	490	2,199
68	40	546	144,914
18	0	357	778
11	16	502	441
29	14	464	557
18	28	484	191

and variable number of parishes at different points in time, and even Southampton by only half of its parishes. This should increase the measured degree of variation from area to area, yet the reality is that households from different urban populations seem to differ somewhat less in certain key respects (in numbers of households with married and nonmarried heads and in the number of offspring they contain) than do households from different rural populations. Of the towns and sections of towns covered in table 3, only those in Holland really stand out on account of their low numbers of relatives, servants, and other unrelated persons in their exceptionally small households.

Sex ratios. The emphasis on variability is reinforced if we consider the sex ratio of particular categories of people within the household, nonmarried heads, offspring, relatives, servants, and other unrelated persons in the rural populations of Europe. As might be expected, through women generally being younger than spouses on marriage and generally outliving them, most of the nonmarried persons heading households were women. Even here, however, Iceland provides an exception, while two of the three Swiss communities lie at the other end of the distribution, with more than three times as many nonmarried women as nonmarried men heading households.

Sons and daughters who resided with their parents were usually present in almost equal numbers (a sex ratio of around one hundred). Any marked departure from a sex ratio close to a hundred in a population of any size would indicate either a mortality differential by sex or, most probably in these populations, an earlier exit from the parental home either by sons or by daughters. In rural populations, other factors being equal, any desire to retain male family labor in farming and keep the heir in residence, assuming the heir was, by preference a son, would tend to raise the sex ratio. However, the effect on the sex ratio of the entire offspring group (as opposed to offspring over the age of ten) is likely to be muted since the vast majority of offspring would be of an age when both sons and daughters would normally still be in the parental home. Nevertheless, in the case of England, where local censuses giving ages have been analyzed, it emerges that prior to the late eighteenth century it was sons and not daughters who were first to leave the parental home.

Whether this is the same elsewhere would merit investigation. What is already evident is that the majority of the young rural labor force recruited in the form of servants was male. Many of these servants, of course, were the offspring who were "missing" from the homes of their parents. The surplus of male ser-

of course would be the lodgers and boarders traditionally associated with town life. Overall, urban households, even including lodgers, were generally smaller than rural households. As with the rural households, however, there is also evidence of considerable variation from place to place. The households of the inhabitants of Norwegian towns, for example, were most likely to have married couples as heads. Households in Bruges, Gouda, and Zurich were more likely than those of other towns to contain offspring. Relatives, other than members of the head's own nuclear family, were most often to be found in the households of the inhabitants of Bruges and Fribourg. Servants turn up most frequently in Norwegian and Swiss towns and in Konstanz, and unrelated persons in Rome, Bruges, and Fribourg. Yet despite this variation in the composition of the urban household, the association of specific types of households with particular towns is not an easy task. In part this reflects the very fragmentary nature of the evidence currently available. London, for example, is represented only by one of its central and wealthier parishes, Rome by a handful

TABLE 3
PERSONS PER HUNDRED HOUSEHOLDS BY RELATIONSHIP TO HOUSEHOLD HEAD, EUROPEAN URBAN POPULATIONS

Country	Town	Dates	Household Heads		Offspring	Relatives
			Married Couples	*Others*		
Belgium	Bruges, southeast	1814	134	33	190	42
England	London, St. Mary Woolchurch	1695	142	29	146	9
	Southampton	1695–1696	116	42	162	12
Germany	Konstanz	1774	109	46	167	14
Italy	Rome	1653–1659	95	52	120	47
	Rome	1700–1701	104	48	128	20
	Rome	1800–1827	129	37	153	27
Netherlands	Leiden	1581	124	38	159	18
	Gouda	1622	171		207	9
	Gouda	1674	161		171	7
	Delft	1749	159		127	11
	Leiden	1749	167		142	2
Norway	Main towns	1801	152	24	142	18
	Other towns	1801	146	27	160	21
Spain	Cuenca	1724	140	30	159	20
	Cuenca	1800	138	32	140	19
Switzerland	Zurich	1637	138	31	193	12
	Geneva	1720	134	33	153	19
	Fribourg	1818	114	43	176	36

Source: Wall, 1995, p. 33.

vants shows up strongly in West Flanders in 1814 and in England before 1750. However, the surplus is less marked in Denmark at the end of the eighteenth century and is reversed in two of the Swiss communities and in Iceland, indicating considerable differences in the way in which these societies used service as a source of labor. Comparable differences occurred in the sex ratio of the groups of related and unrelated persons in the household. In a number of the populations, for example, such as rural Denmark in 1787, female relatives outnumbered male relatives by more than two to one, whereas in West Flanders there were considerably more male relatives than female.

A glance at the sex ratio of the urban populations suffices to show that females predominated in the majority of towns that it was possible to examine (few data sets, unfortunately, were available). Females were generally in the majority among the nonmarried heads of households and among relatives, servants, and other unrelated persons to a much greater extent than was the case with the rural populations. The effect of this excess of females (in Bruges, for example, there were only six males over fifteen to every ten females) on the economic and social life of certain towns was considerable. Through their preponderance in the population these women made a major contribution to the economic vitality of these towns, and their networks of contacts with other women, both relatives and nonrelatives, were an important feature within the social structure.

Not all city populations, of course, were like this. The City of London parish of St. Mary Woolchurch, for example, had a marked surplus of men among the nonmarried household heads. However, of all the urban populations examined, it is those from Rome which are most distinctive on account of the

Servants	Other Unrelated	All	Total Households
36	99	524	1,516
213	161	700	69
42	20	394	317
72	20	427	948
95	117	526	273
27	140	467	762
20	78	443	2,333
25	23	386	2,985
9	28	425	3,503
10	6	355	2,632
23	28	347	3,433
23	28	362	9,778
78	55	469	8,462
53	45	452	10,188
45	3	395	1,046
42	10	380	815
65	29	468	752
60	37	436	3,031
62	91	522	1,194

relative preponderance of males in all constituent parts of the household, at least in the first two of the periods studied (1650s and 1700s). In the case of Rome, there is no reason to doubt the representative nature of these results since year by year through the course of the seventeenth century a marked surplus of males was recorded in the total population of the city.

THE FORCES SHAPING EUROPEAN FAMILY AND HOUSEHOLD SYSTEMS

To explain the essential elements of the family system at the earliest point at which its workings can be observed, different scholars have pointed to the significance of a broad range of economic, cultural, and demographic factors. Economic forces have probably commanded the greatest attention in the attempts to explain historical family structures. In contrast, con-

temporary household structures, particularly supposedly new forms such as nonmarital cohabitation and "living apart together," as well as the increased numbers of lone parents and persons living alone, are seen as the result of the exercise of personal choices on the part of those concerned—in other words, as cultural preferences, although with the economic wherewithal to live in the desired way taken as a prerequisite.

The capacity of economic forces to shape family and household patterns is self-evident and can take a multitude of forms. For Pier Paolo Viazzo and Dionigi Albera, environmental factors, particularly the varying labor requirements of different mountain communities of northern Italy, explained the variations in their demographic and family patterns. The significance of the local labor market is also stressed by Michael Mitterauer for Austria, by John Rogers and Lars-Göran Tedebrand for Sweden, and by James Lehning for the Loire region of France, among many others. More generally, economic factors appear to underpin the marriage and household patterns of northwest Europe. According to this scenario, the timing of marriage and the formation of a new household were postponed until a suitable farm became available, sufficient savings had been accumulated, or an appropriate skill gained on the labor market. In eastern Europe, on the other hand, the serf owner, together with the village community, occasioned the formation of complex households.

In societies where land was a key resource, a shortage of land, whether as a result of population growth or landlord restrictions on land use, could occasion the formation of more complex households. However, greater security of tenure could also encourage the formation of more complex households, even when the economic situation of the farming population was, relative to other sections of the economy, in decline, as in Hruni, Iceland, between 1880 and 1930. Hruni provides a particularly interesting example, as early in the nineteenth century the structure of households in Hruni had became less complex during a period of severe economic hardship resulting from disruption to trade and depleted catches of fish, even though the crisis was less severe in its impact in Hruni, an agricultural parish, than in parishes whose inhabitants depended on fishing.

The role of demographic factors as determinants of family patterns is also very evident. High mortality limits the opportunities for parents to coreside with their adult children. A rise in life expectancy at older ages, a rise greater for women than for men, as in the twentieth century, increases the numbers of persons at risk of living on their own. The growth of population may also strain the existing family system, directly or indirectly: directly by forcing parents to ex-

Servants. *The Governess,* painting (1845) by Richard Redgrave (1804–1888). VICTORIA & ALBERT MUSEUM, LONDON/ART RESOURCE, NY

port children to the grandparental home, indirectly by promoting the subdivision of landholdings, thereby making complex households less viable. The demographic impact of male migration, rather than a set of inheritance rules, is cited as the factor occasioning the presence of extended households in Lanheses, Portugal.

Much more difficult to identify with any degree of precision are the norms and expectations influencing residential choices. However, most interpretations of historical household structures, even while according preeminence to economic factors, have awarded at least a minor role to cultural forces. For Mitterauer, for example, cultural forces limited the explanatory power of eco-types (local economies that suited the topography) as determinants of household patterns in the extreme east and west of Austria. According to Inez Egerbladh's account of the family patterns of landed peasants in coastal areas of northern Sweden, cultural influences such as a strong regional church helped to shape family patterns within the context established by demographic and economic factors. Cultural influences lie embedded in the ways in which property is transferred between generations and in whether the care of the elderly is assumed almost entirely by the family or is shared with the community.

Admittedly, there have been some dissenting voices. Smith and Verdon have separately argued that there was a natural preference in historical populations for the formation of simple, noncomplex households. Smith saw it as natural because the of the resemblance between the simple family and the basic biological unit, and Verdon because of the "natural" preference for every adult not part of a couple to maximize their individual autonomy. These accounts at first sight leave no room for the forces of cultural change, although it would seem that both Smith and Verdon see culture as the prime determinant of a presumably universal family system. Other factors, primarily economic but also including, at least for Smith, well-established behavioral patterns, feature only in the role of constraints which prevent individuals from following what would otherwise be their natural inclinations to live separately from other adults.

Smith and Verdon assume a major disjuncture between the real (but largely unexpressed) preferences for particular types of living arrangements and the households that are actually formed. In this respect they are in agreement with Laslett, but with the important difference that Laslett saw the familial normative structure as enabling individuals to survive demographic and economic crises and ideological transformations. Verdon and Smith, by contrast, see the natural preferences of populations as completely subverted by economic and other constraints. Others have predicated a more harmonious relationship between economic and demographic realities and the familial system, in which choices are framed taking account of the options available. Such arguments have been advanced to explain the evolution of family patterns in a specific microregion in Croatia after the defeat of the Ottomans, the long-term persistence of simple-family households in the Spanish province of Cuenca, and the continued dominance of the northwest European household system. The significant factors shaping family patterns in northeast Croatia were, according to Jasna Capo Zmegac, the timing of resettlement, the amount of land available, and the family patterns of the first settlers. These factors acted in combination to establish preferences for particular types of household. In a similar vein, David Reher has argued that in Cuenca relatively early and universal marriage, neolocal household formation, and property transfers through inheritance ceased to be demographic, social, and legal acts and became normative cultural behavior. Finally, Mitterauer traces the origins of the northwest European household system back to the early Middle Ages and the combined influences of the Catholic Church and a tighter control over access to land consequent on a deterioration in the land-labor ratio. According to Mitterauer, therefore, the northwest European household system was the joint creation of economic circumstances and a specific institutional structure (which was itself embedded in a number of cultural values). These forces then shaped the cultural preferences of various European populations which kept the system in place thereafter.

See also **The Population of Europe: Early Modern Demographic Patterns** *(volume 2);* **The Population of Europe: The Demographic Transition and After** *(volume 2);* **Preindustrial Manufacturing** *(in this volume); and other articles in this section.*

BIBLIOGRAPHY

Alderson, Arthur S., and Stephen K. Sanderson. "Historic European Household Structures and the Capitalist World-Economy." *Journal of Family History* 16 (1991): 419–432.

Andora, Rudolf, and Tamás Farragó. "Pre-Industrial Household Structure in Hungary." In *Family Forms in Historic Europe.* Edited by Richard Wall, Jean Robin, and Peter Laslett. Cambridge, U.K., 1983. Pages 281–307.

Andorka, Rudolf, and Sandor Balazs-Kovács. "The Social Demography of Hungarian Villages in the Eighteenth and Nineteenth Centuries (with Special Attention to Sárpilis, 1792–1804)." *Journal of Family History* 11 (1986): 169–192.

Benigno, Francesco. "The Southern Italian Family in the Early Modern Period: A Discussion of Co-Residence Patterns." *Continuity and Change* 4 (1989): 165–194.

Brettell, Caroline B. "Emigration and Household Structure in a Portuguese Parish, 1850–1920." *Journal of Family History* 13 (1988): 33–57.

Caftanzoglou, Roxanne. "The Household Formation Pattern of a Vlach Mountain Community of Greece: Syrrako, 1898–1929." *Journal of Family History* 19 (1994): 79–98.

Capo Zmegac, Jasna. "New Evidence and Old Theories: Multiple Family Households in Northern Croatia." *Continuity and Change* 11 (1996): 375–398.

Egerbladh, Inez. "From Complex to Simple Family Households: Peasant Households in Northern Coastal Sweden 1700–1900." *Journal of Family History* 14 (1989): 241–264.

Friedman, Kathie. "Households as Income Pooling Units." In *Households and the World-Economy.* Edited by Joan Smith et al. Beverly Hills, Calif., 1984. Pages 37–55.

Guinnane, Timothy. "Coming of Age in Rural Ireland at the Turn of the Twentieth Century." *Continuity and Change* 5 (1990): 443–472.

Gunnlaugsson, Gisli Ágúst. *Family and Household in Iceland, 1801–1930: Studies in the Relationship between Demographic and Socio-Economic Development, Social Legislation, and Family and Household Structures.* Uppsala, Sweden, 1988.

Hajnal, John. "European marriage patterns in perspective." In *Population in History: Essays in Historical Demography.* Edited by D. V. Glass and D. E. C. Eversley. London, 1965. Pages 101–138.

Hajnal, John. "Two Kinds of Pre-Industrial Household Formation System." In *Family Forms in Historic Europe.* Edited by Richard Wall, Jean Robin, and Peter Laslett. Cambridge, U.K., 1983.

Henderson, John, and Richard Wall. *Poor Women and Children in the European Past.* London, 1994.

Kertzer, David I., and Dennis P. Hogan. "Reflections on the European Marriage Pattern: Sharecropping and Proletarianization in Casalecchio, Italy, 1861–1921." *Journal of Family History* 16 (1991): 31–45.

Laslett, Peter. "The Character of Familial History, its Limitations, and the Conditions for its Proper Pursuit." *Journal of Family History* 12 (1987): 263–284.

Laslett, Peter. "Family and Household as Work Group and Kin Group: Areas of Traditional Europe Compared." In *Family Forms in Historic Europe.* Edited by Richard Wall, Jean Robin, and Peter Laslett. Cambridge, U.K., 1983. Pages 513–564.

Laslett, Peter. *Family Life and Illicit Love in Earlier Generations: Essays in Historical Sociology.* Cambridge, U.K., 1977.

Laslett, Peter. "Introduction: the History of the Family." In *Household and Family in Past Time.* Edited by Peter Laslett and Richard Wall. Cambridge, U.K., 1972.

Lehning, James R. "Socioeconomic Change, Peasant Household Structure, and Demographic Behavior in a French Department." *Journal of Family History* 17 (1992): 161–181.

Marchini, Antoine Noble. *À Propos de la Casinca, Mediterranéens, Corses, des Gens et des Pays de France, L'Histoire (1770–1968). Individus, Familles, Cours de la Vie dans les Aléas de la Transition.* Université de Nice Sophia Antipolis: Thèse de Doctorat d'État, 1996.

Martinez Carrión, José Miguel. "Peasant Household Formation and the Organization of Rural Labor in the Valley of Segura during the Nineteenth Century." *Journal of Family History* 1 (1988): 91–109.

Mitterauer, Michael. "Medieval Routes of the European Family Development." Unpublished Paper presented at the conference Where does Europe End?. Budapest, 1994.

Mitterauer, Michael. "Peasant and Non-Peasant Family Forms in Relation to the Physical Environment and the Local Economy." *Journal of Family History* 17 (1992): 139–159.

Mitterauer, Michael, and Reinhard Sieder. *The European Family: Patriarchy to Partnership from the Middle Ages to the Present.* Translated by Karla Oosterveen and Manfred Hörzinger. Oxford, 1982.

Moring, Beatrice. "Household and Family in Finnish Coastal Societies, 1635–1895." *Journal of Family History* 18 (1993): 395–414.

Morris, Lydia. *The Workings of the Household.* Cambridge, U.K., 1990.

Papataxiarchis, Euthymios. "La Valeur du Ménage. Classes Sociales, Stratégies Matrimoniales et Lois Ecclésiastiques à Lesbos au XIXE Siècle." In *Espaces et Familles dans l'Europe du Sud à l'Âge Moderne.* Edited by Stuart Woolf. Paris, 1993.

Reher, David Sven. "Household and Family on the Castilian Meseta: the Province of Cuenca from 1750–1970." *Journal of Family History* 13 (1988): 59–74.

Rogers, John, and Lars-Göran Tedebrand. "Living by the Sea: Farming and Fishing in Sweden from the Late Eighteenth to the Early Twentieth Century." *Journal of Family History* 18 (1993): 369–393.

Sabean, David Warren. *Property, Production, and Family in Neckashausen, 1700–1850.* Cambridge, U.K., 1990.

Schiavoni, C., and A. Sonnino. "Aspects Généaux de l'Évolution Démographique à Rome: 1598–1826." *Annales de Démographie Historique* (1982): 91–109.

Segalen, Martine. "Nuclear is not Independent: Organization of the Household in the Pays Bigouden Sud in the Nineteenth and Twentieth Centuries." In *Households: Comparative and Historical Studies of the Domestic Group.* Edited by Robert McC. Netting et al. Berkeley, Calif., 1984.

Smith, Daniel Scott. "American Family and Demographic Patterns and the North West European Model." *Continuity and Change* 8 (1993): 389–415.

Smith, Joan, et al. eds. *Households and the World-Economy.* Beverly Hills, Calif., 1984.

Verdon Michel. *Rethinking Households: An Atomistic Perspective on European Living Arrangements.* London, 1998.

Viazzo, Pier Paolo, and Dionigi Albera. "The Peasant Family in Northern Italy, 1750–1930: A Reassessment." *Journal of Family History* 15 (1990): 461–482.

Wall, Richard. "Historical Development of the Household in Europe." In *Household Demography and Household Modeling.* Edited by Evert van Imhoff, Anton Kuijsten, Pieter Hooimeijer, and Leo van Wissen. New York, 1995.

Wall, Richard. "Leaving Home and the Process of Household Formation in Pre-Industrial England." *Continuity and Change* 2 (1987): 77–101.

Wall, Richard. "Mean Household Size in England from Printed Sources." In *Household and Family in Past Time.* Edited by Peter Laslett and Richard Wall. Cambridge, U.K., 1972.

Wall, Richard. "Zum Wandel der Familienstrukturen im Europa der Neuzeit." In *Historische Familen-forschung.* Edited by Josef Ehmer, Tamara K. Hareven, and Richard Wall. Frankfurt, 1997.

Wall, Richard et al., eds. *Family Forms in Historic Europe.* Cambridge, U.K., 1983.

Wong, Diana. "The Limits of Using the Household as a Unit of Analysis." In *Households and the World-Economy.* Edited by Joan Smith et al. Beverly Hills, Calif., 1984.

INHERITANCE

Julie Hardwick

In the narrowest sense, inheritance concerns the transmission of property from one person to another, whether that property is money, real estate, personal possessions, titles, or kingdoms. This very specific process has, however, the broadest of implications. Every person in European society—men and women, rich and poor, young and old, urban and rural, Catholic and Protestant—was affected by the transmission of property through inheritance. Relations between people, whether parents and children, siblings, or men and women, have influenced and been profoundly influenced by the way inheritance worked. The giving of property provided a symbolic as well as material means for family members to express their affection for each other or to designate their preferences for some family members over others. Moreover, patterns of inheritance were determined by many factors, such as laws, economic practices, social customs, and demographic patterns, as well as personal preferences. Because exploring the way inheritance worked in a particular historical community reveals many different aspects of that community, European social historians have found inheritance to be an invaluable topic.

The approaches of historians to the study of inheritance have changed focus in significant ways since the 1970s. They have moved from examining what might be called the mechanics of inheritance, looking at issues like what the pertinent laws were and what wills of individual testators suggest about how those laws were observed (or not) in practice, to trying to place inheritance more broadly in the context of social relations. In this more recent phase, social historians have looked at inheritance as a key strategy that family members used to deal with the various challenges they faced—to ensure they had support in old age, to provide for all their children, or to guarantee that social status was maintained. This conceptual approach encourages historians to examine the many ramifications of inheritance. As David Warren Sabean has observed, "The way that property is held gives shape to feelings between family members, territorializes emotion, establishes goals and ambitions, and gives to each a sense

of dependence and independence" (Medick and Sabean, 1984, p. 171).

Key variables in inheritance practices include laws, timing, the nature of the property, and the status of men and women. The legal regimes governing inheritance varied enormously from country to country or even region to region within countries. Yet as social historians have shown in many studies, families did not always seem to follow the dictates of laws when it came to transmitting their property. They pursued a variety of strategies that tried to ensure that their own goals were met even while legal requirements were being observed or circumvented.

The timing of the transmission of property was enormously influential, shaping individual fortunes and family relationships. Parents might transfer property, in the form of dowries, gifts, or postmortem bequests, to one or more of their children at almost any time between the children's marriages and the parents' deaths. The consequences of these decisions over timing were enormous. A son who had to wait until his parents died to receive his inheritance might, for example, continue living with them and delay marriage. In turn, that pattern of delayed marriage for men was often accompanied by high rates of illegitimacy or prostitution.

When laws required that all children inherit equally or constrained parental testamentary discretion in other ways (as in England, where in many cases the law of thirds prevailed, whereby a widow would get a third, the children would get a third, and the father could dispose of the other third as he chose), parents could still privilege one child over another either by differential timing or by the kinds of property assigned to each child. One child might, for example, receive a substantial portion of their inheritance years earlier than a sibling.

The character of the property that was transmitted—that is, whether it took the form of movables (cash, tools, linen and other household goods, or personal items) or immovables (usually land or houses)—was also a key element in inheritance. When property

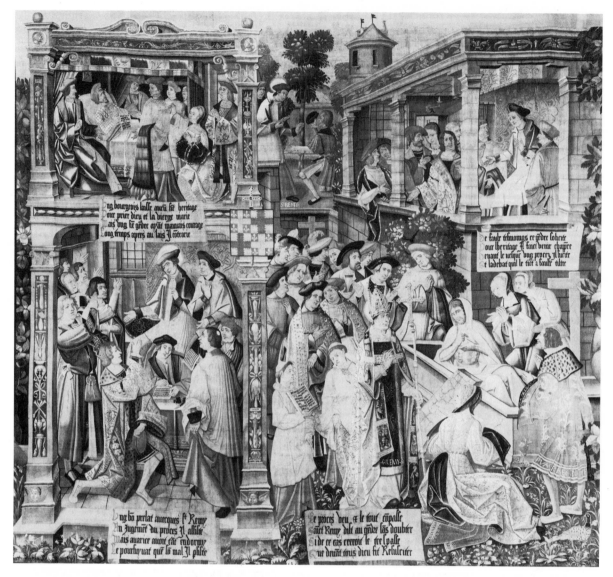

Making a Will. A bourgeois makes a will *(lower left)*, but it is contested by members of the family gathered around his deathbed *(upper left)*. Flemish tapestry of the life of St. Remigius, 1531. MUSÉE DE SAINT-REMI, REIMS/GIRAUDON/ART RESOURCE, NY

was transferred on the marriage of a child, it was more likely to be in movables than in real estate.

Gender was another critical element in inheritance: men's and women's right to property often differed, whether as widows and widowers or as sons and daughters. It was possible, for instance, that in a family where the parents' property appeared to be divided equally among all children, sons might receive a preponderance of the land and daughters a preponderance of the movables. In some early modern communities, daughters who received dowries at the time of their marriages were subsequently excluded from any further claim on their parents' estate. Early modern women who were widowed often found themselves in very precarious financial situations because they had to divide their household property with the other heirs.

EARLY MODERN EUROPE

Inheritance shaped the prospects of most early modern Europeans in very profound ways. Although laws about the transmission of property varied enormously, in early modern society a person's life was profoundly shaped by what property he or she might receive through inheritance. The impact was not only economic but also social, framing household structures and kinship relations.

126

Renaissance Italy. Renaissance Italy provided one of the earliest and most fertile grounds for historians' studies of inheritance. Although the territory of Italy was divided into myriad self-governing republics, Venice and Florence have dominated scholarly attention. In Venice, patrilineal ties (where kinship was figured through the male line) were especially strong. The most striking institutionalization of this dynamic came in the form of the *fraterna,* a legal device that gave sons equal and joint shares of their fathers' estates while excluding daughters, who had rights only to dowries. Traditionally, this inheritance system was viewed as the key to the persistent close ties between male kin, especially in the Venetian elite, and to the marginalization of women.

Yet as historians have studied inheritance in practice as well as law, a more complex view has appeared because Venetian women's dowry rights were strongly protected, and elite women were key links in the kinship networks that underlay political and economic success. Persistent dowry inflation through the fourteenth and fifteenth centuries made daughters ever more expensive. While some families responded by coercing their girls to pursue the cheaper course of becoming nuns, other families met the clear obligation to dower daughters at whatever cost by drawing on an ever wider group of kin to raise the money.

In Florence, broadly similar inheritance practices prevailed in the fourteenth and fifteenth centuries. Patrilineal tendencies were reinforced as new elite families of merchants and bankers emulated traditional aristocratic practices by giving themselves a family name that was transmitted by male heirs. The marginalization of women was given more material form when families used dowries to fulfill their obligation to daughters while sons were given equal shares of all remaining property. The close ties between brothers that resulted were evident, for example, in the establishment of fraternal communities where all brothers and their families lived together in the same large household, even after the father had died. Even when these groups broke up and siblings established their own households, they often lived in very close proximity, building complex webs of kinship ties that underpinned much economic and political activity. Sisters meanwhile found themselves in limbo, regarded as only temporary members of either their birth families or the families of their husbands.

Partial inheritance. Just as inheritance contributed to the distinctive characteristics of Renaissance Italian city-states, different inheritance laws and practices were similarly pillars that profoundly shaped daily life in the rest of Europe from the late fifteenth to the late eighteenth century. In many parts of Europe, rural and urban, partible inheritance prevailed as a matter of both law and practice. In these kinds of inheritance systems, the property was divided up more or less equally among all heirs. Families observed versions of partible inheritance in much of England, in slightly

A Woman's Inheritance. Dowry of a woman of Lucerne, Switzerland. Engraving, nineteenth century. ©Swiss National Museum, Zurich

different forms in western and northern France, and in much of Germany.

In some partible inheritance regions, the commitment to absolute equality was extraordinary. In western France, for example, customary law set very egalitarian standards for inheritance. Daughters as well as sons had equal claims on non-noble estates, and the principle of forced return to the succession required that all property received previously be declared so that the final portion each claimant received would reflect long-term equality. Heirs met to report what each had already received (whether as dowries, loans, or gifts of other kinds), and then the lots were made. Again elaborate safeguards ensured that equality among heirs was preserved. Heirs selected lots according to their sex, with all sons choosing first, and their age, with the oldest having the first pick. This pattern might seem to give the oldest son considerable advantage over the youngest daughter. Yet the person who would choose last was charged with making up the lots from which the heirs would chose, an ingenious device that gave him or her clear incentive to make the lots as fair as possible.

In other partible inheritance regions, the division of property followed what might be termed a different-but-equal pattern. In England, for instance, where many peasant families practiced partible inheritance, an alternative strategy was usually pursued. One heir alone would receive the land, while the others received movable wealth of various kinds.

The consequences of partible inheritance were complex. While it ensured equality among heirs, the constant fragmentation of property endangered the financial viability of family members. Social historians studying some areas, such as rural societies in early modern Germany, have argued that partible inheritance caused intense competitiveness and tension between siblings, whereas elsewhere, as in early modern French towns, it seems to have fostered cooperation. In England, partible inheritance that limited land transfers to one child left the other heirs detached and free to pursue their lives elsewhere, in towns, cities, or even the emerging colonies. In many parts of France, where land was assigned to all children, peasant ties to the countryside remained strong, contributing to greater reluctance to emigrate. Many commentators and historians have linked these differences to subsequent differences in national histories, such as rates of economic development or successes with colonization.

Primogeniture.

In other regions, families followed versions of inheritance systems based on the principle of primogeniture, in which one child (usually the eldest son) inherited the bulk of the landed property.

Primogeniture was especially widespread among elites throughout European society and in areas where Roman law prevailed, such as southern France and Spain. In Roman law regions, testators had broad discretion to distribute property as they saw fit, which allowed them to concentrate their estate in the hands of a single heir.

Yet even in areas where a basic commitment to primogeniture prevailed, in practice most families showed a clear desire to provide for all of their children. Daughters received dowries and younger sons were helped with education or apprenticeships to provide them with means to make a living otherwise than off the family land. In such areas, families may not have been committed to equality, but they seemed to have pursued equity in their efforts to ensure to the best of their abilities that each child received help. Thus for most nonelite families the legal differences between partible inheritance and primogeniture were not as important in practice as they might seem. Families used inheritance along with many other aspects of their lives to weave strategies that met the varying needs of parents, children, and siblings.

In the late nineteenth century, a French sociologist, Frédéric Le Play, hypothesized that the practice of primogeniture led to the formation of a particular kind of household structure that he called "the stem family." Le Play suggested that in families where only one son would inherit the land, the heir's marriage usually coincided with the retirement of his parents. Subsequently, the two married couples shared a multigenerational household while other noninheriting siblings either went off to establish their own households or remained unmarried in the household of their brother and parents. Since the 1960s, social historians have endeavored to investigate the validity of this thesis, and many doubts have been raised. Historians now think household structures were less stable than this model suggests. Multigenerational households were common experiences at some point for many people, but their formation represented particular moments in the life courses of families. Moreover, families adopted multigenerational households for many reasons besides inheritance systems, including caring for the elderly, redistributing labor needs, and providing child care.

Dowries and inheritance.

Marriages were also important moments of property transmission, primarily through families' provision of dowries to their daughters as they married. Realistically, a girl could not marry without a dowry in this period. If a young woman's parents could not afford to provide her with one, she needed to work to save her own dowry. Many female servants, for example, used the payment they received at the end of their term of employment to fund dowries for themselves. (Early modern servants were usually paid only when they left their employers' households, not on a regular weekly or monthly basis.) Most nonelite families seem to have taken their dotal obligations to their daughters very seriously, however, and provided contributions to dowries if they could.

For newly wed couples, dowries were critical elements in establishing the long-term prospects for married life. Young men could use the cash injection dowries represented as an important means of promoting their careers, allowing them to fund their occupations by buying tools or positions. Even the poorest women's dowries also usually included the essential goods to set up a new household—items like a bed, some pots and pans, a stack of linens, and some clothes.

The effect of giving dowries on women's right to inherit varied considerably. In some areas, families considered that their obligations to their daughters had been met by the provision of dowries, and such "dowered off" daughters gave up any further claim on family property. In these cases, dowries were probably a means by which daughters' claims on family property were limited, and consequently girls received smaller shares than their brothers. Elsewhere, though, daughters who had been dowered were still entitled to participate in the division of property after their parents' deaths.

Legally, in most countries, husbands became the managers, if not the outright owners, of their new wives' dowries (and of any other property their wives subsequently inherited). Nevertheless, women's ability to have access to their own property varied from place to place. In England, a married woman's legal identity was consumed by her husband's as she became a *feme covert*. In the countries of continental Europe, women's dowries were often divided into lineage property and community property, even in nonelite families. Husbands managed both, but could only inherit community property: women's children became the heirs to lineage property, and if wives died childless, husbands had to return lineage property to their in-laws. Everywhere courts were careful to protect women's dowries from the threats posed by husbands who might squander the money.

Noble inheritance patterns.

For elite families across Europe, the situation was different. Even in regions where partible inheritance prevailed for commoners, laws permitted noble families to practice primogeniture in some form. Such families often pursued versions of primogeniture most ruthlessly because they felt that their status, with all the privileges it carried, would be jeopardized by dividing their patrimony—their family property in all its forms—among many heirs. The most striking practitioners of primogeniture were of course the European monarchical dynasties, who bequeathed not only personal property but kingdoms, and the contrast between the fortunes of the child who would inherit and other siblings was very dramatic in terms of political power as well as material comfort. The eldest son was the preferred heir in all royal families, and all sons were preferred to all daughters. In France, the early modern observation of Salic law meant in fact that women could not inherit the throne.

Other aristocratic families adopted a number of strategies to circumvent the perils of multiple heirs. The proportion of never married sons and daughters in elite families was high, a tactic that reduced the number of heirs and limited the financial burdens that dowries presented. In many Catholic countries one or more children were encouraged to take religious orders, a step that invalidated their right to inherit. As a result of choices like these, in eighteenth-century Venice, for example, 64 percent of the sons of elite families never married, while in France at the same time 42 percent of the sisters of dukes and peers likewise remained single. The numbers were similarly high throughout European aristocracies.

From the sixteenth century onward elite families also increasingly developed new legal means to avoid the division of their estates. These practices (known as *mayorazgos* in Spain, *fideicommissa* in Italy, *substitutions* in France, and strict settlements or entails in Britain) all sought to preserve intact the landed estate that usually provided the core of both the wealth and the status of great families by forbidding the division of land and putting it beyond the claims of creditors.

All such efforts to preserve the wealth of aristocratic families intact privileged the status of the family as a lineage or dynasty over the interests of individual heirs. Even the son who inherited such an estate was effectively a tenant for life rather than an owner, as his ability to manage the property was severely restricted. He could not, for example, sell the estate, and his ability to mortgage it to raise money was also strictly limited. Younger sons often found themselves with few prospects and needed to seek their fortunes in the army or church. Some historians argue that daughters may have fared better, at least if they were permitted to marry. Although dowry inflation was rampant across Europe in the seventeenth and eighteenth centuries, with the result that the high costs of dowries threatened to ruin many families, the alliances daughters made were essential for the building of kinship and political networks. A daughter who

129

Father and Heir. The first marquis of Santillana at prayer; behind him is his first son and heir, who became the duke of Infantado. Anonymous Spanish painting, sixteenth century. MUSEO DEL PRADO, MADRID/INSTITUT AMATLLER D'ART HISPÁNIC

was married with a dowry sufficient to attract a suitor of appropriate status could expect to live a life that was more on a par in material terms, at least, with that of her inheriting oldest brother than her younger brothers could.

Widows. Women who were widowed were also a distinctive group in terms of inheritance. In most countries, widows were entitled to a specific share of the property they and their husbands had accumulated. That share was determined either by law or by specific arrangement at the time of the couple's marriage. It was often around a third, although it could be much less. Although this provision was meant to give widows financial means to support themselves, the splitting of household property between widows and all other heirs left many widows in dire financial straits, as tax rolls from communities across Europe show.

Wills offered one last means for testators to shape the disposal of their property. Historians have shown that besides the practices already described that took care of the majority of property, men and women also used small gifts of personal property, like jewelry, clothes, linen, or books, as a way of expressing particular ties. Women especially seem to have been likely to remember their sisters or nieces, emphasizing a continued sense of the importance of extended kinship beyond the conjugal families they had established with their husbands.

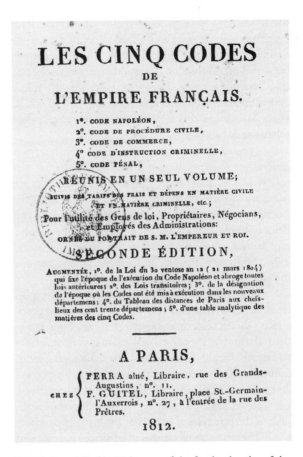

French Legal Codes. Title page of the five legal codes of the French Empire, second edition, 1812. The first section contains the Napoleonic Code, which established French inheritance law in the period after the French Revolution. BIBLIOTHÈQUE NATIONALE DE FRANCE/©COLLECTION VIOLLET

MODERN EUROPE SINCE 1789

The two hundred years or so since the late eighteenth century have seen many dramatic shifts in European society that have had enormous impacts, both directly and indirectly, on the practice and significance of inheritance. These changes have included not only obvious developments like the passage of new laws that explicitly impacted how inheritance worked but also the emergence of new economic and political patterns that have transformed the role of inheritance in most communities.

The era of the French Revolution marked a watershed in many ways, as political changes in many countries were accompanied by shifts toward industrialization, albeit at different rates and by different means in different countries. In France itself, many revolutionary leaders were quick to insist that all children should have equal inheritance rights. The commitment to equal shares for all heirs became a cornerstone of revolutionary legislation, and was enshrined with little alteration in the Napoleonic Civil Code of

1804. For those seeking to reform France, equality of inheritance had political as well as familial goals because they foresaw newly egalitarian families as the building blocks of a democratic nation. This Civil Code, with its emphasis on equal shares for all heirs, became enormously influential in other continental countries in the nineteenth century, providing a model for legal reform. Even regions where its introduction was not the result of Napoleon's conquests chose to adopt the Code, as in the case of the Netherlands, where it became law in 1838.

As Western industrial societies evolved, four key developments dramatically reduced the traditional importance of inheritance in determining individual wealth and life course for all but the richest of families. For most young people, education rather than inheritance became the key to their life fortunes. With the rise of wage earning, children became more independent of their parents. The emergence of a variety of social security systems as elements of welfare state programs also reduced individual dependency on inheritance. The most important of these perhaps has been the establishment of national pension schemes that provide income during old age. Finally, many governments introduced new fiscal regimes, of which estate taxes were the most significant for the role of inheritance.

Nevertheless, the property families transmit from generation to generation still has important material and symbolic roles. Although laws about inheritance still vary from country to country, with France, for example, insisting that all children inherit equally and Britain giving parents the right to divide their property as they wish, in practice equity among all inheriting children, both sons and daughters, has become the rule in all but the most elite families.

Since World War II, as life expectancy has increased, parents have increasingly chosen to pass property to their children at many different stages rather than at the traditional pivotal moments of marriage and death. Parents have underwritten the costs of education as that has become an increasingly important determinant of success for large parts of populations, and offered financial help at many other moments, such as the purchase of houses or the birth of children.

The situation of widows in particular has changed dramatically in many regions since World War II. Increasingly, in countries like England that give wide latitude over the disposal of property, when one spouse dies, the surviving partner, man or woman, inherits the entire estate, leaving the next generation to receive their ultimate share only after the death of both parents. Even in areas like the Netherlands, where inheritance laws are still heavily influenced by the provisions of the Napoleonic Code that were introduced in the nineteenth century, husbands have moved toward choosing to protect the rights of their surviving wives to have at least use of all the property. This pattern, which privileges the interests and competence of both spouses, marks a dramatic change from earlier practices, when widows' portions were assigned along with those of other heirs on the death of the father.

In the countries of Eastern Europe, meanwhile, the post–World War II transition to socialism revolutionized inheritance along with many other aspects of family life. The abolition of private ownership of the means of production ended the role of inheritance as a means by which wealth was transmitted from one generation to the next.

In sharp contrast, elite families have continued to incline toward preserving their estates intact. The legal strategy of entail survived most powerfully in England, where the nobility, like other testators, enjoyed few restrictions on the transmission of their property. For continental nobilities, however, the egalitarian intentions of the French Revolution and Napoleonic Code produced powerful impetuses toward division. Since the early nineteenth century, elites in France and Spain have had only very limited abilities to keep their estates intact. Even in countries like Prussia that at first shared with Britain the survival of the right to entail, noble estates were being divided by the later nineteenth century.

Even in the most aristocratic circles, where primogeniture seems to prevail most stoutly in the transmission of titles and estates, changes in progress suggest that the dramatic transformation of inheritance practices of the last two centuries are reaching the highest levels. In 1999, the British government was preparing a constitutional revolution that designated birth order alone, regardless of sex, as the key to inheritance of the British monarchy. Should a future monarch see a daughter as the firstborn, she will become queen ahead of any subsequently born brothers.

See also **Gender History; Patriarchy** *(in this volume); and other articles in this section.*

BIBLIOGRAPHY

Burguière, André, Christiane Klapisch-Zuber, Martine Segalen, and Françoise Zonabend, eds. *A History of the Family.* Volume 2: *The Impact of Modernity.* Translated by Sarah Hanburg-Tenison, Rosemary Morris, and Andrew Wilson. Cambridge, Mass., 1996.

Chojnacki, Stanley. "Dowries and Kinsmen in Early Renaissance Venice." *Journal of Interdisciplinary History* 5 (spring 1975): 571–600.

Desan, Suzanne. "'War between Brothers and Sisters': Inheritance Law and Gender Politics in Revolutionary France." *French Historical Studies* 20 (fall 1997): 597–634.

Goody, Jack, Joan Thirsk, and E. P. Thompson, eds. *Family and Inheritance: Rural Society in Western Europe, 1200–1800.* Cambridge, U.K., 1976.

Gullestad, Marianne, and Martine Segalen, eds. *Family and Kinship in Europe.* London, 1997.

Kertzer, David I., and Richard P. Saller, eds. *The Family in Italy from Antiquity to the Present.* New Haven, Conn., 1991.

Klapisch-Zuber, Christiane. *Women, Family, and Ritual in Renaissance Italy.* Chicago, 1985.

Medick, Hans, and David Warren Sabean, eds. *Interest and Emotion: Essays on the Study of Family and Kinship.* Cambridge, U.K., University Press, 1984.

Shammas, Carole, Marylynn Salmon, and Michel Dahlin. *Inheritance in America: From Colonial Times to the Present.* New Brunswick, N.J., 1987.

Spring, David, ed. *European Landed Elites in the Nineteenth Century.* Baltimore, 1977.

THE FAMILY AND THE STATE

Roderick Phillips

The family has historically been central to European social systems. In the early modern period and during much of the modern age it was the main institution for reproduction and the raising of children, the principal means by which property was transferred (by inheritance) from one owner to another over time, and it frequently provided services, such as the care of the sick and old, that in modern times are more commonly associated with other social institutions. The family economy, to which all members of the family contributed labor and resources, was the main unit of production in the preindustrial European economy and it remained important well into the industrial era.

The family was also perceived as critical to the maintenance of social stability and the moral order. Sexual activity was generally defined as permissible or illicit by its relationship to family relations: sex within marriage was permitted while sex before or outside marriage was frowned upon. Children were socialized into gender and other roles within the family; and in many respects authority within the family was portrayed as mirroring the exercise of power in society at large. Marriage breakdown, disobeying parental authority, the reversal of gender roles, dishonoring the family, and other disruptions of patterns of normative family relationships were often perceived as real threats to social stability.

Given the importance of the family to so many dimensions of society, the economy, and the polity, it is not surprising that any institutions that wanted to control the social order, either by changing it or maintaining the status quo, had a particular interest in all aspects of the family.

During the Middle Ages the church progressively appropriated control of the family, sexuality, and morality from secular authorities that had regulated family relationships and behavior through customary legal codes or legislation based on Roman Law. For example, laws and customs that permitted divorce were steadily replaced by church decrees and council decisions against divorce until finally, by the thirteenth century, the canon law of marriage was triumphant throughout most of Europe (although it was weak at the peripheries). Divorce was effectively denied to European populations until the Reformation.

By the end of the Middle Ages the church regulated the formation and dissolution of marriage and a broad range of behavior within the family, particularly as they related to sexuality. Some spheres of family life evaded church regulation more than others, however, and in general the church had less success in gaining jurisdiction over property matters than over individual behavior and family relationships. There were also class differences in that the church made exceptions for the wealthy and powerful. For example, the church often waived prohibitions based on consanguinity and affinity, which ruled out marriage between a man and a women who were too closely related, to enable royal or aristocratic families to arrange marriages that served political or dynastic ends.

The emergence of the nation-state in the early modern period challenged the dominance of the church over many areas of law, including the family, and the sixteenth to the nineteenth centuries can be seen as a period in which the state progressively undermined the authority of churches to regulate the family. Although it was by no means a steady, linear trend, the general trajectory of change is clear throughout much of Europe, and by the second half of the nineteenth century the primacy of the state in regulating the family in Europe was established. Even though much of the substance of family law and policy continued to express principles that drew on Jewish and Christian teaching on the family—biblical texts frequently remained points of reference for legislation related to marriage, divorce, and sexuality until the late twentieth century—the power to legislate and competence to judge family matters were progressively transferred from church to state.

The distinction between church and state should not always be drawn too starkly, however, because as much as there was conflict between these two institutions for power to regulate the family, there was often cooperation. In England, where the church retained much authority over the family until well into the nineteenth century, it did so at the behest of the state. When a commission was set up to revise the canon laws of the Church of England after the Reformation, it was appointed by the king, who was head of the church. Similarly, in eighteenth-century France the royal government set down the rules by which the church kept records of baptisms, marriages, and burials. The process by which the state assumed legislative power over the family from the religious authorities was sometimes sudden and dramatic, as during the French Revolution. But for the most part it was a slow evolution that combined both cooperation and tension between the two bodies.

There are three broad areas in which the state related to the European family in the early modern and modern periods (1500 to the present). First, the state attempted to regulate the family by means of laws, especially those dealing with marriage formation, stability and dissolution, sexuality, parental authority, inheritance, and adoption. Second, the state developed policies in other social spheres that affected the family directly. For instance, states frequently sponsored measures to increase population size by encouraging (and sometimes even coercing) procreation using fiscal and other means. Third, models of state power sometimes drew directly on images of family authority. The clearest example is patriarchalism, where the monarch's relationship to his subjects is likened to that of a father's to his children, a relationship that was considered natural (even when it was created by adoption) and was therefore deemed to be beyond challenge.

The social history of the family has related unevenly to the evolution of the state's attempts to regulate family relationships. Although the state, like the church before it, prescribed rules and norms of behavior, many were widely disregarded by populations in their everyday lives. Court records dealing with family issues—such as litigation concerning inheritance, suits by one engaged person to force the other to fulfill a promise of marriage, or prosecutions for domestic violence—reveal challenges to legal prescriptions.

For all that the state had an interest in regulating the forms of the family—who could marry whom, what circumstances might justify a divorce, how property ought to be divided—and for all that it gradually accumulated authority over them, it has historically been reluctant to legislate or intervene judicially in some areas. A prime example is domestic violence. According to the doctrine of "moderate correction" that was enshrined in many European codes of law, a husband was permitted to "correct" (punish) his wife physically when he had good reason and when the violence he used was "moderate"—that is, when it did not draw blood or threaten the wife's life. Because much domestic violence was thus legally permissible, court records do not reflect its incidence and there is no way to ascertain how common violence was. It is quite possible that the principle of "moderate correction" expressed a position broadly accepted by men as a means of maintaining authority within the family.

The law established the boundaries of many areas of family life and at times compelled individuals to observe the outward forms of acceptable behavior. Inheritance laws established the identity of heirs and their rights, and these rules appear to have been observed; they were enforceable by law. On the other hand, rules of partible inheritance, which mandated the division of property among more than one heir, could be circumvented if some heirs wished to sell their share (or exchange it for goods or services) so as to allow one person to consolidate ownership of all or most of the property.

In some respects the social history of the family is the story of the struggle of social groups or individuals to maintain their autonomy to observe cultural or individual forms of behavior despite the demands of the state. It is important to bear class distinctions clearly in mind here. State-sponsored regulations often expressed the values of one particular class, such as the bourgeoisie. Workers or peasants might well ignore attempts to interfere with patterns of behavior to which they were accustomed. For example the high rate of premarital pregnancy in some parts of Europe in the early modern period (about a fifth of English brides were pregnant when they married in the seventeenth century) might well have reflected a continuing pattern where couples began to have a sexual relationship as soon as they were engaged and married when the woman became pregnant. Such an attitude to the relationship of marriage and sexual activity would give a premarital pregnancy a completely different (and acceptable) meaning than in a culture or class where a sexual relationship was expected to begin only after marriage and where premarital pregnancy was evidence that the principle of premarital chastity had been breached.

THE EARLY MODERN PERIOD

The intrusion of the state into family affairs began in earnest with the development of the nation-state at the beginning of the early modern period, and a number of centralizing monarchies, such as those in France and England, began to legislate on family issues. Paradoxically, state regulation was boosted by the Protestant Reformation, which shattered the unity of the medieval church and led to the creation of state-sponsored churches in northern Germany, Switzerland, Scandinavia, Scotland, the Netherlands, and England. In Protestant states the church continued to play an important role in some aspects of the family, but Protestants generally accepted that the secular authorities, increasingly the nation-state, had authority and jurisdiction over many family matters. They rejected the Catholic doctrine that marriage was a sacrament, and believed that even though marriage was ordained by God, it should fall within the jurisdiction of the state.

John Calvin, for example, argued that marriage was a civil contract under the jurisdiction of the secular authorities, and Martin Luther likewise insisted that it was a "worldly thing" and that the state should regulate marriage and divorce. In Sweden, the basic reforming law of the Lutheran Church in 1572 specified that marriage was an issue for the civil law.

Even so, Protestant states were generally slow to assume the power to regulate the family, and in most countries churches continued to play important legislative and judicial roles in family issues. The canon law adopted by each church continued to be important and the church courts continued to adjudicate in many matrimonial issues in England until the mid-nineteenth century. In parts of Protestant Switzerland, marriage courts were mixed tribunals of clerical and lay judges from the sixteenth through the eighteenth centuries. In Scandinavia, church courts handled marriage cases but turned them over to secular courts if they were unable to reconcile the parties.

Although the Reformation opened the way for the state rapidly to increase its regulatory activities over the family, there were fewer differences between Catholic and Protestant states than might be expected. Throughout Europe, regardless of the dominant confession, states progressively gathered legislative power into their own hands at the expense of the religious authorities. This was the case in Catholic France, where the royal government steadily eroded the legislative and judicial powers of the Church. The indissolubility of marriage was affirmed by the Catholic Church in one of the decrees of the Council of Trent in the 1560s, but because the French monarchy claimed primacy over the church in France, it issued its own declaration to the same effect, the 1580 Edict of Blois.

French royal judges also began to use a legal instrument known as *appel comme d'abus,* which was a declaration that a church court hearing a case was acting beyond its authority. From the sixteenth to the eighteenth centuries the royal courts used this action to gain jurisdiction over a wide range of family issues: the marriage of minor children, bigamy, impediments to marriage, and broken engagements, as well as all property questions that affected spouses, parents, and children.

The state also gained legal and judicial authority over the family from the Catholic Church in the Habsburg empire. In 1784 Emperor Joseph II forbade the church courts to exercise any jurisdiction over the validity of marriages, legitimacy of children, promises of marriage, engagements, or any other matrimonial matter. The 1784 law declared that marriage was a civil contract and that power over it lay solely with the civil power (the state) and the civil courts.

The same process was evident in Protestant states. In Sweden the state (through the monarch) began to override the Lutheran Church's marriage laws almost as soon as they were issued in the late 1500s. By the 1630s the practice had developed whereby the Swedish king could grant divorces by dispensation in circumstances other than desertion and adultery, the only grounds recognized by the church. Grounds for divorces by royal decree included ill-treatment, frequent drunkenness, and the presence of "hatred and bitterness between the spouses."

Faced with the Church of England's refusal to allow divorce (it was unique among Protestant denominations in this), the English state began to grant them instead. From 1670 until 1857 (when a divorce law was passed), English men who could prove their wives were guilty of adultery (and English women whose husbands were guilty of aggravated adultery) could have their marriages dissolved by private Act of Parliament. The church was not excluded entirely from such cases, however, because it was necessary for a petitioner to obtain a separation from an ecclesiastical court before obtaining the parliamentary divorce.

Within this broad trend of growing state intervention, it is possible to detect a number of recurring patterns. One was the tendency of the state to intervene in the family in order to achieve certain broader social and political goals. In the seventeenth and eighteenth centuries there was widespread concern in governments about what was thought to be sluggish or nonexistent demographic growth. This was an important matter in a period when economic and military power were more directly related to population size than they are today. In late-seventeenth-century France the government of Louis XIV tried to stimulate the birthrate by providing tax concessions to large families. This was the beginning of persistent attempts on the part of the French state to employ fiscal and other inducements to encourage procreation. In the eighteenth century the French monarchy tried to re-

Polyphiloprogenitive. Captain Simon Maire, founder of the Popular League of Fathers and Mothers of Large Families, with his family in 1912. The league, founded in 1908, was open to heads of families with at least four children (or three if the head of family were young). ©COLLECTION VIOLLET

duce infant mortality by such means as sponsoring courses in midwifery, requiring unmarried pregnant women to register their pregnancies with the authorities, and reforming the laws related to the treatment of abandoned children.

Divorce was sometimes used for the same demographic purpose. In Prussia, Emperor Frederick William II designed a divorce policy in part with demographic purposes in mind. In 1783 he issued instructions to judges stating that "in matters of divorce one ought not to be so easy going as to further abase [marriage]; but one should not be too difficult either, because that would impede population." When divorce was legalized in France in 1792, one argument was that it would allow unhappily married (and presumably nonprocreative) couples to remarry and have children with their new partners.

The progressive secularization of family law and policies from the seventeenth century onward typically shifted the balance of regulation from churches to the state. Many Enlightenment writers were critical of the continuing influence of religion over law and society, and because they had no wish to see these issues unregulated, they urged their respective states to take over jurisdiction from the church. Faced with

specific problems, governments enacted legislation and adopted policies that extended their power. In England, where the Anglican Church controlled marriages, a Marriage Act was passed by parliament in 1753 in order to combat the increasing incidence of clandestine marriage. In France, where in the eighteenth century only marriages performed by a Catholic priest were recognized in law, the state unilaterally improved the position of Protestants with respect to the legitimacy of their families. From mid-century royal judges tended to consider Protestant marriages valid for the purpose of inheritance, and in 1787 King Louis XVI issued an Edict of Toleration that extended legality to marriages by Protestants.

Within the evolution of state power over the family in Europe, there were periods of acceleration, generally associated with revolution or political upheaval. During the English Revolution the republican government of Oliver Cromwell passed laws dealing with a variety of marriage issues. Civil marriage was legalized in 1653 and in 1650 an Adultery Act provided for capital punishment in certain cases. A married woman who committed adultery could be hanged along with her accomplice, but a married man who committed adultery with an unmarried woman was liable only to imprisonment for three months. In this case the limits of state law were determined by juries which, clearly thinking that the penalty was far too severe for the crime, refused to convict married women of adultery in all but a handful of cases during the ten years the Adultery Act was in force.

THE FRENCH REVOLUTION

The French Revolution (1789–1799) provided a particularly striking example of the emerging role of the state in attempting to regulate the family and establishing family policy as part of a broader agenda for social transformation. Revolutionary legislators accelerated the process of secularization that had been evident under the Old Regime and deprived the church of any legal authority over the family. As for the substance of Revolutionary law, two aims appear to have been uppermost. The first was to make family relationships more consensual and equal than they had been under the Old Regime and the other was to use the family for broader demographic, social, and political purposes.

Greater legal equality within the French family was achieved by a series of legal reforms. The authority of fathers and husbands to control their children and wives was steadily reduced, beginning with the abolition in 1789 of *lettres de cachet,* arrest warrants that could be obtained from the royal bureaucracy in order to imprison any family member whose behavior threatened the honor or financial security of the family. The following year, a new family court was established to deal with litigation or other issues involving family members. In the constitution of 1791, marriage was declared to be a civil contract, and in September 1792 a wide-ranging law made marriage easier (the range of impediments was reduced and the age of majority was lowered to twenty-one years from the twenty-five or thirty years then current in various regions of France) and divorce legal for the first time in France. Women and men were given equal access to divorce either by mutual consent, for reason of incompatibility, or for a number of specific grounds that included violence, insanity, immorality, and desertion.

The reform of family law under the French Revolution also transformed property relationships. In 1792 married women were granted property rights and in 1793 a new inheritance law mandated equality of inheritance among all children to replace the unequal distribution that had been the case in much of France before 1789. Earlier in the Revolution, the rule of primogeniture (inheritance by the firstborn) that had applied to noble estates was replaced by equality of inheritance in order to break up the financial power of the aristocracy.

The effects of these legal reforms on behavior varied. The marriage rate increased in many places, although it rose most dramatically in 1793 when the government introduced conscription and drafted bachelors before married men. Under the divorce law, which remained in force until 1803, there were perhaps as many as twenty thousand divorces, two-thirds of them in Paris alone. Given that France had a population of 28 million at the end of the eighteenth century, the number of divorces was low by modern European terms, but it was astonishingly high for the time. Outside Revolutionary France, divorce was either not available or, when it was permitted (in Protestant states), it was difficult to obtain and correspondingly rare. In England there were only 325 parliamentary divorces (including four by women) in the whole period from 1670 to 1857.

In France there was a surge of divorces in the first years the Revolutionary divorce law came into effect, as thousands of couples who had separated informally when divorce was not available took advantage of the new law to put their status on a legal footing. In the Norman city of Rouen, divorces averaged 161 a year during the first three years of the 1792 law, but the annual average fell to 67 in the following years. Some of the early divorces regularized separations that dated back decades. In Rouen one of the first divorces, in December 1792, dissolved the marriage of a woman whose husband had been missing more than thirty years: he had not returned from service in the Seven Years' War (1756–1763).

French Revolutionary law reforms generally improved the legal status of women within the family, a stark contrast to their continued exclusion from many other citizenship rights (such as the right to vote). Within the family, women gained equality of inheritance, and married women could own property in their own right and sue for divorce. Still, material circumstances often inhibited many women from using their new rights. Most divorces were sought by urban wives, who had the possibility of finding accommodation and work when they left their husbands. In contrast, divorces in rural areas were not only less common, but they were more likely to be sought by husbands.

French Revolutionary legislators not only reformed the law to reduce what they considered the tyrannical authority the Old Regime had given husbands and fathers but they aimed to foster harmony within the family. Divorce itself was viewed as a last resort, and it was hoped that its simple availability would lead husbands and wives to settle their differences amicably rather than persist in domestic conflict. Similarly, one of the purposes of giving all children an equal share of their parents' inheritance was to eliminate the jealousy and hatred that inequality of inheritance was believed to have fostered among siblings.

By these reforms of family law in the 1790s, and by other measures that included national festivals in honor of family values (such as fidelity within marriage and respect and obedience toward parents) the Revolutionary legislators intended to create the legal framework for a new family. In it the parents would remain married because they wanted to, not because they had no alternative; spouses and children would be treated as equals; and harmony, not conflict, would reign supreme. The Revolutionary family would thus embody the virtues of Liberty, Equality, and Fraternity that underlay the Revolution more generally. As a microcosm of the new state and society, the family would socialize and prepare men and women for their roles in the regenerated nation.

It was expected that a morally regenerated family would also lead to a higher marriage and birth rate and would thereby serve the demographic policies of the period. Improvements in family life would make marriage more attractive but, in case things did not work out, divorce provided a means of escape. Partly in order to boost the marriage rate, bachelors were subjected to policies that would induce them to marry. They were taxed more heavily than married men, levied at higher rates when forced loans were imposed to pay for the costs of war, and were conscripted before their married peers. The sentiment was often expressed that men who did not marry were asocial at best and antisocial at worst because they lived solitary, selfish lives and did not contribute fully to society or to population growth. Revolutionary legislators rejected proposals that bachelors be humiliated into marriage by being forced to wear ridiculous headgear or that any man not married by the age of thirty should be executed.

There is little evidence of much success in the goals that French Revolutionary family law set out to achieve. The marriage rate did rise in some years, but there is no reason to think that the character of relationships within the family was affected by the new policies. Even so, the French Revolution was an early and striking example of a state attempting to remodel the family and to align it with broader social and political agendas. Napoleon revised family law in a different direction to foster broader social and political agendas. The Code Napoléon (1804) made divorce more difficult to obtain, especially for women, and generally strengthened the authority of the father over his children and the power of a husband over his wife, reforms that reflected the authoritarian Napoleonic regime.

NINETEENTH CENTURY

Elsewhere in Europe state intervention in the family increased at a more sedate pace. The nineteenth century was a particularly important period, for it saw a virtual revolution in statistics and measurement that enabled states to produce national censuses with greater precision and to collect social statistics of all kinds. As state bureaucracies expanded steadily and there was a dramatic extension of state activity in all areas of economic, social, and cultural life, the state regulation of the family intensified in many European countries. In England the first comprehensive marriage legislation was enacted in 1837, and twenty years later divorce was made available from the civil courts for the first time. A wave of secularizing and liberalizing legislation on marriage, separation, and divorce swept through Europe in the second half of the nineteenth century. Included were laws granting married women varying degrees of property rights.

The creation of new unified states in the nineteenth century intensified the role of the state. The unification of the German states under Prussian leadership led to the extension of secular law and, by the turn of the century, the promulgation of a uniform code of laws—including family law—for the German empire. For the most part the new imperial law was based on existing Prussian code, which tended to be more liberal than laws that had been in force in many other states that became part of the empire. In Italy, too, unification led to the passage of standardized state laws related to the family, a major source of conflict between the nation-state and the papacy.

State-sponsored education could also affect family relationships, particularly by the end of the nineteenth century. Governments used education to encourage women to be good wives and mothers, for example, reinforcing this emphasis in family ideology. Regulations in hygiene, infant feeding, and other matters, pushed through schools and some welfare agencies, could also constrain family behavior.

TWENTIETH CENTURY

It was in the twentieth century, however, that the most serious attempts to regulate the family in the interests of the state were undertaken. Paradoxically, some of these attempts often involved weakening the family in order to reduce its effectiveness as a rival to the state in claiming the loyalty of individual citizens. There were hints of this tendency during the French Revolution, for during the Terror (1793–1794) the Jacobin regime introduced policies that were at odds with the more general tendency of Revolutionary policy of strengthening family relationships and the family as an institution. Jacobin legal innovations included making divorce much easier and removing procedures of the 1792 law that were designed to prevent the abuse of divorce; giving inheritance rights to illegitimate children; encouraging loyalty to the nation at the expense of family relationships if necessary; and framing educational reforms that would have children live in state boarding schools rather than with their parents. In the first half of 1794, during the radical phase of the Terror, thousands of children were given names (such as Liberté, Égalité, and even Guillotine) that linked them to the state rather than their families.

Underlying these policies (which were repudiated and repealed when the Jacobins were overthrown) was the belief that family sentiments inhibited the development of concern for society more generally. This belief was expressed early in the nineteenth century by a number of utopian socialists, including Robert Owen and Charles Fourier, who fostered alternative family systems in the model communities they devised.

A more sophisticated analysis of this sort was developed by Frederick Engels and Karl Marx, who argued that both the state and the family system at any given historical period reflected existing economic relationships. The nineteenth-century family reflected the values of the dominant bourgeoisie, and state and family would be transformed when the working class seized political power. Early in the 1917 Russian Revolution the Bolshevik government implemented family laws that reflected the Marxist view that the bourgeois family would disappear. Divorce was made available at the request of either or both spouses and contraception and abortion made freely accessible. The result was a high rate of divorce and a decline in the birthrate during the 1920s that so concerned the regime of Joseph Stalin that in the mid-1930s family policy was reversed: divorce was made much more difficult to obtain and contraception and abortion were officially regarded as antisocial because they ran counter to the state's need for a growing workforce.

Other authoritarian regimes of the interwar period also paid attention to the family. In Germany the Nazis manipulated family law for a variety of state purposes following Hitler's declaration in *Mein Kampf* that marriage "must serve the greater end, which is that of increasing and maintaining the human species and race. This is its only meaning and purpose." The 1935 Nuremberg Laws forbade marriage and sexual intercourse between a Jew and an "Aryan," while other laws prohibited the physically or mentally "unfit" from marrying. While groups classed as undesirable were thus excluded from the state-recognized family system, "Aryans" were encouraged to marry and procreate. A system of marriage loans was established, with a quarter of each loan being canceled with the birth of each child. Nazi divorce law also reflected the regime's demographic agenda. Grounds for divorce included not only disparaging Hitler, but also premature infertility and using illegal means (abortion had been banned for "Aryans") to terminate a pregnancy.

Extreme family policies and rigorous family laws were imposed by a number of authoritarian states in the first half of the twentieth century in order to achieve racial or demographic goals. Most governments opted for more moderate policies, even if their goals were often similar. Many states introduced laws based on eugenics principles that were designed to improve the physical and mental health of the population. In France, anyone intending to marry had to obtain a certificate that showed their health and family history of physical and mental disease so that the prospective spouse would be fully informed about potential risks to any children they might have.

Most governments attempted to encourage a higher birthrate, by some combination of family aid and regulation of certain types of birth control such as abortion. Fascist states went farthest in this direction, along with the Soviet Union after the more experimental 1920s, but France and other democracies joined in. Rarely, however, did these interventions affect family behavior, as birth rates continued to drop.

From the late 1960s, which ushered in a period of liberalization in social policies of all kinds, European states began to reduce the level of family regulation. A notable example was the introduction of no-fault divorce laws, under which divorce was available not on grounds (or faults) set out in law but after the couple had lived apart for a certain length of time. The effect of this legal reform was to allow spouses themselves to decide what grounds justified separating and, in the course of time, divorcing. Rather than be required to prove violence, drunkenness, cruelty, persistent drunkenness or some other state-designated ground, spouses could decide what circumstances or behavior were so intolerable as to make living together impossible.

States also accorded children greater rights with respect to their parents. Some, such as Sweden, went so far as to allow children to "divorce" their parents, but even where this was not possible, state agencies became far more willing to intervene to protect children when they appeared to be at physical or emotional risk if left in their families.

States also began to adopt more tolerance toward diversity in family forms. In the late twentieth century governments throughout Europe considered the issue of same-sex marriage. By the end of the twentieth century no state had given same-sex partners the right to marriage in exactly the same form as different-sex couples, although some (including the Netherlands, Denmark, and Sweden) permitted same-sex couples the same pension and fiscal rights. Among others, France had created state-registered unions or partnerships that had many of the financial and fiscal effects of marriage.

Trends in family policy in the late twentieth century have run in several directions simultaneously. On the one hand there has been a tendency not to interfere in aspects of family and marriage such as sexual behavior and to allow married couples to make their own decisions about divorce based upon their individual expectations and experiences. Similarly there has been a tendency for the state to blur the distinction between marriage, a state-sanctioned institution, and cohabitation, which historically has existed in tandem with but apart from the official family system.

While the state may be seen to be deregulating the family in these respects, it became more intrusive in others. Intervening to assure the rights and well-being of children is one example, as is the greater willingness of the state to have its police and courts intervene in domestic violence, an issue in which the state has historically been reluctant to intervene.

CONCLUSION

Since 1500 there have been many points of contact between the social history of the family and the history of the state's relationship to the family. The persistent aim of the state to regulate marriage, filiation, and family relationships has provided historians with vital documentation on the family, but it is necessarily biased in favor of the state's perception of the institution. Marriages are documented, but rarely are cohabiting couples. Divorces are recorded, but not couples who separated informally unless they came to the attention of a state agency.

Records of courts and other state agencies offer privileged insights into many aspects of the family, and they are the core of historical studies of themes such as divorce, domestic violence, and inheritance. Censuses and records of vital events (births, marriages, deaths, and divorces) provide the basic source material for the study of family demography and enable historians to determine such important information as marriage and birth rates, family size, age at marriage, the duration of marriages before divorce or death, and rates of remarriage.

This is not to discount the important records maintained by churches, nor the myriad other sources that are often useful to historians of the family: personal papers, family archives, and the records kept by institutions such as guilds. But state records, like the church records that preceded or ran parallel to them, have certain advantages. They tend to be maintained relatively intact and concentrated in accessible locations in state or regional archives. They also often offer series of documents (like court records that extend over centuries) that enable historians to track changes over the long, medium, and short term and to identify historical trends.

At the same time, it is important to recognize the limitations of any sources. Court records of family behavior highlight breaches of the law or challenges to legal prescriptions, but we cannot say with any certainty how representative they were of more general social behavior. Very few cases of domestic violence reached the courts because a degree of violence was permitted under the rubric of "moderate correction" and because women, who were most often the victims, were seldom in a social or economic situation to prosecute their husbands even if they wanted to. A woman whose family depended upon her husband's work and income for its survival had little interest in seeing him imprisoned or fined, for either penalty deprived the family of vital resources. In this respect, as in many others, the material and cultural circumstances of family law tended to neutralize many attempts the state might have made to change family relationships. They also mean that historians must always be very cautious about interpreting and generalizing from records of such cases.

Nonetheless, the relationship between state and family is an important one for social historians, not least in that it can provide historical indicators of the extent to which family-specific behavior can be influenced by state policy. Overall the conclusion must be that states have experienced little success in encouraging rates of marriage formation or fertility. Legal restrictions on divorce in the past might well have kept the number of divorces low, but they did not necessarily have much impact on informal separation.

Research on the history of the state, the law, and the family is more than an integral part of the history of the family because so many historians rely on state-generated documentation as their primary sources of evidence. In order to read them effectively they must understand the legal, judicial, and political contexts that produced the documentation. Although the state may have become so intrinsic to family systems as to be an invisible partner to those involved in historical families, it is an institution that historians of the family must confront explicitly in their research.

See also **The Welfare State** *(volume 2);* **Patriarchy; Sex, Law, and the State; Sexual Behavior** *(in this volume); and other articles in this section.*

BIBLIOGRAPHY

Abbott, Mary. *Family Ties: English Families, 1540–1920.* London, 1993.

Brundage, James. *Law, Sex, and Christian Society in Medieval Europe.* Chicago, 1987.

Burguière, André, et al., eds. *A History of the Family.* 2 vols. Cambridge, Mass., 1996.

Donzelot, Jacques. *The Policing of Families: Welfare versus the State.* London, 1980.

Duby, Georges. *Medieval Marriage: Two Models from Twelfth-Century France.* Translated by Elborg Forster. Baltimore, 1978.

Fuchs, Rachel Ginnis. *Abandoned Children: Foundlings and Child Welfare in Nineteenth-Century France.* Albany, N.Y., 1984.

Gauthier, Anne Hélène. *The State and the Family: A Comparative Analysis of Family Policies in Industrialized Countries.* Oxford, 1996.

Gillis, John. *For Better, For Worse: British Marriages 1600 to the Present.* New York, 1985.

Goody, Jack. *The Development of the Family and Marriage in Europe.* Cambridge, U.K., 1983.

Graveson, R. H., and F. R. Crane, eds. *A Century of Family Law, 1857–1957.* London, 1957.

Grossman, Atina. *Reforming Sex: The German Movement for Birth Control and Abortion Reform, 1920–1950.* New York, 1995.

Hammerton, A. James. *Cruelty and Companionship: Conflict in Nineteenth-Century Married Life.* London, 1992.

Hanawalt, Barbara. *The Ties that Bound: Peasant Families in Medieval England.* New York, 1986.

Hunt, Lynn. *The Family Romance of the French Revolution.* Berkeley, Calif., 1992.

Koven, Seth, and Sonya Michel, eds. *Mothers of a New World: Maternalist Politics and the Origins of Welfare States.* New York, 1993.

Lacey, T. A. *Marriage in Church and State.* London, 1947.

Lynch, Katherine A. *Family, Class, and Ideology in Early Industrial France: Social Policy and the Working-Class Family, 1825–1848.* Madison, Wis., 1988.

Moeller, Robert. *Protecting Motherhood: Women and the Family in the Politics of Postwar West Germany.* Berkeley, Calif., 1993.

Outhwaite, R. B., ed. *Marriage and Society: Studies in the Social History of Marriage.* London, 1981.

Ozment, Steven. *Ancestors: The Remaking of the Premodern European Family.* Cambridge, Mass., 2000.

Ozment, Steven. *When Fathers Ruled: Family Life in Reformation Europe.* Cambridge, Mass., 1983.

Phillips, Roderick. *Family Breakdown in Late Eighteenth-Century France: Divorces in Rouen, 1792–1803.* Oxford, 1980.

Phillips, Roderick. *Putting Asunder: A History of Divorce in Western Society.* New York, 1988.

Safley, Thomas Max. *Let No Man Put Asunder: The Control of Marriage in the German Southwest: A Comparative Study, 1550–1600.* Kirksville, Mo., 1984.

Staves, Susan. *Married Women's Separate Property in England, 1660–1833.* Cambridge, Mass., 1990.

Stone, Lawrence. *The Family, Sex, and Marriage in England, 1500–1800.* London, 1977.

Stone, Lawrence. *Road to Divorce: England 1530–1987.* Oxford, 1990.

Traer, James F. *Marriage and the Family in Eighteenth-Century France.* Ithaca, N.Y., 1980.

Usborne, Cornelie. *The Politics of the Body in Weimar Germany: Women's Reproductive Rights and Duties.* Ann Arbor, Mich., 1992.

Watt, Jeffrey R. *The Making of Modern Marriage: Matrimonial Control and the Rise of Sentiment in Neuchâtel, 1550–1800.* Ithaca, N.Y., 1992.

COURTSHIP, MARRIAGE, AND DIVORCE

Joanne M. Ferraro

Marriage in European society was the basic unit of social organization and was believed to form the fabric of society, giving it cohesion and stability as well as a legal structure to govern inheritance and reproduction. In some European towns and villages marriage also conferred political rights on men. For both women and men it was a rite of passage to social adulthood. First and foremost, marriage forged the alliances, inheritance practices, and patronage systems that permitted generations of family lineages to endure over time. Nonetheless, prior to the nineteenth century many people either chose not to marry or more commonly could not afford to marry. About 10 to 15 percent of the overall population in northwestern Europe during the early modern period did not marry at all. The percentage was higher for southern Europe. Thus marriage was a privileged status often made possible by inheritance. Those who had nothing to inherit did not necessarily feel compelled to establish a legal, conjugal bond and so experimented with other forms of family life based on informal arrangements. The proportion of people who married in western Europe in the nineteenth and twentieth centuries increased significantly from that of the early modern period. The change was linked in part to the transformation of the family from an economic unit into an affective household.

THE SIGNIFICANCE OF MARRIAGE

Any discussion of European marriage must take into account its demographic and economic context, social and cultural attitudes about age and sex, and the constructed norms of masculinity and femininity that affected the marriage process. John Gillis's findings for early modern England may be extended to the Continent as a whole. The conjugal ideal best served people of economic substance. Moreover it reflected a gender-bound view of relationships between women and men. Finally, the values and patterns of behavior attached to marriage differed according to social and economic standings.

Marriage in the cities, towns, and villages of early modern Europe was a recognized community affair rather than the more private agreement between individuals that developed in modern times. Rites and festivities evidenced its public nature. Betrothals, marriage contracts, and weddings involved complex relationships with kin, friends, and community that in turn helped sustain the conjugal bond over time. Courtships, betrothals, and weddings were occasions of social drama in which family patriarchs forged new social and political ties with compatible families. Both the social activity leading up to the wedding and the actual ceremony furnished occasions to publicize these new relationships of solidarity. The public announcement of the bride and groom's consent, the exchange of rings and gifts as symbols of the new union, and the public affirmation of the marriage by family and community were as important as the actual legal procedures that established the bond. Thus church, state, family, peers, and community participated in this collective process that ultimately validated a new economic, social, and legal unit.

The breakup of rural communities during the modern era, in contrast, profoundly changed the relationship between a marrying couple and local society. A more commercial economy reduced traditional ties and constraints. One result was an increase in the number of illegitimate children from 1750 onward. Urban growth later furthered the increase. In Britain by 1830 rural areas witnessed marked depopulation as more people moved into manufacturing towns. They left their community ties behind for a more impersonal urban environment. At the same time the enclosure movement in the countryside furthered the breakdown of the rural household and, in turn, the cohesion of the rural community. Late nineteenth-century industrialization solidified this overall trend, bringing strangers together in marriage or common law relationships without the participation of the wider community. Far from family, community, and religious counsel, couples might also form relationships that left unmarried women abandoned with child.

Marriage in European society held profound religious significance. It was one of the seven sacraments of the Catholic Church, and its essential function, according to Catholic dogma, was reproduction. Sex for pleasure alone was a sin; the couple's purpose was to procreate and suitably educate children. Protestants took this argument in another direction by actually devaluing celibacy and asserting that marriage was the spiritually preferable state. They praised the patriarchal nuclear family as a liberation from the celibacy idealized by Catholic thinkers. Husbands and wives were more highly regarded in principle than monks and nuns. Protestants such as Martin Luther claimed to have released Catholic clerics from the regulated life of a cloister or monastery and sexual repression and to have freed children from the involuntary celibacy that accompanied family practices of restricting marriage. Luther and later other Protestants maintained that marriage stabilized both partners sexually and, by extension, society as a whole, creating households, communities, property, and honor. Maintaining principles of good household government would in turn impart good government on society at large. The home thus founded good citizenship, good habits, and virtue.

Both Protestant and Catholic courts regarded mutual consent as the essential requirement for a valid marriage. Church services celebrated the union, making it public and secure under law, but it was the couple's mutual agreement that made it binding in the eyes of God. Strasbourg law explicitly stated in 1534 that a church ceremony was not obligatory to make a marriage valid or legal. Despite this stance, it was recognized that church ceremonies performed the important function of putting marriage on public record. Registering nuptial vows systematically could help prevent the breach of promise cases women more often than men brought to the courts.

While marriage was a sacrament in Catholic theology, for Protestants it was not. However, some still regarded it as a spiritual bond, and for Luther it was a divine ordinance. Martin Bucer took a different view, regarding marriage as a civil matter devoid of spiritual content save for the church's blessing. He maintained that marriage was a secular bond legitimized under secular authority. It was the church's duty, however, to set up and uphold the moral standards associated with marriage, just as secular authorities enforced them.

THE DEMOGRAPHIC AND ECONOMIC CONTEXT OF EUROPEAN MARRIAGE: VARIATIONS IN PLACE AND TIME

Regional, demographic, and economic factors affected marriage patterns in Europe. Historians have identified a European marriage pattern in northwestern Europe, which included England, Scandinavia, France, and Germany. Age at marriage in these areas was linked to the idea that couples should be economically independent before setting up their own households. Thus couples married in their mid- to late twenties and immediately established independent, nuclear households. It was preferable that husband and wife be close in age, with perhaps a two- to three-year difference between them. Women in their twenties were regarded as better suited for marriage because they brought both maturity and experience to it. Some women at the lower levels of society worked as domestic servants prior to marriage. Women who married in their twenties were less dependent on their husbands than women who were significantly younger than their spouses. In a nuclear household older brides were also freer from the authority of mothers-in-law.

The northwestern pattern differed from practices in southern and eastern Europe, where some couples married in their teens and lived under the authority of one set of parents well into adulthood or, typically, a teen bride wed a man in his late twenties or even thirties. Young Jewish women in Italy were engaged at puberty and usually married between the ages of fourteen and eighteen, while their grooms were between twenty-four and twenty-eight. Christian girls in Florence, according to the tax survey of 1427, married young, between thirteen and sixteen, while their husbands were from eight to twenty-five years older. Urban areas witnessed wider gaps in age between couples than rural ones. The delayed age at marriage of urban males helps explain the presence of prostitutes as well as concubinage and secret marriages. Younger wives were frequently at a disadvantage in their relationships with their spouses. However, if they outlived their husbands, inherited wealth, and did not remarry, they achieved financial independence relatively early in their life cycles.

Household structure in southern and eastern Europe also varied from the northwestern model. Depending on demographic trends and economic means, a household could be multigenerational rather than nuclear. Extended families with grandparents, multiple siblings, uncles, and aunts were common in rural areas, where successful farming depended in part on a steady supply of labor. Wealthy families as well had the capacity to house several generations in one household in both the city and the countryside. Children married early, seventeen for grooms, fifteen for brides. Age at marriage rose slightly after 1860. In extended families the practice of married children living under the authority of a father until his death emancipated them delayed social adulthood and often created tensions within the household. In contrast, the urban worker or shopkeeper could not afford to maintain an extended family nor supply employment to all offspring. Thus his or her household did not extend beyond its nuclear origin. Sons and daughters married if they could establish separate households, the groom with secured work, the bride with a dowry. If not, they remained unmarried.

Besides regional variations, demographic and economic trends also affected marriage patterns. Marriage rates usually rose following the catastrophic mortality resulting from famines and epidemics. The reduced population made the resources needed to set up new households, including land, employment, and possibilities for profit, more readily available. The average age at marriage plunged during these cycles, a reflection of the urgency of replenishing numbers. The earlier age at marriage increased the number of childbearing years. In contrast, in periods when the population was swollen and landed resources did not match demand, the marriage rate dropped and age at marriage rose. More people remained unmarried during these demographic cycles. This was generally the case during the sixteenth century, a period of dramatic demographic growth accompanied by inflation. The period witnessed a decline in the number of extended family households. The last three decades of the century, however, brought religious war, plague, and famine, relieving population pressure and encouraging earlier marriages. The seventeenth and eighteenth centuries also experienced cycles of economic hardship that impinged on marriage rates.

In contrast, from about 1750 to 1914 the European population grew dramatically, from 140 million in 1750 to 266 million a century later and 468 million on the eve of World War I (1914–1918). While early modern societies had suffered high natality and mortality rates, societies of the modern era experienced an overall reduction in the incidence of mortality. Once again living standards declined in rapidly growing towns and cities, limiting marriage rates. Although poverty constrained marriage, many couples established common law unions. France was an exception to the growth trend, as were areas where landowning peasants practicing partible inheritance attempted to limit births. In these cases couples still took into account economic considerations when deciding whether or not to marry. Dowries and marriage

contracts remained important. Men married later than women, upon establishing financial independence, and the age gap among couples was sizable.

In the early modern period many women and men who did not marry spent their lives in convents or monasteries in the Catholic areas of southern and eastern Europe. This was often not out of choice but out of necessity. Sometimes parents could not provide a daughter with a dowry commensurate with their social class, or parents restricted the number of sons who could marry for financial reasons to preserve the wealth of the lineage over time.

In Catholic Italy the growing number of women who could neither afford to marry nor enter a convent prompted the city-states to found special asylums for women. These institutions provided food and shelter, while residents earned their keep through spinning or sewing. This was a way, according to the views of both secular and ecclesiastical authorities, to protect a woman's virtue and the honor of her family. In many instances lay donors provided small dowries for these women so that eventually they could leave the asylum for marriage. Poor unmarried women who did not enter asylums or convents generally ended up working as domestic servants if they were fortunate or as prostitutes if they were not.

COURTSHIP

Dating did not exist in early modern European society. Forms of courtship were determined in part by social standing. At the upper levels of society marriage was primarily a business arrangement. Parents, not spouses, made the match, generally employing such criteria as status, wealth, family reputation, and religion. Family patriarchs, taking into account the standing of the family in political and social life as well as the preservation and expansion of its wealth, arranged betrothals with the help of friends, kin, and marriage brokers. Children had at best minimum input in these negotiations. Sometimes the betrothed did not meet until formal contract negotiations were finalized. At that point the prospective groom was permitted to visit the bride during the period leading up to the wedding. At other times the couple did not meet until the actual wedding day.

Lawrence Stone hypothesized that betrothal practices for upper-class English families evolved between the sixteenth century and the eighteenth century from the "restricted, patriarchal, nuclear" family to the "closed, domesticated, nuclear" one. By the late seventeenth century and the eighteenth century children chose their partners but asked for parental con-

Engagement. *The Fiancés,* painting (1519) by Lucas van Leyden (1494–1533). MUSÉE DES BEAUX ARTS, STRASBOURG, FRANCE

sent. Marriages determined by economic and social interests waned. By the end of the eighteenth century affection and companionship became decisive criteria in making the match, and husbands and wives manifested strong affective bonds. This process, Stone maintained, advanced by the upper and middling strata of English society, trickled down to the lower classes.

Stone's hypotheses have not remained unchallenged. Perhaps the greatest adjustments have come from new research on the values and behavior of the mass of the English population. Historians have argued that popular experience in England differed from that of the aristocracy, upper gentry, and urban plutocracy and that popular experience did not necessarily derive from upper-class models of behavior. Moreover even within the upper levels of society, some evidence points to courtship or input from children, modifying the argument of strict parental absolutism in the sixteenth and seventeenth centuries. Young people's initiation of marital agreements, however, apparently had more success farther down the social ladder, where wealth and standing were lesser concerns. Still parental consent was desirable, and property was an important consideration. Parity in the match remained the most common criterion for suitability. In early modern France dowries and marriage contracts governed the joining of families through wedlock. Financial concerns led men to marry late, after reaching a state of economic security. Women married considerably earlier, joining with husbands in the service of lineage and family estate management.

The less-formal arrangements of meeting at social occasions and forming attractions was more prevalent or at least socially acceptable among the peasant and working classes. Young people met at dances and celebrations. It was acceptable for them to pair up in a large group at festive occasions but not to pair off. One reason for this was to protect the young woman's honor; unaccompanied dating was unacceptable. Another reason was that, until couples were ready to make a serious commitment, they preferred to keep their courting relationship private. Thus most serious courtship went on at night, out of sight of others. The suitor brought the woman gifts. Among the English lower classes these included stay busts (corset stays) and love spoons. Gifts had significant symbolic value. They could signify whether the pair were friends or lovers, whether the relationship was honorable or licentious, or whether the relationship was getting serious or not. Friends and servants sometimes acted as go-betweens during the courting process.

When couples expressed mutual consent to marry, their casual courtship was transformed into a serious relationship that now involved a wider circle of family and friends in the alliance. Consent had to be expressed in front of public witnesses before it was taken seriously and considered a binding promise. Various rituals allowed the community to recognize publicly the new commitment. One was hazing, which, Gillis has argued, expressed the intense feelings of jealousy and loss aroused any time a friend became engaged. It meant these single people were about to withdraw from their unmarried friends and join the circle of married couples. Charivari was another rite that neighbors engaged in to express disapproval of unusual betrothals.

Protestant theologians and jurists held that secret marriages were valid if not licit and urged parental acceptance since these unions had already been consummated. Conversely, parents also were urged not to coerce children into arranged marriages. Luther denounced excessively authoritarian parents in this regard and urged civil authorities to punish them. In Catholic territories boys and girls of canonical age, fourteen and twelve, respectively, had the right to refuse arranged marriages.

Clandestine marriage in France presented a highly different case. Sarah Hanley's research has demonstrated that marriage was regulated in lockstep with the growth of political absolutism and specifically served the secular interests of the French *noblesse de robe* (judicial nobility). At the Council of Trent, French delegates differed from their Italian and Spanish counterparts by insisting that the church sanction parental control of marriage. But the opposition, rather than capitulate, countered that parental consent was not required for a valid marriage to take place. French lawmakers continued to institute legislative changes that secured parental authority, arguing that it was critical to safeguarding natural and legal propriety. The Parlement of Paris thus implemented legal reforms. In 1556 it overturned canon law with a royal edict decreeing that parents could disinherit children who married without their permission. It also established the legal age for marriage without parental consent as thirty for men and twenty-five for women. The edict was an effort to exercise social and political control and to protect property. The Ordinance of Blois followed in 1578, requiring the officiating priest to have proof of the ages of the couple and the consent of their parents. Violators of the ordinance were charged with forced abduction or willing elopement, crimes punishable by death.

Legalists continued throughout the seventeenth century to tighten patriarchy, strengthening the power of husbands over wives. In 1629 and 1639 the requirement of parental consent was reiterated with further restrictions. Thus the French absolutist state created its own civil laws on marriage, curtailing ecclesiastical jurisdiction and claiming that marriage was a civil contract, not a religious one. Violators of the rules on parental consent would be tried in the secular courts. Determined couples in both Protestant and Catholic areas, however, managed to defy parental wishes despite efforts to restrict them. Romantic love may not have been practical in early modern Europe, but it was a powerful force that sometimes overrode the principles of property and standing that propelled arranged marriages. Both marriage and divorce in early modern Europe were more the concern of the propertied than of the humbler folk, whose values and behavior were guided by other, less-restricting principles.

Courtship and engagement in Jewish families shared some of the characteristics of Christian practices, but Jewish women might play a greater role in the matchmaking procedures. While it was traditional for fathers to arrange marriages, at times mothers, theoretically in the presence of witnesses, made the matches and concluded the symbolic exchange of property. The marriage contract provided for the costs of banquets, lodging, transportation, and clothing. The betrothed exchanged gifts and sometimes love notes. They, too, played some role in choosing whether to marry or not. Jewish women came to marriage with dowries, but so did grooms. The *ketubah* was the debt a man owed his wife in the event of divorce, imprisonment, or death.

Courtship obviously changed as a result of industrialization and urbanization. Parental controls less-ened. Among the working classes and some peasants it was increasingly common to engage in sexual intercourse before marriage, and marriage might occur only if a woman became pregnant, with pressure from her family to match. Middle-class arrangements remained more formal with strong economic overtones as families sought to assure the financial viability of a new family through a proper blending of resources by the bride and groom. But a culture of love, which could complicate expectations in courtship, also gained ground, widely touted in novels and popular reading.

MARRIAGE RITES

Throughout the Middle Ages and into the early modern period practices varied according to region, social class, and religious affiliation. In 1562–1563 the Catholic Church, through the Council of Trent, attempted to regularize and unify rites of marriage in Catholic areas of Europe. The council mandated that couples announce their banns in advance, publicizing them at least three times in their community; that they marry before their parish priest and at least two witnesses; that they affirm and publicize their mutual consent; and that they register the marriage. These requirements were formulated in response to the widespread confusion over what constituted marriage, for a wide variety of customs had prevailed in western Europe, developing over time in an autonomous and haphazard manner. Although by the fourth century A.D. the church had proclaimed that consent was the basis of Christian marriage, requiring that rites demonstrate the wish to join together, consent had not been attached to any specific protocol. French authorities, unlike their neighbors in England and on the Italian Peninsula, aimed to standardize marriage rites early on, from the eleventh century. They emphasized the sacramental nature of the bond and monitored the requirement of mutual consent attentively. Elsewhere, however, a freedom of form prevailed until the last decades of the sixteenth century.

Form was determined by socioeconomic level as well as by regional custom because marriage was a primary instrument of property relations. Marriage among humbler folk may not have entailed formal negotiations, and some couples may simply have started living together with or without a church ceremony. The man publicly kissed the woman and presented her with a gold ring or some other gift, whereupon they proceeded to have a sexual relationship. Some evidence suggests that communities recognized these unions and did not stigmatize their offspring. Brides may have gone to their weddings in the early stages of pregnancy. Marriage arrangements of this nature, however, were forbidden at the Council of Trent and were condemned as sinful. The council mandated that all marriages must be performed by a priest in a church. The Anglican Church was more lenient in these matters, while the Puritans concurred with the Catholic stance that marriage be formally blessed by the church.

In the sixteenth and seventeenth centuries the English upper and middle classes, in contrast with the lower strata of society, followed some protocol of arranged marriage. The groom's father wrote to the bride's father asking permission for the son to court the lady. After several visits, if the potential groom found the woman appealing, he gave her gifts of gold, a ring, or a pair of gloves over a period of about six months. Once the fathers agreed to the betrothal, the bride's father visited the groom's father, and the fathers agreed to a dowry. A ceremony and celebration followed, yet the bride did not leave her natal family for several weeks. The groom fetched her in the presence of family and friends, and the couple began their life together. Of course, these are just a few examples among many variations.

In the Italian regional states marriage contracts often preceded any clerical benediction of the match and were of utmost priority. Even artisans, workers, and peasant farmers went to notaries to record dowries, the exchange of consent, and the gifts of wedding rings. But the social orders with political weight and financial substance paid the closest attention to the contractual nature of marriage and to the financial terms of the union, for marriage was of deep importance to the socioeconomic structure of society. In many Italian cities, such as Florence, Venice, and Brescia, oligarchs constituted a hereditary elite, and endogamy was essential to the lineages' preservation and expansion of power over time. The secular dimension of marriage rites reflects the importance of patrilinear descent and of the disposition of dotal property within urban lineages. Marriage created a new economic unit linked to a network of other units that affected the cohesion of society. Negotiations between the allying families, who were normally entering into a political as well as a social consortium, were mediated by common friends. The fathers, or alternatively the male kin of the future spouses, met accompanied by close family and friends. At this meeting the terms of the marriage were set down in writing, and they were formally finalized at a later date in a notarial document. This betrothal ritual was as binding as the wedding ceremony. The size of the dowry, the terms of dowry payment, the living facilities and clothes the husband promised to provide, and an itemized account of what the bride would bring to the marriage were all stipulated in the contract. Marriage was indeed an economic arrangement.

Until at least the early twentieth century women of all classes, Jewish or Christian, were expected to provide dowries that might consist of some clothing and household items, usually including the marriage bed and bedding, for poor women, or vast amounts of cash, goods, or property for wealthy ones. The dowry was a statement of the bride's social status, publicizing her place in society as a whole. The dowry often substituted for a daughter's share of the family inheritance and increasingly did not include the land earmarked for the patrilineal lineage. Often that land was entailed, a legal restriction that made its recipient, through primogeniture, its custodian over his lifetime with the obligation to pass it on to the first male in the line.

The dowry was the central concern of contract negotiations. While in Roman times its purpose was to aid the groom with the expense of matrimony, in medieval and early modern times it was the bride's right to a share of her natal family's patrimony. Her husband could not alienate or consume it, and his own property was in jeopardy if he transgressed these rules. Legal restrictions over the governance of dotal resources varied from region to region. The dotal share might be equal to that of male siblings' inheritances, or it might amount to more or less. Fathers, brothers, mothers, aunts, and other kin contributed to dowry resources, for a well-dowered bride became a family's social asset with which to make a beneficial matrimonial alliance. If an unmarried and undowered woman lacked parents or paternal ascendants, responsibility might pass to her maternal ascendants, for jurists, clerics, and secular authorities considered dowry provision fundamental to the welfare of women. Laws regarding a woman's control of her dowry varied from region to region. In general a husband had use of it but not ownership during his wife's lifetime. In some areas a widower was entitled to one-third of the dowry, and the rest went to surviving children. Women who thought their husbands were wasting their dowries could sue them. Courts in many areas protected women, taking control of the dowry out of the husbands' hands. The Republic of Venice established a special tribunal for this in 1553. Women might bequeath their dowries, and in some areas they were obliged to leave them to their children. The dowry's importance was so fundamental to both the married woman and her wider kinship network that in Florence a public Dowry Fund was established at the birth of a daughter so deposits could accumulate over time and secure for her a place in the marriage market.

Eighteenth-Century Marriage Contract. *The Marriage Contract* (before 1743), the first painting in the series *Marriage à la Mode* by William Hogarth (1697–1764). NATIONAL GALLERY, LONDON/THE BRIDGEMAN ART LIBRARY

Moreover many cities established charities to help with the dowries of the indigent.

In the Italian states the sixteenth century was characterized by dowry inflation, making women and women's property increasingly important to marriage negotiations. Only after the details over the dowry were ironed out could the future groom visit his intended, bring her gifts, and dine with her family. At times the wider kinship group and their friends gathered publicly to celebrate the betrothal and to voice doubts or objections before the final arrangements were made. The marriage contract was a binding document, and guarantors and arbiters were appointed to implement its terms and to supervise its proper execution.

Following the establishment of a marriage contract, the rites of engagement unfolded at the bride's house, where friends gathered and gifts were delivered. The future husband visited, bringing friends and family. A notary asked the couple the questions relating to mutual consent prescribed by the church to con-

firm their agreement to an alliance formed by the families. The husband gave his new wife a wedding ring and gifts, and a wedding banquet followed. Wedding banquets could be quite lavish and last for days, with large feasts, dancing, games, and other festivities. By the end of the day of the verbal promise and exchange of rings, the union had to be consummated to be valid. The consummation could also be accompanied by festivity, called charivari. Typically the couple was serenaded but also inundated with noise made with drums, bells, and horns. Widows who remarried were also subject to this social ridicule and festivity. In Florence this was called *mattinate*.

The newlyweds might reside with the bride's family during the initial stages of the relationship. When the new bride left her natal home for that of her husband, further ceremonies might follow, such as riding through the town by torchlight escorted by friends and family. This was a way to notify the entire community of the couple's consent.

A Wedding Banquet. A Finnish bride sings farewell to her family. *The Bride's Song* by Gunnar Berndtson, 1881. FINNISH NATIONAL GALLERY/ATENEUM, HELSINKI, FINLAND/ANTELL COLLECTION/PHOTO: CENTRAL ART ARCHIVES

THE RESPONSIBILITIES OF HUSBANDS AND WIVES

Early modern Catholic marriages have largely been characterized as patriarchal arrangements in which husbands exerted paternalistic authority over wives. These models come largely from moral treatises and other prescriptive writings that in fact may not reflect social reality or the variety of experiences of the historical past. Protestant writers took a slightly different stance from their Catholic counterparts, emphasizing companionship, but in principle both denominations advanced the same patriarchal model of marriage. Protestants, Catholics, and Jews stressed shared responsibility between husbands and wives. A husband was required to sustain the upkeep of his wife and children, to protect them from harm, and to guide them. The husband was expected to be a role model for his family and servants, exercising self-control and good wisdom. He was to be God-fearing and disciplined so he might rule firmly but gently over his family. Excessive eating or drinking was frowned upon; abusive authority, violence, and infidelity were condemned. A husband was to exercise goodwill and concern for the welfare of his wife and family. The marital bond was to be based on mutual respect and love, though wives were asked to defer to the authority of their husbands.

A wife was responsible for governing her household and servants and for feeding and disciplining her children. She was her husband's co-worker and companion but was required to respect his authority. In Protestant areas women were usually in their twenties when they married so they would be mature enough to take over the responsibilities of running a household. A wife was expected to perform the conjugal duty of having sex and procreating, though her refusal was not grounds for divorce. Infidelity was condemned, and a woman was obliged to carefully guard her honor and reputation by behaving in a modest and civil manner and not indulging in excess.

The marriages considered to work best, according to prescriptive writings, were those in which husband and wife were close in age, both shared the same religion, both had similar economic means and social status, and the union enjoyed the approval of parents and friends. It has been argued that a wide age gap between spouses brought less parity to the marriage and at times less compatibility.

Ideas of greater parity in marriage found their way even into Russia's highly patriarchal pattern around 1700, with the partially westernizing reforms of Peter the Great. In a traditional custom the bride's father passed a whip to the groom as a symbol of the transition of male disciplinary authority. Peter outlawed this custom and in general promoted greater independence of wives among the upper classes.

The age of industrialization in the nineteenth century brought marked changes to the division of labor between husbands and wives. Husbands worked farther away from the home, becoming wage earners in factories and offices. Wives remained at home to supervise households and children. Only married women from poor families worked outside the household. Legal changes in the status of husbands and wives subordinated married women to their husbands. Wives did not enjoy the same legal rights as their spouses. For example, in England they did not have the right to hold property in their own names. In France the Napoleonic Code gave married men the preponderance of the rights to property, divorce, and custody of children. Most everywhere middle-class women lacked basic legal rights, whether under English common law, the Frederician (Prussian) Code, the Napoleonic Code, or Roman law. Husbands had the legal right to control wives' property, to determine their standard of living, and to make all decisions regarding estate management and the upbringing of children. In eastern Europe paternal authority was even more absolute.

Feminists of the late nineteenth and early twentieth centuries fought to redress the legal subordination of wives to husbands. Some political activists, liberal politicians, and demographic specialists, preoccupied with declining birthrates, joined them. Together these groups argued for the basic rights of married women, such as the right to their wages, to own property, and to share the governance of children with their husbands.

In western Europe the role and status of wives during the early twentieth century began to slowly change. As they became better educated, women acquired more control over their homes and their children. Some managed the family budget, the children's schooling, and religious instruction. Married couples developed stronger affective ties to each other as the home increased in emotional importance. More marriages were based on affection and sexual attraction than the formal arrangements of previous centuries.

The world wars of the twentieth century further advanced the rights and opportunities of women both at home and in the labor market, although in interwar periods married women were encouraged to leave the workforce to men. As the century progressed growing numbers of women acquired white-collar jobs, giving them independence and the possibility of dramatic change in lifestyles. More married as well as unmarried women worked and supported themselves, family size became smaller, and husbands increasingly shared family and household responsibilities.

REMARRIAGE

The likelihood was greater that widowers would remarry than would widows, especially if widowers were left with children who needed maternal care. Conversely, widows with children were more unlikely to remarry. Older women were at a greater disadvantage than younger ones, whereas age did not appear to make as much difference among widowers. For example, in seventeenth-century France only 20 percent of widows remarried, while half the widower population took new spouses. For women economic status played a role both in their desirability and their own wishes to remarry. A rich widow had a better chance of finding a new husband but might resist the pressure of remarriage in favor of enjoying her newly gained economic freedom. Her in-laws also might discourage remarriage lest the property be dispersed. Pressure for young widows of economic substance to remarry was high, both for the wealth they had to offer and because their independence and sexual experience were disturbing to a predominantly patriarchal society. The same did not apply to widowers, who were socially desirable but free to do as they chose.

THE QUALITY OF MARITAL RELATIONSHIPS

Historians have explored both the ties of affection that bound married couples and the tensions that divided them but have come to no consensus over the quality of early modern marital relationships, most of which were arranged. One part of the debate has hinged on property arrangements and inheritance patterns that restricted marriage. Some historians have stressed that parental authority over marriage delayed social adulthood and prevented ties of affection between parents and children. Moreover Philippe Ariès, Jean-Louis Flandrin, David Hunt, and Stone found affection absent in early modern couples. They characterized relations between spouses and between parents and children as distant and cold, for arranged marriage was a product of relationships based on property and not on love. The findings of other historians challenged this thesis, primarily by making it class specific. Steven Ozment's research on burgher society in Reformation Europe reveals intense emotional relationships between husbands and wives as well as between parents and children. Michael MacDonald's study of depression in early modern England finds spousal loss a common cause. He argued that affection was important and expected in marriage. Moreover several historians pointed to the writings of Lutherans, Puritans, and other Protestants during the Reformation that stress the importance of companionate marriage and mutual affection between spouses while still sustaining patriarchal principles.

Physical attraction and emotional love were not prerequisites for arranged unions. However, the potential development of love and affection played a critical part in keeping a marriage together. Sentiments are not always easy to document. Whether love developed in marriage or not, a successful union was one that developed respect and trust and in which spouses shared responsibility and were willing to work and sacrifice for the good of the household.

Another part of the debate over the quality of marital relationships revolves around the contention that dramatic changes in the history of sentiment took place from the eighteenth century onward. Flandrin and others argued that the family took on greater emotional importance for its members as early industrialization created a less emotional or psychologically satisfying environment. The growth of domestic manufacturing and the expansion of market relationships created sterile, competitive relationships among individuals and social classes, and the family became the center of emotional life. The relationship between husband and wife became less authoritarian and more affectionate. Evidence for this position is in family advice literature published during the Enlightenment. Writers urged the expression of greater affection and love in place of anger. This has been interpreted as the first steps toward the modern, middle-class ideal of the loving home. It seems, however, that this thesis is based primarily on prescriptive literature and applies best to the aristocracy and the middle class. In contrast, critics of this view, who have studied social experiences at other levels of society and through other sources, have argued that love may have thrived beneath the principally economic relationships produced by arranged marriage. Some sixteenth-century studies have concluded that the nuclear family increasingly became a focus of loyalty and was upheld in the Protestant ideal of the companionate marriage. During the Reformation the home displaced the church for some religious activities, such as reading the scriptures and prayer. Whether or not major changes in the emotional lives of husbands and wives, parents and children, took place during the eighteenth century is still debated.

Yet another historical controversy revolves around whether a married woman maintained close ties with her natal family or simply came under the custodianship of her husband's family. The answer may be linked to customary practices. Christiane Klapish-Zuber found that fifteenth-century Florentine families detached themselves from married daughters, while Joanne Ferraro's evidence for sixteenth- and seventeenth-century Venice indicates parents continued to be actively involved in their married daughters' lives, especially if their sons-in-law were failing in their duties as husbands. Moreover both Stanley Chojnacki and Ferraro have found that in Venice and Brescia, respectively, women made bequests to members of their natal families and provided female kin with dowries, signs that they continued to maintain close kinship ties throughout their lives. In early modern Jewish families, however, women were expected to leave their natal families behind both emotionally and physically so husbands rather than fathers would have the final say over their married lives.

Again industrialization and urbanization would change family dynamics in the nineteenth and twentieth centuries. Many urban working-class men spent much of their time outside the home at work and in male comradeship. Wives often preserved intense contacts with their mothers, sharing a variety of activities and household chores even when living in separate residences.

ANNULMENT, SEPARATION, AND DIVORCE

Because divorce was not permitted and separation was discouraged, the Catholic Church devoted a great deal of attention to regulating marriage at its inception to prevent the conflicts that ultimately might lead to petitions for annulment. The church meticulously defined the impediments to marriage that invalidated any claims to a legitimate union. An invalid marriage was grounds for annulment, in canon law signifying the marriage never took place and the parties involved were still free to wed. Couples obtained annulments in cases of forced unions, incapability of consummating the marriage (premarital impotence), and consanguinity and affinity in relationships of third cousins or closer. The Catholic Church also found marriages between people of different religions inappropriate unless the non-Christian converted. Taking vows of chastity or holy orders impeded marriage, as did secret vows to wed someone else or sexual relations with another person after one was engaged. Godparents and godchildren were forbidden to marry because they shared a spiritual affinity, and a godchild could not marry the child or sibling of a godparent. Legal guardianship created the same impediments. It was, moreover, inappropriate to marry someone convicted of fornication, adultery, or planning to murder a married lover's spouse. Life-threatening coercion also invalidated the consent to marry. In a number of cases that came before the courts of early modern Venice adult children lamented that they were forced into the arrangements of their parents with threats of violence. The Catholic Church maintained that parental consent was not a prerequisite for valid marriage and that these unions had been forced against the will of one or both of the spouses.

The discussion of divorce in Catholic circles was far less detailed than the subject of impediments. While Eastern Orthodox courts allowed divorce for adultery or taking religious vows, the Roman Catholic Church did not permit this solution for failing marriages. Canon law defined marriage as a permanent union before God and the church, based on Matthew 19:6, "What God has joined together, no man may put asunder." However, under specially defined circumstances couples in failing marriages were allowed separations of bed and board. This signified they would not cohabit, but they could not remarry. The circumstances under which the Roman church allowed separation included life-threatening abuse, leprosy, and adultery. Battered wives in early modern Venice found the Patriarchal Court sympathetic to their grave circumstances. The court acted as a place where women could seek redress and hope to dissolve a failing union. Often women in bad marriages in early modern Venice and elsewhere in the Italian regional states retreated to one of the many asylums established through law and ecclesiastical charities. In this way the *malmaritate* (badly married) safeguarded their honor and reputations before their communities. Husbands were ordered by secular tribunals to sustain the cost of living of separated wives and to be responsible for the care of the children. Adultery was also just cause for separation in Catholic courts. A guilty husband was responsible for the support of an injured wife. In the reverse case, however, a wife might be obligated to forfeit her dowry as punishment for this serious moral offense.

In early modern France the Roman Catholic doctrine of marital indissolubility was staunchly defended by the Gallican church and the monarchy. As in Italy, separations were permitted. However, the control over this process came increasingly under the civil courts because of property considerations. Separations had far-reaching effects, unraveling ties between kin groups and political oligarchies, rearranging or canceling property transfers, forcing friends and relatives to adjust to a new social situation, and generally upsetting the life of the community. Consequently this solution to failing marriage was highly discouraged and rarely occurred before the eighteenth century. More women than men sought separations in the French ecclesiastical courts because they needed the assistance of the law against tyrannical husbands. Separations in France were granted when the wife was in physical or moral danger, if she was falsely accused by her husband of adultery, or if her husband was insane, attempting to murder her, or expressing deadly hatred of her. On the other hand, wives with adulterous husbands were generally expected to endure poor marital relations.

Ecclesiastical authorities in France increasingly lost jurisdiction over the regulation of marriage and separation to secular authorities. Ultimately a partnership developed between the Gallican church and the absolutist state that marked the beginning of secularization and the laicization of family law. The trend spread throughout many parts of western Europe. Gradually, from the eighteenth-century onward, French monarchs and their counterparts in Sweden, Denmark, Prussia, and Catholic Austria, had a hand in dissolving marriages, as did republican Venice's Council of Ten, the oligarchy's supreme judicial organ.

In eighteenth-century France the grounds for marital dissolution expanded from adultery and desertion to emotional incompatibility. Most thinkers during the ancien régime opposed divorce until the Enlightenment, when philosophers rejected the theological assumptions of the Middle Ages in favor of natural law and secular ideas receptive to divorce doctrines. Some argued that divorce would promote population growth, regenerate morality, and increase happiness and harmony within families. The subject of divorce was prominent in the depopulationist literature emphasizing both reproduction and regeneration. Its prohibition reputedly caused adultery and illegitimacy as well as child and spousal abandonment and poverty. Divorce and remarriage would make families happier. Moreover, writers such as Montesquieu and Paul-Henri-Dietrich d'Holbach argued that it would be beneficial for women, who could use it as a counterweight to the authority that their husbands wielded within marriage.

Not just in France but throughout the Catholic regions of Europe separation was generally discouraged by the church courts, and couples were urged to work out their differences. This was true in Anglican England, where marriage differences came under the jurisdiction of ecclesiastical courts that continued to administer medieval canon law. The Reformation had

Revolutionary Wedding. The marriage oath is taken in the presence of a French municipal official before a statue of the goddess of Reason. Engraving by Maradan after a painting by Senave. BIBLIOTHÈQUE NATIONALE, PARIS

not revised canon law in England save for reducing the number of proscribed degrees of incest. The Anglican Church, unlike other Protestant denominations, did not permit divorce with permission to remarry but, as in Catholic areas of Europe, granted separations of bed and board in cases of adultery and life-threatening danger as a result of physical abuse. As the idea of companionate marriage diffused throughout Reformation England, wives requesting separations as a result of cruelty received more sympathy.

Before 1657 the ecclesiastical courts in England had sole jurisdiction over marital break up. The church courts were administered by men trained in the civil law over property matters who in marriage cases applied canon law as well. By the late seventeenth century English common law courts became increasingly involved in breach of promise suits, and these slowly replaced marriage contract suits before the ecclesiastical courts. English criminal courts also became involved if either of the parties chose to sue the other for bigamy or sodomy. Finally, Parliament had a hand in marriage disputes in the late seventeenth century. It passed private bills of full divorce with permission to remarry for wealthy husbands.

England instituted many deterrents to suing for separation, particularly if the wife was initiating the dissolution. Stone wrote that significant numbers contrived to escape their marital bonds without going to court. Only 10 percent of the cases involving legal proceedings came to trial and sentence. Stone contended that wives, made docile by the ideology of female subordination and inferiority, were reluctant to sue for separation. Moreover for them separation meant near certain financial hardship or destitution.

When the husband was found guilty, the alimony was generous, amounting to a third of his declared net income. However, it was hard to enforce payment. Another serious deterrent was that wives could also loose contact with their children. Fear of publicity also discouraged petitions to separate. The situation of English women, as presented by Stone, is in stark contrast to the sympathy for abused wives expressed by the ecclesiastical court in early modern Venice.

Nonetheless, reasons to separate in England did arise, among them the physical separations and outright desertions caused by war, infidelity, financial quarrels, ruptures between the husband's kin and the wife's kin, physical cruelty by the husband, and adultery by the wife or husband, although generally the double standard made only adultery by the wife legitimate grounds for separation. Marriage ties in early modern England could be broken in a variety of ways, such as through desertion, wife sale among the lower classes, and separation by private deed. In the last instance the husband and wife made a private agreement in which the husband assured his wife alimony. The wife was subsequently financially free to act. Divorce as a legitimate remedy for failed marriage only came to England after 1660, and until 1820 it was class specific. Only the rich, landed elite and merchants could afford to pay the personnel involved in formal litigation.

In other Protestant areas of Europe marriage regulations differed from both Catholic and Anglican ones on several points. First, they stressed the importance of parental consent more than Catholic regulations did and allowed for the possibility of divorce with remarriage for adultery, impotence, refusal to have sex, abuse, abandonment, and incurable diseases. Second, Luther reduced the large number of legitimate impediments to Catholic marriage to two or three, including impotence, marriages made in error, and the twelve kinship barriers stated in Leviticus 18.

Protestant reformers, however, were not in consensus over what constituted a legitimate impediment to marriage. In Strasbourg and Constance the tenets of canon law still essentially informed rules about marital impediment. In conservative Nürnberg, however, reformers not only sustained the kinship barriers that had been outlined by the Catholic Church but further multiplied them. The theologian Andreas Osiander established nineteen kinship barriers from Leviticus 18 and 20, fifteen from the laws of Moses, and sixteen from the kinship ties traced from grandparents.

In principle Protestants made divorce and remarriage possible for those with legitimate cause. Reformers, such as Luther and Bucer, and theologians, such as Johannes Brenz in 1531 and Johannes Bugenhagen in 1540, rejected the Catholic solution of separation of bed and board for failing marriages. Without cohabitation, they maintained, no marriage existed. Moreover they rejected the Catholic notion of marriage as a sacrament, viewing it instead as a secular commitment. Its purpose extended beyond procreation to that of creating a harmonious hearth and home through mutual commitment. French Reformed Protestants and English Puritans took a similar stance.

Perhaps the most compelling cause for divorce in Protestant areas was adultery, which liberated the innocent spouse from the union. Lutheran theologians also recognized emotional incompatibility and hatred as causes for marital dissolution but not religious differences. In extreme cases couples could be granted a separation, but the husband retained the right to summon the wife back into his house if he could not manage it by himself. A grant of separation, however, did not sanction dating or remarriage. Brenz cited other unusual circumstances that might lead to divorce, including threats of murdering a spouse or of practicing dangerous magic, but none was as powerful as adultery in arguing for divorce. A marriage that was not consummated after three years could also be dissolved, but not if the marriage had been consummated and then serious illness impeded sexual relations. Desertion was also legitimate reason to divorce, as it certainly did not live up to the ideal of companionship in marriage. The abandoned spouse was allowed to remarry a year after his or her partner's disappearance.

Divorce in Protestant areas of Europe came under the jurisdiction of secular tribunals rather than the clergy. Lutheran clergy could advise the court, but they neither made marriage laws nor judged marital litigation. Luther called on civil magistrates to establish divorce courts that would use both scripture and secular law as their legal and moral guidelines. Protestant courts tended to be cautious in granting divorces. Nürnberg judges in particular resisted divorce and remarriage, fearing it would encourage adultery and abandonment. Conservative reformers voiced these concerns in Basel as well. John Oecolampadius advocated that only adultery should be valid cause for divorce. But these conservative views were balanced with more liberal ones, such as those of Bucer, who recognized leprosy, madness, impotence, and abandonment as just causes for the dissolution of marriage. Thus in Basel both men and women sought divorce on these grounds. Refusal of the conjugal duty, however, was not just cause for marital dissolution.

Ozment collected important information on the activities of the Protestant courts. A Zwinglian church court was established in Zurich in 1525, replacing the bishop's court in Constance. Two clerics and four lay authorities sat on the six-member team that dealt with contested marriages and requests for divorce. While this court could make judgements, their enforcement was exclusively in the hands of the city councils, which also served as appellate courts. The Zurich court heard petitions mostly from women, who were sometimes represented by lawyers, and supporting testimony from parents, guardians, and other witnesses. The court recognized six grounds for divorce, specifically adultery, impotence, willful desertion, serious incompatibility, a sexually incapacitating illness, and deception. The court also attempted to end lay concubinage, prostitution, and breach of promise to marry and to regularize secret marriages, perhaps to protect the reputation of pregnant women by obtaining a firm marriage commitment for them. It denied private unions and required credible witnesses at the marriage ceremony as well as public declarations of mutual consent. Betrothed couples were urged to postpone cohabitation until after public vows and a church-recorded marriage ceremony.

In Basel five laymen and two clergymen heard divorce cases. The court recognized adultery, impotence, willful desertion, capital crimes, leprosy, and deadly abuse as grounds for divorce. Convicted adulterers were fined five pounds. The fine was doubled for a second offense, and the offender was given a six-day jail sentence. Repeated offenses increased the punishment. Zurich had similar punishments. An offender could be banished from the church, his or her right to hold public office withdrawn, and his or her eligibility to join guilds and societies removed. Remarriage was not permitted until one to five years after the divorce. Basel was more severe, forbidding remarriage. The injured spouse in adultery cases received a cash settlement as well as property.

Divorced people were expected to wait at least one year before remarrying. The ceremony for a second marriage for Lutherans had to be a private affair before civil authorities rather than a public church occasion. The couple made their commitment before civil magistrates and then perhaps spent an evening with family and friends and a pastor who concluded the new union. The remarriage of a widow or a widower was also a private occasion.

Besides petitions for separation or divorce, church courts heard cases that challenged arranged marriages. In Venice these petitions were often brought by women in defiance of parental authority. Life-threatening coercion or disinheritance, if convincingly demonstrated, gave cause for invalidating an unwanted marriage. In Zurich parental challenges to secret mar-

riages of children under nineteen came to the court's attention, but these marriages were not automatically annulled.

Under certain circumstances, such as infidelity or violent abuse, divorce was permitted in Jewish law, though wives did not have the right to initiate the petitions. Still, cases were brought before rabbinic courts by women accusing men of various deficiencies that were acceptable grounds for divorce according to rabbinic law.

DIVORCE IN THE MODERN ERA

In terms of the law, the modern history of divorce began with the French Revolution. Enlightenment ideas about the family gained prominence, and for several years divorce was legalized, open to action by wives as well as husbands. Although the rate was not massive, a number of divorces ensued, often initiated by women. Napoleonic legislation then closed off many opportunities. During most of the nineteenth century divorce remained highly circumscribed throughout Europe, particularly for women. But changes in laws, usually associated with the discussion of new rights for women, altered the situation late in the century.

By 1900 divorce had spread dramatically throughout Europe. Only a few Catholic states (Spain, Portugal, Italy, and Ireland) made no legal provisions for divorce. Elsewhere civil courts made it readily available, and the laws governing marital dissolution were generally liberalized. England founded a Court for Divorce and Matrimonial Causes in 1857. France, having suspended divorce laws in the second decade of the nineteenth century, reintroduced them in 1884. Meanwhile nineteenth-century ideologies of domesticity and femininity urging equal access to divorce courts for women made a notable impact, so much so that divorce became a subject of debate in the years leading up to World War I. Framed as "the marriage question," the broad and lively discussion encompassed such issues as free love, polygamy, fertility, contraception, the liberties of women, and the social and moral issues of divorce. Conservative efforts to restrict divorce faltered as many countries either legalized or liberalized it. Divorce increased in the Soviet Union in the 1920s, when experiments in family law were widespread. Nevertheless, great efforts to maintain family stability characterized the Stalinist era.

In the second half of the twentieth century divorce was accessible to all social groups. As the century progressed divorce rates soared. It is difficult to attribute this dramatic rise to any one cause. Explanations have linked a number of important transformations in twentieth-century life, including attitudes toward sexuality, morality, and religion; the relations of men and women; and social, economic, and demographic conditions. The late twentieth century brought change both in the expectations of marriage and in the attitudes toward divorce. Premarital pregnancy, which previously had propelled couples into marriage, lost its social stigma, and single parenthood gained recognition. In Scandinavia a growing number of people, including parents, did not bother with marriage at all. Further, increasing numbers of women entered the labor market, achieving the financial independence that gave them choices about whether or not to marry and whether or not to remain married. Legal changes also facilitated divorce for women, giving them property rights and the possibility of alimony and child support. The late twentieth century was thus a vital transition period that broadened the opportunities to marry and at the same time made divorce more commonplace. Divorce rates varied by region, however, and the United States outnumbered all others.

See also other articles in this section.

BIBLIOGRAPHY

Adelman, Howard. "Italian Jewish Women." In *Jewish Women in Historical Perspective.* Edited by Judith R. Baskin. Detroit, Mich., 1991. Pages 135–158.

Ariès, Philippe. *Centuries of Childhood: A Social History of Family Life.* Translated by Robert Baldick. New York, 1962.

Boxer, Marilyn J., and Jean H. Quataert, eds. *Connecting Spheres: European Women in a Globalizing World, 1500 to the Present.* 2d ed. New York, 2000.

Boxer, Marilyn J. and Jean H. Quataert, eds. *Socialist Women: European Socialist Feminism in the Nineteenth and Early Twentieth Centuries.* New York, 1978.

Burguière, André, et al. *Family and Sexuality in French History.* Edited by Robert Wheaton and Tamara K. Hareven. Philadelphia, 1980.

Chojnacki, Stanley. "Dowries and Kinsmen in Early Renaissance Venice." *Journal of Interdisciplinary History* 4 (1975): 571–600.

Davis, Natalie Zemon. "City Women and Religious Change." In *Society and Culture in Early Modern France.* Stanford, Calif., 1975. Pages 65–96.

Ferraro, Joanne M. *Family and Public Life in Brescia, 1580–1650. The Foundations of Power in the Venetian State.* New York, 1993.

Ferraro, Joanne M. "The Power to Decide: Battered Wives in Early Modern Venice." *Renaissance Quarterly* 48 (1995): 492–512.

Flandrin, Jean-Louis. *Families in Former Times: Kinship, Household, and Sexuality.* Translated by Richard Southern. New York, 1979.

Gillis, John R. *For Better, for Worse: British Marriages, 1600 to the Present.* New York, 1985.

Hanley, Sarah. "Family and State in Early Modern France: The Marriage Pact." In *Connecting Spheres: Women in the Western World, 1500 to the Present.* Edited by Marilyn J. Boxer and Jean H. Quataert. New York, 1987. Pages 53–63.

Herlihy, David, and Christiane Klapish-Zuber. *Les toscans et leurs familles: Une étude du catasto florentin de 1427* (Tuscans and their families: A study of the Florentine catasto of 1427). Paris, 1978.

Hunt, David. *Parents and Children in History: The Psychology of Family Life in Early Modern France.* New York, 1970.

Klapish-Zuber, Christiane. *Women, Family, and Ritual in Renaissance Italy.* Translated by Lydia Cochrane. Chicago, 1985.

Laslett, Peter. *Family Life and Illicit Love in Earlier Generations.* Cambridge, U.K., 1977.

MacDonald, Michael. *Mystical Bedlam: Madness, Anxiety and Healing in Seventeenth-Century England.* Cambridge, U.K., 1981.

Macfarlane, Alan. *Marriage and Love in England: Modes of Reproduction, 1300–1840.* New York, 1986.

Marshall, Sherrin. *The Dutch Gentry, 1500–1650: Family, Faith, and Fortune.* New York, 1987.

Mitterauer, Michael, and Reinhard Sieder. *The European Family: Patriarchy to Partnership from the Middle Ages to the Present.* Translated by Karla Oosterveen and Manfred Hörziner. Chicago, 1982.

Offen, Karen. "Depopulation, Nationalism, and Feminism in Fin-de-Siècle France." *American Historical Review* 89 (1984): 648–676.

Ozment, Steven. *When Fathers Ruled: Family Life in Reformation Europe.* Cambridge, Mass., 1983.

Phillips, Roderick. *Family Breakdown in Late Eighteenth-Century France: Divorces in Rouen, 1792–1803.* Oxford, 1980.

Phillips, Roderick. *Putting Asunder: A History of Divorce in Western Society.* Cambridge, U.K., 1988.

Ruggiero, Guido. *Binding Passions: Tales of Magic, Marriage, and Power at the End of the Renaissance.* New York, 1993.

Ruggiero, Guido. *The Boundaries of Eros: Sex, Crime, and Sexuality in Renaissance Venice.* New York, 1985.

Stone, Lawrence. *Broken Lives: Separation and Divorce in England, 1660–1857.* New York and Oxford, 1993.

Stone, Lawrence. *Family, Sex, and Marriage in England, 1500–1800.* London, 1977.

Stone, Lawrence. *Road to Divorce: England 1530–1987.* New York and Oxford, 1990.

Tilly, Louise A., and Joan W. Scott. *Women, Work, and Family.* New York, 1978.

Traer, James F. *Marriage and Family in Eighteenth-Century France.* Ithaca, N.Y., 1980.

Trumbach, Randolph. *The Rise of the Egalitarian Family: Aristocratic Kinship and Domestic Relations in Eighteenth-Century England.* New York, 1978.

Wiesner, Merry E. *Women and Gender in Early Modern Europe.* Cambridge, U.K., 1993.

Wrightson, Keith. *English Society, 1580–1680.* New Brunswick, N.J., 1982.

MOTHERHOOD

Ellen Ross

Motherhood, as defined here, is the cultural process of locating women's identities in their capacity to nurture infants and children. As a set of concepts it dates only from the late eighteenth century or the early nineteenth century in Europe. English dictionaries do not make these distinctions, yet "motherhood" can be differentiated from mothering, actually caring for children, and also from the biological events, pregnancy, birth, and lactation, associated with maternity. The panorama of changing discourses and practices offered by social history vividly demonstrates the error of conflating motherhood, mothering, and maternity.

Four main eras are identifiable in the history of mothers' child rearing practices and in dominant ideas about women and their mothering capacities:

(1) the early modern period, with its shifting and contradictory narratives and images of mothers and communal child care patterns;

(2) the late eighteenth century and the nineteenth century with their elaboration of motherhood as a sacred female calling;

(3) the twentieth century from 1918 to about 1970, when birthrates plummeted, psychological constructions of motherhood dominated the helping professions and the mass media, and motherhood as a symbol was central in the formation and reconfiguration of war-torn nations; and

(4) the late twentieth century, characterized by a dramatic reconfiguration of the material experience of motherhood.

This entry covers both the discursive aspects of motherhood as eventually constructed by the literate elites as well as the phenomenology of mothering among the peoples of Europe—strands that are deeply intertwined. Meanings of motherhood and motherly roles have been communicated to the inhabitants of Europe in a variety of ways. Communities have informally enforced their own norms through gossip, shaming rituals, or exhortation. Voluntary associations accepting foundlings or offering aid to mothers have played major roles in communicating principles of motherhood. As Jean-Louis Flandrin and Michel Foucault have pointed out, clergymen, especially in the early centuries, have been central in establishing the discussive outlines of motherhood and fatherhood. State legislation on such issues as compulsory education, child custody, child labor, and workplace protection are also powerful statements about parental duties. The mass media, of course, have also played an incalculable role in propagating models of motherhood.

WIFE, MOTHER, WITCH: THE SIXTEENTH CENTURY THROUGH THE EIGHTEENTH CENTURY

Europe's Catholic heritage offered an ambivalent view of mothers. Celibates were the holy ones, and not until the late Middle Ages were married people considered for sainthood. Christ's mother Mary, whose cult was promoted by the twelfth-century church as a way of stimulating lay piety, was different from all other mothers—not only because of her lifelong virginity but because of the enraptured devotion to a single child with which she was often depicted. Late medieval and humanist writers often preferred Anne, the mother of Mary and the matriarch of a large extended family, as a more familiar model of maternity.

With the Reformation, the saints lost both their shrines and their vivid personal presence. The new moral center of the Christian universe was the family. Though Martin Luther revered maternity and women's nurturing of children, in Protestant countries marriage rather than motherhood dominated female identities. In the public rhetoric of Reformation-era Augsburg, for example, a woman was almost always referred to as a Frau or *Weib,* almost never as *Mutter,* which referred to the uterus.

In both Catholic and Protestant countries, families were patriarchal. In law and to a great extent in custom too, children belonged to their fathers, whose

Maternal Devotion to the Child. *Madonna and Child with Cherubim,* glazed terra-cotta relief by Andrea della Robbia (1435–1525). NATIONAL GALLERY OF ART, WASHINGTON, D.C., ANDREW W. MELLON COLLECTION

duty it was to raise them to be decent, God-fearing, and self-supporting. The Renaissance Florentine system of placing infants with wet nurses was organized through fathers, who often negotiated with the *balia* or her husband and who decided when the child should be weaned or transferred. In Samuel Richardson's *Pamela,* Part 2 (1741), Pamela's husband and former master autocratically insists on a wet nurse for their new baby despite Pamela's strong desire to breast-feed, another indication that wetnursing signified paternal power more than maternal indifference. Patriarchy did not always mean a stern and remote father, of course. Dutch fathers were depicted in seventeenth-century paintings playing with or teaching children, even infants.

Being a mother—giving birth or caring for children—was the destiny of European women in the early modern era and fully occupied the adult lives of most of the female population. In early eighteenth-century France approximately five children per family survived, and about two more did not live beyond childhood. For the average European in 1700, life expectancy was only about twenty-five years, and few lived past age forty. A woman marrying in her mid-twenties or a little later would most likely die with young children still in the home.

Not all children's births have been welcomed. Women have always tried to limit births that would cause hardships, and recipes for abortifacients were

part of folk knowledge and the more specialized knowledge of healers. In some of the poorest regions of the world even in the twentieth century, to be a mother could involve a form of triage, the selection of some children for neglect or abandonment and nearly certain death. Very poor or unmarried woman were more likely to abandon their newborns. This practice had become so common by the Middle Ages that special homes for foundlings, whose death rates were extraordinarily high, proliferated in major European towns. The number of foundlings increased whenever economic conditions deteriorated.

Wife, housekeeper, and breadwinner were identities that competed with and often overshadowed that of mother. For the poorest women, the preoccupations of income earning and the price of the grains that made up family diets were far more central than the development of each child. Household survival was based on "an economy of makeshifts" (Hufton, 1974, pp. 69–127), such as begging, thieving, charity, or street selling. The collective desperation of poor mothers entered the historical record through the bread riots of the seventeenth and eighteenth centuries, including the October Days in 1789, which constituted a crucial stage in the French Revolution. Mothers' sense of "food entitlement," to use the term of the economist Amartya Sen, brought women into the streets well into the twentieth century, most famously in Saint Petersburg in March 1917 but also in early twentieth-century Italy and in Germany during World War I.

Mothers were extremely important as educators of the children in their care, especially girls. Literate mothers produced literate children. Mothers also taught daughters household skills, such as growing vegetables, keeping hens, feeding pigs, making cheeses, or simply preparing meals. Sewing—fancy or plain depending on the status of the household—constituted another important set of skills mothers imparted to their daughters. The poorest mothers often made their daughters partners in subsistence activities, such as selling milk or vegetables at market or even begging. Mothers sometimes managed to save enough money from their own by-employments of fattening chickens or rabbits or selling honey to help daughters accumulate dowries that would dramatically improve their marriage prospects.

The biological mother and child pair that seems so natural today received relatively little cultural emphasis. Both urban and rural women in the early modern period supervised and befriended many who were not their biological children. Households exchanged children, especially teens, as apprentices and servants. In eighteenth-century Paris, for example, domestic servants, workshop apprentices, and local neighborhood children and young people circulated constantly through both domestic and work spaces. Servants sometimes inherited from their masters as if they were kin. The formal adoption of children, while difficult in this period when blood lineages were essential to definitions of family, did take place, at least in France, under a variety of legal fictions.

For artistocratic and bourgeois women of the seventeeth and eighteenth centuries in many parts of Europe, breast-feeding by the biological mother of an infant was not considered essential. Wetnursing, especially common in France among the well-off and those of moderate means, meant that a woman might spend little time with her biological children during the first few years of their lives. Wetnursing apparently was the norm in eighteenth-century Hamburg, where a surprising five thousand of its ninety thousand inhabitants were wet nurses by profession.

To say that the construction of motherhood is a twentieth-century phenomenon is not to claim that fertility, birth, or children received no cultural emphasis in the early modern period. They were in fact at the center of elaborate systems of folk magic and storytelling. Themes related to motherhood are also prominent in definitions of witchcraft, in many regions a capital crime, for which at least 200,000 were executed between about 1450 and 1725. Men constituted under 20 percent of that number. The witch, as the definition was formulated over many generations in clerical treatises and court transcripts, was a distorted mother. She was betrayed by her "witch's teat," any extra fold of skin upon which the devil could suck. The ingredients of the brew served at witches' weekly sabbats included dead babies, and witches killed or caused to sicken animals and children, especially babies. A witch's daughter or granddaughter might well become a witch. Court records and trial transcripts reveal the jealousies, grudges, and fears generated by issues of fertility and childbearing that often were the motives for denunciations and may have given the crime of witchcraft its vivid inverse relation to motherhood. The accused included a disproportionate number of midwives and lying-in assistants.

Perhaps the inchoate mother of this era is most easily seen in folktales, which portray a wide range of mothers and stepmothers, loving, cruel, witchlike, strong, clever, and stupid. Tellingly, in the nineteenth-century Jacob Grimm and Wilhelm Grimm, whose versions of these tales became widely read, turned the jealous and vicious biological mother of Snow White into a stepmother. By this time cruelty and envy did not square with notions of selfless motherhood.

THE CULT OF MOTHERHOOD: 1760–1918

The cult of motherhood developed in the context of a new anatomy and physiology. Late eighteenth-century anatomists broke with the "one-sex" view that had dominated the study of anatomy since the Renaissance, in which the female was simply an imperfect or perhaps inverted version of the male. Medical writers began to stress the anatomical differences between women and men and to detail female reproductive anatomy and menstruation, a trend that was accentuated with the early twentieth-century discovery of the endocrine system and hormonal differences between women and men. Physicians and other Enlightenment authors, most famously Jean-Jacques Rousseau in *Émile* (1762), claimed breast-feeding and a mother's full-time care of her infants and children was "nature's will," using as models both animal mothers and aboriginal peoples in Africa and South America. Though some of the new arguments outlined the health advantages of mothers' milk and maternal care, the feeding method represented a new, idealized mission for leisured woman free of other

Mother as Educator. *Maternal Instruction,* painting by Caspar Netscher (c. 1635–1684). NATIONAL GALLERY, LONDON

163

Breast-feeding. An upper-class woman feeds her own child rather than sending it to a wetnurse. Illustration from *The Elegant Mother,* by James Gillray (c. 1796).

demands. Their pleasure and fulfillment was to come through motherhood.

Indeed motherhood became, in advice books for women, the central female identity. The touch of the child was supposed to bring out the latent, intensely tender feelings in women. As the nineteenth-century British physician P. H. Chevasse put it: "The love of offspring is one of the strongest instincts implanted in women; there is nothing that will compensate for the want of children. A wife yearns for them; they are as necessary to her happiness as the food she eats and the air she breathes" (Oakley, 1980, p. 9).

In Victorian ideology motherhood was associated with the home, which was distinguished from the public world of politics and industry. The private realm was the special arena of mothers, who presided there as "the bright spirit of the home" or as "our warming sunshine," as middle-class Swedes stated (Frykman, 1987, p. 121). Family events, such as dinners and holiday celebrations, revolved around the presence of the mother, then seen as the only such figure in a child's life. Conceptions of the central place of female nurture in children's spiritual

development circulated in thousands of middle-class advice books. Many well-off mothers closely charted their children's motor skills, language, and social development and were deeply involved in their achievements.

In France the cult of motherhood was heavily accented with populationism and, given France's low birthrates, had official government support. The long-lived Bordeaux Society for Maternal Charity offered material aid and close surveillance and was typical of nineteenth-century French voluntary and government organizations formed to promote the new motherhood and to encourage procreation. The upper-class volunteers of the society accepted only women of demonstrated respectability, cleanliness, and thrift but supported them with generous cash payments. Meanwhile French statisticians adopted new ways of charting population size that focused on classifying women in terms of their childbearing potential and counting the babies born to women in their "fertile" years. Although government and private agencies in France offered a number of services to pregnant women and new mothers, they also treated women with small families almost as traitors undermining the nation's vitality.

The new motherhood doctrines were by no means fully instituted in wealthy women's daily lives, though there they had the greatest chance of acceptance. To be sure the practice among the comfortable classes of hiring wet nurses gradually died out everywhere in the nineteenth century, as much the result of the feasibility of bottle-feeding because of antisepsis as of new desires for intimacy with infants. In Paris by the nineteenth century the majority of wet nurse patrons were poor working women. Wealthy women continued as wives and socialites first, mothers second. In the early nineteenth century many mothers in the Nord province in France continued to run family textile businesses and visited their infants and children on Sundays at their wet nurses or boarding schools. Many dissenting voices throughout the nineteenth century challenged the new motherhood paradigm. Feminists harshly criticized their own mothers' lives and motherhood as an institution more generally. To take just one example, Florence Nightingale loathed domestic life and suggested that there should be "crèches for the rich as well as the poor."

For the bulk of the population, the experience of mothering was little changed by the new doctrines. Being a mother meant, as it had in the past, the struggle to feed and dress a large family on an economy of makeshifts. Fatalism about frequent pregnancies predominated, and families were especially large through most of the nineteenth century. Even the best-educated women in most of Europe did not limit their births significantly in the first half of the nineteenth century. Britain between 1800 and 1850 and Russia between 1850 and 1900 averaged completed family sizes of over six children plus stillbirths and child deaths. Maternity constituted a physical feat, as it had in earlier times. Even though life expectancy increased substantially in the richest European countries by the nineteenth century, only a few mothers lived long enough to see all of their children grow up and leave home.

If domesticity and motherhood were the only appropriate callings for women, the vast majority of the female population was stigmatized as unwomanly. As industrial capitalism developed in the early nineteenth century, more mothers and nonmothers became waged workers, though at about only half of men's rate of pay, rather than creating subsistence goods for their own families. In rural Hungary and England women plaited straw in their homes for national markets. In Danish villages women shaped and fired clay pots. Throughout Europe women were farm laborers. They were forced to work for landlords in eastern Europe, where serfdom existed until the middle of the nineteenth century in the Hapsburg lands and until 1861 in Russia. Urban mothers toiled in factories and workshops, worked at home on piece rates, took in lodgers, sweated in industrial-sized laundries, or took in washing at home.

In much of rural Europe women were still agricultural workers under the discipline of a father, a husband, a father-in-law, or in feudal regions a landlord. Under these conditions women's maternal functions were considered secondary. In late nineteenth-century Russia, for example, breast-feeding was the rule, but as new mothers quickly returned to the fields, babies were fed several solid meals each day. Often pacifiers of cloth filled with grain and bacon rind, often prechewed by an adult and obviously quite deadly, were given to babies. Folk sayings such as "It's better to lose an egg than a chicken" minimized the loss that an infant death represented and also stressed the importance of the mother as a worker.

In urban working-class households, motherhood, whether accompanied by waged work or not, involved hard physical work and careful budgeting rather than finely tuned child nurture. What would have been called "mother love" by Victorian middle-class observers was, as understood by poor mothers and children, embodied in the mother's physical exertions, such as frantic bargaining for discount food, after-hours factory piecework done at home, late-night hours spent sewing or ironing children's clothing, and bedside vigils with sick babies. Indeed moth-

"Our Warming Sunshine." *Roses and Lilies,* painting (1897) by Mary MacMonnies (1868–1946). MUSÉE DES BEAUX-ARTS, ROUEN, FRANCE/ROGER-VIOLLET

ers' incessant work is central in French and German nineteenth-century working-class autobiographies. The daughter of a Paris lace maker wrote that it was her mother "who with her needle and agile fingers built a wall against misery" (Maynes, 1995, p. 79).

Children in these urban settings were expected to repay their mothers' efforts back in cash or in kind. They minded younger siblings, did household chores, helped with mothers' home manufacturing, or freed their mothers from the costs of their keep by taking jobs as servants or factory hands. In late nineteenth-century London they ran household errands and often were sent to fetch things that required a long wait in line, such as the penny-a-quart soup served by a local mission, where one autobiographer often waited in the 1890s with his empty jug. As their children grew though their teens and earned higher wages, mothers claimed a diminishing share of this cash, though sons kept more pocket money than did daughters.

These patterns of mother-child reciprocity became strained, especially in the early twentieth century. Compulsory education, introduced in some of the German states as early as the eighteenth century, represents one of the tensions. In northern and western European countries the years of required schooling expanded in the late nineteenth century or the early twentieth century. The French system, which from 1833 had educated only boys, included girls after 1881. In Britain after 1881 all children between five and ten were expected at school, and the years of compulsory schooling gradually increased thereafter. Mothers' rights to children's services were thus defied by national education systems. Educators, for their part, sometimes attacked maternal claims on the time and loyalty of their children.

The new classification of women as mothers is evident in a variety of nineteenth-century institutions and was sometimes beneficial to women, sometimes not. Unions fought to keep women workers out of their shops in the name of their motherhood capacity, legislators enacted special conditions for hiring women workers, and pregnant or lactating women had claims on particular state or municipal services in many countries. A German law of 1878, for example, mandated unpaid maternity leave for factory workers for three weeks after a birth. Otto von Bismarck's health insurance scheme of 1883 included short-term maternity benefits, though the payment was at the discretion of the funding agency.

For many suffragists and feminists, motherhood provided the basis for claims to citizenship and voting rights. The former seamstress Jeanne Deroin, a utopian socialist and feminist inspired by Olympe de Gouges, argued in 1848 for women's right to work and for full political participation by stressing their importance to fulfilling a mother's "duty." Deroin said, "It is especially the holy function of motherhood, said to be incompatible with the exercise of the rights of the citizen, that imposes on the woman the duty to watch over the future of her children and gives her the right to intervene, not only in all acts of civil life, but also in all acts of political life" (Scott, 1996, p. 70). Deroin was imprisoned in 1850 for her political activism.

The infant welfare movement of the early twentieth century, an international campaign for infant and child health led by medical and social work professionals, added new meanings to motherhood. For the first time it was not only a special kind of female nurture but a highly complex and technical calling. The campaign introduced new knowledge about nutrition, vitamins, for example, and the measure of food energy in calories; bacteriology; statistics on infant death rates; and new data on child development. Professional journals and popularly written pamphlets offered mothers practices, such as antisepsis in the home, that could improve the health and survival of their children. Anna Fischer-Dueckelmann's *The Housewife as Doctor,* first published in German in 1910, included detailed information on the home, health, pregnancy, and birth. Eight full pages were devoted to the chemical composition of dust. Infant welfare activists were successful in getting European legislators of this era to pass such measures as licensing childbirth personnel, tighter supervision of foster parents, and free or subsidized medical care for working-class mothers and infants.

The turn of the century's increased public attention to motherhood and infant care heartened those feminists who had long been concerned with the needs of working mothers but with little legislative success. French feminists openly played on population fears to improve the situations of mothers and of women in general. Maria Martin said in 1896, "If you want children, learn to honour the mothers" (Cova, 1991, p. 120). Feminists of varying positions combined suffrage agitation with proposals for government support for working mothers, mothers' child custody rights, and support from fathers of illegitimate children. Others developed this preoccupation with mothers' importance in a more radical direction. For instance, the Norwegian feminist Katti Anker Moeller argued in the first decades of the twentieth century that mothers should not be dependent on husbands but, single or married, should be paid by governments to raise their children independently. Furthermore, she thought without reproductive choice for women, motherhood would simply be "slavery."

Women should be able to choose or reject childbearing with available contraception and abortion. Moeller's international contacts with feminists of similar views, Helene Stoecker, head of the German *Mutterschutz* movement in particular, suggest the vitality of "maternalist" feminism in this important era in the social history of motherhood.

MID-TWENTIETH-CENTURY MOTHERHOOD: FROM RECIPROCITY TO MATERNAL LIABILITY

For the majority in western Europe, the sheer physical work of mothers—childbearing, child care, and probably also housework—began to decrease in the interwar period. Most obviously, child care declined along with birthrates in most of Europe, including Poland, Yugoslavia, Norway, Britain, France, Switzerland, Germany, and Austria. Only Ireland maintained its prewar birthrates through the 1920s. In the interwar years workers' birthrates began to approximate those of artisans and the professional and middle classes, which had begun, in general, to decline in the second half of the nineteenth century. Caring for two or three children was surely less taxing than caring for five or six. The expansion of social infrastructures also helped to ease the mother's burden, especially with municipally supplied clean and plentiful water, indoor plumbing, electric lighting, gas stoves, and in the 1930s antibiotics to treat children's illnesses, such as pneumonia, rheumatic fever, and bacterial infections.

The expansion of a mass consumer culture in the 1920s brought new kinds of proscriptions for mothers, however. New behaviorist ideas about the importance of "training" children, transmitted through advice literature and medical personnel, paralleled the movement to rationalize industrial production. The experts of the interwar period, including the Australian doctor Truby King and Americans L. Emmett Holt and John Watson, advocated efficient child rearing methods, such as rigid "habit training" and avoiding germ transmitters like kissing and cuddling. The U.S. home economics movement positioned mothers mainly as efficient homemakers and consumers of household cleaning supplies, packaged foods, and small appliances like toasters, radios, and irons. Scholars have explored some of the paradoxes of an American-born trend when electrification and income levels in Europe were considerably lower than those in most of the United States. Even in Berlin fewer than half of the homes had electricity in 1928. The campaign to modernize the home in Weimar Germany did little more than accentuate the domestic sexual division of labor, conflating motherhood and housekeeping.

Developments in psychology were crucial to twentieth-century motherhood. Particularly after World War II, psychoanalytic thought was popularized through many service professions, including social work, psychology, and psychiatry. In mid-twentieth-century Britain, as Denise Riley noted, psychology was a major "historical actor" in the postwar re-creation of gender and motherhood. Initially Sigmund Freud had remarkably little to say about mothers and certainly did not blame them for the problems of his analysands. However, in his writings of the 1930s, the decade of his death, Freud reassessed his thinking on gender. The girl's discovery of her "castration," her readiness to blame this on her mother, her wish for a baby as a substitute for the "lost" penis were the ingredients of a psychoanalytic position that postulated motherhood as a basic need of all women. D. W. Winnicott, on the other hand, put mothers and their mothering at the center of his writings beginning in the 1930s. He viewed infant development as a social as opposed to an instinctual process, but this "society" included only the mother and child. The emphasis, in all the schools derived from Freud, on invisible and unconscious forces irrevocably shaping children's personalities together with the Winnicott-inspired concentration on mother-infant interactions made a close social scrutiny of women's child care inevitable. Motherhood had become associated with continuous contact between mother and child, and other potential caretakers, such as fathers, siblings, grandparents, or neighbors, were viewed as secondary figures in a child's emotional world. Mothers' obligations to their children were expanding markedly, while those of the child were dropping away.

The twentieth century's many episodes of deadly violence on European soil, two world wars, at least three episodes of genocide, and many fascist or totalitarian regimes with their huge casualties, brought a distinct kind of suffering to mothers perhaps unprecedented in its severity. The Turks' forced marches of Armenians in 1915 killed hundreds of thousands of women and children. Famines generated by World War I and its aftermath killed many more among the Central Powers and in the Soviet Union. The World War II bombings of civilians and the Nazi genocide did not guarantee respect or protection to mothers. Indeed mothers with infants and small children were usually executed first in concentration camps. In the Bosnian Civil War of the early 1990s, Serbian soldiers systematically raped Muslim female civilians, intending to force them to bear their captors' offspring.

Enforced Motherhood. In Nazi Germany, as in Mussolini's Italy, a woman's highest duty was defined as the production of children for the Fatherland. *Family Portrait*, painting (1930s) by Wolfgang Willrich (1897–1948). BILDARCHIV PREUSSISCHER KULTURBESITZ, BERLIN

Being a woman at home in wartime meant both material hardships and perpetual fears for the safety of husband or son. The soldiers' death tolls of the two world wars, between 9 and 10 million in World War I and about 22 million in World War II, left millions of widows with young children and populations with long-lasting sex-ratio imbalances. World War I killed nearly a quarter of the Serbian male population aged fifteen to forty-nine. In 1950 women headed a third of German families, and the Soviet Union in 1959 had seven women to every four men in the age group thirty-five to fifty. In the two decades after World War II the revival of early marriage, high birthrates, and intense female domesticity constituted in part an effort to reestablish some form of normality.

Twentieth-century states sometimes enforced "normal" motherhood with a vengeance. Benito Mussolini, ruling over an overpopulated country whose emigration route to the United States had just been cut off, nonetheless promoted "births, many births" (De Grazia, 1992, p. 41) as a way to restore the con-

ventional gender relations that had been shattered in the aftermath of World War I. Mussolini defined all women in terms of motherhood, implementing new penalties for abortion, the repression of birth control, the exclusion of women from many professions, and discrimination against girls in secondary and higher education.

Similarly motherhood figured prominently in the reconstitution of West Germany after 1945. With so many soldiers dead or still prisoners of war, the new state was a "country of women." High proportions of women lived alone or with their children, and the illegitimacy rate was over 16 percent in 1946. Even in 1950 the country counted 130 women to every 100 men aged 25 to 40. The few women who were feminists before 1933 and survived the Nazi years hoped that Germany's new constitutional order would include more egalitarian family law and welfare measures to benefit married and single mothers. But West Germany was constructed as a patriarchal state, a link in cold war Europe's anticommunist chain. The conventional two-parent family with a Hausfrau mother became the symbol of the "free" Germany.

Post World War II state welfare programs expanded in much of Europe. Though based on a variety of views of women's capacities, these programs included family allowances, maternity leaves, medical care, and in some countries state-run child care and after-school centers for all children of working or nonworking mothers. Sweden provided a salary and housing allowance to women whose partners did not offer child support. Although postwar government policy in France continued to be based on efforts to encourage population, the socialists and communists who helped formulate the French policies in 1945 also strongly supported women's and mothers' rights to work and to equality in the workplace.

THE RECONFIGURATION OF MOTHERHOOD: THE 1970s, 1980s, AND 1990s

By the last decades of the twentieth century, motherhood had been transformed yet again. A majority of mothers, even those with young children, had broken with Winnicott's dicta and were now in the labor force. Taboos on births outside of marriage had waned, and with highly reliable birth control methods and legal abortion in the great majority of European countries, the one-child family became the new norm in many regions.

One departure from the European past was the proportion of mothers not married to their children's fathers, though in many cases the parents were co-habiting. In western Europe as a whole and world-wide, about a third of households were headed by women. The proportion of births to single women in Britain, for example, shot up dramatically in the 1980s, reaching about one-third of all births in the early 1990s, the highest in its history to that date. In Denmark and Norway the proportions approached 50 percent in the mid 1990s.

The completed fertility rates of European women in the late twentieth century were at a historical low. In the late 1990s the Italian rate was under 1.2 children per woman. An Italian sociologist commented, "The ethic of sacrifice for a family" has dissipated (Spector, 1998, p. 6). The highest European Union rates were those of Ireland and Norway at slightly under two children. Spain and Italy had the lowest. European Muslim countries had higher fertility rates, 2.5 in Albania and 2.7 in Azerbaijan, than their Christian neighbors, but these were considerably lower than in the Muslim parts of Africa. European conditions, attitudes, freedoms, and services quickly transformed the birthrates of North African immigrants to France, which declined steeply during the 1980s, and of West Indian, Indian, and Chinese immigrants to Britain.

Mothers' work outside the home lost much of its stigma in the late twentieth century. Indeed among the best-educated mothers, over 90 percent of those with postgraduate degrees had jobs in virtually every country in the European Union according to 1995 figures. Although mothers' job holding varied from country to country, rates were high, partly reflecting the fact that most of the jobs generated in late twentieth-century decades were "female" ones. Among the women between twenty and fifty-nine years old with at least one child under the age of eleven, proportions in the labor force ranged from a high of 89 percent in Denmark to a low of 67 percent in the western states of Germany in 1992. Labor force rates were about as high among mothers of children under seven years of age.

Not surprisingly, motherhood as a doctrine faced lively challenges in this period, beginning in the 1970s with the objections of Ann Oakley, Adrienne Rich, Jessie Bernard, and Christine Delphy. Motherhood's overwhelming demands were among the elements critiqued. As Rich wrote in *Of Woman Born* (1976), "The institution of motherhood finds all mothers more or less guilty of having failed their children." At about the same time the wages for housework movement, with Italian roots, attacked the association of mother with socially dependent homemaker. Activists argued that housework and

child care, productive activities beneficial to society as a whole, ought to be waged by governments or husbands, a position that had not been enunciated since the 1900s. In her 1947 *Housewife*, a sociological study of mothers' attitudes, Oakley continued this line of argument: that love of children was by no means equivalent to enjoying housework. The two needed to be separated. In the 1970s and 1980s, the growing acceptance of fathers as capable of child care, supported by parental leave in several states, further shifted what it meant to be a mother. In the 1990s the acceleration of genetic research also challenged the older concept of motherhood. Researchers in many scientific disciplines found that personality traits of all kinds have genetic bases and may have little to do with the quality of a person's mothering. Finally, the reproductive technologies available to at least some European women, separating conception, pregnancy, and birth, shook the biological foundations of motherhood.

Twentieth-century feminists attempted to move motherhood from the realm of the private and culturally invisible into the center of culture and politics. Feminist environmentalists defined the Earth as a mother and viewed women as more respectful of nature because of their experiences of pregnancy and childbirth. Other feminist activists, with a revived sense of mothers' social importance, attacked welfare-state bureaucracies for failing to provide housing and quality medical services for mothers and children. They demanded public support for those, mainly women, caring for dependents of all needs.

It would be wrong, of course, to see the patterns of the late twentieth century as the end of motherhood discourses or of female mothering. In general child care continued to be socially coded as female. In two-parent, two-earner families, including those in Denmark and Sweden, where fathers were most involved with their families, the preponderance of both child care and housework is done by women. Single parents are overwhelmingly women. Raising children alone, while relatively free of the disgrace of "bastardy," often means poverty. Welfare benefits declined in the European Union during the 1980s and had never, in most countries, offered parity for those not fully in the workforce. As a result, from about a fifth to a quarter of female-headed households in Europe were poor. Proportions were higher in Ireland and lower in Sweden. Poverty rates for such households appeared somewhat larger for some groups of immigrants and ethnic minorities.

Elisabeth Badinter, in her social history of motherhood, *Mother Love: Myth and Reality* (1981), implied that the regime most "natural" to women was the era of casual care and benign neglect destroyed by

Rousseau's writings on motherhood and childhood in the 1760s. It is tempting to suggest that the contemporary European regime comes closer to meeting women's fundamental needs as mothers. After all, it includes the ability to limit conceptions, end pregnancies, and maintain small families and offers opportunities for economic independence and job holding while raising children. History, however, is not the place to look for hypothesized natural human tendencies. Instead history offers a range of material possibilities that enables us to interpret our own lives with clarity and wisdom.

See also **The Population of Europe: Early Modern Demographic Patterns; The Population of Europe: The Demographic Transition and After** *(volume 2);* **Women and Femininity; Gender and Education; Childbirth, Midwives, Wetnursing** *(in this volume); and other articles in this section.*

BIBLIOGRAPHY

Adams, Christine. "Constructing Mothers and Families: The Bordeaux Society of Maternal Charity, 1805–1860." *French Historical Studies* 22, no. 1 (Winter 1999): 65–86.

Allen, Ann Taylor. *Feminism and Motherhood in Germany, 1800–1914.* New Brunswick, N.J., 1991.

Atkinson, Clarissa W. *The Oldest Vocation: Christian Motherhood in the Middle Ages.* Ithaca, N.Y., 1991.

Badinter, Elisabeth. *Mother Love: Myth and Reality.* Translated by Roger DeGaris. New York, 1981.

Caine, Barbara. *Destined To Be Wives: The Sisters of Beatrice Webb.* Oxford, 1986.

Central Intelligence Agency. *The World Factbook 1999.* Washington, D.C., 2000.

Cole, Joshua H. "'There Are Only Good Mothers': The Ideological Work of Women's Fertility in France before World War I." *French Historical Studies* 19 (Spring 1996): 639–672.

Cova, Anne. "French Feminism and Maternity: Theories and Policies, 1890–1945." In *Maternity and Gender Policies: Women and the Rise of the European Welfare States, 1880s–1980s.* Edited by Gisela Bock and Pat Thane. London, 1991.

De Grazia, Victoria. *How Fascism Ruled Women: Italy, 1922–1945.* Berkeley, Calif., 1992.

Duncan, Carol. "Happy Mothers and Other New Ideas in French Art." *Art Bulletin* 55, no. 4 (December 1973): 570–583.

Fildes, Valerie A. *Breasts, Bottles, and Babies: A History of Infant Feeding.* Edinburgh, 1986.

Fildes, Valerie. *Wet Nursing: A History from Antiquity to the Present.* Oxford, 1988.

Frykman, Jonas, and Orvar Löfgren. *Culture Builders: A Historical Anthropology of Middle-Class Life.* Translated by Alan Crozier. New Brunswick, N.J., 1987.

Fuchs, Rachel Ginnis. *Abandoned Children: Foundlings and Child Welfare in Nineteenth-Century France.* Albany, N.Y., 1984.

Fuchs, Rachel G. *Poor and Pregnant in Paris: Strategies for Survival in the Nineteenth Century.* New Brunswick, N.J., 1992.

Gillis, John R. *A World of Their Own Making: Myth, Ritual, and the Quest for Family Values.* New York, 1996.

Gillis, John R., Louise A. Tilly, and David Levine, eds. *The European Experience of Declining Fertility, 1850–1970: The Quiet Revolution*. Cambridge, Mass., 1992.

Greenfield, Susan C., and Carol Barash, eds. *Inventing Maternity: Politics, Science, and Literature, 1650–1865*. Lexington, Ky., 1999.

Gutton, Jean-Pierre. *La sociabilité villageoise dans l'ancienne France*. Paris, 1979.

Hufton, Olwen H. *The Poor of Eighteenth-Century France 1750–1789*. Oxford, 1974.

Jacobus, Mary L. "Incorruptible Milk: Breast-Feeding and the French Revolution." In *Rebel Daughters: Women and the French Revolution*. Edited by Sara E. Melzer and Leslie W. Rabine. New York, 1992. Pages 54–75.

Jenson, Jane. "Both Friend and Foe: Women and State Welfare." In *Becoming Visible: Women in European History*. 2d ed. Edited by Renate Bridenthal, Claudia Koonz, and Susan Stuard. Boston, 1987. Pages 535–556.

Kaplan, Marion A. *Between Dignity and Despair: Jewish Life in Nazi Germany*. New York, 1998.

Kent, Susan Kingsley. *Gender and Power in Britain, 1640–1990*. London, 1999.

Kiernan, Kathleen, Hilary Land, and Jane Lewis. *Lone Motherhood in Twentieth-Century Britain*. Oxford, 1998.

Kitzinger, Sheila. *Women as Mothers*. New York, 1980.

Klapisch-Zuber, Christiane. *La maison et le nom: Stratégies et rituels dans l'Italie de la Renaissance*. Paris, 1990.

Klaits, Joseph. *Servants of Satan: The Age of the Witch Hunts*. Bloomington, Ind., 1985.

Laqueur, Thomas. *Making Sex: Body and Gender from the Greeks to Freud*. Cambridge, Mass., 1990.

Lastinger, Valerie. "Re-Defining Motherhood: Breast-Feeding and the French Enlightenment." *Women's Studies* 25 (1996): 603–618.

Lewis, Judith Schneid. *In the Family Way: Childbearing in the British Aristocracy, 1760-1860*. New Brunswick, N.J., 1986.

Lundell, Torborg. *Fairy Tale Mothers*. New York, 1990.

Maynes, Mary J. *Taking the Hard Road: Life Course in French and German Workers' Autobiographies in the Era of Industrialization*. Chapel Hill, N.C., 1995.

Moeller, Robert G. *Protecting Motherhood: Women and the Family in the Politics of Postwar West Germany*. Berkeley, Calif., 1993.

Moscucci, Ornella. *The Science of Woman: Gynaecology and Gender in England, 1800–1929*. Cambridge, U.K., 1990.

Mulder-Bakker, Anneke B., ed. *Sanctity and Motherhood: Essays on Holy Mothers in the Middle Ages*. New York, 1995.

Nolan, Mary. *Visions of Modernity: American Business and the Modernization of Germany*. New York, 1994.

Oakley, Ann. *Becoming a Mother*. New York, 1980.

Oakley, Ann. *Woman's Work*. New York, 1975. Originally published in 1974 as *Housewife*.

Ozment, Steven. *When Fathers Ruled: Family Life in Reformation Europe*. Cambridge, Mass., 1983.

Peretz, Elizabeth. "The Costs of Modern Motherhood to Low Income Families in Interwar Britain." In *Women and Children First: International Maternal and*

Infant Welfare, 1870–1945. Edited by Valerie Fildes, Lara Marks, and Hilary Marland. London, 1992. Pages 257–280.

Perkin, Joan. *Women and Marriage in Nineteenth-Century England.* Chicago, 1989.

Perry, Ruth. "Colonizing the Breast: Sexuality and Maternity in Eighteenth-Century England." *Journal of the History of Sexuality* 2, no. 2 (October 1991): 204–234.

Parekh, Bhikhu. "South Asians in Britain." *History Today* 47, no. 9 (September 1997): 65–68.

Ransel, David L. "Infant-Care Cultures in the Russian Empire." In *Russia's Women: Accommodation, Resistance, Transformation.* Edited by Barbara Evans Clements, Barbara Alpern Angel, and Christine D. Worobec. Berkeley, Calif., 1991 Pages 113–132.

Re, Lucia. "Fascist Theories of 'Woman' and the Construction of Gender." In *Mothers of Invention: Women, Italian Fascism, and Culture.* Edited by Robin Pickering-Iazzi. Minneapolis, Minn., 1995. Pages 76–99.

Rich, Adrienne. *Of Woman Born: Motherhood as Experience and Institution.* New York, 1976.

Riley, Denise. *War in the Nursery: Theories of the Child and Mother.* London, 1983.

Ruggiero, Guido. *Binding Passions: Tales of Magic, Marriage, and Power at the End of the Renaissance.* New York, 1993.

Roper, Lyndal. *The Holy Household: Women and Morals, in Reformation Augsburg.* Oxford, 1989.

Roper, Lyndal. "Witchcraft and Fantasy in Early Modern Germany." *History Workshop Journal* 32 (Autumn 1991): 19–43.

Rose, Nikolas. "The Pleasures of Motherhood." *m/f* 7 (1982): 82–86.

Ross, Ellen. *Love and Toil: Motherhood in Outcast London, 1870–1918.* New York, 1993.

Schama, Simon. *The Embarrassment of Riches: An Interpretation of Dutch Culture in the Golden Age.* New York, 1987.

Scott, Joan Wallach. *Only Paradoxes to Offer: French Feminists and the Rights of Man.* Cambridge, Mass., 1996.

Sen, Amartya. *Poverty and Famines: An Essay on Entitlement and Deprivation.* Oxford, 1981.

Smith, Bonnie G. *Ladies of the Leisure Class.* Princeton, N.J., 1981.

Smith, Bonnie G. *Changing Lives: Women in European History since 1700.* Lexington, Mass., 1989.

Southgate, Walter. *That's the Way It Was: A Working Class Autobiography 1890–1950.* Oxted, U.K., 1982.

Specter, Michael. "The Baby Bust: A Special Report. Population Implosion Worries a Graying Europe." *New York Times,* 10 July 1998. New York Times qpass Archives on line.

Thurer, Shari L. *The Myths of Motherhood: How Culture Reinvents the Good Mother.* New York, 1994.

Tilly, Louise. "Food Entitlement, Family, and Conflict." *Journal of Interdisciplinary History* 14 (Autumn 1983): 333–349.

"Trend Watch: One-Child Families Are Not New." *Market—Europe* 10, no. 10 (October 1999): 1–2.

Trumbach, Randolph. *The Rise of the Egalitarian Family: Aristocratic Kinship and Domestic Relations in Eighteenth-Century England.* New York, 1978.

Watson, Sophie, and Lesley Doyal, eds. *Engendering Social Policy.* Philadelphia, 1999.

"Women in the European Union." Christina Institute, University of Helsinki, www.helsinki.fi/science/xantippa/wee.

CHILD REARING AND CHILDHOOD

Colin Heywood

Can there be a history of childhood? Until the late twentieth century most people apparently thought not. The temptation was always to think of childhood as a natural and universal phenomenon. The members of any society tend to consider their own particular arrangements for childhood as rooted in nature, having been steeped in them all their lives. At the same time it is easy to assume that the overriding influence on childhood will always be the biological immaturity of children. It will therefore be broadly similar in all societies and of limited interest to scholars. Some have even suggested that a male-dominated academic profession for decades contemptuously dismissed child rearing as beneath its dignity, a humdrum matter left to wives and mothers. Historians face the additional problem of assembling evidence on a section of society little seen and almost never heard in the surviving documentation. Not surprisingly, as late as the 1950s the history of childhood could be described as almost virgin territory. An extensive literature addresses child welfare, outlining the efforts of philanthropists, charities, and above all the state in this sphere. Such an approach, however, has done little to show how people conceptualized childhood as a distinct stage of life and even less to illuminate the experiences of children themselves.

Two developments in historiography have brought the subjects of childhood and children more firmly into focus. First, historians and social scientists in general grasped the important cultural dimensions of childhood. Far from a natural and universal model of childhood, each society, each class, perhaps even each family constructs its own image of the child. Some, for example, consider children naturally depraved from birth, and others see them as naturally innocent. The physical immaturity of children is undeniable, of course, but it is no longer considered a determining influence. As the sociologists Allison James and Alan Prout wrote, "The immaturity of children is a biological fact of life but the ways in which this immaturity is understood and made meaningful is a fact of culture" (James and Prout, 1990, p. 7).

Second, a number of researchers set out to recover the experience of growing up in various social and geographical settings in the past. In so doing they reacted against the older habit of depicting young people as putty in the hands of adults, with all the emphasis on development and socialization. Instead they looked for the ways in which children have been active in carving out their own place in the world, noting their interactions with parents and other forms of authority. Locating and interpreting sources in this area poses problems. It is not hard to find examples of manuals giving advice to parents on how to raise their offspring, but whether anyone took any notice of them is another matter. Members of the educated elite may have left traces of their feelings for their children in diaries and autobiographies, but how the mass of peasants and laborers felt must remain largely a matter of conjecture. Nonetheless, the basis exists for understanding social constructions of childhood in the past and for what might be called a social history of children.

CHANGING CONCEPTIONS OF CHILDHOOD

Philippe Ariès and the "discovery" of childhood. In 1960, with his *Centuries of Childhood,* Philippe Ariès launched the history of childhood with a bang. Ariès made the striking assertion that "in medieval society the idea of childhood did not exist." By this he did not mean that people had no affection for children, but rather that they lacked "an awareness of the particular nature of childhood, that particular nature which distinguishes the child from the adult, even the young adult" (Ariès, 1996, p. 125). The result was that medieval civilization failed to perceive a transitionary period between infancy and adulthood. Around the age of five or seven, as soon as they could survive without the constant attention of their mothers, the young were launched into the world of adults. They joined in the games and pastimes going on around them and learned their trades working beside fully trained practitioners. Children were simply thought of as miniature adults.

The "discovery" of childhood had to await the fifteenth, sixteenth, and seventeenth centuries. Ariès discerned two phases in this process. To begin with, in the fifteenth and sixteenth centuries women looking after children took the initiative by treating them as a source of amusement and relaxation, delighting in their "sweetness, simplicity and drollery" (Ariès, 1996, p. 126). Ariès conceded that "mothers, nannies and cradle-rockers" (p. 125) must have always found the little antics of children touching, but he suggested that they had hesitated to express their feelings. The second, and for Ariès more significant stage, began in the seventeenth century. At this point reformers replaced the "coddling" of children with "psychological interest and moral solicitude" (p. 128). A small group of lawyers, priests, and moralists came to recognize the innocence and weakness of childhood. Gradually, starting with the middle classes, these reformers imposed the notion that children needed special treatment, "a sort of quarantine" (p. 396) before they were ready to join the world of adults. What Ariès envisaged, therefore, was a huge shift in the cultural sphere, attributable to the growing influence of Christianity and a new respect for education.

Moving on from Ariès. Like many other pioneers, Ariès found his work at once praised for its originality and sniped at on all sides by the next generation of researchers. Few historians after Ariès accepted that there was a complete absence of any consciousness of childhood in medieval civilization. Certainly medieval authors did have a tendency to gloss over childhood and adolescence. Even in the early modern period, children were still largely absent from literary works, as both the French and the English cases attest. Insofar as authors did focus on the young, it was often the child prodigy, the *puer senex,* a child who already thought like an old man, who interested them. For example, Thomas Williams Malkin, born in 1795, started his career at age three, became an expert linguist at four, was a profound philosopher at five, read the fathers of the church at six, and died of old age at seven. Nonetheless, medievalists were quick to demonstrate at least some recognition of the "particular nature" of childhood during their period by examining law codes, for example, or medical treatises. They also drew attention to the extensive treatment of the notion of the ages of man inherited from classical antiquity. During the late medieval and early modern periods, such ideas and the images associated with them, including the swaddled baby or the frolicsome child, were widely disseminated in the vernacular.

However, these schemes were largely academic exercises that owed more to the ingenuity of philosophers in relating the human life cycle to the natural world than to any direct observations of children and others. Besides the seven ages familiar from Jaques's speech in Shakespeare's *As You Like It,* popular interpretations embraced three, four, and six ages. It all depended on the author's intention to draw parallels between the stages of life and, for example, the four humors or the seven planets.

The sweeping changes during the early modern period proposed, but not very convincingly documented, by Ariès also made the majority of historians uncomfortable. For a while some accepted the notion of a discovery of the particular nature of childhood but claimed to locate it in another period or a more specific one. Pierre Riché, for example, went back to the sixth century among teachers of the young oblates in the monasteries. John Sommerville contended that "sustained interest in children in England began with the Puritans" of the sixteenth and seventeenth centuries, for they were "the first to puzzle over their nature and their place in society" (Sommerville, 1992, p. 3). According to many historians, in the eighteenth century the French philosophe Jean-Jacques Rousseau was perhaps the first thinker to consider childhood worth studying in its own right.

Scholars began to diverge even further from the Ariès approach by doubting the appropriateness of thinking in terms of a definitive discovery of childhood at some point in the past. Critics of Ariès, notably Adrian Wilson, accused him of extreme "present centeredness" (Wilson, 1980, p. 147). That is to say, Ariès looked for evidence of twentieth-century French ideas of childhood in medieval Europe, failed to find it, and then leaped to the conclusion that the period had no awareness of this stage of life at all. It is conceivable that the Middle Ages had a consciousness of childhood so different from the familiar modern one that it is unrecognizable. The suggestion of some fixed and stable notion of childhood "waiting in the wings of history for just recognition" (Jordanova, 1989, p. 10) then becomes difficult to sustain. Instead it may be more illuminating to seek various cultural constructions of childhood in the past. These invariably competed with each other at any particular period and did not necessarily evolve in one direction. Indeed many historians have noted the ambivalence of adult attitudes to childhood. There is in fact a whole repertoire of themes in the construction of childhood worthy of exploration.

Nature versus nurture. One reason why medieval writers paid scant attention to children was that they

Children's Games. Painting (1560) by Pieter Brueghel the Elder (1530–1569). Kunsthistorisches Museum, Vienna/Erich Lessing/Art Resource, NY

did not share the modern view of the early years of life as critical for character formation. They considered the nature a child is born with the most important influence, the raw material without which the finest nurturing would be wasted. Hence Middle High German texts assume that a base character like Judas, brought up to be a noble, was bound to turn out badly. Conversely, a young man responds almost instantly to instruction in his true calling, as Parzival became an accomplished knight relatively late in life after a few words of instruction from the hermit Gurnemanz.

This particular balance in favor of nature over nurture gradually shifted in the opposite direction from the Renaissance onward. The Dutch humanist Desiderius Erasmus (1466–1536) hinted at the common notion that a child's mind was a blank sheet on which teachers could write whatever they considered suitable. He noted the "quality of rawness and freshness" in a child's mind, which had to be molded to produce a fully human soul rather than a "monstrous bestiality." The English philosopher John Locke gave

the image of the child as a tabula rasa a further boost when he published *Some Thoughts Concerning Education* (1693). In the final paragraph he admitted that he had considered the gentleman's son for whom it had been written "only as white Paper, or Wax, to be molded and fashioned as one pleases" (Locke, 1989, p. 265). The middle and upper classes in particular began to pay more attention to this "molding" of the young and to the detailed advice on child rearing and education provided by moralists. The idea that "the hand that rocks the cradle rules the world" became received wisdom. Locke summed up the increasingly environmentalist perspective by asserting, "Of all the Men we meet with, Nine Parts of Ten are what they are, Good or Evil, useful or not, by their Education" (p. 83). At the same time he noted that tutors needed to pay close attention to the "various Tempers, different Inclinations and particular Defaults" found in children (p. 265).

Hereditary influences made something of a comeback in certain scientific circles during the late nineteenth and early twentieth centuries. The Italian

177

Cesare Lombroso claimed that some people were born criminals. Fortunately, an "anthropological examination" would expose these criminal types, explaining their "scholastic and disciplinary shortcomings" so they could be segregated from their better-endowed companions. Meanwhile a number of educational psychologists in England and Germany asserted the hereditary nature of intelligence. In 1906 Karl Pearson stood Locke on his head by writing, "the influence of environment is nowhere more than one-fifth of heredity, and quite possibly not one-tenth of it." Three years later his colleague Cyril Burt concluded that intelligence is innate after finding that boys from a small sample of upper-class families in Oxford performed better at his tests than those with a lower-middle-class background. He spent the rest of his career campaigning for selectivity in education on the grounds that most of the population could never develop much in the way of intelligence. What mattered, in his view, was to identify and nurture that small elite "endowed by nature with outstanding gifts of ability and character."

Depravity versus innocence. The origin of the view that children are naturally depraved goes back to St. Augustine, who asserted in the fourth century that the taint of sin was passed down from generation to generation by the act of creation. His firm line that infants are born in sin generally prevailed over the opposing one of infant innocence until the twelfth century. It was also taken up again with a vengeance from the sixteenth century onward by Protestant reformers and their Catholic counterparts, both heavily influenced by Augustinian theology. A German sermon dating from the 1520s contended that infant hearts craved after "adultery, fornication, impure desires, lewdness, idol worship, belief in magic, hostility, quarrelling, passion, anger, strife, dissension, factiousness, hatred, murder, drunkenness, gluttony" and more. The English Presbyterian Daniel Williams was equally forthright in the eighteenth century, telling his juvenile readers, "Thou by nature art brutish and devilish." Yet for all their insistence that children were born with evil in their hearts, Puritans were at least willing to envisage them as vessels "ready to receive good or evil drop by drop," or as young twigs ready to be bent the right or the wrong way. Catholics of this same era continued the Augustinian tradition with no less vehemence. As Pierre de Bérulle, leader of the Oratorians in France, magnificently put it during the 1620s, "Childhood is the vilest and most abject condition of human nature, after that of death." At the same time they were prepared to argue that the very weakness of children made them model Christians insofar as they were in no position to resist the Divine Will.

Catholic and Protestant writers also liked to compare children to wild, undomesticated animals. Both Erasmus and Martin Luther, for example, characterized bad behavior as animal-like. Small children, according to the historian David Hunt, were seen as intermediate beings, not really animals but not really humans either. This tradition died hard. The English Evangelical movement of the late eighteenth and nineteenth centuries was perhaps most explicit in reasserting the idea that children are by nature evil. Its last gasp around 1900 took the form of recapitulation theory, whereby each child growing up follows the stages of civilization experienced by human beings. Childhood was of course akin to savagery.

The contrasting belief in the original innocence of children was also deeply rooted in the Christian tradition. As early as the fifth century Pope Leo the Great preached, "Christ loved childhood, mistress of humility, rule of innocence, model of sweetness." During the early modern era notions of infant depravity continued to hold sway, though most authors softened the original Augustinian position. A full blast against it came with the eighteenth-century Enlightenment, and the most forceful opponent was Rousseau. He made his position perfectly clear in *Emile* (1762), which begins with the famous line, "Everything is good as it leaves the hands of the Author of things, everything degenerates in the hands of man" (Rousseau, 1979, p. 37). As innocents, children could be left to respond to nature, then they would do nothing but good. 'Respect childhood," he counseled, and "leave nature to act for a long time before you get involved with acting in its place" (p. 107). The romantic conception of childhood, which first appeared during the late eighteenth and early nineteenth centuries, continued in this vein. It depicted children as "creatures of deeper wisdom, finer aesthetic sensibility, and a more profound awareness of enduring moral truths" (Grylls, 1978, p. 35). Childhood had become a lost realm that was nonetheless fundamental to the creation of the adult self. For the poet William Wordsworth, in his "Ode: Intimations of Immortality" (1807), "Heaven lies about us in our infancy!" For the German romantic Jean Paul Richter, in *Levana* (1807), children were "pure beings" sent to earth from the unknown world above.

It was one thing to proclaim the angelic nature of childhood in a poem but quite another to create plausible characters in a novel or to deal with hardened street urchins. Charles Dickens (1812–1870) may occasionally have lapsed into sentimentality when describing children, such as Little Nell (from *The Old Curiosity Shop*) or David Copperfield. More characteristically, as Peter Coveney observed, in his strongest depictions of childhood Dickens achieved a powerful mingling of pathos and idealization with the squalid (Coveney, 1967, p. 159). By the twentieth century the association of childhood with innocence was firmly embedded in Western culture, though the excesses of Victorian sentimentalization of childhood did not survive the appearance of Freud's theories on the human personality.

Helplessness versus dependence. All infants are born helpless, but when they should start becoming independent is an open question. As late as the nineteenth century the majority of children in Europe were encouraged to begin supporting themselves at an early stage. The age of seven was an informal turning point when the offspring of peasants and craftspeople were generally expected to start helping their parents with little tasks around the home, the farm, or the workshop. By their early teens they were likely to be working beside adults or were established in apprenticeships. They might have left home by then to become servants or apprentices. This is not to say that they were treated as miniature adults—they certainly were not required to do the same work as older people—but they were expected to grow up fast. The young may also have discussed sexuality quite openly with adults during the medieval and early modern periods. The sociologist Norbert Elias argued that boys lived from an early age in the same social sphere as adults, and the latter did not feel it necessary to restrain themselves "in action or in words" as in modern times. He cited *Colloquies,* a schoolbook written by Erasmus in 1519, which includes sections on a young man wooing a girl, a woman complaining about the bad behavior of her husband, and a conversation between a young man and a prostitute. (Elias neglected to mention that the book was condemned by the theologians of the Sorbonne and eventually put on the Catholic Church's Index of Forbidden Books.) How much of a sex life young people had in the past is a matter of controversy among historians. Low rates of illegitimacy during the seventeenth and eighteenth centuries may provide evidence of sexual austerity outside marriage. Alternatively, Jean-Louis Flandrin argued from French evidence that youthful libido found various outlets short of full intercourse, especially through homosexuality, masturbation, and intimate courting customs.

Since the sixteenth and seventeenth centuries, the middle-class desire has been to isolate children and, later, adolescents from the world of adults. Young people have been increasingly infantilized by efforts to keep them out of the workplace, to repress their sexuality, and to prolong their formal education in schools and colleges. Ideally such feeble creatures

would be removed from all temptation, constantly supervised, and subjected to an endless round of rigorous rules and exercises. Hence learning languages would feature prominently. To put it another way, the child would be kept apart and preserved by living in Latin among the idealized figures of antiquity. Yet it was one thing for Rousseau to recommend that the young remain continent until their twenties and quite another to prevent them from masturbating or experimenting with the opposite sex. Efforts to prevent children from earning a wage also clashed with peasant and working-class notions of early independence. These tensions came to a head in many countries during the nineteenth and early twentieth centuries, as governments attempted to impose the new model through factory legislation and compulsory schooling. The notion of a long childhood finally prevailed, perhaps at the cost of underestimating the capacities of children.

Age versus sex. How did people in the past combine their perception of age, a child as opposed to an adult, with that of sex, a male as opposed to a female? During the Middle Ages, when they used the word "child" in written sources, they usually appeared to have a boy in mind. In the Occitan literature of the twelfth and thirteenth centuries, for example, girls were virtually invisible. For centuries the prevailing mode in literary sources provided advice on the rearing of young males from the elite. Locke's *Some Thoughts Concerning Education* was a particularly illustrious example. Rousseau's *Emile* reflected something of a turning point in the eighteenth century by introducing Sophie beside Emile, though the subordinate role envisaged for her hardly endeared Rousseau to feminists or to modern sensibilities. The romantic movement brought the child rather than the boy to the forefront. Indeed the tendency was for that stock character in Victorian fiction, the child redeemer who reconciles estranged members of families or helps adults see the error of their ways, to be a girl. One thinks of Sissy Jupe, Little Nell, or Florence Dombey in the work of Dickens. Advice on the dress, diet, and exercise appropriate for children and infants in Victorian England minimized sex differences. Parents were probably relaxed about this, according to Deborah Gorham, because they were certain about innate differences between males and females. Nonetheless, they hoped that, as the two sexes played together, the supposed weakness of the girl would be strengthened and the roughness of the boy softened.

Conclusion. It appears from the available sources that a generalized interest in childhood was slow to emerge in Europe. This might be linked to underlying socioeconomic conditions. In an agrarian economy, predominant in much of Europe until the nineteenth century, children were inserted gradually into the world of adults from an early age. Childhood and adolescence meshed progressively and almost imperceptibly into adulthood. This does not necessarily mean swallowing the Ariès thesis whole and asserting that people in early modern Europe were unaware of different stages of development among the young. For example, the responsibilities with which young people were entrusted at the workplace were graded until the youngsters reached full maturity as workers in their late teens. They played their own games, apart from those of adults, and legal codes recognized their need for protection under certain circumstances.

Nonetheless, under these conditions childhood and adolescence did appear less structured and special. Most young people followed in the footsteps of their parents, so one generation shaded unobtrusively into the next. The strict age grading introduced by the modern school system was a late-nineteenth-century development. Also a raft of cultural influences from antiquity and Christianity lent themselves to a negative view of childhood. These were challenged under the humanist banner during the Renaissance, allowing the more sympathetic perspective on childhood, which was also part of the Christian tradition, to come to the fore. Changing material conditions also fostered an interest in childhood, notably with the rise of capitalism between the fifteenth and eighteenth centuries. Various historians have noted how an increasingly commercialized and urbanized society required more investment in the young. The urban labor market was more diverse than that of the villages, the element of choice and experimentation became more critical during the early years, and education was established as a channel to success in business and above all the professions. The welfare of children became a matter of intense interest, which immensely complicated the whole business of child rearing.

CHILD REARING PRACTICES

Bad parents, good parents. Parents have received a bad press in much of the historical literature on child rearing. In *The History of Childhood,* Lloyd deMause went further than most in a ringing denunciation: "The history of childhood is a nightmare from which we have only recently begun to awaken. The further back in history one goes, the lower the level of child care, and the more likely children are to be killed, abandoned, beaten, terrorized and sexually abused" (DeMause, 1974, p. 1). To his critics, deMause had

in effect written little more than a history of child abuse. He was, however, in good company during the 1970s. Lawrence Stone asserted that, during the sixteenth and seventeenth centuries, children in England were "neglected, brutally treated, and even killed" (Stone, 1977, p. 99). Edward Shorter contrasted the indifference of mothers to the development and happiness of infants in traditional society with the "good mothering" of the modern period. Later studies of parent-child relationships generally took a more tolerant line on past practices. Steven Ozment deflated earlier claims, observing, "surely the hubris of an age reaches a certain peak when it accuses another age of being incapable of loving its children properly" (Ozment, 1983, p. 162).

Historians have attempted to distinguish more carefully between practices considered in the best interests of the children at the time, even though they might appear wrongheaded in hindsight, such as swaddling, and others, such as infanticide, condemned outright in the past as in the present. The general drift of the revisionist argument has been that continuities in parenting are more in evidence than any dramatic turning points. Examples of cruel and abusive parents can be found in any age, they have suggested, but the vast majority probably felt affection for their offspring and did the best they could for them. Linda Pollock, for instance, denied that the young were neglected or systematically ill treated in the past because of an alleged inability to appreciate the needs of the young. Her bold counterassertion, based on British and American material, was that there were "very few changes in parental care and child life from the 16th to the 19th century in the home" (Pollock, 1983, p. 268). The problem of finding evidence to settle what appears to be two plausible but contradictory cases has presented an interesting agenda for debate.

Caring for infants: food, clothing, and hygiene. A compelling case can be made to show that the alleged indifference to childhood in the medieval and early modern periods resulted in a callous approach to child rearing. Infants under two years of age in particular were thought to suffer appalling neglect because parents considered it unwise to invest emotional or material resources in "poor sighing animals" who were all too likely to die young. Hence they often were denied their mother's milk and instead were sent to mercenary wetnurses. Imprisoned for hours in their swaddling bands and tight little cribs, they were left to stew in their own excrement and other filth. At the very worst, they were killed or abandoned to a charitable institution. Only with the more enlightened views on childhood of the eighteenth century did par-

Changing Diapers. Engraving from *Emblemata of Zinne-werck* by De Brune (Amsterdam, 1624). DEPARTMENT OF PRINTING AND GRAPHIC ARTS, THE HOUGHTON LIBRARY, HARVARD COLLEGE LIBRARY

ents begin to adopt more "modern" approaches to child care. Certainly moralists and physicians gave ample testimony on parents' lack of interest in their youngest children. Yet some historians possibly have sided a little too hastily with Enlightenment reformers in denigrating parents influenced by the traditional popular culture.

On the matter of feeding infants, at first sight nothing would appear more heartless than to snatch a newborn babe from his or her mother. Indeed a tradition among physicians and theologians favoring maternal breastfeeding was established well before the famous interventions of Rousseau and his contemporaries during the eighteenth century. The seventeenth-century Dutch writer Jacob Cats, for example, entreated young mothers to "give the noble suck to refresh your little fruit." Yet in much of Europe, notably in France and Italy, wealthy families turned to wet nurses, women paid to suckle someone else's child. Wetnursing took on a whole new scale in many cities during the eighteenth and nineteenth centuries. In 1780 the lieutenant general of police estimated that only 1 in 30 of the 21,000 babies born each year in Paris was nursed by its mother. The rest went to wet nurses in the suburbs or the surrounding countryside. By this period in France the very wealthy had been joined on the market by large contingents of artisans, shopkeepers, and even servants. Contemporaries accused mothers of refusing to breastfeed because they

were more concerned about their figures and the social round than the welfare of their children. Fathers were considered no less selfish, circumventing the recommended abstinence from sexual intercourse during breastfeeding (it was thought to spoil the milk).

As for the nurses, they supposedly acted as true mercenaries, treating their tiny charges as a commodity like any other. According to their critics, they deceived parents in their letters on the condition of their charges, offered milk to their own children before the little intruders, and supplemented their overstretched milk supplies with pap made from flour or breadcrumbs and water. Above all they allegedly deprived infants of the care and attention they needed. In eighteenth-century England, John Stedman complained bitterly of his four wetnurses:

> The first of these bitches was turn'd off for having nearly suffocated me in bed. . . . The second had let me fall from her arms on the stones till my head was almost fractured, & I lay several hours in convulsions. The third carried me under a moulder'd old brick wall, which fell in a heap of rubbish just the moment we had passed by it, while the fourth proved to be a thief, and deprived me even of my very baby clothes.

To clinch the case, an appalling "massacre of the innocents" occurred in the villages. George Sussman suggested three levels of infant mortality among those born in French cities during the eighteenth century. The lowest and rarest rate, 180 to 200 per 1,000 live births, was registered among those breast-fed at home by their mothers. A medium range of 250 to 400 per 1,000 occurred among those put out to nurse in the countryside. Finally, a catastrophic rate of 650 to 900 per 1,000 struck foundlings who also were placed, several to each nurse, in rural areas.

This grim version of events, however, risks distorting the overall perspective on infant feeding. To begin with, the consensus among historians is that most mothers in the European past breast-fed their own offspring at home. Wetnursing, generally confined to the larger, older cities of Europe, was rare in villages, small towns, and the new industrial centers of the nineteenth century. It was also quite rare in Germany and Holland and perhaps in England. Evidence from Germany supports marked regional variations in feeding practices. A 1905 survey shows that infants in the northern and western sections of Bavaria and Baden and in Hessen usually were breast-fed, while the majority in southern and eastern Bavaria were fed artificially. But data for such maps of breast-feeding practice are rare.

The traditional custom was to wait a few days before putting babies to the breast because mothers thought the first milk was a bad substance. Newborn infants were given a range of substitutes, such as milk from another woman or a purge. (The benefits of colostrum were not recognized generally until the French surgeon François Mauriceau turned the tide in the late seventeenth century.) Nurslings were generally fed on demand at all levels of society. The German physician Friedrich Hoffmann reported in the 1740s that "for the most part the breast is given in the first months every two hours; after three or four months, six or seven times a day; and at length only twice or thrice a day." Even wetnurses apparently suckled their own children for nine or ten months before taking on another for money. Weaning was an important rite of passage that varied considerably according to such considerations as the wealth of the parents, the health of the mother, the sex and size of the infant, and local customs. It generally occurred somewhere between six months and two years.

A further point to bear in mind is that, until the "Pasteurian revolution" of the late nineteenth century, wetnursing was the safest alternative to maternal breastfeeding. Some wealthy mothers may have believed that peasant women were healthier than they were and that the country was a more suitable place for children than the city. What counted therefore was finding and maintaining a good nurse. Many in the middling ranks of society had little choice in the matter. Wives were essential in running a small workshop or business, as among the silk weavers of eighteenth-century Lyon and Milan, and the families could not afford to spend much on a nurse. The wealthy, who could choose from the best wetnurses, were in an entirely different position. Most of them probably took for granted the privilege of handing over child-care responsibilities to someone else, whatever the dangers. Above all the urban elites could secure nurses who lived in or near their homes and who therefore could be supervised easily. Memoirs written by children from noble families in imperial Russia describe the serfs who nursed them as loving and attentive; the poor women were in no position to be anything else.

Providing children with enough food was the overriding problem facing poor families well into the nineteenth century. Pierre-Jakez Hélias remembered that large families in the Pays Bigoudin area of Brittany during the first decade of the 1900s still measured food sparingly and that children squabbled over crusts of bread. Keeping children warm was a further challenge. For the first month or so of their lives children were tightly bound with strips of cloth; after that their arms and heads were left free until they were ready for the little robes that both boys and girls wore. Medical opinion became hostile to swaddling during the eighteenth century. Critics argued that it restricted the freedom of young limbs, risked constricting the breathing of the child, and left it wrapped up with its own urine and feces for long periods. They also felt that hanging a swaddled child from a nail for hours was negligence. Yet they were bound to recognize that, besides keeping infants warm, these practices helped protect the young from being bitten by domestic animals, pigs especially. The popular belief was that the bands and tightly fitting cribs helped the child develop strong bones and an upright posture. The lower orders also diverged from educated opinion on matters of hygiene. Many mothers believed that a layer of dirt on the head protected the fontanel and that it was better to dry diapers than to wash them because of the healing powers of urine. Such practices gradually died out during the eighteenth and nineteenth centuries as the medical influence on childhood became more prominent. The resultant changes, in terms of child development and adult attention, were considerable.

Infanticide and abandonment. The parent-child relationship sometimes broke down completely, most dramatically when infants were killed or abandoned by their parents. Charges of infanticide were rare in the law courts, but occasionally evidence surfaces hinting that newborn infants were quietly disposed of in some numbers by mothers and their accomplices.

During the 1720s, for example, when a drain was opened in the Breton town of Rennes as part of a construction program, the tiny skeletons of over eighty babies came to light. Judicial records reveal that those caught by the authorities were almost invariably unmarried women, mothers who had killed their illegitimate offspring shortly after birth. It may be that married couples managed to rid themselves of unwanted infants by surreptitiously starving or suffocating them. Because infant mortality remained high until the late nineteenth century, such criminal acts were difficult to detect. Servant girls, the occupational group most often prosecuted for infanticide, were more vulnerable, because they were constantly supervised by their employers and associated with this type of crime in the common mind. Since good character was all-important for a servant, the pressures on these young mothers were enormous. If discovered as the mother of an illegitimate child, a servant faced instant dismissal from her job, poor chances of future employment, and reduced prospects for a respectable marriage partner. The risk of shame and impoverishment was therefore particularly acute for a servant with a solid reputation; a more dissolute woman had less to lose.

Infanticide would probably have been more common in the European past had it not been relatively easy during many periods to abandon a child. The scale of abandonment in certain towns was simply staggering, particularly after the middle of the eighteenth century. In Paris during the early nineteenth century, approximately one-fifth of all babies born in the city were abandoned. In St. Petersburg during the 1830s and 1840s, the figure was between a third and a half, and in Milan up until the 1860s it was between 30 and 40 percent. Few of the foundlings were in fact discovered on the streets in this late period. Most were deposited with foundling hospitals and other charitable institutions. By the nineteenth century boys were as likely to be abandoned as girls, and legitimate as well as illegitimate children were included in considerable numbers.

Initially these decisions by parents appear cruel, especially given that mortality rates for foundlings reached 80 or 90 percent during the first year of life. Doubtless some unscrupulous parents took the opportunity to off-load unwanted children onto a charitable or state-run institution. The occasional doctor, lawyer, artist, military officer, or noble who turned up as a father—perhaps rejecting the outcome of an illicit liaison—in the records of the Hôpital des Enfants-Trouvés (Foundling Hospital) in eighteenth-century Paris surely was open to the common accusation of debauchery.

A closer look at the evidence on abandonment suggests two further considerations, however. First, the familiar combination of shame and poverty bore down upon young, single women from the working classes who were contemplating parenthood. A number of studies have revealed close links between surges in the abandonment of children and periods of economic crisis. In the Norman town of Caen a rise in the price of wheat was soon followed by an increase in abandonments during the eighteenth century. In Russia the *soldatki,* the wives and daughters of men drafted into lifetime military service, were prominent as abandoning mothers during the early nineteenth century. Second, parents often made it clear that they hoped to reclaim their children at a later date, when their circumstances improved. They frequently slipped little forms of identification into the babies' clothing, such as ribbons, medals, playing cards, or plaintive notes explaining their predicaments. They may have believed that their babies would have a better chance of survival in the foundling hospital than at home, apparently unaware of the lethal conditions in the hospitals and among the hard-pressed wet nurses. Volker Hunecke showed that in nineteenth-century Milan large numbers of poor families treated the local foundling hospital as a source of free nursing for their legitimate children. He cited, admittedly as an extreme case, the handloom weaver Maria G., who in twenty-eight years produced twenty-two children, all but the last nursed by the hospital.

The second phase of childhood: age two to seven years. After weaning, children moved into the second phase of childhood, commonly perceived to last until around the age of seven, the age of reason. The specter haunting the young during this stage of life was the intrusive rather than the indifferent parent. According to the historian Bogna W. Lorence, many parents in the eighteenth century insisted on complete control of their children in a bid to subdue their spirits and harden their bodies. Indeed, throughout the early modern period, parents often set out deliberately to break the will of their offspring. The more fervent Protestants usually emerge as the villains. In 1732 Susanna Wesley wrote in a letter to her son John Wesley, the future founder of Methodism: "In order to form the minds of children, the first thing to be done is to conquer their will and bring them to an obedient temper." Evidence from continental Europe, however, suggests that Catholics as well as Protestants thought in terms of breaking in the young. Child rearing then became a grim story of cold and formal relationships between parents and children, rigid rules, harsh punishments, and heavy-handed moralizing. It is tempting to contrast this type of regime with the gentler one, based on mutual affection between parent and child, documented in a minority of upper-class households from the late seventeenth century onward. Twentieth-century historians attempted to present a more sympathetic view of puritan parents and to locate them more precisely in particular social milieus. They noted that even the most austere evangelicals were moved by the desire to save the souls of their children and that rigorous theory was usually softened by more flexible practice.

During early childhood children were mainly in the hands of women—mothers, aunts, grandmothers, nurses, governesses, and older sisters. Some mothers, particularly those in aristocratic circles, doubtless remained indifferent to the fate of their offspring at this stage. The French statesman Charles-Maurice Talleyrand claimed never to have slept under the same roof as his mother and father. Children in this milieu were routinely handed over to a governess, often remembered by Russian nobles as an arbitrary and punitive character. At the other end of the social scale, mothers from the laboring classes struggled with difficult material circumstances, which may have strained relationships with their sons and daughters. Children were a potential nuisance for women who had a heavy routine of work on a farm or in a workshop and the tightest of budgets to manage. Many working-class autobiographies from the nineteenth century recall with some resentment the lack of physical warmth in relationships with mothers. At the same time the writers generally recognized that their mothers were trying to look after their interests as best they could. Adelheid Popp, born near Vienna in 1869, claimed that she had been deprived of a childhood guided by motherly love. "In spite of this, I had a good, self-sacrificing mother, who allowed herself no time for rest and quiet, always driven by necessity and her own desire to bring up her children honestly and to guard them from hunger."

Similarly, pious mothers who believed in innate depravity, typically women from lower-middle-class backgrounds, were not necessarily unsympathetic to young people. A woman like Susanna Wesley might display a steely determination to break the wills of her progeny, but she also provided a caring and supportive environment. Stone argued that mothers and fathers who attempted a more affectionate, child-oriented approach first appeared among the English landed and professional classes during the late seventeenth century; the approach then spread to the Continent and to other classes. This may underestimate parental interest lower down the social scale, but certainly it helped to have material security and support from servants.

One of the earliest tasks of child rearing was toilet training. Modern authors have often expressed surprise at the relaxed attitudes that prevailed in this area until the late nineteenth century. For the mass of the population living in the countryside, a mess on a beaten earth floor was easily cleared up with the help of some ashes. Even in more bourgeois circles, judging from diaries, it often passed without comment or was treated lightly. During the 1680s a Dutch authority counseled parents to avoid frightening infants during the process and to treat bed-wetting merely as a passing phase. Parents might prove more anxious when teaching their children to walk, since tradition associated crawling with animals rather than humans. They resorted to leading strings attached to clothes and little frames to encourage children to remain upright as early as possible. Sometimes those in middle- and upper-class circles inflicted various iron collars and backboards on girls as a follow-up to swaddling.

To help teach children to talk and to count, mothers relied on a repertoire of lullabies, nursery rhymes, riddles, and counting games. Lullabies, curiously enough, often dwelled on the harsh realities of life. A German one, presumably from the time of the Thirty Years' War in the seventeenth century, urged the child to go to bed because Count Oxenstierna and his Swedish army would be coming in the morning:

Bet' Kinder, bet',
Morge kommt der Schwed'.
Morge kommt der Oxestern,
Der wird die Kinder bete lern.

Pray children, pray,
The Swede will be here in the morning,
Oxenstierna will be here in the morning,
And he'll teach the children to pray.

Counting and word games usually were playful, as in the French counting game that played on the pronunciation of "assassin," "*assa un, assa deux, assa trois, assa quatre, assa cinq.*" Others were parodies, such as "*Dominus vobiscum, mangez les poires, laissez les pommes*" (the Lord be with you, eat the pears, leave the apples).

Peasant families in addition had to think about keeping youngsters out of danger while adults were busy. They generally relied on fear, threatening their charges with an assortment of bogeymen, trolls, fairies, werewolves, and the like lurking around water and forests. In Brittany, for example, Hélias remembered warnings of the man with carrot fingers, a tall figure in a cloak who liked to play tricks on travelers. The vibrancy of this culture is difficult to determine. Folklore collections give the impression that many regions had a rich heritage, while studies of modern industrial towns sometimes leave a bleaker impression. A selec-

Nursery Songs. Frontispiece to the selection of nursery songs in *Des Knaben Wunderhorn* (The boy's magic horn), a collection of songs by Achim von Arnim and Clemens Brentano (Heidelberg: Mohr und Zimmer, 1808).

tion of autobiographies of working-class childhoods in Vienna around 1900 indicate that the use of language was reduced to the bare essentials.

Parents also turned to a range of toys and books for children to help with their intellectual and physical development. However, the main developments here did not occur until the eighteenth and nineteenth centuries. In all periods children improvised toys from everyday materials and created their own fantasy worlds. In the seventeenth century, for example, John Dee mentioned in his diary, "Arthur Dee and Mary Herbert, they being but 3 yere old the eldest, did make as it wer a shew of childish marriage, of calling ech other husband and wife." Besides traditional playthings, such as tops, marbles, and dolls, the toy industry supplied young people with innovations that included board games, jigsaw puzzles, automata, and

model soldiers. The earliest board games certainly trumpeted their educational content. Titles of early English games included A Journey through Europe (1759), Royal Geographical Amusement (1774), and Arithmetical Pastime (1798). By the middle of the nineteenth century manufacturing centers such as Nürnberg in Germany and the Black Country in England turned out huge quantities of cheap wooden and metal toys, and evidence suggests that even some working-class households could afford to buy them.

The production of books for children also took off in the eighteenth century. For a long time the heavy-handed moralizing of an earlier tradition loomed large. The most infamous example is the passage in Mary Martha Sherwood's *The History of the Fairchild Family* (1818), in which the parents react to a squabble between siblings by imposing an evening walk to see the rotting corpse of a man hanged for murdering his brother. More appetizing fare for children soon appeared, however. German authors, like the brothers Jacob and Wilhelm Grimm, mined a rich vein of fairy tales and folk poetry, while American and English authors, including James Fenimore Cooper and Frederick Marryat, became renowned throughout Europe for their adventure stories.

The most challenging role for "intrusive" mothers was passing on moral and religious values. In the sixteenth and seventeenth centuries, when most people still believed in the innate depravity of children, the only way they saw to break in such creatures was to draw up a tight set of rules and strictly enforce them. A German discipline manual dating from 1519 barked out its orders to children: "Sleep neither too little nor too much. Begin each day by blessing it in God's name and saying the Lord's Prayer. Thank God for keeping you through the night and ask his help for the new day. Greet your parents. Comb your hair and wash your face and hands." Even babies and toddlers who broke the rules risked fierce retribution. During the 1600s the future king Louis XIII of France was first whipped by his nurse when he was only two years of age. Susanna Wesley noted in a sinister passage concerning her offspring, "When turned a year old (and some before) they were taught to fear the rod and to cry softly."

Whether many parents stayed the course in crushing the will of their children is a matter of speculation. The constant complaint from moralists that mothers loved to spoil their children may hint that they avoided the extremes. Doubtless the widespread custom was "beating, whipping, abusing and scolding children and holding them in great fear and subjection," as Pierre Charron observed in 1601. Yet advice manuals advised using corporal punishment as a last

Discipline. Parents distribute gifts to their children on 5 December, the eve of *The Feast of St. Nicholas* (painting by Jan Steen, 1626–1679). The boy on the left has received a switch, the traditional gift for a naughty child, but from behind the curtain in the background, Grandmother—perhaps with a present—beckons. ©RIJKSMUSEUM, AMSTERDAM

resort and disapproved of immediate, ill-tempered responses to childish faults. What mattered was that the child develop a conscience and internalize the prevailing norms. English Puritan testimony suggests that this group may not deserve its fearsome reputation in child rearing. Ralph Josselin's diary, written between 1641 and 1683, gives no hint of harsh and authoritarian attitudes toward his sons nor of physical punishments. The historian Simon Schama noted that Dutch Protestants in the seventeenth century followed the alternative humanist tradition of cajoling children into learning. Moreover adults always faced the likelihood that excessive discipline would provoke resistance. In her memoirs, Madame Roland, famed for her association with the French Revolution, con-

trasted her "sagacious and discrete" mother with her "despot-like" father. Her mother realized that the young Jeanne-Marie needed to be governed by reason and affection. Her father failed miserably, and his recourse to the rod converted his gentle daughter into "a lion."

The third phase of childhood: age seven to twelve or fourteen. The age of seven, as noted above, marked a significant turning point in the life of a child in early modern Europe. The future Louis XIII discarded his robe for a doublet and breeches, and the sons of Russian nobles moved from the female to the male quarters in the home. Children faced new responsibilities as they became involved in formal education and the world of work. Gender differences, never far below the surface in infancy, became more pronounced. Fathers took over prime responsibility for sons, while mothers continued their instruction of daughters. Agricol Perdiguier, brought up on a small farm near Avignon early in the nineteenth century, remembered that his father considered reading and writing a waste of time for girls (though he was scarcely more ambitious for boys) and that the two youngest daughters at least were spared from work in the fields. Children might be educated at home, by a tutor in elite families, or by parents, but the latter sometimes found this a daunting task. There were books to help them, such as *The Rules of Christian Propriety and Civility, Very Useful for the Education of Children and for People Who Lack Both the Good Manners of Society and the French Language*, published in 1560 in France, but parents with rudimentary educations must have struggled to achieve much.

Growing maturity did not necessarily mean that children were freed from demands for unquestioning obedience. Highborn families might insist on elaborate signs of deference. For instance, the daughter of a Russian noble family recalled that "children kissed their parents' hands in the morning, thanked them for dinner and supper, and took leave of them before going to bed." Working-class families, faced with overcrowded lodgings, bore down on the young in their own way to ensure that fathers were not disturbed when they returned from work. In Vienna parents often imposed silence at mealtimes and punished children by making them kneel quietly. Some children had to leave home at this stage, but this was the exception rather than the rule. In preindustrial times most waited until their teens, when they went to a boarding school, for example, started an apprenticeship, or entered domestic service. Children of a poor family might have to depart at a more tender age, possibly temporarily, usually to work as a servant of some kind.

Older children usually escaped from the clutches of the family to spend much of the day in the company of their peers. Boys and girls played together in the fields or on the streets of a town, but mostly they went their separate ways. Young males tended to form gangs, profiting from their greater freedom to roam away from the house. It seems that young lads drifted into these gangs at around the age of ten and gave them up when courtship took over during their late teens. The gangs had their own codes of conduct. Members solemnly supported their oaths with a "cross my heart" or, in the French version, "Boule de feu, boule de fer / Si je mens, j'irai en enfer" (Ball of fire, ball of iron / If I lie, I go to hell). Gangs demanded

absolute loyalty and punished sneaks and traitors mercilessly, as demonstrated by the fate of Bacaille in Louis Pergaud's novel *La guerre des boutons*. For betraying his comrades' camp to a rival gang, Bacaille was stripped, beaten, and spat upon, and his clothes were returned heavily soiled, with all the buttons missing.

The climate of the urban street gangs, as Michael Mitterauer noted, was dominated by a strong sense of machismo. The gangs carved out their identity by defending their "patch" against incursions from rivals in neighboring parishes or sections of town. According to a report from Cologne in 1810, repeated brawls during the summer months prevented young lads from venturing unaccompanied into another district. In Lancashire this custom of "scuttling" involved much ritualized abuse and brandishing of weapons, though in the end the lads preferred to rely on fists and boots in a fight. A gang member from Manchester insisted that, from his experiences in the early twentieth century, "It wasn't too serious; every party was more or less satisfied with a black eye or a nose bleed." Public authorities regarded male juveniles with a jaundiced eye because of their rowdy street games, their petty thefts, and their pranks to annoy adults. Such antics have a long pedigree. In the 1590s complaints were recorded of boys breaking windows and disturbing services at St. Paul's Cathedral in London.

Girls were more inclined to group together in twos and threes, defiantly observing and mocking the males. Parents tied them more closely to the home, especially in Mediterranean cultures. Even farther north, custom demanded that they behave modestly and make themselves useful. A study of the village of Minot in Burgundy revealed that, among the young shepherds in the fields, boys played around while girls knitted, made lace, or mended clothes.

Last but not least, young people spent as much time as they could playing games among themselves. These activities display a remarkable continuity. Iona Opie and Peter Opie remarked in *Children's Games in Street and Playground* (1969) that "if a present-day schoolchild was wafted back to any previous century he would probably find himself more at home with the games being played than with any other social custom" (Opie and Opie, 1969, p. 7). They noted that the Elizabethans played bowls, "king by your leaue" (a version of hide-and-seek), and "sunne and moone" (tug-of-war). Other familiar games can be traced back to the Middle Ages and even into antiquity, encouraging the pleasing notion of a particular culture of childhood. Thomas Jordan talked in terms of a lost tribe of children, which the historian must

Pretending. *Playing at Doctors,* painting (1863) by Frederick Daniel Hardy (1826–1911). ©CHRISTIE'S IMAGES, LTD.

investigate like an anthropologist to understand how it transfers the lore of the group to its newest and youngest members; for it is children, not adults, who teach the rules. The danger is sidelining the young into a ghetto, ignoring the fact that from the beginning they acquire their language and patterns of thought from adults. Nonetheless, children undoubtedly liked nothing better than to roam unsupervised in the fields, in vacant lots, or around the streets of a town. Georges Dumoulin remembered marauding the gardens of his village in the Pas-de-Calais with friends during the 1880s. Their favorite occupation was killing the cats of wealthy old women and turning them into a stew. The young also played games with scrupulous attention to tradition. Karl Friedrich Klöden recalled from his childhood in late-eighteenth-century Germany, "One knew that 'Kühler' [marbles] was played only in early spring, ball only at Easter time, kite-flying in the autumn." The Opies classified the games under various headings, including chasing, hunting, racing, daring, guessing, and pretending. Sporting activities, which were not universally codi-

fied until the nineteenth century, included football (soccer), hurling, hockey, and tennis.

Child rearing is a matter of interaction between adults and children. Parents invariably start out with ideas about how they want to bring up their children, influenced by religious beliefs, standard of living and occupation, region, and family traditions. Yet they quickly confront manipulation or even outright resistance from their progeny. As indicated, nurslings had some control over their mothers when they were fed on demand, young children might provoke rivalry for their affections between their mothers and their wet nurses, and older children rebelled against overly intrusive parents. The question is whether historians should look for continuities or discontinuities in the history of parent-child relations. Clearly children had some capacity to shape their own lives.

CONCLUSION

The quality of life for children has in many respects improved almost beyond recognition since the Middle

Ages, at least in western Europe. The crippling death rates, when a quarter or more of all babies were dead within a year and another quarter failed to reach adulthood, have ended. The painful and disfiguring diseases, such as rickets and tuberculosis, have receded, and although glaring disparities in income and wealth have persisted, most children are probably better fed, clothed, and housed (not to mention entertained) than in the past. The period of quarantine from adult life, so precious for Ariès, has become well entrenched, notably with the triumph of free, compulsory education. Perhaps a long line of humanists from the time of Erasmus onward encouraged a more sensitive handling of young people. It is uncertain how children reacted to separation from parents, whippings, cold baths, threats of bogeymen, and meditations on death, but perhaps a measure of resignation was the best that could be expected.

Yet progress has its costs. Child rearing became a more daunting experience for parents in the late nineteenth century, as experts from the medical profession and others turned it into a science. Young people have been deprived of many of the responsibilities they took on in earlier centuries. In 1979 Martin Hoyles wrote indignantly, "Our present myth of childhood portrays children as apolitical, asexual, wholly dependent on adults, never engaged in serious activities such as work or culture" (Hoyles, 1979, p. 1). It is perhaps fortunate that children have an impressive record of subverting adult intentions.

See also **Birth, Contraception, and Abortion; Farm Families and Labor Systems** *(volume 2);* **Patriarchy; Motherhood; Youth and Adolescence; Generations and Generational Conflict; Puberty; Childbirth, Midwives, Wetnursing; Child Labor** *(in this volume);* **Schools and Schooling** *(volume 5).*

BIBLIOGRAPHY

Ariès, Philippe. *Centuries of Childhood.* Translated by Robert Baldick. London, 1996. Truly a seminal work; originally published in French in 1960.

Becchi, Egile, and Dominique Julia, eds. *Histoire de l'enfance en Occident.* Vol. 2: *Du XVIIIe siècle à nos jours.* Paris, 1996.

Coveney, Peter. *The Image of Childhood: The Individual and Society: A Study of the Theme in English Literature.* Harmondsworth, U.K., 1967.

Cunningham, Hugh. *Children and Childhood in Western Society since 1500.* London, 1995. Fine introduction to the subject.

DeMause, Lloyd, ed. *The History of Childhood.* New York, 1974. Interesting collection of essays ranging from the early Middle Ages to the twentieth century.

Elias, Norbert. *The Civilizing Process.* Vol. 1: *The History of Manners.* Translated by Edmund Jephcott. Oxford, 1978.

Fildes, Valerie A. *Breasts, Bottles, and Babies: A History of Infant Feeding.* Edinburgh, Scotland, 1986.

Flandrin, Jean-Louis. *Families in Former Times: Kinship, Household, and Sexuality.* Translated by Richard Southern. Cambridge, U.K., 1979.

Fuchs, Rachel Ginnis. *Abandoned Children: Foundlings and Child Welfare in Nineteenth-Century France.* Albany, N.Y., 1984.

Gorham, Deborah. *The Victorian Girl and the Feminine Ideal.* London, 1982.

Grylls, David. *Guardians and Angels: Parents and Children in Nineteenth-Century Literature.* London, 1978.

Haas, Louis. *The Renaissance Man and His Children: Childbirth and Early Childhood in Florence, 1300–1600.* London, 1998.

Habermas, Rebekka. "Parent-Child Relationships in the Nineteenth Century." *German History* 16 (1998): 43–55. Part of a special issue on childhood in Germany.

Hawes, Joseph M., and N. Ray Hiner, eds. *Children in Historical and Comparative Perspective: An International Handbook and Research Guide.* New York, 1991. Helpful collection of essays on various countries.

Hélias, Pierre-Jakez. *The Horse of Pride: Life in a Breton Village.* Translated by June Guicharnaud. London, 1978.

Hendrick, Harry. *Children, Childhood, and English Society, 1880–1990.* Cambridge, U.K., 1997. Useful survey of recent literature.

Heywood, Colin. *Childhood in Nineteenth-Century France.* Cambridge, U.K., 1988.

Hoyles, Martin, ed. *Changing Childhood.* London, 1979. A radical critique of notions of childhood placed in historical perspective.

Hufton, Olwen H. *The Poor of Eighteenth-Century France 1750–1789.* Oxford, 1974. Final chapter covers parent-child relationships.

Humphries, Stephen. *Hooligans or Rebels? An Oral History of Working-Class Childhood and Youth, 1889–1939.* Oxford, 1981. Interesting material on street gangs in England.

Hunecke, Volker. "Les enfants trouvés: Contexte européen et cas milanais (XVIIIe–XIXe siècles)." *Revue d'Histoire Moderne et Contemporaine* 32 (1985): 3–29.

Hunt, David. *Parents and Children in History: The Psychology of Family Life in Early Modern France.* New York, 1970.

Hürlimann, Bettina. *Three Centuries of Children's Books in Europe.* Translated by Brian W. Alderson. London, 1967.

James, Allison, and Alan Prout, eds. *Constructing and Reconstructing Childhood: Contemporary Issues in the Sociological Study of Childhood.* London, 1990. Interesting ideas for historians to explore.

Jordan, Thomas E. *Victorian Childhood: Themes and Variations.* Albany, N.Y., 1987.

Jordanova, Ludmilla. "Children in History: Concepts of Nature and Society." In *Children, Parents, and Politics.* Edited by Geoffrey Scarre. Cambridge, U.K., 1989. Pages 3–24.

Locke, John. *Some Thoughts Concerning Education.* Edited by John W. Yolton and Jean S. Yolton. Oxford, 1989. First published in 1693.

Lorence, Bogna W. "Parents and Children in Eighteenth-Century Europe." *History of Childhood Quarterly* 2 (1974): 1–30.

Malcolmson, R. W. "Infanticide in the Eighteenth Century." In *Crime in England, 1550–1800.* Edited by J. S. Cockburn. London, 1977. Pages 187–209.

Maynes, Mary Jo. *Taking the Hard Road: Life Course in French and German Workers' Autobiographies in the Era of Industrialization.* Chapel Hill, N.C., 1995. Interesting point of entry for study of childhood.

Opie, Iona, and Peter Opie. *Children's Games in Street and Playground.* Oxford, 1969. Introduction is informative on the historical dimension.

Ozment, Steven. *When Fathers Ruled: Family Life in Reformation Europe.* Cambridge, Mass., 1983. Mainly focused on Germany with some comparative material.

Pollock, Linda A. *Forgotten Children: Parent-Child Relations from 1500 to 1900.* Cambridge, U.K., 1983. An influential counterblast against earlier works by Ariès and deMause.

Ransel, David L. *Mothers of Misery: Child Abandonment in Russia.* Princeton, N.J., 1988.

Ransel, David L., ed. *The Family in Imperial Russia: New Lines of Historical Research.* Urbana, Ill., 1978. Contributions cover parent-child relations and child welfare developments.

Rousseau, Jean-Jacques. *Emile.* Translated by Allan Bloom. New York, 1979. First published in 1762, this work incorporates many ideas of the eighteenth century but with more panache than any of its rivals.

Schama, Simon. *The Embarrassment of Riches: An Interpretation of Dutch Culture in the Golden Age.* London, 1991. Includes a fascinating survey of children in the seventeenth-century Dutch Republic that uses both visual and literary sources.

Shorter, Edward. *The Making of the Modern Family.* New York, 1975. A wide-ranging and influential study, though many of its conclusions have been disputed by historians.

Sieder, Richard. " 'Vata, Derf I Aufstehn?': Childhood Experiences in Viennese Working-Class Families around 1900." *Continuity and Change* 1 (1986): 53–88.

Sommerville, C. John. *The Discovery of Childhood in Puritan England.* Athens, Ga., 1992.

Stone, Lawrence. *The Family, Sex, and Marriage in England 1500–1800.* London, 1977. More persuasive on the upper than the lower classes.

Strauss, Gerald. *Luther's House of Learning: Indoctrination of the Young in the German Reformation.* Baltimore, 1978.

Sussman, George D. *Selling Mother's Milk: The Wet-Nursing Business in France, 1715–1914.* Urbana, Ill., 1982.

Thomas, Keith. "Children in Early Modern England." In *Children and Their Books.* Edited by Gillian Avery and Julia Briggs. Oxford, 1989. Pages 45–77 Excellent grass-roots view of childhood.

Wilson, Adrian. "The Infancy of the History of Childhood: An Appraisal of Philippe Ariès." *History and Theory* 19 (1980): 132–153. A critique of *Centuries of Childhood.*

YOUTH AND ADOLESCENCE

Andrew Donson

Social historians have taken an interest in youth in part because of their numbers: Those age fifteen to twenty-nine comprised 26 percent of the population both in France in 1776 and in England in 1840. While the decline of fertility in the nineteenth century limited this preponderance, modern states recognized that they needed youth to establish their legitimacy. Governments, aware that they did not lack competition for the allegiance of this crucial group, engaged in massive projects to make young people reliable citizens. For revolutionaries, the rough and energetic behaviors of male youth—their predilection to engage in violence and radicalism—proved instrumental. Social history has established that youth played a pivotal role in the development of European polities.

Because modern states and reformers left voluminous source material in their drive to reinforce citizenship and morality, we know far more about the modern than the premodern period. But social historians have been successful in applying their main approach—identifying the norms, behaviors, and institutions that correspond to the stage of the life course marked by growing independence from the family—to all periods. In Europe before the modern era, the stage of youth distinguished itself by its rites and rituals. By contrast, youth in the modern era was far more defined by leisure, secondary schooling, and the norms and behaviors that social scientists called "adolescence."

THE CONTINENT IN THE RENAISSANCE AND THE REFORMATION

The most celebrated argument in the social history of youth was Philippe Ariès's thesis in *Centuries of Childhood* that French society in the fifteenth century made no distinction between adults and young people. Ariès contended that youth—as a concept and a stage in the life course—emerged out of developments in the sixteenth and seventeenth centuries, when parents began to express affective bonds to their children and a growing literature presented youths as imperfect, weak, and in need of education. His narrative explored the pedagogical implications of socializing youth in such works as Jean-Jacques Rousseau's (1712–1778) *Emile* (1762). Much research in social history confirmed that German Protestantism in the Age of Reason demanded diligent raising of children. The debate against Ariès hinged on whether youth as a stage in the life cycle existed in traditional rural Europe.

Against Ariès, the scholarship of Natalie Zemon Davis and Andreas Gestrich borrowed methods from anthropology and made clear that European villages had rituals where single young men regulated the pools of marriageable young women. In France, the young men in these charivaris, the carnivalesque hordes, donned masks and publicly humiliated those perceived to be disrupting the marriage market. In Germany the *Katzenmusik* (cat howls) of male youth humiliated adulterers, as well as men in second marriages and women who failed to become pregnant. Humiliation was administered with loud shouting or singing to debase the putative miscreants.

Most importantly, this rough courtship ritual was often organized in formal youth societies, like religious orders and trade associations. Upon church confirmation at fourteen years of age, members entered the organized male youth abbeys in parts of France and the brotherhoods and boys' clubs in Germany. From this age until twenty-five to twenty-nine, the age of marriage, young men in these groups issued statutes, held meetings, marched in parades, and upheld financial regulations. On the Continent more generally, fraternal and journeymen's associations segregated young people by age, developed elaborate initiation rituals, and enforced rules of celibacy. Their members fostered strong corporate identities linked to age during their itinerant period, their *tours-de-France* or *Wanderjahre*. Of course, age segregation in these rites and organizations was far from strict. Examples abound of adults who engaged in the rough and carnivalesque behavior alongside male youths. "Youth" was a flexible category in the early modern period,

Early Modern Courtship. A bawdy "spinning room," engraving (1524) by Barthel Beham.
GERMANISCHES NATIONALMUSEUM, NÜRNBERG

and the age at which it began varied with locale and time.

The rough practices of youth had a long tradition of tacit support in European villages, but with the growth of cities in Renaissance Italy, charivaris became more mixed-age or disappeared altogether. Because governments wanted to solidify their rule, they could not condone the arbitrary justice meted out by the rough behaviors of male youth. In addition, demographic and financial changes in Florence made fathers absent in the raising of children. As Richard Trexler argued in *Dependence in Context in Renaissance Florence,* for these reasons many grew anxious about masculinity and the leanings toward debauchery among male youth. In 1396, these conditions induced petitioners to found a confraternity, the first formal institution outside the nobility aimed at socializing youth in restraint and dutifulness (Renaissance schools never undertook such moral aspirations). By the mid-fifteenth century, numerous such groups for boys age thirteen to twenty-four staged political and religious dramas. These youth groups also provided supervised leisure activities, competed for positions in public processions, and held elections for officers. In their probity they cast themselves as the pious saviors of society. As such, these organizations influenced local politics in fifteenth-century Italy, and the charivaris disappeared.

Still, the rougher traditions of male youth were integrated into the new youth groups. Italian tyrants organized boys into brigades during festivities, having them light bonfires and fight on the street as a way to reinforce authority. Likewise, between 1497 and 1502 the confraternities under the preacher and reformer Girolamo Savonarola (1452–1498) appointed themselves the roles of moral guardians, burned books and paintings, emitted sulphur and manure during sermons, and attacked girls whom they perceived as shameless. In Europe after the Reformation, religious holidays and other festivities were opportunities for male youth to wrestle married men, set fires in fertility rituals, and on Mardi Gras play *soules,* a violent form of football. It was expected that during weddings youths would fire salvos, extort drink money, obstruct processions for ransom, and ferret out the couple in their conjugal bed. Youths also made themselves conspicuous outside festivals by playing pranks. They scared people, jumped off bridges, threw benches in churches, and rolled large stones down hills.

Gender, the relations of power among the sexes, strongly informed the stage of youth. Courtship and sexuality needed to be regulated for at least a decade: Europeans had exceptionally late marriages—the average age of marriage was much higher than most other cultures in the world. Youth, the stage between leaving home and marriage, was therefore particularly long. Though young women certainly participated in the charivaris, research shows that rough behaviors were practiced primarily by young men who asserted their authority over the pools of marriagable young women. Female youths found more equanimity in the rituals regulating courtship in the village spinning or light rooms (*Spinnstuben* in Germany, *veilles* in France, *posidelki* in Russia). The practical use of these rooms was to conserve light and warmth while sewing and doing handicraft in winter, but the rooms also developed into spaces attended exclusively by young people where they could drink heavily, discuss villager misconduct, organize mixed-sex charivaris, and engage in physical and erotic contact.

The modern age ultimately brought the decline of charivaris, spinning rooms, and other rural traditional practices. Furthermore, the category "youth" became more distinct. States and voluntary associations began to organize their activities according to age, determined by state-issued birth certificates. More rigorous segregation by age was also a consequence of urbanization, public schooling, voluntary societies, military conscription in nationally led armies, and the consequent politics of nations. As the categorization of youth developed, more stringent regulations and hierarchies of age followed. In Germany in the eighteenth century, enlightened state and ecclesiastic officials strove to end the free sexuality in the spinning rooms and replace the arbitrariness of the *Katzenmusik* with a rational form of adult justice. Of course, state and civil society arrived late in rural Europe: We still find the traditional rough practices in the German countryside in the period before World War I and in France after World War II. But though the date of the arrival of modern youth culture differed in countries, regions, and times, scholars agree that across Europe youth became a more regulated stage in the life course, and traditional rural practices faded.

EARLY MODERN ENGLAND

England is a well-studied case in the early modern social history of youth. England in the sixteenth and seventeenth centuries lacked the age-segregated charivaris and organized youth groups common on the Continent. But apprenticeships segregated female youths age fifteen to twenty-five and male youths age fifteen to twenty-nine. These youths were single, in dependent relationships, and performed service as domestics, apprentices, or farm laborers. Though Ariès contended that an extended adolescence was a privilege only for the upper class, almost all subsequent scholarship has established that most youth in early modern England had a particularly long period of dependence—as long or longer than in the modern period. Though the time spent under the care of biological parents was short, masters acted in *loco parentis*.

In general these relationships of dependency were short-term with any individual master, however. Because labor was in high demand, rural youths in early modern England had considerably high mobility, working in one apprenticeship for only a period of months or weeks before moving on to benefit from skills in a different one. In this regard, youths enjoyed a fairly large degree of independence in making decisions about where to work. The two features of high mobility and short-term dependence on masters marked youth as a particular stage in the life course.

Although Lawrence Stone argued in *The Family, Sex, and Marriage* that the removal of children from their biological parents demonstrated the lack of affective ties in the early modern period, few scholars now agree with this thesis. Masters were far less sadistic than historians initially assessed them to be. Low rates of illegitimacy tend to indicate that communal supervision limited the abuse of female apprenticeships by male masters. Furthermore, parents and kinship networks continued to provide financial and logistical support for apprentices after leaving home. Of course, public bureaus to support youths—clubs, voluntary associations, parish-relief systems, and philanthropic societies—expanded in the late seventeenth century. Furthermore, provincial attorneys, registry offices, newspaper advertisements, and hiring fairs in the countryside provided new institutionalized support to apprenticed youths. But ultimately biological parents and kin remained the single most important source of aid.

While England lacked the formal youth groups of the Continent, certain rites were similar to those in the rest of Europe: Youths had particular roles in such holidays as Shrovetide and May Day. They engaged in contests, cockfights, revels, and games such as football, skittles, archery, cudgel, and sword play. The ale house served as the place where youths developed an informal associational life and discussed their own ideas about recreation, literature, sexuality, and riotous behavior.

As with the charivaris on the Continent, these activities often involved adults, as the distinctions in age created by the state did not yet have their import. Ilana Krausman Ben-Amos pointed out in *Youth and Adolescence in Early Modern England* that variations in levels of literacy and in regional practices tended to splinter youth cultures. In general, the value systems of youths and adults converged, and youths lacked social institutions and spaces separate from adults. The hallmark of the early modern period, Michael Mitterauer claimed in *A History of Youth,* was the relative absence of competition between the family and the peer group.

This condition was nevertheless coterminous with the high mobility that demarcated youth from the adult world. Arguing against the view that early modern England lacked a cohesive youth culture, Paul Griffiths emphasized in *Youth and Authority* the informal rituals of age, such as the pranks, licentiousness, and fighting condemned in a large body of pamphlet and advice literature. The needs of high mobility—the life on the road—brought a separate set of interests for youth, which then shaped their recreation, support, and companionship.

THE REVOLUTIONS AND MODERN YOUTH

What distinguished youth in the modern from the early modern period were the national and social revolutions that brought military conscription, voluntary societies, and public schooling. While our understanding of youth more broadly in the French Revolution (1789) is still limited, the violence of male youth clearly proved instrumental to tyrants, reactionaries, revolutionaries, and other radicals. After the fall of Robespierre (1758–1794) in July 1794, for example, gangs of young men calling themselves the Gilded Youth attacked members of the radical Jacobins and forced actors to sing counterrevolutionary tunes in Parisian theaters. On the left, the need to have youth participate in the violence—in the wars and the intimidation—boded well with the political demand for reform, that is, for rejuvenation and renewal. Article 28 of the Constitution of 1793 guaranteed "one generation cannot subject a future to its laws." The concept of youth was grounded firmly into the French Republic.

The most important legacy of the French Revolution for the social history of youth was not its violence but its introduction of age regulation by the state. The need for conscripted soldiers to fight the Republic's wars complemented the codification of age in state citizenship and eligibility to hold office. Furthermore, the new Republic set up a pedagogical policy that emphasized the collective over the individual—citizen-soldiers needed to be loyal. As early as the Reign of Terror (1793–1794), there were demands that sixteen- and seventeen-year-olds be trained in patriotism, martial arts, and hatred of tyranny. The Republic also introduced a host of civil ceremonies, the *fêtes de jeunesse,* which celebrated the ages of citizenship (twenty-one) and bearing arms (sixteen).

The pedagogical goal of creating loyal citizens in turn ceded to the right to receive an education. Consequently, new distinctions of age were produced in the *lycées,* faculties, and *grande écoles* of the national university system after Napoleon. These schools, whose first graduates Alan Spitzer called the *French Generation of 1820,* concentrated boys of the same age in youth barracks, thereby increasing the importance of the peer group. They produced a cohort of young men who expressed their awareness of their youthful identity on the editorial boards of journals and in discussion circles, Masonic lodges, and political groups. They turned in the 1830s to the "Young France" movement, established ties to Saint-Simon (1760–1825) and other Utopian Socialists, and reproduced the theme of revolution, rejuvenation, and renewal. But France in 1806, a country of 25 million, had only 50,000 pupils receiving secondary education. Much about the ancien régime persisted: The *Wanderjahre* and *tours-de-France* of apprentices flourished on the Continent after Napoleon.

During the industrial revolution Britain saw a slow decline in apprenticeships and the youth culture they had produced: The new jobs in factories did not demand that youths be itinerant and gain skills in short-term, dependent relationships at work. Furthermore, factory labor offered youths independence and so gradually ended the early separation from the family that so strongly characterized the early modern period. Consequently, youths working in factories now lived at home until they married; patriarchal migrant apprenticeship in Britain declined. Though wages offered a modicum of independence to youths, volatile industries like weaving brought instability, misery, and discontent—in short conditions that abetted rough behaviors of youth in gangs and popular movements like Captain Swing (1830). The radicalism of youths of the lower social classes in Britain in turn frightened an increasingly influential middle class, which held a more restricted view of youth independence, education, respectability, and other distinctions. While the rough traditions of youth proved useful in political revolutions, liberal politicians shunned youths' violence.

THE MIDDLE CLASS AND THE BIRTH OF ADOLESCENCE

John Gillis argued in *Youth and History* that adolescence denoted a particular stage in the life cycle of middle-class families in England after 1870 and in Europe more generally. Adolescence was characterized by the pressure of being middle class—of securing professions, trades, secondary schooling, or perhaps admission to university. At the same time, it was a stage in the life course with increasing leisure time, as middle-class youths had the privilege to learn and play, in contrast to adults and working youths. Because increased leisure time led to independence, the discourse on adolescence in Europe after 1870 expressed concern of this stage in the life cycle and called for more controls (Gillis, 1974, pp. 95–183).

Thus despite the privilege of an adolescence of learning and leisure, middle-class youths faced controls, such as the time discipline enforced in the secondary school regimes of the new European middle classes (see sidebar). Secondary schoolboys in both England and Germany faced a particularly brutal world, with the liberal use of corporal punishment. Suicide notes of middle-class teenagers in Germany identified their despair with the strict and demanding conditions in school. As John Neubauer has made clear in *The Fin-De-Siècle Culture of Adolescence* (1992), the woes of the privileged secondary-school boy and his contrast to the working class usually orphaned boy became a familiar theme in literature. Youth as a particularly trying time in the life cycle was depicted in novels by Charles Dickens (1812–1870), Honoré de Balzac (1799–1850), and Gustave Flaubert (1821–1880), and in the poetry of Arthur Rimbaud (1854–1891), Paul Valéry (1871–1945) and Hugo von Hofmannsthal (1874–1929). In the visual arts, the gaze turned toward youth most introspectively in Edvard Munch's (1863–1944) painting *Puberty* (1895), a subject that medical science had openly discussed for the first time in the 1870s.

Some historians have disagreed with Gillis that a concept of adolescence had developed before the turn of the century. As Harry Hendrick pointed out in *The Male Youth Problem,* the term "adolescence" did not come into wide usage among social workers in England until after the publication in 1904 of G. Stanley Hall's (1844–1924) *Adolescence.* Adolescence was largely a concept of Hall's influential work, which had borrowed heavily from Freud and the discussions of the celebrated case of Dora in 1901. As Mitterauer has argued in *A History of Youth,* the grounding of the term "adolescence" in psychology related to the new social scientific discourse of youth that emerged at the turn of the century. Though German social scientists never widely adopted the French and English term *Adoleszenz,* they produced a large body of studies on youth and developed powerful pedagogical models that predicted the speed of learning and acquisition of practical skills. Influenced by the progressivism of Ellen Key (1849–1926) in *Century of the Child* (1893, Swedish; 1902, German), German pedagogues addressed issues of motivation and self-determinism. And as in Britain, social scientists in all European countries turned to a concept of adolescence as a vulnerable period to create categories of youth deviance.

THE DAILY SCHEDULE OF STUDENTS IN THE COLLÈGE DE TULLE IN THE SUMMER OF 1864

5:00 A.M.	Arise
5:30–7:15 A.M.	Study period
7:15–7:45 A.M.	Breakfast
7:45–8:10 A.M.	Review of study period
8:10–10:10 A.M.	First lesson
10:00–10:15 A.M.	Recreation
10:15 A.M.–12:00	Second lesson or study period
12:00–1:00 P.M.	Lunch followed by recreation
1:00–2:10 P.M.	Study period
2:00–3:00 P.M.	Lesson
4:00–5:00 P.M.	Snack
5:00–7:30 P.M.	Study period
7:30–8:00 P.M.	Soup followed by a walk
8:00 P.M.	Bed

Corbin, Alain. *Archaisme et modernité en Limousin aux XIXe siècle, 1845–1880.* Paris, 1975. Page 374.

Modernization involved imposing more regulation on the work and leisure schedules of youth. In the premodern period, the seasons tended to regulate the rough rites of saints festivals and other holidays. But with the invention of the clock and the ascendancy of the middle class ideal of productivity, schools organized according to time discipline. At the same time, however, regulation in schools produced more influential peer groups.

Gillis pointed out that because application of these categories of youth deviance enforced greater conformity in comportment and appearance, adolescence became universalized for all social classes, even though its model was clearly a middle-class youth.

The concept of adolescence reproduced femininity for middle-class youth and made categories of gender more rigid. As Carol Dyhouse made clear in *Girls Growing Up in Late Victorian and Edwardian England,* the British middle-class families disapproved of women who worked outside the home; a sexual division of labor asserted middle-class respectability. Consequently, when secondary schooling did become acceptable, it aimed to prepare girls for matrimony. The separate sphere of domesticity was also institutionalized in public elementary schools that expected schoolgirls to become mothers or domestics.

THE YOUTH MOVEMENTS

The sine qua non of adolescence was leisure, but the leisure of working adolescents, with its rough practices of marking territory and participating in courtship parades, distressed the middle class. Consequently, a vigorous reform movement developed after the 1870s in Europe to educate, train, and above all enforce morality. Reformers set up clubs, youth centers, apprentice homes, and sports associations. Uniformed youth movements, such as the Boys Brigade (founded in 1883), evolved into organizations with the goal of furthering the empire, Christian manliness, and youths' efficiency and reliability.

The influence of uniformed youth movements was limited, however. As Michael Childs pointed out in *Working-Class Lads in Late Victorian and Edwardian England,* these organizations failed to attract the vast majority of working-class male youths whom the movement was supposed to reform. But the British youth movements presented a model of social control highly attractive to states and reformers: The more time a youth spent in supervised activities, the less likely he or she was involved in activities deemed delinquent. As John Springhall has argued in *Youth, Empire, and Society,* the combating of deviance also pleased a state that saw the advantages of nationalism, militarism, and imperialism—ideologies central in the founding of the Boy Scouts in 1908. The goal of the Scouts, like the ambition of the pedagogues in the French Revolution, was to create the citizen-soldier.

Youth organizations in Germany at the turn of the century were particularly well developed. Secular clubs for youths—crafts, gymnastics, and other sports—flourished. The availability of rail transportation to rural areas led to the growth of hiking organizations for urban middle-class youth. In addition, Germany by 1918 had 350,000 members in Catholic youth groups and boasted an even larger network of Protestant organizations. Further making Germany unique were the growth of large socialist and patriotic organizations: The Socialist Youth Movement, with an estimated 250,000 members in 1914, and the Young German League, a patriotic umbrella organization with 750,000 members. In contrast to Britain, these last youth movements followed a politics opposed to the social order. The right followed the left's lead in viewing youth as a regenerative social and political force.

The most celebrated of the German youth movements at the turn of the century were the *Wandervögel* (wandering birds), the hiking organization. Though it had fewer than 50,000 members, the *Wandervögel* were important in asserting the demand for youths' self-expression and self-realization, a demand that then influenced a wide range of youth organizations, from socialist to conservative ones. Furthermore, they presented a challenge to the strict and drab academic system: They set up youth hostels, held "nest" meetings, and performed folk music on the lute and the guitar.

France too had an expanding youth movement at the turn of the century. The French Catholic Youth Association, founded in 1886, had 140,000 members by 1914. In addition, French youth groups supported hosteling, football, bicycling, and socialist and communist politics. When Henri Massis and Alfred de Tarde published the survey *Les jeunes gens d'aujourd'hui* (Young People Today) under the pseudonym of Agathon in 1913, they made France aware that youths wanted their own organizations. Furthermore, Catholic youth rejected pacifism and showed a disdain for intellectual introspection. They wanted national renewal, even if that meant a war to win back Alsace and Lorraine. Above all, the associations that grew out of this youth movement, Maurice Crubellier has argued in *L'Enfance et la jeunesse,* constituted peer groups and made age more salient.

Segregation by age, peer groups, and leisure offered the opportunities to cultivate youthful identities that were then addressed by a popular commercial press. In Britain as early as the 1830s, cheap domestic romances and sensational stories—the "penny bloods"—flooded the bookstores for youth. Youths wanted fantasies, and the religious monthly's appeal was simply no match for the penny hero Sweeney Todd, the demon barber of Fleet Street. As the Danish anthropologist Kristin Drotner showed in *English Children and Their Magazines,* Britain in the 1880s in particular saw a more expansive and open youth reading culture with the publication of the durable youth magazines, *Boys Own Magazine* (1879–1967) and *Girls Own Paper* (1880–1908). These magazines were the first popular literature to address a variety of leisure and work activities: skating, angling, photography, hygiene, body building, career advice, and rabbit feeding. Advanced literacy and a commercial mass book market had addressed the adolescent.

In addition to age, this popular reading culture was clearly distinguished by gender. As Sally Mitchell demonstrated in *Girl's Culture in England, 1880–1915,* male youths were cast as active movers and shakers and had a masculinity where emotions were absent or minimal. Female youths by contrast had intellects appropriate not for creating but for ordering and making decisions, for purity, service, sacrifice, and domesticity. But girls' magazines in Britain also addressed the promising female professions and oc-

Scouting. French boy scouts, 1960s. ©ROGER-VIOLLET

cupations, such as nursing, teaching, and clerical work. The first generation of women with secondary schooling produced a pool of writers who filled voluminous pages of school stories, holiday adventures, advice on careers, and tales of heroism and misfortune. Together these produced a modern girl caught between the expectations of domesticity and the fantasies of independence.

WORKING-CLASS YOUTH

The nineteenth century saw a long and gradual decline in apprenticeships for working youths. Apprenticeships brought more security for youths in the long term but made them more dependent on their families in the short term. Wage labor, on the other hand, offered immediate independence and financial relief for poor families. Furthermore, with the successive child-labor laws, the pool of cheap labor shrank, and the demand for the labor of male youth swelled. A buoyant labor market for youth—a condition that characterized Britain from the 1890s to the Great Depression and Germany from the 1890s to the end of World War I—in turn raised the status of the young workers in the family, as they had more money to control and spend.

The youth movement was stimulated in part by the middle class's desire to reform the consumer habits of working-class youths. Although most youths in industrial Europe still worked more than forty hours per week, the growing number of high-wage jobs increased the leisure time and pocket money available

to spend on consumer pleasures, such as alcohol, tobacco, football, cinemas, cafés, billiards, penny bloods, amusement fairs, and dance and music halls. With money for clothing, social types with distinctive dress styles emerged. In German cities, there was the *Halbstarke* (ruffian), with his weapons, sported insignias, bright colors, fantastic hats with feathers, and other distinctive raiment. In Paris, there was the *apache* (savage), who rejected work, stood in conflict with his family, scribbled graffiti, dressed well in a silk scarf and a cap, and spent his days wandering coolly through the streets. Formal working-class youth organizations, though growing rapidly, were still incipient in comparison to the middle-class youth movements. Much of working-class culture thus continued to reproduce the rough traditions of youth: Youths in working-class neighborhoods formed gangs and fought on the street. Courtship came to be regulated by youths in the Monkey Parade, the trains of male and female youths who dressed in their weekend best and picked each other up. These behaviors alarmed a set of middle-class reformers, who sought to impose respectability on working-class youth.

As vigorous as the youth movements in trying to impose this respectability were the organizations that addressed the so-called "boy labor" problem, the masses of male youths who became porters, messengers, newsboys, vanguards, and errand boys. These "blind alley" jobs, as they were called in Britain, were chosen because they offered wages that in the short term were far higher than traditional apprenticeships. They also had better working conditions, with more independence and less monotony. Concerned about the reliability of these male working-class youths "between school and the barracks," between the ages of fourteen to eighteen, Germany became the first country to found obligatory vocational schools aimed at both the practical and moral welfare of youth in these jobs. It also set up advice and job exchange centers.

In all European countries, discipline in school was the response of the middle class to the growing independence of working-class youth. The oral interviews collected by Stephen Humphries in *Working Class Childhood and Youth* showed that though school offered the possibility to achieve literacy, the classroom demanded strict obedience and gave little room for creative self-expression. As in the rest of Europe, teachers in Britain meted out brutal punishment against violation of regulations or resistance to authority. All European countries founded juvenile detention centers, which kept boys deemed deviant in isolation in order to develop their piety, moral integrity, and self-control. British working-class schoolboys harbored deep resentment against the educational regime and the class inequalities it produced. Poor families looked upon obligatory grammar schools as an imposition because they limited the wage-earning potential of sons and daughters.

Working-class youths gained leisure as industrialization progressed, but they still spent a significant amount of time at work, in addition to commuting and doing household chores. Work also started early: A 1908 survey in Vienna revealed that over 40 percent of eleven- and twelve-year-olds had jobs, and this figure did not include informal modes of work. Furthermore, all but the very poorest working-class families encouraged their daughters to stay at home to shop, care for siblings, and do housework. A survey in Vienna as late as 1931 discovered, for example, that 45 percent of all girls were kept home from school regularly. The case was similar in England. Nevertheless, as Robert Wegs has argued in *Continuity and Change among Viennese Youth,* the general trend after 1870 was for working-class youths to spend less time with families and more time with one's peer group in school, youth organizations, and public sites. Without a doubt, working-class youth after 1900 in Paris had a repertoire of associations and leisure activities to shape a youth identity.

Despite many attempts to limit the independence of youth in England, France, and Germany, spaces for youth separate from adults widened in the 1920s. Public consumer venues—theaters, cinemas, automats, jazz clubs, sport clubs, hiking and hosteling organizations, and dance halls especially—offered opportunities wherein the absence of adults established norms and hierarchies. The demise of the calling system, where parents had regulated courtship, and the broad adoption of the dating system, where youths themselves determined the rules of wooing, is perhaps the most lucid example of how this new recreational world gave youths greater opportunity to shape their social world. As David Fowler established in *Young Wage-Earners in Interwar Britain,* working youths showed a defiance of their parent's call for respectability. They fashioned their own teenage culture in leisure activities and the new objects of consumption. Cinemas, spaces that youths visited on average three times per week, became the venues where rival gangs toughed out hierarchies of status and established the turf of youth. In France too, consumer items like the "show me bracelet" offered possibilities to create youth identities.

SOVIET YOUTH

It was a hallmark of totalitarian regimes in the twentieth century that they introduced national youth organizations with the goal of socializing youth in political loyalty. Just as the requirements of conscription induced new pedagogical goals after the French Revolution, these national youth organizations proved essential in producing ideologically reliable soldiers on a massive scale. For example, the 400,000 members in the Soviet Komsomol (Young Communist League) filled the ranks of the Red Army in the civil wars after 1917, and at least 10 million of its members fought in World War II. In Germany, the Hitler Youth served as a conduit for the elite Nazi groups, just as the Free German Youth in East Germany cultivated future Communist Party members. While the success of the Italian Fascist organization is doubted, historians agree that the Hitler Youth, the Komsomol, and the Free German Youth were essential in establishing the legitimacy of European totalitarian states.

On the eve of the Revolution, Russian youths were still largely integrated into the world of adults. Like their counterparts in rural western Europe, they participated in the rough music rituals of villages and regulated courtship in the light and spinning rooms. In the cities, however, industrialization clearly placed new interests on the labor of youth. The liberalization following the February Revolution in Russia in 1917 led to a blossoming of autonomous youth groups, including the Socialist ones that pioneered the strategy of using youth cells in factories to protest those in the worker's movement who ignored them. The programs of the Communist Party in June 1917 included concrete demands for improving youths' social and economic standing.

The Komsomol, Ralph Fisher argued in *Congresses of the Komsomol,* demonstrated that a successfully run state youth organization in totalitarian regimes secured the loyalty of future soldier-citizens. The first national youth institution of its size and complexity in the history of the world, the *Komsomol* was imagined to be the vanguard of the social revolution. After the civil war, it cast itself as a bulwark against the decadence of the West, expelling its members for bourgeois attitudes and demanding a plain style of dress. It grew rapidly, incorporating previously independent youth organizations, which had flourished after the Revolution, into a vast network of recreational and political clubs. Youth organizations that resisted its march were banned, and great efforts were made to organize rural youth, despite the protest of village leaders. Memoirs attest that the mission of the *Komsomol* was greeted enthusiastically by its members, who felt hopeful it would bring social justice and better education and employment. Membership rose to 2 million at the announcement of the first Five Year Plan in 1928. But the Komsomol's commitment to improving youths' social and economic standing was weak. Its higher priority was to secure ideologically reliable members for the Communist Party.

A singular phenomenon in the European experience of youth was the displacement in the Soviet Union of 9 million youths, a consequence of World War I, the civil war, and the subsequent famine and orphans they produced. Like western European cities, Soviet cities had a vibrant subculture of youth gangs that engaged in brawls, public courtship displays, and promenades around streets, gardens, taverns, and dance halls. But this subculture of displaced youth also differed markedly from European youth by its independence and its identity with wandering: Initiation rites into gangs included clinging to the underside of trains. A strong counterpoint to the organized youth in the Komsomol, these youths were viewed in theory by the Party as victims of capitalist oppression. In practice, it dealt with them as hooligans, forcing them into working and attending vocational schools. By 1938, two-thirds of those arrested were sent to work camps. The same draconian treatment applied to dissident members of the Komsomol, which purged its ranks.

YOUTH UNDER FASCISM

Like the Communists in the Soviet Union, the Fascists in Italy presented themselves as a continuing revolution whose dynamism stemmed from its youth. Indeed, fascist martyrology in 1925 claimed one-half of its saints were under twenty years old. Youth were

Hitler Youth. Propaganda poster (c.1940) proclaims "Youth serves the Führer" and "All ten-year-olds in the Hitler Youth." BUNDESARCHIV, KOBLENZ, GERMANY

by all measures disproportionately represented in the party. In the early 1920s the average *squadrista,* the fascist fighter, was scarcely over twenty years old. In 1922, when the Fascists became a mass party, the average age of its members was just twenty-five.

The goal of creating the citizen-soldier led the Italian Fascist Party to use schools as an agency of indoctrination. Benito Mussolini's (1883–1945) education ministers introduced state textbooks in the fascist spirit and eliminated academic freedom for teachers. Emphasis was on blind obedience to the Leader. The Italian Fascist state-run youth organization, Opera Nazionale Balilla (National Youth Works), functioned much like the Komsomol. It organized schoolboys under eighteen years of age into leisure activities like sports and paramilitary training and countered refusal to join with demands for a written explanation. As in the Komsomol, membership was also a prerequisite for advancement in careers. The Italians also pioneered a political aesthetic for their youth: Sleek uniforms, athleticism, singing, glorification of war, and rites of the Party. By 1930, premilitary training for boys was obligatory. In certain respects, the Opera

Nazionale Balilla expanded opportunities to working-class Italians: At least 4 million youths participated in the fascist culture courses, most in rural areas, in 1939. But the socialization project, Tracy Koon has argued in *Youth in Fascist Italy*, ultimately failed to provide Italy in World War II with a mass of loyal soldiers, as the 1930s saw a growing dissidence among youth against Mussolini and his project.

In contrast to Britain, which had little youth protest and generational conflict after World War I, Germany had political and independent associations for youths that practiced violence and radicalism. Of course, most youths preferred the state-supported sport and recreation associations, as the welfare of youth was guaranteed by the Weimar Constitution (Articles 119–122). But Germany was the country in Europe with the most splintered and politically charged youth organizations: paramilitary Protestant groups; Nazi, Socialist, and Communist Party associations; and the peculiarly German autonomous male youth groups, the Bünde, who aspired to an idealistic atavism of mythic knights and masculinity. Suffering tremendously under the inflation and the unemployment, youths turned to violence and radicalism and played a significant role in the downfall of the Weimar Republic.

Before 1933, the Hitler Youth was a relatively small organization not rigidly controlled by the Nazi Party. But like the Komsomol in the Soviet Union, the Hitler Youth owed its success to intimidation and violence: Its members swallowed older youth organizations and beat up those who resisted. In addition to its predatory tactics, the Hitler Youth's growth also stemmed from its popularity, especially among right-wing groups in rural Protestant organizations and also among the working-class youth. Its maxim, "youth must be lead by youth," had much affinity to the early youth movements. It also attacked hierarchies within the educational system, as its leaders goaded members to challenge the authority of teachers and the traditional curricula. The organization promoted camping, hiking, and physical fitness and gave recognition to the efforts of working-class youth, developing the immensely popular competitions in craftsmanship and technical skills in which 3.5 million participated. Membership grew to 7.7 million members in 1939, making it a rival to the Komsomol. Like the Komsomol, the Hitler Youth provided the state with an ideologically reliable cohort: The broad reach of the Hitler Youth made it one of the central institutions that popularized racism, anti-Semitism, violent nationalism, and the Hitler myth. As a general trend, the fascist and communist models of national youth organizations lessened the significance of school and family in the socialization of youth. Both placed youths under the guidance of state-sponsored, ideologically driven youth groups.

YOUTH IN THE COLD WAR

The history of totalitarian regimes is also about the resistance from urban youth subcultures: In Germany, youth gangs with names like Edelweiss Pirates and a Swing scene of high school jazz parties together formed an underground, illegal protest of the morality and politics of the Nazis. Subcultures flourished in the Soviet Union after World War II as well. The era of Nikita Khrushchev (1894–1971) was marked by a new youth counterculture distinct from the Komsomol. Calling themselves the *stiliagi* (the "stylish"), they were the sons and daughters of the elite urban class who cast their identity in their dress and preference for jazz. Subsequent to the *stiliagi* were other subcultures: the *bitniki* (beatniks) and the rock, punk, and heavy metal aficionados. Nevertheless, youth culture remained dominated by the Komsomol, whose membership grew to 19 million by 1962. The Komsomol continued to block avenues of dissent against the Communist system and its Marxist-Leninist ideology. It persecuted the *stiliagi* and threatened to send them to work camps. In contrast to the West, youth in the East were neither subject to a secondary labor market nor influenced by a consumer-oriented culture. Furthermore, the Komsomol provided a single and ideologically unified organ of social control. Even the discourse of youth, including its sociological study, were coordinated by the policies of the Komsomol.

In East Germany, the state-sponsored Free German Youth was a central institution that solidified communist rule as well. It had quickly gained 1 million members by 1949, filling the void vacated by the Hitler Youth. Its popularity stemmed in part from its promotion of games, dances, and sports and its project of building a socialist consciousness in volunteer work projects on dams, buildings, and farms. As important, however, was that membership in the Free German Youth improved chances in receiving advanced education and choice apprenticeships. By 1977 more than 50 percent of all eligible youths age fourteen to twenty-five were participating. Even if informal youth organizations flourished despite the Free German Youth, it remained a durable institution of the Eastern system. It also complemented schools, which had their pupils take oaths against fascism, sanctify socialist heroes, and condemn capitalism under the maxims of Marxism-Leninism.

In many ways, Western Europe after 1945 saw trends similar to the interwar period: The traditional

Mods. British teenagers outside a pub in Canning Town, 1979. HULTON GETTY/ARCHIVE PHOTOS

practices of rural youth disappeared; secondary schools absorbed greater numbers of youth; affluence made working unnecessary for the growing middle class; sport and confessional youth associations thrived; youths visited cinemas, cafés, and dance halls. But in other ways, ties of Western Europe with the United States introduced the American culture of consumer goods, such as radios, motorcycles, automobiles, cameras, jazz, rock and roll music, and record players—status symbols that defined youthful identities. Still, youths in Central Europe in the 1950s were remarkable for their conservative apoliticism. Surveys showed that their primary concerns were employment, inflation, and other economic matters. This stance stood in contrast to the highly politicized and confident youth culture of the 1920s and 1930s.

In all European countries in the 1960s, however, a generation of youths who had not experienced the war became active politically, particularly against the spread of nuclear weapons, relationships with the East, the Vietnam War, and the conservative academic and educational establishment. These more liberal views also altered sexuality, impelling the vast majority to support premarital sex. In Britain, peer groups that stood in opposition to state institutions

and formal youth associations proliferated. Stuart Hall and his colleagues have argued in *Youth Subcultures in Postwar Britain* that these groups—the Mods and the Rockers, the Teddy Boys, the Skinheads, and the Rastas—were an effect of the growth of leisure in Britain after World War II and the ascendancy of universal secondary schooling. Furthermore, mass culture (entertainment, art, communication) produced styles of dress (shaved heads and black suits) and expressions of musical taste (jazz or rock) that asserted an identity separate from the adult value system.

Youth has existed as a stage in the life course throughout European history, but a youth subculture based on style and dress had its origins in the modern transformation that introduced consumer goods and commercial locales. Modernity also made the boundaries between youth and adulthood more distinct. Furthermore, it made peer groups more influential insofar as the stage of youth shifted away from work and toward leisure and age-structured institutions like school. At the same time, states and politicians recognized the importance of winning youth to establish their legitimacy and created highly influential institutions of socialization.

See also **The Life Cycle** *(volume 1);* **Students; Juvenile Delinquency and Hooliganism** *(volume 3);* **Puberty; Child Labor** *(in this volume);* **Schools and Schooling** *(volume 5); and other articles in this section.*

BIBLIOGRAPHY

Ariès, Philippe. *Centuries of Childhood: A Social History of Family Life.* Translated by Robert Baldick. New York, 1962.

Ben-Amos, Ilana Krausman. *Adolescence and Youth in Early Modern England.* New Haven, Conn., 1994.

Brigden, Susan. "Youth and the English Reformation," *Past and Present* 95 (1982): 37–67.

Childs, Michael James. *Labour's Apprentices: Working-Class Lads in Late Victorian and Edwardian England.* Montreal, 1992.

Crubellier, Maurice. *L'enfance et la jeunesse dans la société française, 1800–1950.* Paris, 1979.

Davis, Natalie Zemon. "The Reasons of Misrule: Youth Groups and Charivaris in Sixteenth-Century France." *Past and Present* 50 (1971): 41–75.

Dowe, Dieter. *Jugendprotest und Generationskonflikt in Europa im 20. Jahrhundert: Deutschland, England, Frankreich und Italien im Vergleich.* Bonn, Germany, 1986.

Drotner, Kirsten. *English Children and Their Magazines, 1751–1945.* New Haven, Conn. 1988.

Dyhouse, Carol. *Girls Growing Up in Late Victorian and Edwardian England.* Boston and London, 1981.

Fisher, Ralph Talcott. *Pattern for Soviet Youth: A Study of the Congresses of the Komsomol, 1918–1954.* New York, 1959.

Fowler, David. *The First Teenagers: The Lifestyle of Young Wage-Earners in Interwar Britain.* Portland, Ore., 1995.

Gestrich, Andreas. "Protestant Religion, the State, and the Supression of Traditional Youth Culture in Southwest Germany." *History of European Ideas* 11 (1989): 629–635.

Gillis, John R. *Youth and History: Tradition and Change in European Age Relations 1770–Present.* New York, 1974.

Griffiths, Paul. *Youth and Authority: Formative Experiences in England, 1560–1640.* New York, 1996.

Hall, Stuart and Tony Jefferson, eds. *Resistance through Rituals. Youth Subcultures in Post-War Britain.* Boston and London, 1989.

Hanawalt, Barbara, ed. *The Evolution of Adolescence in Europe.* Special issue of *Journal of Family History* 17 (1992).

Hendrick, Harry. *Images of Youth: Age, Class, and the Male Youth Problem, 1880–1920.* New York and Oxford, 1990.

Humphries, Stephen. *Hooligans or Rebels?: An Oral History of Working Class Childhood and Youth 1889–1939.* Oxford, 1981.

Koon, Tracy H. *Believe, Obey, Fight: Political Socialization of Youth in Fascist Italy, 1922–1943.* Chapel Hill, N.C., 1985.

Laqueur, Walter. *Young Germany: A History of the German Youth Movement.* London, 1962.

Levi, Giovanni, and Jean-Claude Schmitt, eds. *A History of Young People in the West.* Translated by Camille Naish. Volume 1: *Ancient and Medieval Rites of Passage.* Volume 2: *Stormy Evolution to Modern Times.* Cambridge, Mass., 1997.

Mitchell, Sally. *The New Girl: Girl's Culture in England, 1880–1915.* New York, 1995.

Mitterauer, Michael. *A History of Youth.* Translated by Graeme Dunphy. Oxford, 1992.

Peukert, Detlev. *Jugend zwischen Krieg und Krise: Lebenswelten von Arbeiterjungen in der Weimarer Republik.* Cologne, Germany, 1987.

Pilkington, Hilary. *Russia's Youth and Its Culture: A Nation's Constructors and Constructed.* New York, 1994.

Spitzer, Alan B. *The French Generation of 1820.* Princeton, N.J., 1987.

Springhall, John. *Coming of Age: Adolescence in Britain, 1860–1960.* Dublin, Ireland, 1986.

Springhall, John. *Youth, Empire, and Society: British Youth Movements, 1883–1940.* London, 1977.

Stachura, Peter. *The German Youth Movement 1900–1945: An Interpretative and Documentary History.* New York, 1981.

Stone, Lawrence. *The Family, Sex, and Marriage in England, 1500–1800.* London and New York, 1977.

Trexler, Richard C. *Dependence in Context in Renaissance Florence.* Binghamton, N.Y., 1994.

Wegs, Robert J. *Growing Up Working Class: Continuity and Change among Viennese Youth, 1890–1938.* University Park, Penn., 1989.

WIDOWS AND WIDOWERS

Sherri Klassen

Through most of European history, the death of a spouse created a crisis in social identity. Widowhood for both sexes called into question alliances between families that were forged in marriage, threatened the continuity of patrilineal wealth, and reduced the emotional and economic support for the surviving partner. Widowers could emerge with a relatively unscathed identity, their wealth and family intact. Widows, however, embodied many of the contradictions in European attitudes toward women and marriage. Widows were both the weakest and the most powerful women in their society, both dependent and independent, the least respectable of women and the most.

DEMOGRAPHICS AND THE MEANING OF WIDOWHOOD

Widowhood refers to the state of being unmarried due to the loss of a spouse through death. In most legal and cultural definitions, remarriage terminates widowhood. The size of the population of widows and widowers, therefore, depends both on the frequency of deaths of spouses and on the frequency of remarriage. Before the twentieth century, marriages rarely lasted longer than thirty years and were almost as likely to be dissolved by the death of a wife as of a husband. The European population, however, contained more widows than widowers because the latter were likelier to remarry.

Estimates place the percentage of widows in Europe between the sixteenth and nineteenth centuries close to 11 to 14 percent of the female population. The visibility of widowers was much smaller; rarely would more than 5 percent of the male population be widowed at any given time. Fifteenth-century Florence provides an informative exception. Recording almost as much information as a census, the tax records there show that 25.1 percent of the female population over the age of twelve in 1427 was widowed. The large number of widows reflects a pattern in which women married very young to much older men, a pattern common to much of Renaissance Italy and perhaps more prevalent than once assumed.

Increasing female longevity combined with decreasing remarriage rates kept between 10 and 17 percent of the population of European women widowed through the nineteenth and twentieth centuries. The two world wars of the twentieth century produced an increase of 5 to 7 percent in the number of widows. The proportion of widowers also dropped as women increasingly outlived their partners in the late nineteenth and twentieth centuries.

As life expectancy increased in the nineteenth and twentieth centuries, the age of widows also soared. The proportion of widows and widowers always increased with age because young men and women whose spouses died were more likely to remarry than were their elders. A sharp decrease in mortality in the nineteenth and twentieth centuries meant that the death of a spouse became a much rarer experience for men and women under the age of sixty. On the eve of the French Revolution, 42 percent of the women in France who died between the ages of twenty and sixty were widowed at the time of their death; in the most recent census of France, only 1.9 percent of the women under the age of sixty were widows. This meant a reduction in the number of widows and widowers left supporting young children and an increased cultural equation of old age with widowhood. The diversity of widowhood decreased as a result. Previously, age and marital status had interacted in the social definition of womanhood; the experiences of widowhood depended on the age of the widow as well as on her class or social standing. By the late twentieth century, widowhood disappeared as a social and cultural category, though it remains a demographic one.

Widowers and relatively young widows frequently ended their widowhood with remarriage. Between the sixteenth and nineteenth centuries, approximately 30 percent of all marriages in France involved a widow or a widower. Fourteenth-century Tuscany shows the tendency for remarriages to be greater in the countryside than in urban centers, but this does

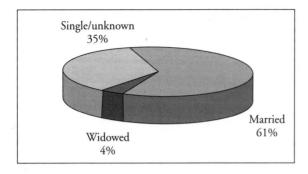

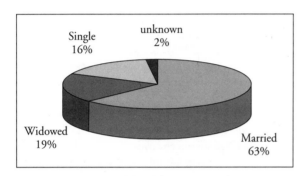

Figure 1. Marital status in Renaissance Tuscany. The charts demonstrate the disparity between male and female marriage patterns. The high rates of single males and widowed females reflect the unusual custom of young girls marrying men considerably older than they and not remarrying upon being widowed. *(Top)* Marital status of men over age twelve, 1427. *(Bottom)* Marital status of women aged twelve and older, 1427. Adapted from David Herlihy and Christiane Klapisch-Zuber, *Les Toscans et leurs familles* (Paris, 1978).

Demographics formed one of many factors determining the likelihood of widows and widowers to remarry. In European history since the Renaissance, the population's sex ratio was rarely imbalanced enough to alter marriage patterns considerably. Such an influence was evident in periods of high migration. Since men tended to emigrate in greater numbers than women, these periods showed unusually low rates of remarriage for widows. Apart from such aberrations, economics, legal systems, and family structures played a more powerful role in deciding whether widows would live independently, with family, or remarry.

ECONOMICS, INHERITANCE LAW, AND THE HOUSEHOLD

In premodern Europe the loss of either spouse brought economic as well as personal suffering. The household, existing as an economic unit, relied on the contributions of at least two adult members. This was true for members of all levels of society. Though the wealthy were rarely threatened with starvation at the loss of a spouse, widows and a certain number of widowers in these classes felt their resources diminish. Peasant households and city dwellers alike could face severe economic dislocation when death deprived the household unit of one of its breadwinners. Widowers were most likely to overcome this economic dislocation by marrying again; widowers with young children often married within months of the death of their spouse. Widows might remarry, but they more often found other recourses in response to the economic strains of widowhood.

Widowers benefited economically as well as personally from remarriage. A new wife brought with her a new dowry or marriage portion—wealth that the widower could use for as long as they were married. Among the elites the portion a wife contributed to the marriage could be considerable, and family businesses often relied on the dowry as capital. A widower without children was usually required by law to return his wife's marriage portion to her family. Those who fulfilled this obligation saw their capital dissipate at the moment of widowerhood. A widower with children would not normally lose control over his first wife's dowry—this would remain in his trust until his children would inherit—but he gained a second dowry and a valuable assistant with a subsequent marriage. Though the marriage portion could significantly affect the household economy of artisans, the urban poor, and the peasantry as well as the wealthy, widowers from these classes also sought to replace the lost income provided from the deceased wife's labor.

not appear to have been the case in other regions of Europe. Eighteenth-century data confirm that widows were likely to relocate upon the death of a husband, but these moves were not always from the country to a town or city. In this period, one-half of all widowers and one-third of all widows remarried after the death of a spouse. The percentage to remarry dropped in the nineteenth century when increased life expectancy diminished the number of younger widows and widowers. Not only age but also the number of dependent children appears to have affected the widow or widower's decision to remarry. The vast majority of remarriages studied in sixteenth- to nineteenth-century France involved the marriage of one party with children to a spouse who had no children. Marriages were frequently made between partners of disparate ages throughout the period; instances where both partners were over the age of fifty became less rare in the early nineteenth century.

A widow suffered greater economic loss with the death of her spouse than a widower of the same social standing. Though the legal regimes varied, widows were often excluded from any inheritance from their husbands' estates. Both Roman law and common law, the two systems that predominated in European legal practice, dictated that a certain amount of the estate must be assigned to the widow. Under Roman law widows were entitled to the dowry that they brought with them into the marriage. The heirs were obligated to liquidate enough of the estate in order to return the portion to her. Under common law the heirs needed to provide the widow with one-third of the couple's common goods.

Occasionally, the wealth that the widow could claim through her marriage portion was considerable. In Renaissance Italy merchants married young women with exorbitant dowries and used this wealth to establish their businesses. In the highly volatile family clan system operating in the Renaissance Italian city-states, large amounts of wealth transferred at marriage served to bond families together. When a woman was widowed young, her family saw an opportunity to create new, advantageous matrimonial ties. Far from being empowered by the wealth they controlled, these widows had few choices but to follow the dictates of their families since their wealth had made them vital to the family status. The men who relied so heavily on their wives' income feared this outcome. A widow's remarriage deprived her children by the first marriage of the use of her wealth. Disputes broke out when the husband's family refused to pay the widow the amount she had brought into the marriage for fear she would leave the children of this marriage destitute.

The property that widows controlled bolstered their authority in the family and helped them economically maintain the family unit. In addition to the portion due back to widows in their marriage contracts, some women gained property or assets of their own through inheritance. Though some of the legal regimes excluded women from their husband's estates, other relations and friends frequently bequeathed items or money to women. These amounts remained theirs alone when the women were widowed. Where the law did not forbid it, husbands sometimes bequeathed the bulk of the estate to their wives. When this was the case, and the widow controlled considerable wealth, her children relied on her for their economic future since she controlled the inheritance that would allow them to establish themselves in a trade or take over the family plot of land.

When not awarded a full estate, widows were frequently awarded the rights of usufruct during their widowhood. Under Roman law, when the heir was a minor, the testator could name a guardian in his will who would manage both the finances of the estate and make decisions regarding the child's education and upbringing. In most cases the heir would be the couple's eldest son and the widow would be named guardian. This allowed her control of her late husband's wealth for as long as her son was a minor and guaranteed her custody over her son. If she chose to remarry, however, the guardianship would pass to one of the child's paternal relatives. This restriction on

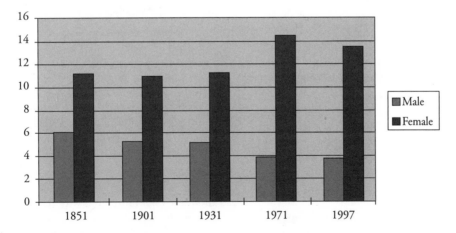

Figure 2. Proportion of men and women widowed in England and Wales, 1851–1997. The proportion of the population widowed over the course of the nineteenth and twentieth centuries is relatively stable. The high percentage of widows in the 1971 census reflects the combined factors of women widowed during World War I or World War II and increasing female longevity. Source: Great Britain, Census Bureau, *Population and Vital Statistics,* 1998.

WIDOWS AND CHILD CUSTODY UNDER THE NAPOLEONIC CODE

When Napoleon conquered new lands, he imposed the French Civil Code, or Napoleonic Code, on much of continental Europe. Most of these countries maintained remnants of this civil law well into the twentieth century. The following passage outlines the restrictions placed on widows with regard to their children. Although this law broke with the Roman law tradition allowing fathers to name a guardian other than the children's mother, it still allowed the fathers to name an assistant, and it required a family council meeting before widows could remarry and maintain custody. The passage is from chapter 2, section 1 of the 1930 version of the Civil Code.

> Article 389. The father is during the lifetime of the husband and wife the legal administrator of the property of their children who are under age, and are not emancipated. . . . When the father is deprived of the administration, the mother becomes the administratrix in his place and stead. . . .
>
> Article 390. After the dissolution of the marriage by the natural or civil death of the husband or wife, the guardianship of the children who are under age and not emancipated belongs as a matter of right to the survivor of the father or mother.
>
> Article 391. The father nevertheless may appoint a special adviser to the surviving mother as guardian, without whose advice she cannot take any steps in connection with the guardianship. If the father specifies the purposes for which the adviser is appointed, the guardian shall be able to act without his assistance in all other matters.
>
> Article 395. If the mother who is guardian wishes to remarry, she must call together the family council before the celebration of the marriage, and such council shall decide whether she may retain the guardianship. . . .
>
> Article 407. A family council shall be composed, in addition to the Justice of the Peace, of six blood relatives . . . of whom half shall belong to the paternal side and half to the maternal side, following the proximity in each line. . . .

Source: The French Civil Code, 1930

the widow's custody of her children remained in effect in many parts of Europe until legal reforms in the late nineteenth and twentieth centuries. Occasionally, nineteenth-century women petitioned to be allowed to remain the guardians of their children even after they had remarried, arguing that they had needed

to remarry in order to support the children who were now being denied them. These women were caught in a bind—while the legal system pressured them against remarriage, economic survival pressured them toward it.

The rights of usufruct afforded the widow less power over her children than outright ownership, but even in these cases widows controlled the purse strings of the family. The practice of widows claiming the usufruct of the estate sometimes exceeded the boundaries of the law. This is particularly true of France, where adult children tried in vain to gain access to their paternal inheritance while their mothers were still alive and living on the wealth of the estate. In addition to providing the widow with a home and economic well-being, the use of the estate gave her the power, by passing on (or withholding) necessary amounts of capital at opportune moments, to determine the education and training of her children, set the amount of her daughters' dowries, and influence the timing of their marriages and professional decisions.

Napoleon's legal reforms brought legal consistency to the inheritance and custody rights of widows across most of Europe, and the resulting legal system remained in effect until the late nineteenth and early twentieth centuries. The Napoleonic Code ensured widows a portion of the joint estate but gave fathers control of the custody of their children and allowed the patriarch the power to dictate educational and other life choices of his heirs in his testament. Widows also needed to obtain permission from a family council before they were permitted to remarry while maintaining custody of their children. Property disputes between widows and their children continued throughout the nineteenth century, dying down as a result of demographic shifts rather than legal adjustment.

THE PRIVILEGES OF WIDOWHOOD

Efforts to strengthen the position of the household patriarch in sixteenth- and seventeenth-century legal reforms bolstered the widow's legal position. Over the course of these centuries, the household acquired a more significant legal role, with the head of the household wielding power as the monarch ruling over his or her subordinates. A widow with dependent children ruled her household with most of the same rights and authority that her late husband had exercised. Unlike a married woman, a widow could engage in business in her own name, form contracts, speak in court, and make decisions with regard to the other members of her household. Economic power bolstered the widow's moral authority over her children and generally provided her with a level of respect from her children that rivaled the respect given to her late husband.

Before the emergence of the modern state, citizenship was often defined by household status. Such a definition allowed the women who headed their households to enjoy the same privileges and partake in the same responsibilities as the men who headed households. In some towns and corporate bodies, this included voting privileges and eligibility to hold minor offices. As the heads of their households, widows also paid taxes and contributed to the funds for maintaining a military force.

As head of the household, a widow with the usufruct of her husband's estate governed the estate in his absence. Noble widows governed the people on their lands in addition to administering the lands. Under feudal systems, a widow could administer justice and resolve disputes, control the various monopolies, arrange for relief in times of famine, and raise her own army. As feudal systems gradually disintegrated over the early modern period, noble widows lost their position as rulers. The centralized monarchies that emerged offered no equivalent position for noble or royal widows. With the exception of Catherine II (the Great) of Russia, sovereign power was never passed to a king's widow in the early modern period. When a royal widow ruled, she did so as a regent for an un-

derage son. Though royal governments spawned bureaucracies with officials whose offices were passed from one generation to the next, widows played no role in this transmission and were excluded from offices and bureaucratic work.

Though barred from the government, widows did have special privileges allowing them to operate their deceased husbands' businesses and trades. Widows were particularly active in moneylending and banking, dominating these fields especially if they had no adult sons to usurp their roles. Artisan women had the right to take over the family business and participate in the guilds or trade associations as full members. Some of their rights were gradually reduced between the sixteenth and nineteenth centuries, but for as long as an artisan economy remained, widows operated workshops on much the same footing as masters. These women became masters in the trade through their connection to their deceased husbands. In regions where a married woman could not engage in financial transactions or conduct business in her own name, widowhood provided her with commercial independence. Artisan businesses could, however, be difficult for a widow to operate alone. Since artisans generally established their businesses and married at approximately the same time, their businesses relied on the work of both partners. While a widower might remarry to replace the labor of his wife, a widow re-

Royal Widow. Catherine de Médicis *(in black, left)* dominated the French monarchy from the death of her husband, Henry II, in 1559 to her own death in 1589. Detail of *The Tournament,* one of the Valois Tapestries in the Uffizi Gallery, Florence. GALLERIA DEGLI UFFIZI, FLORENCE, ITALY/ALINARI/ART RESOURCE, N.Y.

CHOOSING TO REMAIN A WIDOW IN FIFTEENTH-CENTURY FRANCE

In 1405 Christine de Pisan, herself a widow, wrote a book of advice to Frenchwomen of various social standings. The following passage complements the statistical information that suggests that widows who could manage financially frequently preferred to avoid a second or subsequent marriage.

Of Widows Young and Old

Because widowhood truly provides so many hardships for women, some people might think it best for all widows to remarry. This argument can be answered by saying that if it were true that the married state consisted entirely of peace and repose, this indeed would be so. That one almost always sees the contrary in marriages should be a warning to all widows. However, it might be necessary or desirable for the young ones to remarry. But for all those who have passed their youth and are sufficiently comfortable financially so that poverty does not oblige them, remarriage is complete folly.

Source: Christine de Pisan, *A Medieval Woman's Mirror of Honor: The Treasury of the City of Ladies,* trans. Charity Cannon Willard (New York, 1989), 200–201.

tained her business only so long as she remained a widow. Widows, then, relied heavily on assistance from their children and from paid laborers or journeymen, who replaced some of the labor lost by the husband's death. In some of the legal regimes, a widow could pass her business to a new husband if this husband was a journeyman in the same trade. Many widows, however, chose not to remarry and preferred to continue their family trade as the head of both the household and the family workshop.

The growing cult of domesticity and a shift toward industrial work patterns in the early nineteenth century combined to eliminate privileges afforded to widows in business and the trades. When the guild system dissolved, the opportunities for widows to operate small businesses faded. The industrial employer preferred unmarried women whose place in industry was short-term. Widows were likelier to find employment in domestic service or retail trades. The middle classes and the nobility had, by the nineteenth century, embraced an ideal of female domesticity. Though middle-class families built businesses upon marriage

alliances, these alliances provided widows with no place in the family firm. In the nineteenth century widows, as much as married women, resided within the domestic sphere.

THE SOCIAL SAFETY NET

While the privileges afforded widows allowed some to succeed, others lived on the brink of destitution. Both artisan widows and widows of the laboring classes keenly felt the economic dislocation that accompanied widowhood. Widows with small children and elderly widows without children were particularly vulnerable to poverty—the first because they needed to support dependents and the second because they needed to support themselves. Widows fought poverty with the labor of their own hands. Research for seventeenth-century London shows that only 15 percent of all widows were unemployed. Widows became destitute when work was insufficient for economic survival.

If a widow's income was insufficient, she first turned to family members for assistance. Those who had only young children or none sought aid from their siblings and cousins, occasionally gaining help from the families of their husbands. Older widows relied on their own children for assistance; far more elderly women than men could be found living as dependents in one of their children's homes. Widows with land or businesses relinquished control of this wealth by signing it over to one of their offspring in return for a promise of care in old age. A successful widowhood depended upon a strong relationship between the widow and her adult children.

When family support was lacking, widows, who had long been recognized as members of the "deserving poor," turned to charity for assistance. Biblical exhortations urged Christians to give alms to assist poor widows and orphans; widows appeared in disproportionately large numbers on the English Poor Law lists and in Catholic countries received parish charity. Widows could depend on assistance from their local churches, the sympathy of their neighbors, and private charities. Guilds and mutual aid societies maintained funds to assist the widows and orphans of their members, though these funds rarely provided more than funeral expenses. In Victorian England, when etiquette even for the poor demanded funerary pomp, mutual aid burial societies grew into organizations of mammoth proportions.

In exceptional cases, pensions and insurance schemes assisted some widows as early as the eighteenth century. The Netherlands and Prussia were pioneers in this area, but other countries followed over the course of the nineteenth century. The early schemes usually provided pensions for the widows of civil servants and soldiers. The size of the pension was based on the husband's rank and the value of his service to the state. French Revolutionary widows petitioned the government for pensions by citing both their own poverty and the exemplary service performed by their late husbands. The practice continued into the twentieth century. The widows of veterans received pensions after each of the two world wars—an expense that asked the states to dig deep into their national pockets.

Despite a continued recognition of the needs of the widow and the growth in their numbers, social welfare reforms in the late nineteenth and early twentieth centuries did not address widows as a unique category of women. Reforms aimed at increasing the birthrate provided benefits to young mothers. Though the reforms were geared toward married women, since they were enacted in the interwar years, many of the young war widows with children would have benefited as well. Older widows benefited from old age pensions but, unless they had contributed with their own wages to the insurance schemes, they received a much smaller allowance than their husbands received in their own old age. In Britain after World War II, William Beveridge's social insurance plan provided need-based relief for widows with children who were seeking training or employment. The plan included both a cash payment and child-care subsidies.

In the late nineteenth and early twentieth centuries, husbands also began to plan more diligently for the support of their widows. Life insurance offered planning and security to working- and middle-class couples. Moreover, inheritance practices no longer excluded widows from their husbands' estates. Husbands felt a keen sense of responsibility; providing for a secure widowhood had become a matter of masculine pride. Private responsibility continued to supersede state responsibility in the case of impoverished widowhood. When the state did provide assistance, this was offered for the travails of old age or maternity and was not tied specifically to widows.

SOCIAL AND CULTURAL IDENTITY

The widow's social and cultural identity was shaped by her relationship to her deceased spouse. Trappings of widowhood reminded society that the widow was not truly independent, that her apparent independence derived from her unrelenting bond with the husband beyond the grave. Widows defined their so-

cial and cultural identities in a terrain dominated by two opposing stereotypes—that of the virtuous and dependent widow and that of the powerful, independent, and licentious widow. The widower occupied a very different land. While a woman's identity has, to varying degrees throughout European history, been tied to her relationship with a man, the reverse was not true for male identity. Thus the loss of a wife impinged on a man's identity to a much smaller degree than the loss of a husband impinged on a woman's.

In having been joined and subordinated to her husband through marriage, a widow became a liminal character upon her husband's death, existing between death and life. Even the name by which the widow was known reasserted this liminality. Although naming patterns varied, widows normally continued to use their dead husband's name as their own and were identified as "the widow Brown," either as their whole name or as an appendage to their birth name, as in the French pattern: "Marie Petit, veuve [widow of] Bonhomme." Research on seventeenth-century England has shown that women who were widowed twice chose to identify with their more prestigious dead husband, whether or not this was their more recent marriage. This practice demonstrates that widows consciously exploited their relationship with deceased husbands to build up their own prestige and status.

MOURNING

Widowhood began with a period of mourning replete with the symbolic liminality of widows, who withdrew from the world of the living, rejecting social life, sexuality, and sumptuous goods. In the sixteenth and seventeenth centuries, aristocratic widows underwent a period of isolation in their houses or bedchambers upon the death of their husbands, often resting on particular beds and chairs taken out of storage only in times of mourning. Pious widows in mourning rejected any hints of sexuality, and custom forbade remarriage and flirtation during that period.

Better than any of the other mourning customs, widow's weeds demonstrated the widow's position between life and death. Mourning dress, common in European history from at least as early as the fourteenth century, imitated the garb of the monastic communities and originally placed equal demands on male and female mourners. Black was adopted as a color for mourning by the sixteenth century as an imitation of the religious habit first worn by the Benedictine monks. Just as monks and nuns ritualistically

Mourning. Commemorating the dead on *All Saints' Day* (1888) by Émile Friant
(1863–1932). In the Roman Catholic calendar of feasts the day following All Saints' Day
(1 November) is All Souls' Day (Commemoration of All the Faithful Departed, 2 November).
MUSÉE DE BEAUX-ARTS, NANCY, FRANCE/PHOTO ©LL-VIOLLET

enacted a death to the world, so too did mourners ritualistically reject the world of the living for their period of mourning. Both men and women in mourning wore long robes with hoods, usually in black, through most of the early modern period.

While mourning was ungendered in the sixteenth century, three centuries later mourning etiquette had become distinctly feminine. As regular fashions diverged, mourning clothes became less imitations of the monastics and instead somber reflections of everyday clothing. By the nineteenth century men wore black suits and women dressed in silk or wool black dresses suitable only for mourning. Women withdrew from social life for several months, whereas men simply attached a black armband to their sleeves and carried on their business. The greatest difference between male and female mourning was the length of time each was to dedicate to grief. Eighteenth-century French court etiquette dictated that widows mourn their husbands for a year and six weeks; widowers wore mourning for six months after the death of their wives. Mourning for women reached its grandest scale in the mid-nineteenth century, when widows were expected to be in various stages of mourning for two and a half years and widowers for only three months. Many older women continued to wear mourning beyond the prescribed period. In so doing these widows

continued to express their marital status in their personal appearance, representing themselves as defined through their spouse and his death.

For royal and aristocratic widows, representations of their marital identity could help confirm their status and establish their authority. Queen regents in particular wore opulent mourning clothes that explicitly reminded their subjects that their authority was derived from their connection to the deceased king. Obedience to the mourning queen depended on her connection to this past as much as on her role as mother of the next king. Mary, queen of Scots, arrived in Scotland as a widow and drew the entire Scottish court into mourning with her—a fine emblem of the unity of the court behind her. By the nineteenth century, however, mourning no longer evoked authority. When Queen Victoria went into mourning, politicians feared that she would destroy the position of the English monarchy by withdrawing so completely from politics and world affairs.

PIETY AND VIRTUE

In addition to asserting a connection to a deceased spouse, mourning clothes indicated virtue, and many wealthy widows chose to emphasize this aspect of their widowed identity. Retirement had been a common preference for aristocratic women from the early Middle Ages. Church fathers admonished widows not to remarry, and widows who remained faithful to their dead husbands enjoyed a certain prestige throughout the history of Christian Europe. Many of the first women's convents were founded by widows and indeed housed more widows than never-married women. By the sixteenth century, convents frequently took in wealthy widows as lodgers; they followed a less rigorous rule than the nuns but lived within the walls of the convent and participated in parts of the liturgy.

While some widows were drawn to the radical movements of the Protestant Reformation, the Catholic Reformation of the seventeenth century saw much wider-scale involvement of widowed women. The Catholic Reformation movements seemed to allow widows to work in the world without divorcing themselves from their families and community. Such women had found retirement to a convent impossible because of their duties to their children and obligations to manage estates. Groups of pious, wealthy widows banded together in seventeenth-century Italy, Spain, and France to do good works and minister to the urban poor in the growing cities of the early modern period. Such pious women had found marriage restricting their devotional lives and welcomed the freedom that widowhood offered. Together with St. Vincent de Paul, the widow St. Louise de Marillac established a group of laywomen, both widows and unmarried women, who visited the poor and tended the sick. These "daughters of charity" administered a good deal of the local parish charities from the seventeenth into the twentieth century. Likewise a group of widows gathered in Paris with the assistance of St. François de Sales to form a moderate religious community known as the Sisters of the Visitation. The order was designed with the particular needs of widows in mind—the members were permitted to leave the community periodically in order to deal with their family obligations. Through these activities, religious widows formed a niche for themselves that relied on their independence, control of wealth, and moral status as widows.

The independence even of virtuous women in widowhood was, however, frequently a contentious issue. Most of the religious movements that involved widows in active work in the early seventeenth century were within decades converted into contemplative orders—convents in which nuns engaged in very limited work and restricted themselves to life within the confines of convent walls. These nuns might teach or nurse the sick within a hospital, but they lost the flexibility that had made the orders particularly attractive to the independent widow. When widows began to participate in ministering to the poor in the late nineteenth century, they did so alongside married women and under the leadership of younger, unmarried women. Though many widows still devoted themselves to their faith, they found no institutional expressions for it and no active ministry.

DANGEROUS WIDOWS

Independent and solitary widows posed threats to the male social order. While some social structures sought to confine widows in remarriages or within the families of their birth, for most of the European past widows headed their own households and acted as free agents. Though many of these widows won sympathy and respect, others garnered suspicion and censure.

Though widows were not to be found in large numbers in the criminal elements of society, numerous widows in premodern Europe developed a reputation for dabbling in the occult and wielding power

A Widow's Devotion. Queen Victoria and Princess Alice (Victoria and Albert's second daughter) with a bust of Prince Albert, the prince consort. Victoria and Albert were married in 1840; Albert died in 1861. Victoria wore widow's weeds until her death in 1901. Photograph by Prince Alfred (Victoria and Albert's second son), 1862. THE ROYAL ARCHIVES ©HM QUEEN ELIZABETH II/PHOTOGRAPHER PRINCE ALFRED

through witchcraft. Even before the rage of witchcraft trials in the seventeenth century, various widows were credited with manufacturing and selling charms or divining the future. Approximately half of the individuals prosecuted in the early modern offensive against witchcraft were widows, most of them childless and between the ages of forty and sixty. Many of these widows had built up reputations as witches over the course of a decade or longer. Neighbors, long wary of these solitary figures with their sharp tongues and vague threats, eventually denounced the women when the legal system turned its attention to witchcraft as a crime.

Though the denouncing neighbors feared the widow's muttered curses, the judicial witch-hunters suspected her unbridled sexuality. The most pernicious stereotype of widowhood was that of the independent and sexually licentious widow. According to the witch-hunter's manual *Malleus maleficarum* (The hammer of witches; 1486), older women without legitimate sexual outlets engaged in intercourse with the Devil so as to satisfy their insatiable sexual desires. Medical theory supported the belief that the female sexual appetite grew with age and that widows, having tasted the pleasures of sexuality, became voracious in their desires after being denied them by the death of their spouse. In addition to erudite theory, popular fears and fantasies created images of wanton widows. The widow's uncontrolled sexuality remained a topic of humor and anxiety throughout most of European history, appearing as a trope in the theater of the seventeenth century, the libertine novels of the seventeenth and eighteenth centuries, and cartoons and pornography in the nineteenth. The libertine widow was seen as controlling her own sexuality, disregarding her connection to her late husband and manipulating the minds and bodies of the men around her.

A widow's sexuality called into question her fidelity to her late husband. Because widows acted as liminal beings—their identity depending on the bonds that transcended death—their sexuality was still liminally owned by their husbands. The power of this bond was reflected in remarriage taboos that existed in various degrees of strength in most places and periods of the European past. In Renaissance Italy both widows and widowers broke taboos when they remarried. Custom dictated that widowers pay a sum of money to their neighbors when remarrying to compensate for disrupting the social order through their act of pseudobigamy. Remarriage to a widow required a larger payment. Refusal to pay resulted in rough music and vandalism. On the other hand, observers of nineteenth-century French peasantry were astonished to see widows and widowers arrange new mar-

THE LIBERTINE WIDOW

One of the most famous literary widows is the marquise de Merteuil of Choderlos de Laclos's epistolary novel *Les liaisons dangereuses* (1782). The widow here is in complete control of her sexuality and manipulates the people around her through deception and sexual power play. By the late eighteenth century, libertinism portrayed a widow's sexuality as dangerous not because of her unbridled and voracious appetite but because of the control it could hold over men and the havoc created by a widow whose sexuality was not channeled through male ownership. The following passage is a letter from the marquise de Merteuil describing her early life as a widow.

> Monsieur de Merteuil's illness interrupted these soft occupations; I had to follow him to town whither he went for medical aid. He died, as you know, shortly afterwards; and although, taking it all round, I had no reason to complain of him, I felt nonetheless keenly the value of the liberty my widowhood would give me and I promised myself to make good use of it.
>
> My mother expected I should go into a convent or return to live with her. I refused both courses; all I granted to decency was to return to the country again. . . .
>
> I began to grow weary of my rustic pleasures, which were too monotonous for my active head; I felt a need for coquetry to reconcile me with love, not to feel it veritably but to inspire and to feign it. In vain I had been told and had read that this sentiment could not be feigned; I saw that to do so successfully one had only to join the talent of the comedian to the mind of an author. I practiced myself in both arts and perhaps with some success; but instead of seeking the vain applause of the theatre, I resolved to employ for my happiness what others sacrifice to vanity.

Source: Choderlos de Laclos, *Les liaisons dangereuses*, trans. Richard Aldington (New York, 1962), 180–181.

riages on the occasion of the deceased spouse's funeral feast. Elsewhere, remarriage taboos were expressed in the amount of time a widow or widower was required to remain unwed. The period was generally longer for women than men. In late seventeenth-century England, remarriage within ten months of the death of a husband could bring charges of petty treason against the widow-bride. By the late nineteenth century, widows who remarried within the prescribed two and a half years brought scandal upon themselves. Only through the ritualized transitions within the mourning period was the widow's sexuality freed from the grasping hand of her buried spouse.

THE DECLINE OF THE WIDOW

Although the number of widows increased, widowhood lost much of its cultural meaning in the twentieth century. Demographically, even with the surge of young widows produced by the two world wars, widowhood continued to be increasingly confined to the latter two or three decades of life. Widows, then, became part of an already marginalized population in European society, and age became the more significant category defining them both legally and culturally. In combination with altered definitions of marriage and womanhood, the aging of the widowed population deprived widowhood of much of its earlier cultural meaning.

A watershed in the decline of the significance of widowhood occurred with the two world wars of the twentieth century. Already before the outbreak of war, women had begun to construct their identities with less attachment to their matrimonial ties. The war accelerated this process by producing a great number of widows at the same time that it demanded women perform war service and recognized women's actions quite independently from their positions as wives and widows. In responding to the demands of total warfare, women dropped their mourning rituals and costumes. Women in World War II were warned that to wear mourning clothes displayed a lack of patriotism; each fallen husband was to be applauded as a hero rather than mourned as a personal loss. When war widows did band together to seek pensions or attend memorials, they were invariably conservative women, holding onto a cultural identity marker that was quickly growing irrelevant. For the majority of widows, although they continued to mourn privately, their authority and independence no longer bore any connection to their special bonds to men who rested on the other side of death.

See also other articles in this section.

BIBLIOGRAPHY

Bideau, Alain. "A Demographic and Social Analysis of Widowhood and Remarriage: The Example of Castellany of Thoissey-en-Dombes, 1670–1840." *Journal of Family History* 5(1979): 28–43.

Blom, Ida. "The History of Widowhood: A Bibliographic Overview." *Journal of Family History* 16(1991): 191–210.

Bremmer, Jan, and Laurens Van den Bosch, eds. *Between Poverty and the Pyre: Moments in the History of Widowhood.* London and New York, 1995.

Diefendorf, Barbara B. "Widowhood and Remarriage in Sixteenth-Century Paris." *Journal of Family History* 7(1982): 379–395.

Hufton, Olwen. "Women Without Men: Widows and Spinsters in Britain and France in the Eighteenth Century." *Journal of Family History* 9(1984): 355–376.

Klapisch-Zuber, Christiane. *Women, Family, and Ritual in Renaissance Italy.* Chicago, 1985.

Klassen, Sherri. "Old and Cared For: Place of Residence for Elderly Women in Eighteenth-Century Toulouse." *Journal of Family History* 24(1999): 35–52.

Lanza, Janine. "Family Making and Family Breaking: Artisan Widows in Eighteenth-Century Paris." Ph.d. diss., Cornell University, 1996.

Prior, Mary, ed. *Women in English Society, 1500–1800.* London and New York, 1985.

Taylor, Lou. *Mourning Dress: A Costume and Social History.* London, 1983.

THE ELDERLY

David G. Troyansky

At the turn of the twenty-first century, as European states tinker with the social security systems their populations have come to treasure, "the elderly" present a variety of faces. Naming them poses a problem. The word "elderly," like "the aged," carries with it an odor of condescension, fragility, and passivity. "Elders" implies wisdom, "seniors" a certain activity and privilege in the marketplace, "older people" a category that avoids categories. Distinctions between the "young old" and "old old," or "third age" and "fourth age," register the impact of demographic, medical, socioeconomic, political, and cultural changes as well as the separation of retirement from old age. Such diversity of names and categories, which exists in other European languages as well as English, reflects cultural choices but also social historical changes. People live longer in our present "age-transformed" populations (Peter Laslett's phrase), claiming entitlements, consuming medicines, and forming new social, cultural, and political groups.

Social historians have sought to understand these transformations and have shared their labors with historical demographers, cultural historians, and political economists. Their concerns have included demographic aging, family and household structures, work and retirement experiences, state support systems, medicalization and institutionalization, cultural representations, and popular attitudes. Those concerns are best addressed through their own chronologies, approaches, and examples. At the most general level, however, the literature on old age and the elderly can be divided between social and cultural history.

SOCIAL AND CULTURAL APPROACHES

The general tensions between social and cultural history are visible in the literature on the history of old age and the aged. As Paul Johnson has explained, social historians who made the elderly a subject of historical interest favored such themes as participation,

well-being, and status, and addressed them in studies of employment, political activity, property ownership, health, and the transmission of household authority. The earliest efforts tended to follow an already creaky "modernization" scheme. For some, the modern world rendered the elderly marginal. For others, it was premodern society that had no use for them and modernity that invented them as a group.

Such simple choices proved unsatisfactory. The history of old age would not be contained in a one-directional master narrative of either progress or decline. Social historians have examined the age structure of limited populations, the shape of peasant households, entries to and exits from hospitals, age consciousness in official records, and the development of social policies concerning old age and retirement. But no overarching model has emerged.

Cultural history provided a possible solution. European culture has long examined the ages of life. Religious, philosophical, and scientific texts provided prescriptions for aging well, often connected with related themes of vanity, honor, and preparation for death. Religious retreat and humanist retirement to the study were among the recommended options for the fortunate minority, but there was no formal marker of entry into a new lifestage. Literary and artistic materials offered descriptions of experience but tended to repeat traditional tropes and images among representations of the elderly. Cultural historians recognized the predominance of certain images, from the ridiculous, lascivious graybeard or crone to the dignified wise man or woman.

These images have changed with successive periods of cultural history. The Protestant Reformation and the growth of the early modern state have been associated with the rise of patriarchy. The Enlightenment has been associated with a softening of the image of the patriarch and a process of de-Christianization that focused new attention on the last years of earthly existence and harmony between old and young. Nineteenth-century middle-class culture further developed eighteenth-century sentimentality, announc-

Image of the Elderly. *An Old Man and His Grandson* by Domenico Ghirlandaio (1449–1494). MUSÉE DU LOUVRE, PARIS/ERICH LESSING/ART RESOURCE

ing the great era of grandparenthood, and also produced a powerful image of the indigent elderly. In all those periods, one found nostalgic evocation of a time in the past when elders were respected.

Cultural historians paid attention to representations of the ages of life, often in the form of a ladder or series of steps ascending by decade to fifty and descending to one hundred. Such images hardly conformed to typical human experience; they are best read as allegorical renderings of the life course that urged adherence to prescribed roles and attention to the omnipresence of death. In the sixteenth and seventeenth centuries, flames of hell beneath the steps warned of the punishment for straying. In the eighteenth, the images turned secular. Other sources suggest a very old tradition of seeing sixty, sixty-five, or seventy as the threshold of old age. Some historians have asked when people began to see each other as old, placing the emphasis on physical appearance, and some suggest menopause as a female threshold. Institutions such as hospitals and hospices often settled on sixty or seventy, but labor and environmental conditions more commonly placed the beginning of old age closer to fifty. Still, the elderly have been identified more in terms of physical and mental condition, household authority, and cultural status than numerical age. Awareness of chronological age mattered little to most premodern Europeans.

The greatest contribution of cultural history was to make clear that old age has meant many different things in different historical settings. It might have to do with authority and its loss. It might come with the marriage of children. It might bring honor or ridicule. It was already an object of study. More people in the contemporary world can experience it, and although cultural historians found much to examine in the early modern period, some social historians and historical demographers insist on the unprecedented nature of modern demographic aging.

DEMOGRAPHIC AGING AND INCREASING LIFE EXPECTANCY: TWO PROCESSES

Recognition of demographic aging lay behind some of the growth in historical literature on aging and the aged. Some historians have considered the aging of populations on a par with the demographic transition that has traditionally been described simply as a decline in mortality and fertility. It was the fertility decline, principally in the nineteenth and twentieth centuries, that resulted in demographic aging: an increased percentage of people over the age of, say, sixty or sixty-five within a population. Thus the age pyramid was broadened at the top, the eventual result of narrowing at the bottom. Even the post–World War II baby boom failed to reverse a process that has had a lasting impact on Europe and much of the world. Peter Laslett has demonstrated that there is no going back. The "fresh map of life" for the majority of Europeans includes a long period (the "third age," as the French named it) from retirement to the time of sickness, decline, and death.

In early modern European countries, between 7 and 10 percent of the population was over the age of sixty. France reached 12 percent by the last quarter of the nineteenth century. Sweden reached that level in 1910, when England and Germany still had just under 8 percent. England attained 12 percent in 1931, Germany in 1937. Experiencing the demographic aging that transformed Europe in the second half of the twentieth century, England had 16 percent over the age of sixty in the 1950s and 17 percent by the 1980s. These figures were significantly higher for women, lower for men (table 1). Socioeconomic differences were apparent, as they had been in the early modern period as well.

220

The Ages of Life. Italian representation of the stages of life from the early modern period. The flames of hell are above and to the right of the steps. CABINET DES ESTAMPES, COLLECTION HENNIN, NO. 11737. BIBLIOTHÈQUE NATIONALE, PARIS

Local economic differences render "national" figures in the earlier period misleading. Thus eighteenth- and nineteenth-century cities receiving large numbers of young immigrants had relatively few elderly (sometimes under 4 percent), while depressed rural areas experiencing out-migration might for a time reach as high as 20 percent. The early modern elderly often had a small female majority, but that gender gap grew to be very significant in the modern and contemporary periods.

The female role in demographic aging (a merely perceived role if fertility decline is not only women's responsibility) and the fact that female life expectancy has exceeded male life expectancy led some early demographers to blame women for what they saw as a symptom of national weakness. In this way, demographic aging has been given political and cultural meaning, symbolizing national decline. Beginning in the 1920s, the work of French demographer Alfred Sauvy expressed that common conservative fear and provided a very influential model for social scientific thinking about aging. It need not have been that way. Aging could have been seen as a sign of progress in the battle against disease and premature death. Whether survivors of disease constitute a healthy population is another matter that has been debated. James Riley's discussion of "insult accumulation" dares to make projections about unhealthy survivors among elders in the future, but most historians of aging have avoided the alarmist language of Sauvy.

Declining mortality had some impact on the aging of populations, particularly in the more contemporary period, but its more important result was increasing average life expectancy. In general that meant more children reached adulthood. Only in the most recent period has mortality among older people fallen significantly. But even in the early modern era, some periods were clearly healthier than others, and socioeconomic standing almost always had an impact on survival into old age. The wealthy and

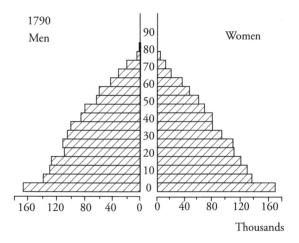

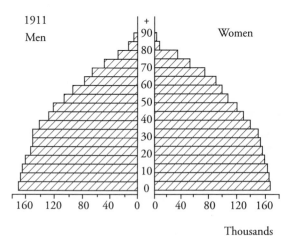

Figure 1. French Age Pyramids. *(Top)* Age structure of the French population, 1790. *(Bottom)* Age structure of the French population, 1911. Adapted from Jacques Dupâquier et al., *Histoire de la population française,* vol. 3: *De 1789 à 1914* (Paris: Presses Universitaires de France, 1988), p. 234.

privileged were therefore overrepresented in the elderly population.

Historical studies of life expectancy have mostly provided figures for life expectancy at birth. In England, whose population history has been most thoroughly studied, life expectancy at birth was around thirty-five from the sixteenth through the mid-nineteenth century. Progress was apparent in the late nineteenth century and dramatic in the twentieth. European women reached a life expectancy of 50 in the 1910s, 57 in 1930, 71.5 in 1960, 74.1 in 1970, and 77.5 in 1985, when men lagged farther behind at 70.6 (table 2).

Historians of the elderly have discovered the advantage of studying life expectancy in youth and

adulthood, thus eliminating infant and child mortality. It is clear that once they survived childhood, reaching middle age was common for early modern young people. In France from the 1740s to the 1820s, the probability of a twenty-year-old's reaching age 60 went from 41.9 percent for men and 43 percent for women to 59 percent and 58.1 percent. But socioeconomic differences were crucial. In seventeenth-century Geneva, those probabilities for men and women can be divided into three classes. At the highest social class, the probability was 51.7 percent for men and 52.1 percent for women; in the middling classes, 38.8 percent and 40.5 percent; in the lower classes, 31.9 percent and 33.9 percent. Thus European elites had an experience of what their cultures considered old age long before the transformation of entire populations and the generalization of retirement.

Placing the emphasis on the contemporary period, Peter Laslett has created a "third age indicator," a measure of the moment when at least half of a country's male population can expect to survive from twenty-five to seventy. Patrice Bourdelais, criticizing demographers' arbitrary choice of a threshold of old age, opted for a moving threshold based upon probabilities of living five years between the ages of sixty and seventy-five and upon the chances of living another ten years. He recognized that chronological age does not correspond simply to "biological age," that a sixty-year-old person in the twentieth-century was not the equivalent of a sixty-year-old person two centuries earlier. His approach, lowering the age of entry into old age while moving back in time, resulted in the claim that old age was almost as common in the early nineteenth century as in the twentieth. In effect, he was telling demographers to tone down their alarm.

Even before the big transitions, within the context of the old demographic regime, situations have varied. Relatively small demographic alterations and migration resulting from regional economic developments may have contributed to social stresses. And we find life expectancy after childhood that is surprisingly long. Old people, in short, were visible in all historical times. They are mentioned in high cultural sources referring to continued political and administrative activity or the awarding of honorary posts, legal sources regarding exemption from military or state service, and notarial archives for premortem transmission of property. In some historical settings before the great transitions, peculiar household structures influenced the nature of the aging process. In Renaissance Florence, for example, husbands were on average thirteen years older than their wives. But even elsewhere, old men might have

TABLE 1
PERCENTAGE OF ENGLISH
POPULATION OVER AGE SIXTY

Year	Male	Female
1881	6.9	7.8
1891	6.8	7.9
1901	6.8	8.0
1911	7.3	8.6
1921	8.7	10.0
1931	10.7	12.3
1951	14.6	17.7
1961	15.3	17.9
1971	15.9	21.9
1981	16.2	22.7
1991	16.5	23.1

Source: Kertzer and Laslett, p. 19.

young children, especially as widowers remarried much more frequently than widows.

FAMILY AND HOUSEHOLD STRUCTURES

The elderly were not the primary concern of the early family historians, who tended to emphasize childhood and marriage. But eventually it became apparent that family history was a possible approach to the elderly. Just as historians found a predominantly nuclear family model in northwestern Europe and a variety of extended forms to the east and south, so they have described a range from independent elders to older persons living within more complex households. As they turned from static descriptions of households at particular moments to more developmental life course approaches, they found more complicated and gradual transitions from one generation to another.

Some parts of Europe were characterized by co-residence between adult generations, and local custom indicated whether the younger resident was an older or younger child, a boy or girl. Inheritance customs and laws, whether demanding division of property or permitting a favored heir to hold the patrimony together, played a major role in determining the residence pattern. In southwestern France, for example,

the oldest child, regardless of sex, was the heir, and patterns varied dramatically from one microregion of Europe to another. Rudolf Andorka found great "generational depth" in the household system of four Hungarian villages in the eighteenth and nineteenth centuries. Households there went through stages and changed shape, as children matured, left, and sometimes returned, but three generations coresided in the vast majority of households containing aged individuals. This may have been a cultural choice, but it may also have been the result of land shortage or the lack of charitable institutions.

By contrast, independent households remained the norm for the elderly in much of western Europe. In some cases, that may have meant abandonment and neglect, but most scholars have assumed that elders living on their own, then as now, did so by choice. And independent households did not preclude assistance from relatives, particularly at moments of emergency. Such assistance, moreover, may have continued to flow from elders to their children and other kin. We should not assume that the elders were necessarily poorer than their adult children. But widows and infirm widowers who did not manage to remarry might be in a difficult position. Even in England, in situations of need or where property was involved, the elderly might join or be joined by adult offspring in a stage of what David Kertzer calls a nuclear reincorporation model.

For knowledge about the elderly without property and without children, the best historical sources concern charitable institutions. In England the des-

TABLE 2
LIFE EXPECTANCY
AT BIRTH IN EUROPE

	1910	1930	1960	1970	1985
Men	46.7	53.6	66.4	68.0	70.6
Women	49.7	57.0	71.5	74.1	77.5

Source: G. Caselli, F. Meslé, and J. Vallin, *Le triomphe de la médecine. Evolution de la mortalité en Europe depuis le début du siècle,* INED, Dossiers et Recherches, 45 (February 1995), p. 9, cited by Feller, ''La construction,'' p. 294.

Grandmother. *Grandmother's Birthday Cake* by Fritz Sonderland (1836–1896). JOSEF MENSING GALLERY, HAMM-RHYNERN, GERMANY/THE BRIDGEMAN ART LIBRARY

titute elderly were supported partly by the poor-law system and partly by relatives. One kind of support might complement the other. Lynn Botelho has found a significant percentage of seventeenth-century elderly receiving assistance in two small villages of Suffolk, but discovered that the amounts provided were considerably less than for the younger poor. She also found that one community was more generous than the other, probably because it was wealthier, but possibly because of greater religious motivation. Continental Europeans dealt with the poverty of the elderly in a variety of ways. Catholic charity was often based upon the activities of confraternities. German assistance to the aged tended to be local, while some French institutions were supported by the monarchy. Sherri Klassen has looked at urban elderly women in eighteenth-century France and found a variety of ways in which neighbors and coworkers met the impoverished elderly's minimal needs.

Culture undoubtedly played some role in determining patterns of residence, but structures varied according to the local economy. Thus, separating family from work history is artificial. Families were work-units, and the modern tendency to separate interest and sentiment is an obstacle to understanding the past. Within generally prescribed patterns of residence and inheritance, families worked out labor responsibilities and expectations for succession. Sharecropping

households in southern Europe often joined together generations and kin. Feudal landlords sometimes forced transmission of limited authority from a less productive older generation to the next. In a very different spirit, some northern European elders chose retirement at their children's expense.

WORK AND RETIREMENT EXPERIENCES

Preindustrial populations were overwhelmingly rural, and transmission of property usually took place gradually. But there were exceptions. Thus it is possible to speak of peasant "retirement." At a time when the "empty nest" was not yet a common experience—in recent times property tends to flow from the very old to the fairly old or to skip a generation—transmission of authority and individual retirement primarily involved aged parents and young adults. In many parts of Europe, the "old person's portion," room, field, or bench, was commonplace. Notarized maintenance provisions have led historians to speculate about the need for such assurances. Did the stipulation that adult children owed so much firewood or food indicate the absolute need for such provisions? Would children have neglected the elderly if not legally bound to care for them? Or did it simply set forth sensible guidelines? Whether they were effective or even needed, such legal agreements continued to be drawn up in rural areas into the nineteenth and early twentieth centuries. Eventually, rural exodus and changes in occupation rendered them less important. So did the rise of private and public pensions. Over the long term, individual arrangements were replaced or accompanied by transfer payments involving large bureaucracies that may well have shifted the locus of intergenerational tension from individual families to entire societies. One consequence may have been greater intergenerational solidarity within families, but that is hard to know.

Artisanal experience was occasionally comparable to peasant experience in terms of transmission of the patrimony. Tools and shops replaced tools and fields in notarized settlements. Workers' own organizations sometimes addressed issues of dependency. Provident funds, mutual aid or friendly societies, and savings banks had early origins, but they were more concerned with meeting short-term emergencies such as temporary disabilities and burial costs than with a long-lasting old age, which became more important in the nineteenth century. Such organizations always favored men over women.

With demographic aging, workers often tried to hold onto their jobs or shift to less burdensome tasks. Adaptation to new tasks indicates a traditional approach that continued even into the era of industrialization. It has been suggested that elderly industrial workers were not a problem because aging workers tended to move into other occupations. The notion of career was not yet fully formed, especially among proletarians. Thus old age pensions for industrial workers often struck those workers as deferred payments they would never see.

Workforce participation was high for the elderly in the nineteenth century, higher perhaps than in preindustrial Europe. In such circumstances, retirement came only with disability or a downturn in the economy. It was not a condition to be sought. Participation of the elderly in the workforce fell dramatically in the twentieth century. In England, for example, 73.6 percent of males aged 65 and older were defined as "economically active" in 1881; that figure fell to 56.9 percent in 1911, 31.1 percent in 1951, and 8.7 percent in 1991. It was not a consistent decline, as wartime demand temporarily reversed the trend, and interwar rates of labor force participation remained exceptionally high in France, but in general (and especially in the second half of the century) healthier elderly, physically capable of working longer, retired. Historians have debated the degree to which this was a matter of choice. They have also debated the role of business and of the state in the spread of retirement. Were

systems of social security largely responses to national emergencies, or did the creation of social security systems encourage retirement? Both situations can be found, and particular political parties, unions, and interest groups pushed differently for state pensions.

The Bismarck pensions in Germany are often described as the policy of a conservative politician seeking to steal an issue from the socialists. It was not an issue that was high on the socialist agenda before the late nineteenth century, but it had appeared from time to time on the European left since the French Revolution. Nineteenth-century political thinkers spoke about a social debt to the aged, but little was actually done for elderly other than soldiers or civil servants. By the late nineteenth century, a right to retirement was proclaimed from many quarters. Bismarck's state socialism developed out of an awareness of how private pensions served to discipline workers. Social welfare systems financed by general revenues are commonly assumed to be most highly developed in Scandinavian countries as a result of social democratic activism in the 1930s; however, Peter Baldwin has argued that in the late nineteenth century Danish and Swedish agrarian middle classes demanded universalist and solidaristic social legislation so as not to be denied benefits socialists were demanding for urban working classes.

STATE INTERVENTION

Before the spread of social security, European states addressed issues of aging and retirement at two levels: rewards to civil servants in the form of pensions and assistance to the poor. The structure of pension systems was elaborated in the world of the relatively privileged public servants. Formulas for arriving at payment schedules were worked out long before the social security era. Early modern pensions had usually been paid at a wide range of ages for services rendered, not as a reward at the end of a career. Dock workers in the English customs service (1684–1712) and tax farmers in France (1768) were early beneficiaries of retirement systems, but military pensions in the eighteenth century provided the most influential models for civil service pensions in the nineteenth. Different government ministries often set up their own systems, which were eventually standardized and centralized in France in 1853, Great Britain in 1859, and the German Empire incrementally in the 1870s and 1880s.

Salaried industrial workers were next to receive pensions, and miners tended to be first in that group: 1854 in Prussia, 1894 in France. Railroad workers followed. Meanwhile, private pensions continued to

Old Men at Leisure. *Old Men in Rockingham Park* (1904) by Walter Bonner Gash (1870–1928). ALFRED EAST GALLERY, KETTERING, NOTTINGHAM, U.K./THE BRIDGEMAN ART LIBRARY

play a role, paternalistically aiding and disciplining a minority of workers. In Britain friendly societies were more common, thus maintaining the middle-class ideal of the provident worker. But that image changed as social investigations, similar to those conducted on the continent, revealed a significant population of aged poor. Social insurance was passed in Germany under Bismarck in 1889, in Britain in 1908, and in France in 1910, but coverage varied: the Germans covered white-collar workers, the British focused on the poor, and the French included farmers. Coverage of the self-employed and professionals generally awaited the welfare state legislation following World War II. Private pension schemes, far from being replaced, continued to grow in the welfare state era. Income packaging was more common than dependence upon a single source of support.

The image of the retired worker included the Bismarck pensioner who was really a victim of disability rather than age and the French pensioner who had a "right" to leisure at a particular age, but the image was always male, and all across Europe state pensions were designed for older men. Women were offered widows' pensions or their own, usually at

lower rates. Age at retirement varied as well, but national systems tended to imitate each other. The Bismarck pensions had an impact throughout Europe, and the return of Alsace and Lorraine to France after World War I resulted in the continuation of German rules in French territory.

Studies of state pension systems indicate the eventual emergence of retirement as a way of managing old age, but that stage was reached incrementally. Often parties of the Left avoided the issue, seeing forced retirement as a trap and old age pensions as devices for cutting wages. They were particularly hostile to contributory pensions, demanding instead noncontributory pensions paid out of general revenues. Businessmen and civil servants saw contributory pensions as fiscally responsible and providing a clearer individual right; they saw noncontributory ones as open-ended, too expensive, and overly redistributive. Members of friendly societies feared losing control of pension funds. But they eventually compromised, and the late nineteenth and early twentieth centuries saw the development of social welfare policies that dealt with old age, retirement, widowhood, and medical care.

Over the long run, social security systems contributed to the development of a three-stage life course: training, work, and retirement. Particular debates about retirement pensions revealed serious disagreements over issues of equity and purpose. Pensions based upon male breadwinner assumptions marginalized women, who were consistently the majority of the elderly. Age of eligibility and requirements to leave the workforce were hotly contested. Did pensions exist as insurance for the aged poor or as a right for all elderly?

MEDICALIZATION AND INSTITUTIONALIZATION

As European welfare states created greater coherence out of individual institutions dealing with income, housing, and health, attention focused on the medicalization of old age. The process was not completely new. A medical literature on preventing aging and works addressing the diseases of the aged go back to the ancients; like other wisdom from the classical past, these ideas were revived in the Renaissance. The eighteenth century saw a western European campaign for public health, the beginnings of a long-term professionalization of health practitioners, a greater differentiation between age groups in medical publications, and the proliferation of projects for hospitals and hospices.

Institutions changed slowly, but hospitals and workhouses assigned different roles to people of different ages. Nineteenth-century poorhouses were transformed into old age homes. Nursing homes and other facilities emerged in the twentieth century, and hospitals themselves, overcoming popular fears that they were essentially places to die, witnessed a dramatic aging of their populations. Young men were more likely to be found in French and German urban hospitals than old men or women at the beginning of the twentieth century. All that would change. In a sense, the popular turn to medicine still preceded the medical profession's discovery of its new clientele. Consuming medicines, paid for by the state, became the norm for the European elderly in the second half of the twentieth century. An unmedicalized old age became virtually unthinkable.

Geriatrics has proved successful, but it has hardly shared the heroic image of other specializations. A medical practice that emphasizes treating chronic illness, easing pain, improving quality of life, and observing the process of dying was often less attractive than one that cured acute illness and restored patients to youthful vigor. Gerontology, resulting from the fusion of different strands of the social and health sciences, has perhaps been more successful than geriatrics, which developed as a branching off from mainstream medicine. We are back in the realm of culture.

CULTURAL REPRESENTATIONS AND POPULAR ATTITUDES

Some historians have moved relatively easily between cultural representations of old age and popular attitudes about it. *King Lear* provides a lesson about the risks of premortem transmission both for kings and farmers. It has spoken to rather diverse audiences ever since Shakespeare wrote it, and it derived from earlier tales. But as paths of inheritance in the twentieth century have tended to skip generations, and as aging Europeans depend more upon state-administered transfer payments and less upon private patrimony, that great tragic expression has probably come to be more about intergenerational sentiment than property, which long remained a subject for peasant proverbs. Throughout Europe one might have heard that a father can raise one hundred children, but not one of a hundred children can support an aged father. Such folklore survived into the twentieth century.

Stereotypes of the elderly still abound. Modern Europeans have an entire menu of possibilities. Attitudes toward the elderly are multiple, but emphases have been different at different times. In the early modern period, witchcraft became associated with elderly women. Even when witch-hunting came to an end, the image survived. The respected elder emerged as a common figure in eighteenth-century culture, which frowned upon traditional ridicule. It is possible to recognize an emphasis on both the decrepit aged in certain discussions of the welfare state and the young old in appreciations of the positive features of age-transformed populations.

A significant change occurred in the last quarter of the twentieth century, when retirees could look back on an earlier generation that had pioneered retirement. Expectations changed accordingly. Retirees not only traveled and became active consumers, but increasingly changed residence after retiring from the workforce. But knowledge of what previous generations have achieved is tempered by the various ways in which aging people move from the "active" life to the third age. Some still experience retirement as disability. Others experience it as a choice and a cultural opportunity. They take up serious projects and participate in "universities of the third age." Still others approach it through premature unemployment, which is a challenge for individuals and for social security systems. The unemployed may become the retired long before becoming elderly.

The third age is the happy side of contemporary European aging. It combines health, wealth, and possibilities for cultural enrichment. The fourth age, looking much like indigent old age of a century ago, but lasting longer, poses challenges of a philosophical as well as economic and political nature. Social history suggests that neither broad demographic changes nor individual predicaments can be understood in isolation. It is hard to imagine a reversal of demographic aging, and demand for labor in countries with large numbers of elderly will result in population movements. The twentieth century has seen immigration to Europe from the former colonial world—that was

the specter for some of the conservative demographers who first noticed the phenomenon of demographic aging. The formation of the European Union is accelerating another historical trend, the migration of Europeans from countries of relatively high fertility and unemployment to other parts of Europe. And yet fertility declines in Italy, formerly sluggish economies develop, and European governments, recognizing the historic trend of increasing productivity, are experimenting with cuts in working hours. Leisure becomes as much of a problem as work. Questions of intergenerational equity, not as yet so explicitly posed as in the United States, force their way onto political and social agendas. And the institutional challenges of the very old may test European ideals of intergenerational solidarity.

See also **The Population of Europe: Early Modern Demographic Patterns; The Population of Europe: The Demographic Transition and After; The Life Cycle** *(volume 2); and other articles in this section.*

BIBLIOGRAPHY

Andorka, Rudolf. "Household Systems and the Lives of the Old in Eighteenth- and Nineteenth-Century Hungary." In *Aging in the Past: Demography, Society, and Old Age.* Edited by David I. Kertzer and Peter Laslett. Berkeley, Los Angeles, and London, 1995. Pages 129–155.

Bois, Jean-Pierre. *Les vieux de Montaigne aux premières retraites.* Paris, 1989.

Borscheid, Peter. *Geschichte des Alters.* Münster, Germany, 1987.

Botelho, Lynn. "Aged and Impotent: Parish Relief of the Aged Poor in Early Modern Suffolk." In *Charity, Self-Interest, and Welfare in the English Past.* Edited by Martin Daunton. New York, 1996.

Bourdelais, Patrice. *Le nouvel âge de la vieillesse: Histoire du vieillissement de la population.* Paris, 1993.

Conrad, Christoph. *Vom Greis zum Rentner: Der Strukturwandel des Alters in Deutschland zwischen 1830 und 1930.* Göttingen, Germany, 1994.

Dumons, Bruno, and Gilles Pollet. *L'État et les retraités: Genèse d'une politique.* Paris, 1994.

Ehmer, Josef. *Sozialgeschichte des Alters.* Frankfurt, Germany, 1990.

Feller, Elise. "La construction sociale de la vieillesse (au cours du premier XXe siècle)." In *Histoire sociale de l'Europe: Industrialisation et société en Europe occidentale, 1880–1970.* Edited by François Guedj and Stéphane Sirot. Paris, 1997.

Gutton, Jean-Pierre. *Naissance du vieillard: Essai sur l'histoire des rapports entre les vieillards et la société en France.* Paris, 1988.

Hannah, Leslie. *Inventing Retirement: The Development of Occupational Pensions in Britain.* Cambridge, U.K., 1986.

Johnson, Paul, Christoph Conrad, and David Thomson, eds. *Workers Versus Pensioners: Intergenerational Justice in an Ageing World.* Manchester, U.K., and New York, 1989.

Johnson, Paul, and Pat Thane, eds. *Old Age from Antiquity to Post-Modernity.* London, 1998.

Kertzer, David I., and Peter Laslett, eds. *Aging in the Past: Demography, Society, and Old Age.* Berkeley, Los Angeles, and London, 1995.

Klassen, Sherri. "Old and Cared For: Place of Residence for Elderly Women in Eighteenth-Century Toulouse." *Journal of Family History* 24 (1999): 35–52.

Laslett, Peter. *A Fresh Map of Life: The Emergence of the Third Age.* Cambridge, Mass., 1991.

Macnicol, John. *The Politics of Retirement in Britain, 1878–1948.* Cambridge, U.K., 1998.

Minois, Georges. *History of Old Age: From Antiquity to the Renaissance.* Translated by Sarah Hanbury Tenison. Chicago, 1989.

Pelling, Margaret, and Richard M. Smith, eds. *Life, Death, and the Elderly: Historical Perspectives.* London, 1991.

Quadagno, Jill S. *Aging in Early Industrial Society: Work, Family, and Social Policy in Nineteenth-Century England.* New York, 1982.

Riley, James C. *Sickness, Recovery, and Death: A History and Forecast of Ill Health.* Iowa City, 1989.

Stearns, Peter N. *Old Age in European Society: The Case of France.* New York, 1976.

Stearns, Peter N., ed. *Old Age in Preindustrial Society.* New York, 1982.

Troyansky, David G. *Old Age in the Old Regime: Image and Experience in Eighteenth-Century France.* Ithaca, N.Y., and London, 1989.

GENERATIONS AND GENERATIONAL CONFLICT

Elizabeth Townsend

"Generation" is a term that indicates identity with a particular age group. Although it may refer to any age, this term has most often been associated with youth. Generation X, the Lost Generation, the Beat Generation, the "1989" generation, the Pepsi generation, the Baby Boomers, the Sixty-Eighters, the German Youth Movement, the Hitler Youth Movement, and the French bohemians are all examples of youth generations. As a term, "generation" seems familiar, easy to comprehend, self-evident. Yet "generation" can stand for a theoretical concept, a thirty-year age group in society, a student movement, a literary group of friends, a grandchild, youth at war, youth making war. This essay will explore the historical uses of the term "generation," both in social history and in related disciplines.

Generational history has been explored by social historians from several vantage points. It is not, however, an analytical staple, and may well deserve more attention than it has received. The factors that shape a generation vary with time, and generational identity is not a constant. This has been true even in the past two centuries of European history, when the generational concept has been particularly deployed.

DEFINITIONS OF GENERATIONS: BIOLOGY AND HISTORY

The study of generations can be seen as many-layered, but its basic components are the biology and history of individuals within groups. Biology refers to an individual's particular life cycle—birth, growing up, aging, and dying. History refers to the historical placement of the life lived. Historical generations are formed by combining the two. To better see how the term "generation" is used in different contexts, it might be helpful to recognize the mixture of history and biology within each type of use.

First, biological family-based generations can be seen as relationships between father, son, and grandson. Second, genealogical generations can be seen as biological generations used as markers of his-

torical time. In the most famous example, the Old Testament, one biological generation begets another to show how much time passes. Third, a generation can be seen as a group of people born around the same time (a number of painters born during the 1950s, for instance). Often these groups of people know each other (friends, schoolmates) and it is that relationship that is the focus of the study (and how that relationship affects what they do and how they view the world around them). Fourth, "generation" can be used in a broader context to understand larger societal groups. These groups are made up of individuals who do not know each other but nevertheless feel a particular bond because of the time in history that they were born and the events they have lived through.

In some instances, a person could belong to all four types of generation simultaneously. For instance, British writer Robert Graves, born in 1895, lived in a family made up of his parents, his siblings, and grandparents, an example of a biological family-based generation. One could confine a study of Graves to understanding the relationships between the generations of his family. Second, his birth could be used as a marker of the next generation of Graveses or of British upper-class society. This is what a demographer who studies populations, or a genealogist, would do. Third, historians could look at his school friends and see how they viewed the world. This study would be broader than the Graves family study, but would be confined to the relationships of the group he spent his life with. Art historians and literary historians often use the term "generation" in this way, to describe a group of artists working in the same circles, influenced by the same movements, and developing new works within the context of a group consciousness. Fourth, Robert Graves could be seen in the larger context of people born in the 1890s who served in World War I. The members of this larger generation type do not know each other, but they have common ties nevertheless. Born around the same time, they usually experienced the same kinds of events and cultural experiences growing up. Because of this, their reactions to large, often catastrophic events tend to fall within a particular range that makes them identifiable as a group. Graves identified himself as part of the World War I generation.

The concept of generation has been used as far back as the Old Testament, Homer, Herodotus, Plato, and Aristotle. Even this early, "generation" was used in a variety of ways. For instance, Genesis describes biological generations—relationships between parents and children (Adam and Eve with Cain and Abel)—and uses genealogical generations to mark time, as described above. Also, the book of Job contains elements of generational conflict, where one generation does not agree with the next. The Middle Ages with their feudal primogeniture laws of inheritance could also be seen as promoting generational study. But it was not until the nineteenth century that modern theories and examples of generations began to emerge.

THE NINETEENTH CENTURY

Before the industrial revolution, social and technological change moved slowly, with few upheavals that drastically altered circumstances from father to son to grandson. As feudal systems were replaced by capitalist and industrial societies, scientific, industrial, and democratic revolutions changed the structure of society and of historical time, including interaction within the family. Sons and daughters no longer necessarily followed the same life path as their parents and often moved away to industrial jobs or educational opportunities. Thus, the growth of generational consciousness can be seen as a by-product of the growth of industrialization, modernization, urbanization, democratization, and nationalism. Generational identity was a product of a quickly changing society, and came to be seen as synonymous with youth confronting and/or hastening that change.

By the nineteenth century, notions of progress and change had enveloped society. At this time new emphasis was placed on childbearing and childhood, and the idea emerged of "youth" as a distinct time between childhood and adulthood. This time, often spent in new cities or at universities, far from parents, gave youth a time to gather together in coffeehouses and bars, to discuss the new ideas they were being exposed to. They began forming bonds of a generational sort.

Nineteenth-century generations in this context became narrowly defined as conflictual youth movements of the male, educated elite at universities. Some of these students were political, even violent activists.

Others withdrew from society, creating their own alternative bohemian ways of life. This elite expanded during the nineteenth century to include more middle-class men, and many of the student movements rallied for greater access to education for women and for the rights of other groups in society, including peasants. The university became a site of agitation for increased democracy, and the students saw themselves as the generation to bring about that change. They longed to modernize, liberalize, democratize, and radicalize. The German student movements of 1815 and the Russian student movements of the mid-1800s exemplified this desire to change existing institutions and prevailing attitudes. What is interesting about generations is that often the "new" generation builds on the frustrations and dissatisfactions of the old "new" generation. Each successive generation builds on the success or failure of the previous generation, trying to be more modern, more industrialized, and more successful.

Post-Napoleonic student movements. In many ways, generational identity began with the defeat of Napoleon in 1815. As examples, student generations of Germany and France are polar opposites, as one responded to victory over Napoleon and the other to his defeat.

The German student movement, centered in the *Burschenschaften* (youth associations), is considered the first student revolt in western history. Anthony Esler's *Bombs, Beards, and Barricades* describes the movement, one centered on the idea of nationalism and a "united Germany." The movement involved university students, many of whom had just returned from having volunteered in the German Wars of Liberation against Napoleon (1813–1815). These young men typically came from middle-class Protestant families from northern Germany. Their anger was directed at Metternich and other politicians, for their lack of commitment to nationalist aims once the war had ended. The sense of a generation emerged as interested students formed reading groups at the universities. This segued into public demonstrations, which culminated in mass public events like the Wartburg Festival. While this generation of students did not find immediate success, their actions spurred other student movements in Germany throughout the nineteenth century, and their dreams were realized when Germany became unified in 1871.

In contrast to the post-Napoleon generation in Germany, with its activism, public protest, and dynamic leaders, the post-Napoleon generations in France took a different path. Alan Spitzer's *The French Generation of 1820* explores the incongruencies this generation felt, as they found themselves faced with a far different world than they had been prepared for. As nineteenth-century Europe faced repeated challenges of revolution and revolt, successive generations of youth came to identify with the particular cause at hand.

Anthony Elser also explores the post-Napoleon generations in France, calling them the romantic generations. The first romantic generation, of 1820, set the stage with new ways to think about and view the world, and included writers, painters, and composers like Alexandre Dumas, Honoré de Balzac, Hector Berlioz, Eugène Delacroix, Victor Hugo, and George Sand. The second romantic generation, of 1830, adopted these views and embodied the romantic way of life in dress, style, and attitude. Born around 1810, this was the first bohemian generation. Far from being militant rebels, these youth withdrew from society and created a subculture of their own. Esler describes them as the first modern counterculture.

France and Germany were not the only countries to experience the rise of generational consciousness. In Austria, a generation of 1848 made its presence known, and in Italy the youth played an important part in all steps of unification. Russia also experienced significant generational movements, as the youth sought to move the country into a more democratic era. As populist university students tried unsuccessfully to include peasants in their movement, disillusionment set in, leading to more radical actions.

Interestingly, the German Student Movement, the French bohemians, and the Russian populists were all inspired to action in part by literature. The eighteenth-century poet Johann Wolfgang von Goethe's novel *Sorrows of Young Werther* (1774) articulated the frustrations, feelings, and desires of the German students. The work has been identified by scholars as one of the first to inspire a modern generational consciousness. Joachin Whaley's "The Ideal of Youth in Late-Eighteenth-Century Germany" (Roseman, 1995), looks at the works of Goethe, J. C. F. Schiller, and Friedrich Hölderlin in generational context, noting that they reflected a Sturm und Drang generational consciousness that was adopted by subsequent generations as part of their own identity.

Like Goethe, Victor Hugo inspired a generation. His novel *Les Misérables* is supposed to have presented the first portrait of student revolutionary leaders, which became a universal type taken by subsequent student movements as models for action and style of dress. Esler describes scenes of the 1830 French bohemian generation waiting for hours to see a new play by Hugo, and emphasizes the importance of Hugo's fiction in the development of this generation's conception of itself.

In contrast to Goethe and Hugo's novels, Ivan Sergeyevich Turgenev's *Fathers and Sons* (1862) both embodied the complaints of the Russian nihilist generation and inspired individuals to act like the characters. The relationship of literature and generations continued to be important, but it changed with time. This first set of modern generations in the nineteenth century used literature as a model for their action, thoughts, and behavior.

Generational theories. As generations became identified with revolution and change, in a separate arena theories developed to explain the movement of history by identifying generations. During the nineteenth century, demographers, philosophers, and French historians took up the idea of the generation to categorize humanity, to explain larger questions of society, and to understand the impact of political changes. Auguste Comte used generations to study the "velocity" of human evolution. John Stuart Mill built on Comte's work, and also devoted a few pages to understanding the empirical laws by which society changes with each age. Émile Durkheim examined the influence of generations in times of accelerated change, particularly as men moved to urban areas, where they were less bound by traditions. Justin Dromel sought to organize French history in generational groupings, although he later abandoned the genealogical approach to the idea of collective identity. Other nineteenth-century generationalists include Antoine Cournot, Leopold von Ranke, Giuseppe Ferrari, Gustav Rümelin, Wilhelm Dilthey, Wilhelm Pinder, and Julius Peterson. But it was not until the early twentieth century that modern generational theories were developed. The two major twentieth-century theorists, who sought to understand the nature of the historical or social generation, were the Spanish philosopher José Ortega y Gasset and the Austrian-born German sociologist Karl Mannheim. They developed notions of generation that are still used by scholars today.

THE TWENTIETH CENTURY

The twentieth century also saw a change in emphasis within generations themselves. Where in the nineteenth century generations had comprised university students and young bohemian intellectuals struggling to change the culture and institutions of their society, the twentieth century saw generational identity developing around the events of war itself. For many twentieth-century generations, their identity would be forever linked with blood, death, and destruction. The World War I generation, in many ways, became the

World War I. Wounded soldiers at the Somme, 19 July 1916. IMPERIAL WAR MUSEUM, LONDON

model for the characteristics and qualities of a war generation.

World War I.

Erich Maria Remarque is the most widely read World War I generationalist. His novel *All Quiet on the Western Front* describes the war and how deeply it affected his generation. Unlike the older generations at the front, with careers and lives to return to after the war, his generation had just graduated from high school, had not begun careers, and had not married or started families. Just when his generation entered the world of adults, they marched off to fight the war. They knew nothing but war. In his novel, Remarque wonders how they will ever fit back into society. He contrasts his generation with the schoolteachers who preached to them of the honor and glory of war—Remarque's generation had believed their teachers and felt betrayed. His parents and grandparents' generations were no better than the schoolteachers; they sat at home gossiping about the war, seeing it more as a chess game than as the reality Remarque's generation experienced. Finally, Remarque describes the generation too young to fight as strong and confident, unblemished by war, which has crippled and worn out his own generation.

A number of scholars, including Robert Wohl, Paul Fussell, Samuel Hynes, and Eric Leeds, have looked at this World War I generation. The genera-

tion itself produced many novels and memoirs, including Robert Graves's *Goodbye to All That,* Vera Brittain's *Testament of Youth,* Edmund Blunden's *Undertones of War,* Irene Rathbone's *We That Were Young,* and R. C. Sherriff's *Journey's End.* Compared to the nineteenth-century generations, which used literature as a battle cry, the war generation used literature as a healing process for their wounds. Instead of looking to others for models, they wrote stories of their own war experiences. Their literature solidified their identity as a generation.

Out of the aftermath of World War I, Hitler and Mussolini, who both identified themselves as part of the war generation, used the fuel of their broken generation to embark upon their rise to power. The Hitler Youth Movement in Nazi Germany created an institutional identity for a new generation of youth. In this way, generational identity became a tool for military might. One could say that the British had tried this earlier in the century, after they realized they had been unprepared for the Boer War. They started the Boy Scouts to produce men who were fit and healthy for military service in the future. By the 1930s, generational identity was being used as an institutional tool of political control in both Germany and Italy. Literature also played a role in the formation of generations in fascist Europe, in the form of propaganda promoting appropriate behavior and views.

This institutional generation faced reconstruction of generational identity upon Germany's defeat in World War II. Alexander von Plato, Dagmar Reese, and Michael Buddrus have written about the difficulty of this transition in a collection of essays edited by Mark Roseman entitled *Generations in Conflict: Youth Revolt and Generation Formation in Germany 1770–1968.*

World War II. World War II produced identifiable generations associated with resistance, occupation, allies, and Holocaust survivors. In identifying one's own generation age was less important than the activities one was involved in, and the generational aspect played less of a role than in previous instances. And yet, views on politics and visions of what the postwar world should look like were deeply colored by one's generational perspective. Henry Rousso describes this phenomenon in *The Vichy Syndrome: History and Memory in France since 1944.* Angela Dalle Vacche also describes a generational progression of visions of Italy's past in *The Body in the Mirror: Shapes of History in Italian Cinema.* Neither book foregrounds generations as the motivation behind changes in history, but both recognize that with each generation new influences arise and a rewriting of history takes place. In some way, these books mimic the place generation holds in the post–World War II era. No longer the

individuals central focus, as in the nineteenth and early twentieth century, the concept of generation is nevertheless still present.

The 1960s marked a resurgence of generational identity and conflict in Europe and America. The 1970s found scholars once again interested in writing about generations, both describing current events as well as investigating past generations. Like the nineteenth-century student movements, the May 1968 student rebellion in Paris and the other student movements throughout Europe and the United States signaled a return to the activist university population, out to change the institutions and culture of society. A great deal has been written on the subject. Ronald Fraser's *1968: A Student Generation in Revolt,* using interviews with participants in the 1968 revolts as a basis, compares the rebellion in six countries: the United States, West Germany, France, Italy, Britain, and Northern Ireland. Esler and Lewis Feuer also devote chapters to the 1968 student uprisings in their studies of student movements. In relationship to literature, scholar John Hazlett sees the generation as writing their autobiographies and forming their generational identity in the midst of the events themselves, a process he traces in *My Generation: Collective Autobiography and Identity Politics.*

In the late twentieth century the notion of generational identity was embraced by American adver-

Institutional Generational Identity. German youth march in Berlin, 1934. UPI/CORBIS-BETTMANN

tisers, who targeted baby boomers and generation X, for example, in their ad campaigns. But unlike earlier generations, centered around activist activities or around war and other types of catastrophic events, these generations were centered around consumerism and economics. In "The 'Generation of 1989': A New Political Generation?" Claus Leggewie demonstrates the difficulties of discussing these generations in the terms used to describe earlier generations.

Leggewie discusses the fall of the Berlin Wall in 1989, which should have been a marker of identity for a new generation of youth. The participants, however, were well established, middle-aged professionals who, instead of coming from a common socioeconomic background, represented all kinds of social movements, the church, the governing classes, and artistic and intellectual groups. If they were a generation in the previously accepted sense, this group might be called the "eighty-niners," but they do not fit the traditional profile of youth in conflict and revolution. So, instead of looking at the cohort that toppled the wall, Leggewie turns his attention to the youth in 1989, to see if he can fit them into the category of generation. Leggewie's concentration on youth points to the self-inflicted inflexibility felt by those using generation as a category. The youth of 1989 were not active participants, but instead experienced the events as a "community of TV consumers." No longer conflict or war generations, the new generations are defined by their consumerism. This change in orientation in how generations are defined can be seen particularly in studies of the baby boomers and generation X.

APPLICABILITY BY
SOCIAL CLASS AND GENDER

Robert Wohl, in *The Generation of 1914*, sets out the three elements necessary for a historical generation: age, common experiences, and self-conscious identity as part of a generation. Neither social class nor gender is included in this or any other of the standard definitions of generation. Yet the well-known generational studies have concentrated on upper-middle-class, educated male youth during particular times of cultural and political societal change. Charles Rosen's *The Romantic Generation* provides an example. In his preface, Rosen explains that he excludes women composers from his study because their work and their notoriety are not sufficiently up to the standards of the more well known men composers of the 1820s and 1830s.

Generational histories of war have also focused primarily on men. War brings specific generational identity not merely to those who fight in the battles, but to those who are children during the war, those who care for the combatants, and those who wait, worry, and pray for the safe return of loved ones. Lynne Hanley's *Writing War: Fiction, Gender, and Memory* explores this theme. Parents, grandparents, and children too young to participate all have experiences, specific to the historical period, that could be categorized from a generational perspective. Too often, though, only the soldiers have been studied.

Feminist scholars have not readily used the generational structure either. Jennifer E. Milligan's *The Forgotten Generation: French Women Writers of the Interwar Period* presents one example. Her study looks at women writing during the interwar period, regardless of age, to reinscribe them into history. One of her goals is to provide the missing links of collective identity and continuity in women's writings. But her work does not look at a group of women of a particular age, experience, or self-consciousness. Rather she focuses on the writings of women during a period of time, without regard to their historical generational identity. Mark Roseman's 1995 collection *Generations in Conflict: Youth Revolt and Generation Formation in Germany 1770–1968,* includes two essays specifically on women and generation, as well as essays on Jewish political generational identity, and working-class generational identity. While these essays constitute a good beginning, more studies of generational identity in a myriad of groups are needed to understand better the relationship between class, gender, and generational group formation.

FAMILY-BASED BIOLOGICAL
GENERATIONS AS HISTORICAL

For a long time, historians felt that the biological categories of parent, child, and grandchild were ahistorical. Generational histories could not be based on these categories, because no definitive dates existed for clumping people together. Every day a new child is born, making it impossible to distinguish between one historical generation and the next.

And yet, the story of the family within a historical framework has provided a great deal of interest, especially in the form of memoirs and novels. These stories take intergenerational experiences as their focus, shedding light onto larger, historical generations. These types of works provide the opportunity to view generations without focusing on the

The Romantic Generation. *Franz Liszt at the Piano,* painting (1840) by Josef Danhauser. Inspired by the leading romantics of the early nineteenth century, Lord Byron (the portrait in the center) and Ludwig van Beethoven (the bust above the piano), Liszt plays for the leading romantics of the mid-nineteenth century: the French writers Alexandre Dumas and George Sand (wearing men's clothing) *(seated at left),* and the French writer Victor Hugo and the composers Niccolò Paganini and Gioacchino Rossini. On the floor next to the piano with her back to the viewer is Liszt's mistress, Marie-Cathérine-Sophie d'Agoult; their daughter Cosima later married the leading romantic composer of the next generation, Richard Wagner. STAATLICHE MUSEEN ZU BERLIN/ BILDARCHIV PREUSSISCHER KULTURBESITZ, BERLIN

male elite of society. In fact, many of the most prominent works of this kind have focused on the relationships between mother, daughter, and granddaughter. The most famous of these is American novelist Amy Tan's *The Joy Luck Club* (1989). European examples also exist. British writer Vera Brittain's *Honourable Estate* (1936) documented in fictional form three generations of her family and the place of women in society—in the suffrage movement, in marriage, in politics, and in war. Her novel *Born 1925: A Novel of Youth* (1948) explores the relationship between a World War I veteran who began as a pacifist with the next generation's desire to participate in World War II. Marianne Fredriksson's novel *Hanna's Daughters: A Novel of Three Generations* (1998) spans one hundred years of Scandinavian history and looks at the relationship of mother, daughter, and granddaughter in terms of the interrelationship of choices and opportunities for each.

Another interesting development in generational studies comes from Holocaust scholars, who use the family-based biological category of generation to understand the impact of the Holocaust survivors' experiences on their children and grandchildren. In this way, generational studies look beyond the generation that experienced events firsthand to see what impact their memoirs and experiences have on the next generations.

SOCIAL HISTORY: APPROACHES TO GENERATION

Social historians tend to rely on Karl Mannheim and José Ortega's concepts of generation as the basis for their work. These early-twentieth-century theorists tried to determine the parameters of what makes up a generation. Building on their work, Alan Spitzer, Robert Wohl, Anthony Esler, Lewis Feuer, and Hans Jaeger are among scholars who have investigated the concept of generation. Anthony Esler has quantitatively done the most work on generation, covering a wide variety of subjects, including an introductory history to the concept. Spitzer's "The Historical Problem of Generations," and Jaeger's "Generations in History: Reflections on a Controversial Concept" survey the work on historical generations, and are critical to understanding generation scholarship. Both pieces look at Mannheim and Ortega's theories in the context of other studies on generations.

Robert Wohl and Alan Spitzer both conducted studies on specific generations that led to a deeper exploration into the meaning and theory of generation. In particular, Robert Wohl's work looks at the development of the concept of generation in theoretical terms, and includes detailed chapters on Ortega and Mannheim. Anthony Esler and Lewis Feuer have each written substantial survey works on student and youth generations over the last two hundred years.

Bloomsbury. Virginia Woolf (1882–1941), seated before a fresco by her sister, Vanessa Bell (1879–1961). Woolf and Bell were daughters of Sir Leslie Stephen (1832–1904), the English critic and biographer. © GISELE FREUND/PHOTO RESEARCHERS

OTHER DISCIPLINES AND APPROACHES TO GENERATIONS

Generational historians look at groups of people born around the same time who experienced similar events and circumstances that informed a generational consciousness. But, as this essay points out, the notion of generation has been used in other ways as well, both by historians and in other disciplines.

Artistic and literary scholars have often used the term "generation" when describing a particular art or literary movement—usually referring to a group of friends or people that knew each other. Their point is to confine their study to those who created a particular genre of art. Generation is a structure that helps them define the parameters of their project. Although literary and artistic groups are found throughout both the modern and pre-modern periods, these twentieth-century scholars have conceived of such groups within a generational context.

Samuel Hynes's *The Auden Generation* depicts a group of friends that developed a prominent British literary movement during the 1930s. Hynes is not concerned with depicting a larger historical generation (such as the war generation) nor is he concerned with intergenerational relationships within the individuals' families. Yet for Hynes the concept of generation is important in defining his project. He begins by defining a literary generation born within a particular range of years (between 1900–1914), who developed with a particular consciousness and in particular circumstances. Although his project aims to better understand English culture during the 1930s, he confines his study to this small group.

Charles Rosen's *The Romantic Generation* presents examples in the field of music. He studies the music of composers whose style was defined in the 1820s and 1830s, including Frédéric Chopin, Franz Liszt, Hector Berlioz, Felix Mendelssohn, and Robert Schumann. He suggests that after Beethoven's death in 1827, this new generation gained a sense of freedom from his shadow. Rosen deliberately excludes

Giuseppe Verdi and Richard Wagner, because their musical style became fully developed in the 1840s, rather than in the 1820s and 1830s. He seeks to understand how these composers' music is bound to the literature and science of their time.

Leon Edel's *Bloomsbury: A House of Lions* is a biography of the Bloomsbury group, which included Virginia Woolf, Leonard Woolf, Clive Bell, Virginia's sister Vanessa Bell, Lytton Strachey, John Maynard Keynes, Duncan Grant, and Roger Fry. Although Edel never identifies this group as a generation, his work parallels the generational studies of Rosen and Hynes. He presents a group of artists (some family-related) who worked within the same cultural context, were born around the same period, and grew up under the same circumstances. Thus, Edel looks at the Bloomsbury group in what might be called a generational perspective.

Finally, Gertrude Stein's "Lost Generation" in 1920s Paris is an interesting case. The famous label is supposed to identify a generation lost because of their experiences in World War I. However, a number of the most prominent members of this Lost Generation never actually fought in the war. They might more appropriately be called the "expatriate generation." *Sylvia Beach and the Lost Generation: A History of Literary Paris in the Twenties and Thirties* by Noel Riley Fitch chronicles the world surrounding Shakespeare and Company, Beach's English bookstore and lending library located in Paris. Like Edel, Hynes, and Rosen, Fitch sets out to paint a portrait of a group of artists, including Ernest Hemingway, William Carlos Williams, James Joyce, and Ezra Pound.

Sociologists and other social scientists study generations as well. In both his 1951 dissertation, *The Cohort Approach,* and his 1965 essay, *The Cohort as a Concept in the Study of Social Change,* Norman Ryder was the first to substitute the word "cohort" for generations. Usually using birth-years as a marker, Ryder pointed out in his essay that a cohort can be defined by an infinite number of markers, such as marriage year, graduation year, or even all those who published a novel in a particular year or set of years. He discarded the notion of a collective generational self-consciousness, pointing to the homogeneity within a cohort group. Yet he believed that cohorts powered social change. Cohorts are determined by temporal, rather than qualitative, subjective data. In 1997 Melissa A. Hardy compiled a series of sociological essays, *Studying Aging and Social Change,* beginning with classic essays by Mannheim and Ryder, and including later developments in specific sociological areas of cohort analysis, aging, and social change.

Other disciplines that use the concept of generations are anthropology and gerontology. The life-course approach focuses on shared experiences at particular stages in life. Life-course scholars focus on all stages of life, rather than the narrow focus on youth often taken by generation scholars. Life-course scholars often, but not exclusively, use a biographical approach to their subjects. Age-groups and age-systems are a related area of study used by sociologists, anthropologists, gerontologists, and other scholars. An example of such studies is *The Changing Contract across Generations* (1993), edited by V. L. Bengston and W. A. Achenbaum.

CONCLUSION

Generational studies tend to track change—whether within families, over long historical periods in the form of statistics, in small intimate groups, or in large social groups. Change is often created by the generation's reaction to larger events that have changed their circumstances within society. Generations can be active artistic and political movements, or they can be passive or consumer groups. What they have in common is that they alert us to some kind of change. They are like barometers measuring the pressure of change on society, yet they also exert pressure, influencing the particular changes a society makes in its institutions and culture.

See also other articles in this section.

BIBLIOGRAPHY

Baird, Allen Jan. *Family Life Course and the Economic Status of Birth Cohorts: The United States and Western Europe, 1950–1976.* New York, 1989.

Bertman, Stephen, ed. *The Conflict of Generations in Ancient Greece and Rome.* Amsterdam, 1976.

Esler, Anthony. *Bombs, Beards, and Barricades: 150 Years of Youth in Revolt.* New York, 1971.

Esler, Anthony. *Generations in History: An Introduction to the Concept.* N.p., 1982.

Feuer, Lewis S. *The Conflict of Generations: The Character and Significance of Student Movements.* New York, 1969.

Furness, Raymond. *Zarathustra's Children: A Study of a Last Generation of German Writers.* Rochester, N.Y., 2000.

Hass, Aaron. *In the Shadow of the Holocaust: The Second Generation.* Ithaca, N.Y., 1990.

Hazlett, John Downton. *My Generation: Collective Autobiography and Identity Politics.* Madison, Wis., 1998.

Herlihy, David. "The Generation in Medieval History." *Viator* 5 (1974): 347–364.

Hynes, Samuel. *The Auden Generation: Literature and Politics in England in the 1930s.* London, 1976.

Jaeger, Hans. "Generations in History: Reflections on a Controversial Concept." *History and Theory* 24, no. 3 (1985): 273–292.

Leggewie, Claus. "The 'Generation of 1989': A New Political Generation?" In *Rewriting the German Past: History and Identity in the New Germany.* Edited by Reinhard Alter and Peter Monteath. New Jersey, 1997.

Mannheim, Karl. "The Problem of Generations." In *Studying Aging and Social Change: Conceptual and Methodological Issues.* Edited by Melissa A. Hardy. Thousand Oaks, Calif., 1997.

Marías, Julián. *Generations: A Historical Method.* Translated by Harold C. Raley. University, Ala., 1967.

Mushaben, Joyce Marie. *From Post-War to Post-Wall Generations: Changing Attitudes towards the National Question and NATO in the Federal Republic of Germany.* Boulder, Colo., 1998.

Passerini, Luisa. *Autobiography of a Generation: Italy, 1968.* Translated by Lisa Erdberg. Hanover, N.H., 1996.

Pilkington, Hilary, ed. *Gender, Generation, and Identity in Contemporary Russia.* London and New York, 1996.

Roseman, Mark, ed. *Generations in Conflict: Youth Revolt and Generation Formation in Germany 1770–1968.* Cambridge, U.K., 1995.

Spitzer, Alan B. *The French Generation of 1820.* Princeton, N.J., 1987.

Spitzer, Alan B. "The Historical Problem of Generations." *American Historical Review* 78:5 (1973): 1353–1385.

Winston, Stuart Conrad. *Hemingway's France: Images of the Lost Generation.* San Francisco, 2000.

Wohl, Robert. *The Generation of 1914.* Cambridge, Mass., 1979.

Section 16

SEXUALITY

SEXUAL BEHAVIOR AND SEXUAL MORALITY

Lisa Z. Sigel

Two conflicting beliefs dominate discussions about sexuality. On the one hand, people think sexuality is innate and unchanging. On the other hand, many believe that Freud's era brought sexual diversity. Neither is in fact true. Although sexuality might appear inherent, historians have shown that it, like most aspects of human life, has developed over time. Sexual behaviors, orientations, and identities and even the understanding of the fundamentals of physiology have been shaped and molded by historical factors. Rather than being intrinsic to the individual, sexuality is affected by everything from food production and family systems to social class and psychological theories. In turn, rather than being segregated into a small and private area of people's lives, sexuality has shaped historical processes from systems of governance to styles of worship.

In excavating these patterns, historians have confronted the second misconception that dominates popular perceptions about sexuality. Many people believe that men worked, women stayed home, and a combination of "nature" and the church constrained sexual behaviors until the 1960s. Sexual diversity, including single motherhood, sexual experimentation, and homosexuality, supposedly began in the twentieth century. This cluster of beliefs formed a progressing narrative from repression to liberation that Michel Foucault decisively undermined in his series on sexuality. To help understand the past on its own terms, historians demonstrated that sexuality is neither static nor easily influenced. The reciprocal process between large social forces and the formation of the individual at his or her most basic level makes the history of sexuality particularly important to social historians who try to understand the relationship between individual choice and broad social change.

To document sexuality in the past, historians have grappled with gaps in the sources and learned to use sources in new ways. Traditional sources, like government documents, newspapers, and memoirs, tend to say little about sexual practices. In spite of the centrality of sexuality to people's lives, few individuals wrote about their sexual desires or sexual activities, and those who did often fit their experiences into pre-existing narratives about temptation, love, or adventure. In addition the proportionally small category of literate people who left accounts of their lives, sexual or otherwise, were overwhelmingly from the aristocracy or bourgeoisie, which makes their documents exceptional rather than representative. The literacy campaigns of the nineteenth century did not focus on individual self-expression. When working-class people began to write their own stories, few wrote their sexual stories in any detail, and even fewer disregarded the morality campaigns that made sexual acts something to regret. Thus memoirs and autobiographies reveal little about sexuality for the majority of the population. Historians have had to resourcefully overcome these gaps in the sources.

Historians have augmented firsthand accounts with legal codes, criminal records, literature, art, medical tracts, and psychiatric testimonies. When using such sources, historians learned to read them as carefully constructed narratives that reveal as much about social expectations and prejudice as actual behaviors. Thus women who abandoned their children at foundling homes told careful stories of their own sexual experiences to fit with the demands of charity. Few bragged about their sexual exploits, instead relying on stories of seduction and abandonment. Decoding such information offers hints rather than certainties about people's lives. While social historians have learned a great deal about how Europeans saw themselves, their bodies, and their sexual partners, correlating thought with deed and belief with practice has proven difficult. Charting the history of sexuality is no easy task, and despite the proliferation of fascinating accounts, much work remains.

THE RENAISSANCE

One of the first findings people need to confront about the history of sexuality is the frequently overlooked tie between sexuality and reproduction. Because sexual reproduction in the twentieth century was a choice and generally a positive choice at that, the lack of choice makes sexuality in the premodern world look a bit dismal. The limits on birth control and abortion made sexual intercourse fraught with economic and social consequences. The differences among European societies are the second issue that deserves consideration. Region, religion, social class, and urban or rural settings all effect patterns of sexual morality and behaviors and make universal generalizations impossible. Nonetheless, some broad patterns are discernable, and after the shock of sexual limitations, the ways that sexuality worked in European society before the twentieth century seem flexible, even though the constraints that influenced individuals and society were different than those operating in the twentieth century.

The church, the family, and the community were the three main regulators of sexual morality in the premodern world. The Catholic Church before the Reformation provided a theological basis for sexual standards across western Europe, even if the interpretation and implementation of theology varied from region to region. The standards set by the church included celibacy and sex within marriage. St. Paul, in his famous injunction that "it is better to marry than to burn," provided an illustration of the Catholic model of sexuality. Christian society saw sexuality as a powerful force that needed to be eliminated or, if that was unfeasible, channeled into marital procreation. Although priests continued to marry and have concubines until the eleventh century, by the Renaissance the church had developed a more uniform standard of sexual restriction.

In practice the family and the community saw to much of the informal and daily policing of sexual behaviors, working to maintain economic and social stability. The community regulated premarital and extramarital intercourse as well as nonprocreative intercourse, like bestiality and homosexuality. Because most Europeans lived in agricultural communities and depended for their livelihoods on the land—a limited and often unpredictable resource—they tended to delay marriage, a pattern which encouraged the curtailment of sexual activity generally. Women experienced menarche or onset of menses in their late teens, and the community further shortened their procreative years by not marrying them off until their mid-twenties. Most women went through menopause in their early forties, creating a window of roughly a decade and a half of fertility. Women spaced their reproduction through prolonged lactation after childbirth, herbal remedies, and mechanical devices.

By limiting reproduction, families sought to conserve their resources and thus to guarantee generational stability. But reproduction remained critical to the agricultural community. Thus premarital sexuality was tolerated in many areas when it was clearly "premarital." Often the community allowed couples some sexual interactions once a marital contract or promise was established. In some regions in Germany and the Low Countries, a couple married only when the woman proved her fertility by becoming pregnant. The lack of other economic options guaranteed that the suitor would fulfill his promise and honor his implicit contract.

The demands of survival in closely knit agricultural communities encouraged careful regulation of other sexual practices as well. The charivari, for example, disciplined extramarital affairs. Bands of young men paraded through the streets, stopped at the houses of cuckolds or May-December marriages, and demanded payment in coin. The community called attention to sexual deviance and insisted on sexual standards and sexual reform. The charivari also provided young men yet unable to marry with an outlet for their resentments against those who already enjoyed sexual relations.

Often the church and community worked together to police sexual morality. Although medieval legends attributed the origins of the Danish royal family to the sexual congress of a farm girl and a wild bear, by the sixteenth and seventeenth centuries such legends of human-animal copulation, no longer suggestive of strength and virility, rapidly went out of favor. The church proclaimed bestiality a sin against nature, and the community responded with surveillance and turned perpetrators over to religious and state authorities. In seventeenth- and eighteenth-century Sweden cases of bestiality accounted for 25 to 35 percent of capital punishments, and even more men were sentenced to flogging, hard labor, and church penalties. Because herding was a young boy's occupation and milking was the labor of women, the Swedish community grew wary of interactions between adult men and animals, often watching at chinks in the barn and examining men's clothes for evidence of inappropriate animal matter. Families, servants, and friends were so horrified at finding perpetrators that they experienced fits and seizures and felt polluted. Wives of bestial men worried that they would give birth to monsters, and even the perpetrators believed they needed to practice coitus interruptus lest their sperm impregnate animals. Although the church set the doctrine, the community and the family regulated the individual.

In eastern Europe a similar cooperation between the church, the state, and the community controlled

Courting. A *veillée,* or evening gathering, offers opportunity for young people to show their affection for one another, to the accompaniment of rough music. Engraving, eighteenth century. BIBLIOTHÈQUE NATIONALE, PARIS

sexuality. Slavs did not become Christian until much later than western Europeans, but by the Renaissance paganism had been curtailed, at least on the surface, in eastern Europe. The Orthodox Church, which dominated a large part of eastern Europe, concurred with the Catholic Church in a number of important aspects of its conception of sexuality. Virginity and abstinence were favored in both variants of Christianity, though Orthodox religion stressed abstinence even within marriage. While Slavs recognized the relationship between intercourse and conception, they separated sexual desire, which came from the devil, from procreation, which was a blessing from God. Sexual impulses came from outside humanity and only brought evil to the individual and the community. In contrast, western Europe saw a rise of romantic and courtly love from the twelfth century onward that legitimated sexual impulses. Slavs tended not to connect love with sexual desire. Instead love remained tied to generosity rather than physicality, at least until the importation of Western culture by Peter the Great. However, the apparent harshness of these beliefs was tempered by a greater pragmatism than in the West. Orthodox theology judged on the basis of actions rather than thoughts, allowing individuals a less stringent standard of observance. Furthermore, while ideals for behavior remained high, expectations of observance remained low. Orthodox priests could marry even though celibacy remained the ideal.

In Mediterranean cities the traditional protectors of sexual morality, most notably the family, the community, and the peer group, were weakened by urban anonymity, economic opportunities, and population change. City life offered more room for sexual variation than did life in the village. Population losses from the plague encouraged the migration of the young with their unruly desires to urban areas, where they encountered a proliferation of prostitutes, courtesans, slaves, and servants and opportunities for seduction, fornication, and gratification of homosexual desire. These sexual options particularly benefited young noblemen, who could gratify their sexual desires down the social hierarchy with little interference. Although a woman could use sexuality as a way to influence her life course by copulating with a man on the understanding that it would cement their future marriage, the repercussions of the loss of virginity if such a method failed made the strategy quite dangerous.

Women were often victims of circumstances and status. Postpubescent women had far fewer opportunities than their male coevals, because society believed they should be daughters, wives, or widows, though even the last carried a certain instability. The

Ideals of Marriage. *The Arnolfini Betrothal,* painting (1434) by Jan van Eyck (before 1395–1441). NATIONAL GALLERY, LONDON/ALINARI/ART RESOURCE, NY

other option for those whose families could afford it was joining a nunnery. That route did not always guarantee an end to sexual intercourse, as cases of nuns bearing children demonstrate. But even without actual intercourse the rhetoric of the church made nuns brides of Christ and infused spiritual life with sexual meanings. Life in the nunnery thus mirrored life outside the nunnery in its understanding of women as sexual creatures, even though it granted them a greater opportunity for autonomy. In the secular world marriage and the family continued as the

central institutions upholding social stability, and city governments stepped in to guarantee the smooth functioning of those institutions. In cases of rape, seduction, and fornication, for example, the Venetian government often demanded that the perpetrator supply the woman's dowry and marry her or serve time in jail. The government assured that sexually active women did not become a burden on society by guaranteeing them a place within the institution of marriage. While urbanization and trade offered more opportunities for sexual congress, the ideals of marriage and family as the central organizing principles that guaranteed stability remained intact.

Paradoxically, the Protestant Reformation ended the sacrament of marriage but elevated the importance of marriage within society. Protestant theologians argued that celibacy brought hypocrisy rather than spiritual enlightenment and that all should marry, including clerics. Conflicts over sexuality and gender formed an important component of Protestant criticism of the Catholic Church. Their attacks on Catholicism emphasized the irregularities of contemporary moral life and encouraged the purification of society. Clerics railed against prostitution and in many places expelled prostitutes for the frequency of their sinning, while they generally only fined their clients. The metaphor of the whore as a symbol of evil spread beyond women, and the pope became known as the archwhore in antipapal polemics. In these polemics sexual irregularities and sexual chaos caused by the inappropriate insistence on celibacy in the Catholic Church were contrasted with proper Protestant sexuality regulated by the family. In regions that became Protestant, the end of the monastery, priesthood, and nunnery brought the reintegration of the spiritual into the familial world.

The opportunities for female autonomy and asexuality guaranteed by the nunnery ceased in the Protestant world and diminished even in the Catholic world, which tightened the constraints around nuns in reaction to the Protestant Reformation. The Reformation insisted that all women existed within a sexual domain and that all should be placed under the hierarchy of the family. In the realm of symbols, the Protestants deemphasized the Virgin Mary, who had allowed a place for the mysteries of sexuality to receive a measure of contemplation, and, their suppression of the cults of both male and female saints—whose sexual renunciation, even if fictive, had often been a facet of their spiritual ascension—diminished the variety of available religious symbols. By minimizing Mary's place in theological discussions, removing the saints from contemplation, and eliminating the option of separate, celibate life as a spiritual path, Protestant theologians left procreative, marital sexuality as the most viable model for synthesizing spirituality with sexuality.

While mainstream Protestant thought used rhetoric about sexuality to distinguish itself from Catholicism, it maintained a sexual morality linked to the family and community. Familial control of sexuality characterized premodern social regulation across the Orthodox, Catholic, and Protestant worlds. Even in rapidly changing urban environments, the family and community were the central institutions impos-

ing sexual morality. The church and government reinforced the family and community in the maintenance of sexual stability even though religion and systems of governance varied from region to region. The insistence on stability implies a recognition that sexuality could bring economic, cultural, and social chaos. The sheer force and power attributed to sexuality as a disruptive agent demonstrates its centrality to the Renaissance world.

THE ENLIGHTENMENT

Although the Enlightenment questioned established belief in the area of sexuality, the period experienced a tightening of legislation and a criminal crackdown on perceived deviance in sexual and gender roles. For example, the eighteenth century saw a reaction against

Prostitution. Anonymous woodcut on the title page to the French edition of *Amsterdam's Whoredom,* (The Hague, 1694). KONINKIJKE BIBLIOTHEEK, THE HAGUE, THE NETHERLANDS

sodomite practices. In the Dutch Republic a total of forty-four executions took place between 1233 and 1729, but roughly two hundred executions were carried out between 1729 and 1803. The most enlightened areas, including France, Britain, and the Netherlands, experienced the harshest administration of such laws.

Historians have debated the causes of the criminalization of sexual deviants and the relationship between sexual conservatism and Enlightenment thought. In general they tie changes in enforcement of sexual norms to the increased reliance on biology and science, on the ways that sexuality stood in for discussions of traditional authority (such as in the attribution of sexual immoralities to authorities of the ancien régime), and on new forms of gender differentiation. The application of reason to human behavior was supposed to clarify and expose where human nature ended and cultural forms began, allowing society to strip away those perversions that impeded its progress. Instead of presenting firm conclusions, the Enlightenment encouraged European society to question. The church's relationship to sexuality, the sanctity of marriage, and the relationship between the sexes could no longer be accepted as given, but all became subject to critical inquiry. As the Enlightenment stripped away the legitimacy of old authorities, it enthroned new ones, such as reason, nature, freedom, and the individual, that shaped in both constructive and destructive ways people's sexual options.

Most historians see the Enlightenment as a time when gender and sexual norms underwent radical revisions. Thomas Laqueur has shown that before the eighteenth century biological sexuality was conceptualized as a matter of degree. During the Enlightenment the sexes became antithetical, and gender became wedded to biological sex. In medical texts and anatomical drawings female genitalia began to look distinct from male genitals rather than as internal versions of male organs. Along with their new look, female genitals gained their own nomenclature, like ovary and vagina, rather than derivatives from male organs, like stones and shafts. The egg became a miniature version of the female, passive, waiting, and monogamous, while sperm became the active agent of reproduction. Science ceased to see maleness and femaleness as related in a hierarchy of perfectability and instead began to examine them as wedded to an incontrovertible biology. Women could not become men through the sudden descent of a penis because women and men were constitutionally different from the ovaries outward.

As science differentiated male from female on the basis of biology, social philosophers like Jean-Jacques Rousseau and Mary Wollstonecraft Godwin emphasized the innate differences between the sexes. These authors overturned the traditional ideas that women were the more lusty partners and instead emphasized their maternal urges. Both writers argued that social fripperies and sexual intrigues led women astray, although their conclusions about how to provide women with a meaningful role in society differed. Wollstonecraft put forth a program of education for women that would allow women to develop their potential outside of sexuality. If given the chance, women could put aside coquetry and vanity and contribute to a sound home and a sounder society. Rousseau, on the other hand, believed that women should stay in the home and follow their maternal impulses. Education would harm women and lead society astray. As this example demonstrates, Enlightenment thought did not provide a single, clear line on sexuality or procreation but provided an impetus for debate and argument.

These debates, which took place in reading groups or clubs and through essay prizes (a common Enlightenment convention), centered on ways to differentiate the natural sexual drive from sensuality. Essay prizes encouraged extended discussions on topics like masturbation (1785), sexual control (1788), the ruination of servants (1790), and celibacy (1791), the last apparently funded by the king of England. And as Isabel V. Hull pointed out, the reading groups, clubs, and lodges that formed the foundation of a German civil society during the Enlightenment took sexuality seriously as an avenue for thought. Extended explorations of the "normal" preoccupied these groups, and the main concerns of citizenship, adulthood, character, and marriage overlapped with the issue of sexual maturity, potency, and restraint. Even the issues of abnormality, in particular masturbation and infanticide, became grounds by which to differentiate the positive effects of marital procreation from the sexual degeneracy associated with absolutist and aristocratic ruin. The discussion and elaboration of sexual standards thus played a pivotal role in the formation of a German civil society.

In France the relationship between sexuality and politics received even greater scrutiny. The Enlightenment's questioning of tradition opened clerical, aristocratic, and absolutist norms to debate. European aristocratic society was more sexually permissive than other classes. Extramarital affairs, concubinage, sexual clubs, intellectual salons, early marriage, and early widowhood allowed both male and female aristocrats a great deal of leeway for sexual dalliances. Enlightenment thinkers used those pleasures as a way to delegitimize traditional authority by focusing on the themes of corruption, profligacy, and the pitfalls of the social hierarchy. The disavowal of tradition, however, did not function just as a thinly veiled class-based attack on aristocratic behavior and privilege. In fact, the aristocracy who benefited sexually from their social privileges were often at the forefront of Enlightenment intellectual life, and thus party to the process of defining new forms of liberty. Aristocratic women provided the philosophes with financial, political, and social support and used their salons to popularize radical ideas and to encourage intellectual life. The philosophes' writings on sexuality took multiple forms, including attacks on religion and the sexual profligacy of clerics, mockery of the monarch's sexual peccadilloes, philosophic inquiries into the nature of sexuality, and anticlerical and antimonarchal pornography, which encouraged rethinking traditional sources of authority over sexuality. The French government saw the implicit threat in these philosophic and sexual writings and responded by outlawing them. Philosophes and pornographers were drawn closer together as they sought to escape prosecution and to earn profits from their writings. The combination of high political philosophy and low pornographic innuendo became a powerful way of stirring public opinion and fomenting change.

The changes inspired by such works took numerous directions. The Enlightenment encouraged freethinking, as the example of the English radical Richard Carlile demonstrates. Carlile advocated birth control so both men and women could engage in sexual intercourse and pleasure without fear. On the other hand, the marquis de Sade took liberty and freethinking to its most radical conclusions. His version of untrammeled liberty in sexuality meant that the pursuit of pleasures and liberties should allow no barriers, including the recognition of the personhood of others. The emphasis on reason and freethinking allowed people to reconsider the impact of sexuality on the individual outside of the traditional restraints of family, the church, and the community; from this starting-point, individuals arrived at radically different conclusions.

Freethinking in matters of sexuality and politics overlapped in low circles as well as in the salon. John Gillis has demonstrated that plebeians followed a pattern of informal marriage that received legitimacy from Enlightenment debates. Elites institutionalized marriage in the eighteenth century and attempted to impose new standards of betrothal, ceremonies, and bastardy on English society. However, plebeians resisted this imposition, and between the late eighteenth century and the early nineteenth century informal marriages reached new heights. In resisting marriage

fees and clerical control over marriage, individuals avoided religious and political control over sexuality. They wedded and bedded according to their own dictates. Informal marriage and equally informal divorce were popular practices that Enlightenment thinkers followed rather than initiated. In advocating individual freedom to marry and divorce based solely on affection, Enlightenment and revolutionary thinkers like Thomas Paine articulated patterns of sexual freethinking already in place.

Paine justified his marital freethinking and his own de facto divorce with the model of Native American practices. The establishment of empires after the Age of Discovery allowed the European world much greater contact, however unequal, with regions throughout the Atlantic world and across the globe. The vast cultural differences between Europe and other regions gave rise to speculation on the state of nature, and many Europeans contrasted their own decadent society with the supposedly more primitive and natural societies abroad. European philosophes used travel narratives, like Denis Diderot's *Supplément au voyage de Bougainville* (written 1772, published 1796), and their own fantastical portrayals to discuss sexuality in nature as a way to undercut cultural corruption in Europe. European projections about Polynesian, Amerindian, and Turkish sexuality offered utopian models of sexuality without corruption. However, it is important to recognize that "utopia" means no where, and these ideas spoke more to a rejection of European norms than to any recording of sexual practices elsewhere. Europe's fixation on Turkish sexuality and the pleasures of the harem, for example, did little to elucidate day-to-day life within the harem. Instead, such accounts provided ways to think about the pleasures and dangers of sexual variation, like anal sexuality, within an absolutist society, where men ruled and women submitted. The range of places explored in such narratives speaks to the wide-ranging interactions that Europe had with the rest of the world in the eighteenth century. While in many cases Europeans argued for toleration and admiration for the "noble savage," they also exported their beliefs about the sodomite, the tribade, polygamy, and polyandry to the areas they explored and colonized. In North American areas where Europeans gained dominance, practices such as polygamy were outlawed, and the berdache was persecuted.

The Enlightenment left numerous contradictions in European society around the issue of sexuality. While it secularized issues of gender and sexuality, in essence delegitimizing religious authority over them, it also laid the groundwork for state control of such matters. It shifted rather than eliminated social control over sexuality. Many of the progressive impulses of the Enlightenment, like pleas for tolerance, helped root out older patterns of prejudice, like the illegality of sexual relations between Jews and Christians. But Enlightenment thinkers also contributed to new stereotypes, like the "noble savage" and the amorous Turk. Such stereotypes carried great weight and influenced social and political relationships between Europeans and other peoples. The triumph of science and the scientific method associated with both the scientific revolution and the Enlightenment offered new ways to envision sexuality and sexual biology and in the long term contributed to improved sexual health. However, the rise of science also endowed biology with a new importance that made male and female inextricably different. This turn to biology to explain the world allowed continuing inequalities on the basis of sex. These enduring contradictions set the stage for future conflicts between sexual morality, sexual deviance, and sexual behaviors.

THE LONG NINETEENTH CENTURY

As a result of the French Revolution, the Napoleonic Code, which affected much of the Continent, replaced laws on sodomy with laws on public indecency and the corruption of minors. These laws institutionalized the distinction between private home, ruled by the father, and the public spaces, ruled by the state. While previous legislation made little distinction between public and private spaces, the new laws focused on the state's role in encouraging marriage and propagation. The more liberal-sounding laws did not decriminalize sodomy or other acts of sexual deviance. Instead, they shifted the rhetoric of prosecution from sin to antisocial behavior. Because much homosexual activity took place in parks, bathrooms, and other public places, the new laws about public indecency, exhibitionism, and corruption of minors became a way to control and penalize homosexual acts and practices. Although most European states ceased to execute individuals for acts of sodomy, the nineteenth century remained a period of repression for same-sex desires.

After the French Revolution legislation regarding adultery tightened. After the initial liberalization of laws between 1789 and 1795 allowed the redefinition of marriage as a civil contract, the Napoleonic Code of 1804 reintroduced a sexual double standard. Divorce legislation instituted during the high point of the French Revolution insisted on equality and freedom and allowed both men and women to sue for divorce on the basis of incompatibility or moral of-

fenses. However, the Napoleonic Code, while maintaining the secular state of marriage, allowed a man to sue on the basis of adultery but a women to sue only if her husband committed adultery in the marital household. A man's sexual irregularities occurred because of his perpetual quest for freedom according to the new formulation, but a woman's adultery negated her essential maternal qualities as constituted by Enlightenment thinkers such as Rousseau.

A similar double standard prevailed across Germany with regard to female sexuality. A Prussian decree of 1854 insisted that any woman who had sexual relations with a married man forfeited claims to paternity and support. Both Prussian and French legislators, justifying changes in laws surrounding divorce and adultery, argued that women's sexual infidelity disrupted the public realm. Demands for order in the public realm reinforced the sexual subservience of women in the private realm. For both sodomy and adultery, the period of questioning and liberalization during the Enlightenment that culminated in the French Revolution gave way to a later reactionary regime that intended to suppress these supposed disorders of sexuality and gender. As part of this reaction, nineteenth-century society invented a tradition of continuity even though patterns of regulation, beliefs about sexuality, and sexual behaviors had changed. By linking sexuality to fictive traditions, nineteenth-century society developed a way of thinking about sexuality that seemed universal, intrinsic, and natural.

As part of the new natural order, new marital ideals developed. In the new model man ruled the household as the representative of reason, and woman submitted as appropriate for emotion. The two spheres joined through affection, compassion, and mutuality. The rise of the compassionate marriage among the middle classes in the eighteenth and nineteenth centuries brought new expectations to marital intercourse. No longer was intercourse supposedly based on physical hungers that made it necessary for good health. Instead, a new model of sexuality emerged in which intercourse became an expression of love akin to spiritual communication. The model of affectionate marriage brought new power dynamics to sexuality. If marriage was based on mutuality and love rather than patrimony, then forced sex within marriage broke the fundamental emotional exchange of affection and respect. Women's reform efforts stressed "voluntary motherhood," meaning that a husband should control his passions rather than expect sexual congress as a right of marriage. The model of affectionate marriage combined with the expense of raising children among the bourgeoisie, who clothed, fed, and educated their children until their twenties rather than sending them out to work, made birth control an economically prudent action. The falling birthrates in western Europe, particularly among the middle class, testify to the effectiveness of these economic and ideological changes, even though different societies used different means to achieve the decrease. By the mid–nineteenth century France achieved low marital fertility through prostitution, coitus interruptus, and nonprocreative sexual practices. In England delayed marriage continued to be the norm.

Regardless of the effectiveness of the informal and formal control over marriage, conflicts between compassionate marriage as a model and the desires for sexual pleasure as practice created tensions in the nineteenth century and helped contribute to an increased focus on sexual deviance. Medicine, social scientific theory, legislation, moralism, and popular accounts all contrasted the purified home as the emotional center of the family with the polluted world of public life, where sexual deviancy took place. Although sexual deviance in these formulations began to look like the opposite of sexual morality, the two reinforced each other at a number of fundamental levels. Sexual murder provides a clear example of this process. Although serial killers murdered before the nineteenth century, sexualized serial murder seems to be a particularly modern phenomenon related to new gender roles and the development of sexual and social autonomy for women. As the historians Judith Walkowitz and Angus McLaren have shown, sexual violence intensified existing gender and sexual relationships. The famous case of Jack the Ripper, in which an unidentified person murdered and eviscerated five London prostitutes in 1888, encouraged the policing of streetwalkers and raised tensions and concerns about single and independent women. Rather than working to make the streets safer for women, urban reformers worked to clear out the transients in the Whitechapel area in response to the murders, which dispersed support networks for women. The media and the police told women to remain at home, where the levels of sexual and other violence remained high throughout the century. In Victorian England, sexualized murder reinforced gender control and state surveillance of sexual deviants like prostitutes. Victorian society's use of a violent rhetoric against prostitutes and other independent women at some level contributed to actual violence against such women.

More routine examples also illustrate the relationship between sexual morality and deviance. According to medical authorities, the prostitute functioned as the main vector of sexual disease. Across Europe the state tried to stamp out syphilis and gonorrhea, even though the two were not yet fully differentiated, by controlling prostitutes, regulating the sex trades, and introducing coercive measures against "loose" women identified as carrying the diseases. Doctors and moralists contrasted the long-suffering wife with the degraded prostitute to justify these coercive measures but generally ignored the role of men in spreading the disease. Many doctors kept the information about a husband's infection from his wife even though that meant that she would receive little or no medical help or attention. The issue of public health elevated the home even while sexual deviance infected it with disease. The contradiction was noted by feminists and socialists, who focused on the husband's sexual philandering.

Feminists attempted to reroute the conversation about sexuality toward discussions of the implicit flaws in the marital contract, while socialists emphasized the economics of poor women prostituting themselves for rich men. The rhetoric about prostitution and syphilis from each side, whether conservative, liberal, or revolutionary, pitted ideals about sexual morality against problems of deviance. In each model, sexual morality needed to be reformed to combat greater problems in society. Ridding society of social problems like loose women, gender inequalities, or economic inequalities was supposed to make the problems of sexual deviance wither away. The Victorian world, which became in the modern formulations synonymous with repression, spent a great deal of time and energy focusing on sexuality. If sexuality was a secret, then it was a secret invested with enormous powers.

The home and family as the center of procreative sexuality received additional relevance with the development of eugenics. Eugenicists, building on Charles Darwin's theories about the evolution of species, developed a science of race. They believed that populations and races competed against each other in a struggle for survival. This struggle took place between nations and races through battles over fecundity. According to eugenicists, falling birthrates among the middle class and the proliferation of the unfit boded ill for the continued progress of society. Eugenicists attempted to counter the problem by encouraging births among the fit, a program called positive eugenics, and discouraging births among the unfit, or negative eugenics. Fitness in both the positive and negative eugenics programs remained a nebulous quality that often stood in for race and class and ignored environmental causes of ill health and debility, like malnutrition, work conditions, and impure food.

The eugenics program also overlooked the real reasons that people had for limiting their fertility, like limited economic resources. The fears about decadence and the decline of the white race across Europe encouraged greater control of sexuality in the public realm. Both national and international campaigns against abortion and birth control, both of which were said to contribute to race suicide; pornography; the white-slave trade; and homosexuality and other forms of so-called perversions were part of the eugenics program. In addition to discouraging practices that curtailed fertility, eugenicists tried to encourage procreation by linking it to patriotism and national duty, by providing tax incentives and social programs to help the fit raise children, and by providing scientific knowledge about ways to increase marital pleasure. The science of sexuality thus received legitimacy because of its links to nationalist and imperialist concerns. Eugenics demonstrates that issues of sexuality defy traditional political categories. Although in the twentieth century eugenics was most often associated with the far right of the political spectrum, most notably fascism, in the nineteenth century it was associated with the political left.

Nationalist concerns about fitness also contributed to new models of sexual deviance. Although the Enlightenment advocated sexual tolerance, nineteenth-century and early twentieth–century medical science more effectively promoted reforms if not tolerance by stressing the physiological character of homosexuality. According to these early sexologists, sexual perversion had two causes, environmental, which included habitual masturbation, and hereditary. Just as evolution caused heterosexual desire, so devolution caused homosexual desire. The stresses and strains of modern life and the availability of physical stimuli weakened individuals, making them susceptible to sexual diseases. Once introduced as pathologies into families, they caused devolution. The early focus of medicine and psychiatry on homosexuality, alternately called sexual inversion or uranism, had progressive motivations that nonetheless produced a number of negative consequences for homosexuals. Sexologists, including K. H. Ulrichs, Richard von Krafft-Ebing, Magnus Hirschfeld, and Havelock Ellis, tended to see sexual deviance as a medical problem that could be cured rather than as a legal problem that deserved punishment. In shifting the focus of homosexuality from the law court to the doctor's office, these reformers stigmatized the homosexual, however, creating a model predicated on mental illness that lasted well until the late twentieth century.

The increased focus on the origins of sexual inversion in the medical community was matched by a series of court cases that raised the issue of homosexuality in the law, the press, and the popular imagination. The cases of Oscar Wilde in England, Baron Jacques d'Adelswäärd-Fersen in France, and Philipp Eulenberg in Germany publicized homosexuality in each of those countries and contributed to the notoriety of the developing gay subculture. A gay culture flourished in homosexual balls, bars, and brothels in Europe's large cities. The negative outcome of these cases combined with the increased visibility of homosexuality made homosexuals increasingly vulnerable. Nonetheless, the late nineteenth century and early twentieth century saw an outpouring of literature for and about homosexuals. Memoirs and novels raised the issues of same-sex desires and allowed homosexuality to become more central to the cultural life of Europe. Lesbians also developed their own cultural life. While the notoriety of male homosexual subcultures and literature has frequently overshadowed the development of a lesbian culture and literature, with the possible exception of Radclyffe Hall's *The Well of Loneliness* (1928), the increased opportunities for independence, education, and professional development allowed middle-class women to escape the familial home and live in same-sex relationships. The continued belief that women were less beset by sexual desires than men masked much of lesbian life under the rubric of spinsterhood.

In spite of the period's reputation for stifling sexuality, Europe between the French Revolution and World War I experienced major transformations of sexual ideals, legislation, and behaviors. Enlightenment ideals, like the freedom of the individual, a naturalistic interpretation of sexuality, and the turn away from tradition, continued to affect much of society. Governments across Europe attempted to stabilize society after the outbreak of the French Revolution and the Napoleonic Wars, but despite new legislation and policies, ideologies like nationalism, socialism, and feminism swept across western Europe and further reworked sexual behaviors and models. Women and workers began to fight for a greater role in society, and they saw sexuality as an emblem of the need for social, economic, and political reform. The rise of nationalism contributed to a race for procreation. Large urban centers that allowed extensive sexual variation in turn encouraged reformers to develop new models for dealing with sexual deviance. The extensive and often acrimonious discussions about sexuality demonstrate not only the central place that sexuality had in the Victorian world but also how political and social changes played out along a sexualized fault line.

EUROPE IN THE AGE OF THE WORLD WARS

In post–World War I Europe, sexuality remained a central metaphor for discussing changes in society.

The extreme conditions during the war years allowed women to develop new roles and to take advantage of new economic opportunities. As young women from all classes stepped out of the paternal home, they developed their own sexual standards rather than inheriting them from their parents' generation. Dating, premarital sex, and a rise in illegitimacy became a facet of youth culture. In many ways the development of a mass society during the war gave rise to a liberalization of sexual culture after the war. The deepening of democracy as a result of the war made the state more accountable to the political and social desires of a broad section of European society, and as a result shifts in sexual morality occurred fairly rapidly.

The flourishing of film, jazz, flappers, modern art, and modern dance testified to the daring sexual culture of the age. Josephine Baker appeared seminude in cabaret shows across Europe. Marlene Dietrich, the German film star, dressed in a man's topcoat and tails and publicly inverted male dress patterns, hinting at the emerging butch-femme cultural formations in the lesbian community. Film, public dances, and seaside bathing resorts exposed even the poor to the emerging pleasure culture that flirted with sexual titillation.

Modernism, as both an artistic and an intellectual movement, began to confront sexuality head-on. The surrealists took up themes of unconscious sexuality and confronted the nonprocreative and nonmarital aspects of sexuality. Salvador Dali's *Lugubrious Game* (1929) used the themes of coprophilia and masturbation to provoke viewers. Although they based their art on Freudian psychology, surrealists' interpretations of the relationship of sexuality to the unconscious bore only a surface resemblance to that of Freud's. In the world of the surrealist little made sense, and certainly sexuality was not an orderly phenomenon. In contrast, Freud saw sexuality as integral to human development and believed that perversion only resulted when the orderly processes from oral, anal, to genital development went awry. His theories and the advocacy of the "talking cure" demonstrate the new place sexuality held in the culture of the interwar period. Although earlier sexologists like Krafft-Ebing had discussed sexuality and perversion, their work mattered to a fairly small section of interested scholars, doctors, and writers. During the interwar years, in contrast, the overt discussion of sexual themes became more central to conversations across European society in a wide variety of contexts, from the death impulse to the meaning of civilization. Freud's popularity as a theorist owes something to his emergence during this particular period. His theories of the Oedipus and Electra complexes, his beliefs that babies had sexual urges, even his advocacy of the vaginal orgasm legitimated sexuality as a central part of the human experience and moved ideas aboveboard that appeared perverse just a generation before.

Despite the rhetoric of conservatives who were affronted by these changes, the 1920s did not just advocate hedonism. Instead, sexuality took an integral part in the many struggles over the direction of society. Sexual themes in modern art criticized the hypocrisy of the prewar world and the atrocities of the war. Sexual autonomy became linked to the increased rights of the individual. Sex reform and access to birth control information became part of a cross-European effort to enact progressive social reforms. In contrast, sex education, stressing premarital abstinence, morality, and the basics of reproduction, using plants and lower animals as examples, was occasionally incorporated into schools, generally in classes on ethics and biology. The church continued to argue that sexuality was a product of lust and thus to be fought against. In 1929 and 1931 Pope Pius XI warned against sex education, while the left successfully lobbied for greater access to information about sex. In the Soviet Union the revolution gave rise to increased access to birth control, divorce, and abortion, which allowed women to define their own sexual destinies. Early Soviet policy allowed women to take control of their own fertility as part of a broader policy of social reform. However, prostitution and homosexuality were repressed, and little was done to insure the sexual safety of women in prison and work camps. The steps toward greater flexibility in promoting women's independence were curtailed by the 1930s, when Joseph Stalin stressed the need for raised birthrates to advance the state. Other sexual matters received even harsher treatment. In 1933 homosexuality was recriminalized, in 1935 pornography was banned, and in 1936 abortion was outlawed.

The importance of the state over the individual became symptomatic of the political shifts of the 1930s. Many of the programs and beliefs about sexuality that gained momentum during the 1920s came under attack during the 1930s. The rise of fascist regimes in Italy, Germany, Spain, and Portugal and conservative regimes across much of eastern Europe were in part predicated on the supposed social disorders of the preceding generation. In attacking these disorders, fascist ideology singled out sexuality and gender as key elements. Fascist regimes across Europe reacted to changes in society by targeting the supposedly decadent and degenerate sexual culture of the 1920s. In practice this meant outlawing birth control in Spain, insisting on the procreative role of women in Italy, and attacking homosexuals in Germany. Roughly ten thousand gay men went to concentration camps in Germany, where 60 percent of them died. Spain and Italy sought to eliminate the modernization of sexuality and return to a family-oriented state. In contrast, Germany developed a new ideology that stressed the state over the family. The Nazi Party incorporated eugenics into its political platform and sterilized roughly 400,000 people on the basis of the Law for Prevention of Offspring with Hereditary Diseases (1933). The Nazis also removed the stigma in laws regarding illegitimacy in 1940 to promote the birth of racially pure offspring within or outside of marriage. The Nazi agenda was by far the most radical and far-reaching in its attempts purify Aryan race lines and to eliminate the bloodlines of those who supposedly tried to pollute the Aryan body, in particular Jews who, according to Nazi propaganda, lusted after Aryan women. In conceptualizing sexuality as a race for reproduction, Nazi theorists took eugenics to its extreme conclusions and on that basis justified the murder of millions of people.

As conservative governments aggressively pursued population programs, democratic governments scrambled to find consensus to counter the threat of the right's military strength. For the most part, the search for consensus meant moderation or silence in the area of sexuality. Legislation and social programs took a backseat to the recovery from the Great Depression then preparation for war.

THE POSTWAR WORLD

In issues of sexuality, World War II did not end in 1945, according to a Dutch saying. In the Netherlands 250 homosexual men were castrated to avoid prison sentences between 1937 and 1967. While political conservatism was largely discredited at the war's end, sexual conservatism stayed intact until the 1960s. The sexual conservatism had real implications for people's lives that should not be overlooked. At the same time, though, this conservatism masked larger changes that allowed the transformation of sexual behaviors and morality in the next generation.

Individual states returned to prewar policies on sexuality. Germany returned to stressing sex within marriage and retreated from the intrusive stance toward the family it developed under the Nazis. Other European states emphasized family, population, procreation, and heterosexuality. The French focus on population and procreative sexuality continued unabated as it had since the nineteenth century. In England sexual conservatism existed side-by-side with rising illegitimacy and women's continued participa-

tion in the workforce. In Italy prewar conservative tendencies prevailed. However, the world after the war was not the same as the one before. Prostitution became a problem as a result of the war and occupation. The church reacted by reemphasizing the family, but the position of the church shifted slightly when it advocated sexual harmony within marriage as a way to maintain marital resilience. In 1948 the church opened a Catholic marriage counseling facility to combat the growing secularization of society. The church's new stance revealed a larger accommodation to secularization of sexuality.

Although the secularization of sexuality varied from region to region and from religion to religion, European states largely separated church and state and individuals increasingly tended to see spirituality and sexuality as separate realms. In part this shift had been building since the Enlightenment, which delegitimized the church's traditional authority over sexuality. With secularization and the rise of the state as a secular authority also came the growing distinction between public and private. This division contributed to the waning influence of the church over public behavior and public morality, as people believed that church teaching no longer necessarily applied to the public sphere. If the dictates of one church or another concerning sexual morality held any validity, they generally did so within the realm of the individual conscience, the family, or the religious community, no longer coterminous with the state or any other public authority. Regulation of sexual behavior continued, but it was now for the state to decide—its reasoning stripped of explicitly religious content—what types of behavior constituted a threat to society and how they should be dealt with.

These long-term trends toward secularization were augmented by a number of fairly rapid changes that occurred as a result of World War I and World War II. The impact of communism in Eastern Europe and a large socialist presence in Western Europe delegitimized religion and religious control of sexuality in much of Europe. Additionally women's continued participation in the workforce across Europe and the resulting female independence laid the groundwork for shifting sexual mores across Europe. As women became more economically independent, they could decide their own sexual destinies. The dominance of the mass media and American culture and the postwar economic recovery also made many changes possible. Because of the American servicemen and servicewomen stationed in Europe, American youth culture, including rock and roll, films, and dating, began to influence European society in the 1950s. This transatlantic pattern of cultural interaction intensified dur-

Sexuality in Youth Culture. Couple kissing on New Year's Eve in Trafalgar Square, London, c. 1975. IAN BERRY/ MAGNUM PHOTOS

ing the 1960s and continued into the twenty-first century. Medical advances separated sexual intercourse from the physical repercussions that society had used to tie sexual actions to sin and deviance. Syphilis and gonorrhea, the scourges of sexuality in the past, became curable with penicillin in 1943, leaving a window, before the onset of AIDs in the 1980s, in which sexual intercourse seemed disease-free. The apparent end of sexual diseases followed by the widespread availability of the birth control pill in the 1960s promised to liberate sexuality from its previous constraints.

During the 1960s the feminist movement, the gay liberation movement, and the youth movement rapidly transformed sexual morality and sexual behaviors in Europe. In many ways the 1960s signaled a return to the issues of the 1920s, which had been discarded amid the extremes of World War II. These movements were self-conscious attempts to transform society and also the culmination of slower changes in European society. The 1960s had far-reaching consequences in terms of individual behaviors and state

policies. Sexual intercourse ceased to be predicated on an implicit premarital contract. Men and women began to have intercourse at younger ages as part of dating and early adulthood. The stigma against women's unmarried sexual activity lessened, so young women as well as young men envisioned sexual intercourse as an individual right and pleasure that did not involve marital intentions.

Across Europe marriage as an institution became less important. However, unmarried couples behaved in very similar ways to married couples, exhibiting patterns of monogamy, procreation, and mutual economic support. It appears as if the informal aspects of marriage mattered more than the formal institution of marriage, particularly since the economic, social, and legal stigmas against bastards were lifted. In many ways this model continued the longer trend of informal marriage among the working classes before the twentieth century. Formal marriage from the Renaissance forward was often a luxury that workers could not afford. The falling marriage rates in Europe did not signal the end of the heterosexual couple. Instead, an additional stage of life, in which young people lived together rather than married, became more standard.

In Western Europe states liberalized laws on sexuality and lifted restrictions on birth control, abortion, homosexuality, and pornography. During the 1960s the Labour government in Britain decriminalized homosexuality between consenting adults in private, began subsidizing birth control under the National Health Service (NHS), and allowed the NHS to cover abortions. Contraception, which was severely curtailed in France until 1967, became legal, and limited abortion rights were passed in 1975. In Germany the reassessment of the past encouraged a rejection of the earlier generation's sexual behaviors and morality as the two "dirty secrets" combined into one. German students rejected the double standard, premarital purity, and the linking of promiscuity and sin. West Germany legalized the birth control pill, abortion, and pornography. East Germany connected sexual liberalization with capitalism and American culture and did not respond as favorably to changes in youth culture. Nonetheless, East German young people pushed for similar adaptations, and across Germany beliefs and behaviors changed rapidly.

Along with new behaviors and regulations, new theories of sexuality took hold during this period. Theology began to emphasize the dignity and wellbeing of parishioners' lives as essential to Christian teachings. Partly in response to internal changes in the church and partly in response to the broader secularization of society, the Catholic Church and many Protestant denominations reexamined their own tra-

255

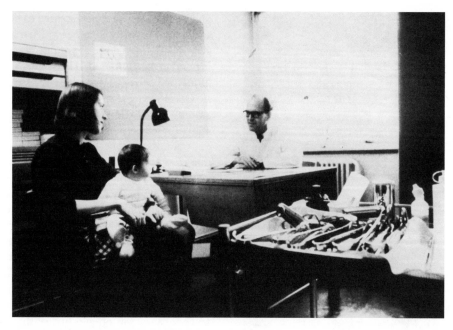

Contraception and Family Planning. Danish family planning office. WHO PHOTO BY E. MANDELMANN/NATIONAL LIBRARY OF MEDICINE

ditional stances towards sexuality. Because of the liberalization of abortion laws in many countries, the Catholic Church muted its message of the sinfulness of unmarried mothers. In contrast to abortion, bearing an illegitimate child seemed like the lesser sin. In turn this position promoted a more relaxed stance on premarital sex. Sexual purity no longer carried the force it once did. Even in Ireland, where Catholicism was the semiofficial religion, churchgoers relaxed attitudes on sexuality after the 1970s. In a poll taken in 1973 and 1974, 87 percent of those over fifty-one years of age thought premarital sex was "always wrong," whereas only 44 percent of those aged eighteen to thirty agreed. Moreover theology considered fair negotiation and trust in sexuality equally important as procreation. Abuses of power like rape and molestation violated these principles and seemed more compelling problems to individual priests, ministers, and members of the laity than sexual purity. The long-term impact of this focus created conflicts over abortion, sexual abstinence of clerics, and homosexuality within Catholic and Protestant Churches and divided Christian communities across Europe.

Other controversies, apparent at the origins of these rapid changes, became embedded in sexuality and continued to affect it. Most notably the relationship between the nature of biology and the social restrictions around sexuality called for new theories and new legislation. An identity politics that emerged from the Western European focus on individual rights legitimated alternative sexual desires. The contradictions between commercialization and sexual liberation raised important questions about what purpose sexuality should have in society.

Feminist scholars examined the relationship between sexuality and women's second-class status, which did not guarantee them the same rights, responsibilities, and freedoms as men. They noted that much of the theory about the biological origins of sexual impulses and behaviors guaranteed men's freedom at women's expense. The theory that women's sexuality was organized around maternity rather than orgasmic pleasure received particular opprobrium because it overlooked women's physical desires, justified the division of women into whore-madonna dualities, and legitimated legislation promoting maternity rather than protection of women as equal citizens. Feminists affirmed women's sexual desires as legitimate in and of themselves and lobbied for access to birth control and abortion to free those pleasures from reproduction. Reassessing the Freudian theory that posited the vaginal orgasm as the mature orgasm and the clitoral orgasm as immature, they argued that the theory promoted male pleasure through heterosexual coitus rather than female pleasure through manual stimulation. The continuing controversies around these theories pointed toward the gaps in understanding female and male sexuality. If biologists, psychologists, and doctors cannot agree on the physiology of sexual pleasure, then separating biology from culture remains impossible.

The gay liberation movement also attacked the theoretical underpinnings of sexuality. The disease model of homosexuality did not allow individuals to build an identity that incorporated their sexual preferences. Instead, it argued that same-sex desire was a pathology, even though no adequate treatment existed. Citing the work of Alfred Kinsey, whose book on American men, *Sexual Behavior in the Human Male* (1948), demonstrated that a significant proportion of the male population had same-sex desires and experiences, gay activists argued that homosexuality was not pathological but normal and as a normal desire deserved recognition rather than imprisonment, electric shock therapy, and other dubious treatments. If homosexuality is intrinsic and natural, then social restrictions against it are unnatural according to the new model. Feminist and queer theories redrew the boundaries of nature and culture and, in the process, threw into doubt the basis of previous legislation.

A third area of reconsideration developed around the issues of capitalism and sexuality. The commercialization of sexuality became an important issue to progressives and conservatives alike. Political differences over what to do about the issue persist, and many see problems in the economics of sexuality. For example, the use of women in sexually suggestive advertisements raises the question of whether women have been liberated sexually or made into another commodity. Similarly, the decriminalization of pornography, initially touted as a step away from state censorship, promised to liberate sexuality, political opinions, and artistic sensibilities. In 1960, for example, Penguin Books won a censorship case against the British government concerning D. H. Lawrence's *Lady Chatterley's Lover* (1928). The relaxation of old standards seemed to liberate art from the vise of Victorian morality. However, the distinction between art and pornography remained shaky, and standards based on the idea of socially redeeming value permitted states to err on the side of free speech rather than censorship. First soft-core then hard-core pornography gained legal status across Europe over the objections of feminists and traditional conservatives alike. Especially in Britain and the United States, feminist work in the area of pornography has raised the ques-

tion of whether legalization liberates both men and women or it only provides a way for men to conceptualize women's subjugation. Conservatives argue that pornography inspires perversions and desacralizes what should remain sacrosanct. In spite of these concerns, pornography has become an international phenomenon through the rise of film, television, and video. The breakdown of Communism in Eastern Europe and the economic instability it engendered encouraged a rise in the sex trades across national borders, including the manufacture of pornography. Pornographic production companies use actors from across Europe and sell the products to an increasingly international audience. The poverty in eastern Europe encouraged many women to sell their only asset, themselves, in spite of the equally international spread of diseases like AIDS. The transition to capitalism in eastern Europe demonstrates the problems of commercialization at its most profound levels.

As these issues demonstrate, sexual morality has slowly emerged from the province of the church, the family, and community, and the regulation of morality and behaviors has shifted to the state and the individual. This shift, though promising in its inception during the Enlightenment to free individuals from the chains of tradition and allow them to find more reasonable accommodations for their passions, created as many confusions and controversies as previous systems. Sexual behaviors transformed along with systems of regulation. The two seem mutually dependent, though their relationship is not as straightforward as many might believe. For example, in spite of the enormous pressures toward marital procreation in the nineteenth century, individuals practiced family planning and curtailed the number of their offspring. Regulation attempted to control behaviors but to little avail. Religion and family did not successfully control sexuality before the Enlightenment, but the state and secular authorities also failed after the Enlightenment. Instead, systems of regulation seem to provide individuals with models that they build upon, reject, and accommodate. People's diverse reactions to changes in sexual regulation demonstrates the complexity of sexuality. As an identity, a practice, and a biological phenomenon, sexuality contravenes legislation and easy answers. Nonetheless, as the history of sexuality demonstrates, large changes reverberate through the individual, making it unclear where an individual's sexuality ends and social forces begin.

See also other articles in this section.

BIBLIOGRAPHY

Eder, Franz X., Lesley A. Hall, and Gert Hekma. *Sexual Cultures in Europe: National Histories.* Manchester, U.K., 1999.

Eder, Franz X., Lesley A. Hall, and Gert Hekma. *Sexual Cultures in Europe: Themes in Sexuality.* Manchester, U.K., 1999.

Hull, Isabel V. *Sexuality, State, and Civil Society in Germany, 1700–1815.* Ithaca, N.Y., 1996.

Laqueur, Thomas Walter. *Making Sex: Body and Gender from the Greeks to Freud.* Cambridge, Mass., 1990.

Levin, Eve. *Sex and Society in the World of Orthodox Slavs, 900–1700.* Ithaca, N.Y., 1989.

Liliequist, Jonas. "Peasants against Nature: Crossing the Boundaries between Man and Animal in Seventeenth- and Eighteenth-Century Sweden." *Journal of the History of Sexuality* 1, no. 3 (1991): 393–423.

Maccubbin, Robert Purks, ed. *'Tis Nature's Fault: Unauthorized Sexuality during the Enlightenment.* Cambridge, U.K., 1987.

McLaren, Angus. *A Prescription for Murder: The Victorian Serial Killings of Dr. Thomas Neill Cream.* Chicago, 1993.

Roper, Lyndal. *Oedipus and the Devil: Witchcraft, Sexuality, and Religion in Early Modern Europe.* London and New York, 1994.

Rousseau, G. S., and Roy Porter, eds. *Sexual Underworlds of the Enlightenment.* Manchester, U.K., 1987.

Ruggiero, Guido. *The Boundaries of Eros: Sex Crime and Sexuality in Renaissance Venice.* Oxford, 1985.

Vogel, Ursula. "Whose Property? The Double Standard of Adultery in Nineteenth-Century Law." In *Regulating Womanhood: Historical Essays on Marriage, Motherhood, and Sexuality.* Edited by Carol Smart. London, 1992. Pages 147–165.

Walkowitz, Judith R. "Jack the Ripper and the Myth of Male Violence." *Feminist Studies* 8, no. 3 (Fall 1982): 542–574.

ILLEGITIMACY AND CONCUBINAGE

Anne-Marie Sohn

From the eighteenth to the twentieth century, the public view of illegitimacy and concubinage (or cohabitation) changed radically. Once marginalized and ostracized, these behaviors became common and tolerated. Thus abstinence gave way to the right to sexual fulfillment for all, and the bastard, once despised and condemned to an almost certain death among the poorest, became the illegitimate child who is both desired and cherished, as the boundaries between concubinage and married life disappeared.

FROM ABSTINENCE TO THE ACCEPTANCE OF ILLEGITIMATE BIRTHS

If this long-term change is unquestionable, numerous national and regional exceptions reveal the complexity of factors that influenced sexual freedom.

Chastity established as an expected virtue. It is incontestable that the Reformation and especially the Counter-Reformation introduced a rupture in social perceptions and controls. Certainly, Christianity had always upheld the family as the sole venue for reproduction and fought unceasingly against extramarital sexuality, although it never succeeded in eradicating it.

In Catholic countries, the post-Tridentine reaction hardened the marriage doctrine of the church, devalued love except in marriage, and reinforced the repression of extramarital sexuality because the new solemnity of the sacrament of matrimony rendered transgressions more difficult. The effects were immediate. Around 1560 the rate of illegitimacy fell dramatically. In France it was on average 1 percent, and even less for the rural parishes; but it was higher in the cities, to which young peasant women, anxious to hide their "mistake," flocked in order to give birth. Prenuptial conception fluctuated between 3 and 4 percent in the countryside. In England, on the other hand, the decline came later, contemporary with Oliver Cromwell's Commonwealth; the rates of illegitimacy in rural areas actually grew from 1560 to 1620,

reaching between 2.3 and 3.5 percent. Beginning in the 1660s, the English and French situations were comparable, with illegitimate births not exceeding 1 percent. On the other hand, England distinguished itself by its frequency of prenuptial conceptions, which occurred in 10 to 40 percent of marriages, depending on the region.

Loosening constraints (1750–1850). Beginning in 1750 most European countries saw illegitimate births rise dramatically. In England the rate of illegitimacy reached 3.3 percent in 1741–1760 and 4 percent in 1761–1780; it exceeded 5 percent by 1781–1787. In France the rate increased fivefold in one century, and the rise, though coming later, was just as regular, reaching 1.8 percent in 1760–1769, 2.6 percent at the eve of the Revolution, 4.4 percent in 1810, 6.6 percent in the 1820s, and stabilizing at over 7 percent in 1860. The upsurge was even greater in the cities, where on the eve of the Revolution illegitimate births stood at between 8 and 12 percent, and at 30 percent in Paris. From 1790 to 1830, the average reached 16.2 percent for small cities, 20 percent for medium-sized cities, and 22.5 percent for large cities.

The phenomenon also reached Scandinavia and exploded in Germanic countries in the first half of the nineteenth century. In Austria the rate of illegitimacy wavered between 10 and 30 percent in 1870. It reached 40 to 50 percent in Styria and 68 percent in Carinthia; hence the expression "Carinthian marriage." In some districts it reached 60 percent. In short, Austria surpassed all European and urban records, with illegitimate births reaching 50 percent in Vienna and 69 percent in Klagenfurt. This peak was followed by a decline in the twentieth century.

Illegitimate birth in the twentieth century. The increase in illegitimate births in the twentieth century was real, although it occurred more or less early in the century. However, the statistics do not represent the phenomenon with complete accuracy because of contraception. Thus in France, for example, the recorded rate of illegitimacy does not reflect a sexual freedom that was increasing but was masked by the association, common since the Belle Époque, between coitus interruptus and, when that failed, abortion. Thus only 8.7 percent of children were illegitimate in 1900–1914, increasing to only 11 percent in 1978. But more revealing is the fact that between the two world wars 20 percent of newlywed women were pregnant and 12 percent were already mothers. In England from the 1840s to the 1960s the rate of illegitimacy, except for the periods just after the world wars, remained stable around 3.4 to 5.4 percent. Prenuptial conceptions never dropped below 16 percent, and prenuptial relationships increased rapidly: 16 percent of women born in 1904 had experimented with such relations, compared with 36 percent of the generation born between 1904 and 1914. On the other hand, in the Netherlands, where the power of religious parties was great and their influence reinforced by the practices of the coalition government, the prudish atmosphere restrained the liberalization of morals so well that in 1955 the rate of illegitimacy reached its lowest level. Likewise, in Ireland, where Catholicism shaped the national identity, the rate of illegitimacy stagnated at around 2 percent and in 1961 fell to its lowest level, 1.6 percent, even though contraception remained taboo.

During the 1960s, however, all European countries experienced a "sexual revolution," accompanied by the massive diffusion of contraception, which permitted the avoidance of unwanted pregnancy. Nonetheless, beginning in 1970 Europe saw a new explosion in illegitimacy. Denmark and Sweden were at the peak of this development, followed by Great Britain and also by France, where the change accelerated: in 1991 one-quarter of births occurred outside marriage, 37.6 percent in 1997, and 40 percent in 1998, with a rate of over 50 percent for firstborn children. Illegitimate births thus became a major component of demography, attesting to the overturning of traditional standards of behavior.

ILLEGITIMACY AND PREMARITAL SEX

The rate of illegitimacy reveals the degree of tolerance for nonmarital relationships, but it still needs interpretation. Edward Shorter imputes the "first sexual revolution" of 1750 to 1850 to industrialization. Capitalism overturned attitudes by valuing profit and by creating the autonomous worker whose choices were no longer subordinated to traditional rules and authorities. If the economy played a role, however, its role was much more complex than Shorter claims, and

in any case the economy was not the only cause of change. The erosion of religion and the transformation of the family were also significant. The legal system also directly and indirectly influenced individual choices.

Historians have debated the various causes of the rise in illegitimacy, as they combined to produce some striking changes but also great regional and class variations from the late eighteenth century onward. A key issue involves gender: obviously, both men and women participated in premarital sex, but quite possibly for different reasons and from very different positions of power. Weaker job opportunities for women may have increased a woman's felt need to use sex to try to cement a link with a man, while men's concerns about eroding status may have made sexual conquest a more desirable expression of masculine prowess.

Illegitimacy and the law. In the early modern era laws prohibited extramarital sex. In Germanic countries the Reformation codified sexual norms through ordinances of morality (*Sittlichkeitsordnungen*). Catholic states, in the wake of the Council of Trent, criminalized concubinage and sexual relations between fiancés. In France the declaration of pregnancy, instituted in the edict of 1556 by Henry II, was intended to prevent infanticide but also sought to restrain passions by rendering the father responsible for his child and its upkeep. Similarly in England in 1733 women were given the right to bring suit against the father of their children, to secure marriage or the confiscation of his goods if he refused to pay alimony, and even to send him to prison if he was penniless. In the Germanic countries the legal framework of marriage hardened toward the end of the seventeenth century. Severe limits were imposed on the marriage of house servants.

Legislative restraints endured, and indeed grew, into the nineteenth century. In France the Civil Code (1804), in defining the legal obstacles to marriage, placed certain couples in inextricable situations. Dispensations accorded for marriage between an aunt and a nephew related by marriage, or between a stepfather and stepdaughter, were extremely rare and were the product of prolonged negotiations. Furthermore, until the Lemire law of 1898, the acquisition of the administrative documents necessary for marriage was difficult for peasants who moved to the city and who were often illiterate, and the cost was frequently prohibitive for the poorest of them. The society of Saint-François Régis was founded in Paris in 1826 in order to facilitate these procedures and to permit the legalization of stable concubinages. In Germany and Austria the legal restrictions inherited from the seven-

Seduced and Abandoned. *The Letter,* painting by Domenico Induno (1815–1878). Museo Nazionale di Capodimonte, Naples/Scala/Art Resource, NY

teenth century were reinforced into the 1820s and 1830s. Thus developed the policy called "consent to marry," which aimed at preventing concubinage and illegitimate birth but had the paradoxical effect of making them more widespread. Workers who were not landowners were required, in effect, to have a stable income, irreproachable conduct, and to possess some goods to be able to marry. These restrictive laws survived until the creation of the German Empire in 1870 and until 1868 in Austria, with the exception of the Tirol, which did not repeal them until 1921.

Socioeconomic structures and illegitimacy. While cities differed from the countryside in socioeconomic conditions, rural areas themselves were often quite distinct in their attitudes to illegitimacy. In France and Germany, for example, there were both permissive and restrictive regions. In France rural illegitimacy was particularly strong in the northeast half of the country, where it reached 5 percent by 1820–1829. In 1914 one-quarter of Alsatian marriages were celebrated after the conception of a child. The Hautes-Pyrénées and Basses-Pyrénées were second, always

261

staying two percentage points above the national average. In the valley of Campan (Hautes-Pyrénées) the proportion of illegitimate births even reached 18.3 percent. Added to this is the fact that prenuptial conceptions were rarely lower than 5 percent. This phenomenon was even more accentuated in the German Alps.

Thus geographical contrasts often arose from different social structures. In regions like the Pyrenees, where the eldest son traditionally inherited the bulk of a family's wealth, the younger sons often remained bachelors in order to keep the family property intact, and the poorest younger daughters could not find a husband for lack of a dowry. The exclusion from inheritance explains the extramarital outlet before the rural exodus reduced the demographic pressure that reached its peak in 1848. But the ostracism that weighed on young single mothers persisted to the point that within three generations distinct lineages were established of single mothers, who were relegated to the bottom of the social ladder. The right of the eldest (*Anerbenrecht*) also existed in Germany and led to similar situations. Furthermore, in areas of large-scale farming, which in Germany and Austria beginning in the eighteenth century employed a large working class, servants and dispossessed youngest sons were too poor to marry. As they were also very mobile, they escaped the scrutiny of the neighbors and had elevated rates of illegitimacy.

On the other hand, in "democratic" societies such as Savoy, and even in regions like the Parisian basin, where the peasants were leaseholders and not landowners, the decision to marry rested on personal qualities. Consequently, all suitors were considered equal, familial pressure was weak, and the freedom accorded to the young was great. In 1910 Arnold van Gennep concluded that, at the most, 10 percent of young women of Savoy entered marriage as virgins. *Kiltgang*, the generic name given to the practices of youth in the French, Swiss, and Germanic Alps, as well as in Scandinavia and England, reveals the correlation between economic equality and premarital sex. In these regions, young men would prolong the evening by visiting young women in their homes. They could demand shelter and in that case would sleep next to the young women, fully dressed and generally on top of the covers. They could even go to a woman's room in a group and stay there alone or in turns without compromising her reputation. It goes without saying that when these young people got engaged, the *Kiltgang* gave way to proper and decorous courtships. This rite codified the freedom of youths, but under the double control of their peers and of adults, who remained vigilant though in the background. In effect, a young woman who mixed courting with debauchery lost her chance at matrimony.

In cities and villages dedicated to protoindustry, a similar situation produced the "immorality" of the working woman, denounced vehemently by both the French and the English bourgeoisie in the nineteenth century. Laborers, who were deprived of any inheritance and indifferent to the strategies of social status, became involved very early with their chosen loves, since at the age of eighteen a young man earned as much as an adult. Pairing off was thus a natural occurrence. In the principality of Neuchâtel in Switzerland, the increase in illegitimacy—31 percent of births after 1760—was a result of the flood of cotton textile manufacturing into the villages. The introduction of cotton manufacturing, which recruited its labor force from among poor peasants and proletarianized farmers, brought increased sexual freedom as cohabitation was based on salaries and hard work. Thus, the bonds that tied marriage to the inheritance of land were loosened.

Generally, illegitimate births were limited to the working classes until the twentieth century. A census of France during the Third Republic (1870–1940) confirmed that nearly 87 percent of young women who had had nonmarital relationships were wage earners: 35 percent were laborers, 29 percent were house servants, and 22.7 percent were agricultural day workers or farm servants. As under the ancien régime, servants, frequently uprooted to an unknown city, appear to be the primary victims of this system: they were 3 times less likely to marry and 2.5 times more likely to commit infanticide than workers. As for female agricultural workers, if they managed to obtain a shotgun marriage as often as factory workers, they were nonetheless twice as likely to commit infanticide. But economic constraints are only part of the story, and the comparative ease of city-dwelling women was due more to the attitudes that prevailed in the city than to their financial independence.

Attitudes toward illegitimacy. Wherever the teaching of the churches was respected, chastity was established as an absolute. Take for example the courtship practices of the early modern era. An engagement, also called *don de foi* (gift of faith) or *promesse à main* (promise of the hand), was common in England. It rested on a public agreement between families with witnesses and symbolic gestures such as the kiss and an exchange of gifts, most often a gold ring. Still, this agreement did not take effect until after sexual relations. The banns (official public announcement) of marriage therefore served only to confirm the engagement of the spouses and their parents.

These engagement practices were not abolished until 1753 with the Hardwick Marriage Act, which had little effect on them. The Catholic Church, on the other hand, prohibited them as early as 1564. This explains the lower number of prenuptial conceptions on the Continent than in England.

Dechristianization also eroded moral prohibitions. Evidence shows that the development of concubinage and illegitimate births in Germanic countries beginning in the eighteenth century coincides with an erosion of the influence of churches. In France, where Jansenism and above all the Revolution were accompanied by a decline in religious practice, the Catholic Church in the nineteenth century no longer had the means to make its sexual standard respected. Priests were denounced for their rigidity and for the hidden influence they exercised in their confessionals over the lives of couples. Men turned away first from the confessional, then from the altar. The French who remained practicing Catholics freed themselves rapidly from sexual prohibitions, to the point that confessors opted for caution through the 1930s. Despite the development of the cult of the Virgin Mary and the exaltation of feminine virginity through sodalities such as the Enfants de Marie, the secularization of society permitted the emancipation of single men and women.

The value accorded to virginity, however, could be independent of religious precepts. To take the French example, in Flanders, Artois, and Picardy virginity was not valued in the least. In Gravelines a virgin could even be referred to as "rien qu'une merde sur une pelle" (nothing but shit on a shovel). In Burgundy the subject was never even taken up. As for the Normans, they did not criticize the unmarried mother, as they were happy to verify her ability to bear children. Peasants were always torn between a respect for chastity and a rejection of barrenness. There were, by contrast, until the period between the two world wars, areas that were hard on young women who had "erred." In these places even prenuptial conception was criticized, and weighed as an indelible stain on the wife. Furthermore, in certain southern rural regions masculine honor and feminine virginity were conflated. There, a prenuptial relationship was experienced as a dishonor that began with the first suspicion of immorality, and the punishment was public. The charivaris (noisy rituals that expressed communal disapproval of perceived violators of social norms) that targeted "loose women" were common in Charente and in Limousin until 1914, in Brittany during the period between the wars, and in Languedoc into the 1950s. The rejection of illegitimacy thus led either to rapid marriage or to infanticide, which is reflected in the statistics, although in the north both shotgun marriages and infanticide were rarer.

The geography of intransigence takes on the appearance of a mosaic. The laxity of the Basques, for example, contrasts with the rigidity of the Ossau valley and of the eastern Pyrenees. In Mâconnais girls were rarely scrutinized, while the reverse was true in neighboring Bresse. In Alsace, where, in the case of birth before marriage, they said "the papers were late," there were communes that conserved the *Krönel-Hoschzit* (virgin marriage crown) that was passed on with pride from mother to daughter. And in the Bas-Rhin, Catholic parishes, isolated in Protestant lands, were particularly cruel to "dishonored girls," who were relegated to a pew of infamy at the back of the church. The weight of regional attitudes could prevail over national trends, sometimes with unexpected reversals. Savoy, long indifferent to feminine virtue, aligned itself with the bourgeois model after World War I and required virgin marriage from then on.

In the cities, tolerance prevailed among the populace, which joked that one must lose one's virginity as quickly as possible to avoid being taken for a half-wit. Far from wanting to marry a virgin, many men preferred experienced women. An illegitimate child was better received and a single mother, if she was not promiscuous, could be wed. Shotgun marriages were common. But there were also workers and artisans, often from the south, who retained the ideology of honor from their village life, and who believed the virtue of the fiancée guaranteed the future wisdom of the spouse. And the middle-class cult of virginity remained unshakable at least until the 1920s among the lower middle class. Nevertheless, the transformations of the couple and the family prevailed over this resistance in the twentieth century.

From illegitimacy endured to illegitimacy proclaimed.

In France patriarchy eroded in the nineteenth century. Maternal and paternal love bloomed, and a wave of tenderness washed over familial relationships. Unquestioned obedience to the father's command gave way to persuasion, and children gained more freedom. The reduction in parental authority went hand in hand with the rapid decline of arranged marriages. After World War I marriages of love triumphed even in the most resistant regions, if only because heavy demographic losses prohibited excessive restrictions. These marriages rested on the union of two individuals who took a chance at happiness with a freely chosen partner. In this framework, happiness depended on love. One had to seduce one's future spouse, and the progression from tender words to sexual relations became inescapable.

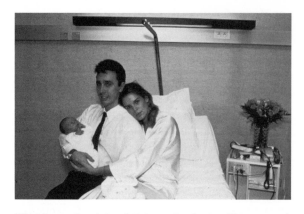

Illegitimacy Proclaimed. Princess Stéphanie of Monaco and her bodyguard, Daniel Ducruet, with their newborn son, Prince Louis, 26 November 1992. ©GAMMA/LIAISON AGENCY

Certainly, young girls could say no, but refusal passed more and more often for frigidity. Between the two world wars 30 percent of couples consummated their union before their wedding night. Although it was still possible before World War II, refusal became archaic in the 1950s and 1960s, when the one-night stand became an obligatory rite of initiation. In 1959, 30 percent of women admitted to prenuptial relations, and 12 percent refused to respond to a question about them. Things then accelerated: from 1968 to 1989, the age at which a young person first had intercourse dropped five years for women and six years for men. By 1989, 90 percent of young women were no longer virgins by the age of eighteen. In Denmark, while 40 percent of female students were still virgins in 1958, only 3 percent were in 1968. In Sweden 68 percent of women born between 1905 and 1935 and 86 percent of those born between 1935 and 1950 were no longer virgins at the time of their marriage. Thus sexual relations became the norm for single young people between 1920 and 1968, but they resulted less frequently in unwanted pregnancy because of progress in contraception.

Beginning in the 1970s, the new phenomenon of the planned illegitimate child emerged, attesting to the dissociation of reproduction from marriage and contributing to a decline in marriage. The changes in concubinage were the ultimate proof of this.

CONCUBINAGE BY DEFAULT AND BY CHOICE

Concubinage (also called cohabitation) is not well understood because it is difficult to pinpoint. Its history is therefore a developing one. The French example,

however, reveals that in the recent past concubinage changed from a marginal practice to an official way of life.

The social milieus of concubinage. During the Restoration in France (1815–1830), one out of five households in Paris lived outside the bonds of marriage. This was far less than alarmist contemporary witnesses claimed. Furthermore, Parisian cohabitants were not as overwhelmingly working-class as has been thought. Nonlaborers made up, depending on the quarter of the city, 33 to 40 percent of cohabitants. If concubinage was indeed one of the "forms of working-class civilization," it thrived equally on the anonymity and freedom that the capital offered.

The study of concubinage under the Third Republic confirms the change. Of recorded cohabitants, 80 percent lived in cities, with half in large cities, and 15 percent in Paris. A comparison of the maps of concubinage and industrialization is equally striking. Concubinage thrived in modern France along the Paris-Lyon-Marseille axis extended to the Belgian border. Conversely the west, the Alps, the Massif Central, and Languedoc had little cohabitation. Also, in villages cohabitants were less numerous—9 percent—and were generally day laborers. Rural France tolerated social mistakes, preferring prenuptial pregnancy to a barren woman, but unanimously rejected a public attack on the norm. Thus concubinage remained overwhelmingly a characteristic of the working class into the period between the two world wars: 60 percent of men were artisans or laborers, and 48 percent of women were laborers, 28 percent working in textiles. Generally, cohabitants also came from the urban lower classes, which mixed laborers and the lesser trades, from bread sellers to upholsterers and ragmen. Privileged circles represented at best 10 percent of male cohabitants, for while concubinage was unthinkable for a middle-class woman, it seduced certain middle-class men. One-quarter of the cohabitants of single young women came from well-to-do circles. That said, the working-class character of concubinage increased from 1840 to 1940.

A multifaceted concubinage. In the Third Republic concubinage involved partners with varied levels of sexual experience. Among women, 56 percent had been or were still married and only 44 percent were unmarried. Cohabitors who had been married were older, since 64 percent moved in with their partner after thirty years of age. They also controlled their fertility well: one-third had no children, 43 percent had one or two children, and 67 percent—72 percent among widows—had no illegitimate children. Unmarried cohabitors, on the other hand, were younger: 82 percent were younger than thirty-five, and 20 percent were minors. They were also less experienced: 54 percent failed to avoid pregnancy. The concubinage of unmarried women was thus similar to prenuptial relationships, although 30 percent of them lived with men at least ten years older than they and of a different social class.

When the motives that prompted couples to live together outside of marriage are taken into account, the situation becomes even more complicated. For 10 to 25 percent of couples, concubinage was lived as though it was a preface to marriage. This phenomenon concerned only marriageable couples, half at best of those living in concubinage. It was most often young single people who found themselves in this situation, sometimes because their parents disapproved of the union, sometimes because the promise of marriage, or engagement, was enough of a union, sometimes because the women involved secretly hoped to legalize their union. Without the pressures of society and especially the family, this situation could drag on for long periods of time. Young couples whose four parents were still alive were rare in the nineteenth century, at most one-quarter in Beauce near Orléans. Further, the parents of young cohabitants seemed particularly patient and tolerant, even agreeing to house the young couples. On the other hand, cohabitants who had previously been married, primarily women who were separated, divorced, or abandoned, were not always in a hurry to enter into a binding relationship, and remained satisfied with a situation that preserved their freedom. They did not discard the possibility of legalizing their union, however, primarily for reasons of inheritance; thus toward the end of their lives, older couples would often marry in order to settle legal questions of inheritance. On the other hand, after 1918 war widows remained inflexible for fear of losing their pension.

In one out of four cases, however, cohabitation resulted less from choice than from necessity or instability; 12 percent of cohabitations reveal marginality and poverty. Abandoned women with children agreed to concubinage because of a lack of resources. This was also true of unemployed women. Victims of their sex in the workplace, young underpaid women would live with a man just to survive, and would leave him when they found work. Concubinage between a servant and her master, in the city or in the country, was not always forced on the woman, and there were servant-mistresses who commanded respect, but that situation more often arose from the economic subordination of women; a servant who refused the sexual overtures of her master would be fired. Certain un-

derprivileged and scorned professions existing on the margins of society, such as ragmen or fairground entertainers, made concubinage a way of life. Some cynical men preyed upon mildly disabled women, imposing themselves and taking advantage of these women who could not protest. Four percent of cohabitants came from the circle of ex-convicts, prostitutes, and pimps. Marginal society was frequently indifferent to moral norms.

But most cohabitants, at least half, moved in together as good spouses. The most common face of concubinage was that of cohabitants regarded as married couples. A shifting vocabulary was daily proof of this, particularly with the change from *concubine* and *concubin* to "wife" and "husband" and, for the woman, the use of "Madame" followed by the man's name. It was also common for neighbors to be ignorant of the legal status of cohabitants whom they believed to be married. Confusion was particularly strong in the case of young couples, couples who had been together five years or less, and women who had been married and retained their married name and behavior. In order for this assimilation to be possible the couple had to live quietly and project honorable conduct, without scandal. Contemporaries praised supposedly married couples for their good rapport, hard work, and the love they had for each other. Cohabitants were esteemed because they were respectable. They gauged their own conduct against that of married couples and concluded that their irregular situation with regard to legal status could in no way dishonor them. Since they conducted themselves as responsible and moral citizens, and were supported by the praise of their contemporaries, they had little reason to go before the mayor to be married. On the other hand, those who refused on principle to marry were rare. Until World War II concubinage was not the free union advocated by anarchists; it appeared more often as a substitute for married life.

Therefore it is not surprising that the behavior of cohabiting couples was similar in all points to that of legitimate couples of the same working-class circles. There were no more bad male cohabitants—violent, alcoholic, "bad providers"—than there were bad husbands. The tacit contract that made up concubinage seems even to have protected women from abuse because a husband could use his status as head of the family to exercise unchallenged tyranny. In particular, concubinage took women away from the domination of a jealous man or "master." It did not prevent love from blossoming, sometimes in forms more exalted than in the framework of marriage, nor did it prevent adultery from occurring with the same reactions as in married couples. Cohabiting women were judged like wives, according to their domestic and professional talents. They were not worse housekeepers than married women and did not complain more about serving their partners. They were not worse mothers. For example, they rarely abused their children. Their role was even more important than that of a mother in a legitimate family, in which attachments could be lukewarm compared to the love an unmarried woman had for her children. The only difference between legitimate and illegitimate couples was that cohabitants suffered, beginning in the interwar period, under the increasing spread of "social hygiene," a more particular scrutiny. Suspected a priori of immorality, and put at a disadvantage by their low income and poor living conditions, they were judged incapable of educating their children. Thus 47 percent of unmarried parents were deprived of their parental rights and authority on grounds of immorality, compared to 25 percent of married parents.

Although three-quarters of cohabitants lived peaceful daily lives, concubinage was not generally accepted, a fact to which public reprobation bears witness. Primarily verbal, this criticism denounced the "false household" and even became xenophobic when the cohabitants were ostracized foreigners, as were the Yugoslavs, Portuguese, and Algerians in the interwar period. It could even compel certain couples to hide their legal status. But in the twentieth century no one dared vilify the bastard child, whose interests had been protected by the authorities since the 1870s because of the collapse of the birth rate.

From prenuptial relationships to accepted concubinage. In the late twentieth century, as soon as a couple began an extramarital relationship, the question of living together arose.

In France, 12 percent of future spouses already lived together at the time of their marriage in 1965, 17 percent in 1968, 43 percent in 1977, and 87 percent in 1997. Living together served as the framework for prenuptial relationships, and marriage, which was no longer obligatory, often intervened only after the first birth. The rate of illegitimacy coincided thenceforth with the rate of concubinage. Further, the law confirmed these evolutions by giving any natural child, whether of a married couple or of a single person, the legal right to social services. More than two million couples, one out of ten, thus lived without legal ties. From 1985 to 1999 nearly all couples lived this way, at least at some point in their relationship. Also, public disapproval was no longer an issue. That said, the acceptance of concubinage undermined the institution of marriage. Couples thereafter had many options in choosing their social status: free union, marriage, PACS (*pacte civil de solidarité*). PACS, debated in Parliament in the late 1990s, created a contract, primarily aimed at establishing inheritance, between cohabitants, whether heterosexual or homosexual. On the eve of the year 2000, recognition of homosexual concubinage was the order of the day.

Thus the circle of a long history, beginning in 1750, is completed that allowed public opinion to tolerate and then to accept as normal both sexual relations outside of marriage and concubinage.

Translated from French by Sylvia J. Cannizzaro

See also **Orphans and Foundlings** *(volume 3);* **Courtship, Marriage, and Divorce** *(in this volume); and other articles in this section.*

BIBLIOGRAPHY

Barret-Ducrocq, Françoise. *Love in the Time of Victoria.* Translated by John Howe. London, 1991.

Breit, Stefan. *"Leichtfertigkeit" und ländliche Gesellschaft: Voreheliche Sexualität in der frühen Neuzeit.* Munich, 1991.

Caspard, Pierre. "Conceptions prénuptiales et développement du capitalisme dans la principauté de Neufchâtel (1678–1820)." *Annales ESC* (November–December 1982).

Dupâquier, Jacques, ed. *Histoire de la population française.* Vols. 2, 3, and 4. Paris, 1988.

Duprat, Catherine. *Usages et pratiques de la philanthropie.* Paris, 1996. See chapter 1, "*Famille.*" Pages 589–670.

Eder, Frantz. "Sexual Cultures in Germany and Austria, 1700–2000." In *Sexual Culture in Europe: National Histories*. Edited by Lesley A. Hall, Gert Hekma, and Franz X. Eder. Manchester, U.K., 1999. Pages 138–172.

Frey, Michel. "Du mariage et du concubinage dans les classes populaires à Paris (1846–1847)." *Annales* (July–August 1978): 803–829.

Fuchs, Rachel G. *Poor and Pregnant in Paris: Strategies for Survival in the Nineteenth Century.* New Brunswick, N.J., 1992.

Gennep, Arnold van. *Manuel de folklore français contemporain.* Paris, 1977. Original edition 1937–1953.

Knodel, John E. *Demographic Behavior in the Past: A Study of Fourteen German Village Populations in the Eighteenth and Nineteenth Centuries.* Cambridge, U.K., 1988.

Laslett, Peter. *Family Life and Illicit Love in Earlier Generations: Essays in Historical Sociology.* Cambridge, U.K., 1977.

Laslett, Peter. *The World We Have Lost.* London and New York, 1965.

Mossuz-Lavau, Janine. *Les lois de l'amour: Les politiques de la sexualité en France de 1950 à nos jours.* Paris, 1991.

Phan, Marie-Claude. *Les amours illégitimes: Histoire de séduction en Languedoc (1676–1786).* Paris, 1986.

Shorter, Edward. *The Making of the Modern Family.* New York, 1975.

Sohn, Anne-Marie. *Chrysalides: Femmes dans la vie privée (XIX–XX siècles).* Paris, 1996. Pages 549–633.

Sohn, Anne-Marie. *Du premier baiser à l'alcôve: La sexualité des Français au quotidien (1850–1950).* Paris, 1996.

Sohn, Anne-Marie. *Les rôles féminins dans la vie privée à l'époque de la III République: Rôles théoriques, rôles vécus.* Thèse d'État, Université de Paris I, 1993. See chapter 8, "La jeune fille et les écueils de la fréquentation," and chapter 14, "De l'épouse à la concubine." Pages 974–1038.

Tilly, Louise A., and Joan W. Scott. *Women, Work, and Family.* New York, 1978.

PUBERTY

Alexandra M. Lord

Europeans have traditionally regarded puberty as a dangerous demarcation point between adulthood and childhood. Much of this anxiety has stemmed from the fact that puberty signals the emergence of adult sexuality. But concerns about puberty have also been linked to medical and lay perceptions of the mature and immature body. As a transition point between adulthood and childhood, puberty has often been characterized as a period of "great weakness." In becoming an adult, the adolescent was believed to experience a radical physiological transformation. For boys, this transformation was defined in terms of the emergence of sexual desire, the appearance of body and facial hair, a deepening of the voice and a growth in height. For girls, puberty has been defined first and foremost in terms of menarche. This emphasis on menarche has been widespread despite the fact that Europeans from the ancients onwards have recognized that other factors—the appearance of body hair, the emergence of breasts and the development of sexual desire—are also linked with female puberty.

A PERIOD OF DIFFERENTIATION AND DANGER

Because physical maturity is linked to socioeconomic factors, ages at puberty have fluctuated from region to region and from period to period. In general, European women appear to have experienced menarche relatively late, at anywhere between fourteen and sixteen. Instances of women experiencing puberty at the age of twelve and thirteen can, of course, be found, but these cases are relatively uncommon and appear to have been regarded as highly unusual by contemporaries. Ages at menarche appear to have remained fairly constant before the nineteenth century; beginning in the late nineteenth century, improved nutrition, especially in Western Europe, began to have an impact upon the emergence of maturity. Ages at menarche then began to drop, with women experiencing

their first menstrual cycle at anywhere between twelve and fourteen.

In the absence of such a clear marker as menarche, calculating men's ages at puberty is difficult. However, the link between sexuality and puberty may provide some insights into this subject. Medical texts, contemporary literature, journals, inquisition records, and a variety of other sources indicate that many boys began experimenting sexually around the age of twelve or thirteen. Religious rituals marking the emergence of adulthood, such as the Christian practice of confirmation and the Jewish bar mitzvah, would also seem to indicate that most Europeans viewed the emergence of adulthood as occurring between twelve and fourteen. This age appears to have been fairly constant. But in view of the role nutrition plays in the development of puberty, it is possible that physical maturity occurred later in preindustrial than in industrial Europe.

Occurring as they did at similar ages, male and female puberty were often seen in complementary terms. Thus the ability to produce semen was often viewed as a parallel process to the ability to produce menstrual fluid. Discussions of the changes in a women's breasts and nipples were often paralleled by discussions of the changes which occurred in a young man's nipples. And just as a young man's voice became deeper with the emergence of puberty so too did a young woman's voice become higher. These similarities did not, however, mean that female and male puberty were seen as being analogous. According to both lay and medical writings, female puberty resulted in an overall weakening of the body, with the end result being that women became both physically and mentally weaker than their male counterparts. Conversely, male puberty led to an increase in both physical and mental strength. In other words, rather than illustrating the similarities between the sexes, puberty underscored the differences between them.

Even in medical models that elided the differences between the sexes, such as Aristotle's one-sex model, puberty was seen as a pivotal point in differentiating between male and female traits. According to the Aristotelian schema, the primary difference between men and women was one of heat. Women, being colder, lacked the external genitals that characterized the male body. But puberty—among a range of other activities such as jumping or active sex—could transform the female body by causing an increase in heat, resulting in the emergence of male genitalia. Women could thus become men. Men could not become women as all creatures strove toward perfection. Being already perfect, the male body remained static, even during puberty. In medical texts and lay literature, this point was best illustrated by the story of Marie-Germain Garnier. Garnier had lived as a girl until, at the age of fifteen, she experienced puberty. This, combined with the violent and highly physical act of jumping across a ditch, caused a rupturing of Garnier's internal ligaments and, ultimately, the emergence of a penis. Garnier was now publicly acknowledged to be a man and his/her story was widely circulated. The famous sixteenth-century surgeon Ambroise Paré (1510–1590) claimed to have met Garnier, and he used the story to demonstrate the fungible nature of sexual difference in his medical text, *On Monsters and Marvels* (1573). Garnier's story also appeared in Michel de Montaigne's *Travel Journal* and *Essays* (1580), while a folk song insured that the story remained well known among both the literate and illiterate. Other less well known but equally graphic examples of women becoming men during puberty can be found in medical literature dating back to the ancients.

While this transformation from female to male was the most dramatic evidence of the body's instability during puberty, it was not the only sign of the body's precarious state during this period. Beginning with the ancient Greeks, medical practitioners routinely emphasized the role puberty played in initiating diseases. According to Hippocrates, adolescents experiencing puberty could expect to suffer from not only the diseases associated with childhood but from a range of other diseases as well, most dramatically prolonged fevers and epistaxis (bleeding from the nose). Later practitioners echoed this sentiment, arguing that puberty was often characterized by the onset of consumption (tuberculosis), convulsions, or epilepsy. On the positive side, puberty could also signal the termination of childhood diseases—in particular, the termination of epilepsy and the disappearance of testicular dropsy (an enlargement of the testicles). However, practitioners were more inclined to emphasize the relationship between puberty and the onset of new diseases; the termination of childhood diseases, while a characteristic of puberty, was often downplayed or even ignored. Puberty thus came to be more commonly viewed in negative rather than positive terms.

FEMALE PUBERTY

While both male and female puberty were characterized as periods of dangerous instability, female puberty was widely regarded as the more dangerous of the two. The reasons for this belief stemmed, in large part, from the emphasis which Europeans placed on the appearance of a young girl's first menses. Because the Jewish, Christian, and Islamic traditions all saw menstruation as a fundamentally unclean process, a young girl's first menstrual cycle marked a negative transition point in her life. Leviticus detailed the restrictions to be placed on a woman once she had experienced puberty; menstruating women were prohibited from engaging in any type of intercourse with men and from participating in various religious rituals. Nowhere was the stigma associated with menarche more evident than in the Eastern Orthodox Christian tradition; before experiencing puberty, young girls were allowed to participate in a range of religious rituals as well as allowed freedom of movement within the church. The emergence of menarche, however, put an end to this freedom. While the Western church was not as consistent in forbidding menstruating women from full participation in various rituals, western theologians routinely portrayed menstruating women as unclean. Outside of the Christian tradition, adherence to Leviticus was even stricter. For Jewish women, puberty meant that a woman was now required to attend the *mikvah,* the ritual bath which cleansed a woman after her menses. And among Islamic gypsies, menstruation was also seen as a form of pollution—a clear indication that, while puberty might bestow adult status on a young girl, it also carried negative overtones.

This negative view of puberty was not limited to the realm of theology; it was endorsed by medical theory as well as folk beliefs. For pre-nineteenth-century medical practitioners, menstruation and its causes were regarded as inexplicable. While the theories explaining the reasons behind this process were myriad, the menses was almost always defined in terms of the weaknesses of the female body. Thus, in experiencing menarche, a young woman's body presented evidence of not only her unclean and therefore sinful state, but also of her physical inferiority.

Although menstruation was typically regarded within the context of physical inferiority and/or of a woman's sinful nature, folk practices that stressed the supernatural aspect of menarche were only slightly less disparaging. In preindustrial Europe, menstrual blood was traditionally viewed as having magical properties such as the ability to tarnish mirrors or to cause flowers to wilt. While these attributes did not necessarily have positive connotations, they did accord the female body some measure of power. This emphasis on the supernatural powers of menstrual blood was reflected in attitudes toward menarche. Not surprisingly, a woman's first menstrual blood was believed to be especially potent; it was often collected and used in the concoction of various potions. Because menstrual blood was often viewed in conjunction with a woman's power over a man, this fluid was believed to be especially effective when used in love philtres. Mothers in medieval France, for example, collected their daughter's first menses to create a charm which would ensure that the girl's future husband would remain faithful to her.

Variations and abnormalities in menarche. Despite its unique and magical properties, medical theorists and folk healers maintained that menstrual blood was prey to a variety of external influences. Paramount among these was climate. Women living in southern and tropical climates were believed to experience an earlier puberty than their counterparts in northern and colder regions. According to this schema, southern women—women living in Italy and Spain—experienced puberty at the age of twelve or thirteen. In tropical regions, the age of puberty was believed to drop even lower; women in Africa were widely held to experience menarche at eight or nine. Northern women—women living in Britain or the Netherlands—experienced puberty at the age of fifteen or sixteen. In arctic regions, there was even some debate as to whether women *ever* experienced menarche. Women in Lapland, for example, were sometimes characterized as suffering from a permanent form of amenorrhea (an absent menses). Although there was no evidence to support this view of climatic influences and although medical practitioners began to dismiss this theory in the nineteenth century, this belief lingered among lay people. As a result, there is and always has been a tendency to regard women from southern regions as experiencing sexual maturity at an earlier age than their counterparts from northern regions. As an early puberty has often been linked to a greater sexual awareness and sexual promiscuity, this belief has led many Europeans to argue that women from southern or tropical regions are more inclined to sexual passion and sexual activity than their "colder" counterparts from northern Europe.

This link has also led many practitioners to argue that sexual maturity and morality are strongly connected. During the eighteenth century, the noted French physician Jean Astruc (1684–1766) echoed the concerns of many of his contemporaries when he argued that an early menarche could be precipitated simply by the reading of obscene books or by unchaste touching. Astruc's theory was endorsed by a variety of physicians and found additional support among clergymen and moralists. This view continued to hold sway among lay people throughout the nineteenth and twentieth centuries. Thus, in European culture, a late puberty has typically been regarded as preferable to an early one, since a late menarche is often viewed as evidence of a young girl's greater sense of delicacy and modesty.

While an early puberty was not desirable, most medical practitioners and lay people agreed that an excessive retardation in puberty was also best avoided. Young girls who reached the age of seventeen or eighteen without a menses were characterized as suffering from primary amenorrhea or chlorosis, a term which referred to the greenish cast the skin assumed. This greenish coloring was, in fact, believed to be so pronounced that lay practitioners often called the disease "the green sickness." Throughout the Middle Ages and early modern period, chlorosis was believed to stem from one of two causes. In the first case, the body produced menstrual fluid, but because there was no egress for this fluid, blood accumulated within the body. This form of the disease was regarded as dangerous; although menstrual fluid was not believed to be toxic, its retention within the body could cause it to *become* toxic. In the second case, chlorosis was the direct result of a malformation within the hypersensitive uterus. This form of chlorosis was believed to be even more dangerous than the first. Practitioners and even lay people commonly maintained that this disease resulted in death if not properly treated. Possible causes for either form of primary amenorrhea were numerous, but beginning in the eighteenth century, medical practitioners began to argue that affluent and urban lifestyles were among the primary causes of this disorder. Although widely accepted, this theory was contradicted by the evidence, as most women who suffered from primary amenorrhea were drawn from the working classes.

To cure this disorder, practitioners advocated several different remedies. In cases where the fusion of the hymen prevented menarche, practitioners were told to pierce the hymen to allow the blood to escape. But while this treatment was frequently recommended, this procedure was rarely performed, undoubtedly because of concerns regarding a young girl's chastity. Although Europeans were aware that a torn hymen did not always indicate that a girl was not a virgin, most parents were reluctant to allow their daughters to undergo this procedure. Actual treatments for amenor-rhea were, as a result, often less dramatic. Emmena-gogues—medications which were believed to provoke the menses—were commonly used, and adolescents' diets were closely monitored under the belief that a proper diet would foster the growth of the womb. Young girls were also warned of the dangers associated with indolent and excessively affluent lifestyles. Some historians have argued that this attack on affluent life-styles is evidence of a class hostility on the part of medi-cal practitioners, who were often from the lower middle class.

The medicalization of "normal menarche." Hos-tility and criticism of their patients' lifestyles may also have reflected practitioners' uneasiness in discussing menarche with female patients. While historians have argued that there was no real taboo on discussions of menstruation in preindustrial Europe, the care and treatment of women experiencing menarche had tra-ditionally been confined to the female-dominated practice of midwifery. Beginning in the seventeenth century, however, male medical practitioners began to argue that the dangers presented by menarche were such that medical assistance was necessary. Male prac-titioners now began to inquire about their patients' menstrual cycles, often noting the patient's age at menarche and using this age to predict and assess the patient's health. While some doctors argued that a woman who never experienced menarche was still a woman, the growing consensus held that a "normal menarche" was the primary hallmark of good health.

But even a "normal menarche" entailed the be-lief that women were more fragile and less stable than men. William Osborn, an eighteenth-century British medical practitioner, argued that a young girl's first menses was lightly colored. Her second and later men-ses assumed darker colors as a result of the fear that she experienced upon receiving her first menses and noting the external changes that puberty had wrought upon her body. Descriptions of puberty echoed such sen-timents by describing it as a "crisis" and defining it as the result of vessels being "forced open" by an excess of blood. The emphasis on the violent nature of pu-berty may explain why so many girls were unprepared for menarche. Fear, combined with a growing prud-ery—especially during the nineteenth century—fed a vicious cycle: Many mothers were reluctant to dis-cuss menarche with their daughters, and as a result some girls seem to have been caught unaware by their first menses. Their reactions of fear and distaste con-firmed many practitioners' belief that menarche was an especially traumatic and turbulent period for a young girl.

In the nineteenth century, the British psychia-trist Henry Maudsley took this argument a step fur-ther, arguing that the onset of menstruation was so draining that girls needed to be cautioned against the overexpenditure of energy during this crucial period. According to Maudsley, the physical drains on the body during puberty were so great as to preclude any type of intellectual activity. Competition was to be avoided, as it could damage a young girl's nerves, push-ing her over the edge into insanity. Overall, any over-expenditure of energy during puberty could, Maudsley insisted, result not only in amenorrhea and sterility but even the atrophying of the breasts. Thus, young girls who were careless of their health during this period would never become women; instead they would be-come "sexless beings" whose monstrous nature and inability to reproduce would result in race suicide. Al-though vigorously refuted by many of his contempo-raries, Maudsley's argument was used throughout the late nineteenth century to justify the exclusion of women from higher education.

Hysteria and other disorders of female puberty. Concerns regarding puberty were not limited to dis-cussions about menarche. From the classical period into the twentieth century, female puberty was asso-ciated with a range of disorders. Among the best known of these were hysteria, insanity, and anorexia nervosa. The profound psychological and physiolog-ical changes which occurred at puberty were also be-lieved to accentuate a tendency toward epilepsy, con-sumption, and convulsions. Experiences at puberty also shaped a woman's interaction with the supernat-ural: throughout the Middle Ages and most of the early modern period, young girls who were between twelve and sixteen were believed to be especially vul-nerable to possession by demonic spirits. And in the nineteenth century, most famous female mediums claimed to have experienced an especially traumatic puberty.

Of all the diseases associated with puberty, hys-teria has had the strongest and longest connection. This strong connection stems in large part from the fact that hysteria has traditionally been viewed as a disease of the womb. While the causes assigned to this disease have not always remained constant from pe-riod to period, most medical practitioners have asso-ciated the disease primarily with women. When prac-titioners have sought to disassociate this disorder from the womb, the implication has always been that hys-teria was a gynecological problem—a disease rooted in uniquely female organs. Thus, puberty, the period when the womb underwent the most dramatic change, was traditionally linked with hysteria. Even doctors who claimed that hysteria stemmed from neurological causes were inclined to see a connection between puberty and hysteria. Typically, Robert Whytt, an eighteenth-century professor of medicine at the University of Edinburgh, argued that hysteria was a nervous disorder but then went on to link the disease with adolescents and menstrual disorders. According to Whytt and many of his contemporaries, primary amenorrhea could and often did initiate an attack of hysteria. Even the fright which a young girl experienced upon her first menses could trigger an hysterical episode. Later medical practitioners took a more sophisticated approach, linking hysteria and puberty with a growing sense of sexual awareness. Sigmund Freud (1856–1939), for example, claimed that girls who expressed boyish attributes as children were most likely to experience hysteria at puberty. This hysteria was directly caused by the repression of a young girl's masculine desires; this repression, while presenting dangers to a young girl's health, was necessary if feminine desire was to emerge.

While alarming, hysteria was not the most significant threat which faced a young girl at puberty. According to many Victorian doctors, insanity posited one of the greatest dangers of adolescence. Mental breakdowns during puberty were always explained in biological terms—they were, in other words, a result of the physical changes associated with puberty. Yet evidence suggests that the insanity exhibited by many pubescent girls stemmed from the restrictions placed on them during this period. Certainly, the onset of menstruation and the corresponding development of breasts and body hair sharply limited the activities which a young girl could pursue; travel, exercise, and physical activities were often prohibited. Given the intense scrutiny which young girls underwent at this point in their lives, it is not surprising that many of them rebelled and that their rebellions were often couched in terms of mental instability.

Like insanity, anorexia nervosa has often been characterized as one of the most serious illnesses associated with adolescence and puberty. Varying forms of this disorder can be found throughout European history; however, it was not until the nineteenth century that Europeans began to make a strong connection between puberty and anorexia nervosa. Several instances of "fasting girls" received widespread press attention in the early part of this century, but it was only in 1868 that the British practitioner William Gull isolated and named the disease. While Gull did not make a direct equation between anorexia nervosa and puberty, he argued that the disease was common in young girls between the ages of sixteen and twenty-three, ages commonly associated with sexual matu-

ration. In 1873, the French physician Charles Lesègue termed the disease hysterical anorexia and claimed that food refusal stemmed from a conflicted relationship between a maturing girl and her parents. According to Gull, Lesègue, and their contemporaries, puberty was characterized by peculiar cravings and irregular eating patterns. In both medical and lay literature, these bizarre eating patterns were often taken as evidence of unnatural sexual appetites. Masturbation was not uncommon among these girls. To prevent this type of behavior, parents were told to monitor their daughter's health before it deteriorated. Again, the implication was clear; without proper care, a young girl's experience of puberty would be a negative one. This trend and view continued into the twentieth century. Although perceptions of anorexia nervosa shifted during this century, the disease continued to be associated with girls experiencing and/or completing puberty. In fact, some theorists began to argue that girls experiencing anorexia nervosa were attempting to retard or reverse their sexual maturation.

A host of other disorders—epilepsy, consumption, "long-continued fevers," and convulsions—were also linked to puberty. The causes of these diseases were believed to be myriad. But most medical theorists linked these disorders with menarche. In those cases where the menses was absent or retarded, practitioners argued that any one of a range of illnesses could be expected. Consumption, for example, might occur because, lacking a natural egress, menstrual fluid would accumulate and collect in the weak and maturing lungs of adolescents. Consumption was also linked to the vanity which most young girls began to experience at puberty; according to some practitioners, the pre- and postpubescent girl's desire for a slim figure led to irregular eating which led, in turn, to consumption. Epilepsy and convulsions, both of which were seen as separate and distinct disorders, were often linked to the instability caused either by puberty itself or by the onset of new passions during this period.

While medical discussions such as these always cast puberty in dire terms, religious and lay perceptions of female puberty did little to contradict this view. It might be argued, in fact, that medical practitioners took their cue from Judeo-Christian doctrine; as evidence of a woman's sinful nature and impurity, the menses and its onset could never be regarded with equanimity. But even in lay terms, the onset of menarche would always be a troubling issue. While puberty signaled the emergence of womanhood, it also signaled the advent of a restricted life. Before the development of the tampon and effective birth control in the twentieth century, menarche and menstruation would always circumscribe a woman's activities.

MALE PUBERTY

Male puberty has traditionally received less attention from medical, lay, and religious writers than its female counterpart. To some degree, this more limited emphasis may have been the result of the more diffuse nature of sexual maturation in men. Although many ancient and medieval writers argued that male puberty began at a specific moment (most typically at the age of fourteen), and that the production of semen paralleled the onset of the menses, the process of maturation is not as clearly delineated in men as it is in women. This lack of a clear demarcation point for male puberty was not, however, the only reason for limited discussions of this topic in religious, lay, and medical literature. A young boy's sexual maturation, while not without dangers, carried less negative overtones than that experienced by his sister. For theologians, a young boy's maturation might incline him toward masturbation and other forms of illicit sexual activity, but it did not automatically render him impure. In fact, religious rituals commemorating a young boy's coming of age were often couched in highly positive terms. For lay writers, male puberty entailed the emergence of adulthood—and as male adulthood brought freedom, not restrictions, male puberty was often depicted in relatively positive terms. Medical writers agreed, presenting puberty as a period when a young boy came into his full strength. Viewed from this perspective, it is not surprising that most Europeans regarded male puberty with less concern than they did its female counterpart.

This did not mean that Europeans completely ignored male puberty. From the ancients onwards, the subject was discussed in both medical and lay texts—although always as a subsidiary to female puberty. The relative absence of medical literature on male puberty stems from the fact that the male body was never medicalized to the extent that its female counterpart was. While the female body was the focus of midwifery and gynecological texts, the male body was usually discussed within the context of general medicine. As a result, the unique nature of male biology was often ignored.

Concern over male sexuality. According to many ancient and medieval medical practitioners, the key difference between the sexes lay in one of heat. Men were hotter than women, a characteristic which enabled them to grow facial hair and extensive body hair. Although some practitioners speculated that men matured at a slower rate than women, this type of speculation often took a back seat to more general discussions of sexual maturation. For early medical writers, as for their later counterparts, male puberty was often directly linked to a young boy's emerging sexuality.

During the Middle Ages, writers as varied as Hildegard of Bingen and Albertus Magnus agreed that the production of semen was not necessary for a boy to experience sexual pleasure. Puberty did not, in other words, result in the emergence of sexual desire. However, puberty did mark an increase in this desire. The release of this passion—through masturbation and even intercourse—was regarded with some ambivalence. Albertus Magnus argued that moderate sexual activity during this period would enable the body to grow faster. Sexual intercourse could also contribute to the greater nourishment of the body as the ejaculation of semen entailed the expulsion of "humidities" which impeded the body's heat. But while Albertus Magnus and other writers might argue that sexual activity was natural and to be encouraged during this period, this did not mean that medieval writers called for unlimited sexual activity. Most lay and medical writers agreed that excessive intercourse during this period could harm a young boy. But if excessive sexual activity could damage a young man's health, so too could sexual inactivity. Medieval writers warned their readers that an inability to produce semen at this period denoted a lifetime of impotence.

The dangers of masturbation. Beginning in the eighteenth century and stretching into the Victorian era, practitioners began to be more condemning of the dangers associated with sexual activity during puberty. As numerous historians have pointed out, the Enlightenment signaled a shift in thinking about masturbation, illicit sexuality, and, therefore, puberty. Beginning with the publication of the anonymous *Onania* (c. 1710) and S. A. Tissot's *Onanism or a Treatise upon the Disorders Produced by Masturbation* in 1760, masturbation by young boys came under increasing attack. By the nineteenth century, it was commonly accepted that the temptation to masturbate was especially prevalent in young boys experiencing puberty; according to most medical literature, this activity could and did permanently damage a young boy's health. Even writers such as the Victorian physician George Drysdale, who maintained that the generative organs required "due exercise" from puberty onwards, spoke of the dangers associated with "self-pollution."

Resulting as it did in the wasting of semen, this practice was commonly believed to cause incurable nervous and hypochondriac complaints as well as an overall "constitutional weakness." These fears regarding adolescent masturbation stemmed from a variety of factors. Beginning in the eighteenth century, a growing number of medical and lay texts began to explore the moral welfare of children and adolescents. Texts condemning adolescent masturbation were, then, a part of a wider publishing trend in which the experiences of childhood and adolescence were being prioritized.

Although sexual maturation could, at least in biological terms, enable young men to marry and produce children, Europeans did not encourage young men to marry immediately after puberty. The reasons for delayed marriage were, of course, economic, but medical writers provided a justification for later marriages by viewing sexual activity during and immediately after puberty in nonreproductive terms. Condemnations of masturbation may have been linked to fears that young men were marrying later; without the natural outlet of marriage, young men were believed to turn to masturbation for relief. It was not until the late nineteenth and early twentieth century, with the publication and acceptance of works by writers such as Havelock Ellis (1859–1939) and Sigmund Freud, that masturbation during puberty came to be viewed in less negative terms.

Puberty and the attributes of masculinity. The external changes wrought by puberty also reflected a young man's sexuality. Typically, the appearance of facial and body hair was seen as a mark of virility. Both medical and lay literature claimed that the hairier the man, the more powerful was his libido. Thus, both the quantity and location of the hair which appeared on a young man during puberty were viewed as evidence of his sexual temperament. As men from southern Europe were often believed to be more hirsute than their counterparts from northern Europe, this connection between hair and sexuality was undoubtedly behind the belief that southern men were more sexually active than their northern counterparts. While the sexuality of southern women was depicted in negative terms, the virility of southern and hirsute man was widely admired.

Concerns regarding puberty and the physical changes which occurred during this period were not linked solely to sexuality. Before puberty, young men were believed to possess a feminine appearance; in lay literature, prepubescent boys, with their smooth skin and high voices, often played upon their sexual ambiguity by assuming feminine personas. This type of gender distortion was frowned upon in postpubescent boys, and concerns regarding sexual ambiguity can be found in the writings of moralists and medical practitioners. Of particular concern to these writers was the descent of the testicles, as the failure of these organs to descend at puberty would result in sterility. But while this aspect of puberty was frequently discussed, treatments for this disorder remained rudimentary and ineffective throughout most of European history. Along with the natural descent of the testicles, practitioners also discussed the external changes which occurred at puberty and the ways in which these changes should be regarded. Medical texts informed readers that, although alarming, the changes wrought by puberty were not to be feared. Thus the appearance of a milky serum in a young boy's breasts during puberty was, medical texts insisted, as natural as the appearance of facial hair. Neither should be regarded as evidence of an abnormality.

In fact, in discussions of male puberty, the emphasis was almost always positive, stressing the naturalness of a boy's physical development. This view reflected the widely held belief that puberty resulted in a surge of strength for young boys. In becoming men, boys left the protected world of childhood to enter into a world of wider opportunities and, on occasion, greater physical activity. Typically, the eighteenth-century French writer M. Brouzet argued that boys experiencing puberty were naturally attracted by activities such as hunting and militaristic games. This attraction was not surprising, as puberty entailed not only a surge of physical strength but also the emergence of greater confidence. While natural and to be expected, this vitality could be sapped if proper care was not taken. Education was especially crucial at this period, as it helped a young boy to become aware of his new masculine role. For many moralists and medical writers, this meant that separation of the sexes was to be encouraged during this pivotal period in a young man's life.

The fear that a young man would fail to assume masculine characteristics even after puberty was, of course, a very real one. The rigid gender divisions of European society required the creation of a clear demarcation point, which differentiated between the masculine and feminine spheres. Young boys who failed to become masculine as teenagers distorted gender roles and were thus feared by their contemporaries. Concerns regarding male puberty were, as a result, most significant at periods when masculinity was in doubt or under attack. Under normal circumstances, however, a young man's puberty was depicted in positive terms, for it opened up for him a world of wider opportunities.

CONCLUSION

Throughout European history, lay, medical, and religious writers have viewed puberty as a period of great instability. These views stemmed in part from the fact that this period was characterized by the creation of a sharp demarcation point between masculine and feminine. Before puberty, gender roles, while distinct, were not always defined in absolute terms. The physical changes wrought by puberty, however, served to accentuate and justify the social divisions of gender within this society. When looked at through the lens of gender, puberty took on sharply different meanings. For women, puberty was often viewed in negative terms, as it marked the end of a young girl's freedom. For men, of course, the converse was true; puberty marked the emergence of freedom. Despite shifts in medical perceptions of the body and despite the changes in religious views which have occurred over the last five hundred years, these views of puberty have remained fairly consistent over time. Only in the twentieth century—and then only gradually and incompletely—did new views of sexuality and the development of new methods of artificial birth control modify traditional concerns to some degree.

See also other articles in this section.

BIBLIOGRAPHY

Ariès, Philippe. *Centuries of Childhood: A Social History of Family Life.* Translated by Robert Baldick. New York, 1962.

Brumberg, Joan. *Fasting Girls: The Emergence of Anorexia Nervosa as a Modern Disease.* New York, 1988.

Cadden, Joan. *The Meanings of Sex Difference in the Middle Ages: Medicine, Science and Culture.* Cambridge, U.K., and New York, 1993.

Crawford, Patricia. "Attitudes to Menstruation in Seventeenth-Century England," *Past and Present* 91 (1981): 47–73.

Duden, Barbara. *The Woman beneath the Skin: A Doctor's Patients in Eighteenth-Century Germany.* Translated by Thomas Dunlap. Cambridge, Mass., 1991.

Figlio, Karl. "Chlorosis and Chronic Disease in Nineteenth-Century Britain: The Social Constitution of Somatic Illness in a Capitalist Society," *Social History* 3 (1978): 167–197.

Fletcher, Anthony. *Gender, Sex, and Subordination in England, 1500–1800.* New Haven, Conn., 1995.

Foucault, Michel. *The History of Sexuality: An Introduction.* Translated by Robert Hurley. New York, 1985.

Laqueur, Thomas. *Making Sex: Body and Gender from the Greeks to Freud.* Cambridge, Mass., 1990.

Le Roy Ladurie, Emmanuel. *Mountaillou: The Promised Land of Error.* Translated by Barbara Bray. New York, 1978.

Lord, Alexandra. " 'The Great *Arcana* of the Deity': Menstruation and Menstrual Disorders in Eighteenth-Century British Medical Thought." *Bulletin of the History of Medicine* 73 (1999): 38–63.

Maclean, Ian. *The Renaissance Notion of Woman: A Study in the Fortunes of Scholasticism and Medical Science in European Intellectual Life.* Cambridge, U.K., and New York, 1980.

Porter, Roy, and Mikuláš Teich, eds. *Sexual Knowledge, Sexual Science: The History of Attitudes to Sexuality.* Cambridge, U.K., and New York, 1994.

Porter, Roy and Lesley Hall, eds. *The Facts of Life: The Creation of Sexual Knowledge in Britain, 1650–1950.* New Haven, Conn., 1995.

Risse, Guenter. "Hysteria at the Edinburgh Infirmary: The Construction and Treatment of a Disease, 1770–1800." *Medical History* 32 (1988): 1–22.

Showalter, Elaine. *The Female Malady: Women, Madness and English Culture, 1830–1980.* New York, 1985.

MASTURBATION

Lesley A. Hall

Masturbation is usually regarded as an asocial, even antisocial act, normally conducted in private (or at least under conditions of some furtiveness) by an individual, without engaging with another person as sexual partner—except perhaps as the object of voyeurism or fantasy. However, because of the social loading with which all sexual acts are freighted, and thus the social implications of even the most solipsistic act of sexual gratification, masturbation (self-abuse, onanism, the solitary pleasure, defilement with the hand, the secret vice, bashing the bishop, squeezing the lizard, spanking the monkey, jerking off, wanking, etc.) has significant claims to be discussed among other manifestations of the sexual urge.

It is probably the most universal of all sexual practices, at least among men. Surveys on the subject since the nineteenth century suggest that well over 90 percent of men masturbate at some time during their lives. However, the figures for women are significantly lower, though different surveys give a much wider range of variation. Women tend to start at a later age than men, and their frequency of masturbation is around half that of men. The practice has not been the subject of legal regulation, though an 1896 British case of a man arrested for "procuring an indecent act with himself" (presumably in public) is on record (*R. v. Jones and Bowerbank*).

Masturbation is of particular interest to the historian since it quite suddenly became the subject of a medico-moral panic early in the eighteenth century. Although this panic underwent mutations over the course of time, it did not disperse until well into the twentieth century. Its repercussions are still making themselves felt.

Allusions to masturbatory activity can be traced back into antiquity, although the most famous ancient example, the crime for which Onan was struck dead (Genesis 38:9), was not masturbation at all but coitus interruptus, when Onan refused to impregnate the widow of his deceased brother according to the levirate requirement. A rather more positive vision was perhaps conveyed by Egyptian myths of origin crediting the creation of the universe to masturbatory acts by divine beings: Ra of Heliopolis, for example, emerged from the primeval swamp, masturbated, swallowed his semen, and impregnated himself with the god Shu and the goddess Tefnut. However, it would appear that in the case of humans, for whom the act was not procreative as it was for deities but rather the inverse, masturbation was, if not completely stigmatized, not approved or recommended. The Greek Cynic philosopher Diogenes is purported to have masturbated publicly, remarking that it was a pity that the pangs of hunger could not be assuaged as easily as the pangs of lust, simply by rubbing the affected part. In classical antiquity masturbation was largely framed within wider discourses of decorum, propriety, and avoidance of excess that were generally applicable to manifestations of sexual desire.

Within Christianity masturbation, which was largely believed to be particularly the vice of the celibate and the young, was included under the heading of sins of the flesh and considered to contravene natural law. However, it was not the subject of particular scrutiny in the confessional, and unlike other sins of the flesh (such as sodomy), it was not penalized under secular law within Christendom.

For many centuries the Western medical tradition considered it to be no more deleterious than any other manifestation of lust—that is, if not indulged to excess. Indeed, within the Galenic humoral system of medicine, excessive continence causing retention of semen was regarded as almost equally damaging.

THE INVENTION OF A MENACE

These attitudes changed some time around the first decade of the eighteenth century, for reasons that are still the subject of considerable historiographical debate. The immediate cause is well known. Sometime during the first two decades of the century an anonymous volume entitled *Onania: or, The Heinous Sin of Self-Pollution, and All its Frightful Consequences, in*

ONANIA:

OR, THE

HEINOUS SIN

OF

Self-Pollution,

AND ALL ITS

FRIGHTFUL CONSEQUENCES (in Both Sexes)

CONSIDERED:

With Spiritual and Physical ADVICE to those who have already injured themselves by this abominable Practice.

The EIGHTEENTH EDITION, as also the NINTH EDITION of the *SUPPLEMENT* to it, both of them Revised and Enlarged, and now Printed together in One Volume.

As the several Passages in the *Former* Impressions, that have been charged with being obscure and ambiguous, are, in these, cleared up and explained, there will be no more Alterations or Additions made.

And ONAN *knew that the Seed should not be his: And it came to pass, when he went in unto his Brother's Wife, that he spilled it on the Ground, lest that he should give Seed to his Brother.*
And the Thing which he did, displeased the LORD; *wherefore he slew him also.* Gen. xxxviii. 9, 10.

Non Quis, Sed Quid.

LONDON:

Printed for H. COOKE, at the R _Correct Sta._ _Fleet-street,_
1756.

[Price Bound   *Shillings* and *Sixpence*]

Onania. Title page of the eighteenth edition, London, 1756. WELLCOME INSTITUTE LIBRARY, LONDON

Both Sexes, Consider'd, with Spiritual and Physical Advice to those, Who Have Already Injur'd Themselves by This Abominable Practice. And Seasonable Admonition to the Youth of the Nation, (of both Sexes) and Those Whose Tuition They Are Under, Whether Parents, Guardians, Masters, or Mistresses was published in London. Its pathbreaking message about the uniquely disastrous consequences of the solitary vice was disseminated throughout Europe. Its claims for the physical deleteriousness of masturbation seem the stranger, given that the anonymous author—possibly a Dr. Bekkers, an obscure figure—appears in fact not to have been a doctor but a clergyman, or at least at one time in orders. Certainly he gave more attention to the sinfulness of the practice than its harmfulness, even while proffering a patent quack remedy. The work probably deserves a place in the history of advertising as an early example of creating anxiety about an alleged affliction while holding out a remedy for it. At this stage, masturbation, besides having terrible spiritual consequences, was presented as the cause of a plethora of physical (rather than mental) ailments, affecting not only the genitals themselves (with stranguries, or the slow and painful emission of urine; priapism, a painful persistent state of erection; impotence; and discharges) but the entire bodily system (with epilepsy, consumption, fainting fits), and causing infertility in both sexes.

The book went into many editions. Letters purportedly from grateful readers (and replies) were published in the later editions. Its actual impact is hard to gauge, but at the very least it was presumably profitable enough to be kept in print promoting the advertised medicines. It was very much part of a subculture of quackery and did not figure in serious medical discourse, although there were a number of imitations as well as counterattacks. In 1724, Bernard de Mandeville, in *A Modest Defence of Publick Stews* (i.e., public brothels), perhaps a satire on the onanism panic, argued that fornication with prostitutes was preferable to masturbation.

Critics argued that naming and describing the loathsome practice was itself a vicious action likely to deprave and debauch. Earlier silence on the subject may have been due to the feeling that it was not for public discussion. The author of *Onania* and his successors, however, claimed that the habit was so widespread, and so deleterious, that outspokenness was the only remedy. Innocence was not its own best preservation; it was better by far to warn the young against this pervasive danger. They advanced the "public interest" argument for speaking about forbidden practices: this was an educational enterprise warning against vicious habits and offering remedies for their

consequences. Some historians have argued that, under the guise of an apparently high-minded agenda of social responsibility, tracts on onanism were in fact a new kind of pornography, inciting the sins they claimed to deplore. While it is hard to imagine luridly gothic accounts of the evils of self-abuse as a turn-on, the existence of the literature may have brought the possibility of the practice to the attention of some who had never previously considered it.

The permeability of the boundaries between commercial quackery, orthodox medicine, and popular anxieties, which is a noticeable theme in the history of this "great fear," as Jean Stengers and Anne Van Neck have called it, is demonstrated by the appearance of a work on the subject by the respectable and reputable Swiss physician Samuel Tissot. Initially published as *Tentamen de morbis ex manustupratione* in 1758, it was reissued in French two years later in 1760 as *L'Onanisme, ou Dissertation physique sur les maladies produites par la masturbation* (Onanism, or a treatise upon the disorders produced by masturbation). It was rapidly translated into English, German, Dutch, and Italian and remained current for nearly a century. It was heavily indebted to *Onania*, in particular relying on a detailed if critical analysis of the letters from supposed sufferers published in successive editions of the latter.

Tissot constructed a respectable theory on the cause of the disease of masturbation by careful and selective citation from texts of the ancients and Renaissance physicians about the evils of excessive lust in general. The effects he described were pervasive, afflicting the digestive, respiratory, and nervous systems, creating debility and pallor, and affecting the faculties and memory. In women it caused hysteria and a plethora of uterine problems. Unlike the anonymous author of *Onania*, Tissot produced physiologically based arguments consonant with current medical theories for the reasons why masturbation had such evil consequences. On the one hand he drew on humoral theory for an explanatory model, making the suggestion (which became an enduring tradition) that the loss of one ounce of seminal fluid was equivalent to losing forty ounces of blood. On the other he proposed that the activity was a damaging expenditure of nervous energy in an artificially caused convulsive spasm, upsetting the natural balance of the bodily mechanism. He did not propose any patent remedy for the affliction, preferring to make recommendations for a regimen, such as cold baths, a healthy lifestyle, exercise, regularity of the bowels, moderate amounts of sleep, and an endeavor to keep one's thoughts pure. However, quinine, iron water, and other strengthening medicines were also mentioned.

Masturbation became universally reprobated in Europe. There seems to have been little difference in response between Catholic and Protestant cultures, although there were local variations. The question that fascinates the historian is why, at this particular juncture, a previously largely ignored sexual practice came to be seen as the root of a massive amount of physical harm. It has been argued that the new view of masturbation provided an explanation for a variety of bodily ills that existing medical science was ill equipped to account for, at a time when an increasingly rationalist climate of thought was rejecting supernatural causality. But this argument does not account for the staying power of the belief in masturbation's ill effects; that belief persisted well beyond the rise of alternative explanations for many of the diseases attributed to the practice, although the catalog of its alleged consequences often altered.

With the development of urbanization, a growing emphasis on privacy, and changing social patterns (for example, increasing differentiation and stratification between family members and servants), old community forms and mechanisms of control were breaking down. Thus self-abuse, it may be argued, threatened social and community ties already seen as precarious. Masturbation may have actually increased during the mid-eighteenth century as a result of the rise of a bourgeoisie promoting repressive sexual morality and foreclosing traditional options for sexual gratification among the unmarried. A rise in the age of marriage also may have contributed. Contemporaries occasionally attributed it—or its increasing prevalence and malignance—to the luxurious habits of new urban affluence, novel reading, tea drinking, and other pernicious manifestations of modern life. It is a curious fact, and possibly not coincidental, that the eighteenth century saw a massive production of erotica, in particular printed pornographic texts, very different from productions of earlier folk traditions of carnivalesque bawdiness.

A psychoanalytically influenced perspective argues that, as the idea of hierarchical authority was subjected to serious erosion in the period between the Protestant Reformation and the French Revolution, individuals were faced with greater responsibility for themselves and their families. The anxieties thus generated fostered the development of phobic and compulsive processes—for example, the panic over this "least controllable, least harmful" manifestation of the sexual impulse—as a psychic barrier against pervasive sexual guilt and anxiety. The shift from a culture of externally imposed "shame mechanisms" of social control to one of internally generated "guilt" during this period might also be invoked. However, the panic

was not coterminous with the most obviously Protestant and modernizing cultures of northwestern Europe but was far more wide-ranging.

The relationship between masturbation and what might seem a far more pressing cause of concern regarding sexual conduct, venereal diseases of epidemic prevalence, is convoluted. Many of the symptoms attributed to masturbation—genital discharges, lassitude and debility, sores, rashes and spots, uterine disorders—could well have been those of syphilis, gonorrhea, or a range of other unidentified venereal afflictions. Alternatively, perhaps the prevalence of venereal diseases led some individuals to take the logical step of resorting to masturbation as a substitute for potentially dangerous copulation for the relief of sexual desire. Yet for well over a century promiscuous intercourse (at least for men) was seen as a lesser danger than masturbation, and resort to prostitutes was sometimes recommended as a "cure."

It has also been suggested that fears about masturbation in children in particular were generated by the greater value being attached to children and childhood and increasing anxiety over their moral and physical welfare. A concern for the problem figures in Jean-Jacques Rousseau's programmatic text on progressive child rearing, *Émile* (1762). Yet the cause and effect of this argument could almost be inverted: that is, it could be said that much of the attentive surveillance of the young by parents or within the pedagogic context was being advocated precisely on the grounds that without stringent attention children might fall into "secret habits" of self-abuse.

The changing status of servants within the household fostered growing concern about entrusting them with the care and upbringing of the children of their social superiors. Anxieties about the possible "corruption" of children by social inferiors who might teach them habits of masturbation were pervasive. The extent of the horror around the issue of children not merely falling through ignorance into a deplorable habit but being inducted into it by adults entrusted with their care was demonstrated (but with a very different social and class slant) in the accusation against Marie-Antoinette in the Revolutionary Tribunal that she had taught and encouraged the dauphin (Louis XVII) to masturbate. Thus, the practice could also be subsumed under a rhetoric of "aristocratic debauchery."

FROM DEBILITY TO INSANITY?

Tissot remained the leading medical authority on masturbation well into the nineteenth century. There was no advance in medical thinking on the subject, although it continued to be a topic of medical concern and pedagogic intervention and the basis of a flourishing industry in quack remedies. The next major shift took place around 1840, as various evolving specialties within medicine took an interest.

Several authorities had already expressed the opinion that masturbation played a significant role in the etiology of insanity. As early as 1816 the French physician Jean-Étienne Esquirol wrote that "masturbation is recognized in all countries as a common cause of insanity." In 1839 Sir William Ellis, in his *Treatise on Insanity,* asserted that "by far the most frequent cause of fatuity is debility of the brain and nervous system . . . in consequence of the pernicious habit of masturbation." However, views among physicians were not monolithic, and a number of German authorities in particular expressed some caution about the actual causal relationship of masturbation to insanity, suggesting that the habit might follow upon the onset of the latter rather than lead to it.

While the above writers assumed that masturbation might provoke various kinds of mental disorder, by the 1870s, predominantly in Britain, the category of actual "masturbatory insanity" was defined. Authorities such as David Skae, T. S. Clouston, and Henry Maudsley argued for a particular form of mental disturbance brought on by self-abuse. While some association between masturbation and insanity, especially in adolescents, was believed to exist, there was a relatively rapid retreat from this extreme position: both Clouston and Maudsley conceded a few years later that the connection was far from clear. But masturbation was still not regarded as innocuous. If not the cause of actual insanity, it was indicted for generating "neurasthenia" and nervous disorders.

No simple shift occurred from the idea that masturbation produced physical symptoms to the notion that it caused insanity. Effects on the brain and nerves were mentioned in the eighteenth century, while the physical debilitation threatening the masturbator remained prominent during the nineteenth century. There were shifts of emphasis rather than radical changes.

One of the works most influential on the perception of masturbation throughout Europe in the nineteenth century was Claude-François Lallemand's three-volume *Des pertes séminales involuntaires* (On involuntary seminal discharges; 1842). He was more concerned with the pathological loss of semen—"spermatorrhoea"—through involuntary causes, which could be brought about through the irritation of the genital organs set up by habitual masturbation. "Spermatorrhoea" was seen as being at least as deleterious as

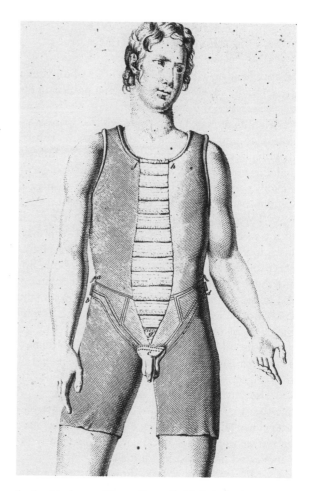

Antimasturbatory Corset. From G. Jalade-Lafond, *Considérations sur les hernies abdominales, sur les bandages herniaires renixigrades, et sur de nouveaux moyens de s'opposer à l'onanisme* (Paris, 1822), plate 13. WELLCOME INSTITUTE LIBRARY, LONDON

masturbation, with the additional horror that it could not be terminated by exercising willpower and self-discipline. It was a godsend to quacks. The imprimatur of Lallemand's name gave it credence within the medical profession, but doctors were careful to differentiate themselves from "advertising quacks" and their often spurious diagnoses of this complaint.

By the last quarter or so of the nineteenth century a few physicians in several European countries were beginning to question the role ascribed to masturbation in the etiology of so many disorders, and some even pronounced it harmless. Sir James Paget, in Britain, suggested during the 1870s that, although a filthy and unmanly habit, it was no more deleterious than sexual intercourse. Like intercourse, it could be debilitating in excess, and because no partner was needed, it was easier to pursue it recklessly.

THERAPEUTICS AND
GENDER ATTITUDES

History has paid a good deal of attention to the brutal prescriptions advocated by the medical profession for the eradication of masturbation (not always adequately differentiated from treatments for spermatorrhoea); around the middle of the nineteenth century, these replaced previous recommendations of lifestyle and dietetic changes. For two or three decades—roughly speaking from the 1850s to 1870s—surgical solutions were proposed to eradicate the peril.

This ruthless agenda may have been the result of the rising belief in the relationship between masturbation and insanity. It may also have been influenced by the advent of the concept of public health and the desirability to the state of a healthy populace. A number of epidemic diseases had been, if not totally eradicated, at least severely curtailed in their effects by programs of sanitary engineering and the enforced quarantine of infectious individuals, while compulsory vaccination schemes seemed to offer the end of the dangerous and disfiguring disease of smallpox. It was also an age of heroic surgery as antisepsis and anesthesia enabled surgeons to go boldly where no scalpel had gone before, a development that may have encouraged belief in surgical cures for previously incurable and intractable conditions.

Most interest has been shown in the relatively rare and unusual operations inflicted on women and girls. The clitoridectomies performed by the British surgeon Isaac Baker Brown during the 1860s in an attempt to alleviate the various disorders in women that he attributed to self-abuse are often cited. Baker Brown's procedures, both operative and in the promotion of his theories, raised an enormous furor within the medical profession, and he was expelled from the London Obstetrical Society after an acrimonious meeting. He subsequently went mad and died shortly afterward. The operation seems to have fallen into more or less total disrepute in Britain. Contemporaneously in France, the eminent French medical scientist Paul Broca argued in a debate at the Société de Chirurgerie de Paris in 1864 that infibulating a girl of five (fastening the sexual organs with a clasp), while a drastic solution to onanism, was preferable to the last resort of clitoridectomy, which nevertheless featured in discussion as a possible expedient.

What gives such cases a possibly undue prominence is their relative infrequency. Masturbation in the male was the object of far greater social anxiety and medico-moral and pedagogic policing throughout the nineteenth century, but it was a constant factor rather than the begetter of scandalous causes célèbres.

Such cases as did arise largely affected quacks rather than legitimate doctors: in Britain following the Medical Act of 1858, some members of the medical profession and moral reform organizations made a concerted effort to prosecute profiteering quacks who drummed up fears of the consequences of masturbation and the dangers of spermatorrhoea and then offered expensive "remedies" (sometimes conjoined with blackmail).

Contemporary accounts suggest that it was very hard for men to avoid the vast amount of propaganda put out by the industry in spurious remedies—posters, handbills distributed in the streets, advertisements in newspapers—even if they managed to spurn the allurements of "anatomical museums," which, with their luridly realistic waxwork representations of the horrific consequences of self-abuse, offered a mix of enlightenment and titillation as a come-on for the sale of patent remedies. In the upper and middle classes public schools provided both a hotbed for the dissemination of masturbatory and homoerotic practices and a source, via schoolmasters' sermons, of more or less explicit horror-mongering about these practices.

There was thus a widespread climate of fear among men about masturbation. This fear-mongering did not just apply to children or young boys but was also aimed at young men, as the increasingly late age of marriage in the middle and upper classes led to concerns about how they managed their sexuality before it achieved a legitimate outlet. Many men were reluctant to take their anxieties to their medical practitioners, fearful of moral condemnation and, perhaps, of the remedies that might be applied. The leading British medical journal *The Lancet* in 1870 mentioned the deployment of caustic preparations and cauterization to render erection painful and guard against improper manipulation, as well as correcting any oversensitivity of the organ in question. Blistering and penile infibulation were also recommended and applied. John Laws Milton's much republished medical tract *On Spermatorrhoea* (1875) included illustrations of toothed and spiked penis rings and electrical alarm systems intended to prevent erection, and thus nocturnal emissions, in sufferers from this dread disease. While similar devices were sold by quacks, they usually purveyed less painful and drastic treatments, such as herbal compounds and "galvanic belts" (which seem to have deployed electricity as a magic revitalizing power, rather than giving electric shocks to the wearer). The topic was also addressed by the proponents of alternative health systems such as phrenology (which held that mental faculties were indicated by the shape of the skull), herbalism, naturopathy (a system of treatment that eschewed drugs and surgery in

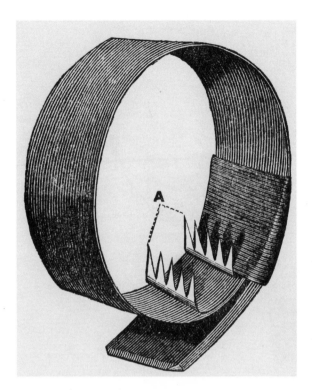

Toothed Urethral Ring. From J. L. Milton, *Pathology and Treatment of Spermatorrhoea* (London, 1887), p. 129. WELLCOME INSTITUTE LIBRARY, LONDON

favor of natural remedies and a healthy regimen), and hydrotherapy.

Parents and teachers were exhorted to employ rigorous surveillance of children (the constant repetition of such exhortations may suggest that this was less practiced than promoted). Corporal punishment and threats of "cutting it off," as well as emphasizing the potential long-term damage to health of playing with the genitals, were recommended. Restraints might also be imposed in cases where the undesirable habit was already established.

MASTURBATION AND NATIONAL DEGENERACY

During the later decades of the nineteenth century a new campaign against the dangers of self-abuse was mounted. Largely directed against the adolescent boy, and initially focusing on the upper and middle classes, it was fed by anxieties about national fitness and the capacity of the existing elite to continue to rule in the face of challenges from rival nations and rising social groups within the nation. The constant subtext of venereal disease, in a period during which clinical observation and investigation were increasingly revealing the long-term and congenital effects of syphilis, was also a factor.

While similar manifestations occurred in other European countries, possibly the most coherent form of this new mutation of masturbation panic can be seen in the "social purity" movement that arose in Great Britain. This movement represented an alliance between feminists who had fought against the regulation of prostitution under the Contagious Diseases Acts of the 1860s, religious interests (provincial nonconformists in particular), public health advocates (medical and nonmedical), and educators.

While "social purity" cannot be reduced to its campaign to purify the nation through the eradication of masturbation, this was a significant element of its strategy. For the feminists within the movement, male lust and its concomitant, the double moral standard (sexual laxity in the male was a peccadillo, in women grounds for social excommunication), was at the root of much that was wrong with society, both on the moral level and in the propagation of disease. It was therefore argued that, since lust was already ineradicably ingrained in the majority of adult males, the target should be youth. Social purity campaigners believed that children should be provided with the clean, pure, true facts about sex and reproduction at an early age, preferably by their mothers, as a counterweight to any misinformation they might acquire from servants or "corrupt companions."

For adolescent boys, however, it was recognized that further warnings were necessary, in particular in the social class in which boys were traditionally sent away to school. This view fit in with the agenda of educators who saw themselves as preparing a new generation of the ruling class of an imperial nation, who needed to be inculcated with the values of self-discipline, self-control, and mastery over the instincts.

Exactly how masturbation endangered the future leaders of the country was not clear-cut. On the one hand, indulgence in self-abuse was seen as fatally eroding habits of self-discipline and resistance to carnal temptation: ultimately the sufferer would be unable to resist the temptations of later life, such as solicitations to fornication and the associated risk of contracting venereal disease. On the other, the traditional discourse of the debilitating effect of masturbation itself was still present, and its ghastly effects on health, sanity, future sexual functioning, and the capacity to father healthy children featured prominently in the growing genre of advice literature.

The awful warnings of social-purity sex educators differed, however, from those of the commercial quacks, who continued to flourish. The social purity

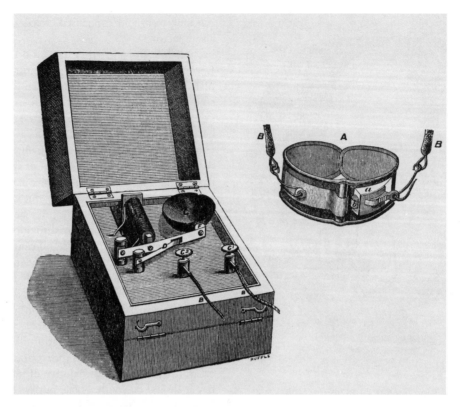

Antimasturbatory Alarm. From J. L. Milton, *Pathology and Treatment of Spermatorrhoea* (London, 1887), p. 132. WELLCOME INSTITUTE LIBRARY, LONDON

campaigners offered the possibility of redemption, condemning the despair created by quack literature so that profit could be made from spurious "cures." The problem was to some extent remoralized, with religion being advocated as a fortifying resource against the habit and prayer commended as a weapon against temptation. The traditional lifestyle prescriptions were made: cold baths, hard beds, early rising, physical exercise, the avoidance of rich and highly seasoned foods as well as alcohol, the distraction of the mind from impure thoughts. In particularly difficult cases, consulting a genuine doctor was recommended.

A vast amount of literature was produced by the social purity movement. In addition to books such as the age-graded works of the American clergyman Sylvanus Stall in his "Self and Sex" series, *What a Young Boy [or Young Man, Young Husband, Man of Forty-Five] Ought to Know* (1897–1907), widely disseminated in Europe, a plethora of pamphlets was produced both by individuals and a range of organizations, distributed free or at a cost of a few pence. These pamphlets found probably their largest outlet in the various youth organizations being established to cope with the newly defined problem of adolescence.

SEXOLOGY AND PSYCHOLOGY

Toward the end of the nineteenth century, a new science of sexology endeavored to investigate sexual behavior, initially in its more anomalous manifestations. Richard von Krafft-Ebing, the Austrian psychiatrist and forensic medicine expert, noted "onanism" as well as degenerate heredity in many cases in his encyclopedic compilation of sexual deviations, *Psychopathia sexualis,* first published in 1886 and subsequently in much expanded editions. However, other writers, notably the British doctor and man of letters Havelock Ellis, drew on anthropological and animal studies to suggest that "auto-erotism" was an almost universal practice. Far from being a uniquely human vice, many animals resorted to analogous behavior, and it was found even among the "primitive" races, contradicting the notion that it was a malign by-product of civilization.

Gradually a somewhat more humane attitude to masturbation emerged. If it was still regarded as reprehensible and not to be encouraged, the horror-mongering of earlier epochs, it was argued, had done much to cause the neurotic sufferings attributed to the practice itself. This new view, however, took quite some time to influence general opinions on the matter. Sir Robert Baden-Powell's *Scouting for Boys* (1908) and *Rovering to Success* (1922) threatened dire outcomes if "beastliness" was practiced, and these texts were published with relevant passages unchanged until well after the Second World War. Leading childcare manuals of the interwar period advised tying children's hands at bedtime to prevent them from masturbating, even as the idea of gently distracting the child's attention, as opposed to threats and punishment, was creeping in as the best mode of handling the "problem." The most progressive works even came to define it as a natural stage in childhood and adolescent development (though "neurotic" in adults).

Marie Stopes, the British birth control advocate and author of the best-selling, widely translated marriage manual, *Married Love: A New Contribution to the Solution of Sex Difficulties* (1918), became a prototypical agony aunt (or advice columnist) for her sexually troubled contemporaries; letters from her male readers suggest that anxieties about the possible damage done by masturbation remained exceedingly prevalent throughout the interwar period. Men of all ages and social classes feared they had affected their health, their ability to father children, and their capacity to function sexually by sometimes very fleeting episodes of adolescent self-abuse. Some of the letter writers specifically cited works such as Stall's and similar social purity literature, but most seem to have picked up their fears as part of the general atmosphere of the time. Occasionally there are faint hints of counterdiscourses—that it was part of the passage to manhood (the social purity literature sometimes suggested that wicked older men might impart this view to boys), that it was preferable to going with prostitutes or ruining good girls. However, in general masturbation for men seems to have become the focus for a range of inchoate anxieties about their own sexuality and sexual functioning, about male desire and "manliness."

What is striking is the lack of any similar anxiety expressed by Stopes's numerous female correspondents. Very few indeed expressed the kind of hysterical fear of ruin characteristic of so many male correspondents. This suggests that whereas male contact with the idea of masturbation was assumed to be almost inevitable, thus requiring the torrent of warning, girls were deemed much less imperiled, and therefore warning them about a vice they had never thought of and were unlikely to come across would be counterproductive. Stopes herself, though reassuring to male fears about lasting damage, was not entirely positive about male masturbation; however, she conceded in correspondence, if not in published works, that masturbation was a possibly permissible expedient for the resolution of sexual tension in the unmarried mature female.

Like a number of her contemporaries, Stopes suggested that masturbation unfitted a person for marriage by accustoming its practitioner to forms of sensation and stimulus unlike those of conjugal sexual intercourse, for the man as well as the woman. Those who were influenced by and sympathetic to psychoanalytic thinking also suggested that the role of fantasy in masturbatory acts might be psychologically deleterious to sexual adjustment. Others suggested that the practice, if overindulged, led to antisocial solipsism. The view, based on a somewhat bastardized popular Freudianism that became prevalent in the 1950s, that clitoral excitation in the woman prevented the transition to the "mature" vaginal orgasm does not seem to have enjoyed much currency outside actual psychoanalytic circles in the interwar period.

THE SECOND HALF OF THE TWENTIETH CENTURY

One might imagine that with the increasing spread, via medical, pedagogic, and child-rearing literature, of the notion that masturbation did no harm, the gruesome history of the "great fear" must have ended about 1950. This was far from the case. While "old-fashioned" fears were scorned, well into the 1970s works of sex education stated that it was much better to try not to masturbate. Older texts with their much less benign messages continued to circulate. The masturbator might not be seen as headed for an early grave or the lunatic asylum, but the British pejorative "wanker" still suggests, at best, a sad loser unable to find a suitable partner. Fears about masturbation long ago took on a life of their own as part of popular culture and urban folklore.

In 1961 Belgian students were questioned about the effects of masturbation. They believed that it retarded growth, weakened the will, and caused blindness, baldness, impotence, sterility, and the procreation of abnormal children. In the early 1990s a group of health-care professionals and educators in Hungary gave "masturbation" as the cause of tabes dorsalis (a spinal disorder caused by tertiary syphilis). No questions on it were included in the British survey *Sexual Behaviour in Britain: The National Survey of Sexual Attitudes and Lifestyles* (1994) because of the distaste and embarrassment the subject caused in respondents. In 1994 the United States surgeon general, Joycelyn Elders, was dismissed for advocating the teaching of masturbation in the context of AIDS prevention. While this concession by President Bill Clinton to the "moral majority" was condemned in European journals, such as *The Lancet,* most European countries were not exactly promoting the practice.

Within the specialty of sex therapy, masturbation has found a medically licit niche. However, while "self-pleasuring" may be recommended to develop responsiveness and familiarize the individual with his or her genitals, in most sex therapy this practice is implicitly a prelude to taking the knowledge and skills thus learned into partnered sex. In the European context, there is no real equivalent to the American Betty Dodson. In 1974, influenced by the sexual revolution and the second wave of feminism, Dodson wrote *Liberating Masturbation: Celebrating Self-Love.* Over twenty years later, her Web site celebrated masturbation's potential for engendering an "erotic renaissance."

The vast proliferation of pornographic Web sites, phone sex lines, and other erotic media suggests masturbation is widely practiced in Europe, but that it is still a "secret vice" exploited for commercial gain—though in rather different ways from those of the advertising quacks of the nineteenth century. After nearly three centuries, *Onania* continues to cast a long shadow.

See also other articles in this section.

BIBLIOGRAPHY

Comfort, Alex. *The Anxiety Makers: Some Curious Preoccupations of the Medical Profession.* London, 1967.

Dodson, Betty. *Liberating Masturbation: A Meditation on Self-Love.* New York, 1974.

Duffy, John. "Masturbation and Clitoridectomy: A Nineteenth-Century View." *Journal of the American Medical Association* 186 (1963): 246–248.

Elia, John P. "History, Etymology, and Fallacy: Attitudes towards Male Masturbation in the Ancient Western World." *Journal of Homosexuality* 14, no. 3/4 (1987): 1–19.

Engelhardt, H. Tristram, Jr. "The Disease of Masturbation: Values and the Concept of Disease." *Bulletin of the History of Medicine* 48 (1974): 234–248.

Gilbert, Arthur N. "Doctor, Patient, and Onanist Diseases in the Nineteenth Century." *Journal of the History of Medicine and Allied Sciences* 30 (1975): 217–234.

Hall, Lesley A. "Forbidden by God, Despised by Men: Masturbation, Medical Warnings, Moral Panic, and Manhood in Great Britain, 1850–1950." In *Forbidden History: The State, Society, and the Regulation of Sexuality in Modern Europe: Essays from the* Journal of the History of Sexuality. Edited by John C. Fout. Chicago, 1992.

Hall, Lesley A. *Hidden Anxieties: Male Sexuality, 1900–1950.* Oxford, 1991.

Hare, E. H. "Masturbatory Insanity: The History of an Idea." *Journal of Mental Science* 108 (1962): 1–25.

Hunt, Alan. "The Great Masturbation Panic and the Discourses of Moral Regulation in Nineteenth- and Twentieth-Century Britain." *Journal of the History of Sexuality* 8 (1998): 575–615.

MacDonald, Robert H. "The Frightful Consequences of Onanism: Notes on the History of a Delusion." *Journal of the History of Ideas* 28 (1967): 423–431.

Mortier, Freddy, Willem Colen, and Frank Simon. "Inner-Scientific Reconstructions in the Discourse on Masturbation (1760–1950)." *Paedologica Historica* 30 (1994): 817–847.

Moscucci, Ornella. "Clitoridectomy, Circumcision, and the Politics of Sexual Pleasure in Mid-Victorian Britain." In *Sexualities in Victorian Britain.* Edited by

Andrew H. Miller and James Eli Adams. Bloomington, Ind., 1997. Pages 60–78.

"The Politics of Masturbation." *The Lancet* 344 (1994): 1714–1715; 345 (1995): 454. Leading article and subsequent correspondence.

Porter, Roy, and Lesley Hall. *The Facts of Life: The Creation of Sexual Knowledge in Britain 1650–1950.* New Haven, Conn., 1995.

Spitz, René A. "Authority and Masturbation: Some Remarks on a Bibliographical Investigation." *Yearbook of Psychoanalysis* 9 (1953): 113–145.

Stengers, Jean, and Anne Van Neck. *Histoire d'une grande peur: La masturbation.* Brussels, 1984.

PORNOGRAPHY

Lisa Z. Sigel

Pornography functions as an umbrella term to cover a wide variety of representations concerned with sexuality, including literature, photographs, illustrations, statuary, and films. An interest in sexuality ties these diverse media together, but in spite of the single predominant theme, pornography has a wide variety of foci and uses—personal spite, political attack, mockery, titillation, and amusement. The realm of sexuality provides fertile ground for depiction, and different ages made use of the raw matter of sexuality within the context of contemporary concerns.

Social historians have begun to chart out how pornography works and what it means within a historical context. Social historians of the 1960s and 1970s began to look at pornography to understand the sexual meanings, acts, and behaviors of the past. While they found these patterns in pornographic texts and images, they also found more than they initially expected. Pornography from the Renaissance, the Enlightenment, the Age of Revolution, the Victorian Era, and the modern world speaks to more than just sexuality. Religion, politics, family, state formation, and gender all figure in and through pornography. In the late twentieth century scholars explored how pornography and sexuality fit into the broader processes that concern the social historian. Neglecting pornography leaves a partial understanding of the past in which culture, politics, and social interactions are curiously fragmented and the understanding of social change is markedly incomplete.

Exploring the history of pornography, scholars have disproved two contradictory popular beliefs. The first belief, that pornography does not change, has been disproved through close explorations of specific periods, through examinations of media, and through deliberations on content. Historians have shown that pornography changes in form, content, and audience. The second popular belief, that pornography is getting worse, either in volume or in content, presents a more complex problem for the historian because of the inability to use quantitative methods on produc-

tion or distribution. While more pornography exists than did a century ago, the sources are not available that would allow a reliable statistical analysis of the ratio of artifacts to individuals. The second aspect of the formulation that pornography is somehow qualitatively worse has been thrown into doubt by historians. Close qualitative analysis has shown that earlier pornography was also a social and cultural problem. Thus social historians have demonstrated that pornography as a phenomenon is rather more nuanced than popular beliefs tend to insist.

THE RENAISSANCE

While pornography in the modern world has connotations of popular rather than learned or "high" culture, during the Italian Renaissance pornography developed within the scholarly world. The renewed interest in classical learning that characterized the Italian Renaissance brought with it writings explicitly focused on sexual themes. The ancient world had an ethos of sexuality different from that of Christian Europe, and the writings of the ancient world reflected this. Homosexuality, a focus on the priapus, and prostitution were integral to the rituals and religions of public life, and the writings, objects, and images of ancient Greece and Rome incorporated these themes. Ancient texts and ancient images had a pagan orientation at odds with the Christian culture of reproductive sexuality expounded by the Catholic Church. These conflicting meanings of sexuality merged to create a dynamic adjustment of ideas through pornography during the Renaissance.

The pornography of the Renaissance took both visual and literary forms. Visual images include paintings, engravings, and woodcuts of the female nude and the act of intercourse. The works emphasize the beauty and perfection of the human form. While these works frequently have allegorical themes, the depiction of coitus places the gods and the heavens within the realm of physical pleasures, and the gods

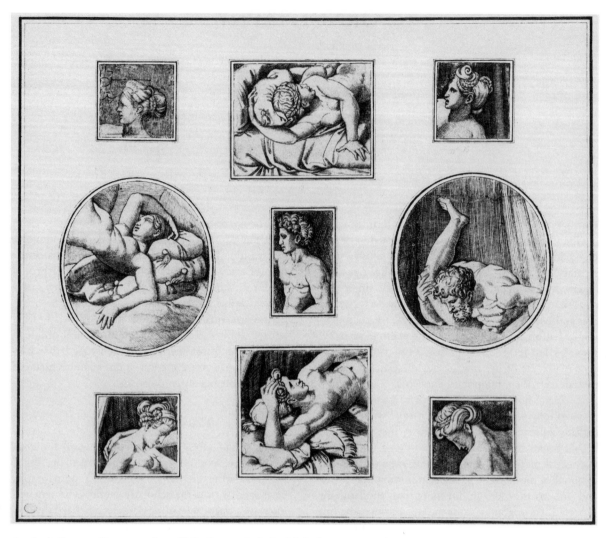

Aretino's Postures. Fragments from Giulio Romano's *Sedici Modi,* the inspiration for *Aretino's Postures.* ©THE BRITISH MUSEUM

have decidedly fleshy tones. The works of Agostino Carracci, Titian, and Perino del Vaga, for example, overturn the medieval tradition of vilifying the flesh. By giving earthy themes and earthy pleasures places within ancient allegories, Renaissance art argued for a corporeality within spirituality and learning.

At the same time the development of the printing press in the mid-fifteenth century allowed a wider dispersal of literary pornography. Italian writers created a pornography built from the ancient texts and contributed to a vernacular and bawdy tradition. Pornography was a form of self-amusement and a political commentary for the most educated in society. Antonio Vignali's *La cazzaria* (1525–1526) and Ferrante Pallavicino's *La rettorica della puttana* (The whore's rhetoric, 1642) were based on ancient styles and were produced in the literary clubs that formed around pa-

trons and styles of learning. However, pornography also functioned as a commercial endeavor, a growth industry perfectly suited to those with skills in wit, satire, and rhetoric, such as Pietro Aretino. Aretino demonstrated his literary skills in *Ragionamento della Nanna e Antonia* (1534) and *Dialogo quale la Nanna insegne* (1536), often jointly published under the title *Ragionamenti,* called *Aretino's Dialogues.* His more well-known work, the *Posizioni* (c. 1527), called *Aretino's Postures,* was inspired by the illustrations of Giulio Romano. Aretino's works have a strong anticlerical focus, in particular satirizing the sexual urges and conduct of priests and nuns. They also stress the voraciousness of women, the sexual incompetence of husbands (perhaps a literary variant of the popular tradition of charivari, the noisy serenade to newlyweds), sexual positions, and details of various ways to

292

please. His dialogues include discussions of intercourse, heterosexual penile-vaginal as well as anal sex, and innuendos about boys. Aretino deliberately violated social taboos and used whores to speak about the delights and malice of sex.

Pornography became so widespread that the Council of Trent (1545–1563) differentiated between ancient texts and more recent writings, like *Aretino's Postures*. The church, functioning as a social regulator, differentiated between licit and illicit writings and enforced sexual norms. The ancient writings could be read because of their eloquence and propriety, but new writings were banned by the papacy for salaciousness. The audience for pornography for the most part remained the learned, while the majority of people in Europe relied on an oral, local tradition for information and amusement about sexuality.

The works of the Italian Renaissance, particularly the literature of Aretino and his imitators, traveled across Europe and became part of a canon of obscenity. Italy was known for its popular pornography, and writers from France and England paid Italy a dubious compliment by setting their fictional erotica in Italy. Authors of other countries also explicitly built on works from Italy. Thomas Nash, the English author of *The Choise of Valentines; or, the Merry Ballad of Nashe His Dildo* (c. 1593), stated that he sought to imitate the style of the Aretines. In his poem, which was circulated in the 1590s, Nash recounted a trip to the brothel to visit a lady's shrine "to see if she would be my valentine." This work builds on Aretino's themes of brothel tours, impotence, and women's insatiability. Nash's use of the style and themes of Aretino demonstrates the circulation of learning during the Renaissance and pornography's integration into bthat circulation.

This international exchange of sexual ideas linked the major centers of developing European economy and culture. Although publications frequently gave false publication information (a practice that bedevils the historian and the bibliographer), the false information marks the rise of particular European centers. For example, *Aloisiae Sigae Satyra Sotadica de Arcanis Amoris et Veneris* (The dialogues of Luisa Sigea) was written by Nicolas Chorier of Vienna, published in Latin in either Grenoble or Lyon in 1659 or 1660. However, Chorier falsely attributed the work to a Spanish woman and the translation to Joannes Neursius, a Dutchman. The text appeared in England and was translated into English and French by the 1680s. The confusing trail of fake names and incomplete publication information should not obscure the links among centers of education, literacy, publishing, and wealth. Spain, Holland, England, and France had reached prominence as centers of the Atlantic world. This world worked not only as an economy but also a place of thinking. The diffusion of knowledge, including the basest sexual knowledge, built on the Renaissance tradition and circulated through the Atlantic world.

THE ENLIGHTENMENT AND THE AGE OF REVOLUTION

The exploration of pleasures of the flesh took on an additional resonance during the Enlightenment's attempt to separate reason from tradition. The pornography of the Enlightenment has been characterized as libertine. The word "libertine" originally meant freethinker but eventually came to connote sexual excess. Libertinism began as an upper-class movement against religious and social customs and gradually spread in the eighteenth and nineteenth centuries. Libertinism applied Enlightenment ideals to sexuality. Belief in rationality and the natural rights of people and skepticism regarding social customs and church mandates made sexual freedom a component of personal freedom, and pornography addressed these issues.

Two prominent social historians, Lynn Hunt and Robert Darnton, demonstrated that the critiques implicit in pornography occurred as part of the broad philosophical discussion. Pornography as a literary phenomenon was tied to the philosophes through critiques of governance in prerevolutionary France. By combining social critiques with sexual allegations, pornography undercut the legitimacy of the French monarchy, the Catholic Church, and the institutions of privilege. In the eighteenth and nineteenth centuries the ecclesiastical systems of social regulation seen in the Renaissance gave way across Europe to state regulation of morality as societies became more secular and were organized around the nation-state. The eighteenth- and nineteenth-century revolutionary sentiment expressed in pornography gave the state good reason to outlaw pornography's dispersal. Pornography not only spoke to sexuality but also to social customs, social regulations, and social relations. The disruptive nature of pornography made the boundaries between "obscene libel" and "treason" nebulous and therefore dangerous. The French monarchy outlawed both pornography and philosophy, cementing the ties between the two as the philosophes had little to lose from the most scurrilous allegations. By the mid-eighteenth century the underground publications of pornography and other bawdy tracts went hand in hand with revolutionary sentiment, and discussions of politics were saturated with discussions of sexuality. Contrib-

Circulation of Pornography. Illustration from a 1775 edition (entitled *L'académie des dames*) of Nicholas Chorier's *Satyra Sotadica,* originally published c. 1660. BY PERMISSION OF THE BRITISH LIBRARY, LONDON

uting to the French Revolution of 1789, pornography critiqued the Old Regime's sexual practices and explored new meanings for sexuality.

Some of the great freethinkers of the Enlightenment wrote pornography. Honoré-Gabriel de Riquetti, comte de Mirabeau wrote *Erotika biblion* (1782), and Denis Diderot wrote *Les bijoux indiscrets* (1748). Freethinking culminated in the works of the Marquis de Sade, who wrote the novel *Justine, ou les malheurs de la vertu* three times. He completed the first manuscript while a prisoner in the Bastille two years before the outbreak of the French Revolution. He published the second version in 1791, then he reworked it to include *Histoire de Juliette* (Story of Juliette) in 1798. The novel of the two sisters "disproves" piety and God's workings on Earth through the reward of vice and the punishment of virtue. Sade takes the pursuit of freedom and gratification to a logical conclusion through rape, child molestation, mutilation, and even necrophilia. His works explore the limits of individual desire in a world unplanned by God and full of maleficence. Philosophers and feminists have used Sade's work to expose the contradictions in the ideals of liberty. Written about women rather than by them, Sade's work employs women's bodies to form philosophies of self and society, limitation and liberty, intrinsic value versus use of the body. Sade bankrupted his estate with his excesses and then demanded that his wife fill his jail cell with expensive delicacies. In his life and in his work, feminists have found important relationships between Enlightenment ideals and female subjugation.

Across the English Channel, England developed its own libertine tradition. Although less philosophic and less violent than Sade, John Cleland produced an equally important text, *Fanny Hill; or, Memoirs of a Woman of Pleasure* (1748 or 1749). This novel features a prostitute, a tour of the brothel, and a series of intertwining stories as each character tells her sexual history. The main story of Fanny Hill, the protagonist of the work, implicitly criticizes the aristocracy as decayed and debauched members of society who prey on the poor. In addition the work criticizes traditional social relations and argues for relationships based on sexual freedom and personal inclination. These elements place the work in the freethinking movement, and as a novel, the work fits into the broader genre formation in England. The model of interlocking letters and dialogues is superseded in *Fanny Hill* by plot, character development, and description. The discussion of pornography as literature is an important counterweight to the idea that a firm line separates popular culture and high culture. Pornography, as an artifact of popular culture, was not an isolated form

of writing, and the pornographic novel rose alongside the more "canonical" novel.

English pornography became more overtly politicized with the outbreak of the French Revolution, as the wave of revolutionary sentiment that crossed Europe influenced texts, writers, and ideas. Iain McCalman, in his study of the English revolutionary world, tied republican agitators to the publication of pornography. The itinerant publishers of revolutionary tracts wrote pornography when the English government cracked down on seditious literature during the French Revolution, and this tradition of revolutionary pornography continued well into the nineteenth century. Radical pornographer-pamphleteers, like William Dugdale and George Cannon, churned out salacious, antigovernment texts during the Queen Caroline affair (1818–1820), when George IV tried to divorce Caroline on the grounds of adultery. These revolutionary pornographers continued to publish a wide variety of pornographic works that destabilized the legitimacy of the British monarchy even though their efforts did not culminate in a radical break with the past like that in France.

THE VICTORIAN WORLD

By the 1840s in England and earlier on the Continent, writers ceased the production of libertine pornography. Pornographers continuously republished the old "classics" in most European languages, but new works excised revolution, philosophy, or critique to refocus in two directions. One applied a greater scientific approach to sexuality, and the other explored titillation and, increasingly, specific sexual fetishes. The process of photography, patented in 1839, contributed to both scientific pornography and fetishistic pornography.

Scientific pornography authors wrote about sexual matters, such as aphrodisiacs, hermaphrodites, sexual techniques like flagellation, biting, intercourse, and sexual practices in distant lands. The scientific aspects did not preclude these works from functioning as pornography, however. They were written, printed, and published by the same people and sold to the same audiences. The development of the social sciences into distinct scholarly disciplines, such as anthropology, sociology, psychology, and sexology, from the 1880s through the 1920s separated works about sexuality from works designed to arouse. This division redefined pornography as based on arousal. Thus Richard Burton and Forster Fitzgerald Arbuthnot's printing of the first English translation of Mallanaga Vatsyayana's *Kama sutra* in 1873 was halted on the grounds of obscenity, but later Burton's translation of *The Arabian Nights* (1885–1888) suffered no such disruption even though the work had equally obscene themes. The growth of the social sciences differentiated works that might have been considered pornographic, like those of Richard von Krafft-Ebing, Havelock Ellis, and Sigmund Freud, from pornographic works.

As the study of sex gained legitimacy, the study of pornography did also. The great bibliographies, central to any historical study of pornography, were written during this birth of sexology. Henry Spencer Ashbee published a three-volume bibliography of pornography in England, *Index Librorum Prohibitorum* (1877), *Centuria Librorum Absconditorum* (1879), and *Catena Librorum Tacendorum* (1885). In 1875 Hugo Hayn published *Bibliotheca Germanorum Erotica,* which he expanded and supplemented between 1912 and 1929. Jules Gay's six-volume work, *Bibliographie des ouvrages relatifs à l'amour,* was published between 1871 and 1873, then supplemented by J. Lemonnyer between 1894 and 1900. These works on English, German, and French pornography, respectively, have formed the backbone for historical examinations.

As the social sciences legitimated the scientific study of sexuality, pornography became a catchall term for items meant to arouse. While the texts produced during the late nineteenth century display a wide variety of interests, individual works are oriented toward a specific sexual activity, such as dominance, submission, children, or flagellation. Each work has its own fetish, and advertisements played up the fetish by de-emphasizing authorship and artistry in favor of fixation. In works like the anonymous *With Rod and Bum* (1898) and *Stays and Gloves* (1919), the narrative is a process of description and culmination, and in each case the process repeats itself. The most well-known work of the period, Leopold von Sacher-Masoch's *Venus im Pelz* (1870), explores male masochism. The main character, Severin, enslaves himself to his mistress Wanda for sexual and psychological gratification. Masoch, a historian, wrote about the problems of liberalism in eastern Europe, and his extended metaphor of dominance and submission integrates the problems of sexuality and gender within contemporary civilization. Only when Severin overcomes the debilitating tendencies of modern society can he assume the male role of dominance. This work became the preeminent source for formulating the psychological motivations of masochism. Sexologists named sadomasochism after Masoch and Sade.

Sexual fetishism in pornography developed against the backdrop of the emerging consumer economy. Consumerism offered new opportunities for sexual exploration divorced from social accountability. For instance, *My Secret Life* (1885–1890), an anonymous pornographic memoir, obsessively documents the male narrator's sexual experiences. The narrator's "real life" of family, community, and work are lost to the "secret life" of brothels, prostitutes, and voyeurism. The author translates the anonymous transactions of a consumer society into impersonal sexual exchanges. The narrator transforms his world into a "pornatopia," a word coined by the historian Steven Marcus to describe the narrator's ability to perceive his world as a utopia of sexuality.

Advancements in photography contributed to the development of pornographic fetishism. Pornographic daguerreotypes appeared by the 1840s, but the daguerreotype allowed only one image per exposure. Later forms of photography allowed more prolific reproductions. The visual pornographic tradition gained a new momentum with photography. Many photographs featured women and intercourse, however, new orientations emerged in the 1880s that played up specific foci, like children, miscegenation, breast size, and underwear. The new orientations were matched by new visuals, including the close-up, the ejaculation or "money shot," and the keyhole, in which the image is bracketed by the shape of a skeleton keyhole, making the viewer a voyeur.

By World War I pornography was traded at a "mass" level as well as a "class" level. These "mass" pornographers took advantage of the mails, and captions for photographs appeared in as many as four languages, usually English, French, German, and Italian. Beginning in the 1890s and culminating after World War I, the rise of a mass consumer culture opened new access to pornography. While previously pornography had broad and diffuse social impacts, the majority of the population, whether peasants in Renaissance Italy, artisans in Enlightenment England, or workers in the French Empire, did not have widespread access to these ideas. But a number of factors, including increased wages, shifting social norms, ever-expanding city life and its subsequent anonymity, and leisure time, fed the rise of mass pornography. The growing number of literates could obtain inexpensive pornography through paperbacks, pamphlets, and cheap magazines, while everyone, regardless of literacy, could find postcards, penny-in-the-slot machines, inexpensive photographs, and films.

Mass pornography built upon older erotic traditions. Photographs, particularly the continental ones in the 1880s and 1890s, had a substantial anticlerical theme, showing the continued relevance of the church even in a more secular society. Postcards used older scatological themes, and penny-in-the-slot machines

Pornographic Postcard. "La Cigale," postcard dating from the early twentieth century. COLLECTION OF THE AUTHOR

and democratic governments insisted on a disciplined populace, and the state began to ferret out sexual and social deviance, including pornography. Boosted by ideas of "respectability" and new interventions in social regulation by the middle class, the state became more concerned with the degeneration, both sexual and social, of the populace. While pornography remained illegal, scientific studies of sexuality were more accepted at the end of the nineteenth century. However, birth control information, abortion advertisements, instruction manuals, and explicit literary discussions of sexuality still came under obscenity legislation. The demarcation of pornography from sexual information and artistry continued as the state, artists, intellectuals, and the marketplace negotiated with each other.

In spite of state control, pornography flourished in many of the major cities of western Europe, including Paris, London, Amsterdam, Rotterdam, Budapest, Lyon, Barcelona, and Zürich. Pornographers produced works for international as well as national audiences and no longer waited for their products to diffuse slowly throughout Europe and America. Instead, they were petty entrepreneurs, using a mail-order system. The international traffic in pornography at both a class and a mass level surpassed the boundaries of state control and state jurisdiction. Voluntary organizations and state agencies across Europe initiated international conferences regarding obscene publications by the 1910s.

sexualized the sentimental narrative of marriage. The recycling of older themes into a visual format brought to the masses the elite ideas of sexuality. The rapidly expanding empires of the 1870s through the 1890s provided new opportunities for a popular, symbolic imperialism. Photographs and illustrations from Asia, Central America, the Caribbean, and Africa flooded back to Europe, exhibiting to all levels of European society concrete images of the benefits of imperialism and European dominion. For example, images of Algerian harem women became common across Europe, making French colonial control more enticing.

The retreat from libertine pornography and the growth of a more popular and less revolutionary version in the nineteenth century did not signal a decline in state legislation against it. The state reconceptualized its concern about matters of morals and increasingly passed laws against the "social evil" of pornography, considered the causal force behind sexual and social deviance. Moreover the growth of nationalism

THE TWENTIETH CENTURY

World War I increased the audience for pornography as the mass migrations of people, the physical and social mobility of men and women, and the disruption of daily life opened new opportunities for exploring sexual material culture. With the end of the war popular and cheap pornography flourished, particularly "girly" photos and motion pictures.

Motion pictures developed in the 1890s, and some early films included female nudity. However, the origins of motion picture pornography generally date to *Le voyeur* in 1907 or to *A l'ecu d'or ou la bonne auberge* in 1908. French filmmakers pioneered the erotic motion picture, but Germans and Italians soon produced their own films. During the 1920s and 1930s France produced a large number of "blue" movies, largely by Bernard Nathan and the anonymous "Dominique." The movies used indoor and outdoor photography and featured heterosexual, group sex, and lesbian scenes. An international trade also developed, and some historians argue that Buenos Aires became a production center for films shown across

Europe. Pornographic films developed well before sound, but the captions for silent films presented few barriers to an international market. Films became a staple fare at brothels, encouraging an overlap between one type of sexual exchange and another. Films also traveled between towns and were semipublically aired, and were sold to private collectors.

The alternate tradition of more expensive literary texts also flourished, as the works of Pierre Louÿs demonstrate. Louÿs wrote poetry, prose, and novels and took hundreds of photographs of young girls. After his death in 1925, his wife sold his papers, which publishers used to produce *Manuel de civilité pour les petites filles* (1926), a sexual etiquette book for young girls, and *Trois filles de leur mère* (1926), a student's experiences with a family of prostitutes. These works built on the themes of older literary pornography, in particular the interest in prostitutes that dates back to the Renaissance and the nineteenth-century fixation on young girls. In comparison, Georges Bataille, a philosopher, used surrealist techniques in *Histoire de l'oeil* (1928), which explores subconscious terrors through the sexual lives of a boy and two girls. The application of modernist techniques in this work demonstrates the continuing ties between "high" literature and pornography.

Because of the complexity of pornography, multiple discussions about it occurred simultaneously within European countries and across Europe. On one hand, lawmakers during the 1920s tried to differentiate between artistic representations of sexuality and pornography, allowing the publication of works like James Joyce's *Ulysses* (1922) as artistry. On the other hand, pornographic production continued to develop its own trajectory in literature, photographs, and films. Lawmakers struggled for a definition of pornography that would allow artists to explore sexuality, while pornographers attempted to widen the definitions of art or circumnavigate them entirely. Finally, a greater acceptance of sexuality in public encouraged a proliferation of semipornographic displays.

Ambiguous definitions of pornography increasingly presented problems as the psychological and cultural dislocations of World War I encouraged the acceptance of Freudianism and modernism. These intellectual attitudes argued that sexuality was central to the human condition, and they inspired new literary and visual movements that stood somewhere between pornography and "the cult of the body." This "cult of the body" withstood the political divisions of the times. Artists, intellectuals, and ideologues viewed the body as a central icon of communication and used the naked body as a symbol of social decay or cultural superiority. Photographic images emphasized hardness, leanness, and youth as symbols of personal and social vitality. The symbol of the body was strengthened by the rise of nudism, the back to nature movement, and the increase in youth groups, all of which legitimized the prevalence of sexuality and the nude in public. Photos, statues, and films featuring nude men and women became more commonplace.

The political right, Nazis in particular, saw Freudian and modernist images as pornographic and symbolic of social decay but developed their own "cult of the body" during the interwar years. The Nazis took power in Germany in 1933, and in one of their first acts to rid society of degenerate sexuality, they burned the Institute of Sexual Science's books and papers. Nonetheless, the male nudity in the public art of the Nazis had strong homoerotic overtones, newly characterized as nonpornographic and wholesome. The Nazis denounced modern art as pornographic, but Nazi representations of bodies remained fluid and incorporated elements of pornography into public art.

The debates over pornography that began during the 1920s and the 1930s persisted into the post–World War II world, but the catastrophic impact of fascism in Europe legitimated political liberalism, including greater freedom of the press. The attitudes of the 1950s encouraged the continuation of older illegal and semilegal forms of pornography in film, photography, and literature, but European governments reversed social policies during the 1960s and 1970s by legalizing pornography. Libertarians argued that free speech worked as a defense against fascism, but in many ways the politics of sexual liberation during this period were far removed from the Enlightenment. While earlier pornography used sexuality to critique old social forms and posit greater possibilities for society, later pornography emphasized sexual pleasures as intrinsically valuable and worthwhile. Pornographic works did not need to speak to politics or redeem society. States defined pornography so that a work with any element of artistic, historical, literary, or social value could not be censored. With the new formulas, a flood of publications, films, and images emerged across Europe, notably in England, France, Germany, and Scandinavia. The policies of legalization moved pornographic films, literature, and photographs from brothels and back rooms to theaters and bookstores, where they were available to respectable society, including women. The legalization of pornography also permitted more aboveboard film production and reduced cottage industry pornographic photography and literature. Certain types of representations, especially glossy magazines and films, predominated, making pornography palatable to a broader consumer culture.

Legalization during the 1960s and 1970s was matched by a growing international feminist movement with increasing concerns about pornography. While pornography has been consumed primarily by men, the dominant images and foci in pornography have been of women. The feminist movement discussed the meanings of these representations of sexuality, particularly the sexuality of women. The American position that pornography degrades and objectifies women, most clearly articulated by Andrea Dworkin and Catherine MacKinnon, was imported into Europe and made notable headway in England. This position received less attention in France, where the works of Anaïs Nin and Pauline Réage resist this feminist analysis of pornography. In Réage's *The Story of O* (1954) the heroine "O" allows herself to be stripped of sexual freedom, personal autonomy, and control over her own sensibilities and pleasures. The story embraces personal renunciation and male dominance. The pseudonymous but apparently female author complicates a feminist analysis of pornography with the complexities of women's desires as Sacher-Masoch did with men. However, as feminists have pointed out, masochism and renunciation for men have been defined as deviant or perverse, while masochism for women has been culturally inculcated. The feminist debates over pornography have suggested possibilities for legislation that uses the standard of oppression rather than explicitness. Although new standards developed in England, most countries after the 1960s opted for increasingly liberalized censorship standards.

With legalization pornography emerged as a viable source of national revenue, and the economics of pornography became a national consideration. World War II encouraged American dominance in Western Europe, and the realm of pornography proved no exception. The pinup girls that American GI's carried with them became models of public representations of sexuality. American "porno" films and magazines followed shortly. The American culture industry dominated during the postwar years, and Americans influenced European pornography as magazines such as *Playboy* reached European markets. When the Scandinavian countries legalized pornography in the late 1960s, American producers heavily entered the market, driving out many local productions. In contrast, France in the 1970s sought to develop its own industry by taxing imports, encouraging a resurgence of the French pornographic film. Hungary entered the international market as a location for film production to stimulate the post-Communist economy. The up-

Cult of the Body. *Nude* by Heinz von Perckhammer, 1935. UWE SCHEID COLLECTION, ÜBERHERRN, GERMANY

heavals caused by the breakup of the Communist bloc encouraged an influx of actors into western European films. The days of national control of pornography, as tenuous as it had been, seemed over, particularly because technological innovations like videos and the Internet distribute pornography rapidly across national barriers. While historians assess the social implications of these developments, pornography has become an international product that reaches an international audience.

Areas for further research on pornography abound, from assessing the meaning of pornography in eastern European countries to documenting the lives of models and actors who took part in production, finding reliable statistics on users, and examining the impact of pornography on people's concepts of sexuality. While social historians since the 1960s have uncovered important relationships between pornography and politics, religion, family, and gender relations, they also have found a dense source that deserves continuing attention and that raises many questions.

See also other articles in this section.

BIBLIOGRAPHY

Alloula, Malek. *The Colonial Harem.* Translated by Myrna Godzich and Wlad Dodzich. Minneapolis, Minn., 1986.

Darnton, Robert. *The Forbidden Best-Sellers of Pre-Revolutionary France.* New York, 1995.

Darnton, Robert. *The Literary Underground of the Old Regime.* Cambridge, Mass., 1982.

Dean, Carolyn. "The Great War, Pornography, and the Transformation of Modern Male Subjectivity." *Modernism/Modernity* 3, no. 2 (1996): 59–72.

Di Lauro, Al, and Gerald Rabkin. *Dirty Movies: An Illustrated History of the Stag Film, 1915–1970.* New York, 1976.

Foxon, David. *Libertine Literature in England, 1660–1746.* New York, 1966.

Frantz, David O. *Festum Voluptatis: A Study of Renaissance Erotica.* Columbus, Ohio, 1989.

Hunt, Lynn, ed. *The Invention of Pornography: Obscenity and the Origins of Modernity, 1500–1800.* New York, 1996.

Kearney, Patrick J. *A History of Erotic Literature.* Hong Kong, 1993.

Kendrick, Walter. *The Secret Museum: Pornography in Modern Culture.* New York, 1987.

Kyrou, Ado. *Amour-erotisme et cinéma.* Paris, 1957.

Marcus, Steven. *The Other Victorians: A Study of Sexuality and Pornography in Mid-Nineteenth-Century England.* New York, 1975.

McCalman, Iain. *Radical Underworld: Prophets, Revolutionaries, and Pornographers in London, 1795–1840.* Cambridge, U.K., 1988.

Noyes, John K. *The Mastery of Submission: Inventions of Masochism.* Ithaca, N.Y., 1997.

Sigel, Lisa Z. "Sexual Imaginings: The Cultural Economy of British Pornography, 1800–1914." Ph.D. diss., Carnegie-Mellon University, 1996.

Slade, Joseph W. "Pornography in the Late Nineties." *Wide Angle,* 19, no. 3 (1997): 1–12.

Wagner, Peter. *Eros Revived: Erotica of the Enlightenment in England and America.* London, 1988.

SEX, LAW, AND THE STATE

Roderick G. Phillips

Sexual attitudes, behavior, and relationships have historically been among the most regulated areas of human activity in Europe. Some sexual relationships, such as those between persons of the same sex (homosexual) or between persons within specified close relationships (incest), have been deemed "unnatural" and socially disruptive insofar as they represented deviations from what is defined as the "natural" order of things. Other sexual relationships, such as those involving unmarried individuals or couples (often called fornication) and sex outside marriage (adultery) have been defined as illicit because they represented deviations from the principle that sex was permitted only between husband and wife. Historically they have been the object of legislation when they were considered threats to the stability of marriage, which was seen as a guarantor of social stability.

Beyond specific kinds of sexual activity and the reasons they have been ruled illicit or illegal by the state and religious authorities, sexual behavior has historically been difficult to regulate. Human sexuality has borne an immense burden of political and cultural significance. Sexual behavior and reputation have defined honor in a way that other human activities have not. More shame has been attached to transgressions of sexual mores than to almost any other social or legal rule of behavior. One result is that sexual slander has been the most effective means of undermining the reputation of a group or individual. Thus many of the marginal religious sects that sprang up during the English Revolution of the mid-seventeenth century were alleged to practice free love.

Certain representations of sexuality also have been subject to regulation in various ways. The explicit depiction of sexual acts in literature, the visual arts, or music may be variously defined as erotic or pornographic. The historical record shows that much of what might be considered pornography in modern society was in earlier centuries intended less to arouse a reader or viewer sexually than to be a means of social comment or political criticism.

REGULATION BY THE CHURCH

Before the rise of the nation-state in the early modern period and the extension of state regulation, most of the oversight of sexual behavior fell within the jurisdiction of the church. While the state progressively extended its secular jurisdiction over a wide range of social behavior and over key institutions such as the family, it was relatively slow and hesitant to legislate on sexuality. Certain forms of behavior that were offenses in church law, such as fornication and adultery, have only rarely been the subject of state legislation. In general the state has preferred to use civil remedies rather than criminal law against sexual activities that legislators considered improper. For example, where church courts often fined, excommunicated, or sometimes imprisoned adulterers, adultery has rarely been punishable under secular law. Instead the aggrieved spouse sought other remedies, such as separation or divorce, and sometimes obtained financial compensation from the adulterous spouse's accomplice in the adultery.

Because church law was the background to state laws and policies regarding sexuality, it is useful to sketch the outlines of sexual attitudes and behavior in ecclesiastical law. The broad rules for sexual behavior embodied in church law were drawn from the Bible, which deals, in several instances ambiguously, with many aspects of human sexuality. Church doctrines were debated and refined by theologians, councils, and popes for centuries, and by the late Middle Ages they reached a broad consensus. Even so various church councils and papal decrees and the many theologians who wrote on sexual issues adopted variations, some minor but some significant, among the policies. One of the challenges facing historians is to define the broadly accepted doctrine on human sexuality without losing sight of the variations. This doctrine was the basis of the secular policies later adopted and adapted by secular legislators who framed state law.

The doctrines of the medieval church on sexuality have been described broadly as negative. Sexuality was considered a gift bestowed by God, but the church preferred the faithful to suppress it if they could. The church valued a life of chastity more highly than one of sexual activity and, following St. Paul, held that Christians ought to remain virgins if they could but that they should marry if they could not. Marriage was deemed an institution ordained by God so men and women could be sexually active in a way that was not sinful. One of the explicit purposes of marriage in church doctrine was to "prevent fornication." In this sense marriage was tainted by its sexual purpose.

On the more positive side church doctrine endowed marriage with the role of procreation because the church insisted on the necessary link between sex and conception. This meant that only procreative sexual activity was permitted in church law, a doctrine that ruled out same-sex sexual relationships and any heterosexual sexual activities, such as oral or anal sex, that could not lead to conception. For the same reason it also excluded techniques such as coitus interruptus (withdrawal by the male before ejaculation), the use of contraceptives in the form of suppositories and condoms, and abortion.

The church placed extensive limitations on procreative sexual activity by a married couple. The church forbade sexual activity at times of penance, such as Advent and Lent, and on certain days that had particular religious significance. Certain coital positions were forbidden. Intercourse with the woman on top was not permitted because it reversed the proper order of society in which men were dominant, and the retro position was condemned because it was too reminiscent of the way animals have intercourse. Sex while standing was discouraged as less likely to result in conception because the semen would flow out of the vagina. What is commonly known as the missionary position was the sole favored position for intercourse.

Although many church writers agreed that sexual relationships might give pleasure, they were generally opposed to having intercourse solely for recreational reasons. The possibility of conception should always be present, which raised the question whether intercourse with a pregnant woman or a woman past the age of conception was permitted. This reinforced the opposition to the use of any contraceptive technique or device, which made intercourse solely recreational by depriving it of any procreative potential. While too-frequent sex was deplored, intercourse was nonetheless considered an obligation within marriage if only to deter either partner from looking for sexual gratification outside marriage. Sex was widely referred to in church literature as "the conjugal [or marital] debt."

The enforcement of these laws by the church courts in the medieval period and beyond varied widely, a pattern that continued when state legislation came into play. In addition to the expected variations according to time and place, the courts tended to treat offenders of various social classes differently and men differently from women. In some instances laws explicitly specified distinctions in penalty between women and men. For example, it was common for laws of adultery to provide more severe penalties for adultery by women, arguing that an adulterous woman risked becoming pregnant and creating the possibility that another man's child would inherit her husband's property. A double standard of sexual morality, which held women to higher standards of sexual behavior, is a persistent theme in the history of sexuality and sexual attitudes, and it was often expressed in laws and their enforcement.

Throughout the Middle Ages the church was the dominant force in the regulation of morality, including sexual morality. It claimed a special role in the surveillance of behavior that threatened the salvation of individuals, and it argued that general disobedience of God's laws as understood by the church would bring God's wrath upon society more generally. In addition sexual offenses were intimately linked to doctrinal nonconformity, and heretics often were alleged to be sexual deviants.

LEGISLATION AGAINST ADULTERY

The Protestant Reformation of the sixteenth century broke the unity of the medieval church and led to the creation of a number of discrete confessions under the protection of secular political authorities. It was accompanied by a shift in attitudes toward sexuality as Martin Luther, John Calvin, and other leading Reformers decried the church's preference for chastity and argued for recognition of sexuality as one of God's gifts to humans. Although Luther's writings at least contained some residual admiration for those who could remain virgins throughout their lives, the Protestants generally argued for the holiness of marriage and for husband and wife to enjoy their sexual activity without sinning as long as they behaved with modesty and the propriety appropriate for using a God-given gift. Protestant theologians were somewhat uneasy about the pleasure that could be derived from sex, but they generally decided that a moderate degree of pleasure was not sinful as long as it accompanied an activity that could lead to procreation and the building of a Christian society.

At the same time that they raised the value of sexuality and marriage, which were intimately linked, the Protestants were trenchant critics of the laxity with which the church, which became known as the Catholic Church to distinguish it from the Protestant confessions, had enforced sexual morality. Reformers such as Luther and Calvin declared that first the church had set impossibly high standards by insisting on the primacy of chastity and celibacy and by making marriage difficult through a range of impediments, and second it had failed to enforce them. The result, they argued, was that sexual immorality was widespread throughout Christian Europe, especially among the clergy, whether they were priests, monks, or nuns. In contrast to the celibate clergy of the Catholic Church, Protestant clergy were permitted to marry.

At the time that state authorities were sponsoring the founding of Protestant churches, this criticism provided an opportunity for the state to begin legislating in matters of sexual morality. But secular legislators, whether monarchs or parliaments, were reluctant to regulate sexuality with the same rigor and enthusiasm that the churches showed. Although a great deal of state legislation on sexuality was enacted between the sixteenth and the twentieth centuries, it was rarely as comprehensive as the purview of the churches. For example, few secular laws paralleled the medieval church's interest in attempting to restrict coital positions.

Because of the relatively restricted scope of state regulation of sexual behavior, churches continued to play an important role through the nineteenth century, just as they did in many aspects of the family. In part this was because the churches could stake a claim to a particular authority over morals, a claim that was not generally challenged by the state because it did not interfere with state policies and even tended to reinforce a particular vision of social relationships and order. Exceptions existed, notably secular laws that aimed to repress homosexuality, but on the whole behaviors such as fornication and adultery have rarely been criminalized. When they have been included in civil law, as grounds for divorce, for example, their application has depended not on state initiative but on the initiative of an injured party.

The history of adultery in England provides an example of the range of legislative options applied to sexual issues over several centuries. Jurisdiction over adultery fell to the courts of the Church of England following the Reformation in the 1530s. It was generally punished by fines, penances, and excommunication in varying combinations and often involved public shame. The guilty parties were compelled to stand in white sheets in the marketplace or in church for two or three consecutive Sundays. Penalties were more severe if adultery resulted in pregnancy. The woman involved was often whipped, half-naked, through the streets of the community and could be imprisoned for up to a year.

On the whole, however, the attitudes of the English church toward common adultery were relatively lenient compared with Calvinist areas like Geneva and Scotland, where in the sixteenth century adultery was made a capital offense. During the English Revolution, when state policy was influenced by Calvinist principles, a more rigorous policy was introduced on the grounds that adultery, incest, and fornication had become widespread and that it was necessary to enforce the biblical rule of death for an adulterous woman. A 1650 law provided the death penalty for a married woman who committed adultery and for her accomplice. On the other hand, a married man who committed adultery would be executed only if he had intercourse with a married woman. If he committed adultery with an unmarried woman or a woman he believed was unmarried, he was liable to a comparatively lenient punishment of three months in jail and a bond of good behavior for the following year. Notably this rigorous law found little support among the men who sat on juries during the 1650s, and not many were willing to convict a woman and send her to her death for committing adultery. Records indicate only a few executions, all of women, under the adultery legislation between 1650 and 1660, when it lapsed. This pattern of convictions reinforces the findings of several historians that adultery generally was not considered a serious offense until it became scandalous or resulted in pregnancy.

When the 1650 Adultery Act lapsed, adultery again fell to the jurisdiction of the church courts, and attempts to recriminalize adultery or to provide other penalties against adulterous couples failed in England. From the 1770s to the early 1800s several "adultery prevention bills" were passed by the House of Lords but were defeated in the House of Commons. Some tried to prevent the marriage of an adulterous couple on the grounds that such marriages effectively rewarded the immoral behavior of the parties concerned. But at least one bill, introduced in 1800, aimed to make adultery a crime punishable by a fine and imprisonment.

Never criminalized in England after 1660, adultery remained a justification for separation in the ecclesiastical courts, and it became grounds for a divorce when Parliament began to grant individual divorces by private acts of Parliament in 1670. Even then the church had a role to play in that a man seeking a parliamentary divorce had first to obtain a separation

The Double Standard. A cuckolded Englishman puts his adulterous wife on sale. The French supposed such customs to exist in England. French engraving, early nineteenth century. MUSÉE CARNAVALET, PARIS

from an ecclesiastical court. Following that, he was required to sue his wife's accomplice in civil court for damages, a suit known as "criminal conversation," meaning "illegal intercourse." The judges awarded damages that were sometimes considerable, in the thousands of pounds, and sometimes a symbolic few pennies. Suits for damages for criminal conversation treated sexual access to his wife as a husband's property and her lover as a trespasser whose action had to be compensated in monetary terms. Often the amount was fixed according to the amount of honor at stake. The higher the social rank of the husband, the greater his loss and the more compensation was appropriate.

Some 325 parliamentary divorces based on adultery were granted from 1670 to 1857. Almost all were obtained by men, but in the nineteenth century three women successfully divorced their husbands. They, however, had to prove not simply adultery but aggravated adultery, that is adultery compounded by another offense such as incest, bigamy, or desertion. This is a clear example of the double standard that held women accountable to higher measures of behavior than men.

This double standard was embodied in the first English divorce law (1857), which allowed men to divorce their wives for simple adultery but required a woman wanting a divorce to prove aggravated adultery. Men and women in England were not put on the same legal footing with respect to adultery until a new divorce law was passed in 1923.

Other states had different legal trajectories with respect to adultery. In France various secular codes dealt with the issue before the French Revolution. The Catholic Church retained some jurisdiction, and under its law an adulterous woman could be confined to a convent for two years. But secular legal codes also dealt with adultery. Among others, the customary law of Normandy allowed a man to separate from his wife for reason of adultery but provided a woman with the same remedy only when she could prove that her husband had committed adultery in their dwelling. If he was unfaithful elsewhere, she had no legal recourse. During the French Revolution men and women had equal access to divorce when it was legalized in 1792, but the double standard did not disappear entirely. A woman divorced for adultery was penalized in the division of property following divorce, but this was not so for an adulterous man who was divorced by his wife.

In general the legislators of the French Revolution, who paid a great deal of attention to the family and social relationships, passed few laws dealing with sexuality, and the regulation of sexuality declined markedly in comparison with the Old Regime. Despite their concern for promoting population growth and thus ensuring that infanticide was limited, the revolutionary legislators suppressed the requirement for pregnant, unmarried women to make declarations of pregnancy to the authorities. Prostitution was criminalized, but mainly because of concerns about the spread of sexually transmitted diseases, especially in garrison towns. Prostitutes were confined, treated for their illnesses, and instructed in the skills that would make them good republican wives and mothers. Sodomy, which had been a capital offense under the Old Regime, did not appear in the criminal or civil codes of the revolutionary period. The Napoleonic period following the Revolution restored the double standard more rigorously. A woman divorced for adultery was sentenced to imprisonment for a period of three months to two years.

Although adultery was thus a matter of concern to the state, which provided either punishment or remedies in civil law, premarital sex was generally deplored but not criminalized. At various times, however, states have developed policies involving unmarried women who became pregnant. In eighteenth-century France, for example, any unmarried woman who was pregnant had to make a declaration of pregnancy (*déclaration de grossesse*) to the police, in which she identified the man responsible and set out the circumstances of the pregnancy, that is, whether she was forced, coerced, persuaded, or willingly agreed to have sexual intercourse. The purposes were not specifically to repress premarital sexual activity or to punish sexually active unmarried women but rather to help the authorities ensure that the father of the child rather than the community paid for the child's birth and upkeep and also to minimize the chances that the woman would try to abort her child or kill it once it was born.

In this case one of the main underlying rationales for the apparent regulation of sexual activity was in fact the state's desire to increase the size of the nation's population. The authorities thought that many women practiced abortion or infanticide to the detriment of the state's demographic interest. They believed one way to reduce the incidences of both was to compel pregnant women to acknowledge their pregnancies and be held accountable if they could not produce a child when the authorities inquired.

A similar concern about burdening communities with illegitimate children was reflected in English legislation of 1576 and 1610. The first law gave justices of the peace the powers to investigate when a child was left in the charge of the parish, to order the parents to support the child, and to punish the parents. The 1610 law allowed justices to sentence mothers of illegitimate children in these cases to imprisonment in a house of detention for a year. Forty years later the law that provided the death penalty for incest and some cases of adultery also allowed imprisonment for three months of couples guilty of fornication.

Clearly it is not possible to generalize about the role of European states in regulating sexuality. In the early modern period immense variations existed among individual states. The rigor of legislation varied from one issue to another, as did enforcement. It can be argued, too, that it is important to consider not only regulations expressed in state law but also those that emanated from the church when the state effectively delegated legislative and judicial powers to it. In other words, state laws were only part of a broader apparatus that defined permissible sexual activities and sought to ensure conformity.

LEGISLATION AGAINST HOMOSEXUALITY

The full force of the state has been felt more frequently in the area of sexual activity between people of the same sex. The word "homosexuality" first appears in the nineteenth century, and until then and even afterward the law focused not on sexual orientation but on specific forms of behavior, generally sodomy or buggery. That is, individuals were defined, for the purposes of the law, not by orientation but by actions.

Secular laws against sodomy date from the Middle Ages. Although the statutes of late thirteenth-century Florence are incomplete and the specific penalties for sodomy are not clear, they did include exile from the city-state. Most secular legislation dated from the sixteenth century, and the first English example was a 1534 law of Henry VIII. Passed on the grounds that existing penalties were too lenient, this act made "buggery committed with mankind or beast" a felony that could be tried only in the secular courts. Conflating buggery and bestiality only highlighted the sense that homosexual activity was deemed an offense against nature.

In one of the most famous cases in early modern England, the earl of Castlehaven was prosecuted in 1631 for, among other offenses, raping his wife and sodomizing two of his male servants. Even then, however, circumstances that were not specifically sexual came into play. Castlehaven had encouraged his male servants, while he watched, to rape his wife and her daughter by a previous marriage, and this breach of the rule of social distance seriously aggravated the charge. Castlehaven and two of his servants were executed. Similar concern for the respective social classes of men involved in homosexual relationships was evident in prosecutions for sodomy in the Royal Navy in the seventeenth century. Sodomy was punishable in its own right but was considered more serious when it involved an officer and an ordinary seaman.

On the European continent other states also legislated against homosexuals in the wake of the Reformation. The 1532 penal code issued by the emperor Charles V included sexual intercourse between men, between women, and between humans and animals in the category of crimes against nature, and it provided the model for later Prussian legislation. Dutch military regulations and secular laws from the same period specified the death penalty for "unnatural misuses," with burning the usual prescribed form of execution. In practice penalties varied. In the eighteenth century only about 10 percent of convictions in the Netherlands resulted in execution. The rest were sentenced to corporal punishment, long periods of imprisonment (up to fifty years), and banishment. The last known execution of a man convicted of sodomy under Dutch law occurred in 1803.

Much legislation was directed at sodomy, and many cases focused on an age or class disparity between the parties involved. Legislation enacted in Florence in 1325 prescribed castration for a man convicted of sodomizing a boy, a fine of 100 *lire* for boys aged fourteen to eighteen who allowed themselves to be sodomized, and a fine of 50 *lire* or being flogged naked through the city for a boy under the age of fourteen who did likewise. The penalties applied to boys younger than fourteen were also applied to women involved in acts of anal intercourse. In the fifteenth century the Republic of Venice issued regulations to try to limit the "abominable vice" of sodomy in schools of music, gymnastics, fencing, and mathematics that brought men, especially older men and young boys, together in close quarters.

Lesbianism has been historically of less interest to legislators than male homosexual activity. It is arguable that lesbian sex was frequently viewed not so much repugnant as symptomatic of more fundamental offenses such as heresy. For this reason it might have been less important to secular legislators than religious legislators. But the use of an instrument that simulated heterosexual sex aggravated the offense of lesbian sex. Spanish law in the fifteenth century varied in its treatment of sexual activity between women depending on whether or not they used a dildo. Two women convicted of having a sexual relationship "without an instrument" were whipped and sent to the galleys, but two nuns who employed a dildo were executed by burning. Generally, however, known prosecutions of women for lesbian sex are few and far between in the early modern period: four in sixteenth-century France, two in Germany, and one each in Italy, Spain, Geneva, and the Netherlands. This is not to say that more did not occur, but the incidence was clearly low. It is notable that women charged as witches or heretics also were charged with related sexual offenses, but they usually were accused of engaging in heterosexual activities, including having sex with the devil.

In some European countries laws against sodomy stayed on the books for centuries with variations over time in terms of their enforcement. The English law of 1534 was reenacted several times, revoked twice, and soon reinstated—all before 1600. But after 1600 it remained essentially unchanged for two and a half centuries, until the late nineteenth century. Even though the death penalty was abolished in the 1820s for more than a hundred crimes, it was retained for buggery, rape, and sex with a girl under the age of consent, then thirteen years. Finally in 1861 legislation abolished the death penalty for sexual crimes, including rape. In 1885 the criminal law was amended to make "acts of gross indecency," which included all sexual acts between males, whether in public or private, and "procuring" males for such acts, punishable by imprisonment for up to two years with hard labor.

Other European states reformed their laws on homosexuality. Prussia abolished the death penalty for sodomy in 1851, and Scotland did so in 1889. But this did not imply toleration of homosexual relationships. The German Penal Code of 1875 punished "criminally indecent activity" with imprisonment for up to five years.

THE NINETEENTH AND TWENTIETH CENTURIES

During the nineteenth century the extension of activity by the state, in the context of growing concern about social stability, led to renewed interest in sexual morals. The broad-based "moral purity movement" focused on issues such as prostitution; white slavery, the insistence that large numbers of young European women were abducted and sold into sexual slavery in the Middle East and elsewhere; and the spread of venereal (sexually transmitted) diseases. Despite strong pressure from this movement, which also pressed for controls on alcohol and gambling, legislators were generally unwilling to attempt to regulate sexuality as broadly as some organizations wanted.

Nonetheless, states enacted legislation on some social issues whose associations were explicitly sexual. Concern about the spread of sexually transmitted diseases, particularly about their effects on military personnel, led the British Parliament to pass the Contagious Diseases Acts beginning in the 1860s. These laws gave the authorities powers to detain women suspected of being prostitutes and to have them examined for symptoms of sexually transmitted disease. The laws were applied with particular intensity in naval towns like Portsmouth, but after an outcry at the discriminatory character of these measures, which ignored the men who were also infected with diseases, the acts were eventually repealed.

In the late nineteenth century, too, eugenics influenced the policies of a number of states with respect to sexuality. Reflecting a widespread sense of a tendency toward physical, intellectual, and moral degeneration because unregulated procreation passed on undesirable traits from generation to generation, many eugenicists argued for education and voluntary restrictions on marriage and fertility. Others, however, urged governments to step in to stop what they called "the breeding of the unfit" that they believed was leading to "race suicide." In the late nineteenth century a number of states, including Sweden, began programs of sterilization to limit the fertility of men and women diagnosed as insane.

Again, however, homosexuality was the main form of sexual activity pursued by the state with much enthusiasm in the late 1800s. At the turn of the century several states were rocked by sensational trials under these laws, including those of Oscar Wilde in England in 1895 and a number of senior military personnel in Germany in the decades before World War I.

Throughout most of the twentieth century European states pursued a variety of policies toward sexuality. The general tendency was toward less intrusive and more liberal policies, in which the state did not try to regulate the parties to sexual activities or the nature of their sexual activities. These trends were by no means linear, nor did they occur at the same rate throughout Europe. Notable exceptions existed. In Nazi Germany laws forbade sexual relationships between "Aryans" and Jews. Although apparently conventional in many respects, Nazi policies on sex and the family were underpinned by racial and demographic agendas. Homosexuality, condemned as degenerate and useless for demographic purposes, was criminalized, and the number of prosecutions rose steadily, reaching eight thousand in 1938. After serving prison terms, thousands of homosexuals were sent to concentration camps. Adultery was retained in Nazi divorce law, primarily because adulterers ran the risk of having sex with unapproved partners. The regime set up a program called *Lebensborn,* under which racially approved women were impregnated by racially approved men to foster the development of a population the Nazis considered racially superior.

Such draconian policies toward sexuality as the Nazis' have been rare in European history. They were echoed in Romania in the 1980s, however, under the regime of Nicolae Ceauşescu. To promote population growth, Ceauşescu forbade the use of contraception and abortion and required women to undergo regular medical examinations to ensure that they were observing the law.

The last decades of the twentieth century witnessed a general decline in state legislation concerning sexuality. Laws against fornication and adultery had long disappeared. From the 1960s onward states liberalized laws concerning abortion and contraception and progressively decriminalized prostitution and homosexuality. Sexual relationships between homosexuals were decriminalized in England in 1967, and by the end of the 1970s they had ceased to be a crime in most West European states. Within another two decades policy shifted toward granting homosexuals positive legal rights, and in the 1990s several states, including Belgium, Denmark, and France, established registered partnerships that gave same-sex couples many of the legal rights and fiscal benefits that different-sex couples derived from marriage.

At the same time specific forms of sexual activity, notably those involving children and young people under the age of sexual consent, child pornography, and pedophilia, gained a higher profile. They evoked legislative responses in a number of European countries where there were well-publicized cases.

Research on the history of sexuality, including its regulation by state law, frequently reflects issues debated in contemporary society. A great deal of research by historians of sexuality in the 1970s and 1980s focused on women and gender. In the 1980s and 1990s more attention was devoted to homosexuality. The work of historians has contributed not only to knowledge of the historical experiences of men and women of all sexual orientations but also to the evolution of social attitudes toward sexuality and their expression in policy and legislation.

Whatever the specific theme they research, historians seek to historicize sexuality and to show that behavior, attitudes, and policies are best understood contextually. One result has been to deny that certain forms of sexuality and some sexual orientations, even if they are by far the most common, are "natural" or "normal." To this extent the historical work has helped inform debates on sexual issues.

As for sources, historians of sexuality are both rewarded and penalized by the place of sexuality in Western culture. On one hand, few dimensions of human behavior have been historically as widely debated as sexuality. Sexual attitudes and behaviors often have been used as surrogate measures for other events and conditions, such as the general level of social order and the state of morality in younger generations, and official documentation and public sources of all kinds provide a wealth of material. Moreover sex has long been a prominent theme in literature and art. All these sources pose problems of interpretation, but they represent a massive database in the search for elusive "social attitudes" toward specific forms of sexuality.

Yet, on the other hand, this mass of documentation deals with one of the most intimate and private dimensions of human activity. Few records of individual sexual lives exist, and few diarists recorded their sexual experiences and thoughts. The single source most commonly used by historians probing the sexual experiences of individuals, specific groups, or whole societies in the past is judicial records. Needless to say, these give invaluable insights into the regulation of sexuality and the ways in which certain offenses were disposed of by the courts. But they seldom reveal how cases were filtered through the policing and judicial processes. That is, no clear sense emerges of the extent to which the extant court cases were representative of more general behavior.

A number of historians have attempted to define certain periods as more permissive and others as more repressive in terms of both social attitudes and the regulation of sexuality. Some have argued that the late seventeenth-century Restoration was a hotbed of sexual activity and that the nineteenth-century Victorian era was one of intense sexual repression on both the individual and the social levels. Neither generalization seems convincing. While some evidence supports broad swings in several countries, the complexity of the issues involved makes generalizations difficult and hazardous. It is arguable that some examples of the regulation of sexuality were actually attempts to regulate the behavior of women. In other instances the rationale behind sexual control was a desire to increase population size or to limit the social implications of increasing numbers of illegitimate children. It is also important to look beyond the terms of legislation to understand the way laws were applied.

The relationship of the state, law, and sexuality is an important historical question, but it is necessary to recognize that sexuality is frequently and intimately associated with other major issues, such as class, gender, and authority. This is not to diminish the importance of the regulation of sexuality as a subject of historical investigation but to recognize its central importance in understanding the links between the private and the public dimensions of European history.

See also other articles in this section.

BIBLIOGRAPHY

Ariès, Philippe, and André Béjin, eds. *Western Sexuality: Practice and Precept in Past and Present Times.* Oxford and New York, 1985.

Boswell, John. *Christianity, Social Tolerance, and Homosexuality.* Chicago, 1980.

Brundage, James A. *Law, Sex, and Christian Society in Medieval Europe.* Chicago, 1987.

Bullough, Vern L. *Sexual Variance in Society and History.* Chicago, 1976.

Bullough, Vern, L., and James Brundage. *Sexual Practices and the Medieval Church.* Buffalo, N.Y., 1982.

Copley, Antony. *Sexual Moralities in France, 1780–1980.* London and New York, 1989.

Dean, Carolyn. *The Frail Social Body: Pornography, Homosexuality, and Other Fantasies in Interwar France.* Berkeley, Ca., 2000.

Duberman, Martin Bauml, Martha Vicinus, and George Chauncey Jr., eds. *Hidden from History: Reclaiming the Gay and Lesbian Past.* New York, 1989.

Hunt, Lynn, ed. *The Invention of Pornography: Obscenity and the Origins of Modernity, 1500–1800.* New York and Cambridge, Mass., 1993.

Ingram, Martin. *Church Courts, Sex and Marriage in England, 1570–1640.* Cambridge, U.K., and New York, 1987.

Kingdon, Robert M. *Adultery and Divorce in Calvin's Geneva.* Cambridge, Mass., 1995.

Laqueur, Thomas. *Making Sex: Body and Gender from the Greeks to Freud.* Cambridge, Mass., 1990.

McLaren, Angus. *Twentieth-Century Sexuality.* Oxford and Malden, Mass., 1999.

Marcus, Steven. *The Other Victorians: A Study of Sexuality and Pornography in Mid-Nineteenth-Century England.* New York, 1964.

Mason, Michael. *The Making of Victorian Sexual Attitudes.* Oxford and New York, 1994.

Mosse, George L. *Nationalism and Sexuality: Middle-Class Morality and Sexual Norms in Modern Europe.* Madison, Wis., 1985.

Nye, Robert, ed. *Sexuality.* Oxford and New York, 1999.

Plant, Richard. *The Pink Triangle: The Nazi War against Homosexuals.* New York, 1986.

Porter, Roy, and Mikulas Teich, eds. *Sexual Knowledge, Sexual Science: The History of Attitudes to Sexuality.* Cambridge, U.K., and New York, 1994.

Rocke, Michael. *Forbidden Friendships: Homosexuality and Male Culture in Renaissance Florence.* New York, 1996.

Tannahill, Reay. *Sex in History.* New York, 1980.

Trumbach, Randolph. *Sex and the Gender Revolutionary.* Vol. 1: *Heterosexuality and the Third Gender in Enlightenment London.* Chicago, 1998.

Turner, James Grantham, ed. *Sexuality and Gender in Early Modern Europe.* Cambridge, U.K., and New York, 1993.

Weeks, Jeffrey. *Sex, Politics, and Society: The Regulation of Sexuality since 1800.* London and New York, 1981.

HOMOSEXUALITY AND LESBIANISM

Randolph Trumbach

Throughout the centuries since 1300 sexual relations between males have been defined by the official cultures of the church and the state as immoral and illegal. From the arrests, trials, and punishment of men who engaged in this behavior it is possible to sketch a history of male homosexual relations. More trials were held in southern than in northern Europe before 1700, and more trials were held in the north than in the south thereafter. Consequently more is known about Italy in the later Middle Ages than about England, France, or the Netherlands, and more is known about these three northern countries than about southern Europe in the subsequent centuries. Nonetheless, some signposts are visible. The nature of sexual relations between males changed profoundly around 1700 as the result of a major shift in all sexual relations, whether heterosexual or homosexual, and significant but lesser changes occurred after 1850 and 1950.

The history of sexual relations between women, by contrast, is much harder to reconstruct. In some places the behavior was illegal, and in others it was not. But the archives have yielded only about a dozen cases before 1500. By the eighteenth century a short history is possible, written from the literary representations of desire between women. But not until the nineteenth century did the diaries and letters of leisured women extensively document actual relationships. After World War II oral histories reconstruct a public sexual culture for women. It is of course likely that significant differences existed throughout these centuries between the sexual behavior of women and men if for no other reason than the domination that men exercised over all of women's activities. But evidence suggests that the significant changes in sexual behavior between men after 1700, 1850, and 1950 had parallels in the behavior between women, since at these points in time the entire Western sexual system, heterosexual and homosexual, changed.

AN AGE-STRUCTURED SYSTEM, 1300–1700

In the years from 1300 to 1700 sexual relations between European males were structured by differences in age. This meant that men past the age of puberty who could grow full beards took sexually active roles with adolescent boys who had entered puberty. Since for reasons of diet and physiology puberty then began later than it did in the twentieth century, boys between the ages of fifteen and twenty-two were anally penetrated by men who were in their mid- to late twenties and sometimes older. This was not, however, the behavior of a minority of 4 or 5 percent of all males, as homosexual behavior was in Western countries in 2000. Instead it is likely that all males experienced conscious desire for other males and that most of them acted on this desire. But these males also desired women. Some of them went to prostitutes, and most of them eventually married women and had children. Among the minority who never married, some were primarily interested in boys, but most were probably restrained from marrying by economic factors that were part of a distinctive western European demographic regime. That demographic regime disappeared over the course of the eighteenth century as marriage became universal except among the small minority of exclusively homosexual men.

More importantly sexual desire in men after 1700 was divided between an overwhelming majority who were exclusively heterosexual and a homosexual minority of less than 5 percent. This can be difficult for Westerners to understand, because in the late nineteenth century a supposedly scientific psychology analyzed the sexual divisions observed in Western societies as moral or biological constants that must exist in all human societies. This psychology invented the terms "homosexual" and "heterosexual" to describe these divisions, unaware that they had only arisen in the first generation after 1700.

Westerners after 1700 had difficulty understanding any sexual system other than their own. This was true even when they read the evidence for earlier Western societies. Despite the great prestige of the classical civilizations of Greece and Rome in Western culture, the literary evidence for their sexual systems, in which men desired both boys and women, was ignored, denounced, or misinterpreted by educated men, who read it as a standard part of their educations. The literary evidence of the Renaissance, whether from Italy or England, was similarly misread in the mistaken belief that Christianity, because it denounced and punished sodomy, had profoundly changed the behavior of European men from what it had been in the ancient pagan Mediterranean. Observing cultures other than their own, in many of which men desired both boys and women, Europeans similarly either ignored the evidence of their own eyes or denounced it as the peculiar degeneracy of inferior races. They understood only Western behavior because that was presumed to be the biological and moral norm. The homosexual minorities of their own societies were categorized as biological and moral deviants, and all homosexual behavior from any time or place was similarly classified.

A comparative perspective. The age-structured system of sexual relations between European males that prevailed between 1300 and 1700 is better understood when compared with similar systems from other cultures and contrasted with gender-structured systems of homosexual behavior. In the Mediterranean world the prevailing systems for sexual relations between males were structured by differences in age. Among the ancient Greeks adult male citizens who had grown their beards courted beardless adolescent boys who were their social equals. It brought great prestige to a beautiful boy like Alcibiades to be desired by many men. But ideally a boy was faithful to one lover, who became his guide. The sexual component of the relationship ended when the boy grew his beard, and his lover married a woman. Boys had to be careful that they were not publicly stigmatized as either passive or mercenary. A free boy who allowed his favors to be bought lost his rights of citizenship, but foreign boys who were slaves or prostitutes were legally bought by their owners or patrons. The transition from passive boy to active man was crucial, and the minority of adult men who continued to be passive were held in contempt even if they married women.

The Roman system was similar yet profoundly different in that relations with free boys were forbidden. Only foreign adolescent slaves or prostitutes were legal companions for men. The Roman material also documents more fully two different kinds of adult passive men. The *cinaedi* married women and remained part of ordinary social life but were held in contempt. The *galli*, by contrast, were given a grudging respect. They left their families and became members of itinerant bands who served a goddess. They danced, begged, sometimes castrated themselves, and were often prostitutes. Consequently men had four different sexual roles in their relations with each other: active man, passive boy, *cinaedus,* and *gallus.* The *cinaedus* and the *gallus* came into existence when a passive boy failed to make the transition to the active role. Passive men from the lower social strata became *galli.* Those who were not prepared to abandon their families and rank became *cinaedi,* the most difficult role of all. But all four roles were parts of a single system in which differences in age ordinarily justified and even gave prestige to some kinds of sexual relations between males. In both Greece and Rome the law and religion therefore took for granted that all men would desire sexual relations with both women and boys.

This age-structured system of four roles (one active, three passive) survived into the world of the Islamic Mediterranean. In the twentieth century in Turkey, for instance, were active men, passive boys, *ibne,* and *köçek.* The *ibne* was the passive man who stayed in society and even married. The *köçek* joined a transvestite band of entertainers and often castrated himself. The *köçek* was admired, and the *ibne* was held in contempt. Similar systems of four roles with different terms for each role existed in Morocco, Iraq, Oman, Saudi Arabia, Pakistan, and northern India. One *hijra,* the northern Indian equivalent of the Turkish *köçek* and the ancient *gallus,* explained that when men could not easily find a woman or a boy, they went to a *hijra.* It is important to notice that, though Islamic religion and law condemn relations between males, adult men are held in honor by their peers when they penetrate a boy, an *ibne,* or a *köçek.* Two systems of sexual morality, the official and the unofficial, therefore coexisted, but the unofficial actually described what men did. As late as 1963, 44 percent of Arab men in advanced psychology classes at the American University in Beirut admitted to having sexual relations with males. The similarity between these Islamic systems and those of ancient Greece and Rome is striking. It raises the question of whether or not the Christian societies that existed between the Roman and the Islamic worlds were any different in this regard, and it outlines the patterns of sexual relations between males that are documented in southern Europe or the northern Christian Mediterranean from the fifteenth through the seventeenth centuries.

Sexual relations between males structured by differences in age is one of two predominant worldwide systems. In the other system relations between males are structured by the presence of a minority third gender role of biological males who have been socialized to combine aspects of the behavior of the two dominant male and female roles of the majority in their societies. This system appeared less frequently than the other, but it has been observed among most of the native peoples of North America, the islands of the Pacific, and sub-Saharan Africa. In age-structured systems all males as adolescents passed through a period of passivity, but most became active once they grew beards. Only two decided minorities remained passive as men. In gender-structured systems most men never experienced sexual passivity. Both as adolescents and as adults they penetrated a small passive minority. This minority from childhood had been socialized into a role somewhere between those of most men and women. Their bodies were strong like men, so they were notable workers, but they did not fight as warriors. Instead they dressed, spoke, and moved as women. In their passive sexual roles with the male majority, they might play the role of prostitute, lover, or wife. They can seem to have a superficial similarity to the two kinds of passive males found in age-structured systems. But unlike the *cinaedus* or the *ibne*, they did not marry women, and unlike the *gallus* or the *köçek*, they did not join liminal groups that served as alternative families. No one expected that they would grow up to be active men, and their sexual partners did not pass through a period of sexual passivity. It is important to understand the differences between these two systems because the major transition in sexual relations between Western males that began around 1700 can be usefully conceptualized as a transformation from a system structured by age to one structured by gender.

These two systems have so far been described only in terms of relations between males because it is primarily those that are described in the historical and anthropological sources. But the two systems also existed among women. Some Native American women became warriors and took wives. The women of Sparta and Lesbos probably took girls as their lovers, and the women of modern Mombasa certainly did. But the age-structured systems of the Islamic world also produced the sworn virgins of Iraq or the Balkans who became men and probably gave up all sexual relations. They neatly parallel the men who became *ibne* or *köçek*. But the women who became masculine were given high status. This was true whether they were the women warriors produced by a gender-structured system or the sworn virgins of a society structured by differences in age. It will therefore be appropriate to see whether these distinctions can be used to understand the history of sexual relations between Western women.

Renaissance Florence. Florence in the fifteenth century provides the most detailed picture of sexual desire between males in the Europe of the late Middle Ages. In the second and third generations of that century at least 15,000 Florentine males were accused of sodomy, and over 2,400 were convicted by the principal magistracy charged with overseeing sodomy. From this Michael Rocke estimated that at least two-thirds of all Florentine males were implicated by the time they reached the age of forty, and these figures do not cover all the magistracies. This strongly suggests that almost all males had sexual relations with other males at some point in their lives and did so repeatedly. The importance of this finding cannot be stressed too much. The most perspicacious readings of the ancient Greek and Roman sources have demonstrated a similar world, and a number of anthropologists who studied societies outside of the West in the twentieth century found the same. But these readings and observations have been challenged or ignored by those convinced that homosexual behavior was limited to a small deviant minority.

Sodomy was nonetheless illegal in Florence. Preachers like Bernardino of Siena regularly denounced it, but Bernardino also accepted that it was widespread. He even said that mothers were proud that their attractive adolescent sons caught men's eyes and deliberately sent them into the streets dressed in the most alluring clothes. The Florentines apparently lived out their sexual lives under two different moralities, a Christian one that disapproved of sodomy and a masculinist and patriarchal one that promoted it. Other facets of the sexual life of Christian Europe exhibited such a contradiction. Christians brought before the Inquisition believed that simple fornication between unmarried men and women was no sin, and married couples divorced each other even though the church held that marriage was indissoluble. Christians also resorted to magic instead of using the channels of grace provided by the Church. These contradictory moralities existed together in the minds of individuals, and at some moments and in some roles one morality prevailed over another in the life of an individual. The presence in all males of sexual desire for other males have to be teased from literary sources. It can be demonstrated statistically.

This must mean that the distinction between a homosexual minority and a heterosexual majority cannot have existed in Florence. If this distinction did not exist in a single European society, it is extremely unlikely to have existed in any of them. Certainly all modern Western societies are organized sexually by the same distinction between homosexuals and heterosexuals. It is true that this distinction became dominant in different Western societies at different moments after 1700, but it is apparent, when Florence is compared with either the ancient pagan or the later Islamic Mediterranean, that the sodomy of Florence was nothing new. It was simply more open and therefore better documented.

The question arises whether or not sodomy became more open in the course of the fifteenth century. There had certainly been relatively few cases in the fourteenth century when the penalties had been far more severe. As the penalties were moderated into a series of graduated fines, which were often not paid, the number of denunciations increased. Many Florentines therefore thought that sodomy was wrong, but they did not think it was so wrong as to merit severe punishment. This was the compromise between the two moralities by which many Florentines lived. But in their adolescence and young manhood, most Florentine males lived entirely according to the masculinist morality and not the Christian one. When Niccolò Machiavelli worried about his son's intimacy with a boy, Francesco Vittori told him: "Since we are verging on old age, we might be severe and overly scrupulous, and we do not remember what we do as adolescents. So Lodovico has a boy with him, with whom he amuses himself, jests, takes walks, growls in his ear, goes to bed together. What then? Even in these things perhaps there is nothing bad."

The sodomy most Florentine males practiced was strictly organized by differences in age. From the time boys entered puberty at fifteen, delayed for physiological reasons, until their beards began to grow at nineteen or twenty, they were anally penetrated by older men. These men were usually unmarried and in their late twenties. Between nineteen and twenty-three came a transitional phase, when a young man could be both active and passive. He was always active with someone younger and passive with someone older. Adolescent boys occasionally took turns being active and passive with each other, but young adult men never allowed themselves to be passive with their adolescents. Older men sometimes fellated their adolescent partners instead of penetrating them. Most men stopped pursuing boys once they married, in their thirties. A few adult men (12 percent) never married, and some had boys throughout their lives. Some men in their twenties had sex both with female prostitutes and with boys. A very few adult men allowed themselves to be penetrated. They presumably failed to

make the transition from passive boy to active man. No adult transvestite men appear in the fifteenth-century records, but the evidence shows such men in the sixteenth century. They certainly appear in the sixteenth- and seventeenth-century records for Spain and Portugal. All of the four positions typical of age-structured systems in the Mediterranean world therefore existed in Renaissance Florence: the active man, the passive boy, the passive man who tries otherwise to live a conventional life, and the transvestite passive man. But as in all such systems, most activity was between men and adolescents. This was not simply a preference for younger partners of the kind found among the homosexual minority of men after 1700. It was instead a desire for the smooth, small, lightly muscled bodies of boys, and it was a desire that was always destroyed, whether in Greece, Rome, Islam, or Christian Europe, by the growth of hair on the thighs and the face.

This world of men and boys could be both highly promiscuous and lovingly faithful. In 1480 sixteen-year-old Andrea was sodomized by forty-two different men in the course of a year, and on average boys, when they were interrogated, confessed to eleven partners. Adult men were as active. A baker admitted having twenty-four boys over seven years, and a butcher admitted having thirty-four boys over twelve years. Sometimes, about one in ten, a boy was voluntarily sodomized by as many as eight men in turn at a time, which occasionally degenerated into gang rape. Some boys were prostitutes. A network of prominent citizens in 1467 sponsored a brothel of boys that a blacksmith ran. Some boys worked for a procurer, or a ring of four boys together worked the taverns, gambling tables, and the houses of female prostitutes, picking up 120 men between them. Boys who were not prostitutes were often given gifts of money at each sexual encounter, which no doubt helped to maintain their honor. Men were often contemptuous of the boys they sodomized, describing them as women, prostitutes, or wives, and this no doubt was part of the source of their sexual excitement. It also explains why some fathers were not anxious that their sons be known as passive. It was acceptable to fathers for their sons to sodomize other men's sons, however. These ambiguities persistently appear in age-structured systems, whether in ancient Greece or the modern Islamic world. Nonetheless, at least a sixth of the men and boys interrogated formed a loving sexual bond that lasted from one to six years. A weaver who worked with his boy and nightly slept with him was said to see "no other god but him." A dyer and an apothecary swore on the gospel book as it lay on the altar that they would be faithful to each other, which would

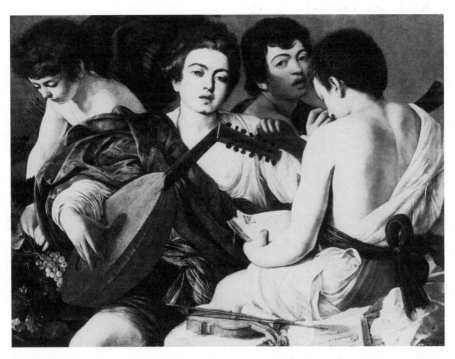

Homosexual Gathering. *The Musicians,* painting by Michelangelo Merisi, called Caravaggio (1571–1610). THE METROPOLITAN MUSEUM OF ART, NEW YORK, ROGERS FUND, 1952 (52.81)

have made a legally binding marriage between a man and a woman.

The rest of Europe. Patterns similar to Florence's turn up throughout southern Europe. Other parts of Italy prosecuted fewer than Florence since the penalties were usually more severe. Venice had known places where men picked up boys. Group sex and gang rape occurred as well as long-lasting love affairs. Occasionally an adult man was sexually passive, and a few men were transvestites. The entire age-structured Mediterranean system was present. The same was probably true of Rome, or so the evidence from Michelangelo Caravaggio's life suggests. But it is instructive to consider the disagreements among his biographers. Some see only the female prostitutes with whom he associated and whom he used as models in his paintings. Others see only the apprentices and adolescent servants with whom he lived and slept and whom he depicted clothed or nude in his paintings. It is clearly difficult to see the women and the boys as inhabitants of a single sexual milieu.

In Spain and Portugal the Inquisition records document similar patterns. In most cases sodomy occurred between men in their twenties and boys between fifteen and nineteen with the men active and the boys passive. These boys were often dressed and painted like women. Florentine boys do not seem to have done this, though at least one of the Roman boys in a painting by Caravaggio was mistaken for a woman. The Iberian material also presents more clearly cases of adult transvestite men, who constantly dressed as women, used women's names, and in some cases even constructed artificial vaginas to conceal their penes. But typically in the Mediterranean pederastical system such men were a decided minority.

Information about northern Europe is much sparser because that area had fewer trials. Basel, for instance, had only eight trials in the first fifty years of the fifteenth century. The penalties were severe. Four were exiled, and three were burned at the stake. In 1475 a chaplain at the cathedral confessed to having sodomized several times a choirboy who lived in his house. The boy claimed that the priest had persuaded him by saying, "If everybody who committed this act was burnt at the stake, not even fifty men would survive in Basel." When read in the light of the southern European materials, these fragments reveal a world of widespread sexual acts between men and adolescents with a great deal of implicit tolerance and few cases brought to trial because the penalties were too severe.

The Reformation in northern Europe apparently made no difference. In Geneva in 1610 a man under torture for high treason and murder confessed to having sexual relations with twenty other males and thereby revealed the existence of a world that usually went undisturbed. England has been studied most extensively. The fragmentary evidence comes in three kinds, including a few trials for sodomy, biographical anecdotes about gentlemen and kings, and plays and poems. Literary scholars who study the third category sometimes claim to find evidence for egalitarian sexual relations between two adult men in some plays from early in the century, but these are certainly misreadings. Those who study the Restoration plays agree that the sodomy in them is structured by differences in age. Every case of sodomy brought to court concerned relations between men and adolescents. Even the most hostile anecdotes about King James I and his lovers took for granted that the king was dominant with younger men. Robert Carr became the king's favorite when he was twenty and "smooth-faced" and fell from favor when he grew his beard, lost his looks, and then married. In England, possibly because of a physiological regime different from that in the south, a young man's passivity could last till the age of twenty-five.

Court factions regularly vied with each other to present the king with a favorite of their choosing. They apparently took for granted that it lay within the power of any handsome young man to satisfy the king's desire, presuming evidently a universal capacity in this regard. The comments on James's behavior could be either condemnatory or noncommittal, establishing in Protestant England the continued presence of two opposing moralities of sodomy. During the years of his marriage, when James evidently slept with his wife because of the cycle of her pregnancies, no evidence indicates that he had male favorites. The favorites came only after he ended sexual relations with his wife. No one thought the king was an effeminate, passive sodomite interested only in men or boys, because such mollies did not appear in England until a hundred years later. The real difficulty with the English material is that the two kinds of passive adult men found in the Mediterranean evidence have not shown up except for the case of John Rykener. He called himself "Eleanor" and was found in women's clothes having sex with another man in a London street on a night in 1394. He worked regularly as a prostitute but also had sex with women. The seventeenth-century populace could conceive of men who were both active and passive and labeled them hermaphrodites, but no actual example has come into view.

Sexual behavior between women. The pattern of sexual behavior between women before 1700 is harder to establish than that of men. If they were structured by differences in age, primarily the small number of adult, masculine transvestite women who penetrated other women with an artificial phallus made it into the legal sources, not the majority of older women who had sex with younger ones. It is as though the sources for men described only the exceptional cases of the two kinds of adult passive men and ignored most of the acts between adolescents and men. Similarly in the twentieth century anthropologists mentioned in passing that many adult women in the villages of Iraq had sex with younger women but then devoted their detailed studies to the exceptional transvestite virgin. In 1560 the Aragonese Inquisition received denunciations of several women for sexual relations with each other enacted "without any instrument." The courts were told not to prosecute because lascivious behavior among women who had not used an artificial phallus was not sodomy. But two Spanish nuns who had used dildos were burned in the sixteenth century. From the sixteenth through the eighteenth centuries in Italy, Spain, France, Germany, the Netherlands, and England women dressed as men, married women, and used artificial penes. Sometimes their wives seem to have been unaware that their husbands were not biological men. In some places these female husbands were punished once they were discovered. Their wives sometimes left them but occasionally stayed in the marriages. Female husbands were part of a larger group of women who for varying lengths of time dressed and lived as men. Some of these women became transvestites as a means of getting better work or while searching for an absent male lover or husband. It is not clear whether those who married women and used a phallus began to dress as men primarily for sexual reasons.

Differences in age seemingly were not an important part of these marriages between women. The literary sources that represent affairs between women indicate that older women took younger ones as lovers without dressing as men or using an artificial penis. Eighteenth-century English erotic novels by Delarivier Manley and John Cleland present such age-structured relations, as does the Italian libertine literature of the previous two centuries. From the arrests of a dozen women in Amsterdam for having relations with each other, it is apparent that as late as the 1790s many of these relationships were partly structured by differences in age. Bartha Schurman, who was thirty-one, murdered Catharina de Haan because she was jealous of her involvement with twenty-three-year-old Bets Wiebes. Maria Smit (forty-six) was observed by neighbors as she made love to Anna Schreuder (seventeen). Gresia Debber, who was twenty-four, was involved with three others, one twenty-seven, close to her own age, but two much older, thirty-seven and forty-six. Two mistresses seduced their maids, who were probably younger women. Christina Knip, forty-two years old, raped a fourteen-year-old girl. Knip used a dildo, but none of the other women did. Some of these women were married, some widows, some single; none was a transvestite. Except for a case in 1750 involving two women (fifty and sixty years old), these prosecutions are the only ones for sexual relations between women during two centuries in Amsterdam. It is not clear why they were prosecuted, but it is likely that they represent the nature of most relations between women in traditional Europe more closely than do the 119 cases of women who lived as men and sometimes married women in the Netherlands in the same period.

A GENDER-STRUCTURED SYSTEM, AFTER 1700

This age-structured system in Europe began to disappear over the course of the eighteenth century, first for men and then for women. It was replaced by a system that structured same-sex relations by gender differences and divided the world into a homosexual minority and a heterosexual majority. In the eighteenth century the change seems limited to northwestern Europe (England, France, and the Netherlands). It reached central Europe by the middle of the nineteenth century, but it did not appear in southern and eastern Europe until the early twentieth century. When it first appeared around 1700, it was probably part of the major societal shift that produced the dominant modern culture of the next three centuries. This likelihood is confirmed by the experience of Japanese society, which between 1910 and 1950 moved similarly from an age-structured to a gendered system that divided the world into a homosexual minority and a heterosexual majority. The beginning of and slow growth of equality between men and women probably account for the change. Certainly in traditional societies, like those of North America, in which same-sex relations were structured by the presence of a third-gender minority, women had relatively higher standing than they did in the age-structured societies of the Mediterranean or East Asia. In neither kind of traditional society was the sexual world divided into a homosexual minority and a heterosexual majority. The modern sexual system was therefore in some respects radically different from all preceding systems.

Mollies. In the thirty years after 1700 it is possible to identify in English society a new kind of sodomite called, in the slang of the streets, a "molly." A molly was an effeminate adult man who desired to have sex only with men or boys. His speech and gait were similar to a woman's, his clothes tended to be elegant, and he occasionally dressed as a woman for a ball. Among his fellow mollies he was often known by a woman's name. Some men, like the Princess Seraphina, always dressed as women, people referred to them using female pronouns, and they lived by prostitution. All mollies differed from the effeminate men of both traditional systems. Their role was closest to the North American berdaches. But whereas it was legitimate for the berdache to be penetrated by the men and boys from the majority, in the modern system the molly was supposed to be strictly avoided by the men and boys from the majority. The molly did desire such men, sometimes as their only objects, but the men who yielded were concerned to hide this carefully since any contact with a molly could be used to put them into that despised category. Mollies also and perhaps mainly had sex with each other, whereas the berdaches strictly avoided each other.

Mollies also differed from the two types of passive men in age-structured systems because in their cases sexual acts between males no longer centered upon men with boys. It is true that adult mollies sometimes pursued boys and that for a while in the early eighteenth century some men continued to desire both women and boys. It was also the case that throughout the next three centuries some men in total institutions like prisons or ships at sea satisfied themselves with the boys who were present. But it was no longer acceptable for a boy to be passive. Boys talked among themselves about mollies with constant horrified fascination, but a boy approached by such a man tended to panic. Masturbation was severely discouraged with threats of mental and physical debility because it led males to a fascination with their penes instead of with women's bodies.

The appearance of the molly was accompanied by the development in the majority of men of a new sexual role that allowed them to desire only women. Men's desire for adolescent males, which had existed as far back as one can go in the history of the Mediterranean, were now taboo. Instead men determinedly pursued the populations of streetwalking female prostitutes, who filled the principal thoroughfares of most Western cities for the next 250 years. They seduced unmarried women with such callous vigor that within a hundred years illegitimacy climbed to unprecedented levels. In the end every sexual act was threatened by the venereal diseases men contracted from prostitutes and passed on to their wives and children. Whoremongering no longer injured a man's reputation. Instead it was crucial not to be known as a molly. Black-

Punishment of Homosexuals. *Justice Triumphant through the Disclosure of Punishment of Terrible Sin.* Anonymous Dutch print, 1731. RIJKSPRENTENKABINET, AMSTERDAM

mailers could terrify a timid man by swearing to charge him with sodomy, since the charge once made was difficult to disprove. But no term distinguished this male majority. They were simply men and not mollies.

Mollies met each other walking in the streets or strolling in the shopping arcades, where it was possible to linger unobtrusively. They met as they turned against a wall to make water, and they met strolling in the parks. In these places they mingled with female prostitutes and with the men who were the prostitutes' customers, and they picked up some of those men. The intermingling of the worlds of prostitution and sodomy lasted for 250 years, until prostitutes more or less disappeared from the streets in the late twentieth century, when premarital sex became common among young respectable women. The molly like the prostitute was promiscuous, and mollies copied the manners of prostitutes. The term "molly," like other subsequent terms, including queer, punk, gay, faggot, fairy, and fruit, was first used for female prostitutes.

The molly and the prostitute in the course of the eighteenth century were the deviant minorities who defined the roles of the respectable majority of men and women. But sentiment and domesticity made women into mothers and destroyed the old presumption that, in Alexander Pope's phrase, every woman was at heart a rake. The male majority's loyalty was contested between the prostitute, with whom they could demonstrate their exclusive interest in women, and the wives, who were the mothers of their children

and the source of domestic comfort. Mollies as men experienced a similar tension between libertinism and domesticity. For the next 250 years they could not legally marry each other or have children, though some mollies married women and had children. In the relative privacy of their molly houses, to which only they had access unless a traitorous molly admitted the legal authorities, they invented rituals that longingly mocked the rituals of marriage and domesticity. Sometimes they conducted marriages with one partner dressed as a bride and with bridesmen and women in attendance. The room in which they engaged in group sex might be called the chapel, the sex called marrying, and a sexual partner called a husband. A man might go into labor and be delivered by a midwife of a wooden doll, his child might be baptized, and his male gossips might visit to drink caudle as a woman's friends waited on her in the real world.

In that real world a molly's life was happiest if he could hide his effeminacy, putting it on and off as he entered and left the molly house. It was sometimes claimed that mollies worked in the trades that dressed women and cared for their hair, but these were simply the men who could not easily hide their effeminacy. Mollies worked in the full range of occupations, and they lived everywhere in town. Men from the middle and upper classes had the most to lose if they were identified as mollies and sometimes tried to hide their effeminacy in an elegant estheticism. But women gossiped about them and their effeminate gestures behind their backs, and men excluded them from political office. If they misjudged and made a pass at the wrong man and were arrested, their families were likely to disown them, and their only option was to flee into exile abroad.

The molly was an English phenomenon, but the life of the new effeminate sodomite remained something like this through the eighteenth and the nineteenth centuries in England, France, and the Netherlands. In eighteenth-century Paris the displacement of the traditional libertine who pursued boys by the new effeminate sodomite can be traced in the police records, with the first predominating early in the century and only the latter present by the 1780s. The legal reforms that came in France with the Revolution did not criminalize sodomy. This sometimes has been mistaken for a new regime of toleration, but the police in both France and the Netherlands simply arrested men for public indecency in the nineteenth century and probably in greater numbers than they had in the previous century. In the 1870s the Parisian police kept a register of sodomites from which a social world rather like that of the eighteenth century can be reconstructed. Of course some changes occurred. Bourgeois propriety no longer allowed men to urinate openly in the street, so the public urinal became one of the main venues for finding a sexual partner and remained so throughout Europe until the 1950s. The young policemen and the telegraph boys in their uniforms joined the soldiers in the streets as objects of men's desire. In the Dutch material from the middle of the eighteenth century men said they were born with their desires and knew they were different from most men. Both the Dutch and the French sources document more readily than the English the male lovers who lived together as couples with varying degrees of fidelity.

Sapphists. Women, on the other hand, were more likely to live as a couple and not move in a public world of meeting places once a new masculinized "sapphist" or "tommy" who was exclusively interested in women appeared in the later eighteenth century. In this respect sapphists had more in common with the majority of women than they did with sodomites, who like other men were likely to pursue sex in public places. The lives of sapphists also differed because the female prostitute, not the sapphist, delimited the respectability of the majority of women, whereas most

Sodomy Punished. Sodomites meet (1) and abandon their wives and children (2). They are arrested (3) and imprisoned (4) and executed by burning (5) or drowning in a barrel (6) before the Amsterdam City Hall. Dutch print, 1730.
RIJKSPRENTENKABINET, AMSTERDAM

319

men measured themselves against the sodomite. None-theless, the gender identities of the sapphist and the sodomite were similarly constructed in that they both combined selected aspects of the gendered behavior of the women and men of the majority. The mascu-linized sapphist emerged one or two generations after the appearance around 1700 of the effeminate sod-omite. She initially appeared among gentlewomen, whereas the poor produced their sodomites from the very first. Why these differences existed is unclear.

To understand the novelty of the sapphist it is necessary to distinguish her from the woman who dressed as a man, married women, and used an arti-ficial penis. These passing women had been the de-viants in a system in which most acts between women were structured by differences in age. In that respect they had been similar to the two deviant kinds of adult passive men when most acts between males had oc-curred between men and adolescents. The sapphist did not wish to pass as a man. She wished to be openly ambiguous, but she hoped that her ambiguity would be stimulating to women's eyes and not to men's. She wore a woman's dress but walked with a man's gait. Seeing Anne Lister in the street, two female prostitutes in the early nineteenth century approached her and touched her breasts to reassure themselves that she was not a transvestite man. Transvestite men in the street were likely to be sodomites engaged in prostitution. In her diary Lister unambiguously established the sex-ual practices of sapphist women in the way that sod-omy trials do for those of men. Her similarities with late-eighteenth-century women like Mrs. Damer, about whom contemporaries gossiped because she wore a dress but with men's boots, help explain the transfor-mation in sexual identity that these women repre-sented. Lister demonstrated that relations between women in the early nineteenth century were some-times genital. These relations were not all romantic and platonic. The late-nineteenth-century discussion about such women did not create them. It merely described them no doubt with the intention of mor-bidifying them.

Lister was a landed gentlewoman who eventu-ally suffered some degree of ostracism because of her perceived tastes, even if the hostility was nothing like the internal exile that the rich young man William Beckford endured because of a scandal over a boy who grew into an effeminate sodomite. Those parts of Lister's diary that detail her sexual feelings and rela-tions with women were written in a secret code. She eventually dressed in black to avoid criticism that she was not fashionably feminine, and she adopted incon-spicuous elements of men's clothes, like braces to hold up her drawers. She disliked masculine manners in women, but her own deep-toned voice frightened other women. She spoke flirtatiously with women the way a man would. Her lover called her "Fred" and "husband." She fantasized that she took a young woman into a shed on a moor and had sex with her using a penis. At thirty she stopped menstruating, and she grew mustaches. Her contemporaries began to os-tracize her, and her lover, who liked what happened in bed between them, became embarrassed to be seen with her. But Lister told her friend that she considered her feelings "natural to me inasmuch as they were not taught, not fictitious, but instinctive." She read the ancient Romans to understand her own relations, but she found the women in Juvenal artificial because they did not form marriages with other women as did the English sapphists, whom she began to recognize and meet in her thirties.

Lister flirted with many feminine women and had sexual relations with most of the sisters in one family. The most important was Marianne Lawton, who had married a man. This marriage Lister dis-missed as mere "legal prostitution." The two women, vowing marriage to each other in bed after a night of lovemaking, agreed to take the sacrament together as a pledge (an old way of making a clandestine marriage between a man and a woman) but to avoid any other ceremony as long as Lawton's husband was alive. When this relationship broke up, Lister went to Paris to recover. She described the sex with women there more explicitly than the "kisses" she wrote about with Lawton. Some people supposed that women who had sex with women had enlarged clitorides for penetra-tion, but Lister explained to one woman that her body was not hermaphroditic, that no one had corrupted her, and that her feelings were "the effect of the mind." Lister would not allow this woman to recip-rocally touch her clitoris or put her finger into her vagina, though she had done this to the woman. That, she said, would be "womanizing me too much." Her male identity allowed her to give pleasure but not to receive it directly. Eventually Lister, when she was forty-one, began a romance with an Englishwoman ten years younger than she, and they lived in a mar-riage until Lister's death.

It is not clear that Lister's feminine partners had the same kind of sapphist identity that she did. Such women may have moved easily in and out of the world of conventional sex with men. It has been suggested that these feminine women did not have a lesbian identity until after the 1950s, when the majority of women took on a heterosexual identity by mastur-bating in increasing numbers and having sex with men they did not mean to marry, behaving as the majority of men had since 1700. Lister's peers turn up elsewhere in Europe in the nineteenth century. The French painter Rosa Bonheur dressed in trousers or the riding habit, a masculine jacket and a feminine skirt, that sapphists often used and lived in marriage with two women in succession. These gentlewomen moved in private networks, however. At the end of the nineteenth century a public sapphist world first appeared in bohemian Montmartre. In literary discussions these women were often portrayed as prostitutes, and some prostitutes, like Thérèse V. in the 1890s, did prefer women. But the working-class sapphist remains hard to find.

Discussions of homosexuality. In the second half of the nineteenth century the lives of homosexual men and women became the focus of an increasingly intense public discussion. Michel Foucault and his followers have claimed that this discussion produced the modern homosexual identity. It is certainly true that the terms "homosexual" and "heterosexual" were coined in the late nineteenth century. As J. A. Symonds put it in *A Problem in Modern Ethics* (1891), "the accomplished languages of Europe in the nineteenth century supply no terms for this persistent feature of human psychology, without importing some implication of disgust, disgrace, vituperation." The words "sodomite" and "sapphist," "molly" and "tommy," could not be used in respectable conversation. These roles, contrary to Symonds, had not always existed, but by the late nineteenth century they were two hundred years old. What therefore needs explanation is why in the 1850s doctors, like Claude François Michéa and Johann Ludwig Casper, who had observed effeminate sodomites from the subcultures of their day, and in the 1860s homosexual jurists and literary men, like Karl Heinrich Ulrichs and Károly Mária Kertbeny, who invented the term "homosexual," drawing on the widespread conviction of sodomites and sapphists that their feelings were inborn, offered a biological origin for the existence of the homosexual minority that came into existence in the generation after 1700.

From the middle of the eighteenth century educated Europeans like Thomas Canon tried to justify modern sodomy by comparing it with ancient pederasty, and they continued to do so into the twentieth century. But a perspicacious reader like Lister could see the difference between herself and the Roman women. Biology may have offered a more modern and convincing basis for Ulrichs and Kertbeny to argue that the state should not punish innate behavior. This was certainly the basis of the first homosexual rights movement that Magnus Hirschfeld launched in 1897, the Scientific Humanitarian Committee. For Ulrichs and Hirschfeld the homosexual was an effeminate man, a third biological sex, an individual with a woman's soul in a man's body. The association of effeminacy seemed to some men deeply discreditable. Consequently in Germany, France, and England groups like the Gemeinschaft der Eigenen and (community of self-owners) and individuals like André Gide promoted an alternative vision of a masculine homosexuality between men and adolescents. By the 1920s Germany had a homosexual rights movement with thousands of members. The dominant role of German thinkers and activists in all these developments remains unexplained, and when in the early nineteenth century the modern homosexual role and an accompanying subculture became identifiable in German society has not been established. It is also not apparent why after 1850 bourgeois homosexual men throughout Europe were moved to publicly justify their behavior in this way. It is certain, however, that the discussion was used against them once the idea of a third sex was presented as a perversion by Richard von Krafft-Ebing (in 1886) and other psychiatrists.

The patterns of homosexuality in the twentieth century and their relationships to the lives of the heterosexual majority are unclear. It is not apparent, for instance, when the modern pattern of gendered behavior, with its division of a homosexual minority and a heterosexual majority, displaced traditional age-structured systems in eastern or southern Europe or in North and South America. In Russia as late as 1860, when the modern system had been fully established for some time in western and central Europe, men were still attracted to both boys and women. But by 1900 something like a homosexual subculture accompanied presumably by a heterosexual majority existed in Moscow and Saint Petersburg. Modern homosexual life was established in North American cities by the 1820s. The difficulty is in understanding the lack of evidence for it in the eighteenth century when the patterns of heterosexuality that accompanied it in England were clearly present in colonial society. The history of Italy, which provides the best evidence for the traditional system, has not been studied since eighteenth century. The legal discussions in Spain between the 1930s and the 1950s make it likely that those were the years of transition for Hispanic societies. Jurists and psychologists in Argentina, Mexico, or Cuba in the early twentieth century used the categories produced in the European discussions at the end of the nineteenth century to describe the sexual encounters between males in the culture of their streets and prisons, unaware that their system of adult men who penetrated boys and passive transvestite men differed profoundly from the homosexuals of their European sources.

In Western and Central Europe from the 1930s to the 1950s homosexuals became a focus of the disputes between fascists, socialists, and communists, each group blaming the others for sexual perversion. The German homosexual emancipation movement was smashed by the Nazis, and thousands of homosexual men were sent to concentration camps. Joseph Stalin conducted his own purges. In Western Europe and the United States homosexuals were labeled security risks during the cold war. But the gains of the earlier German movement were not entirely lost. Danish psychiatrists, one of whom had even joined Hirschfeld's committee, employed the German argument that homosexuality was congenital to justify the decriminalization of homosexual relations between consenting adults as early as 1930. On the other hand, France, which for two centuries had no penal legislation, passed laws in 1942 and 1960 that established a higher legal age for homosexual than for heterosexual acts and stiffer penalties for public indecency when it was homosexual. But by the 1960s most of Europe had decriminalized acts between consenting adults. This granting of respectability to the adult homosexual was often accompanied by two related strategies. Transvestite homosexuals were recategorized as transsexuals and encouraged to undergo surgical transformations of their genitals, and relations between adult homosexuals and adolescent youths or young men in the armed forces were severely policed. In England, for instance, 10 percent of the prosecutions in 1900 were for relations with boys under sixteen, but by the

1950s those were 75 percent of all cases. Having shed its pederasts and transsexuals, a more homogeneous homosexual minority stood poised to enter the brave new world ushered in by the next wave of the homosexual rights movement that arrived from the United States after the Stonewall riot of 1969.

After 1969 homosexual men and lesbian women throughout Europe advocated a move from the private legalization of their consenting relations to a more public acceptance of their right to form legal unions and raise families. From Scandinavia to France and even Spain this was accomplished in an amazingly short period of thirty years. So vast a transformation needs a correspondingly large cause, and changes in the heterosexual identities of the majority of women and men are the likeliest explanation. Most women after 1950 acquired heterosexual identities. Their rates of masturbation nearly matched those of men, and with widely available birth control, they engaged in ever-increasing numbers in intercourse without marriage. These new heterosexual women were firmly demarcated from the feminine partners of lesbian women. At the same moment the sexuality of heterosexual men became domesticated. They ceased to go to prostitutes in any significant numbers, and their sexual contacts with homosexual men also declined. These men and women did not necessarily marry each other. Births outside of marriage and the number of couples living without marriage increased. As a result toleration grew for a homosexual minority that was firmly separated from the heterosexual majority.

See also other articles in this section.

Bibliography

Bergmann, Emilie L., and Paul Julian Smith, eds. *¿Entiendes? Queer Readings, Hispanic Writings.* Durham, N.C., 1995.

Bray, Alan. *Homosexuality in Renaissance England.* London, 1982.

Carrasco, Rafael. *Inquisición y represión sexual en Valencia: Historia de los sodomitas, 1565–1785.* Barcelona, Spain, 1985.

Dekker, Rudolf M., and Lotte C. van de Pol. *The Tradition of Female Transvestism in Early Modern Europe.* Basingstoke, U.K., 1989.

Donoghue, Emma. *Passions between Women: British Lesbian Culture, 1668–1801.* London, 1993.

Dover, K. J. *Greek Homosexuality.* Cambridge, Mass., 1978.

Duberman, Martin Baumly, Martha Vicinus, and George Chauncey Jr., eds. *Hidden from History: Reclaiming the Gay and Lesbian Past.* New York, 1989.

Faderman, Lillian. *Surpassing the Love of Men: Romantic Friendship and Love between Women, from the Renaissance to the Present.* New York, 1981.

Foucault, Michel. *The History of Sexuality.* Vol. 1: *An Introduction.* Translated by Robert Hurley. New York, 1980.

Fout, John C., ed. *Forbidden History: The State, Society, and the Regulation of Sexuality in Modern Europe.* Chicago, 1992.

Fradenburg, Louise, and Carla Freccero, eds. *Premodern Sexualities.* New York, 1995.

Gerard, Kent, and Gert Hekma, eds. *The Pursuit of Sodomy: Male Homosexuality in Renaissance and Enlightenment Europe.* New York, 1989.

Greenberg, David F. *The Construction of Homosexuality.* Chicago, 1988.

Herdt, Gilbert, ed. *Third Sex, Third Gender: Beyond Sexual Dimorphism in Culture and History.* New York, 1994.

Higgins, Patrick. *Heterosexual Dictatorship: Male Homosexuality in Postwar Britain.* London, 1996.

Higgs, David, ed. *Queer Sites: Gay Urban Histories since 1600.* New York, 1999.

Kennedy, Hubert. *Ulrichs.* Boston, 1988.

Langdon, Helen. *Caravaggio: A Life.* London, 1998.

Lever, Maurice. *Les bûchers de Sodome: Histoire des "infâmes."* Paris, 1985.

Licata, Salvatore J., and Robert P. Petersen, eds. *Historical Perspectives on Homosexuality.* New York, 1981.

Lister, Anne. *Female Fortune: Land, Gender, and Authority.* Edited by Jill Liddington. New York, 1998.

Lister, Anne. *I Know My Own Heart: The Diaries of Anne Lister, 1791–1840.* Edited by Helena Whitbread. New York, 1992.

Lister, Anne. *No Priest but Love: Excerpts from the Diaries of Anne Lister, 1824–1826.* Edited by Helena Whitbread. Washington Square, N.Y., 1992.

Maccubbin, Robert Purks, ed. *'Tis Nature's Fault: Unauthorized Sexuality during the Enlightenment.* New York, 1987.

Merrick, Jeffrey, and Bryant T. Ragan Jr., eds. *Homosexuality in Modern France.* New York, 1996.

Murray, Stephen O., and Will Roscoe, eds. *Islamic Homosexualities: Culture, History, and Literature.* New York, 1997.

Norton, Rictor. *Mother Clap's Molly House: The Gay Subculture in England, 1700–1830.* London, 1992.

Norton, Rictor. *The Myth of the Modern Homosexual: Queer History and the Search for Cultural Unity.* London, 1997.

Pflugfelder, Gregory M. *Cartographies of Desire: Male-Male Sexuality in Japanese Discourse, 1600–1950.* Berkeley, Calif., 1999.

Porter, Kevin, and Jeffrey Weeks, eds. *Between the Acts: Lives of Homosexual Men, 1885–1967.* New York, 1991.

Robb, Peter. *M: The Man Who Became Caravaggio.* New York, 2000.

Rocke, Michael. *Forbidden Friendships: Homosexuality and Male Culture in Renaissance Florence.* New York, 1996.

Rosen, Wilhelm von. *Månens Kulør: Studier i dansk bøssehistorie 1628–1912.* 2 vols. Copenhagen, Denmark, 1993.

Ruggiero, Guido. *The Boundaries of Eros: Sex Crime and Sexuality in Renaissance Venice.* New York, 1985.

Schmitt, Arno, and Jehoeda Sofer, eds. *Sexuality and Eroticism among Males in Moslem Societies.* Binghamton, N.Y., 1992.

Smith, Bruce R. *Homosexual Desire in Shakespeare's England: A Cultural Poetics.* Chicago, 1991.

Trumbach, Randolph. "London's Sodomites: Homosexual Behavior and Western Culture in the Eighteenth Century." *Journal of Social History* 11 (1977): 1–33.

Trumbach, Randolph. *Sex and the Gender Revolution.* Vol. 1: *Heterosexuality and the Third Gender in Enlightenment London.* Chicago, 1998.

Weeks, Jeffrey. *Coming Out: Homosexual Politics in Britain from the Nineteenth Century to the Present.* London, 1997.

Williams, Craig A. *Roman Homosexuality: Ideologies of Masculinity in Classical Antiquity.* New York, 1999.

Young, Michael B. *King James and the History of Homosexuality.* New York, 2000.

Section 17

BODY AND MIND

THE BODY AND ITS REPRESENTATIONS

Lisa Z. Sigel

Although the body functions as both a material and a symbolic artifact, it received very little attention by historians until the late twentieth century. The intellectual tradition inherited from Plato, arguing that the physical is just a shadow of the real, as well as the biblical verse "in the beginning was the word" have created a legacy making physicality a mere precondition for the more important matters of mind and soul. Nonetheless, bodies have long dominated European history. Preindustrial bodies remained poised precariously between reproduction and starvation. The rapid changes in agricultural production, hygiene, medicine, and labor since the Renaissance have transformed the body and its impact on society. Bigger, healthier bodies and more of them have remade modern Europe into a mass society with changing aesthetic, medical, and psychological norms that balance population concerns with an increased focus on individualism and new demands of privacy. At the same time that history plays out on and through the body, individuals use their bodies to create their own identities: fashion, clothes, cosmetics, and surgery allow people to create, express, and perform their roles in society.

While bodies have always been available for study, historians have only begun to examine them as separate and equal to the minds that dominated previous discussions. This interest in the body by social historians converged from a variety of directions, many of which have attempted to undermine the mind-body dualism inherited from the Enlightenment. As history has become a more inclusive discipline since the 1960s, historians have tried to historicize their own experiences as embodied beings and have attempted to formulate ways that society has used criteria based on physicality to sort and discipline human beings.

At the most concrete and materialist level, social historians have combined techniques from sociology and physical anthropology to document the body as an artifact. To assess the impact of the industrial revolution, for example, social historians have looked to quantifiable data on the body as a source that would speak beyond the positions laid out by more literate sources. Although those who amassed data on bodies from previous generations rarely did so from an unbiased position, the data itself can be retooled to speak to issues of mortality, illness, and health. The body as material can function as a basic economic indicator that registers wealth and well-being of populations.

Approaching the materiality of the body in a much more confrontational way, women's historians have demonstrated a lack of fixity in the relationship between biological sex and gender, even though women have been conceptualized as limited by their own biological nature in much of Western history. To explore how "biology became destiny," to paraphrase Sigmund Freud, women's historians began to theorize how gender or constructions of femaleness and maleness have been wedded to biology. As part of this project, they examine the ways that societies theorize gender and biology, teach beliefs and practices, and represent them historically.

Scholars of sexuality, in many cases building upon the work of women's historians, have examined the ways that sexual roles and meanings become constituted. Scholars of homosexuality first rediscovered a hidden past, then examined the factors that impeded sexual choice, and finally looked toward processes that allow for sexual and social accommodation. Both women's historians and historians of sexuality have radically reexamined what had been considered unchanging by questioning experiences such as family formation, pain and pleasure, and the biological "urges" of the body.

Cultural historians have built on the methods of literary critics, anthropologists, and art historians to read the body as a sign of society. The debates over language that developed in other disciplines encouraged historians to examine discourse of the body. Rather than seeing knowledge as a form of universal, ahistorical truth, social historians, diverging from the practices of intellectual historians of previous generations, have examined the context of that language to see the emergence of the mind-body split. Thus, they have tried to reinscribe the mind in the context of the world rather than accepting the legacy of René Descartes in the form of the disembodied thinker as absolute. By exploring the development of discourse, cultural historians have demonstrated that the province of "nature" has been largely culturally constructed and thus has changed over time.

These multiple and overlapping directions of scholarship have converged upon the body because it is a central symbol in issues of gender and sexuality, aesthetics and representation, politics and ideas. As society has developed since the Renaissance, the understanding, uses, and meanings of the body have been central to the process of change. As the skeletons of our former selves demonstrate, bodies physically document the effect of big structural changes on the inhabitants of Europe; at the same time, the representations of the body whether naked, clothed, or even unencumbered by flesh show the variety of ways that the body can be conceptualized, perceived, and utilized.

THE RENAISSANCE AND
EARLY MODERN PERIOD

At a basic level, most bodies during the Renaissance were still caught within the demands of subsistence living. On average, the crops failed every sixth year, leaving most people, and particularly the young, a legacy of malnutrition, ill health, and early death. Epidemic and endemic disease, from the periodic episodes of plague that lasted well into the eighteenth century to the continual scourge of smallpox that caused 10 to 15 percent of all deaths in early modern Europe, made attention to the body and its signs of health and illness a central part of everyday life rather than merely the province of doctors, surgeons, and healers. The body as a medical issue mattered across all levels of society. Beyond medical matters, beliefs about other aspects of physicality mattered as well. The study of the body, the schooling of the body, and the relationship between body, mind, and soul all went through incremental changes that heightened the importance of corporeality during the period. While spirit still mattered and older popular beliefs still flourished, new beliefs about physicality emerged between the fifteenth and seventeenth centuries that made the issue of representation as important as the body itself.

Renewed interest in corporeality. During the Renaissance, scholars reexplored beliefs about the body inherited from the ancient world. Some of these be-

liefs, like the medical beliefs of Aristotle and Galen, had influenced European thought throughout the Middle Ages. Others, like the emphasis on personal experience as a method of learning, gained a new respectability. While religion and religious beliefs still governed the conduct of the individual and served as a foundation of education, art, medicine, and philosophy, Renaissance society gave the corporal a new weight in relation to the spiritual. The Church itself rejected the renunciation of the flesh seen in medieval penitents and flagellants who sought to mortify the flesh and renounce its desires. Furthermore, the renewed interest in ancient learning emphasized that the exterior reflected the interior self; thus the physical being of a person spoke directly to their spiritual states. Aristotelian belief emphasized that one's ethics, character, and morality could be read from the physical state because these states were formed by controlling one's passions.

The way anatomists understood the organs and the material matter of the body was based upon a different schema than our current beliefs. The medical understanding of the body was based upon the Hippocratic and Galenic traditions. In these traditions, both the environment and the imbalances in the substances that made up the body caused illness. Health was a matter of maintaining equilibrium. The basic substances of blood, phlegm, black bile, and yellow bile made up the physical matter of bodies and each substance had its own quality that could be read from the countenance of the individual. The preponderance of a substance affected the individual's temperament and health. Sanguineous people had a preponderance of blood—which was hot and dry—and thus they were faster moving and more animated than the phlegmatic. While people's constitutions helped form their temperaments, the environment played a part as well. Heat and cold, moisture, drafts, exercise, shocks, and accidents affected the balance of the humors and caused illness.

Humors, their properties, and their relationships to the environment created the constitution of the body as a sexed organism but, even in the case of sex, biology was a matter of degree and balance rather than a matter of opposition. Women were understood as essentially similar to men though with different predominating humors and internal rather than external genitals. Anatomists saw the vaginal canal as an internal shaft that corresponded to the penis and the ovaries as internal testes. Both sexes produced semen. Without orgasm from both parties, no conception could occur. Similarity in biology, rather than difference, encouraged both learned and popular belief that women needed to orgasm and ejaculate during intercourse to conceive. Coldness and dampness on the part of women and dry heat on the part of men functioned as some of the main markers of biological difference. Thus, women could theoretically become men if heat or shock drove their internal organs outward. Historians have shown by exhuming anatomical drawings and medical beliefs that the simple platform of biology, even in the supposedly clear example of biological sex, remains subject to projection and representation.

At the same time that medicine and natural philosophy formulated these approaches to the body, magic and religion played a role in catastrophe, illness, and the constitution. Though the body's outward appearance spoke to the balance of fluids and organs, it also spoke to the internal state of the soul. Divine intervention could alleviate illness and divine displeasure could cause it. Not only did people believe that the direct will of the Christian creator could affect the functioning of the individual, more accidental influences played a part on the constitution. For example, the experiences of the mother were transferred to the baby because the spiritual was directly tied to the body. Thus, according to popular belief, seeing a deformity while pregnant could give rise to a likewise deformed child. The combination of formal learning and magical belief constructed the body's relationship to the world. As well, the stars played their part in the constitution of the body. The neo-Platonic tradition emphasized that all nature was alive and animate. The placement of the stars affected the physical relationship of the body because macrocosm and microcosm were innately tied, and the most learned in society used astronomy as a way to predict and encourage good health. The conception of the body as a physical being was thus based on many, highly individualized factors, and medicine had the job of peering beneath the opacity of the skin to discover the right balance toward physical health for each person.

The interest in the physical encouraged a new form of exploration into the body based upon observation and personal experience. Renewed interest in corporeality during the Renaissance and the increased interest in philosophical and medical knowledge encouraged the practice of dissection and anatomy, which flourished in Renaissance learning as a way to understand and experience the body firsthand. Artists and naturalists overlapped in their search to see the relationship between the body's interior and its exterior. Both Leonardo da Vinci (1452–1519) and Michelangelo (1475–1564) based their artistic representations of bodies upon detailed anatomical drawings. The bodies they drew were not necessarily the exact bodies they saw but images heightened by beliefs about notions of beauty in the physical form: central to conceptions of beauty were ideas of symmetry, strength, vigor, and grace. Nonetheless, unlike medieval artists, their firsthand knowledge of anatomy gave their works, even those with an allegorical or religious focus, a representational facility that made their conception of the human form more rooted in worldliness and less in the spiritual realm.

Presenting and representing the body. Books on courtesy and manners dictated new ways of schooling the body and its appearance for aristocrats, courtiers, and the bourgeoisie. These books stressed that deportment could be learned, rather than only scrutinized, and the presentation of self could be cultivated as an art. Physical acts of eating, drinking, dressing, speaking, and moving, all of which bespoke character and social status, could be acquired. These accomplishments governed overt physical acts like the use of table implements and the handkerchief and also less tangible ways of controlling the body and wielding it as a predicator of sophistication. For example, movement and dance meant not only steps and timing, but also grace, energy, physicality, control, composure, and expression. One had to know the steps to dances and also know how to deport oneself through the steps. As formal dancing became a social accomplishment and dances began to emphasize the couple instead of groups of three to four, as they had in the Middle Ages, gender behavior and demeanor became a more formal part of dancing as a learned activity. Women needed to learn to demonstrate sweetness, charm, and restraint as qualities in movement; men had to show steadiness, virility, and control.

The schooling of the body as an art thus crossed over between performance and representation. Acts like dancing allowed individuals to perform gender roles and represent themselves as accomplished individuals. Other arts from the Renaissance, like painting and sculpture, incorporated similar ideals of the body as representing the inner workings of character and morality. Artists stylized the human form to create complex aesthetic and moral representations of body that spoke to the internal and external character. Titian's Adonis in *Venus and Adonis* (1551–1554), for example, combined delicacy and vigorous movement. His upright form strides away from the more languorous Venus in movement reminiscent of the male Renaissance dancer.

Older beliefs in the body continued to flourish. The body still had magical properties that gave it curative powers. The live bodies of kings, the dead bodies of convicts, and the body pieces of saints transcended the limitations of physicality and provided a

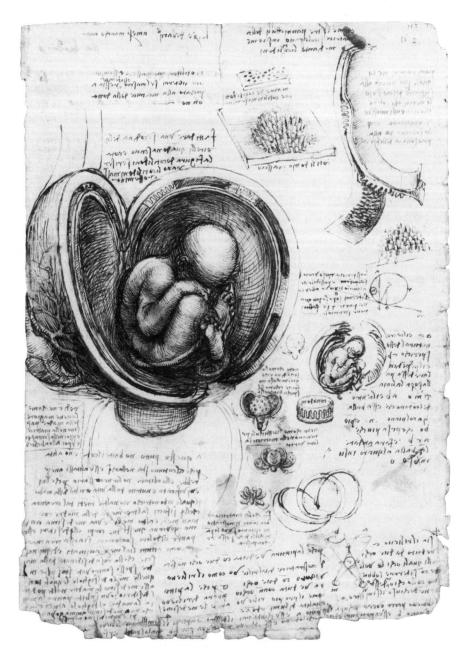

Anatomical Drawing. An infant in the womb. Drawings by Leonardo da Vinci (1452–1519).
©HER MAJESTY QUEEN ELIZABETH II

reservoir of material for spiritual interaction. The touch of the king as well as that of the corpse could cure skin diseases. The transformative powers of bodies as sacred material made the burial sites and the traffic in saints' pieces part of an early tourist trade. The body politic had both material and symbolic power; the term referred to the physical being of the monarch who reflected the domain of the state.

Just as the king's body had divine powers that performed a social role in providing cohesiveness, the convict's body performed justice, retribution, and divine mercy for the benefit of society. Through public torture and ritualized hangings, society could read the effects of crime and immorality upon the countenances of the criminal. The body formed a conduit to the soul. The criminal was made to perform a walk of penitence often carrying the props of his crime. At crossroads, he called out his crimes and sentence, and when arriving at the scaffold, often erected at the site of the crime, he confessed and was executed. The body or its pieces were sometimes left to mark the site of wrongdoing as a rotting marker of justice. If not executed, the marks of criminality were permanently displayed upon the figure of the criminal. Pierced tongues for blasphemers, amputated hands for thieves, and lopped ears for beggars made the stigma of criminality permanently visible as signs of the social order.

The presence of death in everyday life made the corpse a much more significant part of society in the Renaissance and early modern world than in the twenty-first century. Not only did markers of death like the hanging corpse and the weeping, long-dead saint act as conduits to physical and spiritual rejuve-

nation, the idea of the corpse hovered behind the daily acts of life, spurred, no doubt, by the precariousness of existence. The dance of death and the stages of life, two traditional motifs in prints, make it clear that death lurked behind every scene. No matter what station one achieved, death—represented in the grinning skeleton and the waiting coffin—would offer the final embrace. The juxtaposition of life and death, beauty and the grotesque worked as experiential as well as representational motifs. For example, St. Bartholomew's Fair featured an open market, a field for jousting, a hospital, and a gallows. Knights and ladies, cripples and saints mingled with entertainers like fire-

Venus and Adonis. Painting by Titian (Tiziano Vecelli, 1488 or 1490–1576). NATIONAL GALLERY, LONDON/ALINARI/ART RESOURCE, NY

eaters, puppeteers, animal trainers, dwarfs, half men/ half beasts, and other curiosities. The heterogeneity of St. Bartholomew's made it a rich location for the interweaving of commerce and entertainment, physical punishment and physical prowess upon which one could read morality tales in motion.

The protean and ribald body appeared in Renaissance pornography (although the term "pornography" did not itself appear until the nineteenth century). In these representations, the body became a seething mass of profane and spiritual desires that nurtured each other. Through the themes of coitus, bodily evacuation, and the intermingling of orifices, the sexualized body enhanced sexual tensions in society, including the problems of celibacy, the unfaithful wife, the crossed lovers. Through pornography and other representations in the visual and literary arts, men argued about the place and meaning of women and women's bodies in the Renaissance world. Theological understandings of sexuality as well as pornography argued for women's highly sexual nature. Women had the stigma of Eve and were thus biologically insatiable. They needed to be curbed sexually rather than aroused. However, the highly sexed nature of women's bodies offered opportunities as well as problems, and the roles of the courtesan, whore, wife, and mother allowed women to use the social stigmas to their own advantage. Prostitutes in Venice used the rage for small, conical, and firm breasts to advertise their trade by uncovering their breasts in the streets.

The introduction of syphilis to Europe at the end of the fifteenth century (often attributed to Columbus's sailors, as well as foreign troops, Italians, French, or Jews) and its rapid spread brought a physical manifestation of immorality that influenced generations of artists. The rotting nose, open sores, and twisted limbs of the syphilitic and the excessive salivation brought by the treatment of mercury became emblematic of a guilty life and worse death. The importance of physical beauty as indicative of inner purity made the outward manifestations of syphilis markers of sexual immorality. Just as witch's tits spoke of congress with the devil and lopped ears indicated criminality, so the lost nose of the syphilitic announced sexual and moral transgressions. Early attempts to reform and remake the body through surgery began with the reconstruction of the nose to erase the stigma of syphilis. Techniques of skin grafting first developed during the Renaissance, even though they appear largely forgotten until the nineteenth century, when doctors rediscovered techniques of beauty surgery. The mark of the syphilitic continued to counter claims about the progress of humanity even after Enlightenment notions about progress prevailed.

THE SCIENTIFIC REVOLUTION AND ENLIGHTENMENT

While previous generations of scholars saw the scientific revolution as a decisive break marked by scientific advances and a new rationalist approach to the world, social historians who look at actual practice in addition to intellectual changes have some doubts about the clarity of that break. Instead, they tend to see continuity in practice and beliefs. While some large changes in the conception of the body emerged during the seventeenth and eighteenth centuries, these shifts in fact built upon ideas from the Renaissance and were similarly tempered by continuities and contradictions.

At a material level, the world of the body remained limited by a precarious existence. The "little ice age" of the seventeenth century produced famine and starvation. The recovery during the eighteenth century, while allowing for greater agricultural production and a higher population, did not relieve physical misery. In fact, people suffered from the dynamic changes produced by economic development. Growth in the population in the eighteenth century outstripped growth in food production, creating a relative decrease in the standard of living. This resulted in short, sickly bodies suffering from epidemic and endemic disease. The early phases of the industrial revolution and urbanization moved people away from the countryside and its food sources, while higher fertility rates and stagnant mortality rates meant that the population, overall, continued to grow. In late-eighteenth-century England, for example, the rise in population was not offset by an equal rise in food supply, resulting in high food prices, periodic shortages, and frequent riots. Huddled in cities, living in substandard housing, and eating a poor diet overwhelmingly composed of carbohydrates, early industrial workers suffered physically. Up to three-quarters of a worker's income was spent on food in early industrial society, and even with that commitment there was malnutrition and short and sickly bodies. Social class played out in body size and types of diseases. Gout, from rich foods and a heavy diet, affected the wealthy, while scurvy, from too few fresh vegetables and fruits, affected the poor. Thus, notions about progress—a central doctrine of the Enlightenment—need to be weighed against continued physical misery.

While people continued to suffer long-term debility, the elites produced new ideas about the body as a physical organism. William Harvey (1578–1657), in one of the best examples of the revolutionary nature of science, discovered that the heart functions as a pump that moves the blood through the

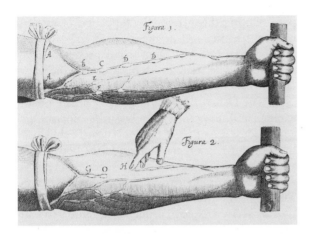

Circulation of Blood. William Harvey's diagram of a bandaged arm, demonstrating the circulation of blood. ©CORBIS

body in a great circle. Harvey, educated in Padua in anatomy and medicine like many Renaissance natural philosophers, saw the soul as a primary force in the body in accordance with Galenic tradition and believed that the blood moved purposefully, rather than mechanically. Thus his ideas seem firmly situated in the Renaissance notions of the body. At the same time, his discoveries, based upon the emerging scientific method of experimentation and observation, contributed to new mechanistic notions of the body.

Even after the idea of the body as a machine emerged, humors and the environment continued to play a large part in ideas of health and sickness. Older conceptions of health augmented the new materialist approach to the body. Theories of miasma and contagion, respectively bad air and the passage of disease between individuals, allowed people to respond to disease by charting weather and draining the swamps. Scientific discoveries based on observation and experimentation yielded results like the discovery of the central nervous system, which contributed to new formulations of ill health. No longer did the spleen predominate in matters of illness, now the nervous system, and particularly the refined nervous system of the upper classes, made certain illnesses more likely.

The scientific revolution and Enlightenment emphasized the process of questioning established belief. The multiple directions of those questions began to pull apart orthodoxies and opened the way for new formulations of the nature of humankind. For example, theories on race, which had emphasized notions of blood, began to examine environmental factors and physiological causes. Competing theories—that all babies are born white but become black within eight days or that the acquirement of dark skin from the African sun was passed from parent to child—implied ways to achieve progress, however dubious and misinformed. Other theories, like that suggesting physiology caused racial degradation, left little room for such improvements. Thus, while attempting to get to root causes of problems, natural philosophers continuously stumbled over the issue of free will versus biology.

As part of the program of mapping the body as discrete and the mind as governed by free will, Enlightenment thinkers tried to do away with superstition, irrationality, spells, faith healing, and magic. In attacking these irrational beliefs and practices, however, Enlightenment thinkers deemphasized the body and its importance in favor of a rational world controlled by the mind. By the eighteenth century the use of religion, astrology, and magic waned in medicine as the body became a more discrete entity that functioned in isolation according to its own laws, rather than one governed by the laws of the cosmos.

The privileging of mind over body, of free will over the symbolics of blood and flesh, however, allowed for a new reliance on the physical and mechanical causes of physical malfunctions. Thus, the body as a mechanical entity came to be seen as causal in "mental" illness. Treatments, from attempts to balance the humors in the seventeenth century to control of the physical and moral environment in the nineteenth century, saw the physical as a conduit to the interior or mental world of the body.

Nonetheless, a new emphasis on biology emerged during the period, influenced in particular by René Descartes (1596–1650), a central figure in the Enlightenment. Descartes's ideas about the body encouraged a new emphasis on the mind as separate from the body. He posited that deceptiveness of sensory data discredited it as a way of knowing one's existence. Instead of believing in the close correlation between soul and body, or even between seeing and knowing that characterized the formulations of many Renaissance scholars and lay people, Descartes saw the mind as paramount and the body, ruled by the mind, as merely responsible for carrying out the animal functions. Because of this formulation, Descartes has been held responsible for the development of the mind-body split characterized as Cartesian dualism and for the ensuing oppositions that have held sway in Europe. As man became characterized by mind and intellect, woman increasingly became seen as antithetical to man, thus more closely aligned to body. Likewise, culture, or the province of the mind, became positioned against nature, the province of the body. These gross divisions were only partially explicated; nonetheless, they affected formulations of the body as a site of meaning and as a physical entity. Later philosophies looked to gender as intrinsic, and natural philosophers developed a standard of biological difference that added to these oppositions.

Anatomists began to draw male and female reproductive organs as incommensurate, and the language for the female organs, terms such as "ovary" and "vagina," entered the European vocabulary. Sex became intrinsic and incontrovertible—heat could not make a woman into a man. As woman became conceptualized as unlike man rather than essentially similar, the role of passion changed as well. Women no longer needed orgasm to conceive, laying the groundwork for later theories that pregnancy could occur through rape and that women's passions were essentially maternal rather than genital. As man and woman became anatomically antithetical, the functions of sex organs became central to an understanding of the natural world. Carolus Linnaeus (1707–1778), a naturalist, developed the classification of mammalia—of the breast—to characterize the animals that suckled their young. Contemporaries pointed out that male mammals did not suckle, but the biological difference between male and female stuck as a central part of biological classification.

The new meanings assigned to men, women, and the body politic reconceptualized maternity. The battle of the breast formed one strand of the decisive differences that emerged during the Enlightenment. While the rich had favored wet nurses in previous centuries to maintain the small, firm breast of the woman, social philosophers argued that maternal nursing was a natural act that cemented the roles of family members. The act of wet nursing, in which the poor suckled the rich, became a metaphor for the larger perversions of the political state. In 1780 only 10 percent of Parisian babies were suckled in their own homes, but within twenty years, roughly half of Parisian babies suckled at the maternal breast. The republican model of nurturing mother, suckling child, and approving father promised a new natural political state of equality for man and domesticity for woman.

THE LONG NINETEENTH CENTURY

The long nineteenth century (1789–1914), marked at the beginning by the French Revolution and the end by the outbreak of World War I, saw a tremendous transformation in bodies and their meanings. New ideas about the equality of "man" gave rise to a variety of revolutionary movements in 1789, the 1830s, and 1848 that demanded greater self-determination but often resulted in greater bureaucratic control of the poor. During this period, the formation of modern nations, scientific racism, the rise of an industrial and consumer culture, and antithetical gender roles all were closely interrelated with the body and the way it was understood.

The French Revolution of 1789 began a reorientation in European politics toward democracy and a mass society. As part of this movement, a shift away from the king as a representation of the body politic and toward the uniformed body of the soldier-citizen worked as a metaphor to reconceptualize the nation. The bodily corruption of the monarchy and the aristocracy served as central themes in satire and caricature to undercut the legitimacy of the ancient regime. For example, the supposed sexual profligacy of Marie Antoinette, the queen of France, became a popular theme in pornographic propaganda. As well as delegitimizing older symbols, the formation of new ideals about the body played out in myriad directions. The guillotine began as a way to minimize the pain of execution and create a uniform system of justice. The kiss of Madame Guillotine, as it became known, supplanted previous crime- and class-specific methods of torture and execution. Men's fashions downplayed the sumptuousness of aristocratic fabrics and offered a new simplicity in the outfitting of men's figures. In spite of the supposed domesticity of women, the female form still had revolutionary potential. The most famous example of this appears in Eugène Delacroix's *Liberty Guiding the People*, also know as *Liberty on the Barricades*. *Liberty* memorialized the uprising of the July revolution of 1830 in which Parisian workers, soldiers, and students overthrew Charles X's monarchy. In the painting, the bare-breasted and barefoot figure of "Liberty" leads the charge through the dead bodies that lay strewn at her feet. She stands a full head taller than her comrades, waving the flag in one hand and holding a rifle in the other. The painting, withdrawn by the French government from public view because of its subversive potential, reemerged during the revolution of 1848. The female form here combined neoclassical elements with a romantic sensibility to express the political demands for a new society. The male and female body thus served as symbolic repositories for thinking through what equality meant to civil society.

Against this backdrop of new ideals of equality, economics still affected the physical form. During the first half of the century, people continued to go hungry as industrialization spread from England to the Continent. The rich continued to be taller, healthier, and less stricken by disease than the poor. Although conditions were alleviated during the second half of the century through improved agricultural techniques,

The Body in the Revolution. *Liberty Leading the People, 28 July 1830,* painting (1830) by Eugène Delacroix (1798–1863). MUSÉE DU LOUVRE, PARIS/PETER WILLI/THE BRIDGEMAN ART LIBRARY

a leveling off of the birthrate, and improved public hygiene, the changes were incremental and the poor still suffered hunger and debility. Widespread industrialization caused its own infirmities, like scalpings when girls' long hair was caught in machines, dismemberment from industrial accidents, and new forms of industry-related disease like black lung and brown lung. Although sanitary measures became a public health concern, crowding, adulterated food, and dirt and disease made the poor seem like a race apart.

Questions of race. The issues of race were exacerbated by new scientific theories and the renewal of European imperialism. Racialism gained new ground with the development of theories of evolution. Charles Darwin's *On the Origin of Species* (1859) examined the way that animal species developed over time. However, his theories were rapidly applied to people. The

problems emerged in deciding who constituted the species of mankind and in what direction that species was heading, as Darwin's *Descent of Man* (1871) made explicit. Concerns with race contributed to two competing theories on the origins of mankind; the first, called monogenesis, posited a single line of descent; the second, called polygenesis, insisted that the races had multiple lines of descent and that each race constituted a different species. Accordingly, each race had different distinguishing marks and scientists developed schemas of body types to classify the races. The Jewish or hook nose, the jug ears of the Irish, the kinky hair of Africans became supposedly scientific facts, rather than mere stereotypes. The science of race tried to document body type and correlate social, emotional, and intellectual factors with the physical form. Eugenicists attempted to sort out the races using basic tools for measurement like calipers, scales, and

335

measuring tapes and tried to assign the races distinct social strengths and pathologies.

The clear diversity of physical forms even amongst whites and fears about what diversity meant for society fostered attempts to fix social ills through breeding. (For example, English aristocrats were almost eight inches taller than working-class men, as recruiters found when trying to enlist soldiers for the Boer War between 1899 and 1902. Out of twenty thousand volunteers, fourteen thousand were rejected on the basis of being unfit.) To combat "race suicide," eugenicists developed two programs. In the negative eugenics program, they believed that if what they considered to be degenerate types could be separated from the rest of society, they would no longer interbreed with the fit and pollute the body politic. They attempted to limit the reproduction of those they identified as social inferiors like criminals, alcoholics, and the insane through voluntary and involuntary birth control. The more positive eugenics program encouraged the proliferation of the fit by promoting reproduction, limiting birth control for the healthy, and providing social insurance programs for children. These positive campaigns became more vehement after World War I, particularly in France and England, because of the enormous death rates both societies suffered and the plummeting birthrates. The search for racial types reached its most radical conclusions under Adolf Hitler, but only after attaining a respectable place in sociology and medicine for almost fifty years from the late nineteenth century until the mid-twentieth century.

As racial types became scientifically defined through body parts, fitness and the development of modern medicine allowed individuals to transform their bodies to fit the new standards. Greater attention to the individual body produced remarkable results in the discovery of antisepsis and anesthetics. These discoveries allowed surgeons to venture beneath the skin to repair and remake the body without killing the patient. The idea that beauty equals health and happiness became paramount. Surgeons could beautify individuals according to the new "scientific" ideals of body standards circumventing the biological standards of race.

Schooling the body. The nineteenth century also saw the rise of physical education, athleticism, sport, and the schooling of the body as an organized educational activity. Although people played physical games and engaged in sport (like boxing and hunting) before the nineteenth century, the nineteenth century characterized these earlier pleasures as barbaric bloodsport and systematized physicality so that control rather than excess became the watchword of exercise. The back-to-nature movement in Scandinavia and Ger-

many promoted heathy exercise for the individual and social renewal for the group. Bathing, in nature and in swimming pools, promoted fitness, vigor, and mental health. Organized hiking allowed people to slough off the pollution and degradation of industrial and urban life and renew their primitive sides. Physical education drew upon military drilling and rhythmic exercises to make children into compliant and productive citizens and workers. The assembly, for example, schooled the body in a posture of discipline, carefully segregated individuals into a uniform mass, and controlled the unregulated habits of children, guaranteeing no kicking, punching, tickling, or other displays of childlike physical pleasures. The careful positioning of bodies made them easy to watch, control, and discipline. The same techniques that applied to children prevailed wherever masses of uniform bodies were needed by the state, such as in prisons, the army, and other institutions.

The overt discipline of the bodies of the poor was matched by more covert ways to discipline according to social class and gender. Changes in fashion begun during the French Revolution continued to heighten the physical differences between men and women throughout the nineteenth century. As men's clothes became plainer with the rise of the ubiquitous black suit that cut across class lines, social class played out on and through the female form. Working-class women's clothes, featuring petticoats, shirts, skirts, shawls, and wooden shoes, marked them as utilitarian working beings. Rich women's clothing guaranteed good posture and a body well-formed for sexual pleasure by straightening the spine, pushing up the breasts, narrowing the waist, and accentuating the buttocks. Corsets and bustles, layers of undergarments, and heavy and expensive cloth marked a rich woman as incapable of work and barely capable of walking. As part of this demarcation, rich women's bodies were transformed by the trappings of their class. They experienced spinal curvatures, displaced internal organs, and a limited physical capacity that hindered their ability to sit, walk, and dance. Fashion magazines and etiquette books offered programs and advice to the parvenue on ways to act, dress, and appear appropriately. Their stylized figures and the mannerisms that emerged to match the clothes demanded the utmost attention and care.

The display of the body. At the same time, however, few people had the opportunity to gaze upon their figures in full. Most peasant villages had only one mirror located at the barbershop, and the urban poor had as little opportunity to see themselves as physical beings. With the rise of a widespread commodity culture in the late nineteenth century, mirrors became more popular even though the tinge of erotic appeal continued to stigmatize them. Gazing at oneself implied a lewdness associated with prostitution and drunkenness because barrooms and brothels featured large mirrors for voyeurism and self-inspection. Parents of respectable girls kept them from viewing themselves as a way to preserve their psychological and physical chastity. Girls washed in light shifts rather than naked and wore costumes for sea bathing that covered their torsos and extremities. The physical form was an object for outward display, rather than close self-inspection.

Against the backdrop of this circumspection, the display of monstrous bodies took on additional potency in the Victorian world. Touring companies and permanent installations of biological curiosities allowed the public to see the supposed wonders from distant (and mostly fictionalized) lands. The "Hottentot Venus" and the "Elephant Man" in England, the "Aztec Twins" and the "Fuegians" in Germany, and the pan-European tours of "Jo-Jo the Dog-Faced Boy" and "Lionel the Lion Man" all brought throngs of spectators to consider the strangeness of biology and the oddity of the physical form. The narratives of the sideshow posited the possibility that these people served as the evolutionary "missing link" between man and animals. These narratives set the people's origins in the remote "jungles" of distant lands where they lived outside modern society surrounded by like individuals. People thronged to such spectacles—a crowd of fifty thousand descended to watch the Fuegians go about their daily lives. They also bought photographs, postcards, and other mementos to remind them of such sights. The fixation on oddities did not stop at casual entertainment; anthropologists debated the origins of such anomalies. Visitors could touch the Hottentot Venus to prove that her rump was unpadded, and scientists wrote papers on the meaning of her genitals. Especially given the close attention to sexual propriety for "normal" female bodies (whose rumps, though padded, were not prodded), the focus on monstrous bodies as entertainment and education in the Victorian world underlined the centrality of the physical form as a basis of meaning. Undergirding the fascination with oddities were questions about the origins of humankind and the meaning of physical diversity.

The eroticism of the naked form and close restrictions on sexuality heightened taboos around sexuality. New injunctions against homosexuality, prostitution, masturbation, and pornography arose during the nineteenth century as a way to channel the energies of sexuality. Behind these conflicts lay a concept of the body as a limited energy system. Masturbation wasted energy and directed sexuality away from marital, procreative sexuality. Furthermore, continued masturbation left the body and mind sapped and impotent resulting in mental and physical illness. Doctors and parents used a variety of methods to discourage the practice. At the simplest level, innuendos and lack of privacy for adolescents discouraged masturbation or at least encouraged the concealment of it. When adolescents continued to masturbate, parents, physicians, and moralists turned to more complicated techniques including sermons and lectures, restraining devices, and physical mutilation to stop the chronic masturbator.

The emphasis on procreative sexuality within marriage should have discouraged prostitution. However, the belief that men needed a sexual outlet meant that men sought prostitutes and that the number of prostitutes continued to rise. European states reacted to the rise in prostitution by alternately outlawing it, regulating it, and ignoring it. The problem of venereal disease kept these problems of prostitution in front of the state. Doctors considered prostitutes one of the main vectors of venereal disease and recommended they be placed in prison or venereal hospitals subject to dubious medical treatment like the ingestion of arsenic and mercury. Feminist campaigns for social purity that emerged across Europe from Britain to Russia built upon the image of the prostitute as the victim of men's promiscuity and the state's unfeeling treatment of women. The prostitute became a powerful icon for addressing male sexual privilege at the expense of women's purity because contemporary theory argued that women had few sexual or economic desires of their own. Often the injunctions against such sexual practices held their own erotic appeal, as can be seen in the white slave trade scandals at the end of the nineteenth and beginning of the twentieth centuries. The popular press reported on the supposed abduction and sexual slavery of young girls. These sensationalist reports heightened concerns about girls' safety and raised the specter of a dark menace that preyed upon the innocence of Western women. Though few cases of sexual slavery were found, and those women who were spirited abroad were generally seasoned prostitutes who went to work in continental brothels, the frisson of fear that accompanied such reports added to the sexual thrills of Victorian and Edwardian society's ideas of race.

THE TWENTIETH CENTURY

The factors that limited bodies in the premodern world, such as inadequate food sources and unhygienic cities, had been curtailed by the beginning of the twentieth century. Bodies grew bigger and people had a greater likelihood of surviving to adulthood. The development of antibiotics during World War II, combined with the nineteenth-century medical advances of antisepsis and anesthetics, promised to wipe out disease and ill health. The great scourges of the past, from smallpox to polio, declined and in some cases were eradicated making it seem as if the precariousness of life and the fragility of the body would end. However, the massive mortality of the two world wars combined with the cataclysm of the Holocaust undermined this vision of progress. Instead, the tension between two opposing ideals of bodies that were established during the nineteenth century deepened during the twentieth. On the one hand, bodies became building blocks of a mass society; on the other hand, the rise of individualism played out in the greater attention to the individual body. The world wars and the rise of mass politics during the twentieth century insisted that bodies mattered mostly in quantity. The numbers game of trench warfare, in which each side attempted to throw the most soldiers "over the top" into no-man's-land, set a standard for mass death and dismemberment that has since characterized the twentieth century. At the same time, the development of commercialization and identity politics insisted the individual is distinct and noteworthy. This contradiction still dominated the politics of bodies at the close of the twentieth century.

World War I brought home the necessity of health and fitness in a mass society. At the same time, it also insisted on a fragility of bodies and established a new relationship between mind and body. The sheer numbers of people needed for mass war in World War I encouraged a new rationalization of resources and manpower. The health of the individual and the meaning of bodily fitness became an essential function of the state. In the front lines this meant a greater uniformity of the individual for the formation of a mass army. As the war devoured men on the front lines, they became interchangeable parts in favor of larger objectives of the war. In a grand irony, this commitment to the masses meant greater caloric intake and better health for working-class soldiers even given the appalling casualty rates. Behind the front lines, the rationing of calories, particularly in Germany, weighed the needs of the individual with the needs of the nation's war machine and left a generation of children with the physical consequences of malnourishment. As the state expanded to meet the needs of "total war," it took greater control of the individual's body, molding, using, and ultimately discarding it in accordance with the demands of the greater society.

As the fighting and horrendous conditions affected men's minds, European society needed to confront the mind-body split in new ways. No longer could insanity and the refusal of the mind to function be blamed solely upon a weak feminized biology that allowed for an easily disrupted body. At the outset of the war, doctors first believed that soldiers were faking their conditions. As more seasoned and decorated soldiers experienced neurasthenia and hysteria, doctors and military officials turned to a biological explanation—a blast from high velocity shells disrupted the nervous system causing "shell shock." However, by the end of the war, psychological explanations gained ground—no longer a conscious or a physical act, the unconscious mind of the soldier took over the body, rendering it incapable of action. Although psychologists and doctors attempted to use moral suasion, firmness, and a controlled environment to convince men's minds that fighting constituted progress, the long-term relationship between mind and body continued to be called into question, raising room for a later acceptance of Freudian analysis.

The massive number of mutilated men returning from the front as amputees, invalids, and victims of shell shock encouraged the development of reconstructive surgery to assist in their return to society. Physical reconstruction, though limited in its ability to restore faces and bodies, attempted to provide the patient some semblance of normality and happiness. The reconstructed face could not "pass" as normal: instead, surgeons tried to create a visage closer to humanity. (A French gibe stated that before the patient was horrible and afterward ridiculous.) The limited efficacy of such procedures encouraged a new modernist sensibility that rejected positivist notions about progress, at least in the artistic community. Representations of the wounded hero and particularly the image of veterans mutilated by face wounds became an important visual and literary element in the promotion of interwar pacifism. Exhibitions of facial casts from military hospitals in Paris, Berlin, and London allowed visitors to experience the horrors of war and scrutinize surgical reconstructions of the wounded. Expressionism in particular grappled with the disfigurement of veterans as a metaphor for the ugliness of society. Surrealists incorporated the rawness of bodily effluvia and perceived bodily urges—blood and excrement, sex and death—into their paintings. The veterans themselves fought to get basic benefits like artificial limbs and pensions and worried less about the symbolic uses of their disfigurement. The schism between high and low meanings of disfigurement in the early 1920s quickly disappeared as life as normal returned and the politics of disfigurement retreated to the background of European society. The disfigured continued to be a large part of the European landscape, however, and as late as 1938, 222 thousand officers and 419 thousand enlisted men received disability pensions in Britain alone because of World War I.

The interwar years. The interwar years continued to transform the roles of women, the meaning of sexuality, and the state's responsibility for health and fitness. The exigencies of war had allowed more female autonomy, in part because the needs for women's productive labor superceded demands for reproduction. While women's roles as wife, mother, and daughter remained important for propaganda purposes, the necessities of war afforded women new opportunities to define themselves. For the most part, this meant taking jobs long denied them, having sex outside of marriage, marrying earlier, or striking out on their own. Across Europe, women's freedom during the war contributed to the subsequent contest over sexuality in the 1920s and 1930s. In a striking example, the need for soldiers during the civil war in Russia allowed women to form an independent unit called the Women's Battalion of Death. The women in the battalion shaved their heads, wore regular army gear, and trained to fight. However, the Red Army used them for propaganda purposes—as a way to raise troops—rather than allowing them to contribute on the front lines. Outside of Russia, caricatures of the battalion insisted on seeing them as sexual creatures rather than as equal citizens and soldiers.

The place of women and the meanings of female sexuality and the female body were much debated on all sides. The falling birthrates, the belief in an abortion epidemic, and rising rates of women's paid labor pitted the new woman, with bobbed hair, shaved legs, and a job, against the idea of the traditional wife and mother. Progressives tended to see women's roles as workers and citizens as important as their roles as mothers and made birth control and abortion more available so that women could control their own fertility. Even with their attempts to alleviate sexual misery from unplanned and unwanted pregnancies, though, sex reformers made sexual health, including the female orgasm, part of a program that would serve the state. They recommended that sex education including technical information would restore marriage and stabilize society. Conservatives and fascists tended to see sex education and birth control in a more negative light and stressed women's social and biological roles within the family as primary. (Mussolini gave medals to mothers with large families who provided many sons for the state.) The female orgasm, no longer necessary to conception according to the more recent understandings of sexual reproduction, mattered less than the social imperative of populations and the state.

Discussions of sexuality included a reconceptualization of homosexuality. Sexologists in the nineteenth century, like Richard Krafft-Ebing (1840–1902) and Havelock Ellis (1859–1939), began to reexamine sexuality through the lens of science. They believed that homosexuality and other so-called sexual aberrancies were medical rather than criminal. Building upon the work of these early sexologists, scientists like Magnus Hirschfield argued that homosexuals were "sick people" with a specific etiology rather than individuals who willfully disregarded morality, theology, and the law. As a "sick" person the homosexual should not be prosecuted, but treated and cured. Hirschfield's Institute of Sexual Science in Berlin bore the slogan "per scientam ad justitiam" (to justice through science). The medical model of homosexuality began to affect legislation during the early 1930s, but the fascist backlash circumvented its acceptance. Hirschfield's institute was one of the first sites of Nazi book burnings in the 1930s as the Nazis sought to make an example of the institute's liberalism and supposed disregard of the family.

Society's concern with health, fitness, and the body gained momentum during the interwar period. The rise of modern dance, nudism, and dieting were all predicated upon new ideals of discipline and display rather than concealment. In France, for example, the new culture of dieting emerged in urban areas, particularly for the middle-class woman. The voluptuousness of the corseted female figure from the nineteenth century gave way to a new angularity of women clothed in outfits more attuned to movement, exercise, and athleticism during the twentieth. Doctors began to prescribe regimes of exercise and restraint, overturning traditional ideas of gluttony and plumpness as indicators of good health. While in rural areas food and fatness continued to signal good fortune, the urban ideal of bodies became one of control and moderation. Even Communist Party newspapers during the interwar years embraced fashion and fitness as legitimate concerns indicating a top-down movement of body image. The shift in ideas about weight demonstrates the centrality of control and discipline to the twentieth-century world.

While immediately after the war a focus on the body included a greater sympathy for the heroically wounded and disabled, the shift toward health and vigor as measures of political strength quickly returned. In Germany, the hard, male body became central to ideals of the fascist state. Leni Riefenstahl's

Riefenstahl's *Olympia.* The German director Leni Riefenstahl *(on ground, center)* films Archie Williams, American gold medalist in the 400-meter run, for the documentary of the 1936 Berlin Olympics, *Olympia.* ©BETTMANN/CORBIS

Olympiad (1938) served as a preeminent attempt to apply modernist techniques of representation to the physical form. Her filming techniques, including a nontraditional narrative, close editing, and the use of multiple camera angles, seem divergent from more traditional aesthetic standards set by Hitler's government, which rejected most forms of modernist representation as degenerate. However, the film's emphasis on beauty, fitness, competition, and the interchangeability of perfect bodies seems emblematic of the Nazi cult of the body. The glorification of raw, male power in her film corresponded with the larger objectives of the Nazi government. As political parties made their bids for control of the vastly expanded state, the issue of body politics made its way to the center of political ideologies.

The continued interest in eugenics during the interwar years made the physicality of the body key to the strength of the state. In the most extreme example under the Nazi government, the characteristics of the body correlated to the individual's' political and social place in society. According to this formulation, Jewishness no longer meant a religion or cultural identity, but a series of physical characteristics (skin color, nose shape, ear proportions) that indicated what the Nazis saw as the deeper Jewish goals of promoting communism or capitalism. Thus, while individuals

might lie about their purpose, the body could not. The Nazis took the idea of bodies laboring for the state and expanded it so that not only the product of bodies but the bodies themselves belonged to the state. These ideas clearly related to earlier ideas about physical fitness and health, in which the state derived its vigor from that of its citizens. For German citizens, this program meant that their primary allegiance belonged to the state, and they owed it to the state to maintain good health and strong offspring. In a great irony, the Nazi regime began an antismoking campaign as a way to maintain good health. What made the Nazi regime's treatment of physicality particularly disturbing was that they extrapolated these ideas so that the body no longer maintained its integrity, particularly for its subjects rather than its citizens. Hair, fillings, physical functions all served the state as raw material. The body became a resource for experimentation and recycling, as the treatment of Jews and other subjects made clear. Until the 1980s, skeletons and preserved tissue samples from the Holocaust victims of the Nazi era circulated in West German universities and laboratories. The impact of earlier policies lingered in the German reluctance to donate organs, as compared with other European countries where harvesting and donation became more routine. The physical integrity of the body has become paramount as a way to reject Nazism. (In contrast, East German society under communism, which saw organ donation as serving the community and state, had much higher rates of donation and transplant. The overtones of Nazi policies in eastern Germany were superseded by the communist ideal that the individual should serve the state before and after death.)

After World War II. In the postwar world, a number of often contradictory impulses toward the body and its meanings predominated in Europe. In Western Europe, the body entered the provinces of commercialization and identity politics even though the two were often at odds. In Eastern Europe, the body remained subordinated to the needs of the state, but the utilitarian nature of communist regimes sometimes afforded more leeway for individuals in terms of choices for the body than liberal regimes in Western Europe; the availability of abortion is one example. The ideas of health and fitness that dominated the interwar years returned after the end of World War II. Rather than being mediated by the economics of a boom economy in the twenties and the bust economy of the 1930s, the economic growth allowed for a more fully commercialized society in Western Europe.

Commercialization encouraged a deepening concern with beauty, as the continued rise of plastic surgery, creams, fads, and potions show. The body continued to be groomed as a sign of health and happiness, and increasingly this sign became available to all classes. State-sponsored social welfare programs that offered adequate nutrition and medical care allowed the physical differences of class—like height and health—to diminish. In turn, this physical equality combined with a greater availability of consumer goods allowed identity to be at once less permanent and more prominently displayed. Not only did clothes become cheaper, allowing people to put on and take off their allegiance to brands and fashions, but the supposedly innate biological markers like lip shape, biological sex, or nose size could be changed.

Sexual health and a focus on the body beautiful made erotic display and erotic pleasure central to new conceptions of identity. The sexual body joined the realm of commercialization as products to enhance erotic appeal were joined by advertising that used sexuality to sell products of all types. A number of factors including greater access to birth control, a loosening of restrictions around pornography, and new conceptions of marriage predicated upon intimacy, partnership, and love, rather than economics or progeny, allowed the erotic body to be separated from the reproductive body. Sexual pleasure became a worthy goal in and of itself. Sexual education, begun in the

interwar years to combat sexual misery, was superseded in the 1960s and 1970s by sexual liberation and the right to sexual pleasure. This conception of sexual pleasures as innately worthy allowed for a further liberalization of laws against homosexuality. Gay activists began to argue that homosexuality was not an aberrancy or pathology but a normal state upon which one's identity rested.

New patterns of formulating life and death, the outermost markers of bodily integrity—demonstrate the continued problems of embodiment and its representations in Europe. Greater control of the body by the medical profession has raised new questions and options toward the body. In vitro fertilization, artificial insemination, and surrogate motherhood further removed boundaries around reproduction. Pregnancy has become a choice, but a choice increasingly made in tandem with doctors and technology. Even death seems fully medicalized. The vast majority of Europeans die in hospitals attached to machines under the watching eyes of the medical community. Medical technology keeps the body alive after severe accidents and organ failure, raising the issue of where the self resides. The older pattern of death as part of life seems to have disappeared. Whether souls reside in the brain, the whole body, or in the beating heart, whether life starts at conception, quickening, or birth, whether cloning replicates the soul as well as the body have become important questions because of developments of technological progress. Whereas philosophers raised such questions during the Enlightenment and saw science as providing new answers, science raises these issues and leaves society struggling to catch up.

On the other hand, older beliefs about death and the body continue to haunt European society. With the breakdown of the Soviet bloc in Eastern Europe, the body has again been reformulated as a symbol of massive political change. In one of the more interesting (and gruesome) examples the political implications of change have played out in corpses and dead bodies through the exhumation and reburying of political figures. The rise in ethnic nationalism in the Balkan region encouraged a grand tour of the bones of Prince Lazar to commemorate the battle of Kosovo in 1389. In 1987, his bones began a two-year tour of Serbian monasteries from Belgrade through Croatia, Bosnia, and Kosovo in an illustration of the belief that Serbia is wherever Serbs are buried. The display of his bones outlined the political geography of greater Serbia. The "politics of dead bodies," to use a phrase by Katherine Verdery, consolidated claims by ethnic national groups in the former Yugoslavia. Mass graves, which had been ignored as part of the formation of the multinational state after World War II, added to the rhetoric of nationalism as each group began to exhume the bodies of their dead. Older beliefs about the body can thus suddenly revive as symbols of massive political change.

The contradiction in the history of the body, as old ideas suddenly reemerge alongside new meanings, demonstrates that conceptions of embodiment are neither integrated nor progressive. Instead, the patchwork of often conflicting beliefs affect bodies and their representations at all levels. The sexual body, the gendered body, the political body, and the commercialized body have all had their own histories that warrant close attention. Historians have only begun to excavate and make sense of the meanings of bodies. Because these beliefs refuse to remain static or stable, work on the topic should continue to preoccupy historians for any number of years.

See also other articles in this section.

BIBLIOGRAPHY

Adler, Kathleen, and Marcia R. Pointon, eds. *The Body Imaged: The Human Form and Visual Culture since the Renaissance.* Cambridge, U.K., 1993.

Bourke, Joanna. *Dismembering the Male: Men's Bodies, Britain, and the Great War.* Chicago, 1996.

Gilman, Sander L. *Making the Body Beautiful: A Cultural History of Aesthetic Surgery.* Princeton, N.J., 1999.

Hogle, Linda F. *Recovering the Nation's Body: Cultural Memory, Medicine, and the Politics of Redemption.* New Brunswick, N.J., 1999.

Komlos, John. *The Biological Standard of Living in Europe and America, 1700–1900: Studies in Anthropometric History.* Aldershot, U.K., 1995.

Laqueur, Thomas W. *Making Sex: Body and Gender from the Greeks to Freud.* Cambridge, Mass., 1990.

Lindemann, Mary. *Medicine and Society in Early Modern Europe.* Cambridge, U.K., 1999.

Rousseau, G. S., ed. *The Languages of Psyche: Mind and Body in Enlightenment Thought.* Berkeley, Calif., 1990.

Stearns, Peter N. *Fat History: Bodies and Beauty in the Modern West.* New York, 1997.

Thomson, Rosemarie Garland, ed. *Freakery: Cultural Spectacles of the Extraordinary Body.* New York, 1996.

Toepfer, Karl Eric. *Empire of Ecstasy: Nudity and Movement in German Body Culture, 1910–1935.* Berkeley, Calif., 1997.

Verdery, Katherine. *The Political Lives of Dead Bodies: Reburial and Postsocialist Change.* New York, 1999.

Yalom, Marilyn. *A History of the Breast.* New York, 1997.

CLEANLINESS

Virginia Smith

In the mid-twentieth century, the subject of "cleanliness" was a footnote to the triumphant history of the British, European, and American public health movements, wherein progress in cleanliness was accepted as a foundation of modern life. Despite the devastation of two world wars and other, more local conflicts, Europe as a whole during the twentieth century was probably a cleaner, better housed, better groomed, less verminous place than in earlier centuries. This situation was largely due to unremitting public policies, high public expenditures on infrastructure and research, and ever-increasing consumer demands for luxury goods. Rats, lice, and fleas were subdued, children were shod and clothed, urban slums were demolished, open sewage was encased, pipes supplied water, skin diseases were treated effectively, vaccinations forestalled pandemic diseases, and general life expectancy increased. In addition during the nineteenth and twentieth centuries Europe and then the United States became preeminent in net world exports and technical developments in hygienic artifacts such as pipes, ventilation systems, sanitary ware, medicines, perfumes, toiletries, clothing, and even architecture. Europe exported the Western hygienic lifestyle worldwide through its self-appointed "civilizing mission" in its colonies. After the missionaries and governors left, the architects and engineers remained.

As a twist in the history of European hygiene, the mid-twentieth century hubris about Western achievements in cleanliness began to fade. Oil spills; atmospheric pollution; food contamination through mass farming and marketing, notably the beef market; and macroenvironmental pollution of seas, rivers, lakes, and forests politicized a new generation of green activists. Many activists were products of postwar universities, but they were joined by church members, farmers, rural workers, and a substantial portion of the general public.

METHODOLOGY

The academic debate on the history of hygiene in Europe has undergone various vicissitudes. For many years it was generally accepted that due to the Fall of Rome, the class to which hygiene had been addressed no longer existed, leaving hygiene in a dark age that lasted until the Enlightenment, leaving the main historical interest centered on the modern revival of hygiene, which began in the mid-eighteenth century. By the 1960s the topic had become loosely attached to what was then called "the standard of living" debate concerning the effects of the industrial revolution. In the 1970s the subject was wiped off the historical map by the new sciences of historical epidemiology and demography. According to those studies, the population rise was not determined by catastrophic filth-and-death rates but by proactive birth-and-marriage rates. While the impact of personal hygiene was assumed to be negligible, public hygiene only became effective in the late nineteenth century, following national sanitary reconstruction by the various European states. Mere personal cleanliness was relegated to the notoriously unscientific behavioralism as one of many secondary factors. It was a low point for cleanliness on the scholarly Richter scale.

In the late 1990s many historical certainties were challenged, notably by the French *Annales* historians, opening up new questions and sources in the history of cleanliness and hygiene. The pioneer German sociological historian Norbert Elias started in the 1930s to trace the development of the psychology of habits of "refinement" from the early Middle Ages through several hundred years of what he called the civilizing process. He ended his career with the study of the formal rituals of the royal bedchamber in the reign of Louis XIV. His work began to bear fruit in the 1960s with a new generation of French scholars (including Alain Corbin on the history of odors and the senses, André Guillerme and Jean-Pierre Goubert on the history of water, Guy Thuilliers and Françoise Loux on rural customs) and English social historians (such as Lawrence Stone on marriage and sexuality). Georges Vigarello, in *Concepts of Cleanliness* (1988), took up the history of cleanliness where Elias had left it (in a long footnote) and studied the change in grooming habits from 1400 to 1700. It is now generally accepted that there was a redrawing of social boundaries during this period toward intimacy and privacy.

There are two ways in which the *Annales* methodology can help fill in what are still the many gaps left in the long history of cleanliness. Firstly, a theory of multiple speeds, or levels of time, is helpful in accounting for the consistently recurring evidence of long-term temporal anomalies—the fact that ancient hygienic customs and technology coexist with modern hygienic customs and technology. Elias gave a good *Annales* description of levels of time existing simultaneously, like "a river with three currents running at different speeds. Seen in isolation the phenomena in each of these streams are unique, and unrepeatable. But in the context of differing rates of change, phenomena in a slower current are apt, from the position of a faster current, to seem immutable, eternally recurrent" (*The Court Society,* p. 14). The slowest current of all is the biogenetic timeframe, which helps harness the physical structure of the contemporary human body to those of its animal ancestors. The next slightly faster current is long-term human social development, which confirms the body-anthropologist's view that layers of social customs and training have polished or finished the original primate body. The fastest current is history as we generally record it, occurring over a few hundred years at most. Increasing historical interest in very early hominid societies and in long periods that left few or no written records (such as the Dark Ages) has tended to make Elias's original *longue durée* seem rather short, and will continue to question conventional assumptions about linear development and linear time.

The second major methodological change produced by *Annales* is that the subject of hygiene is clearly not confined to a single continent, as Fernand Braudel points out in *The Structures of Everyday Life* (1967). The chronology of the conventional texts on European hygiene is altered dramatically if world history is taken into account, particularly early world history. The worldview enables us to appreciate the effects of global climate and topography on hygiene, particularly the significance of the civilization-laden subtropical zones. In light of all this the start date of the fifteenth- and sixteenth-century European Renaissance is late and only relates to one end of the Asian landmass. Prehistory and ancient world history are the foundations on which all later European habits were built. Those foundations operated subliminally throughout this essay's three culturally distinct periods, the Middle Ages–Renaissance, the Reformation-Enlightenment, and the nineteenth and twentieth centuries. This essay highlights four major themes,

grooming, washing and bathing, house cleaning, and popular science. The bibliography of this article recommends sources that discuss precise details concerning this large subject.

PREHISTORY

The basic mammalian needs of the body have remained roughly the same since the Renaissance. People eat, defecate, sleep, work, and play according to the diurnal and seasonal phases of the sun and the moon. Human habits as nesting animals also have changed only slightly. People can still "nest" quite happily in a single room and, like animals, divide the nest into living quarters, or separate areas. The human sense of space is acute. Spatial ability is shown in the animal response of automatic recoil (disgust or loathing) from dangerous dirt and poison and in the danger zones and social exclusion zones practiced within and between species. Like other animals, humans constantly groom themselves. Mammalian grooming is triggered by chemical hormones and endorphins, which ease the body from its alert state into a necessary state of calm relaxation that has been called an opiate rush.

Thus biophysical human cleanliness is an initial judgment via the senses and a subsequent removal of any unwanted matter that is out of place. The anthropologist Mary Douglas drew attention to the psychology of defilement in *Purity and Danger* (1966) and showed how the physical separation from any designated form of dirt acts as a form of social control. Ancient purity rules drew certain social and physical boundaries in and around the body and were part of the classification (ordering divisions) of the cosmos and the social world. Language is a form of classification, and the Anglo-Saxon words "clean" and "dirty" are what linguists call basic level categorizations. The most elaborate and ritualized clean-dirty boundaries or social exclusion zones were devised within the world's ancient religions. Pollution theory and divisions of graded holiness featured more or less strongly in Buddhist, Hindu, Egyptian, Zoroastrian, Greek, Roman, Islamic, and Judeo-Christian religious rituals. Religious psychology appeared as a new rationale for hominid cleansing processes well before 5000 B.C. Subsequently, ideas of pollution were written down and thus entered theology.

Zoological evidence suggests, however, that the hierarchical social model predates the hominid experience. Zoologists have seen exactly how social allogrooming (grooming by others) becomes an exercise in social organization and control. Primates order a

Man-made Sweat Hut. *Russian Bath,* painting by I. Letunov (1814–1841). PUSHKIN MUSEUM, MOSCOW/THE BRIDGEMAN ART LIBRARY

grooming hierarchy according to kinship, gender, and rank, and within this order they exchange services and social favors. For instance, the alpha male and alpha female receive the most grooming attention. In a challenging argument, the primate ethologist Robin Dunbar suggested that the social requirements of communal grooming may well have led to early forms of language—vocal grooming or gossip—as larger hominid groups literally struggled to stay in touch. Much of this zoological evidence fits well with the archaeological evidence suggesting that grooming was also a major preoccupation of early Neanderthal groups.

The history of bathing, the wet toilette beloved by humans and other bare-skinned animals, reveals a further interrelationship between biological continuity and social change. Public bathing has a long history in Europe and formed, in Britain at least, a springboard for sanitary reforms in the nineteenth century. River worship, lustral baths, and holy wells have an ancient pedigree, and they also were connected with healing. On all the continents communal bathing in the world's natural hot springs and hot mud wallows was one of the earliest pleasures of hominids and other species. In Europe as elsewhere tribal festivities often lasted for days. The thermae (hot springs) of the southern Mediterranean (Italy and Turkey) and the hot volcanic springs of northern Europe (especially Germany, Hungary, and Russia) were in use in the Roman period and later became spas.

Where no hot springs existed, tribes on all continents, including the Irish and the Finns in Europe, improvised man-made sweat huts of wood, stone, mud bricks, or thick vegetation, heated inside by small fires or hot stones. Participants followed the sweat with a cold dip in a river, a lake, or a snowdrift. This technique was fully refined in the Roman baths' technology of fierce heat and plunge pools.

MIDDLE AGES TO THE RENAISSANCE

After the Pax Romana ended, civic life disintegrated in the western parts of the Roman Empire. According to Inge Nielsen, a historian of Roman baths, one of the first economic indicators of decline in imperial towns was the failure to maintain the costly public baths. The northern European tribal farmers were not by custom town dwellers. Instead, Europeans built ancient hydraulic devices, such as lavers (washhouses); latrines; conduits; black, white, and gray water drainage; tanks; sumps; and cesspits, into monasteries, castles, palaces, and the small urban areas of medieval and Renaissance Europe. Domestic refuse systems (inflow and outflow) had been developed during the prehistoric millennia, and the dry sewage system, recycling or scavenging collected waste into fuel, fodder, and fertilizer, was used consistently in all rural and semirural areas. Well into the nineteenth and twen-

345

Modern Thermae. Gellert Hotel and thermal baths, Budapest, Hungary. PHOTOGRAPH BY JANOS SZAMOSI/THE BRIDGEMAN ART LIBRARY

tieth centuries the majority of rural or semirural peoples, resembling their nomadic ancestors, lived in a single room with an annex, in which nothing was wasted, all was recycled, and objects were few but essential. During the previous two millennia domestic storage systems and artifacts, such as chests, bags, boxes, barrels, urns, and bottles, and simple cleaning materials, such as sand, salt, soda, and soap, had come into use. In product terms, cleanliness was always a technical necessity, enabling possessions to work bet-

ter, last longer, and look attractive. Though not luxurious, this life was not necessarily unclean. Good or adequate hygiene at all dates depended on the efficiency and good order of the individual household.

Body grooming is not usually featured in histories of human hygiene. In fact, the Greeks regarded it as merely cosmetic or superficial and did not consider it a science. Nevertheless, it was probably the occasion when most prehistoric and early modern bodies were thoroughly inspected and deeply cleaned.

Primate ranking patterns connected with grooming were certainly transferred to hominid tribal units. The alpha male and alpha female primates correspond to tribal chieftains, kings, queens, and emperors. Almost all the basic European tools, skills, and cosmetic ingredients of grooming developed in the palaces of the subtropical Eurasian civilizations that existed from 5000 to 500 B.C. China, India, Mesopotamia, and Egypt initiated body-painting, scarification, tattooing, ornamentation of body parts, and oiling, bathing, powdering, painting, perfuming, robing, and floral decoration reached new heights in the courts of Nebuchadnezzer, Nefertiti, and Cleopatra, and at dinner parties in democratic Greece and republican Rome. The first Eurasian civilization on the European mainland was Minoan Crete (about 2000 B.C.).

The Mediterranean area had long abundantly imported and exported luxury products. Though commerce was reduced in Europe after the fall of the Roman Empire, which had produced safe trade routes and large markets, the east-west trade in rare oils, perfumes, paints, powders, and silks was protected by the Mongolian Empire and was sustained via Byzantium and the Silk Route up to the mid-fourteenth century. After that, European merchant venturers entered shipping. The ancient Asiatic toilette provides the background for later European cosmetics and beauty care, especially the courtly toilette. The towering wigs and headdresses of eighteenth-century aristocratic Europe echo those of aristocratic Middle Kingdom Egypt in 1500 B.C. The most famous recorded toilette of modern European history is that of the French King Louis XIV, who established the etiquette for his *levée* (arising) and *couchée* (bedding) in precise gradations of intimacy and patronage. Like his magnificent predecessors, he wore complete works of body art. The Sun King liked to dress in white satin, glitteringly ornamented, with his great fur-trimmed chieftain's cloak trailing on the floor. He was groomed by his retinue and controlled by his doctors, who always made a grand medical fuss about his bathing regimen.

Far from being careless and filthy, the majority of medieval and early modern populations were equally concerned with their health, beauty, and well-being. They practiced methods of dry primate grooming, keeping their skin clean and healthy by rubbing, combing, and annointing it with unguents. Numerous small physical actions and reactions, such as scratching, stretching, picking teeth, combing hair, rubbing eyes or skin, and inspecting feet, provided essential maintenance and care of the unusually bare hominid skin.

In colder regions much of the skin was protected with clothing. As French historians discovered, people talked quite a lot about clothing, especially during the white linen and undergarment explosion of the seventeenth century that Vigarello vividly portrayed. Clothing was considered a part of dry cleaning and part of the evacuatory system, as it absorbed perspiration and other bodily juices. "I pray you keep your husband in clean linen, for that is your business," ran the advice to a fourteenth-century goodwife. In addition she should provide baths for the feet, cut hair and nails, heal sores, feed, medicate, and generally offer a "remedy for every ill" (quotations from *The Goodman of Paris*, translated by Eileen Power, 1928). By the nineteenth century the immaculate, white linen marriage trousseau that French peasant girls kept could contain hundreds of items.

Daily primate grooming was enshrined in the first and most famous health poem, *Regimen sanitatis salernitanum*. An early medieval digest of six Greco-Roman nonnaturals of hygiene, air, exercise, evacuations, diet, sleep, and passions of the mind, the poem was widely copied in many vernacular European languages and circulated in both manuscript and printed forms. Under the heading of "Sleep," a late-medieval Scottish manuscript regimen suggests:

> When a person rises in the morning, let him stretch first his arms and his chest and let him put clean clothes on and let him expel the superfluities of the first digestion . . . then let him rub his body if he has time . . . then let him comb his head and wash his hands out of cold water if it is summer and out of hot water if it is winter . . . and let him wash his eyes . . . then let him rub his teeth. (*Regimen sanitatis,* translated by H. Cameron Gillies, 1912)

Longer grooming sessions on the parts, hair dressing, nail cutting, body bathing, dentistry, and paintwork, were performed at different times of the day, or on certain days of the week, usually Fridays, Saturdays, or Mondays, before or after the days of religious observances. The male and female heads of households received most of the grooming attention, with or without domestic body servants. All members of the household took time out for festive grooming sessions before important personal rites, such as birthdays or marriages, and probably before the public holidays on the religious calendar.

Special grooming attention was paid to the old, to the young, and to adolescents during their rites of sexual display and courtship, when the body had to appear especially healthy and beautiful. As in antiquity, males could purchase body services, specifically the daily shave, from visiting barber-surgeons, in barbershops, or in bathhouses. The professional reign of barbers lasted from the eleventh to the fifteenth century. Thereafter barber-surgeons became medical surgeons and hid their old cosmetic skills. Delousing was a constant problem. Even with relatively sparse hair, humans offer plenty of opportunities for vermin or parasites, and the most obvious apelike traits humans exhibit are elaborate nit-picking or delousing grooming sessions. Intimate delousing was still common in the twentieth century. Communal delousing occasionally appears in European drawings and paintings from the medieval period onward and in rare literary reference. Similar practices certainly continued in remote rural areas in Russia during the nineteenth century.

Everyone aspiring to respectability in early European society regularly washed "the parts," especially the face and hands. From the earliest times European peoples washed and strip washed in basins or dipped in round tubs, inside or outside the house, depending on climate and custom. Domestic washing was quite distinct from domestic bathing or full immersion. Significantly bathing apparently was not on a daily or weekly rota but was on a calendar month or seasonal rota. Elizabeth I of England, like her bishops, had a monthly bath "whether she needed it or no." As Vigarello emphatically reported from French texts, Europeans widely believed that exposing the naked skin to air and water carried grave dangers, like catching cold, and the colder, temperate areas of Europe did not favor casual exposure of the body. Climate, topography, wealth, knowledge, personal preference, and bodily strength or habit determined bathing practices. On the whole, for most of this period bathing was regarded as an optional extra or a luxury, much valued when available. It was considered especially necessary for filthy and muscle-weary travelers, laborers, and people with certain medical conditions.

New domestic bathing arrangements began to appear between the sixteenth and eighteenth centuries. For example, in Italy, France, and England the aristocracy engineered multiple water conduits and drainage systems and installed fixed stone baths and washbasins in their houses. They manufactured porcelain handbasins and, in France, bidets. In smaller town houses elongated portable tin baths gradually supplanted round wooden tubs. The first domestic, portable showers gained popularity during the nineteenth century.

The old traditions of public bathing for pleasure thrived in the Middle Ages. In the eastern Roman Empire, centered at Constantinople in Asia Minor (now Turkey), public baths were incorporated into Muslim culture when the rising Islamic empire took over those Roman colonies. Through contacts with Arabic baths and Arabic translations of classic texts on balneology, technical knowledge spread to medieval

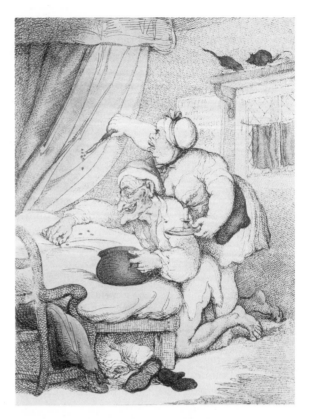

Delousing. "Summer Amusement. Bug Hunting," drawing by Thomas Rowlandson (1756–1827). GUILDHALL LIBRARY, CORPORATION OF LONDON/THE BRIDGEMAN ART LIBRARY

western Europe. Presented as an exotic luxury, bathing remained a part of medieval European court culture, as in the Islamic-style court of the Kingdom of Sicily, which was ruled by a Viking-Norman family during the eleventh and twelfth centuries. The wife of the English king Henry II, Eleanor, originally from French Aquitaine, an old Mediterranean Roman province, made sure she had bathing facilities wherever she held court. Extant pictures depict medieval courtly bath feasts held as receptions for honored guests, with tanks set out in the open air. Similarly embroideries show court ladies bathing in tanks *en pleine air* (in the open air), guarded by female attendants.

The theme of recreational bathing carried into the many medieval town stews, barbers' hot baths, and the custom of "going to the stoves" (or "hot house") with groups of friends who brought in wine and food. In particular, recreational bathing often featured in marriage rites, and was strongly associated with love and courtship. Communal "stoving" remained popular in northern and eastern Europe during the twentieth century.

As to the vexed question of licentiousness, most ancient European public baths were closely controlled by Roman edicts, followed in the early medieval period by locally enforced laws. The early Christian church only condemned public baths that allowed the tribal habit of mixed bathing. Complaints about bawdiness and disorder increased during the fourteenth and fifteenth centuries. Even those houses that practiced single-sex bathing were affected by plague epidemics of increasing severity and by sexually contracted syphilis, which appeared in the 1480s. By the end of the fifteenth century, when fear of contamination drove many customers away, most local public baths closed. Hothouse bathing returned to London in the mid-seventeenth century under a new name, the bagnio.

The larger thermae and cold-water medicinal baths survived, particularly in Italy and Germany, and their healing powers attracted increasing medicoscien-tific observation. After 1553 multiple transcriptions of the Venetian Thomas Junta's authoritative work *De balneis* (1553), appeared in Latin, French, German, and English. *De balneis* comprises a directory of Italian and German mineral baths and a summary of classical and medieval scholarship on bathing. Balneology became a science and outdoor spa bathing an increasingly fashionable pastime for men and women.

THE REFORMATION AND THE ENLIGHTENMENT

During the millennium after the Fall of Rome, tribal populations in Europe slowly multiplied under the ancien régime and in other parts of the world. Toward the end of the eighteenth century the European population grew in a steep upward curve and this growth did not stop. Was the phenomenon attribut-

Communal Bathing. From an illumination made for the duke of Burgundy, c. 1470. Food is set out on linen runner set across the middle of the tub. MS. Valerius Maximus, *Factorum ac dictorum memorabilium.* BILDARCHIV PREUSSISCHER KULTURBESITZ, BERLIN

able to additional food supplies, adaptation to micro-organisms, vaccination, the growth of relatively stable political and economic systems; or public paving, drainage, pest control, and private baths? Microdemographic studies indicate that life expectancy was affected by innumerable factors, and improved personal and domestic hygiene were undoubtedly among them. The European hygienic mentalité developed more quickly between the seventeenth century and the twentieth century than it had in the previous eight hundred years. In some ways nothing changed, but in other ways everything changed, through simple accumulation: more people, more material goods, more words, and more ideas. The Renaissance supplied the words; the Reformation supplied new ideas; and new ideas extended consumer demand and fueled further expansion.

"Rational" hygienic science seems a product of the science of the Protestant North, ambivalently relating to and questioning the old southern masters for their own ends. The printing press was the key technological advance in the development. By the 1480s, during the Renaissance, a complex and coherent ancient scientific cosmology had existed in written form for approximately eighteen hundred years, and the early printers exposed as much as possible to public view and to the public purse. Alongside lucrative work for churches, literature and popular science were their mainstay. Throughout Europe from the fifteenth to the eighteenth century, the Greek hygienic doctrines of temperate regimen were translated from Latin into the vernacular, commented on, and above all experimented with. Seventeenth-century science focused the medical gaze on the body; in the eighteenth century, bodies were counted, measured, weighed, dissected, examined, and analyzed on an unprecedented scale as the scientific Enlightenment spread rapidly throughout Europe.

Many self-employed and semi-employed observers and experimenters in the seventeenth century found in the new "mechanical" or "chymical" physiology simply a new professional opportunity to extend their skills. But for others, especially in Protestant England, Holland, and Germany, the Reformation had touched everything and given natural philosophy a new moral stance. To be a "puritan" meant to take an ascetic view of life. The new science of hygienic physiology was interpreted as a resounding confirmation of God's work and natural proof of the Old Testament hatred of uncleanness and abominations. Like the practices of the Jewish and Christian sects of the late Roman period, with whom the puritans strongly identified, the observance of ascetic purity rules meant a great deal in the daily lives of many

seventeenth-century sectarians. To take one example, the English Anabaptist Thomas Tryon (1634–1703) was a proponent of an ascetic cold regimen, advocating cleanly and godly vegetarianism, fasting, herbal remedies, bathing in cold water and air, and cool beds. He wrote seventeen books on godly hygiene for a new sectarian audience of middle- and lower-class tradesmen, artisans, and housewives. Tryon was just one among many medical Dissenters and visionaries of the period, a hotbed of Protestant ideas described by Charles Webster in *The Great Instauration* (1975). Many of these beliefs and publications crossed the Atlantic with people who settled in America. In Europe they worked their way quietly through eighteenth-century society in the form of a new moral earnestness and reemerged in the grass-roots religious revivals of the nineteenth century.

During the eighteenth century, hygienic ideas advanced on all fronts. By the late eighteenth century, British, French, and German physicians found a ready market for the new cool sanitary regimen, popularized at both ends of the century first by John Locke and then by Jean-Jacques Rousseau. In Protestant Britain it was well bedded in. Cool air found its way into the bedroom in the treatment of smallpox; swaddling bands were discarded, heating drugs were reduced, and cool vegetables found their way onto the table. Domestic cold-water bathing was widespread; it was later modified to more temperate warmth.

The regimen was completed by open-air sports. The Renaissance and Reformation gentry had already promoted sporting exercises such as tennis, golf, and bowls. The eighteenth-century hygienic renaissance added swimming, cricket, archery, wrestling, boxing, and horse-racing. Jogging and gymnastics came in at the end of the century; rugby and football arrived in the mid-nineteenth century. There was also open-air bathing. Cold river bathing became fashionable in Europe during the Renaissance, at a time when the old hot-water public bath system had broken down. Beginning in the late seventeenth century the British began dipping, like the Romans, in the sea. The bracing habit of cool-bathing in spas and coastal resorts spread gradually throughout northern France and Germany in the late eighteenth century, reaching the Mediterranean in the late nineteenth century, and linking up with the old spa bath trade, which was also booming in Germany, Italy, and France. In the mid-nineteenth century mountaintop hydros, or hydropathic treatment centers, were established across Europe following the cold-water-cure craze initiated by German balneologist Vincenz Priessnitz. Eighteenth-century cities like Bath, Brighton, and Budapest developed the mass leisure industries of the nineteenth and twentieth centuries. All these towns and cities were notorious centers of conspicuous consumption and sexual display for the wealthy. Eighteenth-century Europe, following the French lead, developed the new hygienic fashion for clothes and lifestyle *au naturel,* throwing away their corsets, wearing white, and worshiping the ancient Greek purity of line that in architecture was called classicism. In late eighteenth-century Europe much of the increasingly massive gains of the various empires was being poured into housing. The rebuilding of European housing, replacing perishable materials, such as mud or wattle and daub, wood, and thatch with stone, brick, and slates, had begun in the sixteenth and seventeenth centuries and was well under way by the eighteenth century. European architecture lavishly embraced newly designed hygienic conveniences in urban terraces and squares and in suburban villas, mansions, and palaces that slowly covered the countryside. Designs addressed ventilation, heating, cooking systems, larger windows, drainage, plumbing, indoor latrines and bathrooms, and new parks and gardens. The old seasonal and diurnal patterns of house cleaning were codified for the new gentry employers and employees in household manuals published in the mid-eighteenth century. Many new luxuries and new surfaces, carpets, wallpaper, silver plate, ormulu, and veneer, required care. In 1774 a London magazine, the *Annual Register,* complained of "Saturday and absurd cleanliness.... Each day we scrub and scour house, yard, and limb, and on SATURDAY, ye Gods, we swim!" (quotation from *The Spectator, 1711–1714,* edited by H. Morley, 1887, p. 192).

At the other end of the social scale, to have wooden boards or flag floors to scrub at all was, for many in the British Isles and elsewhere in rural Europe, still an unaffordable luxury. The metropolitan rage for cleanliness barely affected rural Scotland in the eighteenth century. Samuel Johnson found the ancient Scottish hut life fully or partially preserved, a precarious survival depending on scant resources. Highland huts, Johnson observed in his *Journey to the Western Islands of Scotland* (1775), "are of many gradations; from murky dens, to commodious dwellings." "Gentlemen's huts" had plastered walls, glass windows, and wooden floors. The clash of cultures is vividly evoked in a wry observation:

> Often ... the house and the furniture are not always nicely suited. We were driven once, by missing a passage, to the hut of a gentleman.... When I was conducted to my chamber, I found an elegant bed of Indian cotton, spread with fine sheets. The accommodation was flattering; I undressed myself, and felt my feet in the mire. The bed stood upon the bare earth,

which a long course of rain had softened into a puddle. (p. 91)

These older ways of life long remained in rural areas of Europe barely touched by the cash economy. Partisans found the same situations in the Italian mountains in the 1940s. Earth floors were common in England and in many other European countries at the end of the eighteenth century. They were less common at the end of the nineteenth century and almost nonexistent in Europe at the end of the twentieth century, even at camping sites.

THE NINETEENTH AND TWENTIETH CENTURIES

Utmost cleanliness, sensibility, and refinement had ruled the drawing rooms of the wealthy in the late eighteenth century, and the old smells and stenches of humanity had begun to be noticed. Greater personal hygiene, and an understanding of its natural causes, led inevitably to steps being taken in greater public hygiene, particularly where bodies were congregated together—notably in the prisons, the army, the navy, and in towns. A new theory of public hygiene at the turn of the century called it "medical police": the quality of public air (in France) and public water (in England) was increasingly discussed and scientifically analyzed. Cholera sharpened health issues in the mid-century. The first civic act was usually to provide paving for the streets; the problem of drainage was addressed next, and then housing. The management of the ever-growing suburban settlements and the removal of the unhygienic urban poor became one of the great political issues of nineteenth- and twentieth-century Europe. Many of the oldest slums and rookeries were not dismantled until after World War II. The rennaissance of public hygiene in the nineteenth and twentieth centuries was complex: the period of elaborate sanitary legislation in Britain, on the Continent, and elsewhere; breaking the codes of the microbiological system and conducting warfare on germs; national insurance schemes and the creation of the welfare state; and Darwininism, Spencerian eugenics, and social hygiene.

Added to this brew of politicians, scientists, and philanthropists was the new breed of religious sectarians that had returned to the old seventeenth-century ascetic beliefs and given them a new twist. From the late eighteenth century onward in Britain and Europe, radical therapies included homeopathy, mesmerism and phrenology, and a new raft of beliefs in "physical puritanism," which included macrobiotic vegetarianism, herbalism, cold-water bathing, air-bathing (i.e.,

Modern Bathroom. Woman in a bathtub, France, 1900.
ROGER-VIOLLET, PARIS

nudism), antivivisectionism, cold-water drinking and teetotalism, and the temperance movement. Dissenters were also prominent in the working-class educational movements, initiating many books and lectures on popular science and popular physiology. The nineteenth century working-class utopia was certainly a hygienic one. In Britain, Quaker and Unitarian philanthropists, communitarian Owenites and early Socialists, and the muscular Christianity school of Anglican clergy promoted the sanitary ideal. The Garden City movement of the late nineteenth and early twentieth century espoused a similar hygienic utopianism.

The many naturist health sects and vegetarian societies of the 1850s, 1880s, 1900s, 1920s, 1930s, and 1950s sought the perfect body through healthy diet and exercise. In fact 1880–1950 was the great era of sports, not only mass, working-class sports but also sports for girls and women. Party-political sports flourished as well. The British Socialists were inveterate bicyclists and walkers, most progressive leagues had a naturist wing, but only the German Nazi Party had that particular blend of tribal body cult and Goethean vitalism.

Extermination of one's neighbors was no novelty in Europe, but the appeal to hygiene was. Blood-tie tribalism, complete with purificatory rites and boundaries, was rechristened racial purity by the Nazis and later was called ethnic cleansing by the Serbs. However, studies have shown that immigrant communities often suffer the same treatment from their host communities, which separate immigrants as "dirty foreigners." In all European colonies, the European immigrants turned host communities into an underclass on grounds of racial superiority. Most immigrants did not go so far as the puritanical Dutch apartheid system in South Africa, which was finally outlawed by world opinion and United Nations sanctions near the end of the twentith century.

The cult of the perfect body became in the second half of the twentieth century, perfectly commercial, and resoundingly secular, and unpolitical except for sexual politics. Dirt and torn clothes, punk, and grunge, became a sign of youthful rebellion. Bodies rarely stank as they had earlier, and the consumption of soaps and cosmetic products per head rose steadily after the 1870s. From the 1920s, first gas and then electricity revolutionized domestic appliances and domestic cleaning. Kitchens had been modernized once in the eighteenth and nineteenth centuries and then again in the twentieth. The modern bathroom arrived with the piped domestic water supplies; at the end of the twentieth century the bathroom was even more well-equipped, but still filled with the same ancient luxury goods. From the 1950s a growing array of cleaning products appeared, mostly derived from the old pharmacopoeia, but less harsh, more perfumed, and increasingly repackaged in a new material, plastic, for consumer convenience: plastic tubing, pots, bottles, sprays, pumps, and so on.

The word "cleanliness" is rarely used in its moral sense and is usually applied to domestic and institutional hygiene. It certainly does not grip the poetic imagination as it did in the twelfth century Anglo-Saxon poem "Cleanness," in which beauty, purity, and cleanliness suggest a glittering, shining, wholesome, and radiant aesthetic with godlike attributes. Television broadcasts instead the daily soap operas, in which no dirt, dust, or facial blemishes are allowed on the screen.

The history of cleanliness is like an iceberg—much of it is submerged below the waterline. The *Annales* methodology has reconstructed what was previously invisible and has greatly extended the historical range. Many gaps in the evidence remain, among them the virtually untapped *longue-durée* history of bathing and cosmetic grooming; Greek, Roman, and medieval hygiene; and Protestant and Catholic hygiene and their local variants. Further research on the main contours of cleanliness will probably confirm much of what has already been written on the subject but in greater detail. Most likely, the economic history of cleanliness and hygiene will prove to be the real eye-opener.

See also **The *Annales* Paradigm** *(volume 1);* **The Population of Europe** *(volume 2);* **Public Health** *(volume 3).*

BIBLIOGRAPHY

Braudel, Fernand. *The Structures of Everyday Life: The Limits of the Possible.* Volume 1 of *Civilization and Capitalism, 15th–18th Century.* Translation revised by Siân Reynolds. New York, 1981.

Corbin, Alain. *The Foul and the Fragrant: Odor and the French Social Imagination.* Leamington Spa, U.K., New York, and Berg, Germany, 1986. Translation of *Le miasme et la jonquille.*

Corbin, Alain. *The Lure of the Sea: The Discovery of the Seaside, in the Western World, 1750–1840.* Translated by Jocelyn Phelps. London, 1995. Translation of *Territoire du vide.*

Corbin, Alain. *Time, Desire, and Horror: Towards a History of the Senses.* Translated by Jean Birrell. Cambridge, U.K., and Cambridge, Mass., 1995. Translation of *Temps, le désir, et l'horreur.*

Douglas, Mary. *Purity and Danger: An Analysis of Concepts of Pollution and Taboo.* London, 1978.

Dunbar, Robin. *Grooming, Gossip, and the Evolution of Language.* London and Cambridge, Mass., 1996.

Elias, Norbert. *The Court Society.* Translated by Edmund Jephcott. Oxford and New York, 1983. Translation of *Höfische Gesellschaft.*

Elias, Norbert. *The Civilizing Process.* Translated by Edmund Jephcott. Oxford, 1994. Translation of *Über den Prozess der Zivilisation.*

Goubert, Jean-Pierre. *The Conquest of Water: The Advent of Health in the Industrial Age.* Translated by Andrew Wilson. London, 1995. Translation of *Conquête de l'eau.*

Nielsen, Inge. *Thermae et balnea.* 2 vols. Aarhus, Denmark, 1990.

Shilling, Chris. *The Body and Social Theory.* London and Newbury Park, Calif., 1993.

Stone, Brian, trans. *The Owl and the Nightingale, Cleanness, St. Erkenwald.* London, 1971.

Stone, Lawrence. *The Family, Sex, and Marriage in England, 1500–1800.* Rev. ed. London, 1979.

Times of London. *The Times Atlas of World History.* Edited by Geoffrey Barraclough. London, 1978.

Vigarello, Georges. *Concepts of Cleanliness: Changing Attitudes in France since the Middle Ages.* Translated by Jean Burrell. Cambridge, U.K., and New York, 1988. Translation of *Propre et le sale.*

Webster, Charles. *The Great Instauration: Science, Medicine, and Reform, 1626–1660.* London, 1975.

Wright, Lawrence. *Clean and Decent: The History of the Bath and Loo and of Sundry Habits, Fashions and Accessories of the Toilet, Principally in Great Britain, France, and America.* Rev. ed. London and Boston, 1980.

THE SENSES

Constance Classen

HISTORICIZING THE SENSES

The senses are not simply biological in nature, they are also shaped by culture. Perception is, in fact, profoundly affected by cultural practices and ideologies. Just as social norms influence how people dress and what they eat, social norms influence how and what people see, touch, or smell. This social dimension of perception makes the senses subject to historical change and thus to historical study.

Culture shapes senses in many ways. The very number of the senses is dictated to some extent by custom. While the senses are generally counted as five—sight, hearing, smell, taste, and touch—their number has risen or fallen at different times according to the interests of the day. For example, in premodern Europe, speech as a supposedly natural faculty was sometimes counted as a sixth sense.

Along with being enumerated, the senses are also ranked according to cultural traditions and values. Such ranking plays a basic role in determining which sensory impressions will be deemed most important by a society and which will be filtered out or ignored. In the West sight customarily has been deemed the highest or most important of the senses, followed by hearing, smell, taste, and touch. This has meant that visual and auditory practices and information usually have been considered of much greater value than those derived from the so-called lower senses of smell, taste, and touch.

The ranking of the senses is congruent with a hierarchy of social values. According to this hierarchy, the higher senses are associated with values highly regarded by society and the lower senses with lower or even negative values. For example, the top-ranked sense of sight has traditionally been linked with the highly valued faculty of reason—intellectual vision. The lowly sense of touch, on the other hand, has been associated with mere physical sensation—the "mindless" pleasures and pains of the body.

The hierarchy of the senses has been subject to some variation in Western history. Within a religious context, hearing, as the sense through which people perceive and obey the word of God, has often been considered the highest sense. For example, in a medieval allegorical epic by Alain de Lille, the senses are depicted as five horses pulling a coach carrying Prudence to Heaven. As the swiftest horse, Sight leads the others, followed by Hearing, Smell, Taste, and Touch. When the coach proves unable to reach Heaven, however, Prudence is persuaded by Theology to unharness Hearing and ride to Heaven on him alone. Here faith—hearing—ascends to spheres where reason—sight—cannot go. Likewise, in certain contexts touch has been called the most fundamental of the senses, while even smell and taste might be given a certain priority as the senses that can most readily access the essence of a thing and thus are least easily deceived. Despite such variations, however, sight and hearing have generally been accepted as "higher" senses and smell, taste, and touch as "lower" senses.

The social values assigned to the different senses are expressed in a variety of ways. The contrast between sight as a supposedly rational sense and smell as an "intuitive" sense is evident in idioms such as "I see what you mean" and "I smell a rat." These different sensory values are also conveyed by associating visual signs (that is, writing, diagrams) with the exercise of reason and olfactory signs (that is, perfumes) with the use of intuition and emotion. The sensory values of a period are further conveyed through such means as stories, myths and religious practices, social customs, and techniques of child rearing and education, in which adults may put much effort into teaching children to understand visual signs but little effort into teaching them to find meaning in odors.

While some senses are ranked higher than others, each sensory field contains both positive and negative sensory values. For instance, although sight has a high social status, certain sights, such as dark colors, or certain uses of sight, such as for personal adornment, may have negative associations. Sensory values, furthermore, must always be understood in context, for what may be a foul sight or smell in one context may be construed as pleasant in another. The smell of urine has generally been associated with negative values. However, within the context of the royal palace of Versailles in the eighteenth century, the strong urinous odor of the grounds owing to a lack of sanitary facilities acquired some of the social prestige of the court itself. This is a good example of how sensory perception is not purely physiological in nature but is informed by cultural values.

The cultural construction of the senses affects not only how people perceive the physical world but also how they relate to each other. While on a practical level of everyday activities it is understood that all people use all of their senses, on a more symbolic plane high-status social groups are associated with the higher senses and low-status social groups with the lower senses. An instance of this comes from the work of the nineteenth-century natural historian Lorenz Oken, who postulated a sensory hierarchy of human races with the European "eye-man" at the top, followed by the Asian "ear-man," the Native American "nose-man," the Australian "tongue-man," and the African "skin-man." Oken's hierarchy of races and senses is based not on any intrinsic characteristics of the races but on their social rankings within the Western imagination.

Aside from its links with particular sensory faculties, each social group is invested with a range of sensory values. Again the more positive sensory values are associated with higher social groups and the more negative ones with groups deemed by the elite as lower on the social scale. Within the domain of smell, for example, high-status groups are customarily typed as fragrant or inodorate, while low-status groups are described as foul-smelling. These associations may be based in part on actual traits of these groups. Persons of wealth have more access to spacious, well-aired homes and costly perfumes, while poor people living in crowded, unsanitary dwellings often have to put up with foul odors. Nonetheless, such sensory social divisions are fundamentally symbolic in nature, depending not on any actual traits of the group in question (that is, unpleasant odor) for their cultural force but on social perceptions that are translated into sensory values. The English author George Orwell wrote in the 1930s, for example, that even those servants whom members of the middle and upper classes knew were quite clean seemed marked by an unappetizing odor (Orwell, 1937, p. 160).

In such cases a general feeling of repulsion based on the low social status of workers is transformed into a bad smell. Under these circumstances even the cleanest, most fragrant member of the working classes may be symbolically typed as malodorous. Conversely, malodor in members of the upper classes does not necessarily detract from their symbolic fragrance.

This sensory categorization of different groups of people enforces social boundaries and hierarchies and rules of social interaction. It signals which groups are thought to uphold the integrity of the social body and which are thought to have an injurious, corrupting effect on the social body. The scheme works well because people often have strong reactions to sensory impressions, such as fragrant or foul odors. When a group has a strong association with positive or negative sensory qualities, positive or negative social and physical reactions follow. Thus Orwell wrote that, even though the stench of the working-class body might be imaginary, it nonetheless induces a physical feeling of repulsion in members of the middle and upper classes that is scarcely possible to overcome (Orwell, 1937, p. 160).

The sensory values propagated by the dominant social group are often internalized to a greater or lesser extent by all groups within society. For example, members of the working classes will come to believe that, no matter how much they wash or what perfumes they use, they are somehow not as clean or as fragrant as members of the upper classes. Members of marginalized groups may also challenge such sensory values, however, and propose alternative schemes whereby "clean-living" workers are contrasted with the "filthy" rich.

The social history of the senses uncovers the different ways in which sensory values have worked to uphold or challenge the social order, shaping the fortunes of groups and individuals. Senses are the means by which people perceive each other and the world. By exploring the ways in which sensory perception has historically been invested with cultural values, scholars can better understand the worldviews of peoples of other eras and at the same time appreciate the social underpinnings of the contemporary sensory universe.

WORK IN THE FIELD

The history of the senses is a broad field with a great range of possible topics for investigation. A work in this field may trace the shifts in sensory values within a society over time, or it may concentrate on an in-depth study of specific subjects, such as the role of hearing in sixteenth-century Anabaptism or the "language of flowers" in Victorian England. Whatever the scope of the subject matter, a sociocultural dimension is essential in a sensory history. A history of perfume, for example, does not constitute a history of the senses unless it relates perfume practices to social trends and ideologies. Similarly the investigation of the sensory worlds of past eras should not merely describe the range of sounds and smells that existed at a particular time, as evocative as that might be, but should uncover the meanings those sounds and smells had for people.

The primary difficulty for the historian of the senses is that sensory environments and the meanings with which they are invested are ephemeral. The changes may be subtle or dramatic, but the world of sensory values is one of constant flux. It is hard to know what or how people of other periods perceived and what these sensations meant to them. Ironically, the most important source for the sensory historian is the seemingly desensualized written text. Learned treatises elaborate philosophies of the senses, letters and diaries describe the sensibilities of everyday life, medical studies praise the healing powers of scents and savors, court records tell of witches condemned for casting an "evil eye," and literary works reveal the sensory priorities of their authors' classes and times. Such written sources may be supplemented by information gleaned from works of art and from items of material culture, such as clothes, furniture, and houses. Where the sources are silent or unclear, a certain amount of conjecture is necessary.

While a broad field in its possibilities for study, the history of the senses has been largely unexplored. Nonetheless, a number of seminal works have contributed to the history of the senses as a vital area of investigation. In the 1940s the cultural historian Lucien Febvre argued that sixteenth-century Europe placed less emphasis on sight and more emphasis on the other senses than did modern Europe. He wrote in *The Problem of Unbelief in the Sixteenth Century* (1942), "A series of fascinating studies could be done on the sensory underpinnings of thought in different periods" (Febvre, 1982, p. 436).

The work of Norbert Elias, the historian of manners, similarly if less explicitly suggests the importance of historicizing sensibilities. Stimulated by Febvre, Elias, and others, cultural historians began to tentatively explore the sensory values of different periods in their writings. Robert Mandrou wrote in 1961 that the senses of hearing, smell, taste, and touch nourished the mental world of sixteenth-century Europeans in ways alien to moderns. Also in the 1960s Michel Foucault aroused interest with his analysis of how sight has served as a medium of social control in institutions like hospitals and prisons.

Influenced by the writings of French cultural historians and by the work of the Russian literary scholar Mikhail Baktin, Piero Camporesi in the 1970s produced a remarkable series of books on the role of the sensuous in the popular culture of premodernity. Camporesi's work focuses on such aspects of material culture as food and the body, with all its fluids and airs, situating each within an intricate web of folk beliefs and practices. However, as Camporesi does not usually look at sensory values separately from particular material objects, such as food or the body, or try to locate his rich source material within a broader scheme of contemporary social values, it could be said that his works offer a sensuous reading of history rather than a historical reading of the senses according to the definition presented here.

The first major exploration within the history of the senses came in 1982 with the publication of Alain Corbin's book *Le miasme et la jonquille* (The foul and the fragrant). In this book Corbin aimed to bring smell out of the historical closet and to demonstrate the importance of odors in eighteenth- and nineteenth-century French culture. Corbin argued that this period saw an intensification of scientific and public concern over the relationship between stench and disease transmission. Strong body odors and perfumes became associated with the working classes, while the elite endeavored to rid themselves of personal odors through increased practices of cleanliness. Smell as a sense declined in utility, save to report disgust. The novelty and wealth of the subject matter together with Corbin's intriguing analysis of the role of smell in contemporary social discourses made *Le miasme et la jonquille* a popular and influential work and helped legitimate future investigations into the history of the senses.

A number of books by Constance Classen explore the cultural construction of the senses in Western and non-Western history. *Worlds of Sense* (1993) investigates such topics as the decline of smell and the rise of vision in modernity and the variation in sensory values across cultures. *The Color of Angels* (1998) delves into the sensuous symbolism of premodern cosmologies, the association of sensory values with traditional gender roles, and the expression and redefinition of sensory norms in modern art. These studies bring out the extent to which sensory perception has been impregnated with social values in different domains of life in different periods and places. Other notable histories of the senses are *Medicine and the Five Senses* (1993) edited by W. F. Bynum and Roy Porter and the literary-historical study *The Smell of Books* (1992) by Hans J. Rindisbacher.

A number of related fields, such as psychology, sociology and literary studies, have contributed to the development of the history of the senses. Anthropology has had the greatest influence on the history of the senses, in fact so much so that, as Corbin has suggested, the social history of the senses might otherwise be called the "historical anthropology of the senses" (Corbin, 1995, p. 181). The anthropology of the senses heightens awareness of the cultural relativity of sensory perception by bringing out the different sensory priorities of different societies. The odors denigrated in one society may be esteemed as sources and symbols of knowledge in another.

Among those who influenced the development of the anthropology of the senses are Claude Lévi-Strauss, who analysed the sensory codes of myths, and Mary Douglas, who explored how "natural symbols," such as the body, can encode a range of social norms. Another influential line of thought comes from the work of the communications theorists Marshall McLuhan and Walter Ong on the relationship between a society's dominant mode of communication (for example, speech or writing) and its sensory model. The foremost exponent of the anthropology of the senses is the Canadian anthropologist David Howes, editor of *The Varieties of Sensory Experience* (1991) and co-author of *Aroma: The Cultural History of Smell* (1994).

As in other fields of social investigation, historians have employed a variety of theoretical approaches to the history of the senses. Among them are a marxist perspective and a feminist perspective. A marxist approach might consider how sensory hierarchies have supported social hierarchies and how class conflicts might be expressed in differing sensory norms. A feminist approach might explore the historical interrelationship of sensory values and gender values and how these affected the lives of women and men.

Twentieth-century feminist theory, as expounded by Luce Irigaray and Julia Kristeva, certainly professed that the senses are strongly imbued with gender values. This notion has been explored within a historical context in *Sexual Visions* (1989) by Ludmilla Jordanova, *Vision and Difference* (1988) by Griselda Pollock, and *The Color of Angels*.

As regards marxism, Karl Marx made the intriguing statement, "The forming of the five senses is a labor of the entire history of the world down to the present" (Marx, 1972, p. 141). Marx's evident interest in sensory perception was taken up by a number of twentieth-century marxist theorists. Walter Benjamin explored how modern capitalist culture was creating a new aesthetic of perception. Max Horkheimer and Theodor Adorno suggested that vision is associated with the upper classes due to its inherent detachment, while the mingling nature of smell makes it a sign for the "promiscuous" lower classes. Even without a marxist history of the senses, marxist theory has certainly influenced sensory historians and cultural historians

in general to undertake a history "from below," from the perspectives of workers and peasants as well as the ruling classes, and to take account of the role of class interests in promulgating social and sensory ideologies.

In a way, looking at the lives of workers and peasants invites an exploration into the culture of the senses because of the traditional association in the West of the "lower" classes with the body and sensuality—the riot of the carnival, the squalor of the hovel, and the earthy rites of hearth and harvest. Similarly the move away from the study of economies, institutions, and public events to study private, everyday life, also found in cultural history, suggests a "descent" from a world of order and reason to the disorderly "underworld" of the senses. Scholars must carefully avoid giving the impression that only the world of the poor is truly sensuous or that sensory symbolism is confined to private life—the kitchen and the bedroom. Sensory values, in fact, shape the worlds of both princes and peasants and permeate the public sphere as much as the private sphere.

Historians of the senses also are cautioned not to impose a personal perceptual model on the sensory experiences of earlier societies. Twentieth-century preoccupations emphasized the importance of both visual culture and sexual culture, and historical studies of sensory life often have been limited to one or the other. An example is Peter Gay's study of Victorian life, *Education of the Senses* (1984), which deals with sexual behavior and attitudes rather than with the senses as such. The social history of the senses, however, should be open to the full range of sensory experiences as well as to the social relations among the various senses. Indeed it should be particularly attentive to those past expressions of sensory life—the odor of sanctity, the king's healing touch, the mythical basilisk's deadly gaze—that, while vital to the popular consciousness of their time, seem most irrelevant to the twenty-first century.

THE SENSORY WORLD OF THE RENAISSANCE

The sensory world of Renaissance Europe, while affected by the shifting sensory values of the modern age, was grounded in traditional practices and beliefs retained from the ancient and medieval periods. Sensory phenomena—colors, odors, sounds—were regarded as potent forces, agents of health or illness, bearers of planetary energy, and symbols of sacred and social order. As in the ancient and medieval periods, during the Renaissance all of the senses were accorded essential cosmological and cultural roles. Thus while

Taste. *Allegory of Taste,* painting by Jan Brueghel the Elder (1568–1625). MUSEO DEL PRADO, MADRID/ALINARI/ART RESOURCE, NY

sight was customarily considered the highest of the senses, it was still insufficient to convey a complete "picture" of the world. The five senses formed a set, like the four seasons or the seven deadly sins. Just as summer or summer and autumn could not by themselves signify a whole year, so sight or sight and hearing could not by themselves accurately convey the nature of the universe.

The "five senses" was, indeed, a popular literary and artistic trope during the Renaissance. A number of plays and stories depicted the senses as each perceiving the world differently and inadequately on its own. Furthermore the medieval and Renaissance predilection for allegory meant that each sensory quality of an object was examined for its symbolic import. The rose was considered an apt symbol of love not only or even primarily because of its beautiful appearance but because of its sweet odor and taste and the poignant contrast between the softness of its petals and the sharpness of its thorns.

Meaning came through all the senses during the Renaissance, and so did pleasure. The Renaissance banquet at its most sumptuous was intended to stimulate all of the senses. Dishes were designed to delight the eye as well as the palate, such as elaborately sculpted confectionaries and peacocks stuffed with spices and adorned with their own feathers. Between and sometimes during courses musicians and actors provided entertainment. The banquet hall was perfumed with rich incense, and at the end of the meal refreshing bouquets of flowers might be distributed. The peasant equivalent to this banquet of the senses was the popular feast, which similarly combined delights for all the senses, from the mouthwatering flavors of ales and pies to the toe-tapping tunes of the fiddler.

In the sacred sphere, both God and the devil were believed to order or disorder the world through a variety of sensory channels. People imagined, based on the ancient notion of the music of the spheres, that a celestial concert of angelic choirs, interrupted now and then by the devil's discordant braying, kept the planets moving along their tracks. Within the realm of smell, people thought trails of odor traveled between heaven and Earth and between Earth and hell, integrating the cosmos in a sacred interplay of scent. Sanctity manifested itself through fragrance and sin through stench. The nose-wise saint could sniff out one or the other, detecting, for example, the pristine scent of virginity or the corrupt stink of carnality.

Accounts of the odor of sanctity were abundant during the Renaissance. The Spanish nun Teresa of Ávila died in 1582, and her corpse became renowned for the fragrance it exhaled, a fragrance that lasted through several inhumations and exhumations. This fragrance was credited with various miracles of healing and added greatly to St. Teresa's reputation for exceptional holiness. A century later in France, Benoîte of Notre-Dame de Laus experienced the olfactory tug-of-war between heaven and hell in her own person. The long-suffering Benoîte reportedly was assaulted with demonic stinks and alternately was rescued by angelic perfumes until she lay in an exhausted stupor. In her most renowned act, she followed a trail of scent left by the Virgin Mary to the divinely chosen site of the future church of Notre-Dame de Laus.

Like the cosmos, the human body, a microcosmos, was ordered or disordered through a multiplicity of sensory channels. As "gateways" to the body, the senses seemed eminently suited to receive influences that could either benefit or injure the body. If poisonous foods could be taken in by the mouth, why not "poisonous" sights by the eye or "poisonous" scents by the nose? Sensory qualities were considered independent forces that served as media of health or illness.

The attribution of agency to sensory qualities made it essential to take such qualities into account when diagnosing disease. A putrid smell emanating from a patient might not simply be a symptom of a particular illness but a primary cause of the illness as well as a vehicle of infection. Likewise treatments might be directed through a variety of sensory avenues. A complaint was often classified and treated in accordance with the hot or cold, wet or dry categories of humoral theory. Thus someone deemed suffering from an excess of "cold" and "wetness" might be treated with herbs considered "hot" and "dry." Music had a range of medical uses, most importantly in treatment for mental disorders. As "air" working on "air," it realigned the disturbed spirit of the patient with the harmonious music of the spheres.

It was believed that fragrant and pungent odors both warded off the contagious odors of disease and alleviated a variety of ailments. The scent of the mandrake cured headaches and insomnia, while rose perfume cooled overheated brains. Violet scent reportedly calmed fits. The alchemical theories of the Renaissance in turn emphasized flavors as basic agents of health and illness. Paracelsus held that the four flavors in the body, sourness, sweetness, bitterness, and saltiness, produced different sorts of physical ills. These "savory" pains, however, could be treated with flavorful remedies, such as salty or sweet elixirs.

The sensory models of the body and the cosmos that underlay much of premodern thought were imbued with ideologies of gender and class. According to humoral medicine, men were positively valued as hot and dry in nature, while women were negatively valued as cold and moist. Indeed the female sex was held to have its origin in insufficiently heated or "undercooked" semen. The most perfectly heated semen always produced males. Heat was held to endow men with courage, strength, and honesty, while coldness made women timid, weak, and deceitful.

Apart from the attribution of different sensory qualities such as temperature to men and women, the senses themselves were coded by gender. Men were associated with the "higher," "spiritual" senses of hearing and especially sight, but women were connected with the "lower," "animal" senses of smell, taste, and touch. This gender division of the senses was linked to a gender division of social spheres. The supposed masculine mastery of sight and hearing was deemed to fit men for such activities as traveling, studying, and ruling (overseeing), while the female association with the proximity senses made women the guardians of the home and mistresses of the kitchen, the bedroom, and the nursery. Such gendered divisions of sensory life were invested with enormous social force and could only be transgressed with considerable difficulty. For example, female writers of the Renaissance period and after, such as Catherine des Roches in France and Margaret Cavendish in England, continually had to justify why they practiced the visual, masculine activity of writing instead of enaging in more feminine sensory pursuits, such as cooking and sewing.

Sensory ideologies of class often paralleled those of gender. Peasants and workers, like women, were allied with the body and the senses, while upper-class men were associated with the mind and reason. The "lower" classes were also customarily associated with the domains of touch, taste, and smell. They were manual laborers preoccupied with the animal necessities of life, that is, food and a warm place to sleep. Increasing contact with the inhabitants of Africa and the Americas led to the symbolic incorporation of these peoples into the European sensory and social order as well. Like the "lower" classes and the "lower" sex, the "lower" races were customarily associated with sensuality rather than reason and in particular with the "lower," "animal" senses.

While much of the sensory symbolism described above prevailed into the nineteenth century, a number of developments during the Renaissance produced significant changes in the Western sensory order. The Renaissance was an exciting period of sensory discovery, with new sights, sounds, and savors entering Europe from the New World. Strange vegetables such as tomatoes and corn appeared on Old World tables. "Native" weavings, carvings, and musical instruments and even natives themselves were displayed for the admiration of Europeans. Enthralling accounts circulated of the curious customs practiced in the newly discovered lands. This cornucopia of exotic stimuli encouraged a fascination with other possible sensory worlds that continued for several centuries. In the sixteenth century Thomas More, inspired by accounts of the Inca Empire, imagined a fragrant commonwealth in which cities were free from stench, meals were perfumed, and neighbors competed in gardening. Intrigued by the Peruvian quipu, a mnemonic device employing knotted strings of different colors, the eighteenth-century English author Horace Walpole saw possibilities for new sensory idioms, such as a language of colors in which puns were made of overlapping hues or a tactile language that could weave poems and knot rhymes.

As the entry of new goods and ideas from the New World increased the possibilities for sensory creativity and enjoyment, the Protestant Reformation, with its backlash against "heathenish" sensualism, had the contrasting effect of sobering European sensory life, particularly in northern Europe. Gaudy clothes, rich foods, and perfumes seemed to the more austere reformers to direct Christians' attention to things of the world rather than the spirit. The church, according to the Reformation ideal, was a place of sensory simplicity, purified of incense and visual displays.

The invention of printing with movable type in the fifteenth century had a profound effect on Western sensory life. The consequent mass production of books made vision an even more important sensory avenue for acquiring knowledge about the world. In religion, for example, literate Europeans relied less on such nonvisual means of accessing the divine as smelling odors of sanctity and tasting the body and blood of Christ and relied more on reading the Word of God.

The Renaissance also saw the beginnings of the desensualized mechanical model of the universe that eventually dominated Western culture. Developing a "scientific" understanding of perception that persisted through the twentieth century, René Descartes reasoned that the senses were purely physical mechanisms designed to convey information about the physical world to the mind. The growing field of quantitative analysis in turn stressed the importance of measure, number, and weight for comprehending and conveying information about the world over such nonquantifiable sensory qualities as odors and music.

Seemingly void of sensuous "coloring," the scientific paradigm of the universe in fact became permeated with visual values. This development was influenced by various factors. Sight had long been associated with the faculty of reason, and as the field of science was based on the exercise of reason, it seemed appropriate for sight to be the sense of science. The scientist did not wish to "smell out" (that is, intuit) the workings of nature or to "taste of" (that is, experience) them but to expose them to the light and see them, to understand them. The invention of "optick glasses," such as the microscope and the telescope, extended the power of sight over the other senses and emphasized the role of vision in investigating the nature of the universe. Furthermore prevalent visual models, such as maps and charts, seemed to adequately represent the world through only one sensory medium, sight. Even mathematics, the most apparently abstract of scientific endeavors, relied on visual signs.

THE SENSES IN MODERNITY

While the old, organic, and multisensory concept of the cosmos lingered in the recesses of the Western imagination, the visualization of the world became pronounced during the Enlightenment in the eighteenth century. As the word "Enlightenment" suggests, this period stressed the value of light and sight. This emphasis was manifested by sight's dominant role in contemporary philosophy and by the widespread attention to scientific advances in the field of optics. In keeping with the male associations of sight and reason, the rise of science was heralded as a triumph of clear-sighted masculine vision over the murky "feminine brew" of superstitions and myths that had previously dominated Western thought.

The ocular obsession of the Enlightenment influenced the domain of aesthetics as well as science and philosophy. During the Renaissance the artistic interest in naturalism and linear perspective emphasized the "realism" of visual images and turned canvases into seeming windows on the world. During the Enlightenment aesthetic attention focused on the organization of space. The eighteenth century disdained the crowded, dark, winding streets of the medieval city and dreamed of wide, bright thoroughfares with open vistas. To give an example of this changing aesthetic, in the Middle Ages the ideal garden was a walled enclosure redolent with the scents of flowers and resonant with singing birds and splashing water. In the eighteenth century the ideal garden became a park, a seemingly infinite expanse of space bounded by no walls or fences, in which odors and sounds were dispersed and the eye was free to roam, seeking the distant horizon. This shift in spatial aesthetics paralleled the changing understanding of the nature of the universe. The Middle Ages and the Renaissance imagined the universe as concentric, an enclosed space of enclosed spaces animated and ordered by a network of multisensory energies. The Enlightenment swept away those old sensory "cobwebs" and opened up the universe to infinite space, a vast visual realm of whirling planets and darting beams of light.

The nineteenth century saw a continuation and extension of most of the visualist trends of the Enlightenment. This century, for example, maintained public order through visual surveillance. These surveillance practices included increased supervision of the population through modern institutions, such as public schools and prisons, and increased monitoring of nocturnal activities made possible by improved street lighting.

Concern for public health in turn led to sanitary reform movements aimed at bringing light and fresh air into the smelly, dark homes and streets of the poor. On the economic front, the intensification of capitalist production and values begun with the industrial revolution emphasized the visual display of goods both to promote sales and as a conspicuous sign of plenty. In the nineteenth century the invention of photography established sight as the sensory repository of the past and the preeminent mediator of reality, while the arrival of electric light extended the domain of sight into the furthest corners of darkness.

One prominent social development of modernity was the rise in importance of the individual as a discrete entity with personal rights and boundaries. In terms of the social history of the senses, this meant that people had to take greater care not to trangress the sensory space of others with untoward odors, noises, or touches. As the most apparently detached of the senses, sight was often the most socially acceptable sense. This was particularly true in the context of urban centers, in which people daily came across strangers whom they could not touch or smell, to whom they could not even speak with propriety, but at whom they could look. In fact the saying "look but don't touch" became a sensory motto of the modern age.

The elevation of sight in modernity was often presented in evolutionary terms as the final stage in a sensory and social development from barbarism to civilization. Civilized people, it was held, perceived and appreciated the world primarily through their eyes. Primitive people, by contrast, were imagined to rely just as much on their noses and fingers for knowledge of the world. Charles Darwin gave this notion of a social progress from the "lower" senses to the "higher" a biological basis by suggesting in his theory of evolution that sight became evermore important to humans as they evolved from animals and learned to

walk upright and take their noses off the ground. Sigmund Freud later psychologized this theory and claimed that individuals went through similar sensory stages in the transition from infancy to adulthood.

As the above indicates, in many cases the elevation of sight was accompanied by a diminution in the importance of the other senses, particularly the proximity senses. Smell, taste, and touch were divested of much of their former cosmological and physical powers and were relegated to the cultural realm of personal pleasure or displeasure. For example, instances of the odor of sanctity were characterized by prominent scientists as hallucinatory episodes or else as ill odors arising from the ravaged body of the saint. Similarly by the end of the nineteenth century the medical profession established that odors could neither cause nor cure disease, thus allotting smell virtually no role in modern medicine.

These shifts in the Western sensory order did not go uncontested. Indeed throughout Western history persons and groups challenged the dominant sensory model with alternative ways of making sense. In the later half of the nineteenth century a significant counterreaction developed to the visualist tendencies of modernity, tendencies associated with scientific materialism and industrialization. This counterreaction was centered in the artistic community, whose members sought to recreate the ideal of a multisensory cosmos through art. The French poet Charles Baudelaire, often considered the forefather of this movement, wrote forcefully that the need to understand sensory phemonena is linked in chains of correspondences due to the essential sensory unity of the cosmos. The correspondence of the senses meant that any sensory impression could and should call up corresponding sensations in other sensory modalitites. A color might remind a person of a sound, or a sound might be described in terms of a fragrance.

Inspired by this multisensory aesthetic, nineteenth- and early twentieth-century artists experimented with creating concerts of perfumes or serving color-coded dinners. The multisensory nature and the popularity of this aesthetic movement meant that it cut across artistic fields. In his influential book *A rebours* (Against nature, 1884), the French novelist J. K. Huysmans described playing "internal symphonies" by drinking a succession of liqueurs corresponding to different musical sounds and creating the impression of a flowering meadow by spraying a room with floral perfumes. The Dutch artist Jan Toorop attempted to portray the auditory and olfactory realms in his paintings by depicting sound swirling out of bells and scent rising up from flowers. The Russian composer Aleksandr Scriabin aspired to engage all the senses in his compositions by including odors, tastes, touches, and colors as part of the performance.

In the twentieth century, however, the notion of a multisensory aesthetic was increasingly dismissed as a quaint, sentimental holdover from *la belle époque* (the beautiful age), unsuited to the brisk nature of modern life. Bold visual lines and colors seemed more in keeping with the characteristics of modernity than clinging fragrances or nostalgic harmonies. With the spread of motion pictures, sight became even more established as the sense of modernity, capable of capturing and acclaiming the rapid pace of modern life. The proliferation of enticing advertising imagery that accompanied the growth of the consumer society indicated that sight was not only the objective sense of science but also the subjective sense of desire.

While the twentieth century saw the virtual end of many earlier ideas about the senses, one sensory ideology persisted—the Western association of women, workers, and non-Europeans with the devalued lower senses. People still deemed men the masters of sight and women the guardians of taste and tact. Workers and "primitive peoples" were still imagined as inhabitants of a dark, odorous underworld of brute sensations. Hence Orwell stated in *The Road to Wigan Pier*, "The real secret of class distinctions in the West" can be "summed up in four frightful words . . . : *The lower classes smell*" (Orwell, 1937, p. 159).

As the century progressed these sensory ideologies of "otherness" came under greater attack, primarily by members of the groups negatively stereotyped. The attack proceeded along several, at times opposing, fronts. One approach resisted any apparent form of sensory ghettoization and asserted the right to equal participation in the "higher" sensory and social spheres of the dominant group. Another positively revalued some of the "lower" sensations and sensory pursuits traditionally associated with a group. Among women, for example, a number of writers and artists chose to explore and celebrate traditional feminine associations with touch, taste, and smell.

At the end of the twentieth century a range of sensory trends existed. The prevalence of visual imagery and of the visual medium of the computer suggests that sight will rule the popular Western imagination for some time to come. However, the spread of alternative medical treatments, such as aromatherapy and acupuncture, signals interests in other avenues of sensory experience. The writings of Oliver Sacks and others have attracted attention to the alternative perceptual worlds of persons with such sensory disabilities as deafness. Regardless of its direction or directions, the Western sensory model provides a rich terrain for cultural investigation.

See also other articles in this section.

BIBLIOGRAPHY

Bordo, Susan. *The Flight to Objectivity: Essays on Cartesianism and Culture.* Albany, N.Y., 1987.

Bynum, W. F., and Roy Porter, eds. *Medicine and the Five Senses.* Cambridge, U.K., 1993.

Camporesi, Piero. *The Anatomy of the Senses: Natural Symbols in Medieval and Early Modern Italy.* Translated by Allan Cameron. Cambridge, U.K., 1994.

Classen, Constance. *The Color of Angels: Cosmology, Gender, and the Aesthetic Imagination.* London, 1998.

Classen, Constance. *Worlds of Sense: Exploring the Senses in History and across Cultures.* London, 1993.

Classen, Constance, David Howes, and Anthony Synnott. *Aroma: The Cultural History of Smell.* London, 1994.

Corbin, Alain. *The Foul and the Fragrant: Odor and the French Social Imagination.* Translated by M. L. Kochan, R. Porter, and C. Prendegrast. Cambridge, Mass., 1986.

Corbin, Alain. "A History and Anthropology of the Senses." In *Time, Desire, and Horror: Towards a History of the Senses.* Translated by Jean Birrell. Cambridge, U.K., 1995.

Elias, Norbert. *The History of Manners.* Vol. 1: *The Civilizing Process.* Translated by Edmund Jephcott. New York, 1982.

Febvre, Lucien. *The Problem of Unbelief in the Sixteenth Century, the Religion of Rabelais.* Translated by Beatrice Gottlieb. Cambridge, Mass., 1982.

Foucault, Michel. *The Birth of the Clinic: An Archaeology of Medical Perception.* Translated by A. M. Sheridan Smith. New York, 1975.

Gay, Peter. *The Bourgeois Experience, Victoria to Freud.* Vol. 1: *Education of the Senses.* New York, 1984.

Howes, David, ed. *The Varieties of Sensory Experience: A Sourcebook in the Anthropology of the Senses.* Toronto, 1991.

Huysmans, Joris-Karl. *Against Nature.* Translated by Robert Baldrick. Baltimore, 1959.

Jay, Martin. *Downcast Eyes: The Denigration of Vision in Twentieth-Century French Thought.* Berkeley, Calif., 1993.

Jordanova, Ludmilla. *Sexual Visions: Images of Gender in Science and Medicine between the Eighteenth and Twentieth Centuries.* New York, 1989.

Mandrou, Robert. *Introduction to Modern France 1500–1640: An Essay in Historical Psychology.* Translated by R. E. Hallmark. New York, 1976.

Marx, Karl. *The Economic and Philosophic Manuscripts of 1844.* Edited by Dirk J. Struik. Translated by Martin Milligan. New York, 1972.

Orwell, George. *The Road To Wigan Pier.* London, 1937.

Pollock, Griselda. *Vision and Difference: Femininity, Feminism, and Histories of Art.* London, 1988.

Rindisbacher, Hans J. *The Smell of Books: A Cultural-Historical Study of Olfactory Perception in Literature.* Ann Arbor, Mich., 1992.

Sacks, Oliver. *The Man Who Mistook His Wife for a Hat and Other Clinical Tales.* New York, 1987.

Sacks, Oliver. *Seeing Voices: A Journey into the World of the Deaf.* Berkeley, Calif., 1989.

Vinge, Louise. *The Five Senses: Studies in a Literary Tradition.* Lund, Sweden, 1975.

GESTURES

Herman Roodenburg

Gestures are perhaps the most ephemeral subject ever studied by social historians. Scholars studying gestures in present-day societies can always photograph and film their subject; historians have to do without such devices. They have to work with texts, not the most convenient medium to capture any gesture, or with such visual media as prints, paintings, sculpture, or, beginning in the second half of the nineteenth century, photographs and films made by other parties. Studying gestures in the past is a complicated but also a very rewarding task. Gestures are not only ephemeral; most of them are also, to the men and women employing them, self-evident and taken for granted. It is the naturalness and unreflectedness of gestures that may offer important and quite unexpected insights in the culture under study. So far most studies have focused on the early modern period. The sources on Antiquity and the Middle Ages are scarce. The relative paucity of studies on gestures in the nineteenth and the twentieth century may be explained by a lesser interest among the historians of these periods in the history of the body and the new cultural history in general.

THE STUDY OF GESTURE

According to the *Concise Oxford Dictionary,* "gesture" refers to "a significant movement of limb or body" or the "use of such movements as expression of feeling or rhetorical device." This is a broad definition, encompassing essentially the whole carriage and deportment of the body. Though this was the original meaning of the term, it generally has been limited to indicating a movement of the head (including facial expression) or of the arms and hands. A gesture may be inadvertent (blushing, fumbling with one's clothes) or deliberate (nodding, making the V-sign). Most scholars agree that a degree of voluntarism should be implied. They also acknowledge that no watertight divisions exist between posture and gesture or between voluntary (or conventional) and involuntary (or nat-

ural) gestures. Indeed these divisions have a history of their own.

Many gestures function independently of the spoken word. A lucid survey of such "autonomous" gestures is in *Gestures: Their Origins and Distribution* (1979) by the ethologist Desmond Morris. The revised edition is *Bodytalk: A World Guide to Gestures* (1994). Particular types of autonomous gestures are the sign languages of the deaf and various tribal and monastic communities.

After the 1970s most studies undertaken by anthropologists, sociolinguists, and social psychologists focused on gestures that accompany speech, or gesticulation. Video and other audiovisual techniques have shown that speech and gesticulation are produced together, as though they are two aspects of a single underlying process. Many studies have been devoted to the nature of this matching, that is, to the question of how phrases of speech production are related to phrases of gesticulation. In addition older classifications of speech-related gestures were qualified and new ones introduced. A well-known classification includes beats, pointers, ideographs, and pictorial gestures. Beats or batons beat time to the rhythm of the words. Pointers or indexical gestures point to the object of the words, either a concrete referent in the immediate environment or an abstract referent, such as a point of view brought forward by the speaker. Ideographs only refer to abstract referents, and they diagram the logical structure of what is said. In contrast, pictorial gestures, essentially the gestures of mime artists, refer to concrete objects and activities.

Gesture has been studied and practiced from many perspectives. Since antiquity speech-related gesture has been a part of rhetoric. For example, both Cicero (106–43 B.C.) and Quintilian (c. A.D. 35–c. A.D. 100) wrote extensively on delivery, in Greek *hupokrisis* and in Latin *actio* or *pronuntiatio.* They deemed it no less important than the other four departments of oratory: *inventio* (invention), *dispositio* (disposition), *elocutio* (elocution), and *memoria* (memory). Quintilian was the first to explicitly distin-

The Fingertips Kiss. Drawing by Jacques Callot (1592 or 1593–1635). ©THE BRITISH MUSEUM, DEPARTMENT OF PRINTS AND DRAWINGS

guish delivery into *vox* (voice) and *gestus* (general carriage of the body). Interestingly Cicero was already using notions such as body language (*sermo corporis*) or the eloquence of the body (*eloquentia corporis*).

FROM THE RENAISSANCE TO THE NINETEENTH CENTURY

Both Cicero and Quintilian's writings were crucial to the flowering of rhetoric in the Renaissance. Delivery, however, had a modest impact. It is true that classical contrapposto was more or less reconquered by Leon Battista Alberti (1404–1472) and later authors, such as Leonardo da Vinci (1452–1519), Michelangelo (1475–1564), Giorgio Vasari (1511–1574), and Giovanni Paolo Lomazzo (1538–1600), on the basis of a passage from Quintilian. However, it is significant that the text in question was not on delivery. It merely

referred to the *Discobolos* (c. 450 B.C.) of Myron (fl. c. 480–440 B.C.), one of the finest examples of classical contrapposto, as an illustration to *elocutio*. Just as this statue, in abandoning the straight line, suggests movement and grace, the speaker, too, should favor an ornate style and introduce grace and variety. Even at the beginning of the fifteenth century, when the complete text of Quintilian's *Institutio Oratoria* and Cicero's rhetorical works became available, scholars complained about the impracticability of classical delivery. They found it hardly conducive to contemporary oratory, and some, including the German rhetorician Philip Melanchthon (1497–1560), disposed of classical *pronuntiatio* altogether.

The tradition of the civilization of manners is another perspective in which the study and practice of gestures has been prominent. In his ground-breaking study on the development of manners, the German sociologist Norbert Elias (1897–1990) strongly emphasized the rules governing the essential activities of life. He discussed the more psychoanalytically significant prescriptions concerning urinating, defecating, and hiding one's nudity and also the lesser ones concerning blowing the nose, sneezing, coughing, and spitting—in short, all those activities that "we share with the animals," as the author of one of the most important manners books, the Frenchman Antoine de Courtin (1622–1685), explained. But the manuals are far richer than Elias, with his strongly Freudian point of view, suggested. They also deal at length with phenomena such as postures, gestures, facial expression, and even paralingual phenomena (the pitch or intensity of the voice). The sixteenth century experienced an explosion of such texts, though many display a disinterest in classical *actio* or *pronuntiatio* similar to that in sixteenth-century texts on rhetoric. Jakob Burckhardt (1818–1897) and several later historians, including Elias, inaccurately said the rules propounded in these manuals originated in the classical or courtly tradition. As the English historian Dilwyn Knox argued, many of these texts derive from the *disciplina corporis* (body discipline), the monastic and clerical precepts of comportment that from the thirteenth century on were communicated to the laity. For example, reaching back to *De institutione novitiorum* (on the instruction of novices) possibly composed by the canon regular Hugh of St. Victor (1096–1142), this tradition provided the framework for Desiderius Erasmus's idea of *civilitas* (civility) set forth in *De civilitate morum puerilium* (On the Civility of Children's Manners) (1530) and the texts based on it, including other manuals on proper comportment, the numerous Latin school curricula, and the regulations of the new Catholic orders, such as the Jesuits.

The second half of the sixteenth century witnessed a new interest in gestures. At this time both the courts and the urban elites in most European countries adopted notions of civility. Generally this development followed a course of restraint compared to the excess of gestures attributed to the peasant population; the inhabitants of southern Europe, particularly the Italians from the seventeenth century onward; and the newly discovered peoples in the East and West. Many of the new codes were adopted in the arts of dancing, acting, painting, and sculpturing. During the seventeenth and eighteenth centuries the concept was increasingly set off against the mere appearance of manners and all exaggerated civility. The background to this was the late medieval aesthetic-cum-moral conviction, already implied in the monastic and clerical codes of comportment, of a close correspondence between physical expression and inner disposition.

The emphasis on the moral or universal rather than the conventional nature of gestures brought civility and the study of physiognomy together. An informative example is *De humana physiognomonia* (On human physiognomy), published in 1586 by the Neapolitan dramatist Giambattista della Porta (1535?–1615). Later studies related physiognomy to the passions, as in the *Conférence de M. Le Brun sur l'expression générale et particulière* (1698) by the French court painter Charles Le Brun (1619–1690), or from a new psychological perspective, related to the so-called moral sentiments, as in the *Ideen zu einer Mimik* (1785–1786) by the German scholar Johann Jakob Engel (1742–1802). These works reveal that gestures were now also studied and practiced from the perspective of contemporary painting and stagecraft.

The late sixteenth century and the seventeenth century also witnessed a philosophical interest in gestures. In 1572, for example, the Spanish scholar Arias Montanus (1527–1598) published *Liber Ieremiae, sive de actione,* (The book of Jeremiah, or on delivery), in which he argued for the universality of gesture. Similarly Giovanni Bonifacio's *L'arte de' cenni* (1616) and John Bulwer's *Chirologia; or, the Naturall Language of the Hand* (1644) were conceived as manuals of rhetorical delivery. However, both authors professed a belief in a natural, universal language of gesture, opining that its often-noted diversity could be reduced to a few general principles and thus facilitate the conduct of trade in Europe, the New World, and the Far East. In the process classical delivery was revalued as natural gesture in contrast to merely conventional gesture and was increasingly identified with the Greco-Roman tradition. Eventually this philosophical interest inspired discussions on universal language schemes in the late seventeenth century and the eighteenth century.

The Neapolitan scholar Andrea de Jorio (1769–1851) offered a quite different, strongly antiquarian approach to classical gestures in *La mimica degli antichi investigata nel gestire Napoletano* (1832). Based on the idea that the lively gestures of his poorer townspeople, the *volgo,* were a direct legacy of the Romans, he interpreted gestures as a key to understanding the mimic codes on antique vases, murals, and reliefs. Offering an extensive survey of all the gestures he witnessed in the streets of Naples, De Jorio's study was highly original. At the same time he was very much a nineteenth-century scholar in his selection of a contemporary phenomenon among the lower classes not for its concrete significance to these individuals but as a relic or survival from the past. In the same decades the romantic folklorists, in particular Jacob Grimm (1785–1863), professed a similar approach aimed at the Germanic past. Later in the century well-known evolutionists, including E. B. Tylor (1832–1917) and Wilhelm Wundt (1832–1920), took an interest in gestures not for their roles in the contemporary culture but for the entry they supposedly afforded into the origins of language. Remarkably both evolutionists were careful not to associate the more lively gesticulation of Italians and southern Frenchmen with a lack of civilization or primitivism.

TECHNIQUES OF GESTURE

In his famous essay "Les techniques du corps" (1935) the French anthropologist Marcel Mauss (1872–

De Jorio's Antiquarian Approach to Gesture. The Neapolitan chin flick. From Andrea de Jorio's *La mimica degli antichi investigata nel gesire neapolitano* (1832).

Superb! French gesture of appreciation, performed by Laurence Wylie. From Laurence Wylie and Rick Stafford, *Beaux Gestes: A Guide to French Body Talk.* PHOTO BY RICK STAFFORD

1950) discussed gesture indepently of any evolutionary schemes. Defined as "the ways in which from society to society men know how to use their bodies" his "techniques" included a wide range of phenomena, from sitting, standing, walking, dancing, swimming, and sleeping to table manners and matters of hygiene. At the same time his comparative approach ranged from the gait of American nurses, whom he observed in a New York hospital, to the delicate balancing of the hips displayed by Maori women in New Zealand. Anticipating the writings of American anthropologists, in particular those of Ruth Benedict (1887–1948), and of Mary Douglas, Mauss was greatly interested in the ways physiology, psychology, and sociology converged in his techniques. He emphasized the role of education, adopting the notion of *habitus* in its Aristotelian and Thomist sense of *hexis* or acquired ability well before Pierre Bourdieu.

Mauss's essay research along with David Efron's *Gesture and Environment* (1941) inspired later research. Reissued as *Gesture, Race, and Culture* in 1972, Efron's work was the first systematic study of cultural differences in gestures. Encouraged by the anthropologist Franz Boas (1858–1942), Efron studied the use of gestures in two ethnic groups, Jewish Yiddish-speaking immigrants and immigrants from southern Italy, in New York City for two years. Using drawings, photography, and film, Efron and his colleagues found some significant differences. The Italians, for example, used both arms, generally needed more space for their gesticulations, and mostly stood apart from one another. In contrast, the Jewish immigrants gestured in front of their faces or chests, stood together in small groups, and touched one another frequently. The Italian immigrants displayed a range of symbolic gestures, many corresponding to De Jorio's inventory, while the Jews displayed a preference for beats and ideographs. Arguing against theories that regarded gesture as racially determined, Efron also showed that the various differences were less conspicuous in the second generation of the two groups, who absorbed much of the American mimic code. Efron's study was also one of the first to focus on speech-related gestures.

In the 1950s a group of anthropologists, sociolinguists, and social psychologists turned to the study of nonverbal communication. The anthropologist Ray Birdwhistell coined the notion of kinesics, the study of communicative body movements. His colleague Edward T. Hall and others introduced proxemics, the study of the distance people keep from each other when talking, and haptics, the study of the way people touch each other during conversations, or social space. In the following decades the fast-growing studies of face-to-face interactions and semiotics gained many insights. In the 1970s art historians, such as Michael Baxandall and Moshe Barasch, studied gestures in Italian paintings of the fourteenth and fifteenth centuries. In the 1980s intellectual historians; literary historians; historians of rhetoric, the stage, and dance; and a wide range of historians of everyday life, including Jean-Claude Schmitt and Peter Burke, developed a much broader interest in gestures, posture, and comportment. Keith Thomas said, "The human body is as much a historical document as a charter or a diary or a parish register . . . and it deserves to be studied accordingly."

See also other articles in this section.

BIBLIOGRAPHY

Barasch, Moshe. *Gestures of Despair in Medieval and Early Renaissance Art.* New York, 1976.

Baxandall, Michael. *Painting and Experience in Fifteenth-Century Italy: A Primer in the Social History of Pictorial Style.* Oxford, 1972.

Birdwhistell, Ray L. *Introduction to Kinesics.* Louisville, Ky., 1952.

Bremmer, Jan, and Herman Roodenburg, eds. *A Cultural History of Gesture.* Ithaca, N.Y., 1992.

Efron, David. *Gesture and Environment.* New York, 1941. Reprinted as *Gesture, Race, and Culture.* The Hague, 1972.

Hall, Edward Twitchell. *The Silent Language.* Garden City, N.Y., 1959.

Jorio, Andrea de. Gesture in Naples and Gesture in Classical Antiquity: A Translation of La mimica degli antichi investigata nel gestire napoletano. Translated by Adam Kendon. Bloomington, Ind., 2000.

Knox, Dilwyn. "Late Medieval and Renaissance Ideas on Gesture." In *Die Sprache der Zeichen und Bilder: Rhetorik und nonverbale Kommunikation in der frühen Neuzeit.* Edited by Volker Kapp. Marburg, Germany, 1990. Pages 11–39.

Le Brun, Charles. *Conférence de M. Le Brun sur l'expression générale et particulière.* Amsterdam, 1698.

Mauss, Marcel. "Les techniques du corps." *Journal de psychologie normale et pathologique* 39 (1935): 271–293. Reprinted in Mauss, *Sociologie et anthropologie.* Paris, 1950. Pages 365–386. Also reprinted in *Sociology and Psychology.* London, 1979. Pages 97–123.

Morris, Desmond, P. Collett, P. Marsh, and M. O'Shaugnessy. *Gestures: Their Origins and Distribution.* New York, 1979.

MANNERS

Cas Wouters

Erasmus, the Dutch humanist, advised his readers in the sixteenth century not to spit on or over the table but underneath it. After that spitting became ever more restricted, until it was banned altogether. In the 1960s most British buses still had "No Spitting" signs. In the West even the very urge to spit has generally disappeared.

Medieval people blew their noses with their fingers. In 1885 Christoph Höflinger, the author of a German manners book, warned his readers not to clean their nose with anything but a handkerchief. Evidently this had not yet become a general habit, for he acknowledges the "courage and mastery over oneself" required to maintain a "decent demeanor."

These examples show some of the changes that have come about in Western manners—changes in behavior as well as in the sensibilities and norms regulating what range of behavior is allowed, what is prescribed, and what is forbidden. Some changes in this range have become formalized as good manners, others as laws. The code of manners and the judicial code supplement and reinforce each other; both provide motives and criteria for punishment and reward. Transgressions against the code of manners are punished in a variety of ways, ranging from assigning blame by means of gossip to excommunication, all involving a loss of face, respect, or status. Manners provide important criteria for social ranking.

THE FUNCTIONS OF MANNERS

Any code of manners functions as a regime, that is, as a form of social control demanding the exercise of self-control. A regime of manners corresponds to a particular network of interdependencies, to a certain range of socially accepted behavioral and emotional alternatives as well as to a particular level of mutually expected self-controls. All individuals are confronted with demands on self-regulation according to the code of manners prevalent in their particular group and society. Thus the history of manners offers empirical evidence for social and psychic processes; that is, for

developments in relationships between individuals and groups (social classes, sexes, and generations) as well as developments in individuals' patterns of self-regulation and personality structure.

As a rule, manners among the upper classes serve to maintain a social distance between those classes and those trying to enter their circles. Manners are instruments of exclusion or rejection and of inclusion and group charisma: individuals and groups with the necessary qualifications are let in while the "rude"—that is, all others lower down the social ladder—are kept out. The dual function of manners is evident in a comment such as "They are not nice people": manners are a weapon of attack as well as a weapon of defense. Any code of manners contains standards of sensitivity and composure, functioning to preserve the sense of purity, integrity, and identity of the group. Incentives to develop "good taste" and polished social conduct further arise from the pressures of competition for status. In this competition manners and sensibilities function as power resources, deployed by the upper classes to outplay and dominate lower classes.

From the Renaissance onward European societies tended to become somewhat more open and socially more competitive. As a result the sensibilities and manners cherished by the established functioned as a model for people from other social groups aspiring to respectability and social ascent. Good manners usually trickled down the social ladder. Only at times of large-scale social mobility, when whole groups gained access to the centers of established power, did their manners to some extent trickle up with them. In contrast to individual social ascent, the ascent of an entire social group involves some mixing of the codes and ideals of the ascendant group with those of the previously superior groups. The history of manners thus reflects the social ascent of increasingly wider social groups in European societies since the Renaissance.

Some changes in manners are symptomatic of changing power balances between states. As France became the most dominant power in Europe, French

Courtly Etiquette. A ball during the reign of Henry IV of France. Painting by Louis de Caullery (d. 1621). MUSÉE DES BEAUX-ARTS, RENNES, FRANCE/GIRAUDON/ART RESOURCE, NY

court manners increasingly took over the model function previously fulfilled by Italian court manners. In the nineteenth century, with the rising power of England, the manners of English "good society" came to serve as a major example in many other countries. After World War II, when the United States became a dominant superpower, American manners served more easily as a model.

THE STUDY OF MANNERS

Interest in the history of manners, a fairly young and as yet understudied discipline, has grown together with interest in the history of emotions, mentalities, and everyday life, all of which became more serious topics of research after the 1960s. Among the studies that prepared the way was the work of the Dutch historian Johan Huizinga, particularly his *The Autumn of the Middle Ages,* originally published in 1919. This book had an unusual focus on manners, emotions, mentalities, and everyday life in the fifteenth century; it presented a lively sketch of the wide range of behaviors, the intensities of joy and sorrow, the public nature of life. Throughout the 1920s this work remained exceptional. In the 1930s the historians Lucien Febvre, Marc Bloch, and others associated with the French *Annales* school again took up an interest in mentalities, lifestyles, and daily life.

The first systematic study of the history of manners, *The Civilizing Process* by Norbert Elias, appeared in German in 1939. This book provided a broad perspective on changes in European societies; pivotal to

Elias's work was an analysis of the extensive European literature on manners from the fifteenth to the nineteenth centuries. The book thus enlarged the empirical basis of cultural history as it had been written thus far. Elias focused particularly on manners regarding the most basic human functions such as eating, drinking, sleeping, defecating, and blowing one's nose. Because these manners are universal in the sense that humans cannot biologically avoid these activities, no matter what society or age they live in, they are highly suitable for historical and international comparison. Elias presented a large number of excerpts from manners books in chronological order, thus revealing an overall directional trend in codes of behavior and feeling. By studying these sources, Elias uncovered evidence of long-term changes in these codes as well as in people's psychic makeup. Elias made connections between the changes in personality structure and changes in the social structure of France and other European societies and offered explanations for why this happened. According to his theory the main motor of the directional process is the dynamic of social relations—that is, in changes in the ways in which people are bonded to each other. Changes in these networks of interdependency are also changes in status competition; they are changes in sources of power and identity, in the ways people demand and show respect as well as in their fears of losing the respect of others and their own self-respect.

On the European map the study of the history of manners has many blank spots. Manners as a serious object of study has faced a major obstacle in the strong social pressures of status competition. No matter what definition of "good manners" may prevail, if these do not come "naturally," that is, more or less automatically, the effect is ruined. Only manners springing from the inner sensitivity of "second nature" may impress as "natural." Otherwise, the taint of longings for status and the fear of losing status attach to an individual, provoking embarrassment and repulsion. Thus, status competition and inherent status fears have exerted pressure to associate the entire topic of manners with lower classes and lower instincts. That is, as good manners themselves were taken for granted, the subject of manners was limited to spheres in which good ones were taken to be absent. Throughout the period from the 1920s to the 1960s, manners were discussed mainly in the context of the behavioral "problems" of lower classes, of children having to learn such things as table manners, as well as of social climbers and *nouveaux riches* who were usually seen as being too loud and too conspicuous. Status fears have thus functioned as a barrier to developing the level of reflexivity needed for serious interest in the history of manners. These fears have impeded the development of a historical perspective by making people less inclined to perceive of their own manners and those of their social group as the outcomes of social and psychic processes.

The social ascent of certain groups—the working classes, women, youth, homosexuals, and blacks—spurred the development of the level of detachment and reflection needed for studies in the social history of manners and mentalities. In the 1960s and 1970s these groups were emancipated and further integrated within nation-states. They succeeded in being treated with more respect. An avalanche of protest against all relationships and manners perceived as authoritarian coincided with the widening of circles of identification. As processes of decolonization took hold, whole populations were emancipated and integrated, however poorly, within a global network of states. Greater interest in the daily lives of "ordinary" people ensued. With increased mobility and more frequent contact between different kinds of people came the pressure to look at oneself and others with greater detachment, to ask questions about manners that previous generations took for granted: why is this forbidden and that permitted? These processes have been the driving forces behind the rising popularity of the study of manners and mentalities.

Existing studies of manners concentrate on changes in upper-class manners. They highlight the ways manners were used to differentiate groups by class, but they do not deal directly with lower-class manners. In particular, the code of manners prevalent in lower classes before they experienced a certain degree of integration into their societies is left unstudied. It is the task of social history to examine how long these distinct lower-class codes of conduct persisted; to what extent they were integrated into the dominant code; to what extent people from lower classes did imitate their "betters"; and when and how these mixing processes occurred to form uniform national codes of manners. The following sketch of changes in European regimes of manners owes a debt to Norbert Elias's *The Civilizing Process* in two ways. First, it uses his theoretical perspective on manners as a model; second, to illustrate changes up to the nineteenth century, it relies on empirical data extracted from his research and presented by Stephen Mennell (1989). For the nineteenth and twentieth centuries, this article draws on studies by Michael Curtin (1987), Leonore Davidoff (1973), Horst-Volker Krumrey (1984), and several by Cas Wouters. The following discussion is a general one; only few remarks indicate variations in the development of manners within western Europe, and differences between western and eastern Europe are neglected altogether. In general, specific national regimes of manners have developed from different national class structures. In each country a national regime of manners emerged out of changes in the relative power of the rising and falling strata, out of their specific forms and levels of competition and cooperation. The ways in which the ranks of falling strata were opened up by and to rising strata appear to have been decisive in the development of distinctive re-

Beatles Fans at Buckingham Palace. By 1965, popular feelings were challenging traditional barriers. The awarding of the MBE (Member of the Order of the British Empire) to the Beatles signified upper-class acceptance of the rebellious culture of rock music. The Beatles had emerged from performing in Liverpool dockside slums only a few years before. ©HULTON-DEUTCH COLLECTION/CORBIS

gimes of manners and to have determined variations in the general pattern set out here.

THE PERIOD OF COURTS AND COURTESY

The manners books studied by Elias included prominent ones that were translated, imitated, and reprinted again and again. These books were directed primarily at the secular upper classes, particularly people living in courtly circles around great lords. Early modern terms for good manners such as "courtesy" derive from the word "courts." With few exceptions, these books address adults and present adult standards. They deal openly with many questions that later became embarrassing and even repugnant, such as when and how to fart, burp, or spit. In the sequence of excerpts Elias presents, changes in feelings of shame and delicacy become vividly apparent. The series on table manners, for example, shows that people at feudal courts ate with their fingers, using only their own general-purpose knife or dagger. The main restriction on using the knife was not to clean one's teeth with it. Everyone ate from a common dish, using a common spoon to put some of the food on a slice of bread. One was advised to refrain from falling on the dish like a pig, from dipping food one has already taken bites from into the communal sauce, and from presenting a tasty bit from one's mouth to a companion's. People were not to snort while eating nor blow their noses on the tablecloth (for this was used for wiping greasy fingers) or into their fingers.

Throughout the Middle Ages this kind of advice was repeated. Then, from at least the sixteenth century onward, manners were in continuous flux. The codes became more differentiated and more demanding. In the sixteenth century the fork is mentioned, although only for lifting food from the common dish, and handkerchiefs and napkins appear, both still optional rather than necessary: if you had one, you were to use it rather than your fingers. Only by the mid-eighteenth century did plates, knives, forks, spoons, and napkins for each guest, and also handkerchiefs, become more or less indispensable utensils in the courtly class. In this and other aspects, the code of these upper classes was then beginning to resemble the general usage of later centuries.

Erasmus wrote that it was impolite to speak to someone who was urinating or defecating; he discussed these acts quite openly. In his conduct manual, *Il Galateo ovvero De' Costumi* (1558), Giovanni della Casa wrote that "it is not a refined habit, when coming across something disgusting in the sheet, as sometimes happens, to turn at once to one's companion and point it out to him" (Elias, 2000, p. 111). This warning is in line with other evidence from early manners books, which indicate that urinating and defecating were not yet punctiliously restricted to their socially designated proper places. Often enough, needs were satisfied when and where they happened to be felt. These bodily functions increasingly came to be invested with feelings of shame and repugnance, until eventually they were performed only in strict privacy and not spoken of without embarrassment. Certain parts of the body increasingly became "private parts" or, as most European languages phrase it, "shame parts" ("pudenda," deriving from the Latin word meaning to be ashamed).

The same trend is apparent in behavior in the bedroom. As the advice cited above indicates, it was quite normal to receive visitors in rooms with beds, as it was very common to spend the night with many in one room. Sleeping was not yet set apart from the rest of social life. Usually people slept naked. Special nightclothes slowly came into use at about the same time as the fork and the handkerchief. Manners books specified how to behave when sharing a bed with a person of the same sex. For instance, a manners book of 1729, as quoted by Elias, warned that "it is not proper to lie so near him that you disturb or even touch him; and it is still less decent to put your legs between those of the other." From the 1774 edition of the same book, an advance in the thresholds of shame and repugnance can be deduced, for this pointed instruction was removed and the tone of advice became more indirect and more moral: "you should maintain a strict and vigilant modesty." The new edition also noted that to be forced to share a bed "seldom happens" (Elias, 2000, p. 137). Gradually, to share a bed with strangers, with people outside the family, became embarrassing. As with other bodily functions, sleeping slowly became more intimate and private, until it was performed only behind the scenes of social life.

In directing these changes in manners, considerations of health and hygiene were not important. They were used mainly to back up—sometimes also to cover up—motivations of status and respect. In all cases restraints on manners appeared first, and only later were reasons of health given as justifications. Nor did changes in poverty or wealth influence the development of manners prior to the mid-nineteenth century, after which their importance did increase.

In general, as Elias's examples showed, what was first allowed later became restricted or forbidden. Heightened sentivity with regard to several activities, especially those related to the "animalic" or "first nature" of human beings, coincided with increasing segregation of these activities from the rest of social life:

they became private. Again and again, what was once seen as good manners later became rude or, at the other extreme, so ingrained in behavior as to be completely taken for granted. Social superiors made subordinates feel inferior if they did not meet their standard of manners. Increasingly, fear of social superiors and, more generally, the fear of transgression of social prohibitions took on the character of an inner fear, shame.

All new prescriptions and prohibitions were used as a means of social distinction until they lost their distinctive potential. Gradually, ever-broader strata were willing and anxious to adopt the models developed above them, compelling those above to develop other means of distinction. For instance, it became a breach of good manners to appear naked or incompletely dressed or to perform natural functions before those of higher or equal rank; doing so before inferiors could be taken as a sign of benevolence. Later, nakedness and excretion not conducted in private became general offenses invested with shame and embarrassment. Gradually, the social commands controlling these actions came to operate with regard to everyone and were imprinted as such on children. Thus all references to social control, including shame, became embedded as assumptions and as such receded from consciousness. Adults came to experience social prohibitions as "natural," coming from their own inner selves rather than from the outer realm of "good manners." As these social constraints took on the form of more or less total and automatically functioning self-restraints, this standard behavior had become "second nature." Accordingly, manners books no longer dealt with these matters or did so far less extensively. Social constraints pressed toward stronger and more automatic self-supervision, the subordination of short-term impulses to the commandment of a habitual longer-term perspective, and the cultivation of a more stable, constant, and differentiated self-regulation. This is, as Elias called it, a civilizing process.

In his explanation, Elias emphasized the importance of processes of state formation, in which taxation and the use of physical violence and its instruments came into fewer and fewer hands until they were centralized and monopolized. Medieval societies lacked any central power strong enough to compel people to restrain their impulses to use violence. In the course of the sixteenth century, families of the old warrior nobility and some families of bourgeois origin were transformed into a new upper class of courtiers, a tamed nobility with more muted affects. Thus the territories of great lords were increasingly pacified, and at their courts, encouraged especially by the presence of a lady, more peaceful forms of conduct became obligatory. Such conduct was a basic part of the re-gime of courtly manners, and its development, including ways of speaking, dressing, and holding and moving the body, went hand in hand with the rise of courtly regimes.

Within the pacified territories of strong lords, the permanent danger and fear of violent attack diminished. This relative physical safety facilitated the growth of towns, burgher groups, commerce, wealth, and, as a result, taxation. Taxes financed larger armies and administrative bodies, thus helping the central rulers of the court societies to expand their power and their territory at the expense of others. The dynamic of the competition for land and money went in the direction of expanding the webs of interdependence, bonding together the people of different territories. Political integration and economic integration intertwined and reinforced each other, culminating in the absolute monarchies of the later seventeenth and the eighteenth centuries.

The inhabitants of these states were increasingly constrained to settle conflicts in nonviolent ways, thus pressuring each other to tame their impulses toward aggressiveness and cruelty. Moreover, families of bourgeois origin had risen in power, enough to compete with the nobility and forcefully to demand more respect. Their former social superiors were obliged to develop the habit of permanently restraining their more extreme expressions of superiority, particularly violent ones. Such displays were successfully branded as degrading. As they came to provoke shame and repulsion, impulses in that direction and the corresponding feelings of superiority (and inferiority) came to be more or less automatically repressed and rejected. Thus, in a widening circle of mutual respect and identification, the more extreme displays of superiority and inferiority were excluded from the prevailing regime of manners.

In the early modern period, the general level of mutual identification was such that, for example, displays of physical punishment and executions were common public spectacles. Moreover, these were still considered necessary to bolster central authority and to seal the transfer of vengeance from private persons to the central ruler. From the early seventeenth century onward, the more extreme, mutilating punishments were mitigated or abolished. During the nineteenth century most corporal punishments were abandoned or, like executions, removed to within prison walls. And in the twentieth century, in most western European countries executions were abolished altogether. The taming of aggressiveness coincided with an increase in sensibility toward suffering, that is, in the scope of mutual identification. Growing sensitivity to violence, suffering, and blood can be deduced also from changes in manners such as increasing restrictions on the use of the knife as an instrument and symbol of danger. For instance, it was frowned upon to eat fish or cut potatoes with a knife or to bring the knife to one's mouth. In a related trend, the slaughtering of animals and carving of their meat were removed from the public scene into slaughterhouses. The carving of large cuts of meat was also increasingly removed from the dinner table to the kitchen.

FROM COURTESY TO ETIQUETTE

In absolute monarchies all groups, estates, or classes, despite their differences, became dependent on each other, thus increasing the dependence of each of the major interests on the central coordinating monopoly power. Administration and control over the state, its centralized and monopolized resources, first expanded and spread into the hands of growing numbers of individuals. Then, with the rise of bourgeois groups no longer dependent on privileges derived from the Crown, in an increasingly complex process royal or "private" state monopolies turned into societal or "public" ones. With the exception of the Netherlands, where monopoly administration had already in 1581 been taken over by merchant patricians, this shift from private to public occurred in the late eighteenth century, first in France and later in many other European countries. This process accelerated in the nineteenth century, with the rising power and status of wealthy middle classes and the declining importance of courts, formerly the aristocratic centers of power.

The transition from the eighteenth-century courtesy genre of manners books to the nineteenth-century etiquette genre expresses this change. The etiquette genre presented a blend of aristocratic and bourgeois manners. The aristocratic tradition continued, for example, in the importance of being self-confident and at ease. Even the slightest suggestion of effort or forethought was itself bad manners. Whereas courtesy books typically advocated ideals of character, temperament, accomplishments, habits, morals, and manners for aristocratic life, etiquette books focused more narrowly on the sociability of particular social situations—dinners, balls, receptions, presentations at court, calls, introductions, salutations. Etiquette books were directed at sociability in "society" or "good society," terms referring to the wider social groups, segments of the middle and upper classes, that possessed the strength of a social establishment. Especially in "society," manners were decisive in making acquaintances and friends, and through manners one could gain influence and recognition. Manners also functioned as a means of winning a desirable spouse. In comparison to court circles, the circles of "good society" were larger, and sociability in them was more "private." In many of those circles the private sphere was more sharply distinguished from the public and occupational sphere.

The life and career of the bourgeois classes both in business and the professions depended heavily on the rather punctual and minute regulation of social traffic and behavior. Accordingly, nineteenth-century manners books placed great emphasis on acquiring the self-discipline necessary for living a "rational life"; they emphasized time-keeping and ordering activities routinely in a fixed sequence and at a set pace. The entrepreneurial bourgeoisie needed to arrange contracts, for which a reputation of being financially solvent and morally solid was crucial. To a large extent this reputation was formed in the gossip channels of "good society" (or its functional equivalent among other social strata).

The reputation of moral solidity referred to the self-discipline of orderliness, thrift, and responsibility, qualities needed for a firm grip on the proceedings of business transactions. Moral solidity also included the sexual sphere. It was inconceivable that any working bourgeois man could create the solid impression of living up to the terms of his contracts if he could not even control his wife or keep his family in order. Therefore, bourgeois means of controlling potentially dangerous social and sexual competition to a substantial degree depended on the support of wives for their husbands. At the same time, these pressures offered specific opportunities to women. Whereas men dominated the courtesy genre of manners books, in the etiquette genre women gained a prominent position, both as authors and as readers. As the social weight of the bourgeoisie increased, middle-class women enjoyed a widening sphere of opportunities. Although confined to the domain of their home and "good society," in the nineteenth century upper- and middle-class women more or less came to run and organize the social sphere. The workings of society in large part took place in women's private drawing rooms. To some extent, women came to function as the gatekeepers of this social formation, as arbiters of social acceptance or rejection.

THE EXPANSION OF "GOOD SOCIETY"

As circles of good society were larger, more open, and more competitive than court circles, the people in them developed increasingly detailed and formal manners for social circulation. Particularly in Britain but also in other countries, a highly elaborate and increasingly formalized regime of manners developed. It consisted of a complicated system of introductions, invitations, leaving cards, calls, "at homes" (specified times when guests were received), receptions, dinners, and so on. The regime regulated sociability and functioned as a relatively refined system of inclusion and exclusion, as an instrument to screen newcomers into social circles, to ensure that the newly introduced would assimilate to the prevailing regime of manners, and to identify and exclude undesirables. A basic rule of manners among those acknowledged as belonging to the circle was to treat each other on the basis of equality. Quite often this was expressed in what became known as the Golden Rule of manners: do to others as you would have them do to you. Others were treated with reserve and thus kept at a social distance. In short, members treated everyone either as an equal or as a stranger; in this way more extreme displays of superiority and inferiority were avoided.

Entrance into "society" was impossible without an introduction, and any introduction required the previous permission of both parties. After an introduction, a variety of relationships could develop, from merely a "bowing acquaintanceship" to one with the "right of recognition," as the English called it. As a rule these differentiations in social distance among those included in "society" ran parallel with differentiations in social status. Thus, even within the ranks of "good society" the practice of reserve functioned to keep people considered not equal enough at a social distance and thus to prevent (other) displays of superiority and inferiority. Procedures of precedence, salutation, body carriage, facial expression, and so on, all according to rank, age, and gender, functioned to regulate and cover status competition within the ranks of "good society."

As large middle-class groups became socially strong enough to compete in the struggle for power and status, they also demanded to be treated according to the Golden Rule. As "good society" expanded in the nineteenth century, circles of identification widened and spread, becoming increasingly multilayered. As ever larger groups ascended into these ranks, status competition intensified, pressuring all toward greater awareness and sharper observation of each other and of themselves. Sensitivities were heightened, particularly to expressions of status difference. As standards of sensibility and delicacy were rising, the manners of getting acquainted and keeping a distance became more important as well as more detailed.

To keep a distance from strangers was of great concern. Especially in cities, the prototypical stranger was someone who might have the manners of the respectable but not the morals. Strangers personified bad company. Their immoral motives and behavior would put the respectable in situations that endangered their self-control, prompting loss of composure in response to repulsive behavior or, worse, the succumbing to temptation. The repeated warnings against strangers expressed a strong moral appeal, revealing a fear of the slippery slope toward giving in to immoral pleasures.

These warnings were directed at young men in particular. Playing a single game of cards with strangers, for example, would "always end in trouble, often in despair, and sometimes in suicide," an early-nineteenth-century advice book warned. By its nature, any careless indulgence in pleasure would lead to "a lethal fall" (Tilburg, 1998, pp. 66, 67). This strong moral advice was intended to teach young men the responsibilities needed not only for a successful career but also, as marriages were no longer arranged by parents, for choosing a marriage partner. Advice betrayed the fear that such choices would be determined mainly by sexual attraction. Social censorship verged on psychic censorship: warnings expanded to the "treacherous effects" of fantasy. This kind of high-pitched moral pressure stimulated the development of rather rigid ways of avoiding anything defined as dangerous or unacceptable via the formation of a rigorous conscience. Thus the successive ascent of large middle-class groups and their increasing status and power relative to other groups were reflected in the regimes of manners and of self-regulation.

THE FORMALIZING PROCESS

Developments from the Renaissance to the end of the nineteenth century can be described as a long-term process of formalizing and disciplining: more and more aspects of behavior were subjected to increasingly strict and detailed regulations that were partly formalized as laws and partly as manners. The regime of manners expanded to include restrictions on behavior defined as arrogant and humiliating, as wild, violent, dirty, indecent, or lecherous. As this kind of unacceptable behavior was sanctioned by increasingly vigorous practices of social shaming, emotions or impulses leading to that behavior came to be avoided and repressed via the counterimpulses of individual shame. Thus, via an expanding regime of manners, a widening range of behavior and feelings disappeared from the social scene and the minds of individuals. In the nineteenth century, among upper and middle-class people this resulted in the formation of a type of personality characterized by an "inner compass" of reflexes and rather fixed habits, increasingly compelling regimes of manners and self-regulation. Impulses and emotions increasingly came to be controlled via

Curtsey. A girl curtseys to a man in a wheelchair. English print, 1850s. ©HULTON-DEUTCH COLLECTION/CORBIS

the more or less automatically functioning counter-impulses of an authoritative conscience, with a strong penchant for order and regularity, cleanliness and neatness. Negligence in these matters indicated an inclination toward dissoluteness. Such inclinations were to be nipped in the bud, particularly in children. Without rigorous control, "first nature" might run wild. This old conviction expresses a fear that is typical of rather authoritarian relationships and social controls as well as a relatively authoritative conscience. The long-term trend of formalization reached its peak in the Victorian era, from the mid-nineteenth century to its last decade; the metaphor of the stiff upper lip indicated ritualistic manners and a kind of ritualistic self-control, heavily based on an authoritative conscience and functioning more or less automatically as a "second nature."

THE TWENTIETH CENTURY: A LONG-TERM PROCESS OF INFORMALIZATION

Around 1900 large groups with "new money" were expanding and rising, creating strong pressures on "old money" establishments to open up. Whole groups and classes still were outspokenly deemed unacceptable as people to associate with, but as emancipation processes accelerated, the old avoidance behavior of keeping a distance became more difficult. People from different social classes had become interdependent to the point where they could no longer avoid immediate contact with each other. Especially in expanding cities,

at work and on the streets, in public conveyances and entertainment facilities, people who once used to avoid each other were now forced either to try to maintain or recover social distance under conditions of rising proximity, or to accommodate and become accustomed to more social mixing. At the same time people were warned against the dangers of familiarity, of being too open and becoming too close. From another direction came attacks on traditional ways of keeping a distance as an expression of superiority. As some social mixing became less avoidable, more extreme ways of keeping a distance and showing superiority were banned. Manners became less hierarchical and less formal and rigid.

The same trend is apparent in manners regulating the relationship between the sexes. From the end of the nineteenth century onward, women gradually escaped from the confines of the home and "good society" (or its functional equivalent among other social strata). Chaperonage declined, and upper- and middle-class women expanded their sources of power and identity by joining the suffragette movement, attending university, engaging in social work, or playing sports. Women, especially young women, wanted to go out, raising the question of whether they were allowed to pay for themselves. The respectability of meeting places and conditions of meeting became more flexible, as young people began to exert control over the dynamics of their own relationships, whether romantic or not.

In the 1920s many newly wealthy families were jostling for a place within the ranks of "good society."

The rise of whole social groups triggered a formidable push toward informalization, and rules for getting acquainted and keeping a distance declined. The expansion of business and industry, together with an expansion of means of transportation and communication, gave rise to a multitude of new types of relationships for which the old formality was too troublesome. New meeting places for the sexes such as dance halls, cinemas, and ice-skating rinks were debated for the freedom they offered. As women entered the wider society by going to work in offices, libraries, and other places, office manners became a topic. The whole trend implied rising demands on the social navigational abilities of the individual, a greater capacity to negotiate the possibilities and limitations of relationships easily without tension.

Until the 1960s some manners books still contained separate sections on behavior toward social superiors and inferiors. Later these sections disappeared. Ideals for good manners became dissociated from superior and inferior social position or rank. The trend was to draw social dividing lines less on the basis of people's belonging to certain groups—by class, race, age, sex, or ethnicity—and more on the basis of individual behavior. The avoidance behavior once prescribed toward people not deemed socially acceptable was increasingly discouraged. No longer could certain groups be legitimately targeted; rather, certain behaviors and feelings—including humiliating displays of superiority or inferiority—were considered inappropriate and could be shunned as such. Avoidance behavior, no longer explicitly set out as rules, thus tended to become internalized; tensions between people became tensions within them. Accordingly, traditional ways of keeping a distance and being reserved when confronted with those outside one's social circles were transformed into the "right of privacy," a concept which lacked a specified class component. The perception was that each individual should have the right to be left alone, to maintain a personal or social space undisturbed by unwanted intrusions.

Restrictions on ways and places of meeting sharply diminished from the 1960s onward. Early in that decade Mary Bolton, in *The New Etiquette Book,* observed (as though with a sigh): "Boy meets girl and girl meets boy in so many different ways that it would be quite impossible to enumerate them." This change in the conditions of "respectable" meeting is in keeping with a general shift in the balance between external and internal social controls. Respect and respectable behavior became more dependent on self-regulation, and self-controls increasingly became both the focus and the locus of external social controls.

In the 1960s and 1970s, with entire groups rising socially, practically all relationships became less hierarchical and formal. The emancipation and integration of large social groups within welfare states coincided with informalization: the regime of manners rapidly lost rigidity and hierarchical aloofness. Many modes of conduct that formerly had been forbidden came to be allowed. Sexuality, the written and spoken language, clothing, music, dancing, and hairstyles—all expressions exhibited the trend toward informality. On the one hand, the spectrum of accepted behavioral and emotional alternatives expanded (with the important exception of displays and feelings of superiority and inferiority). On the other hand, an acceptable and respectable usage of these alternatives implied a continued increase of the demands made on self-regulation.

In increasingly dense networks of interdependency, more subtle, informal ways of obliging and being obliged demanded greater flexibility and sensitivity to shades and nuances in manners of dealing with others and oneself. The rise of mutually expected self-restraints allowed for what might be called a controlled decontrolling. Emotions that previously had been repressed and denied, especially those concerning sex and violence, were again "discovered" as part of a collective emotional makeup: in the emancipation of emotions many emotions reentered both consciousness and public discussion. From a set of rules manners turned into guidelines, differentiated according to the demands of the situation and relationship. This was accompanied by a strong decline in social as well as psychic censorship. Both the fear and awe of fantasy or dissident imagination diminished together with the fear and awe of the authorities of state and conscience. On the level of the personality, an authoritarian conscience made way for a conscience attuned to more equal and flexible relationships. As a psychic authority, conscience lost much of its more or less automatic ascendancy, a change that can be described in shorthand as a transition from conscience to consciousness.

Within families, commanding children and presenting them with established decisions came to be seen as dangerous. Acceptance of peremptory authority—do it because I said so—was seen as a symptom of blind submissiveness, estranging children from their own feelings. Parents more intensely invested in their children's affective lives, and family ties gained in confidentiality and intimacy. Pedagogical regimes stressed mutual respect and affection, and parents and teachers sought to direct children to obey their own conscience and reflections rather than simply obey the external constraints of adults.

Informality. The ubiquity of the cellular phone posed a challenge to traditional table manners at the turn of the twenty-first century. ©HULTON-DEUTCH COLLECTION/ CORBIS

In the 1980s the collective emancipation that had flourished in the 1960s and 1970s disappeared and a market ideology spread. This reflected a change in Western European power structures: politicians and governments came to side less with unions and social movements, and more with commercial and managerial establishments. From the 1980s onward the prevailing power structures allowed only for individual emancipation. Individuals aspiring to respectability and social ascent came to feel strongly dependent again on the established elites and they adjusted their manners accordingly. Thus the sensibilities and manners of the elites again functioned more unequivocally as a model. This shift was reinforced in the 1990s. The events that followed the collapse of the Iron Curtain—breaking out into violence in some cases, such as in the former Yugoslavia—intensified feelings of fear, insecurity, and powerlessness. Increased awareness of European nation-states' lack of control over global processes stimulated a tendency to identify with the established order and to focus with great concern on anything perceived as a threat to it—criminality and bad manners in particular. Accordingly, the whole regime of manners became somewhat more compelling. To a large extent, informal behaviors that had become socially acceptable in the 1960s and 1970s remained so, through their endorsement by and integration into the standard, dominant code of manners.

CONCLUSION

In the twentieth century a dominant process of informalization followed the long-term trend of formalization: manners became increasingly relaxed, subtle, and varied. As more and more groups of people came to be represented in the various centers of power that functioned as models for manners, the more did extreme differences between all social groups in terms of power, ranking, behavior, and management of emotion diminish. More and more social groups directed themselves to uniform national codes of behavior and feeling. Thus, as power inequalities lessened, the Golden Rule and the principle of mutual consent became expected standards of conduct among individual, and groups.

The turn of the twentieth century, the Roaring Twenties, and the permissive decades of the 1960s and 1970s were periods in which power differences sharply decreased. They were also periods with particularly strong spurts of informalization. As power and status competition intensified, and sensitivities over social inequality increased, demonstrations of an individual's distinctiveness became more indirect, subtle, and hidden. References to hierarchical group differences, particularly to "better" and "inferior" kinds of people, were increasingly taboo: social superiors were less automatically taken to be better people. Yet it was not until the 1960s that the once automatic equation of superior in power and superior as a human being declined to the point of embarrassment.

As bonds of cooperation and competition blended, the people involved came to experience more ambivalence in their relationships. At the same time, many people increasingly felt compelled to identify with other people, as was expressed and reinforced by welfare state institutions. Widening circles of identification implied less rigid boundaries of nation, class, age, gender, religion, and ethnicity and provided a basis for a rising societal level of mutual trust. Expanding and intensified cooperation and competition prompted people to observe and take the measure of themselves and of each other more carefully, and to show flexibility and a greater willingness to compromise. Social success came to depend more strongly on a reflexive and flexible self-regulation, the ability to combine firmness and flexibility, directness and tactfulness. As manners and relationships between social groups became less rigid and hierarchical, so too did the relationships between psychic functions such as impulses, conscience, and consciousness. A larger and more differentiated spectrum of alternatives opened up, with more flowing and flexible connections between social groups and psychic functions.

Introducing the term "third nature" as a sensitizing concept can illuminate these changes. The term "second nature" refers to a self-regulating conscience that to a great extent functions automatically. The term "third nature" refers to the development of a more reflexive and flexible self-regulation. Ideally, for someone operating on the basis of third nature it becomes "natural" to attune oneself to the pulls and pushes of both first and second nature as well as the dangers and chances, short-term and long-term, of any particular situation or relationship. As national, continental, and global integration processes exert pressure toward increasingly differentiated regimes of manners, they also exert pressure toward increasingly reflexive and flexible regimes of self-regulation.

See also other articles in this section.

BIBLIOGRAPHY

Curtin, Michael. *Propriety and Position: A Study of Victorian Manners.* New York, 1987.

Daalen, Rineke van. "Public Complaints and Government Intervention: Letters to the Municipal Authorities of Amsterdam 1865–1920." *Netherlands Journal of Sociology* 24 (1988): 83–98.

Davidoff, Leonore. *The Best Circles: Society, Etiquette, and the Season.* London, 1973.

Elias, Norbert. *The Civilizing Process: Sociogenetic and Psychogenetic Investigations.* Translated by Edmund Jephcott. Rev. ed. Oxford, and Cambridge, Mass., 2000. Originally published in German in 1939.

Franke, Herman. *The Emancipation of Prisoners: A Socio-historical Analysis of the Dutch Prison Experience.* Edinburgh, 1995.

Krumrey, Horst-Volker. *Entwicklungsstrukturen von Verhaltensstandarden: Eine soziologische Prozessanalyse auf der Grundlage deutscher Anstands- und Manierenbücher von 1870 bis 1970.* Frankfurt, 1984.

Mason, John E. *Gentlefolk in the Making: Studies in the History of English Courtesy Literature and Related Topics from 1531 to 1774.* Philadelphia, 1935; New York, 1971.

Mennell, Stephen. *Norbert Elias: Civilization and the Human Self-Image.* Oxford and New York, 1989. Rev. ed. published as *Norbert Elias: An Introduction.* Dublin, 1998.

Schröter, Michael. *Erfahrungen mit Norbert Elias: Gesammelte Aufsätze.* Frankfurt am Main, Germany, 1997.

Spierenburg, Pieter. *The Spectacle of Suffering: Executions and the Evolution of Repression: From a Preindustrial Metropolis to the European Experience.* Cambridge, U.K., and New York, 1984.

Swaan, Abram de. *In Care of the State: Health Care, Education, and Welfare in Western Europe and the USA in the Modern Era.* Oxford, 1988.

Swaan, Abram de. "Widening Circles of Disidentification: On the Psycho- and Sociogenesis of the Hatred of Distant Strangers—Reflections on Rwanda." *Theory, Culture, and Society* 14, no. 2 (1997): 105–122.

Swaan, Abram de. "Widening Circles of Social Identification: Emotional Concerns in Sociogenetic Perspective." *Theory, Culture, and Society* 12, no. 2 (1995): 25–39.

Tilburg, Marja van. *Hoe hoorde het? Seksualiteit en partnerkeuze in de Nederlandse adviesliteratuur 1780–1890.* Amsterdam, 1998.

Wouters, Cas. "Changing Patterns of Social Controls and Self-Controls: On the Rise of Crime since the 1950s and the Sociogenesis of a 'Third Nature.'" *British Journal of Criminology* 39, no. 3 (summer 1999): 416–432.

Wouters, Cas. "Developments in Behavioural Codes between the Sexes: Formalization of Informalization, the Netherlands 1930–1985." *Theory, Culture, and Society* 4, nos. 2–3 (1987): 405–429.

Wouters, Cas. "Etiquette Books and Emotion Management in the Twentieth Century: American Habitus in International Comparison." In *An Emotional History of the United States.* Edited by Peter N. Stearns and Jan Lewis. New York, 1998. Pages 283–304.

Wouters, Cas. "Etiquette Books and Emotion Management in the Twentieth Century: Part 1—The Integration of Social Classes." *Journal of Social History* 29 (1995): 107–124.

Wouters, Cas. "Etiquette Books and Emotion Management in the Twentieth Century: Part 2—The Integration of the Sexes." *Journal of Social History* 29 (1995): 325–340.

Wouters, Cas. "How Strange to Ourselves Are Our Feelings of Superiority and Inferiority." *Theory, Culture, and Society* 15, no. 1 (February 1998): 131–150.

Wouters, Cas. *Informalisierung: Norbert Elias' Zivilisationstheorie und Zivilisationsprozesse im 20. Jahrhundert.* Opladen and Wiesbaden, Germany, 1999.

THE EMOTIONS

Rineke van Daalen

Pioneering work in the historical nature of the emotions began in the 1960s and 1970s. At that time interest in aspects of history that previously had been largely unexplored increased, and historians initiated studies of the lives of ordinary men and women, their habits and beliefs, and their attitudes toward birth, marriage, death, and disease. These new topics, especially the study of family life, put researchers on the track of different kinds of emotions. Indeed the sociologist Michael Anderson considered "the sentimental approach" one of the three most important theoretical streams in the history of family life.

The examination of changes in familial emotional standards and experience and in their interactions, has encompassed a broad range, including feelings of honor and gender, honor in relation to parents or to the family, shame and sexuality, and shame in relation to illness. Scholars considered feelings like love and empathy or their absence thoroughly and systematically as topics in their own right, and they have given particular attention to the feelings of affection between men and women and between parents and children. They paid less attention to intersibling dynamics and such feelings as anger, hate, jealousy, grief, shame, and embarrassment, which they studied more obliquely. For the rest, emotion research casts its net to include far more than family life. For example, it may take in attitudes toward political events, the conditions under which anger appeared among the working classes, or the social specificity of fear and phobias.

For obvious reasons, historians are best informed about the feelings of those who are articulate. Adults, members of the elite, and those who were literate clearly generate more sources than do children, peasants, or workers. Personal documents, such as autobiographies, letters, and diaries, provide a many-faceted image of emotional cultures in the past. Parents reflected on the educations of their children and recorded their surprise, pride, or disappointment as they watched their offspring grow up. Adults looked back to their early years and wrote about their emotional lives as children, and in a few instances children wrote diaries.

The interest in emotions went hand in hand with a growth in interdisciplinary methods. Historical approaches combined with sociological, anthropological, and psychoanalytic theories. These disciplines all had characteristic theoretical and methodological traditions, making it difficult to integrate them and take advantage of their individual strengths. During the twentieth century historical research into intimate relations raised theoretical and methodological issues. Aside from the lack of historical sources for the study of emotions, interpreting these sources can be complex. A tension exists between deeply held emotional standards, emotionology, and emotional experience, that is, between the ideals and fantasies of people on the one hand and reality on the other hand (Stearns and Stearns, 1985). That makes it difficult to understand exactly what moral and medical tracts, manner books, religious sermons, legislation, pictures and paintings, biographies, and letters reveal about emotional lives and psychic structures. To what extent do these sources recount reality, or do changes in this material correspond with actual transformations in emotions and in behavior?

Because of the historically and locally bound nature of emotional standards and emotion management, such questions cannot be answered in general terms. Methodological directives and methodological problems are dependent on time and place. Before the late seventeenth century many aspects of social life were public. In interactions between men, women, and children, the role of the community was important in defining and enforcing standards of conduct and emotions. Privacy was a more diffuse concept and did not exist in the modern sense. Thus social historians studying love in the seventeenth and eighteenth centuries have not become much wiser from analyzing diaries or love poetry. Considering the traces of love, which were specific for the early modern period, is more productive. People tended to associate love with the body and with visible and tangible behavior, and

Death and the Child. "Death Taking a Child," engraving (c. 1526–1528) by Hans Lutzelburger after a series of woodcuts, *The Dance of Death,* by Hans Holbein the Younger (1497?–1543). PRIVATE COLLECTION/THE BRIDGEMAN ART LIBRARY

they thought it could be controlled in the same way as other physical functions. They assumed that magic, potions, charms, and rituals could ensure the desired outcome to an amorous encounter. Lore concerning significant objects and customs provides greater insight into such a culture of the emotions than do diaries or autobiographies (Gillis, 1988).

A Dutch study of personal documents demonstrates in another way that each source has its own outlook and limitations. Historians looking for expressions of grief at the death of a child in pre–nineteenth century diaries have found only dryly formulated short notes. But to base observations merely on those brief remarks and to infer that parents were not deeply moved by the death of a child would be inaccurate. Diaries were not where people expressed their mourning. Family happenings and familial emotions were commonly described in topical poems and songs. Indeed epitaphs and printed poetry disclose passionate specimens of grief (Dekker, 1995).

Texts and representations were constructed for different reasons and with a certain intention and public in mind. Parental diaries recording children's educations do not elaborate on severe methods of behavior regulation. But retrospective writing on childhood and youth may reveal a different perspective, recalling harsh treatment and physical punishment (Pollock, 1983). By combining a broad variety of material and the perspectives of different groups, researchers can expand and better substantiate their hypotheses.

Methodological, conceptual, and theoretical problems have induced a great many controversies and disputes and in some cases have resulted in diametrically opposed views on the history of emotions. This tendency has been reinforced by the fragmented nature of emotion research, which is scattered over demarcated studies of intimate relations in different places and among different groups in western Europe. These studies demonstrate the relevance of understanding emotional standards and experiences within the context of broader social, economic, and political relations. They uncover where the first signs of romantic love or modern maternal feelings appeared, in which countries or regions, in rural or urban communities, or among peasants, artisans, the bourgeoisie, or the working classes. But few studies look at the direction, chronology, and origins of change. *A History of the Family* (1986), a systematically comparative family study edited by André Burguière, Christiane Klapisch-Zuber, Martine Segalen, and François Zonabend, elaborates on differences in family life between northern and southern Europe and between eastern and western Europe but without focusing on emotions.

A pioneer work in this area is Norbert Elias's study *The Civilizing Process* (originally published in German in 1939). Examining the relationship between social and psychic processes in western Europe from the Middle Ages to the eighteenth century, Elias developed an inclusive theoretical framework. He demonstrated that changes in personality structure relate to changes in social structure and that changes in emotion management are a function of social interdependencies. This treatment of emotion management contributed a historical and sociological perspective to human psychology and gave the nature of the modern habitus a central place in the history of European societies. It is an example of the interdisciplinary approach required in analyses of changes in emotional behavior and emotional experience.

Studying a variety of European etiquette manuals, Elias identified gradual changes in emotional standards. During the Middle Ages emotions were expressed more violently and directly with fewer psychological nuances and complexities than in subsequent centuries. Manners were less formalized, and fewer aspects of behavior and feeling were subjected to strict regulation. Attitudes toward violence, sexuality, bodily functions, and emotions gradually changed. In the centuries that followed the Middle Ages people exerted stronger pressures on each other, implying self-restraint and a more stable, balanced, and differentiated self-regulation. Aspects of human behavior, especially those associated with bodily functions, such as sleeping or eating, became strictly regulated and were regarded as distasteful. Consequently they were removed to the back stage of social life. Confrontations with people whose manners were less formal produced feelings of embarrassment and discomfort.

Elias related the changes in people's behavioral and emotional standards to expanding social constraints and to the processes of state formation and growing interdependency. He perceived a connection between the level of control of natural and social phenomena at a given moment and the amount of affect and fantasy in a society's thinking. The greater the affective involvement of people, the less their ability to understand and control their world. In his comprehensive study *La peur en occident* (1978) Jean Delumeau also dealt with changes in the relationships among living conditions, the need for security, and sentiments of fear in the "Christianized" Western world between the fourteenth century and the eighteenth century. Elias drew important connections between social and psychological processes. Subsequently developments in different kinds of emotion management have become a major topic of study. Although family life may be seen as the main site for the transmission of the habitus that characterizes a society, feelings between people who are intimate are only one of the many research subjects in this tradition. A variety of other emotions, ranging from changing feelings of solidarity with and compassion for the poor and sick to changing feelings of discomfort with outsiders, also have received attention.

The following paragraphs picture changes in emotion management and deal with various theoretical approaches and controversies. The focus lies on the emotionalizing of family relations, emphasizing love relations and maternal or parental feelings. The central, recurrent theme refers to the most important phenomena in the history of emotions in western Europe, the gradual separation of nuclear families from the wider community and from extended kinship ties; the withdrawal of families from the outside world, including servants; and the individuation of persons with respect to the nuclear family. This extension and differentiation of social networks is related to changes manifested in emotional attitudes toward events, such as birth, death, and marriage, and to shifts in emo-

tional involvement and in feelings of identification and loyalty to the family, the community, and the nation.

This article examines the distribution of emotions and emotional standards and their spread among sexes, social strata, religions, cities, and the countryside by imitation and through disciplining and regulating measures. It also sheds some light on differences in emotion regimes in various regions of Europe.

THE EMOTIONALIZING OF RELATIONS BETWEEN MEN AND WOMEN

The view that romantic love and maternal sentiment are part of modernity is strongly contested by some social historians. They do not observe the emergence of a new emotional style and relativize differences from the past, arguing that relationships between betrothed couples and spouses and between parents and children have always possessed an affectionate character.

As to feelings between men and women, it is difficult to maintain that passionate love is a recent phenomenon found exclusively in the modern period. Sentiments of love have a differentiated and versatile history. Raging love and lovesickness, erotomania, have a long tradition that go back to antiquity (Lepenies, 1969; Wack, 1990). People suffering from these passions were obsessed with the loved object, and in that respect their feelings relate to more modern notions of courtly love and romantic love, which initially were the prerogative of a small, elite circle. In *The Court Society* (1969) Elias considered the development of romantic love relations in France, both reality and ideal, characteristic of the Renaissance. During this period behavior came to be governed less by spontaneous, immediate impulses and more by deliberation and contemplation. Accepted manners became stricter and behavioral codes more regulated. Distance increased between feelings and reason, while at the same time a space arose in which personal and intimate passions could flourish.

Elias observed, first among the courtly elite, a transition from relatively simple and undifferentiated sentiments toward complicated, subtle feelings between men and women. New demands on emotion management for women and even for physically strong men first were formalized into codes of manners and later became unwritten laws requiring self-control. Men and women became more reserved toward each other in matters of sexuality, while their thresholds of shame and embarrassment increased. The growing distance between the sexes manifested itself in the concealment of sexual activity, both in social interac-

Lovesickness. *The Lovesick Woman,* painting by Jan Steen
(c. 1626–1679). BAYERISCHE STAATSGEMÄLDEGALERIE,
MUNICH

tions and in consciousness. Idealizing and refraining
from the loved object and seeking satisfaction in personal melancholy were ingredients of the sentimental
complex of romantic love. Elias considered these alterations in emotion regimes as the symbolic expression of changes in the distribution of power, status,
and respect in the seventeenth-century French court.
The aristocratic circles were especially affected by the
restraints that accompanied centralization of power in
seventeenth-century France.

In a certain sense Mary Wack's observations
concur with Elias's views. She demonstrated in *Lovesickness in the Middle Ages* (1990) that the person suffering from erotic preoccupation was typically a man
of noble birth. His lovesickness resolved the psychological and social tensions facing aristocratic males.
Lovesickness enabled aristocrats to control their own
erotic vulnerability, regarded as feminine, in a rational,
masculine way.

Women in love relations were initially restricted
to the role of the object of desire, but their positions
changed during the Renaissance, when medical writers depicted them as victims of love. Lovesickness, associated with "female disorders," such as chlorosis,
hysteria, and nymphomania, became connected to pathology of the sexual organs. The doctor's visit to the
languishing young woman was a frequent theme in

seventeenth-century Dutch genre painting. Wack attributed this shift in the position of women during
the early modern period to the surplus of young, marriageable women, who confronted a shortage of eligible men. For these women lovesickness was a strategy for finding sexual and romantic fulfillment. Once
the doctor had diagnosed unsatisfied love and discovered the object of this love, the girl's parents could
arrange a marriage and a happy ending.

These studies by Elias and Wack use both a cultural anthropological and a sociological approach to
earlier societies. They try to understand and to reconstruct feelings of love and lovesickness by accounting
for how people perceived the phenomenon of love in
the past and by interpreting it in a historical social
context. They clarify that affective relations between
men and women are part of broader social constella-
tions and that later concepts of romantic love, despite
some similarities, must be separated from courtly passions, which had nothing to do with marriage.

The classic studies of the rise of familial feelings,
including Edward Shorter, *The Making of the Modern
Family* (1975), Jean-Louis Flandrin, *Familles: Parenté,
maison, sexualité dans l'ancienne société* (1976), and
Lawrence Stone, *The Family, Sex, and Marriage in England 1500–1800* (1977), regard romantic love as an
important aspect of the modernization of the familial
emotional culture. They observe during the eighteenth century the replacement of familial and community considerations by romantic sentiments and a
striving for personal happiness. Courtship became a
private affair, in which people did not wish to be restrained by communities, parents, peers, or neighbors.
This privatization reordered priorities in partner selection, which became more personal. People followed
their own inclinations, often at some geographical distance from their home communities. Spontaneity and
empathy rose in importance, and customs and tradition fell to secondary positions. Endogamy declined
along village lines, occupational lines, and class and
status lines, while the ages of partners increasingly approached equality.

Shorter, Stone, and Flandrin located the beginnings of the romantic revolution with different social
strata and interpreted its origin in different ways.
Shorter situated its birth at the same time that affective sexuality was linked to romance, and he saw the
lower classes, who were in the eighteenth century the
first to be caught up in the market economy, as the
vanguard of the sexual revolution. For these new proletarians, capitalist work generated an escape from traditional controls and a wish to be free. Stone located
the rise of "affective individualism" with the key
middle and upper sectors of English society and sit-

uated its establishment half-way through the eighteenth century. The emerging, wealthy entrepreneurial bourgeoisie was especially receptive to the values of personal affections because their way of life was oriented to personal achievement, thrift, and hard work. From the late seventeenth century on their ideas about domesticity, marital affection, and the education of their children spread to other segments of the English elite.

Personal autonomy and romantic love interwove first for young lovers. But love was difficult to reconcile with the social obligations of establishing a household. Feelings of love during courtship were considered a prelude to marriage but a danger during marriage. Thus the transformation of courtship preceded a larger transformation of married life. Men and women defined their marriage relationships not so much in terms of intimacy as in terms of cooperation and mutual sharing (Gillis, 1985). Marrying was a good strategy to guarantee a certain level of prosperity or, for the rich, to preserve the family capital.

Feelings between husbands and wives became less dependent on economic considerations earlier for the higher social classes, while the lower social classes had to wait until the rise of the welfare state. As that happened romantic sentiments more easily spilled over into marriage. It is characteristic for this type of conjugal ideal that love, marriage, and sex are strongly interwoven. The self-evidence of this tripartite unity came to be challenged during the sexual revolution of the 1960s. With the possibility of sex for the sake of sex, men and women who were infatuated slept together, even without considering marriage. By the end of the twentieth century couples chose to live apart, to live together, or to marry. A tension arose between sexual desire and the longing for enduring intimacy (Wouters, 1998).

For couples rich, poor, urban, and rural, in all their variety, ideals of intimacy and love took on importance at every stage of their relationships. Though love was judged a necessary foundation for lasting relations between men and women, the tension between feelings of love during courtship and the reality of running a home and living together did not vanish completely. Consequently Gillis termed the romantic marriage "ideal," often unable to live up to everyday reality and the myth of conjugal love. The myth persists and although most people are aware of its idealized nature, they still behave as if it were viable. The imbalance between feelings of romantic love and worries about everyday life has had a somewhat gendered nature. Although decreasingly in the twenty-first century, young girls remain preoccupied with love. They idealize men, they fall in love more often than boys,

and they have fantasies about dream lovers. These fantasies of heterosexual intimacy have rarely come true (Gillis, 1985), but girls and women expect more empathy and understanding from their lovers and spouses than do men. Women value emotional marriage ideals more than men and show a greater need, willingness, and ability to talk with their partners and to discuss their emotions and relationships. Also they are sooner disappointed and dissatisfied, although men and women both strive for affectionate companionship and shared lifestyles and both have high expectations of each other. People widely hold that once love and infatuation dwindle, the only legitimate reason for staying together has disappeared.

As the supervision of community and family diminished and men and women increasingly regulated their own relationships, their behavior and feelings were subjected to codes and formal emotional standards. But during the twentieth century these standards steadily relaxed, becoming varied and subtle. This trend toward informality may be explained by greater equality in the balance of power between the sexes and by the emancipation of women. For men this process implied increased self-discipline and em-

The Happy Household. *La paix du ménage* (The happy household), engraving by Jean-Michel Moreau le jeune and Pierre-Charles Ingouf, after Jean-Baptiste Greuze. 1766–1767. THE METROPOLITAN MUSEUM OF ART, HARRIS BRISBANE DICK FUND, 1953 (53.600.217)

pathy, while women gained more latitude and greater opportunities. In that sense the distance between women and men decreased. The demands of lovers and partners, male and female, with respect to intimate and sexual relations were heightened. Sincere emotions and authenticity gained importance, while formal manners lost their absolute and discriminatory character. Emotional management came to depend on the situation, and people were expected to assess and understand empathetically which emotional standards were appropriate (Wouters, 1995).

THE EMOTIONALIZING OF RELATIONS BETWEEN PARENTS AND CHILDREN

The historiography of parental attitudes and emotions has been strongly influenced by the work of the French demographic historian Philippe Ariès. *Centuries of Childhood* (1960), a study of changes in manners and feelings of parents and children, reviews the long period of the ancien régime and is based on pictorial representations of family life and a diversity of texts.

Among Ariès's important observations is that the position of infants and small children and the attitude of adults toward children in medieval society were profoundly different from those of twentieth-century society. The idea of childhood as a life stage and the awareness of the particular nature of children did not exist. During the twelfth century children were depicted as adults reduced to a smaller scale with adult expressions and features. As soon as children could walk, talk, and do without constant supervision, they became part of the adult world and participated in adult activities. They did not wear special clothes and did not possess games or toys. At about the age of ten poor children were expected to leave home to work as servants in other households. For them quitting the state of dependence on their parents also meant leaving childhood. The French language made no distinction between children and adolescents. The word *enfant* (child) referred to both categories.

Ariès observed that the pictorial representations of children indicate a gradual transformation in the thirteenth, fourteenth, and fifteenth centuries. The affectionate and naive aspects of the appearance and behavior of children, their special charms, were brought to the fore, first in the religious iconography of childhood and later, during the fifteenth and sixteenth centuries, in the lay iconography as well. The first representations of dead children in the sixteenth century were made on their parents' tombs beside their mothers, but in the seventeenth century the children were

represented by and for themselves. These later portraits indicate that children were increasingly seen as beings with souls of their own.

A growing sensibility appeared among parents, evidenced by their pleasure with the amusing charm and frolicsome behavior of their small children. They expressed their new emotional appreciation of childhood by coddling and playing, yet at the same time they were afraid that too much tenderness could spoil children. Instead of being entranced by the winsomeness of their children, parents should act like educators. For children to mix with adults too much could be harmful to their fragile natures, while too much coddling, though much enjoyed by the parents, was also a risk. Taking the specific nature of each child as the starting point, parents should correct the conduct of their offspring. Accompanying these new ideas, the process of growing from childhood to adulthood became a lengthier one.

Seen from the theoretical framework of Elias, changes in the emotion management of adults are linked with those of children. The differentiation of childhood and changes in the relationship between children and adults suggest a growing distance between adulthood and childhood in their patterns of emotion regulation. Growing up took a longer time because children had to learn more before they could behave as adults. The emotional involvement on the part of parents expanded, while the emotional distance from their children decreased. Both parents and children had to acquire greater self-control and emotion management.

Comparing the medieval ideas and feelings of parents about their offspring with this new parental sensitivity, Ariès observed that the former adult attitude may be considered insensitive or indifferent. But he warned explicitly against confusing this restraint with a lack of affection. Infant mortality was high, and a certain reserve provided a modus vivendi for overcoming grief at the death of a child. Their vulnerability and low chance of survival converted children into anonymous beings waiting for adulthood.

Ariès's work was continued by various social historians and sociologists who emphasized the transformation of parental feelings. While Ariès described the discovery of childhood and its consequences for feelings and manners in a reserved and cautious way, his followers made more radical statements. The classic example is Shorter's *The Making of the Modern Family.* In dealing with the upsurge of parental sentiments, Shorter primarily was concerned with the relation between mothers and infants. Seeing indifference as the traditional attitude of mothers toward their babies and small children, he elaborated this thesis by analyzing

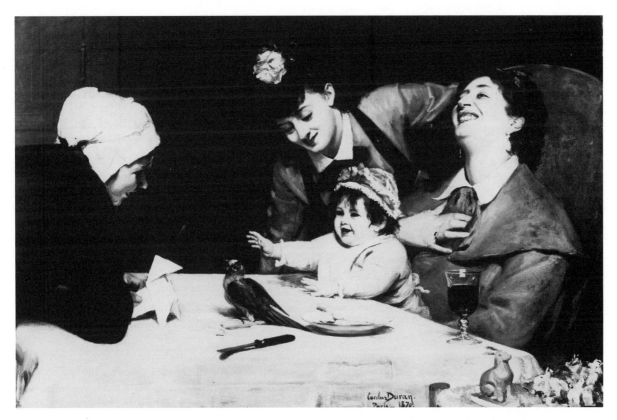

Frolicsome Behavior of Small Children. *Merrymakers (Laughing Women),* painting (1870) by C.-É.-A. Durand, called Carolus-Duran (1837–1917) FOUNDERS SOCIETY PURCHASE, ROBERT H. TANNAHILL FOUNDATION FUND, DETROIT INSTITUTE OF ARTS 1988

eighteenth-century practices like abandoning illegitimate infants, swaddling babies, and sending babies to paid wet nurses, an old custom among the aristocracy that during the seventeenth century trickled down to lower social strata. He considered these practices deliberate, cruel actions in all social classes and an indication of the absence of maternal feelings. He did not observe any signs of mothers coddling and playing with their babies and suggested that mothers accepted even the death of a baby with placid equanimity. Women whose earnings could cover the wet nurse's wages or whose husbands could afford the costs boarded out their children in large numbers; poor women took in nurslings.

Factory workers were the only group that never boarded out their infants or took in nurslings. Shorter saw them as "the spearhead of modernization" in the development of romantic feelings also. He demonstrated that it is impossible to generalize for the whole of France let alone Europe because of vast differences in scale and the pace of change in maternal feelings among social classes, regions, country folk, and urbanites. In general the persistence of traditional in-

difference lasted longer in the heart of the countryside and among the lower classes. Within Europe, France was an anomaly in the number of children sent away from home to live with a wet nurse. In England the custom of swaddling was abolished before the start of the nineteenth century, while the modernization of maternal feelings developed slowly in central Europe (admittedly a broad category). In the Netherlands swaddling never was common, and even wet nurses who came to feed a baby at his or her home were rare (Shorter, 1975; Clerkx, 1985).

For Shorter, Elisabeth Badinter, Stone, and Lloyd deMause this absence of maternal affection caused maternal uninvolvement and poor child care. They regarded maternal feelings as an independent variable. Maternal indifference, common in France and England before the eighteenth century, continued in some circles and in isolated regions well into the nineteenth century, and these scholars held that indifference responsible for the high infant mortality. It seems possible that the rise in maternal emotional involvement and the concomitant increased attention to their offspring may result in a decrease of the rate of infant mortality. This stretches Ariès's argument that parents could not permit themselves to become attached to a child whose risk of dying was so high (Ariès, 1960).

These interpretations of apparently affectionless familial attitudes, particularly the more radical versions, have evoked violent discussion. Historians such as Alan Macfarlane and Linda Pollock have argued the opposite view, claiming that emotional relations have changed little over the centuries and playing down generalizations about dramatic transformations. Macfarlane elaborated this thesis with respect to relations between men and women, while Pollock did the same for parental care and child life from the sixteenth century to the nineteenth century.

The lack of consensus about long-term changes in familial emotions reflects the personal and emotional involvement of the researchers. Scholars accused each other of sloppiness, for example, in selectively reading and quoting their sources without an eye for inconsistencies or for data that did not fit their interpretations. They even claimed willful misinterpretation in "the other camp." Both perspectives have been strongly influenced by the family standards common in twentieth-century Western societies. The emotional involvement of scholars has prevented them from doing justice to the perspectives and perceptions of mothers and from making interpretations in the social context of the times.

Ariès's work was innovative in more than one respect. He wrote his book in a period when the nuclear family was blossoming and booming in the West, when family life centered around children, and when many people considered that living together in strictly private nuclear families was the normal and established way. Ariès, however, demonstrated that attitudes toward childhood are specific to societies at certain moments in time. Age differentiation and the lengthening of the phase called "childhood and youth" should be seen as modern phenomena. Child care and parental feelings also have their own histories. In the 1960s and 1970s Ariès's ideas and even more so the work of the historians who followed him did not, in a sense, fit the current, emotional family ideal. As material security increased, sociologists pointed to the decline of the economic and material functions of the family and situated its major importance in its affectionate functions. Family historians focused on the affective and to a lesser extent on the cognitive aspects of human dependencies and on the relativation of the importance of economic and political aspects of social life. In this respect their perspective has been similar to that of family sociologists. The observation that familial emotions in the past were less affectionate than in the twentieth century was all the more disturbing and surprising.

NETWORKS EXPAND, FEELINGS OF LOYALTY BROADEN, AND REGULATION OF THE EMOTIONS ALTERS

The increasing importance of the conjugal family as a social group has produced important changes in emotional involvement. In the sixteenth century feelings of loyalty were directed to family members, to neighbors in the local community, to mostly homosocial peer groups, and to people of the same religion. Scarcely any sections of the population entertained the notion of an independent nuclear family. The family life of the merchant and ruling classes was embedded in extended families and that of peasants and artisans in the small communities. In the modern period the networks in which people lived gradually expanded, while the family relations of both the rich and the poor moved in the direction of differentiation of the conjugal family as a discrete, private, and revered social unit. Domesticity became an ideal and gradually separated from the interference and concern of family and community. Identifications and feelings of loyalty broadened, while at the same time the emotional attachments between members of the nuclear family became stronger (Ariès and Duby, 1985–1987; De Swaan, 1995).

These processes of inclusion and exclusion embraced a more general process of change within a broad range of intimate and physical human behaviors and mentalities. Family members lived more on their own, and their emotional attachments became strengthened. The consolidation of affectionate bonds between mothers and infants in Shorter's view has crystallized this process of privatization and seclusion of the nuclear family. He drew a correlation between changes in the emotional attitude toward birth and changes in the significance of the community at this event.

Dutch seventeenth- and eighteenth-century genre pictures of *kraamkamers,* rooms specially furnished and decorated for the lying-in period, may be relatively early expressions of this connection. Events in the *kraamkamer* just after birth were a popular theme of Dutch genre artists, some of whom, such as Cornelis Troost, painted a series on this subject. The large number of paintings makes possible a comparison of fifty *kraamkamers* from the beginning of the seventeenth century through the eighteenth century. The most important change in these pictures is increased intimacy and privacy indicated by, among other things, the number of people present. The older illustrations depict crowds of visitors eating, drinking, and making merry. The spaces are relatively open, and windows and doors provide views of the world outside the room or even outside the house. The later pictures, including Troost's, show an intimate circle around mother and infant of at the most five people with no view of the world outside.

The small family scenes and the way they are represented reveal the relatively early private and emotional relations of nuclear families among certain elite circles in the Dutch Republic. Foreign visitors reported that Dutch family life was characterized by a strong attachment to hearth and home and by a close family orientation, especially among burghers, well-to-do citizens such as merchants or patricians (Van Daalen, 1993).

An upsurge of romantic love during courtship and new definitions of love accompanied the nuclear, domesticated family life. The changes in marriage patterns were similar to the privatization of the *kraamkamers*. In the seventeenth century a new couple had to submit to public rites of passage, while betrothal in later times licensed withdrawal from the peer group, which guaranteed some privacy. Traditional marriages were public happenings, creating a new social order where roles were well defined, rituals were firmly established, and feelings were kept well under control. In the course of the seventeenth and eighteenth centuries love became associated with intimacy and was defined as an inner feeling. The new notions of love required new expressions. Verbal utterances replaced traditional customs and ritual practices, and the public rites of betrothal were replaced by the private engagement, witnessed only by the immediate family. These transformations occurred first among the educated elites from the mid-eighteenth century onwards. Smallholders and artisans continued the traditional practices and the old definitions of love well into the nineteenth century. Indeed elements of this constellation still existed in the working-class cultures of industrialized Western countries in the twentieth century (Gillis, 1985).

Such changes in dependency relations and in emotion management may be seen as aspects of the disintegration of preindustrial, small-scale community life and as part of the expanding networks in which people participated and in which their identities were molded. Among these aspects was a growing gap between elite groups and the common people or between a "high" culture and a "low" culture. Pagan feasts and charivaris were condemned along with frightening phenomena like witchcraft and all kinds of blasphemy. The mad and the poor were seen as a public danger and were labeled sluggards, heretics, and disease carriers who should be confined to workhouses. From the sixteenth century on, during the religious reformations, Protestant, Catholic, and civil authorities together increased their efforts to acculturate and normalize deviant people within a Christian moral order. This moral order had a reassuring effect and diminished feelings of fear (Delumeau, 1978).

During nineteenth century state expansion, nation building, and industrialization people became integrated within the framework of the nation-state. The relevance of this frame of reference for intimate relations and emotion management increased with the expansion of collective welfare arrangements, beginning in the swiftly growing cities of the nineteenth century. Large numbers of newcomers seized the new opportunities of the industrializing cities. Local facilities were no longer fit to deal with the urban situations, and municipal institutions tried hard to adapt. People manifested an increasing sensitivity to one another and connected the inconvenience of stench and dirt with fears about infectious diseases and anxieties about "social contamination." Feelings of disgust mingled with concerns about the domestication of bodily functions, public hygiene, and morality. Citizens and municipal institutions demarcated rooms for different functions, separated and cloaked houses from the outside world, and ascribed specific functions to different urban areas. These actions protected domesticity and family life while spatially segregating different classes (Corbin, 1982; Gleichmann, 1977; Van Daalen, 1988). The annoyance and offense of crowds of people intertwined with changes in patterns of stratification. In those nineteenth-century cities physical and social mysophobia should be seen as signs of social and status insecurities.

In the twentieth century the development of the welfare state made poverty less threatening with improved material conditions and institutionalized social security. Thus the vagaries of fate were tempered, which implies a change for the better, especially for the lower social strata. The lower classes gained the possibilities of emancipation and changes in affect control and behavioral codes, which in previous periods had been the standard among the aristocracy and the bourgeoisie. Increased social security in this respect may be considered as a condition of change in emotion management throughout society. But in other respects new forms of emotion management, such as the willingness among people from all social classes to save money, were necessary conditions for the collectivization of social security.

Processes of collectivization also have intentionally promoted affect control, especially among the

Obvious Emotion. *St.-Preux and Julie Embracing*, engraving proposed for Jean-Jacques Rousseau's *La nouvelle Héloïse* by Jean Michel Moreau the Younger (1741–1814). Rousseau rejected this illustration as being too explicit. PRIVATE COLLECTION/©COLLECTION VIOLLET/ THE BRIDGEMAN ART LIBRARY

lower classes. A broad range of professional groups emerged, each with its own discourse and its own emotional and behavioral codes. Their specialized knowledge and their accompanying professional attitudes were more and more taken over by laypeople. Individuals acquired a more deliberate, more calculating, and more detached attitude and approach to their bodies and emotions. Instead of following tradition, intuition, and first impulses, they tried to reflect on their conduct and emotions by looking for orientation among relevant professionals (Donzelot, 1979; De Swaan, 1988).

With regard to the education of their children, parents paid heed to advice from medical doctors, psy-

Emotion Restrained. Illustration for Rousseau's *La nouvelle Héloïse* (engraving) by H. F. B. Gravelot. Rousseau preferred Gravelot's illustration of restrained emotion to Michel Moreau's depiction of the lovers kissing. BIBLIOTHÈQUE NATIONALE, PARIS, EE 8D FOLIO RESERVE

chologists, and professional educators. They sought information about the different emotional stages of growing up and considered this insight necessary for a good, equality loving education. To a lesser extent a comparable process of professionalization accompanied the emotionalization of the relations between men and women. A broad range of experts offered advice and consultation.

Thus the control of emotions and the concealment of reactions are induced on the one hand by more security and on the other hand by professional, formal knowledge and insights. The transformation in emotional culture has occurred along with emotional restraint and a growing reluctance to display emotional intensity (Stearns, 1994). But at the same time it could be said that the growth of arrangements promoting material security established conditions for the increased importance of emotions in social relations. Styles of emotion management became more relevant as a criterion in the process of ranking and in the struggle for status and power (Wouters, 1992).

A comparable link may be seen between the degree of physical safety and material security in societies and the blossoming of sociological and historical interest in emotions and emotion management (Wouters, 1992). In Western societies a relatively high level of safety and security has promoted the study of emotions, especially in the 1970s and the 1980s. After that period the passionate wrangles waned somewhat, and the topic of emotions became a study in its own right. It is a field of research with evident blind spots, such as hate and other emotions that induce aggression and violence in a modern world.

See also other articles in this section.

BIBLIOGRAPHY

Anderson, Michael. *Approaches to the History of the Western Family, 1500–1914.* London, 1980.

Ariès, Philippe. *Centuries of Childhood: A Social History of Family Life.* Translated by Robert Baldick. New York, 1962. First published in 1960.

Ariès, Philippe, and Georges Duby, eds. *Histoire de la vie privée.* Paris, 1985–1987.

Badinter, Elisabeth. *L'amour en plus: Histoire de l'amour maternel, XVIIe–XXe siècle.* Paris, 1980.

Burguière, André, Christiane Klapisch-Zuber, Martine Segalen, and Françoise Zonabend, eds. *A History of the Family.* Vol. 2: *The Impact of Modernity.* Translated by Sarah Hanbury-Tenison, Rosemary Morris, and Andrew Wilson. Cambridge, Mass., 1996. Originally published in 1986.

Clerkx, Lily E. "Moederende minnen en minnende moeders: Elisabeth Badinter construeert een mythe." *Lover* 1 (1985): 3–11.

Corbin, Alain. *Le miasme et la jonquille: L'odorat et l'imaginaire social XVIIIe–XIXe siècles.* Paris, 1982.

Delumeau, Jean. *La peur en occident, XIVe–XVIIIe siècles.* Paris, 1978.

DeMause, Lloyd, ed. *The History of Childhood.* New York, 1974.

De Swaan, Abram. *In Care of the State: Health Care, Education, and Welfare in Europe and the USA in the Modern Era.* New York, 1988.

De Swaan, Abram. "Widening Circles of Social Identification: Emotional Concerns in Sociogenetic Perspective." *Theory, Culture, and Society* 12 (1995): 25–39.

Dekker, Rudolf. *Uit de schaduw in 't grote licht: Kinderen in egodocumenten van de Gouden Eeuw tot de Romantiek.* Amsterdam, 1995.

Donzelot, Jacques. *The Policing of Families.* Translated by Robert Hurley. New York, 1979. First published in 1977.

Elias, Norbert. *The Civilizing Process.* Translated by Edmund Jephcott. Oxford, 1982; 2000. Originally published in 1939.

Elias, Norbert. *The Court Society.* Translated by Edmund Jephcott. Oxford, 1983. First published in 1969.

Flandrin, Jean-Louis. *Families in Former Times: Kinship, Household, and Sexuality.* Translated by Richard Southern. Cambridge, U.K., 1979.

Gillis, John R. *For Better, For Worse: British Marriages, 1600 to the Present.* New York, 1985.

Gillis, John R. "From Ritual to Romance: Toward an Alternative History of Love." In *Emotion and Social Change: Toward a New Psychohistory.* Edited by Carol Z. Stearns and Peter N. Stearns. New York, 1988. Pages 87–123.

Gleichmann, Peter R. "Wandel der Wohnverhältnisse." In *Human Figurations: Essays for Norbert Elias.* Edited by Peter R. Gleichmann, Johan Goudsblom, and Hermann Korte. Amsterdam, 1977. Pages 259–270.

Lepenies, Wolf. *Melancholie and Gesellschaft.* Frankfurt am Main, 1969.

Macfarlane, Alan. *Marriage and Love in England: Modes of Reproduction, 1300–1840.* Oxford, 1986.

Pollock, Linda A. *Forgotten Children: Parent-Child Relations from 1500 to 1900.* Cambridge, U.K., 1983.

Shorter, Edward. *The Making of the Modern Family.* New York, 1975.

Stearns, Peter N. *American Cool: Constructing a Twentieth-Century Emotional Style.* New York, 1994.

Stearns, Peter N., and Carol Z. Stearns. "Emotionology: Clarifying the History of Emotions and Emotional Standards." *American Historical Review* 90 (1985): 813–836.

Stone, Lawrence. *The Family, Sex, and Marriage in England 1500–1800.* London, 1977.

Van Daalen, Rineke. "Family Change and Continuity in the Netherlands: Birth and Childbed in Text and Art." In *Succesful Home Birth: The Dutch Model.* Edited by Eva Abraham-Van der Mark. Westport, Conn., 1993. Pages 77–94.

Van Daalen, Rineke. "Public Complaints and Government Intervention: Letters to the Municipal Authorities of Amsterdam 1865–1920." *Netherlands' Journal of Sociology* 24 (1988): 83–98.

Wack, Mary Frances. *Lovesickness in the Middle Ages: The Viaticum and Its Commentaries.* Philadelphia, 1990.

Wouters, Cas. "Balancing Sex and Love since the 1960s Sexual Revolution." *Theory, Culture, and Society* 15 (1998): 187–214.

Wouters, Cas. "Etiquette Books and Emotion Management in the 20th Century: Part Two—The Integration of the Sexes." *Journal of Social History* 29 (1995): 325–339.

Wouters, Cas. "On Status Competition and Emotion Management: The Study of Emotions as a New Field." *Journal of Social History* 24 (1991): 699–717.

ANTHROPOMETRY

John Komlos and Robert Whaples

Anthropometric history is based on the analysis of the physical characteristics of human beings, especially height, weight, and the body mass index. Beginning in the late 1970s, researchers analyzed such data from historical populations, and their findings have reshaped our understanding of social and economic history in fundamental ways.

The systematic study of the physical characteristics of human beings reaches back well into the eighteenth century. By the 1830s both Adolphe Quételet and L. R. Villermé recognized that biological outcomes were influenced by both the natural and the socioeconomic environment—that innate differences in potential height did not account by themselves for the geographic, social, and temporal differences in physical stature. However, until French historians of the *Annales* tradition began to explore the socioeconomic correlates of human height in the 1960s, the topic interested primarily scholars of nonhistorical disciplines. The explosion of research in the field of anthropometric history has been sparked by cliometricians—economic historians who explicitly link economic models with measurement and statistical techniques. This new field of "anthropometric history" has primarily used human biological measures as complements to (and sometimes substitutes for) conventional indicators of well-being and has also begun to investigate their social consequences.

SOCIOECONOMIC INFLUENCES ON HEIGHT

The relationship between the height of a population and its social and economic structure is based on the biological principle that human growth is related to nutritional status—nutrition intake minus such claims on nutrition as body maintenance, work, and disease encounters. Calories and protein consumption not used for these other purposes during childhood and adolescence are available to enable the human organism to grow. These proximate determinants of stature are themselves determined by socioeconomic factors (figure 1). Since the body's ability to process nutrients is influenced by its disease encounters, the epidemiological environment, hygiene practices, population density, and government policy all have played an important role in determining anthropometric outcomes. The work environment and effort expended prior to reaching adulthood also matter. We now know with certainty that historically the physical stature of a population or subpopulation depended generally on such socioeconomic factors as the level, variability, and distribution of real income, as well as on the relative price and availability of nutrients, particularly of dairy products and other animal proteins. Urbanization and the degree of commercialization of the economy also had an impact on the human growth process, as have, beginning in the late 1800s, such factors as government expenditures on public health and sanitation and the level of educational attainment. In sum, because humans cease to grow after a certain age, the height of a population cohort is a historical record of the nutritional intake in conjunction with environmental factors during the cohort's childhood and youth.

The relationship between nutritional intake and physical growth has been established beyond doubt by medical and biological experimental research, with maternal nutrition also playing a significant role. Genes are important determinants of individuals' heights, but genetic differences approximately cancel in comparisons of averages across most large groups and nations; so in these situations average heights accurately reflect net nutrition.

MEASURES OF WELL-BEING

There are many reasons for integrating human biology into mainstream social and economic history. These include the limitations of using a single measure, such as gross domestic product (GDP) or income per capita, as a proxy for overall welfare, as well as the diffi-

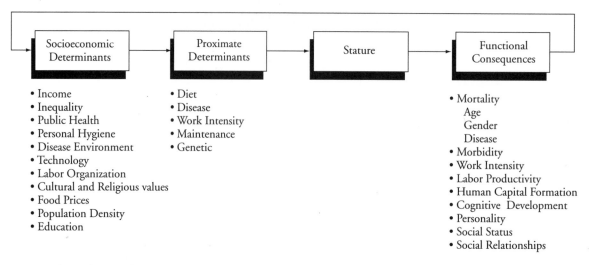

Figure 1. Relationships involving stature. Adapted from Richard Steckel, "Stature and the Standard of Living," *Journal of Economic Literature* 33 (1995), fig. 1. USED BY PERMISSION OF THE AMERICAN ECONOMIC ASSOCIATION

culties associated with deriving income data in historical populations. Human well-being involves such a complicated set of issues that a wide array of concepts and measures is needed to understand it adequately. The best measures of human well-being should meet several criteria: they should have a sound theoretical basis linking them to well-being, they should be concise and easy to understand, and they should be so widely used that new measurements can be easily compared with well-known benchmarks.

Real GDP per capita has been the most widely used measure of the standard of living because it fulfills these criteria: GDP provides a way to aggregate diverse goods produced by the economy using prices (which reflect marginal benefits) as weights; most economic models show that well-being should increase with rising income per capita; and GDP per capita is immediately understood and widely used. However, GDP per capita has many well-known shortcomings as a proxy for welfare. It does not include the value of leisure and other nonmarket activities, does not consider the impact of pollution and other environmental externalities, makes no attempt to encompass distributional concerns, and is plagued by problems of correctly adjusting for inflation and spatial price differences. In addition, income measures are not available for subpopulations in a historical context, including women, children, aristocrats, and slaves, and its distribution within the household is by no means clear.

Biological measures have emerged as an additional tool that meets the above-mentioned criteria. Sometimes called the biological standard of living (as opposed to GDP per capita's material standard of living), height indexes measure how well the human organism itself thrives in its socioeconomic and epidemiological environment and capture the biologically relevant component of welfare. In distinction to other, more direct measures of health, such as longevity and morbidity, average physical stature is relatively easy to compute for many historical populations, and it can be quickly compared to modern distributions. Health measures emphasize that the human experience ought not to be thought of in one dimension: well-being encompasses more than the command over goods and services. Health in general contributes to welfare, independent of income. Stature picks up some of the factors left out by simple income measures, such as work intensity and opportunities to rest, environmental concerns, and even the distribution of resources. Height is also an important determinant of life expectancy.

To be sure, height indexes have their own set of limitations, including the facts that their relevance is confined to the first two decades of life, they cannot easily measure improvements in well-being beyond a certain threshold, and they abstract from the consumption of a wide range of goods and services that people value enough to trade against nutritional status. Both income and stature are correlated with, but distinct from, two of the measures of well-being that are incorporated into the United Nations' Human Development Index (HDI)—education and longevity—as well as such intangibles as freedom, empowerment, capabilities, and spiritual well-being. Hence, neither height nor income is a perfect measure of welfare. Such a measure does not exist. Instead, historians have used these measures in tandem with one another so as better to understand the past. While the two measures are often closely correlated with each other, the exceptions to the rule provide rare insights for our understanding of historical processes.

APPLICATIONS OF ANTHROPOMETRY

Anthropometric measures emerged in the late 1970s, when the primary concerns of economic historians were to extend the existing indexes of living standards backward in time, to illuminate the famous debate about the living conditions of workers during the industrial revolution, and to provide indexes where none existed before. For instance, conventional measures of money income obviously did not exist for American slaves, whose well-being was at the center of a major historical controversy surrounding the publication of Robert Fogel and Stanley Engerman's *Time on the Cross* in 1974. Richard Steckel, a student of Fogel, subsequently explored slaves' physical stature records obtained from slave shipping documents (manifests). His findings turned out to be quite astounding—adult slaves were relatively tall by contemporary standards. In fact, they were taller than most Europeans, and about as tall as American urban workers. Perhaps even more surprising was the finding that despite their heavy work regimen, on American soil slaves actually grew to be taller than the African populations from whence they originated. To be sure, the latter comparison reflects not only the food allotments they received but also the propitious disease environment and resource endowment of the American South.

This was a major finding, and even though subsequent research revealed that slave children were grossly (and perhaps systematically) undernourished, it unleashed a veritable avalanche of research on anthropometric history. Soon thereafter, a large number of new archival sources were explored, including military, criminal, insurance, hospital, and school records, voter registration cards, servant contracts, newspaper advertisements, certificates of freedom, anthropologists' field observations, and even skeletal remains. Anthropometricians have also examined data on birth weight, the body mass index (BMI)—which measures weight divided by height squared (kg/m²)—and various body dimensions such as percent body fat and waist-to-hip ratio. With some half a million observations studied so far, anthropometricians have merely scraped the tip of an iceberg. An impressive array of statistical techniques have been developed to deal with the biases of particular data sets—such as military minimum height requirements—to calculate group means and distributions. Fortunately, the normality of height distributions facilitates this task.

In addition to slaves, there were a number of other subpopulations, such as subsistence peasants, aristocrats, children, and housewives, who were not integrated into the labor market and for whom, therefore, conventional indexes of living standards, such as daily wages, did not exist. The problem of data scarcity also applies to societies in which statistics are inaccurate. This pertains to some degree to most economies prior to the mid-nineteenth century but also to such twentieth-century dictatorial regimes as the Soviet Union or Maoist China. For instance, during Stalin's reign, in spite of the extensive propaganda announcing economic progress, the average height of military recruits increased by only 1.1 centimeters, whereas in the United States the advance was fully twice as large and was even greater in Western Europe. The problem of data representativeness applies also to societies in which the informal sector is a substantial share of the economy but is not part of the official records. In Soweto, for example, anthropometric measures have provided the only reliable information on the well-being of children.

Another important line of research recognizes the significance of physiological development on the course of economic development itself. Drawing on the modern positive relationship between body mass index and mortality, Fogel argues that over half the decline in European mortality that has occurred during the last three centuries was the result of economic and nutritional factors that were associated with increases in body size. John Murray's research shows that the modern relationship between BMI and mortality risk is very similar to that which prevailed in the 1800s, thus supporting Fogel's argument. This implies a positive feedback mechanism: better economic conditions cause greater stature, which makes people healthier and more productive, which in turn strengthens economic growth. The twentieth-century trend in body size also has important implications for future mortality trends and policies regarding aging.

The insights gained thus far from the anthropometric research program have been substantial, and the methodology is widely regarded as one of the most important recent developments in the field of economic history.

LEVELS AND TRENDS IN AVERAGE HEIGHT

Heights have increased steadily in the developed and much of the developing world during the twentieth

TABLE 1
LONG-TERM TRENDS IN THE STATURE OF ADULT MEN (IN CENTIMETERS)

Birth-Decade	U.S.	U.K.	Sweden	Norway	Netherlands	France	Austria	Germany
1750	172	167	167	165	n.a.		165	
1800	173	166	167	166	166	164	163	
1850	170	165	168	169	165	165		163
1900	171	169	173	171	170	167		169
1950	177	174	178	178	178	172	171	176
1970	178		184		185			183

Sources: Nicholas and Steckel (1991); Sandberg and Steckel (1987); Steckel and Floud (1997); Steckel (1995); Komlos (1999); Komlos (1989); Baten (1999).

century. However, this trend ought not be projected backward in time. Prior epochs were characterized by long country-specific fluctuations in physical stature. In western Europe before the twentieth century, adult male heights generally varied between 165 and 170 centimeters, and decadal movements often corresponded well with business cycles. As table 1 shows, Europeans were considerably shorter than their American cousins during the eighteenth and nineteenth centuries. However, by the late twentieth century, the Dutch and Scandinavians were the tallest peoples in the world—between five and seven centimeters taller than Americans.

A significant episode of declining heights occurred in Europe during the late eighteenth century at the beginning of the industrial revolution. Average heights fell in the United Kingdom, Sweden, Austria, Hungary, and Bavaria beginning around the 1760s. Insofar as real wages fell consistently throughout much of that period, the decline in physical stature in the second half of the eighteenth century is not paradoxical (figure 2). The rapid demographic expansion in Europe, coupled with such exogenous factors as the deterioration in weather conditions, brought about diminishing returns to labor in agriculture, making it more difficult to maintain the nutritional status of the population. As long as the agricultural sector was dominant and trading opportunities limited, weather conditions had an obvious impact on nutritional status. Climate affected the length of the growing season and thereby the extent of the harvest. Jörg Baten has shown that physical stature in Bavaria correlated pos-

itively with tithes collected by landlords, and both were affected by mean temperatures. The output of pasture was also influenced by environmental conditions, in turn affecting milk production. Thus the increase in Bavarian heights of the 1730s was accompanied by an improvement in weather conditions, and both downturns in physical stature—in the late eighteenth century and in the 1830s and 1840s—were accompanied by adverse climatic conditions.

Several European countries, as well as the United States, experienced marked downturns in height during the 1830s and 1840s (figures 3 and 4). This pattern is more of an enigma because real wages were generally increasing as average heights fell during the period. These episodes of declining heights were often associated with the beginning of industrialization. Heights fell during the early industrial periods in Austria, Germany, Holland, the United Kingdom, and the United States. Later on in the century, similar downturns were experienced by the populations in Australia and Spain but, notably, not in Japan after the Meiji Restoration and the beginning of industrialization. The diminution in the biological standard of living in the United States was particularly surprising, since per capita output was increasing by some 40 percent per generation. Most spectacularly, average heights of males born in Britain around 1850 were about 2 to 3 centimeters shorter than the average for those born around 1820. Although Britain's industrialization had begun long before, this was the country's most rapid period of urbanization. On the other hand, the evidence on France is as yet inconclusive.

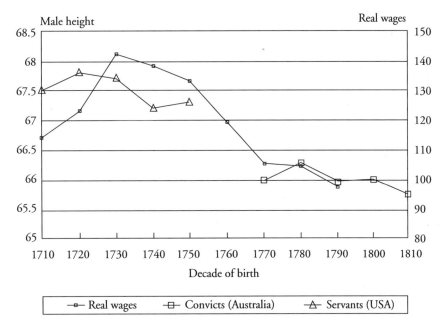

Figure 2. Wages and heights in England, 1710s–1810s.

While the height of military recruits increased slightly (by one centimeter) during the course of the first half of the nineteenth century, that of the students enrolled in the École Polytechnique seems to have diminished.

Richard Steckel and Roderick Floud argue that the timing of industrialization relative to the rise of the germ theory of disease along with public health measures, the extent of urbanization, and diets are the keys to understanding the relationship between stature and industrialization. The germ theory of disease, which became widely accepted by the medical profession by the 1880s, and the subsequent diffusion of public health measures were effective in preventing infection. Exposure to pathogens worsened with industrialization by crowding people together both inside and outside the workplace. Arduous factory work may have been a drain on health. Migration, emigration, and interregional trade brought about by industrialization also increased the exposure of the population to pathogens—as evidenced by the diffusion of epidemics along trade routes. Thus industrialization and urbanization before the development of the germ theory and measures to combat the spread of disease often caused the population to pay a biological penalty, which could not be overcome by rising incomes. After the development of the germ theory, negative health consequences among later industrializers could be largely eliminated, allowing increasing heights. In addition, some early industrializers, such as France, might have been able to avert the urban penalty.

French military heights rose slightly during industrialization prior to germ theory. One reason may be that France's transition was eased by its declining fertility and slower urbanization.

Other explanations for falling heights stress additional economic forces unleashed by the onset of modern economic growth. Much evidence suggests that environmental factors, although their impact varied over time and across localities and they acted in combination with changes in the epidemiological environment, cannot completely explain the decline in health (and the biological standard of living)—that is, the trend in height remains negative even after accounting for changes in the disease environment. Critics of disease-based theories argue that if declines in heights during the 1800s were caused primarily by a deterioration in the disease environment, then one would expect that all segments of society would have been affected; diseases would not have discriminated by gender or by social status to such an extent. Hence, the fact that the physical stature of several groups, including German high-status students, American middle-class cadets, Harvard and Sandhurst students, and male slaves did not decrease at the outset of modern economic growth implies that an increased incidence of disease does not, by itself, explain the diminution in average height. After all, many of the upper- and middle-class youths were of urban origin and were surrounded by the same epidemiological environment as the common man. Moreover, heights increased in some places even as population density,

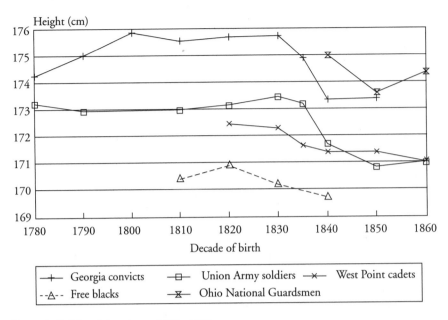

Figure 3. Height of Americans, 1780s–1860s.

urbanization, and commercialization—three important correlates of the ease with which diseases spread—also increased. This line of reasoning implies, therefore, that the decline in heights was caused primarily by a decrease in nutrient consumption and other forces spurred on by economic changes.

One such force unleashed by the onset of industrialization was the skewing of the income distribution in many places in favor of the upper-income groups. This had an adverse effect on average physical stature, inasmuch as the proportion of income spent on food declined as income rose, and the marginal contribution of nutrients to human growth diminished with increasing food intake. A shift in the distribution of income from the lower- to the upper-income stratum caused a decrease in the height of the offspring of the former group, while the height of the children of the upper classes improved by a smaller amount, thus pulling the overall average down.

Moreover, the relative price of nutrients increased considerably with industrialization, partly because technological change and capital accumulation in agriculture were slower than in industry, but also because of rapidly diminishing returns to labor in food production, particularly in Europe, in spite of the spread of the potato. In Britain, for instance, the price of food relative to textiles rose by 66 percent between 1770 and 1795. This induced a replacement of expensive calories and protein with cheaper carbohydrates, even among social groups whose income was increasing moderately. This shift happened partly because the transportation revolution was still in its infancy and methods of food preservation were primitive. Thus less milk, meat, fruits, and vegetables were available for the children and youth of the increasingly urbanized working-class households, despite the considerable advances that were being made in the industrial sector. Consequently, the composition of food intake shifted toward less protein-rich diets. Because the health implications of many consumption decisions were still unknown, some shifts in tastes, such as the increased popularity of white bread, also meant that diets were becoming less wholesome.

With the onset of industrialization, income probably became more variable for a substantial segment of society that had severed its ties to the land. Even if the reduction in food consumption brought about by such adverse developments was temporary, its stunting effect on children could be permanent.

Population growth contributed to the deterioration in nutritional status because of diminishing returns to labor in the agricultural sector in many parts of Europe, where the opportunities for expansion of arable land were quite limited. The increase in both relative and absolute bread prices throughout Europe at the end of the eighteenth century was a direct outgrowth of population expansion. Real wages declined, even in Britain, where agricultural improvements were more advanced than on the Continent.

Furthermore, industrialization and the increased division of labor in turn unleashed other processes, such as the integration of hitherto isolated regions

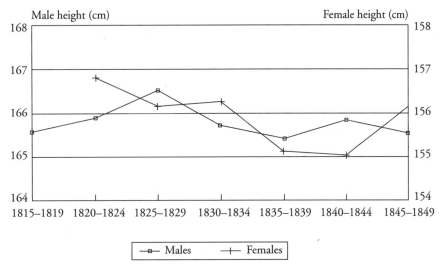

Figure 4. Heights of men and women in Bavaria, 1815–1849. From Jörg Baten, *Ernährung und wirtschaftliche Entwicklung in Bayern, 1730–1880* (Stuttgart, 1999).

into a larger world market, which magnified their impact on nutritional status. In the preindustrial world, remoteness from markets had a propitious impact on nutritional status—probably because almost all the output of the family plot or farm was consumed within the household or perhaps because isolation from the market also meant physical isolation and the more benign disease environment brought about by low population density. No exceptions have been found to the generalization that isolated regions had taller populations: it holds true throughout Europe, North America, and Japan. Yet, once integrated into a larger market, self-sufficient peasants with incomplete knowledge of the fundamentals of health production may have willingly or out of ignorance traded away nutrients essential to the health of their children, who became stunted (and less healthy) as a consequence. In sum, declines in physical stature were associated with economic and epidemiological processes and structural changes that often, but not always, accompanied the onset of modern economic growth.

Heights in the twentieth century were much less susceptible to cyclical fluctuations than in prior epochs, except during the world wars. Markets in food products became better integrated, so that local shortages were alleviated quickly. Child labor declined or was entirely eliminated, freeing up calories for the biological growth process. Because food consumption became a much smaller fraction of family income, it was possible to protect one's nutritional intake from the effects of short-term income fluctuations. The stock of savings increased, so that the reliance on current income was less absolute than before. As a conse-

quence, the impact on heights of even such a major downswing in economic activity as the Great Depression of the 1930s was hardly evident. In contrast, the downturn of the 1890s still had a noticeable impact on physical stature. In addition, government expenditures on welfare programs such as unemployment insurance increased, so that business cycles had a negligible impact on children's heights. For western Europeans the more equal distribution of income, and a social safety net that protects the lower classes from the adverse biological effects of poverty, may have tipped the biological standard of living in their favor relative to the United States. Hence political processes, too, had an effect on human biology through public expenditures on health, unemployment insurance, and welfare.

URBAN-RURAL AND REGIONAL DIFFERENCES

Town dwellers were invariably at a nutritional disadvantage in the preindustrial and early industrial world because they were farther from the source of food supply and, unlike the rural population, were not paying farm-gate prices for agricultural products. Instead, they paid for the costs of transporting food and for the services of the middlemen. Until the invention of refrigerated railroad cars and ships, transportation technology was not advanced enough to ship dairy products and fresh meat over long distances in sufficient quantities, and at low enough prices, to accommodate the biological needs of urban workers. A substantial urban health penalty has been found in widely separated early industrial cities studied such as London, Glasgow, Vienna, Charleston, Philadelphia, and Tokyo. For example, men born in Baltimore in the pre–Civil War era were 3.3 centimeters shorter, and women 1.5 centimeters shorter, than those born elsewhere in the state of Maryland.

The only exception to this generalization found so far is the case of Munich, whose inhabitants were not shorter than those living in the Bavarian countryside in the early nineteenth century. Munich was close enough to the Alps to be supplied with sufficient dairy products on a regular basis. Moreover, the presence of the king's court meant that a large segment of its population was composed of government employees whose income was exempt from cyclical variation. Most urban dwellers were not so lucky.

The above pattern also holds at the regional level: the populations of urbanized or industrialized regions such as New England, East Anglia, or Bohemia were shorter than those of agricultural regions. The accessibility to markets meant that farmers traded away nutrients, and therefore had shorter children, than those agricultural producers who were farther from markets. Prior to the transportation revolution, the availability of milk and meat at the local level had a positive independent effect on nutritional status. The higher income earned in early industrial regions generally did not suffice to offset the longer distances that these perishable products had to travel to reach the consumers.

The relationship between remoteness from markets and urbanization, on the one hand, and physical stature, on the other, changed completely with several social, political, and economic developments that began in the closing decades of the nineteenth century. The beginning of massive public investments into social overhead capital, such as sewer systems and waterworks, meant that a higher degree of cleanliness could develop. Due to these improvements in public health and sanitation, the human organism was less exposed to endemic and epidemic infections. The decline in the cost of long-distance ocean shipping brought the productivity of the American prairies within the reach of Europeans. The invention of refrigerated ships and railroad cars enabled perishable agricultural products and fresh meat to be shipped over longer distances. Then, in the twentieth century, an increase in the number of doctors and a revolution in medical technology made possible by the unprecedented affluence of the West had a major impact on health and biological well-being in the developed world. For all these reasons, by the turn of the twentieth century, urbanites tended to be taller than their rural counterparts, in vivid contrast to the preindustrial and early industrial periods. This is the case in contemporary China as well.

Finally, regional variation in the epidemiological environment had a major impact on height before the twentieth century. Several studies have found a negative correlation between regions' crude death rates, or the infant mortality rates, and adult stature. For instance, men were particularly short in the malaria-infested parts of Murcia (a province of Spain), as were slaves in the disease-ridden rice-producing areas of South Carolina. Hence, prior to the twentieth century, when malaria was brought under control, irrigated agriculture had a negative impact on physical stature. High levels of population density also fostered the transmission of diseases. As noted above, there is some evidence that the increased trade and mobility associated with improved transportation, market integration, urbanization, and industrialization did so as well.

INCOME AND SOCIAL STATUS

In the preindustrial and early industrial periods there was an almost perfect positive correlation between physical stature and income or social status in cross-sectional analysis (figure 5). In the 1840s literate French soldiers were 1.4 centimeters taller than illiterate ones, for example. Aristocrats were taller than the middle class, who in turn were taller than the offspring of the lower classes. In fact, teenage gentry boys around 1800 were taller than the Oliver Twists of London by as much as 15 centimeters, probably the largest such social difference ever recorded. Orphans were also shorter than average: for a typical Slovak male, having his father die before he reached age thirty cost him almost 2 centimeters. However, losing one's mother did not have a significant influence on adult heights. Students were invariably taller than average because, until World War II, education tended to be a privilege rather than a political right. In the United States differences tended to be small by occupation, but slaves were shorter than their owners. No exception has been found to the generalization that in a given time period physical stature rose with income, as long as the groups compared grew up in the same region, faced with the same relative price of nutrients and exposed to the same disease environment.

Across geographic units, however, income did not always correlate positively with physical stature in the early industrial world. Higher income did not always compensate for the higher price of nutrients or

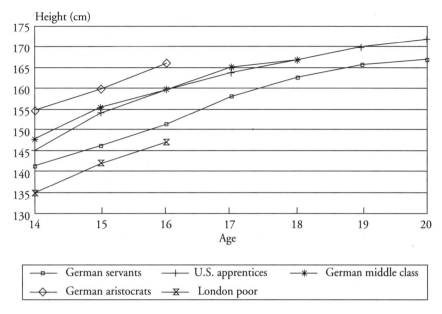

Figure 5. Comparative growth profiles for Germany, Britain, and the United States in the preindustrial period.

higher population density that went hand in hand with economic development. Thus the Irish and Scottish tended to be taller than the English, even though they were poorer on average, and, similarly, Poles were taller than Austrians in the Habsburg monarchy. Bosnians and Serbs were more than 7 centimeters taller than Hungarians, and southerners in the United States were slightly taller than northerners. The tallest white males in the United States in the antebellum period were born in the most isolated states, such as Kentucky and Tennessee, and the shortest in the most advanced region, New England. The Indians of the American prairie were the tallest population on record in the middle of the nineteenth century. However, in the twentieth century the effect of income became more positive at the regional level as well, probably because regional price differences diminished, and the delivery of public health services also correlated positively with per capita income. In the developed world at the turn of the twenty-first century, only very slight differences in physical stature remain by social class, while in the Scandinavian and Dutch welfare states they have disappeared entirely.

GENDER AND FAMILY ISSUES

Before the twentieth century, evidence on the height of females is quite scarce because they were obviously less likely than males to be part of institutions that kept records on physical stature. However, two major sources of female heights of the early nineteenth century do exist—slave and criminal records. These provide conflicting pictures. Sometimes female heights exhibit different trends than male heights. In a couple of cases, females experienced a decline in their physical stature prior to that of males. This was true among the free blacks of Maryland and among Scottish convicts. On the other hand, female heights fell after male heights in early-nineteenth-century England. Some have argued that in times of economic stress boys would have received privileged treatment within the household economy at the expense of girls. However, an examination of the issue for the United Kingdom led Bernard Harris to conclude that it is not possible to infer any significant difference in the treatment of boys and girls from early-twentieth-century height data and that it is impossible to generalize about earlier periods as well. In general, female stature seems to react less dramatically than male stature to disease and nutritional deprivation; thus it is hard to make comparisons across gender.

Research has also examined the impact of adult height on social outcomes in a historical context. Robert Whaples's 1995 study of Slovak immigrants to the United States found that greater height was associated with earlier marriage. Probably because taller men were generally more economically productive and generally earned more, they were more attractive in the marriage market. For example, at age twenty-two, a 149-centimeter-tall Slovak immigrant had a 37 percent chance of being married, while one who was 188 centimeters tall had a 66 percent chance of being married. Likewise, Bavarian women below 150 centimeters were significantly less likely to be married.

CONCLUSION

The nature of human welfare, its components, and its measurement is a philosophical question as old as recorded history. A definitive answer will surely remain elusive. Efforts to supplement conventional economic indicators with biological ones go as far back as the mercantilist thinkers of the seventeenth century who used biological indicators such as population size and life expectancy to gauge the well-being of populations.

Research on the biological standard of living assumes that there is no single measure of well-being. To equate GDP per capita with the standard of living entails a large number of simplifications. Broader measures of well-being, including the Human Development Index, add considerable information to conventional income measures of human welfare—they can unveil the hidden costs as well as the neglected benefits of modernization. In the early phases of modern economic growth, income indexes generally overestimate growth in relation to broader measures of well-being—in the United States by as much as a factor of four. In the twentieth century, however, the reverse is the case. During the decade of the Great Depression, for instance, a Human Development Index for the United States grew twice as rapidly as per capita income. Thus, incorporating such indicators into indexes of well-being can change in fundamental ways our assessment of economic performance.

Because progress is never uniform in all dimensions of human existence, it is useful to supplement conventional indicators of well-being with other measures, including biological indicators. The anthropometric history written at the end of the twentieth century has led to an expanded knowledge of welfare since the eighteenth century. It is now known that the common men and women in many regions of early industrial Europe and North America were, in some ways, worse off than their parents. There was some divergence between their living standard, as conventionally defined, and their biological well-being. The human organism did not always thrive as well in its newly created socioeconomic environment as one might be led to believe on the basis of purchasing power at the aggregate level. According to Steckel and Floud, countries that industrialized and urbanized before the development of the germ theory and public health measures paid a biological penalty.

More careful research is needed to supplement traditional income measures with new indexes, as well as additional investigation of the Human Development Index and its components, particularly on the "noneconomic" aspects of life, both at the theoretical and empirical levels. Though there will be no easy answers, documenting the biological attributes of human beings seems to be a promising way to proceed. As Stanley Engerman suggests, "Given the difficulties in finding an answer to any basic question of differential welfare, perhaps our best strategy is to accept the specific value of particular indicators for answering particular questions but also remain aware of the complexity of the multitude of factors that makes these examinations so difficult and generalization so uncertain" (1997, p. 39). Thus far, anthropometric history affords a much more nuanced view of the welfare of the populations living through the rapid structural changes accompanying two and a half centuries of industrialization.

See also **Racism** *(volume 1);* **Standards of Living** *(volume 5); and other articles in this section.*

BIBLIOGRAPHY

Baten, Jörg. *Ernährung und wirtschaftliche Entwicklung in Bayern, 1790–1880.* Stuttgart, Germany, 1999.

Bogin, Barry. *Patterns of Human Growth.* 2d ed. Cambridge, U.K., 1999.

Crafts, N. F. R. "Some Dimensions of the 'Quality of Life' during the British Industrial Revolution." *Economic History Review* 50, no. 4 (1997): 617–639.

Engerman, Stanley. "The Standard of Living Debate in International Perspective: Measures and Indicators." In *Health and Welfare during Industrialization.* Edited by Richard H. Steckel and Roderick Floud. Chicago, 1997. Pages 17–46.

Floud, Roderick, Annabel Gregory, and Kenneth Wachter. *Height, Health, and History: Nutritional Status in the United Kingdom, 1750–1980.* Cambridge, 1990.

Fogel, Robert. "Economic Growth, Population Theory, and Physiology: The Bearing of Long-Term Processes on the Making of Economic Policy." *American Economic Review* 84 (1994): 369–395.

Komlos, John. *The Biological Standard of Living in Europe and America, 1700–1900: Studies in Anthropometric History.* Aldershot, U.K., 1995.

Komlos, John. *Nutrition and Economic Development in the Eighteenth-Century Habsburg Monarchy.* Princeton, N.J., 1989.

Komlos, John. "On the Biological Standard of Living in Russia and the Soviet Union." *Slavic Review* 58 (1999): 71–79.

Komlos, John. "Shrinking in a Growing Economy? The Mystery of Physical Stature during the Industrial Revolution." *Journal of Economic History* 58 (1998): 779–802.

Komlos, John, ed. *The Biological Standard of Living on Three Continents: Further Essays in Anthropometric History.* Boulder, Colo., 1995.

Komlos, John, ed. "Recent Contributions to Anthropometric History." In *Jahrbuch für Wirtschaftsgeschichte.* Forthcoming.

Komlos, John, ed. *Stature, Living Standards, and Economic Development: Essays in Anthropometric History.* Chicago, 1994.

Komlos, John, and Jörg Baten, eds. *Studies on the Biological Standard of Living in Comparative Perspective.* Stuttgart, Germany, 1998.

Komlos, John, and Timothy Cuff, eds. *Classics of Anthropometric History: A Selected Anthology.* St. Katharinen, Germany, 1998.

Le Roy Ladurie, E., N. Bernageau, and Y. Pasquet. "Le conscrit et l'ordinateur: Perspectives de recherche sur les archives militaires du XIXe siècle français." *Studi Storici* 10 (1969): 260–308.

Mosk, Carl. *Making Health Work: Human Growth in Modern Japan.* Berkeley, Calif., 1998.

Nicholas, Stephen, and Richard H. Steckel. "Heights and Living Standards of English Workers during the Early Years of Industrialization, 1770–1815." *Journal of Economic History* 51 (1991): 937–957.

Quételet, Adolphe. "Recherches sur la loi de croissance de l'homme." *Annales d'hygiène publique et de médecine légale* 6 (1831): 89–113.

Sandberg, Lars, and Richard H. Steckel. "Heights and Economic History: The Swedish Case." *Annals of Human Biology* 14 (1987): 101–110.

Steckel, Richard H. "Stature and the Standard of Living." *Journal of Economic Literature* 33 (1995): 1903–1940.

Steckel, Richard H., and Roderick Floud, eds. *Health and Welfare during Industrialization.* Chicago, 1997.

Tanner, J. M. *A History of the Study of Human Growth.* Cambridge, U.K., 1981.

Ulijaszek, Stanley J., Francis E. Johnston, and Michael A. Preece, eds. *The Cambridge Encyclopedia of Human Growth and Development.* Cambridge, U.K., 1998.

Villermé, L. R. "Mémoire sur la taille de l'homme en France." *Annales d'hygiène publique et de médicine légale* 1 (1829): 551–559.

Whaples, Robert. "The Standard of Living among Polish- and Slovak-Americans: Evidence from Fraternal Insurance Records, 1880–1970." In *The Biological Standard of Living*. Edited by John Komlos. Boulder, Colo., 1995. Pages 151–71.

MEDICAL PRACTITIONERS AND MEDICINE

Matthew Ramsey

Medicine is connected to so many aspects of human experience that we cannot easily isolate it from other areas of social history. Certain key topics are addressed separately in the entries cross-listed below. This article deals primarily with medical practice and secondarily with ideas about health, illness, and the treatment of disease in their social context.

VARIETIES OF EUROPEAN MEDICINE

The first part of this article surveys the kinds of medical practitioners, practices, and beliefs and situates them in the diverse societies and cultures of Europe. It provides a framework for the second part of the article, which describes the evolution of the organized medical occupations, from their appearance in the late Middle Ages through the twentieth century. The emphasis throughout is on medical pluralism: elucidating the many forms that medicine and medical practice have taken has been one of the major contributions that social history has made to the history of medicine.

A diversity of practitioners. Throughout history, family, friends, and neighbors have ministered to the sick, and patients have treated themselves with domestic remedies. In addition, a very heterogeneous group of men and women have offered medical services based on their reputed special knowledge and skills. In Europe some have had formal training and credentials, but many have not. For some, medical practice has been a full-time occupation. For others it has been a sideline or an occasional activity.

The very vocabulary used to refer to medical practitioners reflects this complex social reality. The title "doctor," which derives from a Latin word for teacher, was conferred on holders of the highest university degree. Over time it came to mean, very broadly, a medical practitioner. In this article, it will refer to M.D.s, to distinguish them from other kinds of authorized practitioners. A memory of this tradi-

tional convention has survived in the British custom of addressing surgeons as "mister."

Numerous other terms designated a medical practitioner, who might or might not possess a university degree. In medieval Europe, the Latin term *medicus* (*medica* in the feminine) simply meant someone devoted to the healing arts, as it had in ancient Rome, which lacked a formal system of training and licensure. In the Romance languages, it gave us *médecin* in French, *medico* in Italian, and *médico* in Spanish—the common word for "physician." That English word (and the old verb "to physic") come from a Latin word for natural science and ultimately from the Greek word for natural, recalling the long association between medicine and specialized learning. In medieval texts, *medicus physicus* referred to a well-educated practitioner. The common German term for physician, *Arzt,* also once had lofty connotations; it ultimately derives from a Greek word that designated the chief court physician during the period of the Roman Empire ("archiater" in English).

In contrast, "surgery" and its cognates derive from the Latin *chirurgia*, which in turn comes from a Greek term meaning "working with the hand"; the medieval *medicus chirurgicus* dealt with wounds (an old German word for a simple surgeon was *Wundarzt*), performed rudimentary operations that did not invade the body cavity, and treated "external" disorders, including skin conditions. With some exceptions, surgeons through the early modern period were members of a separate occupation. Some practitioners dealt with a particular condition or part of the body—bonesetters, tooth pullers, lithotomists who cut for bladder stone, oculists who operated on cataracts; midwives are a special case of the same phenomenon. In France before the Revolution, practitioners who concentrated on a particular surgical condition were collectively known as *experts,* from the Latin word for experience, since their competence derived mainly from practical experience of a particular kind.

In the vernacular, there were also a series of terms meaning one who heals: "healer" in English, *guérisseur* in French, *Heiler* or *Heilpraktiker* in German, *curandero* in Spanish, *quaritore* in Italian, and *lekar'* in Russian. Over time these terms came to refer to a practitioner without formal training, though in nineteenth-century Russia the title of *lekar'* was given to a qualified practitioner below the level of the more highly trained *doktor meditsiny,* and Germany has had a system of certification for *Heilpraktiker* since the 1930s.

We now commonly refer to formally trained and certified practitioners as the medical "profession." For the sake of convenience the same term can be applied to practitioners in earlier periods who shared these basic characteristics. It is important to bear in mind, however, that until the nineteenth century the boundaries between "professionals" and other practitioners were poorly defined. The network of approved practitioners encompassed a wide range of occupations and of individuals with uneven training and different types of authorization. The right to practice might be based on anything from a university degree to a privilege accorded by the Crown or by town officials. Itinerant drug peddlers might be authorized to sell and even administer a few particular remedies. Members of the clergy who cared for parishioners and property owners who gave medical assistance to their servants and tenants or to the poor were also an accepted part of the medical scene.

A great variety of other practitioners also sold remedies and offered medical advice. The most colorful were the traveling "charlatans," often accompanied by a troupe of clowns and other entertainers, who set up medicine shows in marketplaces and town squares, where they hawked panaceas and "secrets" for particular diseases. (A less pejorative term for untrained practitioners was "empiric," which suggested that they owed their knowledge and skills to experience—*empeiria* in Greek—rather than formal study.) They flourished in the early modern period, bringing their specialized products and services to out-of-the-way places. In addition, local residents of all descriptions sold a few remedies or were thought to enjoy a special skill to heal particular diseases. Cunning-folk were believed to possess special knowledge or powers, often including an indwelling gift to heal, or to identify and counteract witches whose spells had caused disease and other misfortunes; other magical services might include predicting the future or finding lost objects. In European languages and dialects, these various healers (the preceding is a composite portrait) had a multitude of names, which often suggested esoteric knowledge; the Russian word *znakhar'* (*znakharka,* fem.), like the English word "cunning," comes from a root meaning "to know."

Traditional empirics and healers persisted in rural areas into the twentieth century, though they were to a large extent displaced by mass-marketed proprietary remedies and by practitioners of newer forms of what we now call alternative medicine—magnetizers, for example, the progeny of the Mesmerist movement of the late eighteenth century, who claimed to diagnose and cure disease through a form of animal magnetism. At no point has the profession enjoyed a de facto monopoly of medical practice.

Multiple beliefs and practices. Medical beliefs and practices were similarly characterized by pluralism. A common intellectual thread, however, has run through Western learned medicine since classical antiquity. From the late Middle Ages through the early nineteenth century, the dominant tradition drew on Greek sources mediated first through Arabic translations and then passed on through Latin retranslation to the centers of learning in western Europe. The core of the Greek tradition derived from the body of writings traditionally attributed to Hippocrates, which provided a naturalistic explanation of health and disease without reference to a supernatural realm. The key principle was equilibrium. Four critical humors—blood, phlegm, and black and yellow bile—affected the functioning of mind and body, and an imbalance of these humors produced disease. Therapy, such as bloodletting and drugs that purged, induced vomiting, or otherwise acted on the humors, was intended to restore the equilibrium. Greek learned medicine was codified by Galen (c. 129–199 C.E.) in the second century C.E. in a set of treatises whose extraordinary authority endured for centuries. Although his physiology and therapeutics did not go unchallenged in the early modern period, Galenic principles continued to dominate the university curriculum into the early nineteenth century.

In addition to Galenism, Europe also inherited from classical antiquity an immense body of empirical medical lore concerning the healing properties of natural substances. Some found its way into texts that were integral parts of the Greek medical canon. A different perspective appears in the *Natural History* of Pliny the Elder (23–79 C.E.), a vast and uncritical compendium of miscellaneous information on the properties of animals, plants, and minerals. Pliny shared with some of his Roman compatriots a hostility to the theoretical pretensions of Greek physicians.

Drawing on this tradition, early modern pharmacy incorporated a multitude of plants, as well as animal parts and excreta (the *Dreckapotheke* or filth pharmacy, as the latter sorts of remedies came to be called in German). Even human secretions had a place

Traveling "Charlatan." Itinerant seller of elixirs peddles his wares in a market. Painting by Jan Victors (1620–1676). MUSEUM OF FINE ARTS, BUDAPEST/ARTOTHEK

in the pharmacopoeia, as did human fat and preserved tissue, discreetly known as "mummy," which was typically prepared from the cadavers of executed criminals. The animal products began to disappear from the codices, or official lists of medications, over the course of the eighteenth century. By the early nineteenth century, nearly all were gone and a small number of active ingredients, such as quinine from cinchona bark, had been isolated from a few of the many remaining plant remedies. Although the initial results were modest, pharmacology increasingly relied on chemistry to produce pure drug substances.

Throughout European history, we also find therapeutic practices that we would characterize as magical or religious, though there were no clear dividing lines. These categories would not always have made sense to participants; the potency of a particular herb, for example, might depend on performing a certain ritual or saying a prayer while gathering it. One of the most common magical procedures sought to transfer a disease from the patient to an animal or plant. Religious healing has been even more widely practiced. Greek and Roman patients appealed for divine intervention to cure disease and travelled to shrines seeking cures. Christians did the same, sometimes adapting pagan shrines to their purposes. Many healers, for their part, saw themselves as imitating the

example of Jesus caring for the sick. The cultic veneration of the saints and the concept of patron saints as they developed in western Christianity also became closely identified with healing. The brothers Cosmas and Damian, physicians and Christian martyrs in the third century, became the patron saints of medicine; but many others were invoked for particular diseases, typically associated with an aspect of the saint's life or death. The martyred Saint Apollonia, whose teeth were broken, was invoked for toothache and became the patron saint of dentists.

In the modern period, new types of unconventional medicine emerged, sometimes linked to a form of spiritualism. Their adepts were often well organized, particularly in Germany, Britain, and the United States (which exported its medical movements to Europe), and they explicitly rejected official medicine and its central tenets. Homeopathy, for example, founded at the beginning of the nineteenth century by the German physician Samuel Hahnemann (1755–1843), treated disease with substances that caused similar symptoms, on the principle that like cures like, but in minute doses at very high levels of dilution. Homeopaths contrasted their gentler and (in their view) more efficacious therapeutics with the drastic remedies of the "allopaths"—bleeding, purging, and toxic drugs, such as mercury, the standby against syph-

A Hospital. Interior of a hospital. Woodcut from an edition of Paracelsus's *Opus chirugicum* (1565). National Library of Medicine, Bethesda, Maryland

ilis since the sixteenth century. Rather than disappearing with the rise of modern biomedicine, alternative medicine grew along with it.

Many Europes. The two previous sections have discussed aspects of medicine and medical practice common to many parts of Europe. Both were shaped to a significant degree, however, by particular cultural, social, and political environments.

We tend now to think mainly in terms of modern national cultures. Well into the nineteenth century, however, many Europeans thought of a province or some smaller region as their "country," and might not have recognized themselves as belonging to a nation-state, such as France or Spain. At the same time, many people thought in terms of larger affiliations. For centuries, educated Europeans recognized two great but ill-defined civilizational divides, between north and south, east and west, with implications for medicine and medical practice. The north-south divide was in part the product of climate, geography, and the relationship with the land, reflected in some of the ingredients frequently used in remedies—olive oil for ointments and wine for cleansing wounds and macerating herbs in the south, for example. This division was also cultural and historical, as could be seen, for example, in the prevalence of Roman law codes in the south and customary law in

the north. The Protestant Reformation of the sixteenth century originated and took hold in the north, where it produced distinctive religio-medical practices and sectlike alternative medical movements. In part for this reason, the north has been more tolerant of medical pluralism than the south.

The east-west divide had deep roots as well. The Roman Empire permanently split in two in the fourth century C.E. The Greek eastern half, with its capital at Constantinople, outlasted the Latin empire in the west by a millennium, falling at last to the Ottoman Turks in 1453. Christianity divided along similar lines, with reciprocal excommunications marking the Great Schism of 1054. Eastern Orthodox rites, together with the associated popular religio-medical practices, diffused throughout the Balkans and eastern Europe to Poland and Russia.

A third division followed the emergence of Islam in the seventh century. It spread rapidly outward from Arabia, reaching the Iberian peninsula in the early eighth century. The Christian reconquest of Spain was not completed until the end of the fifteenth century, by which time Constantinople had fallen and the Ottoman Turks had begun to expand into southeastern Europe. Although Ottoman power subsequently declined, the Balkans stayed in Turkish hands. Islam remained a powerful force in this land marked by ethnic and religious pluralism and helped shape

412

the medical cultures of the region. Although the Qur'an has little to say about medicine, subsequent commentators developed a medicine of the Prophet. Something of Arabic popular medicine, with its emphasis on jinns (spirits below the rank of angels) passed into southeastern Europe as well.

As we move forward in time, a fourth distinction between East and West becomes increasingly important. In the Ottoman and Russian empires and many other parts of eastern Europe, limited resources and an undeveloped market economy meant that full-time medical practitioners were thinner on the ground than in the West. The small number of doctors—most of them foreign or foreign-trained—were concentrated in the capital and a few other urban centers.

Finally, Soviet domination of Eastern Europe for nearly half a century after World War II established a fifth east-west divide with important implications for medical practice. Institutions with very different traditions were incorporated into a system of state medicine that greatly diminished professional autonomy.

The rise of the nation-state led to a new set of medical traditions; they most clearly left their mark on institutions and the organized medical profession, which will be discussed in subsequent sections of this article. But it is important to remember that ethnic and cultural divisions often did not coincide with political boundaries, particularly in the east. European Russia, for example, was at one end of a vast region stretching out through Siberia in which the Ural-Altaic peoples practiced shamanism. The shaman owes his healing powers to his ability to commune with the spirit world. Although he undergoes a kind of apprenticeship, his function depends less on acquired learning than on a calling thrust on him at birth. In the West, too, large pockets of cultural difference survived within or astride national frontiers, each with certain distinctive features in its medical culture. Brittany, for example, apart from a Celtic language completely unrelated to French, had an unusually high concentration of prehistoric megaliths (giant stones) known as *menhirs* in Breton. A patient might rub against a menhir or scrape it to obtain a powder for use in preparing medications.

Two widely dispersed groups constituted minorities within every European society. The Jews and the Roma ("Gypsies") shared a long history of diaspora and persecution culminating in genocide at the hands of the Nazis; each also had a distinctive place in the social history of European medicine, though of very different kinds. Jews played a disproportionate role as learned physicians in both Christian and Islamic lands, serving all communities, despite a series of restrictions and prohibitions in the former. Judaism

also powerfully affected views on health and healing within the Jewish community. Although in the Torah only Yahweh appears as a healer, a long tradition supported both learned medicine and popular practices. On the one hand, the revered status of the man of learning demanded respect for the physician (*rofe*) and contempt for quacks. Although the sick and suffering might avail themselves of prayer, they were to rely first of all on natural means. On the other hand, the laws and customs governing hygiene and diet were inextricably linked to religious obligations. Popular medical traditions included magical elements, such as charms. The medieval mystical system called the Kabbalah, which greatly influenced modern Hasidism, was equally non-naturalistic. Hasidism developed in the eighteenth century from a widespread popular revival movement in the Poland-Ukraine region, led by charismatic *tsaddikim,* or holy men. The most celebrated, Israel ben Eliezer (c. 1700–1760), was

ROMANI ("GYPSY") MEDICINE

In the Romani cosmos, the *marime* (morally or physically unclean) is a source of disease; the same term applies to exclusion from the community for violation of purity rules and other norms. Many key practices serve to keep the unclean lower half of the body and its products separate from the *wuzho* (pure) upper half; this distinction applies particularly to women, who are considered potential sources of pollution. Outsiders (*gadje*) who do not observe these precepts are unclean and a source of disease. Such diseases can be successfully treated by outsider physicians, but only *drabarni,* the Roma's female healers, can treat illness originating within the community. The worst of the latter are attributed to the Devil or to Mamioro, a spirit attracted to unclean houses, though they are also the source of powerful remedies. Mamioro's *johai* (ghost vomit), most often found in garbage dumps, is the most potent available remedy. More routine maladies can be treated with herbal preparations. The Roma tend to use the *gadje* health care system only when their own medicine has failed, except for childbirth, which is unclean and would make the home *marime* if the mother delivered there.

called Ba'al Shem Tov (Master of the Good Name) because of his reputation as a miracle healer. The term was also applied more generally to Jewish itinerant healer-magicians, whose gifts were attributed to their mystical knowledge of the secret and unspeakable names of God.

The Roma reached southeastern Europe from the Indian subcontinent by the fourteenth century. Their powerful concepts of purity and impurity and of insider-outsider status, together with the itinerant life some of them led, set them apart from the surrounding society and medical cultures. Because of their distinctive and uncompromising views on health and healing, encounters with physicians often produced a reciprocal sense of dislocation. A similar experience recurred with increasing frequency in the late twentieth century with the arrival of large numbers of immigrants from former colonies and elsewhere overseas—immigrants whose customs contributed to a growing medical multiculturalism.

THE ORGANIZED MEDICAL OCCUPATIONS

The first section of the second part describes the occupational structures that emerged in the late Middle Ages and lasted, with some changes, through the eighteenth century. They were primarily corporatist in organization, with guildlike bodies supervising medical practice. The second section concerns the development in the late eighteenth and nineteenth centuries of many of the features we associate with the modern medical profession, including new forms of organization and licensure. The dominant model in western Europe was liberal in the sense that medical professionals, once certified, were free to practice as they wished. It was also bureaucratic or statist in that government increasingly controlled the process of licensure. The third section focuses on the development in the late nineteenth and twentieth centuries of national health insurance, social security, and other forms of third-party payments, which transformed not just the economics of health care but also its place in the larger society.

The medieval and early modern medical field.
Through most of the Middle Ages, an aspiring physician would have learned medicine at a cathedral school or monastery or through apprenticeship. The first universities appeared in England, France, Italy, and the Iberian Peninsula in the late twelfth and thirteenth centuries, and then in the German lands and central Europe in the fourteenth and fifteenth centuries. The doctorate was the highest degree, normally following the baccalaureate and licentiate, and in some cases came in higher and lower versions; it was not necessarily required for medical practice.

The first medical graduates, many of them members of the clergy, coexisted with the highly diverse network of practitioners described in the first part of this article. Priests and monks made up a sizable percentage of the total number of active practitioners. Their role declined after about 1500, though religious houses continued to maintain dispensaries and care for the poor. Women, though a minority of active practitioners, won public recognition as physicians. They were excluded from the new universities, however, and gradually from the organized medical occupations other than midwifery.

Physicians also shared the medical arena with authorized surgeons and apothecaries, plus the various trades, such as herbalists, spice dealers, and grocers, that sold medicinal plants or other ingredients for making remedies. In principle, the physician, the man of learning, supervised both surgeon and apothecary. The surgeon might bleed a patient at his direction; the apothecary would provide the medication he prescribed, if necessary compounding it according to his directions. This triad was at best an approximation of the social reality; as long as it existed, practitioners regularly complained about boundary violations.

Except in parts of southern Europe, physicians were a distinct minority even of authorized practitioners. In most of eastern Europe they remained scarce; it has been estimated that at the beginning of the seventeenth century, there were perhaps twenty western-trained physicians in all of Russia. Thanks to charity work, sliding fee scales, and public appointments, physicians might treat the indigent and patients of modest means, but the mass of the population did not make regular use of their services.

Physicians did not on the whole enjoy the status or income that we associate with the medical profession today, though it was possible to rise through court appointments and other forms of patronage. In a society of legally defined orders, they usually ranked among the respectable bourgeoisie; the most successful sometimes purchased a patent of nobility where that was possible. In Russia, the Table of Ranks established by Peter the Great (1672–1725) in 1722 placed a university-trained medical doctor at Rank IX, which conferred personal but not hereditary nobility.

The case of surgery is more complex. A tradition of academic surgery existed, mainly in France and southern Europe; in Italy, especially, it gained a place in the university curriculum. "Surgeons of the long robe" as they were sometimes called, in reference to

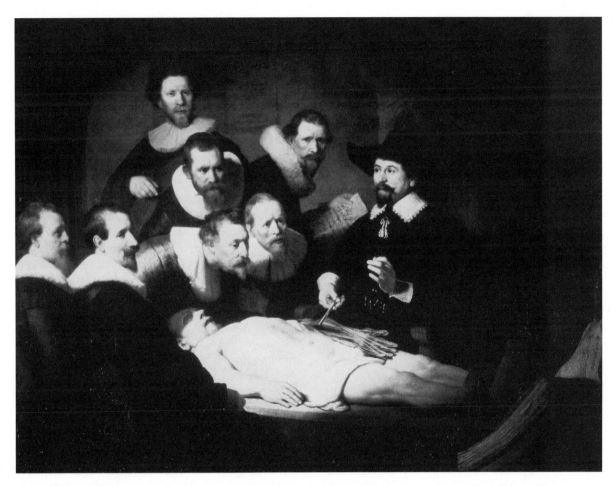

Anatomy. *The Anatomy Lesson of Dr. Nicolaes Tulp,* painting (1632) by Rembrandt Harmensz van Rijn (1606–1669). MAURITSHUIS, THE HAGUE, NETHELANDS/THE BRIDGEMAN ART LIBRARY

their academic gowns, shared the physicians' acquaintance with the Latin corpus of medical texts and a commitment to practice guided by theory. Most surgeons, however, trained exclusively through an apprenticeship system comparable to that of other manual crafts, and many may have been illiterate. At the lower end, surgery was linked to barbering; barbers commonly performed minor operations, pulled teeth, and used their razor for bloodletting.

In most places, lower-level surgeons were the most numerous and widespread of practitioners, serving all the basic medical needs of the population. In central and eastern Europe, one finds special categories, including "practical surgeons" who lacked the full education of master surgeons but could serve the rural population. In the eighteenth century, German states established *collegia medico-chiururgica* to train *Wundärzte* and *Feldscherer* (feldshers). The latter term, which dates from at least the sixteenth century, derives from a German word whose literal meaning is "a mili-

tary man working with shears"—a clear reference to the old association between barbering and surgery. From their origins as surgeons in German and Swiss military companies, the feldshers spread through central, eastern, and parts of southern Europe; they treated increasing numbers of civilians and became the principal providers of medical care to the rural populations.

The more ambitious surgeons aspired to separation from the barbers and autonomy from the physicians. In eighteenth-century France they succeeded spectacularly. The Paris surgeons definitively severed the link with barbering in 1743 and in 1748 won formal recognition of a Royal Academy of Surgery. (Their London counterparts achieved separation from the barbers in 1745.) A decree of 1750 recognized a Paris College of Surgery independent of the University of Paris.

Over the course of the eighteenth century, several other intersecting trends transformed the world of surgery. A growing number of practitioners trained in both medicine and surgery. When the French revolutionaries unified medical and surgical education in 1794, some surgeons regretted the loss of their distinct identity, but the decision simply reinforced and formalized an already well-established trend. Moreover, surgeons increasingly delivered babies, treated teeth, and began to perform and improve operations once generally left to the *experts*. The term "dentist" first came into common use in this period, starting in France. A new conception of specialization was beginning to emerge, in which the specialist would first acquire a general medical education.

Although more clearly tradesmen than surgeons, apothecaries underwent a similar apprenticeship. Most practiced at least a little medicine and surgery, in addition to selling drugs. In England, where apothecary-medical practitioners were particularly numerous, one of them won a notable legal case in 1704, which affirmed their right to treat patients, though they could still charge only for the medicines they sold. A growing number of practitioners qualified as both surgeons and apothecaries, and the "general practitioner" emerged from this dual occupation in the nineteenth century.

In keeping with the legal and social order of the Old Regime, physicians, surgeons, and apothecaries formed corporations—guilds and guildlike organizations—in cities and major towns. The first major urban craft guilds appeared in Italy in the thirteenth century, and the institution subsequently spread throughout southern, western, and northern Europe. The arrangements in the medical field were complex, sometimes bringing together physicians and surgeons, but more often not. Just as surgeons were frequently linked with barbers, apothecaries were often joined with spice dealers. It should be added that universities and faculties were themselves corporations of masters and students, chartered by emperors, kings, popes, and other rulers.

The corporations were probably strongest in France. In England laissez-faire increasingly prevailed, and on the rest of the Continent state and municipal institutions played a larger role in regulating the medical field. The corporations admitted candidates to practice, typically requiring special examinations and fees, and prosecuted unauthorized practitioners, who might include members of another corporation who had crossed the boundary between the two fields. In France, some medical faculties offered little instruction and had become more regulatory than educational institutions. In London, the Royal College of Physicians, established in 1518, theoretically enjoyed a monopoly of medical practice in the capital and its

outskirts, though this did not keep many others from working there.

In most of the rest of Europe, a more bureaucratic regulatory system emerged, though outside the east it often coexisted with fairly robust corporations. In Spain, the Royal Protomedicato, or medical board, conferred licenses and prosecuted those who violated the medical regulations; in many areas practitioners also had to belong to local corporations, but they functioned as mutual-aid societies, religious confraternities, and the like. In Italy, the kingdoms of Naples, Sicily, and Sardinia adopted *protomedicati* on the Spanish model. In the northern and central states of the peninsula, guildlike colleges enjoyed the power to license practitioners since the late Middle Ages. By the sixteenth century, though, some of the colleges had become virtual state agencies; Florence established a state board with licensing powers in 1560. In northern and central Europe, state medical boards *(collegia medica)* emerged in the late seventeenth and eighteenth centuries. In France, although the corporations retained control over practice, the Société Royale de Médecine, chartered in 1778, was empowered to regulate mineral waters and the remedy trade.

Licensure was not the only way in which government impinged on medical practice and practitioners. Physicians found employment with the public health boards pioneered by the city-states of the Italian Renaissance. The northern Italian cities also hired public physicians and surgeons, starting in the early thirteenth century. The institution of the municipal and district physician, who typically treated the poor and discharged certain public health functions, spread widely, especially in the German lands, where he was given the title of *Physikus*. Apart from these official functions, in much of central and eastern Europe the government closely supervised the activities of practitioners after they had been licensed, telling them how and where they could practice and even, in some cases, whether they could marry. In Russia, medical practitioners were formally members of the civil service; very few could have sustained a private practice on the open market. In most German states they were recognized as public health officials. Finally, the military, with its great need for surgeons, played an important role in providing not just employment but also instruction. In the eighteenth century, the Berlin Collegium Medico-Chirurgicum (1724) and the Josephinum Academy in Vienna (1785), both devoted to training future military surgeons, were among the most distinguished surgical schools in Europe.

By the end of the eighteenth century, the corporations were on the defensive, challenged not only by new institutions, but also, in the west, by the burgeoning medical marketplace. Commercialized brand-name remedies, heavily advertised in the new periodical press, sometimes reached an international clientele. The wide dissemination of medical literature at all levels also encouraged new kinds of self-help; in the view of some practitioners, it undermined the physicians' authority over the medical field.

The nineteenth century.

The Revolution (1789) had destroyed the old corporate order in France, including the faculties and guilds. After a period of laissez-faire, which its critics characterized as "medical anarchy," France in 1803 adopted a new medical regime, a cross between a bureaucratic and a liberal model. The state alone would certify new practitioners, but from that point on they were essentially free from government oversight. French military victories during the revolutionary and Napoleonic wars brought analogous reforms to neighboring countries. Some of these changes were reversed after the fall of Napoleon, and in places outside the French sphere of influence many older institutions remained intact. But the deeper transformations reflected in the legislation of 1803 were not unique to France.

In the new model, credentials were standardized and based on uniform examinations. The French not only educated future surgeons and physicians together (a doctorate of surgery was available but required the same basic preparation); they also eliminated the variations in the requirements of the faculties, which had been only partly coordinated by a royal edict of 1707. Doctors could work anywhere in France; under the Old Regime the right to practice in a city required affiliation with a local corporation as well as a medical degree. After some debate, the legislators decided to retain a second tier of practitioners; the *officiers de santé* (health officers) were in theory to meet the needs of rural populations, like the old country surgeons. Although they received a simpler, shorter, and more practical training, they were members of the same occupation as the doctors and were entitled to call themselves physicians.

Henceforth there would be no more special privileges or royal dispensations. There would be no authorizations to practice some part of the medical arts. France led the way in the development of new specialties, including orthopedics and psychiatry, but the M.D. degree was a sine qua non. (The exceptions were midwifery, which had its own diplomas, and dentistry, which remained unregulated until 1892.) Anyone who practiced without an official credential was ipso facto guilty of illegal medical practice. Authorized practitioners now, more clearly than before, embodied what by the mid-nineteenth century had come to be called "official medicine." By the same token, it became easier to identify alternative medicine, especially as unlicenced practitioners and proponents of unconventional medical systems formed their own organizations and even schools.

The new French medical regime became the model for strict regulation of the medical field throughout the Western world, though it was not universally emulated. To some it smacked of Napoleonic authoritarianism. England never imposed a national professional monopoly; indeed, the Medical Act of 1858 rescinded the local monopolies of the old corporations. In Germany, the trades ordinance of the North German Confederation introduced *Kurierfreiheit,* or freedom of healing, in 1869, while lifting the old regulations governing the activities of physicians; it was extended to the unified German Empire in 1871.

France continued to license health officers until 1892. It was the German states that led the way in eliminating the two-tiered system in the 1840s and early 1850s, closing practical schools and making the university essentially the single point of access to the profession. Russia, at the other extreme, retained an elaborate multitiered system. A law of 1838 provided for seven medical degrees (*lekar'* was the lowest). These nice distinctions mattered less among lay people; after around mid-century they generally applied the term *vrach* (physician) to all medical practitioners, as they still do. The feldshers, however, remained a distinct category; they dominated medical practice in many rural areas, resisting efforts by physicians to impose their authority.

In England, the general practitioners trained in hospitals or by apprenticeship formed a broad lower tier compared with the university-educated physicians, especially the elite of the Royal College of Physicians in London. The Medical Act of 1858 created a single register of qualified practitioners without either standardizing education or replacing the old certifying bodies. A conjoint Board of Examinations was created in 1884, and two years later a Medical Amendment Act imposed a general requirement for qualification in medicine, surgery, and obstetrics. The medical field thus had a basic credential, though practitioners remained stratified into general practitioners and hospital consultants. This distinction had parallels elsewhere. Though the degree might be the same, the elite was set apart by hospital and faculty appointments, high government positions, and membership in academies. In France the *internat,* a form of postgraduate hospital training available only to a small cadre chosen by competitive examination, sorted practitioners at a very early stage in their career.

THE FRENCH MEDICAL PRACTICE LAW OF 19 VENTÔSE YEAR XI/10 MARCH 1803

TITLE 1. General Provisions

ARTICLE 1. Starting on 1 Vendémiaire Year XII [24 September 1812], no one may pursue the occupation of physician, surgeon, or health officer, unless he has been examined and licensed as set forth in this law.

ARTICLE 2. Those who are authorized to practice medicine after the beginning of the Year XII will be called *doctors* of medicine or surgery, if they have been examined and licensed at one of the six special medical schools, or *health officers* if they have been licensed by the boards described in the following articles.

. . .

TITLE TWO: Examinations and Licensure of Doctors of Medicine or Surgery

ARTICLE 5. Examinations for doctors of medicine or surgery will be given in each of the six special medical schools.

ARTICIE 6. There will be five examinations: the first on anatomy and physiology; the second on pathology and nosology; the third on materia medica, chemistry, and pharmacy; the fourth on hygiene and legal medicine; the fifth on internal or external clinical medicine, depending on whether the candidate is seeking the title of doctor of medicine or surgery. The examinations will be public; two of them must be in Latin.

ARTICLE 7. After the five examinations, the candidate must defend a thesis written in Latin or French.

ARTICLE 8. Students cannot take the examinations until after they have studied at one of the special schools for four years and paid the appropriate charges.

. . .

TITLE 3. Training and Licensing of Health Officers

ARTICLE 15. Young men who plan to become health officers are not obliged to study at the medical schools; they can be licensed as health officers after having been a private student with doctors for six years, or having worked at a civilian or military hospital for five nyears. Three consecutive years of study in medical school can substitute for the six years with the doctors or the five years in the hospices.

ARTICLE 16. In order to license health officers, a medical board (*jury*) will be established in the capital of each *département* [administrative district] composed of two doctors residing in the *département* appointed by the First Consul [Napoleon Bonaparte], and by a commissioner selected from among the professors of the six medical schools, and appointed by the First Consul.

. . .

ARTICLE 17. The departmental boards will conduct the examinations for licensing health officers once a year. There will be three examinations: one on anatomy; the next on the rudiments of medicine; the third on surgery and basic pharmacy. They will be given in French, in a room open to the public.

. . .

TITLE 4. Registration and Lists of Doctors and Health Officers

[All authorized practitioners must register with the local authorities, who will draw up a list for their district.]

ARTICLE 28. Doctors licensed by the medical schools may practice their profession in every locality in the Republic.

. . .

ARTICLE 29. The health officers can set up a practice only in the *département* in which the board examined them, after registering as has just been indicated. They cannot perform major surgical operations except under the direction of a doctor, where one is available.

. . .

TITLE 5. Training and Licensing of Midwives

ARTICLE 30. In addition to the training conducted in the medical schools, the most frequently used hospice in each *département* will establish a free annual course on the theory and practice of delivering babies, especially intended for the training of midwives.

. . .

TITLE 6. Penal Provisions

ARTICLE 35. Starting six months after publication of this law, any individual who continues to practice medicine or surgery, or to deliver babies, without being on the lists [described in the preceding articles], and without having a diploma, certificate, or letter of licensure, will be prosecuted and sentenced to pay a fine to the hospices. . . . The fine will be doubled for repeat offenders, who in addition may be sentenced to prison for no more than six months.

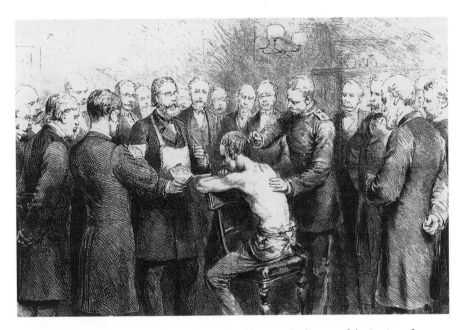

Treating Consumption. Robert Koch (wearing white apron), director of the Institute for Infectious Diseases, Berlin, observes his son-in-law, Edouard Pfuhl, innoculating a patient for tuberculosis at the Royal Hospital, Berlin, 1875. Koch, discovered the bacillus that causes tuberculosis in 1882. PRIVATE COLLECTION/THE BRIDGEMAN ART LIBRARY

In many places, recruitment became less socially exclusive over the course of the century. In Russia, medical education was reorganized in 1856, part of the larger program of modernization and social reform, (including emancipation of the serfs) following defeat in the Crimean War (1853–1856). The changes gave access to many who had previously been ineligible. (See Table 1.) An even more striking development in the last decades of the century was the admission of women to medical training, starting in Switzerland and France. Russian women showed a strong early interest and figured disproportionately among the first female candidates for degrees at Zurich and Paris. Many others qualified as feldshers, a title for which graduates of midwifery schools were eligible. By 1913, 10 percent of Russian medical practitioners were women.

In addition to educational reform, medical practitioners felt a need for new organizations to fill the void left by the passing of many of the old corporations, and by the restricted membership and diminished influence of those that remained. In France, where revolutionary legislation prohibited occupational organizations to defend common economic interests, physicians formed mutual aid societies, which federated in 1858 as the General Association of French Physicians. The whole was greater than the sum of its parts and functioned in many ways as a national profes-

sional association. A generation later, physicians began to form more militant unions—*syndicats,* the same word used for labor unions—though they remained technically illegal until 1892. In that year, the *syndicats* received not only legal recognition but also the right to initiate prosecutions for illegal practice. Germany also had a wide range of voluntary professional organizations, many of which came together in 1873 to form the Federation of Medical Associations. In Britain, the old corporations survived but provided no representation for the rank and file. The British Medical Association (1855) grew out of a Provincial Medical and Surgical Association (1832), an organization primarily for general practitioners hostile to the privileges of the medical elite, on the one hand, and competition from unqualified practitioners on the other. In Russia, the progressive Pirogov Society, named for the celebrated surgeon and scientist Nicholas I. Pirogov (1810–1881), held a series of national congresses starting in 1885 and used a network of local branches to promote medical reform throughout the empire.

In societies where the liberal model of medical practice prevailed, professional misconduct by licensed practitioners posed one of the most troublesome challenges to the new order. In France some physicians called for "disciplinary councils" and other neocorporatist solutions. Later the *syndicats* tried to disci-

TABLE 1
THE NINETEENTH-CENTURY RUSSIAN MEDICAL PROFESSION

Social Origin of 620 Physicians in Three Age Cohorts

| | Year of Birth | | |
	Before 1851 (N = 84)	1852–1863 (N = 229)	1864–1879 (N = 307)
Children of:			
Hereditary nobles	14.3%[a]	9.2%	7.2%
Personal nobles, bureaucrats	33.3	37.6	38.1
Military	6.0	9.2	2.6
Clergy	21.4	23.1	13.0
Honored citizens, members of merchant guilds	7.1	9.2	10.8
Petty tradesmen, artisans, urban laborers	11.9	9.6	22.2
Peasants	–	1.3	5.2
Foreigners, others	6.0	0.9	1.0

[a] This sample may have a disproportionate number of nobles because it includes many physicians of Polish birth, who invariably claimed noble status.

For cases without date of birth, age was computed as 26 at time of graduation from medical school.

The figures show the declining role of foreigners and the gradual opening of the profession to aspirants from more modest social backgrounds.

Source: Frieden, 1981, p. 206.

pline their membership, but the only sanction they could enforce was expulsion. In Britain, the General Medical Council established by the 1858 act could strike errant practitioners off the Register, though they could still practice so long as they did not claim registration. In the German Empire, elected but official chambers of physicians were empowered to police the conduct of licensed physicians; those accused of professional misconduct could be sent before "courts of honor" (*Ehrenräte*). Professional ethics, which became a prominent topic of public discourse at the beginning of the nineteenth century, met a similar need in a less formal way: published codes could take the place of the old corporate statutes in guiding the conduct of practitioners. "Medical deontology," as it was sometimes called, primarily concerned relations with other practitioners; a physician should not lure away a colleague's patients, for example. Increasingly, though, it also emphasized patient rights, such as confidentiality.

Another challenge to the liberal model was the expanding role of government, even outside the countries where the physician was a kind of public servant. Medical practitioners found a growing number of appointments in schools, prisons and other institutions, in public health services, and as physicians to the poor. In Russia, as part of the program of reform that followed the Crimean War, Alexander II (1818–1881) established elective district and provincial councils known as zemstvos. Public health was among their top priorities, and they hired practitioners to provide medical services in the countryside. By the early 1890s zemstvo physicians made up 10 percent of the profession in Russia—a minority, to be sure, but a vocal one, committed to political populism.

Although the principle of government health care programs received wide support from those looking for a middle way between outright socialism and laissez-faire liberalism, the form it should take became a subject of intense debate. The zemstvo physicians, whose position recalled the town and district physicians of the Old Regime, represented only one possible approach. The pioneering system of social insurance established in the German Empire by the Chancellor Otto von Bismarck (1815–1898) in 1883 was another, very influential model. Introduced as part of a campaign of reforms designed to steal the thunder of the left, Bismarck's plan amalgamated a great number of existing local sick funds for workers into a program that employers and employees would jointly administer; workers at the lower end of the pay scale were required to join. The funds signed contracts with individual physicians, who normally received either a fixed salary or an annual payment for each patient covered (capitation). Eventually the system was opened up to all licensed physicians, who would be paid on a fee-for-service basis. In France, a law of 1893 on rural medical assistance left the decision on the form of payment to the districts (*départments*); the great majority chose fee-for-service.

In addition to government programs, a growing number of physicians signed contracts with traditional mutual-aid societies, large employers, and insurance companies, which could use competitive bidding to force costs down. Beyond the economic threat, contracts with third parties, private or public, aroused concerns in western Europe about the future of the liberal physician-patient relationship, in which the two were supposed to agree freely on a service for which the patient would pay directly. More and more often, the purchaser was no longer the consumer. Even though third-party payments benefited the profession by greatly expanding the market for its services, many physicians resisted such proposals, wary of becoming subordinated to lay managers. These fears were a powerful motive behind the drive at the end of the century to develop more effective medical organizations, whether modeled on the old corporations or on the newer trade unions.

The twentieth century. The continued development of ambitious national health care plans was one of the hallmarks of twentieth-century medicine in Europe. Britain established National Health Insurance (NHI) on Bismarckian lines in 1911; compulsory for low-wage workers, and financed by joint worker and employer contributions, it provided sickness benefits and paid for treatment by a general practitioner chosen by the patient from the NHI list—a "panel doctor." Physicians received a capitation for each name on their list. After World War II, the new National Health Service (authorized in 1946, fully implemented in 1948) extended this system to the population at large, funding it mainly with general tax revenues. With the hospital system fully incorporated into the plan, medical care now became famously "free." France followed a somewhat similar path, im-

plementing a social insurance plan in 1930 that included medical coverage; it was compulsory for low-wage industrial and commercial employees. The major difference between this plan and the British model was that patients would pay the physician of their choice and then be reimbursed 80 percent of a standard fee by their chosen insurer; several insurance options were available, including mutual-aid societies, which also offered supplementary policies to reimburse the 20 percent copayment. The Social Security system adopted in 1945 eventually extended coverage to virtually the entire population; it retained the expensive fee-for-service system, but with provisions in-

TRAINING PHYSICIANS IN THE GERMAN EMPIRE: A MODEL OF SCIENCE-BASED MEDICAL EDUCATION

The unification of Germany in 1871 resulted in uniform criteria for medical education and licensure throughout the new Empire, drawn essentially from the Prussian model. Training emphasized both laboratory science and practical clinical experience. Candidates had to possess a diploma from a classical secondary school (*Gymnasium*), study medicine for four years at a university (including two semesters spent in medical and surgical clinics), and deliver four babies. One part of the licensure examination covered the basic medical sciences; it included a demonstration of practical skills in histology, physiology, the preparation of pathological specimens, and the use of the microscope. The remainder of the examination comprised written, oral, and clinical tests on general medicine and surgery, together with ophthalmology, obstetrics, and gynecology. Each candidate had to perform at least one dissection. The clinical work entailed examining and caring for six patients over an eight-day period. The candidate also had to deliver a baby and show on an anatomical model how to deal with different presentations of the fetus. The German standards were generally recognized as the most rigorous anywhere in the nineteenth century.

Bonner, p. 254, citing *Reglemente für die Prüfung der Ärzte und Zahnärzte vom 25. September 1869.* Berlin, 1869.

TABLE 2
SOVIET INTERMEDIATE MEDICAL PERSONNEL BY SPECIALTY IN 1950 AND 1974

Specialty	End of 1950		End of 1974	
	Number	%	Number	%
Feldshers	160,000	22.2	525,100	21.7
Feldsher-midwives	42,000	5.8	78,500	3.2
Midwives	66,500	9.2	244,100	10.1
Assistants to environmental health doctors and assistants to epidemiologists	18,500	2.6	45,500	1.9
Nurses	325,000	45.2	1,185,500	48.9
Medical laboratory assistants	25,300	3.5	105,300	4.3
X-ray technicians and x-ray laboratory assistants	7,500	1.0	29,800	1.2
Dental technicians	6,700	0.9	30,000	1.2
Disinfectors* and disinfectionists	27,000	3.8	87,000	3.6
Residual group†	40,900	5.7	92,300	3.8
Totals	719,400	100	2,423,100	100

* This is a conjectural translation of *dezinstruktori*.
† Not given in source; obtained by subtracting numbers listed under each specialty from the grand total.
Sources: *Narodnoe Khozyaistvo SSSR* for 1970, p. 692; and for 1974, p. 730. Michael Ryan. *The Organization of Soviet Medical Care.* Oxford, 1978, p. 71.

tended to limit physicians' actual charges in most cases to the maximum set in an approved fee schedule. These mechanisms were of some help in protecting patients, but the system as a whole had no budgetary cap. The escalating costs led to further restrictions but not to a capitation system; France clung to its version of socialized medicine with a liberal face.

In Russia, the social insurance law adopted in 1912 was in many ways comparable to the Bismarckian system, but the October Revolution (1917) brought far more radical changes. After initially coopting the insurance system, the Bolsheviks found themselves embroiled in a protracted conflict between proponents of workers' insurance and of a rival vision of universal, state-controlled Soviet medicine. The 1920s were a period of flux, in which Lenin's New Economic Policy (NEP) made room for a significant private medical sector. With the end of the NEP in 1928 came a campaign against private medical practice (though it was not outlawed) and much tighter controls over the work of physicians. The government set up numerous medical centers, dispensaries, and health

stations in factories and on the new collective farms, elements in a comprehensive national health care system. The return to an insurance model started only in 1991, just before the Soviet Union collapsed, part of the broader move away from the planned economy. The basic system introduced in the Russian Federation consisted of national and regional compulsory insurance plans, with the possibility of private insurance as a mostly symbolic affirmation of free-market values.

The October Revolution transformed not just health care coverage but also the entire medical field, particularly after the demise of the New Economic Policy. The Pirogov Society was abolished in 1922; medical personnel in the Soviet Union became "health workers," most of them state employees; a central Health Commissariat was established to oversee public health and medical care; the medical faculties, detached from the universities, became training institutes under the jurisdiction of the Commissariat. Although populist pressures for physician care for the entire population led to a move away from lower-level practitioners in the 1920s, the feldshers became a central part of the new Soviet health program in the 1930s, promoted by the Communist Party as more genuinely proletarian than physicians. (See Table 2).

Under the Soviet system, the medical profession declined to a level of pay and status below that of technical workers. Its position deteriorated further in the unstable economy that followed the disintegration of the U.S.S.R. Soviet medicine also became increasingly feminized, reinforcing the pattern established in Russia before 1917. Generous policies on maternity leave, child care, equal educational opportunities, equal pay, and the theoretical right to hold any job or political office contributed to the trend. But the percentages also reflected a tendency for men to seek more attractive opportunities elsewhere.

The structure of the medical occupations changed in western Europe as well. The number of specialists, on the one hand, and of paramedical personnel, on the other, increased substantially, though not to the same degree as in the United States. Graduates of new nursing schools increasingly replaced the old nursing orders; other auxiliaries provided special services, such as rehabilitative therapy, under a physician's supervision. What the Russians called "intermediate-level practitioners" suffered varying fates but generally declined, apart from midwives, who remained much more strongly implanted in Europe than in the United States.

CONCLUSION: ENTERING THE TWENTY-FIRST CENTURY

At the end of the twentieth century, the European medical scene was not what many would have predicted at its beginning. In 1900, recent advances in the medical sciences, especially microbiology, seemed to promise a new science-based medicine that would dramatically improve the health of the population,

raise the status of the medical profession, and discredit alternative medical systems. These expectations were fulfilled in part. Yet the last years of the century also saw the rise of antibiotic-resistant microorganisms, particularly tuberculosis, and the emergence of frightening new diseases, one of which, acquired immunodeficiency syndrome (AIDS), established a significant presence in Europe. Many other diseases and disorders remained beyond the power of medicine to cure or even to explain, and although life expectancy reached new heights (except in some of the former Soviet republics, where it declined), this was not necessarily true of the quality of life. Moreover, despite the triumphs of biomedicine, alternative medicine flourished as never before, borrowing freely from Chinese, Indian, and other non-Western philosophies and medical systems, as well as from indigenous healing traditions. Medical consumers had a wider choice of therapies for self-treatment than ever before, many of them available on the Internet, or at least the prosperous ones did. Europe still suffered from social inequities in medical care, though they were far less pronounced than in the United States.

Except for a relatively small number of highly paid specialists, most practitioners in the late twentieth century saw their incomes stagnate and their autonomy decline, as the cost restrictions imposed by the various forms of public health care plans began to bite more deeply. In the 1970s, a common radical critique had denounced the excesses of professional and medical power; by 2000 it seemed clear that much of the real power lay elsewhere.

The situation at the beginning of the new millennium confirmed the basic theme of this article. Although the development of modern biomedicine has been a powerful force, medicine is also shaped by larger social, cultural, political, and economic factors. New forms of medical pluralism replaced older ones. The social history of medicine cannot be written simply as a linear story of the rise of medical science and the medical profession.

See also **Professionals and Professionalization** *(volume 3) and other articles in this section.*

BIBLIOGRAPHY

General Works on Medical History

Bynum, W. F., and Roy Porter, eds. *Companion Encyclopedia of the History of Medicine.* 2 vols. London and New York, 1993. Seventy-two articles by specialists on topics ranging from anatomy to war and modern medicine.

O'Malley, C. D., ed. *The History of Medical Education.* Berkeley, Los Angeles, and London, 1970. Based on a 1968 symposium at UCLA. Includes chapters on Italy, France, England, Scotland, Germany, the Netherlands, Scandinavia, Russia, classical antiquity, the Middle Ages, and the Renaissance.

Porter, Roy. *The Greatest Benefit to Mankind: A Medical History of Humanity from Antiquity to the Present.* New York and London, 1997. Best single-volume history of medicine.

Medieval and Early Modern

Brockliss, Laurence, and Colin Jones. *The Medical World of Early Modern France.* Oxford and New York, 1997. Sweeping synthesis of French medical history, with observations on broader European context.

Cook, Harold John. *The Decline of the Old Medical Regime in Stuart London.* Ithaca, N.Y., and London, 1986.

Gentilcore, David. *Healers and Healing in Early Modern Italy.* Manchester, U.K., and New York, 1998. Focuses on the kingdom of Naples.

Lindemann, Mary. *Medicine and Society in Early Modern Europe.* Cambridge, U.K., and New York, 1999. Especially useful introduction for students and the general reader.

Park, Katharine. *Doctors and Medicine in Early Renaissance Florence.* Princeton, N.J., 1985.

Porter, Roy. *Health for Sale: Quackery in England, 1660–1850.* Manchester, U.K., and New York, 1989. Medical practitioners as competitors in the marketplace.

Siraisi, Nancy G. *Medieval and Early Renaissance Medicine: An Introduction to Knowledge and Practice.* Chicago and London, 1990. Very informative survey of medical theory and practice.

Modern: General and Comparative

Bonner, Thomas Neville. *Becoming a Physician: Medical Education in Britain, France, Germany, and the United States, 1750–1945.* New York and Oxford, 1995.

Bonner, Thomas Neville. *To the Ends of the Earth: Women's Search for Education in Medicine.* Cambridge, Mass., and London, 1992.

Bynum, W. F. *Science and the Practice of Medicine in the Nineteenth Century.* Cambridge, U.K., and New York, 1994. Emphasis on Britain.

Ramsey, Matthew. "The Politics of Professional Monopoly in Nineteenth-Century Medicine: The French Model and Its Rivals." In *Professions and the French State, 1700–1900.* Edited by Gerald L. Geison. Philadelphia, 1984. Comparison of regulation of medical practice in Europe, the United States, and other parts of the world.

Modern: National Histories

Britain

Digby, Anne. *Making a Medical Living: Doctors and Patients in the English Market for Medicine, 1720–1911.* Cambridge, U.K., and New York, 1994.

Fissell, Mary Elizabeth. *Patients, Power, and the Poor in Eighteenth-Century Bristol.* Cambridge, U.K., and New York, 1991.

Lawrence, Christopher. *Medicine in the Making of Modern British, 1700–1920.* London and New York, 1994.

Loudun, Irvine. *Medical Care and the General Practitioner, 1750–1850.* Oxford and New York, 1986.

Peterson, M. Jeanne. *The Medical Profession in Mid-Victorian London.* Berkeley, Los Angeles, and London, 1978.

Porter, Dorothy, and Roy Porter. *Patient's Progress: Doctors and Doctoring in Eighteenth-Century England.* Stanford, Calif., 1989. Pioneering study of social history of medicine from the patient's point of view.

France

Faure, Olivier. *Histoire sociale de la médecine.* Paris, 1994. Social history of medicine in France since the eighteenth century.

Gelfand, Toby. *Professionalizing Modern Medicine: Paris Surgeons and Medical Science and Institutions in the 18th Century.* Westport, Conn., and London, 1980.

Léonard, Jacques. *La médecine entre les savoirs et les pouvoirs: Histoire intellectuelle et politique de la médecine française au XIXe siècle.* Paris, 1981.

Ramsey, Matthew. *Professional and Popular Medicine in France, 1770–1830: The Social World of Medical Practice.* Cambridge, U.K., and New York, 1988.

Germany

Broman, Thomas Hoyt. *The Transformation of German Academic Medicine, 1750–1820.* Cambridge, U.K., and New York, 1996.

Huerkamp, Claudia. *Der Aufstieg der Ärzte im 19. Jahrhundert: Vom gelehrten Stand zum professionellen Experten: Das Beispiel Preussens.* Göttingen, Germany, 1985. Social history of the medical profession in nineteenth-century Prussia; useful introduction to German medical institutions.

Jütte, Robert. *Geschichte des alternativen Medizin: Von der Volksmedizin zu den unkonventionnellen Therapien von heute.* Munich, 1996. Wide-ranging synthesis on alternative medicine in Germany since about 1800.

Lindemann, Mary. *Health and Healing in Eighteenth-Century Germany.* Baltimore and London, 1996. Focuses on state of Braunschweig-Wolfenbüttel, but addresses broader questions in history of medical practitioners and practice in eighteenth-century Germany.

Russia/Soviet Union

Field, Mark G. *Doctor and Patient in Soviet Russia.* Cambridge, Mass., 1957.

Frieden, Nancy Mandelker. *Russian Physicians in an Era of Reform and Revolution, 1856–1905.* Princeton, N.J., 1981.

CHILDBIRTH, MIDWIVES, WETNURSING

Amanda Carson Banks

For the majority of western European history, childbirth was viewed as a normal process, and the community was content to allow nature to follow its course. The predominant practices and associated material items and indeed the very language were predicated on this understanding and approach to birth. The *Encyclopaedia Britannica* (1771) reflected such a philosophy by defining midwifery as ". . . the art of assisting nature in bringing forth a perfect foetus, or child from the womb of the mother." Intervention was rare; doctors were called only in the case of an impossible delivery, the death of the mother, or the death of the child *in utero,* and the beliefs and traditions of society governed this process.

Since the Renaissance, childbirth, midwifery, and early infant care in Europe have been influenced and shaped by societal issues, resulting in great changes, new understandings, and different practices. The history of this cycle provides an exciting opportunity to observe how broad changes in a society interact with each other to impact and influence a smaller, specific area. Specifically, these changes include the waning authority of the Catholic Church, the Enlightenment and its emphasis on reason, advances in technology and medical knowledge, industrialization and the move of large portions of the population to urban centers, changes in economic structures and the rise of the middle class, changes in belief patterns and structures in both organized religion and "household" or folk religions, and changing definitions and "new" understandings about women's bodies and health.

This history has been approached in a number of different ways and from a variety of perspectives. Until the mid-twentieth century, the history of birth was presented as a continuum of medical advances, charting the role not of the community but of technological developments in the birth process. Works like Albert Buck's *The Dawn of Modern Medicine* (1920), George Engleman's *Labor Among Primitive Peoples* (1882), and Herbert Spencer's *The History of British Midwifery from 1650–1800* (1927) are examples and were based on a cultural evolutionary understanding of western medicine. Describing practices undertaken and advocated by medical professionals, they did not capture or discuss the experiences of the vast majority of women giving birth, nor did they address the issues of the surrounding society and how these intersected with the process.

In the nineteenth century, early folklorists and antiquarians began to collect what they regarded as "relics of the past," particularly the traditions and beliefs of the more rural areas. Examples associated with pregnancy, childbirth, and infancy were also gathered in this process and included items such as notions about dietary intake and prenatal marking, the divination of the sex of the child, practices and styles of delivery, methods of pain relief, postures for delivery, and the customs and rituals of birth-chamber attendants. These were recorded in large collections of folkways and rural practices and are great resources for historical information.

Later efforts to create a history of birth from a social or cultural perspective placed such traditions and practices in Europe within chronological periods that were seen as having similar or consistent trends and practices. A typical first period begins in the depths of the past with social birth, where women were highly involved in delivery as midwives, mothers, and assistants, practicing a noninterventionist approach that centered around serving the mothers. A second period begins in the mid-1700s with the growing importance of the profession of medicine and the increase in the study and practice of midwifery by male physicians. A third period, from the mid-nineteenth century until the early twenty-first century, is portrayed as a period of consolidation of medical control over birth, with an increasing definition of birth as a pathological, disease state that requires medical control and management.

Midwives Attend a Birth. The midwives deliver the child and comfort the mother while in the background two men cast the child's horoscope. Woodcut (c. 1580) by Jost Amman (1539–1591). [For another scene of the birth chamber, see the article "Birth, Contraception, and Abortion" in volume 2.] PHILADELPHIA MUSEUM OF ART, PURCHASED: SMITHKLINE, BECKMAN CORPORATION FUND

SOCIAL BIRTH— THE RENAISSANCE TO 1700

In the time of "social birth," the process of labor and delivery was a community event. Near the time of delivery the neighborhood midwife was alerted that her services would be required in the days to come. When the moment arrived, the father, another child, or a neighbor was sent to bring her to the home to assist in the delivery. The midwife would bring along the tools of her trade—twine, scissors, cloth, and perhaps a portable birth stool or chair. The birth stool or chair would be assembled and the mother would spend her labor talking with the friends and neighbors who had gathered. When she reached the point of delivery, she would sit upon the birth stool and deliver her child. The birth stool or chair was an important artifact of birth in Europe well into the nineteenth century. It was the implement of choice for midwives, early man-midwives or accoucheurs, and even found popularity among early obstetricians. Birth chairs were used across national boundaries, by rural and urban women, and by both upper and lower classes for delivery. While exhibiting certain common characteristics throughout the continent, such as the semi-

circular opening in the low seat, an open and supportive back, and hand-holds for bracing during contractions, these items of traditional birth bore the distinctive qualities of various areas, including regionally unique ornamentation and construction. In fact, the birth chair was so intimately associated with birth and midwives until the mid-nineteenth century that it was used in both textual references and in art to symbolize the birth act. In some instances, the midwife of a region was recognized for her services to the community and provided with a chair or a stool. For example, an account from the records of Stadt Baden in Switzerland in 1427 records that a midwife was hired to serve the town, and in 1429 a *kindbetterstul*, a birth stool, was purchased for her use.

Midwives and early midwifery texts. Midwives have a long history. They were long considered high-ranking members of their communities and were sources of advice in birth control, pregnancy, child rearing, and conception, as well as all elements of community health care. Midwives had an expansive knowledge of herbal treatments ranging from the early use of ergot, a wheat fungus that stimulates labor (later used and marketed as a medical drug), to anesthetics, aids for relaxation, and herbs to cause the contraction of the uterus. Midwives passed the bulk of their knowledge from one to another through oral communication and informal apprenticeship. Little written material was available regarding midwifery, and the available texts were in Latin (like the works of Hippocrates, Magnus, and Savonarola).

One of the first European books on midwifery written in the vernacular was Ortloff von Bayerland's *Das Frauenbüchlein* (Little book for women; 1500). Eucharius Rösslin, the city physician of Frankfurt-am-Main, soon followed with a similar book, *Der Swangern Frauen und Hebammen Rosengarten* (A garden of roses for pregnant women and midwives; 1513). Like Ortloff and others to follow, Rösslin directed his text to practicing and knowledgeable midwives, offering few suggestions as to actual delivery but rather advising that they follow nature and do what seemed best. The text of Jakob Rueff (1500–1558), director of midwives in Zurich, *Ein schön lustig Trostbüchle in von den Empfangnissen und Geburten der Menschen* (Cheerful, gay, and comforting little book about the conception and birth of people; 1544) is equally revealing of the general practice of delivery in its descriptions and detail about the practice and artifacts of birth, and of the basic tenor of societal attitudes toward the process. He briefly describes the process of birth, suggests some tools, primarily crochets for dissecting a blocked or dead infant *in utero,* and describes the attributes of a model midwife. Louise Bourgeois followed with a casebook of sorts, detailing her experiences as a midwife in *Observations diverses de Lovyse Bovrgeois ditte Bovrsier, Sage-femme de la Royne* (1617).

Of course, just because midwifery writers from various points of the continent were writing similar accounts does not prove that the general practices of birth were universal throughout England and Europe. The proof is in the fact that these were not the only works. Many texts were written throughout Europe that offered the same advice and understanding about birth, and these texts portrayed midwives as serving their community, government, and church and occupying a revered position in society.

Midwives and witchcraft.

Despite the high status midwives held within the community, they also bore the burden of suspicion. Beginning in the Middle Ages, midwives in most European countries were required to be certified by parish priests, or in larger cities such as Paris, London, Frankfurt, and Cracow, by the bishop, as to their upstanding virtue and honesty and their lack of association with witchcraft in order to practice legally. Without this church approval and early licensing, a woman who acted as a midwife or healer was open to charges of witchcraft. The church became involved because midwives were required by law to baptize children, often *in utero,* in the event of a difficult or fatal delivery so the infant could be absolved of original sin prior to death. In addition, part of a midwife's duties, as dictated by church authorities, was to determine the identity of an illegitimate child's father. The Catholic Church was more interested, therefore, in the role of midwives as Christians than in their skills in delivery.

Suspicion related to witchcraft had dogged the reputation and careers of midwives since at least the time of the Dominicans Heinrich Kramer and Jakob Sprenger who wrote in their 1484 *Malleus Maleficarum* (Hammer of witches), "No one does more harm to the Catholic Church than midwives." This suspicion of witchcraft stemmed from various Christian doctrines that loosely supported the interpretation of illness or death as the will of God or the result of sin and association with the devil. In fact, Jacob Rueff believed that "monsters," children with deformities, were begotten by devils. By association, midwives were vulnerable to charges of witchcraft in case of failure to deliver a perfect child. Suspicion was also attached to their free access to objects long considered magical: the placenta, the umbilical cord, and the caul of an infant. In 1555 Würzburg, in Bavaria, instituted regulations that forbade midwives to take the placenta away from a birth and required that they throw it in

running water (for purification) for disposal. As late as 1711 Brandenburg regulations forbade midwives to give away or sell any remains of birth like the membranes, caul, or umbilical cord.

Wet nursing.

While critical to the birthing process, a midwife could do little in the area of feeding or nurturing an infant unless she was also a wetnurse. Typically, a mother would feed her own child. In situations where a mother was unable to nurse, either because of sickness, inability to produce milk, or death, a wetnurse was employed to feed the child until weaning. Broadly conceived, wetnursing—the practice of a woman suckling another's woman's child for pay—stretched well beyond simply feeding the infant. It included all areas of childcare and early infant nurture. The majority of wetnurses in Europe were initially employed by foundling hospitals for the care and feeding of children who had been abandoned or handed over after the death of the mother.

FORCEPS

Obstetric forceps were invented in France in 1588 by Peter Chamberlain (1560–1631). The forceps were shaped like two large spoons and were inserted into the birth canal one at a time around the infant's head and then screwed together. The infant was then pulled out. Use of forceps increased the possibility that the infant might survive a difficult or otherwise impossible delivery, and was a significant improvement over past practices where the child had to be dissected in cases of impaction or impossible delivery. As Hugh Chamberlain, Peter's grandnephew, wrote, use of the forceps dispelled the notion "... that when a man comes, one or both must necessarily die." The forceps brought much honor and business to the Chamberlain family and they were jealously guarded, carried from one job to another in a large, locked, and highly ornate wooden box. When the Chamberlains arrived the mother was blindfolded, all birth attendants sent from the chamber, the room darkened, and bells and noises used to muffle the noise of the forceps. Due to this secrecy, forceps were almost unknown until 1699, when the design was sold to a Dutch college.

Wetnurses. *Arrival of the Wetnurses,* painting attributed to Étienne Jeaurat (1699–1789).
Musée Municipal, Laon, France/Réunion des Musées Nationaux/Art Resource NY

However, the popularity of wetnursing among women who could feed their own infants but for a number of reasons chose not to grew more widespread among royalty and upper classes of Europe between the fifteenth and eighteenth centuries. For these classes, one of the primary reasons for choosing to send a child out to nurse was the need to keep the cycle of ovulation continuing, so that a mother could give birth and quickly conceive again. Often, a wetnurse kept the child in her care long after the actual act of wetnursing ceased, which typically occurred after 24 months. The age that the child was weaned was determined not by a paid wetnurse but rather by the father, and varied according to the sex and birth order of the child. Eldest sons received nursing care the longest and youngest daughters received it for the shortest time. The wetnursing system was well organized early on. Networks of fathers and the husbands of wetnurses almost exclusively negotiated the contracts, and in many cases of extant documentation, theirs are the only names listed on contracts. There were also organized caravans for wetnurses returning from cities with their new charges, and government-managed bureaus. In many cases, at town or village celebrations, holidays, markets, and fairs wetnurses would gather to announce their availability. In Spain,

Portugal, and Germany wetnurses wore special costumes or clothing that indicated their business.

A woman who had recently lost her own child was regarded as the ideal nurse. Second best was a woman who had recently weaned her child, but this was always regarded as a little questionable if the child remained in the home, due to concern that she would continue to nurse both children, thereby affecting the quality and quantity of the milk going to the paying child. Wetnurses were expected to be married women or very recently widowed. Traditional laws, rules, and expectations of behavior were both understood and often captured in the wording of written contracts. For example, nurses were not to associate with their husbands during their tenure as wetnurses. In fact, one of the nurses of the future Louis XIV was dismissed because she was overseen talking with her husband in a garden. This rule was in place because it was believed that the milk of women who engaged in sexual relations was less palatable for infants. Further, the milk of pregnant women was considered of substandard quality, since it was believed that the fetus would draw all the nutrients away from the milk, making it weak and useless to the nursing child. Parents were also upset if their wetnurse turned out to be menstruating while nursing, as this milk was also considered unhealthy and polluted and possibly dangerous for the child. They would often terminate the contract or, if they could not find a replacement nurse, reduce her wages to reflect their opinion about the quality of her milk. While early wetnurses were all married women who either lost a child or had weaned one early, gradually more and more women placed their own children out to poorer, rural wetnurses so that they in turn could take on higher-paying customers for their milk.

Until the mid-eighteenth century medical writers and some midwifery manuals gave advice about the qualities and characteristics to look for during the selection of a wetnurse. It was believed that not only would a child pick up habits from the nurse, such as "coarse behavior," but also that the demeanor, style, manner, and appearance of the nurse could be transmitted through her milk to her nursling. There was also the belief in the sixteenth and seventeenth centuries that the sex of the child the wetnurse had recently given birth to would have an effect on the child she would nurse, in that the milk was designed for a child of a particular sex and could be damaging, or perhaps even deadly, when given to a child of the opposite sex. The belief that children took on the mental and physical qualities of the one providing the milk remained strong well into the eighteenth century. This belief not only influenced the choice of a wetnurse, but also raised some questions and some hesitation about artificial feeding using animal's milk. Stories were told about children becoming goatlike or stupid like sheep for being fed the milk of these animals, and the later midwifery texts advised against anything but mother's milk unless as a last resort. In foundling homes where a shortage of available parish funds for paying wetnurses, or a general shortage of nurses made this necessary, goats, asses, and sheep were kept on the grounds so children could either be fed the milk via carved-out animal horns, or, most frequently, they were held straight to the animal's teat for feeding.

While maltreatment of the infant was rare, since it was a source of income and any damage or death would result in loss of pay, abuse did happen on occasion. The primary danger to nurslings, however, was the threat of being "over-laid," that is, the nurse rolling over onto them and smothering them while asleep and nursing in bed. Devices were designed to prevent this, and parents would often supply the nurse with such protection, along with swaddling clothes and infant wear. Infants also died of the many ailments and diseases that commonly affect children, and the graveyards of rural parishes throughout Europe have a disproportionate number of infant graves given the general population, for if a child died, the nurse would have it buried locally and then would notify its parents.

THE AGE OF ENLIGHTENMENT—1700–1850

With the Enlightenment, the authority of the Catholic Church waned and the pursuit of scientific study and reason increased. Medicine was freed from the outdated notions of Galen and other ancient writers and from the confines of religious orthodoxy concerning illness and health. In midwifery programs, male physicians were at last allowed access to the study of the human body, post-mortem dissections, and attendance and observation of pregnant and delivering women. While initially these physicians had access primarily to the difficult or deadly cases of birth, by the early eighteenth century physicians were attending difficult cases even outside the charity centers of the university, writing midwifery texts, and even founding lying-in hospitals exclusively for the delivery of indigent women.

The practices of birth changed as a result. Most evident are the change in posture for delivery from upright in a birth chair to recumbent in a bed, and the shift toward the male birth attendant. Changes were also apparent in attitudes toward women and in

THE FIRST USE OF A RECUMBENT POSTURE FOR DELIVERY

According to tradition, the first use of a recumbent posture for a normal delivery (and in some versions, the historic first use of a man-midwife by choice for a normal delivery) was by Louis XIV's mistress, Louise de la Valliere, in the late seventeenth century. It is said that Louis insisted that she lie down upon a bed so that he could observe the birth (a socially inappropriate activity of the time) from a hiding place behind the curtains. The legend follows that influential members of the French court then followed King Louis's lead and took to employing man-midwives when they wished to keep their illicit affairs a secret since a midwife's duties, as dictated by the authorities, included determining the identity of an illegitimate child's father.

the language regarding pregnancy and birth. Such terms as "teeming" and "breeding" to describe pregnancy were replaced in contemporary diaries, literature, and other texts with terms such as "sick," "confined," and, tellingly, "ill." A writer in the London *Gentleman's Magazine* in 1791 commented on this.

> All our mothers and grandmothers, used in due course of time to become with child or as Shakespeare has it, *roundwombed* . . . but it is very well known that no female, above the degree of chambermaid or laundress, has been with child these ten years past . . . nor is she ever *brought to bed,* or *delivered,* but merely at the end of nine months, has an accouchement antecedent to which she informs her friends that at a certain time she will be confined.

Midwifery and the rise of obstetrics. The declining influence of the church had made charges of witchcraft less frequent, and midwives continued to practice their art on a large scale throughout Europe. However, doctors began to question the role and ability of midwives. Midwifery manuals soon gave way to obstetrical texts that were less directed toward practicing midwives and more toward physicians. They covered the more fascinating aspects of labor and delivery, and in the titles of these works, pregnancy and birth were increasingly referred to as the diseases of women. The limited exposure of doctors to normal labor, and the popularity of texts that dealt almost exclusively with abnormalities such as poor presentation, impacting, narrow pelvises, and the birth of "monsters" (infants with acute deformities), cultivated an increasingly threatening picture of birth that quickly led to a perception among doctors, and eventually among the population they tended, that pregnancy was anything but normal. The texts that were designed for midwives became more directional and instructive, eventually becoming little more than advice booklets for matrons, not midwives. These books instructed women as to proper behavior during pregnancy examinations and birth, and provided general guidance for the selection and use of doctors. The gradually changing tone of these texts cultivated a changing attitude and approach to midwives and, by association, women. The discovery of the lucrative field of man-midwifery, as well as the growing influence of physicians' guilds and colleges proved to be real threats to the practice of traditional midwifery and to the livelihood of female midwives.

According to William Smellie (1697–1763), a British physician, when the British army and navy surgeons were put on half pay in 1748, many of them attended his lectures on midwifery in order to increase their incomes by practicing as "man-midwives," the

THE ACCOUCHEUR

The term accoucheur was used in reference to man-midwives and appeared in the titles and texts of obstetrical works beginning in the late eighteenth century. The *Oxford English Dictionary* cites the first literary use of accoucheur, the French, and hence polite, term for obstetrician, as Laurence Sterne's 1760 novel, *Tristram Shandy.* "—yet nothing will serve you but to carry off the man-midwife.—Accoucheur,—if you please, quoth Dr. Slop.—With all my heart, replied my father, I don't care what they call you,—but wish the whole science of fortification, with all its inventors, at the devil;—it has been the death of thousands,—." Literary tradition credits Dr. John Burton of York (1710–1771) as the victim of Sterne's satire.

common term of the day. Simply taking the training and advertising their skill was not sufficient for doctors to change the way birth had been practiced for hundreds of years. They accomplished this by increasingly defining birth as a dangerous, pathological crisis that warranted, in fact demanded, their professional services. This undermined the credibility of midwives, compromised society's belief in their skill, and fed the growing conception within society of the fragility of women. Society, led by the tone and tenor of these obstetrical authorities, began to suspect midwives of incompetence, evil, and squalor. Charles Dickens's description of a midwife in *Martin Chuzzlewit* (1843) was typical and reflected his cultural milieu.

> The face of Mrs. Gamp—the nose in particular—was somewhat red and swollen, and it was difficult to enjoy her society without becoming conscious of a smell of spirits. Like most persons who have attained to great eminence in their profession, she took to hers very kindly' insomuch, that setting aside her natural predilections as a woman, she went to a lying-in or a laying-out with equal zest and relish.

By the late eighteenth century, through guild membership and the concomitant persecution of nonmembers who attempted to practice medicine, physicians and surgeons controlled and regulated the medical profession as they saw fit.

Ill health and birth as a pathology. The practice of birth was also affected by shifts in the general attitude of the populace about femininity and womanhood and their role in the birth process. Other important factors included the industrialization of Europe, changing economic structures, and the emergence of the middle class. Each played a significant role in shaping the new beliefs about the process in general. For doctors and scientists in the nineteenth century, birth had come to be viewed as dangerous because women were at last understood to be as weak and fragile as they truly were. Exertion and activity were regarded as dangerous to their health and general well-being. If a woman did not experience illness as a result of such activities, she must not be truly female. Thus, fragility and ill health became acceptable and indicative of refined sensibility and social status. Members of the growing middle class sought to emulate the wealthy classes in all ways, and showing that active economic participation of their wives and daughters was not necessary was critical. Idleness, once considered sinful, was now a status symbol.

The cultivation of upper-class women's ill health as a sign of status and civilized behavior further contributed to the growing conception that the whole process of childbearing was well beyond a refined woman's capability. The social corollary to such thinking was that if a woman did not appear to suffer a difficult, possibly dangerous, labor and delivery, she was in action and demeanor like a "savage." "In proportion as we remove women from a state of simplicity to luxury and refinement, we find that the powers of the system become impaired, and the process of parturition is rendered more painful. In a state of natural simplicity, women in all climates bear children easily, and recover speedily" (Edward Murphy, 1862). If a woman was civilized, it was believed, she needed medical help in delivery.

In the nineteenth century birth did in some ways become more difficult. The idealization of women as fragile created an image of women as inherently unhealthy. Meanwhile, life in the industrialized city and the standards of fashionable dress in many ways made image reality. Years of use of women's undergarments and supports, such as corsets and straitlacing, seriously altered a woman's anatomy, and made delivery difficult or impossible due to a malformed torso and pelvic area, not to mention the damage done to the fetus by their continuous use throughout a pregnancy.

The history of birth has also been shaped by changes in the structure of communities due to industrialization and urbanization. The strong bonds of female community, particularly noticeable through their earlier participation in the delivery of a community member, were weakened by the movement of large segments of the population to cities, where friends, family members, and neighbors were unavailable. Socially, pregnancy became an increasingly unacceptable topic of polite conversation. People rarely spoke about pregnancy and childbirth and when they did, they used euphemisms and told "where babies come from" stories (e.g., the stork and cabbage patches). Even practitioners used such euphemisms when advertising their services. For example, midwives in France had signboards depicting women in cabbage patches with smiling infant faces.

By the middle years of the nineteenth century the general practice of delivery was strikingly different from what it had been a hundred years earlier. Increasingly, birth was seen as a medical specialty that was practiced rather than a natural event that occurred. Birth chairs increasingly became more and more elaborate in order to compensate for the perceived inability of women to labor and deliver effectively alone. New postures for delivery were favored, from horizontal postures in special-made birth chairs to the fully recumbent postures in bed. Drugs were used to hasten delivery, bloodletting was practiced, and the extensive use of obstetrical tools was employed to remove the infant. Such changes made the doctor physically more comfortable and enhanced his feeling and appearance of control, but simultaneously increased the actual burden on the mother and removed control of the event from her. The elements and practices associated with the earlier, more natural, approach came to be regarded with apprehension and dread, representing a period before treatment was available: the dark ages of medicine and a time of "meddlesome midwifery."

Wetnursing in the eighteenth century. While midwifery experienced a great decline in appeal, the popularity of wetnursing reached its peak in the late eighteenth century. The economic and social conditions of the period played a large part in this. Early in the industrialization period, the increase of artisans, shopkeepers, and factory workers in the city expanded the market for the services of wetnurses. Such city workers found the cost of wetnursing was more affordable than the loss of their wives' salaries or labors. Doctors believed a nursing child could drain all the strength and health from a mother, and therefore encouraged women to find wetnurses (this follows the folk tradition that a woman loses a tooth per child nursed). The upper and middle classes, influenced by this thinking and the greater social freedom it permitted, continued to utilize wetnurses. It is notable that Catholic countries (France, Spain, and Italy) had stronger traditions of wetnursing, bureaus to manage the process, and governmental laws and regulations to control it. This wider use of wetnurses was in part due to the larger number of foundling hospitals and the higher number of abandoned infants. In Protestant countries fewer infants were put out to wetnurse; also, fewer children were abandoned. In fact, in countries such as Germany, Norway, Sweden, and Finland, children were not typically sent out to nurse at all. Rather, the nurse was frequently required to be resident in the family home while employed. In some cases, a wetnurse was employed to visit the baby's home once or twice a day to feed the child.

THE CONSOLIDATION OF MEDICAL AUTHORITY—1850–2000

By the mid-nineteenth century, obstetrics had arrived as a legitimate branch of medicine almost entirely male dominated. Maternity hospitals or lying-in centers were first used only by poor women who were delivered for free in exchange for their use as test cases for medical students. However, in the early twentieth century upper-class women and paying customers increasingly gave birth in hospitals following the introduction of obstetrical anesthesia, most particularly, the Twilight Sleep. This method, introduced by Bernhard Krönig in Germany in 1899, used a combination of morphine and scopolamine and caused an amnesiac and unconscious state. It was regarded as a blessing to women since it removed all pain and erased most memory of the process. Like the changes brought about by other medical implements, such as forceps, the use of anesthesia affected the process and practice of birth significantly. It increased the number of medical personnel required for an effective birth; it limited the posture for delivery to a recumbent, often restrained, position; and it strengthened the portrayal of women as too ineffective to manage the process alone. Delivery in hospitals took place in operating rooms or theaters, with the women highly anesthetized on flat tables or hospital gurneys that included arm straps, shoulder straps, and stirrups with leg restraints, attended by licensed medical personnel. Midwives and mothers were literally and symbolically absent. The texts concerning birth were medical ones detailing procedures. The history of birth was written as an example of glorious advances of western civilization. The texts available and intended for women were treatises on home economics, advice for mothering, scientific housekeeping, diapering, and tips for care and nurture.

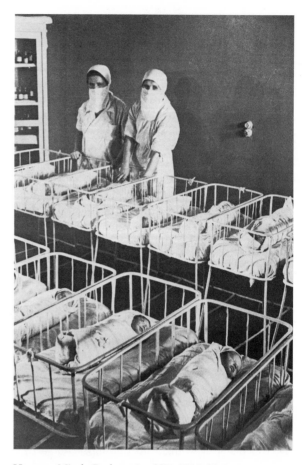

Nursery. Minsk, Byelorussian SSR, 1939. YEVGENY KHALDI/©CORBIS

Renewed communication and alternative birth. Coupled with the growing trend toward forms of socialized or nationalized medicine in European counties, in the mid-twentieth century, women began once again to communicate with one another on the topic of birth. Bolstered by dialogue, women sought out information and brought about the growing popularity in Europe of natural methods of birth like Accouchement Sans Douleur (the Lamaze Method) and the methods of Grantly Dick-Read and Frederick Leboyer, who sought not only to reduce unnecessary intervention in their deliveries, but also to defeat patronizing attitudes of professional medicine toward women. The movement toward more natural birth was popular among both childbearing women and the medical profession as a way to better and more economically care for women in childbirth. Medicalized birth was lessened, and more natural and healthier approaches to childbirth reappeared. In addition, the last three decades of the twentieth century also saw the rise of a small movement for alternative birth. Encompassing a wide variety of natural, alternative, and noninterventionist practices, the movement for alternative birth placed value on the mother's role and strove for practices that worked in concert with birth, rather than attempting to dictate and manipulate it. This movement looked to traditional practices and the growing trend toward self-care for models of practice. Newer approaches were introduced, such as underwater birth, and older practices were revived, like birth as a community-attended event.

Midwives in the twentieth century. In the early years of the twentieth century, midwives in much of Europe, already professionally compromised, increasingly lost access even to indigent women as clients. Hired by governments and municipalities, midwives performed home visits following delivery to check on the mother and to monitor the infant's progress, and were infrequently, if ever, participants in the birth process. Only in very rural areas were midwives still the primary birth practitioners, as need dictated their participation.

With the growth of nationalized medicine, midwives made a return to delivery, caring for the majority of births, those without likelihood of complications requiring significant intervention. As an increase in births crowded available space and resources at hospitals, a trend emerged toward shorter stays, fewer "procedures," and the less expensive attendance of midwives at birth. Midwives practiced in hospitals as certified nurse-midwives, legally licensed and recognized. A large number of lay midwives (unlicensed) attended home births and other alternative forms of delivery. In England and on the continent, midwives delivered a large portion of infants with a physician merely attending, although the control and management of what is considered a normal birth, and what is deemed appropriate care, was still governed by professional medicine.

Wetnursing in the late nineteenth and twentieth centuries. As more and more women delivered in hospitals and stayed for extended periods, they began the process of nursing as advocated by the newer gen-

eration of obstetricians, and wetnursing experienced a demise. With the influence of reformers who campaigned throughout the nineteenth century for a closer mother-child relationship, and the development of adequate forms of artificial feeding, including bottles, infant cups, nipples, and spoons, and sanitary cow's milk, wetnursing was no longer useful, fiscally sound, or any more beneficial than any other means of feeding. While technological advances in artificial feeding did not immediately affect the rate at which children were given over to nurses, they did change the work of the nurse from wetnursing to dry nursing (hand feeding with bottles).

World War I, falling on the heels of decades of campaigning by social authorities about the benefits of mothers nursing their own children, was a primary cause of the demise of wetnursing. During the war, women found that, indeed, wetnursing was far more expensive than the new, alternative forms of infant feeding. After the war, fewer women worked outside the home, making wetnursing unnecessary. It was all but nonexistent in European counties in 2000. Friends and relatives might nurse a child while the mother was away, but there is almost no evidence of a paid market for wetnurses, and the trend toward bottle feeding remained fixed. The advent of effective breast pumps made even bottle feeding with cow's milk unnecessary.

CONCLUSION

While the history of childbirth, midwifery, and early infant-care has changed significantly since 1500, the forces that shaped this history have been consistent. Changes in knowledge and advances in medical science have made a great impact. The economics of the community, societal customs, attitudes about women's roles, changing social classes, and industrialization have also played a significant role in the history of birth. For this reason, the history of childbirth, midwives, and wetnursing provides a vibrant and tangible means of studying the power of cultural and societal norms and attitudes, and the changing face and values of society throughout European history. Likewise, this cycle will continue to reflect the ever-present changes in society.

See also **Birth, Contraception, and Abortion; The Life Cycle** *(volume 2);* **Motherhood; Women and Femininity** *(in this volume); and other articles in this section.*

BIBLIOGRAPHY

Arnup, Katherine, Andrée Lévesque, and Ruth Roach Pierson, eds. *Delivering Motherhood: Maternal Ideologies and Practices in the 19th and 20th Centuries.* New York, 1990.

Banks, Amanda Carson. *Birth Chairs, Midwives, and Medicine.* Jackson, Miss., 1999.

Borst, Charlotte G. *Catching Babies: The Professionalization of Childbirth, 1870–1920.* Cambridge, U.K., 1995.

Donnison, Jean. *Midwives and Medical Men: A History of the Struggle for the Control of Childbirth.* London, 1977.

Eccles, Audrey. *Obstetrics and Gynaecology in Tudor and Stuart England.* Kent, Ohio, 1982.

Edwards, Robert R., and Vickie Ziegler, eds. *Matrons and Marginal Women in Medieval Society.* Woodbridge, U.K., 1995.

Ehrenreich, Barbara, and Deirdre English. *For Her Own Good: 150 Years of the Experts' Advice to Women.* New York, 1978.

Ehrenreich, Barbara. *Witches, Midwives, and Nurses: A History of Women Healers.* Detroit, 1973.

Fildes, Valerie. *Wet Nursing: A History from Antiquity to the Present.* Oxford, 1988.

Forbes, Thomas Rogers. *The Midwife and the Witch.* New York, 1982.

Gélis, Jacques. *History of Childbirth: Fertility, Pregnancy, and Birth in Early Modern Europe.* Translated by Rosemary Morris. Boston, 1991.

Goer, Henci. *Obstetric Myths versus Research Realities: A Guide to Medical Literature.* Westport, Conn., 1995.

Haberling, W. *German Medicine.* Translated by Jules Freund. New York, 1934.

Jarcho, Julius. *Postures and Practices during Labor among Primitive Peoples.* New York, 1934.

Kuntner, Liselotte. *Die Gebarhaltung der Frau: Schwangerschaft und Geburt aus geschichtlicher, völkerkundlicher und medizinischer Sicht.* Munich, 1985.

Kunzle, David. *Fashion and Fetishism: A Social History of the Corset, Tight-Lacing, and Other Forms of Body-Sculpture in the West.* Totowa, N.J., 1982.

Leap, Nicky. *The Midwife's Tale: An Oral History from Handywoman to Professional Midwife.* London, 1993.

Lewis, Judith Schneid. *In the Family Way: Childbearing in the British Aristocracy, 1760–1860.* New Brunswick, N.J., 1986.

Marland, Hilary, ed. *The Art of Midwifery: Early Modern Midwives in Europe.* London, 1993.

Martin, Emily. *The Woman in the Body: A Cultural Analysis of Reproduction.* Boston, 1987.

Murphy, Edward William. *Lectures on the Principles and Practices of Midwifery.* 2d ed. London, 1862.

Oakley, Ann. *The Captured Womb: A History of the Medical Care of Pregnant Women.* Oxford, 1984.

Poovey, Mary. *Uneven Developments: The Ideological Work of Gender in Mid-Victorian England.* Chicago, 1988.

Schrader, Catharina. *Mother and Child Were Saved: The Memoirs (1693–1740) of the Frisian Midwife Catharina Schrader.* Amsterdam, 1987.

Shryock, Richard. *The Development of Modern Medicine: An Interpretation of the Social and Scientific Factors Involved.* Philadelphia, 1936.

Sullivan, Deborah A., and Rose Weitz. *Labor Pains: Modern Midwives and Home Birth.* New Haven, Conn., 1988.

Sussman, George D. *Selling Mothers' Milk: The Wet-Nursing Business in France 1715–1914.* Urbana, Ill., 1982.

Taylor, Lloyd C. *The Medical Profession and Social Reform, 1885–1945.* New York, 1974.

Towler, Jean, and Joan Bramall, eds. *Midwives in History and Society.* London, 1986.

Turner, Ann Warren. *Rituals of Birth: From Prehistory to the Present.* New York, 1978.

Wilson, Adrian. *The Making of Man-Midwifery: Childbirth in England, 1660–1770.* Cambridge, Mass., 1995.

PSYCHIATRY AND PSYCHOLOGY

Roger Smith

"Psychology" denotes simultaneously an expert occupation and the character, mind, feelings, and behavior of individuals. "Psychiatry" denotes the medical specialty concerned with mental illness. The words themselves and the aspects of life they refer to, considered as distinct domains and classes of activity, are modern. The history of psychology and psychiatry encompasses a huge diversity of views about human nature and social relations, and that diversity was present even after psychology and psychiatry became professional occupations in the twentieth century.

Psychology as an occupation is an academic discipline, usually but not always understood to be a natural science, and a cluster of applied specialties. Described this way, psychology is overwhelmingly a twentieth-century phenomenon, a characteristic feature of Western modernity. In the sense of an individual's mental life, however, everyone has a psychology, and it is possible to talk about the psychology of people anywhere and in any period of history. All the same, an intense focus on people's psychology, rather than on other dimensions of the human world, is in fact distinctive of the twentieth-century West.

Psychology and psychiatry are distinct occupations, to the extent that the latter requires a medical qualification and is part of the medical profession. Nevertheless, there is considerable overlap of interest. Clinical psychology has been the largest area of employment for psychologists since about 1950; psychiatry has made significant contributions to psychological ideas, for example, of the emotions. In between psychology and psychiatry lies the history of psychoanalysis, the history of the considerable but controversial impact of the Viennese physician Sigmund Freud on European self-consciousness in the twentieth century.

PSYCHOLOGY AND MODERNITY

The modern history of psychology and psychiatry is bound up with the rise, beginning about 1880, of the professions in the human sciences, the creation of service occupations offering expertise in human affairs—economics, political science, the management sciences, planning, and so on. These professions, and the social, legal, and governmental arrangements that support them, function to offer rational guidance or control in all aspects of human affairs. This contrasts with earlier ages in which it was thought right for order to stem from the interests of rulers, tradition, fate, or God. Psychology and psychiatry are therefore part of what the German sociologist Max Weber analyzed as the rationalization of the modern world.

Like so much European social history, the history of psychology and psychiatry varies considerably with local circumstance. As occupations participating in modernization, psychology and psychiatry fit the pattern in which modern social systems spread outward from Western Europe, in interaction with North America, to southern and eastern Europe. Nowhere in Europe, however, was the scale of development and size of the growing human science professions on a par with the United States. Although many European ideas had earlier crossed the Atlantic and informed American developments, after 1945 Western European psychologists often looked to American leadership in the development of the field as a natural science. Russia shared in Western developments in both psychology and psychiatry in the three decades before the 1917 revolution. Thereafter the Soviet system made any activity concerned with individual consciousness, capacities, and conduct a politically sensitive matter. Whatever the historical diversity, at the end of the twentieth century, psychology and psychiatry were deeply embedded in the experience and expectations of people and in the institutional arrangements of all European countries. Marriage guidance, counseling, market research, child care, education, self-development and self-identity, anxiety, mental breakdown, criminality, aging: every aspect of individual experience and relations between people had its socially embedded psychological or psychiatric reality.

The history of psychology is at one and the same time about what people are thought to share by virtue of a common nature, and how they are thought to differ by virtue of group or individual characteristics. Psychology has never been neutral, because classifying people by difference is the way social values are embedded in policy and action. European countries sought world empires, struggled for national or ethnic dominance, and ordered society by class and gender, and this involved drawing on as well as reinforcing psychology. Psychology provided the language with which to debate similarity and difference. Arguments about what people owe to an original nature as opposed to civilization, or to nature as opposed to nurture, have been a recurrent part of European as well as North American political discourse.

Much of what we associate with psychology is new. In the twentieth-century West there was a marked emphasis on individual qualities and individual subjective experience as the basic fabric on which society is built and in relation to which values must be judged. This stress on the value of individual people and their psychological world correlates with the spread of democracy in politics and competitive individualism in economic life. For example, voting in democratic societies is designed to decide issues according to the sum of individual preferences. Critics therefore draw on descriptions of earlier ways of life in which what was of value in a person was not individual feelings or preferences but rather her or his place in civic society, in God's plan, or in the progress of humanity.

In this regard the Renaissance appears to mark a decisive shift. Early Christians stressed the life and salvation of the individual soul, and Roman law recognized the dignity and responsibility of the individual person. In Europe between 1450 and 1650, however, there is evidence for a new self-consciousness about how subjective life distinguishes people as individuals. The portrait and the self-portrait became genres of painting; autobiography, letters, diaries, and religious interrogation of the soul spread as forms of communication with other people and—more distinctively—with one's self; and essays and philosophy emphasized individual experience as authority for knowledge. In the eighteenth century, the novel began to provide people with a way to fashion their own lives and sensibility. This culminated in romanticism, the Europe-wide culture that established a lasting commitment to individual feeling and creativity and set up the image of artistic genius as a model. If early-nineteenth-century language stressed the richness of the human soul in Christian terms, it also valued the emotional and sensuous experience of embodied individuals.

Romantic ideals shaped human beings as psychological subjects during a century in which the industrial revolution and rapid urban growth gave rise to mass society in cities from Glasgow to Petersburg. When the individual acquired unprecedented freedom and lost identity through city life, psychology came into its own. Italian and French psychologists of the crowd, most popularly Gustave Le Bon, described how in the mass individuals lose autonomy and act by imitation. Social psychology began around 1900 to study the determinants of human relationships. The spread—however uneven—of economically liberal, democratic, and urban society in Europe was accompanied by forms of knowledge and power expressed through the psychology of the individual. When men and women collapsed or degenerated under the strain of the new conditions, or were perhaps ill-equipped at birth to cope, psychiatry provided a social response.

The crystallization of psychology and psychiatry as areas of activity at the end of the nineteenth century also depended on the increasing social authority of the natural sciences. The natural sciences, especially physiology, became the basis for what was claimed as expert knowledge about normal and abnormal individual capacities. Liberal and radical social thinkers turned to psychology and psychiatry in order to replace faith about the soul and God's will with facts about the mind and behavior. Conservative observers feared that the new sciences encouraged materialism, religious unbelief, and social upheaval if not revolution. The acceptance of Charles Darwin's theory of evolution in the second half of the century set such hopes and fears within a framework of belief about natural progress and the place of humanity in the universe. When the communist Soviet state was established in 1917, for a few years some intellectuals thought that the time had arrived when all prejudice about human nature inherited from the past could be thrown away. It was possible, they dreamed, "to engineer the human soul" (in words used at a writers' congress in 1934) and use psychology as the technology to create a new, free man. But for every believer in the inevitable march of scientific progress there was a pessimist who feared the cost. The reported figures for degeneracy, the evidence of alcohol and drug abuse, prostitution, venereal disease, mental deficiency, crime, and class and racial backwardness at the end of the nineteenth century gave substance to these fears and much of the content to modern psychology and psychiatry.

EARLY VIEWS OF HUMAN NATURE

There was no area of learning and no occupation called psychology (or psychiatry) in the Renaissance and early modern periods. There was, however, a rich language for individual character, the language of the humors, temperaments, spirits, and passions, which had originated with the ancient Greeks and been modified by Christian values. This was the language about people used by Shakespeare and Rabelais. It was used both by educated people, including physicians, and by the common people, and it provided a way to describe both human nature in general and individual differences. The language expressed a belief that treated disorders—body and soul were closely linked—as an imbalance in the humors and spirits. Description was as concerned with the moral and religious dimensions of human existence as with physical well-being, since all dimensions were equally real in a world ordained by God. Writers thought it natural to correlate order and disorder in the world and in the individual, to compare the macrocosm and the microcosm, and the body politic (the state) and the body physical. Astrology and magic appeared as reasonable ways of forecasting and intervening in human affairs.

In the second half of the seventeenth century, educated elites began to be skeptical about substantial parts of this belief system, though it retained a large popular following through to the twentieth century. New ideas favored a nonmagical, mechanical ordering of nature and the separation of the soul and the body as different entities (though practical knowledge, not least of madness and passion, held them together). The French philosopher René Descartes championed the idea that the body is fully a machine, and the Englishman John Locke wrote that individual knowledge and character is constructed piecemeal from experienced sensations. These steps seemed to render the study of human nature as much of concern to teachers and natural philosophers (the word "scientist" was not yet invented) as to theologians. Most provocatively, Locke introduced the argument that it is consciousness and memory, the product of experience, rather than a soul, which gives a person his or her identity.

Belief spread that the universe is ordered according to the laws revealed by Isaac Newton at the end of the seventeenth century, and known through experience in the manner analyzed by Locke. This gave intellectual content to the European culture present in the period between Louis XIV and the French Revolution and known to historians as the Enlightenment. Many observers then and later thought of this period as the beginning of the modern secular age, the age in which Europeans sought and made

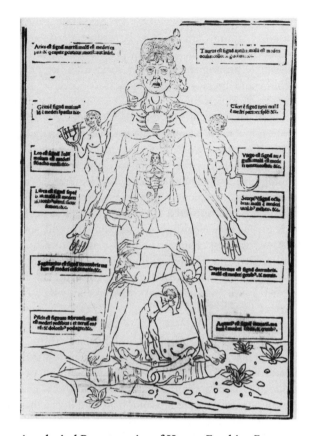

Astrological Representation of Human Faculties. From Johannes Ketham, *Fasciculus medicinae* (1522). BIBLIOTECA CASANATENSE, ROME

progress on the basis of knowledge about nature and human nature alike. The "Enlightenment project," as twentieth-century social critics called it, culminated later in great social movements, both in the marxist form claimed as authority for communism and in the liberal form developed under capitalism, to advance scientific knowledge of human beings and human affairs. In the eighteenth century, meanwhile, the argument that human nature becomes what it is through experience, and through the pleasures and pains of experience leading to one action rather than another, encouraged belief that education and social reform would lead people out of superstition, barbarism, and tyranny. But there remained a vast gap between the aspirations of the educated theorists of progress and the predominantly rural population of Europe. Yet, while Enlightenment ideas were restricted to small aristocratic circles in central and eastern Europe, there were settings where what the eighteenth-century Scotsman Adam Smith identified as commercial society flourished and supported "the science of Man" (to use the contemporary expression). In cities like Edinburgh, London, Amsterdam, Bordeaux, Paris, and Geneva, and later in emerging provincial industrial cities like Birmingham and Lyon, social mobility, new wealth, and literacy opened up society to new and sometimes radical ideas.

In this intellectual and social context, a few writers, like the academic at the Prussian university of Halle, Christian Wolff, and the French-Swiss *philosophe*, Charles Bonnet, began to differentiate psychology as a branch of knowledge. Their interests were philosophical, religious, and moral rather than scientific in the later restricted sense of the term. The Scottish universities taught about the human mind and the formation of character under the rubric of moral philosophy, and they increasingly did so in a manner that separated the subject from theology and hence created more secular ways of thinking about human nature. David Hume's *A Treatise of Human Nature,* published in 1739–1740, was a work in this vein, though it was too skeptical and un-Christian to attract an audience when published. In London and in pre-revolutionary Paris, the reformist Jeremy Bentham developed systematically the opinion that all individual action pursues pleasure or avoids pain, and hence that a calculus of pleasures and pains will make possible a new social order. In the East Prussian center of Königsberg, J. F. Herbart propagated a science of psychology in the service of government in the early nineteenth century. Psychology became differentiated as a branch of knowledge.

Responses to madness and abnormal behavior in the eighteenth century also became less focused on the soul or nonmaterial events and more on the disordered mind. Although it remained common to refer to disordered spirits, Locke's work suggested a view of madness as the wrong working of reflection on experience, a jumbling in the mind of the right order of sensations. Humoral theory continued in practice to underlie much ordinary care, and this was still the case when special homes and asylums for those with mental disorder began to be common in the late eighteenth century. Experience with what, from an educated European perspective, appeared to be abnormal people, gained through travel and encountering different customs, or simply through interacting with children and peasants, sharpened questions about what makes people the way they are. Debates about the origin of language, the state of mankind before civilization, and the effects of education were lively and open-ended, treating psychological ideas as part of discourse about social progress. All this helped shape a modern psychological language; for example, reference to the emotions rather than the passions became common in English in the second half of the eighteenth century.

Contemporary observers of polite society were struck by a new delicacy, reflected in the new fiction, about individual feelings. An interest in sensibility, or claims about the faculty of perceiving beauty, attracted essayists, moralists, and physicians to psychological expression. There was renewed enthusiasm for the ancient and Renaissance art of physiognomy, the art of reading the soul's character from the face. The work of the Swiss pastor Johann Kaspar Lavater was celebrated, and the fashion for the cut-out profile of a person's head, the silhouette, spread through all homes with cultural aspirations. In Paris around 1800, the Austrian physician Franz Joseph Gall elaborated phrenology, the study of individual character by correlating the shape of the head with the underlying brain and mental faculties (like philoprogenitiveness, a polite term for the reproductive instinct). Many people in western Europe and North America learned to anticipate the creation of a science of human nature, accessibly focused on individual differences, by examining the embodiment of mind in the brain. Slightly before Gall, another Austrian physician, Anton Mesmer, introduced in Paris the trance phenomenon that bears his name, mesmerism, which also had a large public audience. When rethought (and called hypnotism), mesmerism suggested that there are hidden or unconscious powers in the human mind. In the late nineteenth century, hypnotism was the direct antecedent of the new science of the unconscious introduced by Freud and the French physician Pierre Janet, among others.

One of the most dramatic of all experiences in human differences, which captured everyone's imagination, was of so-called wild children, children apparently living alone like animals in the countryside. These children posed in concrete form the great political question of the Enlightenment: By what means has man achieved a state of civilization, and is this state natural? Stories of wild children recurred in Europe, even into the twentieth century. Captured in 1724, Peter the wild boy of Hanover was made to tour polite society and even to visit the court of George I of England. In 1801, in what remains the most famous of all experiments on psychological development, Jean Itard, the innovative head of the institute for deaf-mutes in Paris, began the task of bringing civility to the wild boy, Victor, who had lived alone in the woods of the Aveyron region and lacked language, cleanliness, and ordinary sensibilities. It was in these terms, rather than in the twentieth-century language of nature versus nurture, that people faced the challenge of understanding human nature.

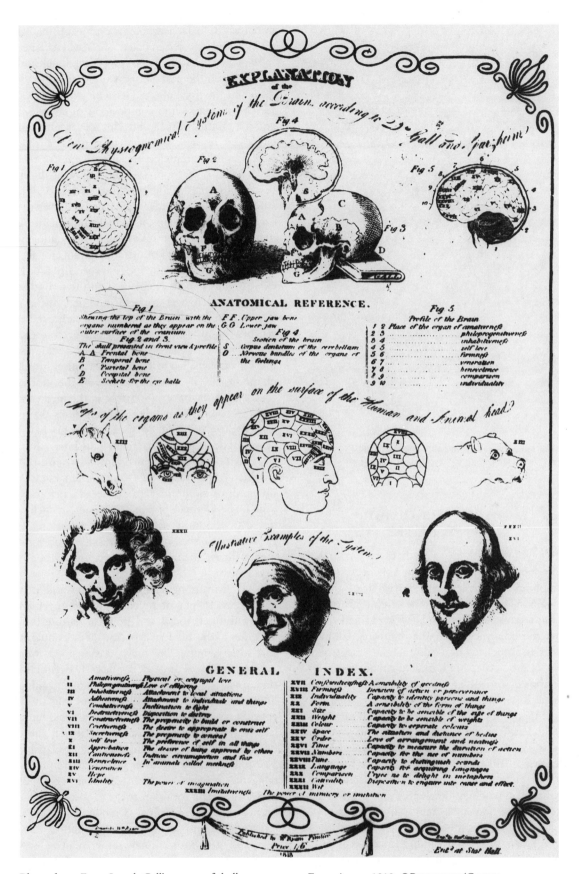

Phrenology. Franz Joseph Gall's system of skull measurement. Engraving, c. 1818. ©Bettmann/Corbis

Mesmerism. Anton Mesmer's theories of mind included notions of animal magnetism. Austrian print, 1780s. BIBLIOTHÈQUE NATIONALE, PARIS/J.-L. CHARMET

MODERN PSYCHOLOGY AND PSYCHIATRY

Psychology and psychiatry thus have very complex roots in many walks of life and not only in academic, philosophical, or medical circles. Two institutional changes in the first half of the nineteenth century had great importance for the consolidation of the fields as distinct social entities. First, the reform of German universities, stimulated by a cultural resurgence under the Napoleonic occupation, created circumstances in which areas of knowledge expanded and flourished as academic disciplines. Other countries imitated the German model or adapted it to local circumstances in the second half of the century. The changes put in place the basis for academic careers, for universities to be accepted as arbiters of knowledge, and for the rapid growth of natural science subjects. The discipline of experimental physiology developed, and it included research on the nervous system and on the senses, systematically studying mind and action in its physical setting. Then, beginning in the 1870s, especially around Wilhelm Wundt in Leipzig and Georg E. Muller in Göttingen, there were new and successful initiatives to make psychology a subject using natural science methods. When taken up elsewhere, especially in the United States, the philosophical dimension was reduced, and the outcome was the modern academic discipline of psychology. German psychological research focused on the composition of consciousness and the rational adult mind. But also in Germany, as elsewhere, research was guided by practical interests in education, commerce, social problems, or the law.

At the same time, especially following the efforts of the physician Wilhelm Griesinger in Berlin, the study of mental disorders entered the university and sought a place as part of scientific medicine rather than as part of asylum management. In gradual ways, varying with local administrative arrangements, this established the academic medical specialty called psychiatry. This step also depended on the second of the institutional changes to be mentioned, the asylum movement of the late eighteenth and early nineteenth century. Across Europe, the asylum became the answer to what was newly perceived as a major social problem and challenge to humanitarianism, the plight of the insane. By the second half of the nineteenth century, the asylums were firmly in the medical orbit and associated with medical organizations that often turned their attention to social problems like alcoholism. The description of mental disorders, the clinical activity that preoccupied late-nineteenth-century psychiatry, was closely tied to moral judgment about the needs of social order. In the decades before World War I, the German psychiatrist Emil Kraepelin, followed by the head of the Zurich institution, Eugen Bleuler, established the basic modern categories of mental illness, the manic-depressive and schizophrenic psychoses.

If institutional changes made possible new academic disciplines of psychology and psychiatry, a widely diffused social and political culture brought attention to the different capacities of individual minds and social groups, like social classes, men, women, nations, and races. Indeed, by the early twentieth century, psychology was well on its way to becoming the lingua franca, the shared language, of human difference. Phrenology had set an early example, but it was largely rejected by scientists by 1850. In the early twentieth century, psychologists began to classify people, and especially children in the classroom, by intelligence, by aptitude, and then, from the 1930s, by personality. The common usage of words like "intelligence" and "personality" is modern: "intelligence" replaced "reason" as it refers to a natural capacity shared in part with animals rather than an abstract phenomenon; and "personality" seemed to be a way to refer to the collective attributes of a person with-

out the old-fashioned moral judgments often implied in a reference to "character."

New work on individual capacities depended on the development and standardization of tests, and the creation of statistics as the means to analyze test results and to relate results to supposed underlying causes of human differences. By this route in particular, psychologists developed an expertise that distinguished psychology as a separate occupation. Statistical analysis was an important British contribution, and in Britain the single most important influence on the academic subject of psychology was Francis Galton, a Victorian obsessed by finding ways to measure human variation. As an academic discipline, however, British psychology developed slowly in the twentieth century, in the interwar years in association with industrial and educational applications; it was only after 1945 that it grew rapidly in size.

In France, Victor Cousin dominated academic philosophy and teacher training for a considerable part of the nineteenth century, and his influence sustained an official view that psychology is the training of the soul in pursuit of the good, the true, and the beautiful. Then, in the 1870s, the concerted efforts of secular and Republican writers like Hippolyte Taine and Théodule Ribot created opportunities for what was called "new psychology," a psychology built on experimental and clinical observation of people. The use of clinical methods, the intensive examination of single, exceptional individuals, gave a special character to French work. Alfred Binet studied hypnotized subjects, his own daughters, and great calculators before undertaking the work on individual children in the classroom that led him to devise the first intelligence tests, published in 1905. The Catholic Church responded to the new psychology, creating an institute that included the field in the University of Louvain or Leuven in Belgium in 1889. Pastors both Catholic and Protestant, as in the Netherlands in the 1920s, turned to psychology in the hope of overcoming the perceived distance of the churches from people's experience of modern life.

Scientific ideas in general, and enthusiasm for psychology in particular, were unevenly spread in Europe. For those committed to modernization, the distribution of psychology mapped the unequal progress made by different countries. Reformers believed that ignorance and resistance to psychology and psychiatry indicated backwardness caused by dogmatic religion, economic and social underdevelopment, and oppressive rule. Progressive intellectuals in Catholic countries like Italy and Spain, or in an autocracy like Russia, therefore often looked to Britain, France, and Germany for advanced ideas and the authority for a

rational and humanitarian order. The evolutionar thought of Darwin and the contemporary socia thinker, Herbert Spencer, was an important mediur of cultural transfer, and both writers clearly supporte a psychology that treated human beings as a part c nature. Students from countries on the margins of Eu rope studied abroad, brought home scientific though and radical ideas, and—frequently associated with na tionalist movements—sought the means to bring thei peoples into the modern age. Much of the idealisr went in fact into practical tasks in education or i medicine, as in the careers of the people who intrc duced modern psychology into Romania, Hungar and elsewhere. Interest in psychology was part of lib eral and radical hopes for change in Russia from th late 1850s. By the end of the century, the early effort of Ivan M. Sechenov to link psychology and th brain were replaced by more recent French and Ger man psychology and psychiatry. The Russian prac titioners, however, faced by the unbending reaction ary politics of the tsars, nearly all linked the futur of their science to the modernization of the countr By the outbreak of World War I, then, Western sec ular ideas about human nature were widely diffuse across Europe, if in some settings restricted to a smal professional class.

Psychology and psychiatry took for granted cer tain norms of mental life and conduct. It was though that divergences from the norms, implicitly under stood to be male, Western, adult, and middle or uppe class, constituted natural experiments, and hence grea value was placed on studying children in contrast t adults, women in contrast to men, Anglo-Saxon in contrast to Italian, and so on. One such so-callec natural experiment, multiple personality, intensively studied in France, appeared dramatically to questior belief that human identity is given by a unitary soul Then, in the years around 1900, Freud developec what he called psychoanalysis, working with the nat ural experiments provided by neurotic cases. He gen eralized from these cases, in the light of his own self analysis, to construct a psychology of the unconscious which argued that irrational feelings and motivation are normal, not abnormal. Immediately before World War I and in the interwar decades, he gained a large public audience for his views, not least because he provided a framework for thinking about sexuality, then becoming a publicly discussable topic. Further, as he pointed to the power of irrational forces in human life, his outlook matched Europe's experience of war and the rise of Nazism and fascism. But even as Freud gained an audience, psychoanalysis split into factions, and his most influential earlier supporter, the Swiss psychiatrist Carl Gustav Jung, left in 1913 to

Sigmund Freud. Photograph by his son, 1914.
MARY EVANS PICTURE LIBRARY

construct his own analytical psychology, which emphasized the reality of a collective unconscious.

All the combatants in World War I centrally organized production and social life in the interest of national efficiency. Opinion was favorable to those who claimed scientific expertise in human affairs, psychologists among them. Psychologists contributed, for example, to studies of industrial fatigue, of great importance to the manufacture of munitions. In the 1920s psychotechnics, the use of psychological tests and experiments to assess personnel and work situations, was widely taken up. The Austrian railways, for example, employed a special train to test its staff. Research on the psychology of children, to create a basis for welfare and education, rapidly expanded. This research involved many women, and in this way as well as through popular texts and advice manuals, motherhood and psychological expertise became closely linked. Child care brought together psychology, psychoanalysis, and psychiatry, as at the Tavistock Institute in London, which became a major center for training people in psychotherapeutic approaches to social questions like marriage, doctor-patient rela-

tions, and delinquency. In the Netherlands and German-speaking countries, psychologists favored character analysis, using handwriting for example, a form of qualitative psychology that was thought to express the unique dignity of each person, in contrast to the quantitative techniques of assessment becoming widespread in the Anglo-American world. In the Soviet Union, by the end of the 1920s the Communist Party was asserting full authority over all areas of intellectual and social life, including the sciences and the professions. During the Stalin years there was suspicion of any practical activity or science not directly serving the communist interest as currently presented by the party. Psychology as a discipline came under suspicion, and in the early 1950s there was a concerted but never fully successful attempt to replace psychology by physiology. In Nazi Germany many psychologists found occupation in personnel testing, and some propagated a form of character analysis sympathetic to racist ends; yet others, many Jewish but also the influential group of Gestalt psychologists, were forced out of work and into emigration.

In the interwar years, psychology became increasingly divided between academic experimental research and the activity (including psychoanalysis) that flourished in practical settings. Many academic psychologists were interested in physiological psychology, the relation of mental events to brain functions, and their research was inaccessible to those not trained in the field. Interest in the brain did link psychology and medicine, especially via the clinical specialty of neurology, the field of brain disorders. Most psychiatrists hoped one day to be able to correlate mental illness and brain disorder, but the early years of the century were filled with pessimism. In the 1930s psychiatrists, almost desperate to make an impact on the seemingly intractable cases in asylums, turned to physical therapies that forcibly intervened in the brain. The effort was international: Manfred Sakel introduced insulin coma in Hungary, Ugo Cerletti used massive electric shock in Italy, followers of Ivan P. Pavlov in the Soviet Union induced deep sleep lasting days, and Egaz Moniz organized the first frontal lobotomy surgery in Portugal. All this was taken up in English-speaking countries before it was substantially displaced in the 1950s by new drug therapies that, for the first time, helped reverse the ever rising number of asylum patients.

Starting in the 1940s, brain research, led by the United States, became a heavily committed and fast-growing area of science, and some scientists claimed it would finally unravel the secrets of the human mind. Skeptics doubted that knowledge would be gained quickly, even when new computing technology suggested powerful models for psychological events

and encouraged what is known as cognitive psychology. Some critics were also opposed on religious or ethical grounds to viewing human beings as material machines. Nevertheless, there was a Europe-wide public following for new ideas about the brain and human identity, an interest taken up in science fiction and films.

While psychology developed very unevenly as an academic discipline and as an occupation in Europe, a large profession became established in the United States. Especially after 1945, United States psychology, which claimed to have established objective methods making psychology a rigorous science, was followed by many European countries, especially West Germany, the Netherlands, and those in Scandinavia. At this time the politics of social democracy and the welfare state supported the provision of psychological expertise and intervention in many areas of life and across the population. Whereas early psychoanalysis was available to a small number of fee-paying individuals, post-1945 psychotherapy became part of the life of ordinary people. Psychologically trained personnel worked on a substantial scale in education, personnel management, counseling, and with difficulties in living of all kinds. It seemed possible to represent the goals of life in psychological terms, and the literature of self-development and personal growth became big business, while many churches rethought pastoral care in a psychological idiom.

In Eastern Europe, following the liberation and then occupation of countries by the Red Army, psychology, like every other area of activity, was forced into conformity with the current policies at the center in Moscow. This imposed an approach given legitimacy by reference to Pavlov's name in the 1950s, the evidence of which was still evident much later, though many intellectuals learned to live with a split between overt conformity and covert independence. Nevertheless, in the 1970s Soviet psychology itself began to diversify and expand, often drawing strength from marginalized earlier work, notably by the Marxist psychologist, Lev Vygotsky, who had died in 1934. With the breakdown of the Soviet empire in 1989 and the virtual ending of funding for science in Russia itself, Eastern European psychologists looked to the West for professional standards or for employment, or responded to a new private clientele.

In summary, the conspicuous twentieth-century growth of psychology in North America as well as in Europe means two things: It means, first, the establishment of a service occupation, which is itself divided between academic psychologists, who view psychology as a scientific discipline, and applied psychologists who view psychology as an expertise in the care and management of individual and interpersonal problems. Second, this development means a shift in beliefs and values, so that it is now widely and unthinkingly held that an expressive life in terms of individual psychology is what accords dignity to existence. A European culture, and more generally a Western culture, has emerged in which psychological knowledge is thought to give access to the good life, and critics have variously judged that this conviction is at the expense of political engagement, spiritual

Pavlov's Laboratory. First experiments of Ivan Pavlov (1849–1936) at the physiology department of the Military Medicine Academy, St. Petersburg, Russia, 1911. SOVFOTO

concern, civic consciousness, and nonpersonal values generally. More positive observers note the humane values that appear to tie together democracy, systems of social welfare and individual support, and psychological activity, giving people knowledge and power to govern their own lives.

See also other articles in this section.

BIBLIOGRAPHY

Ash, Mitchell G., and William R. Woodward, eds. *Psychology in Twentieth-Century Thought and Society.* Cambridge, U.K., 1987.

Danziger, Kurt. *Naming the Mind: How Psychology Found Its Language.* Thousand Oaks, Calif., and London, 1997.

Ellenberger, Henri F. *The Discovery of the Unconscious: The History and Evolution of Dynamic Psychiatry.* New York and London, 1970.

Fox, Christopher, Roy Porter, and Robert Wokler, eds. *Inventing Human Science: Eighteenth-Century Domains.* Berkeley, Calif., Los Angeles, and London, 1995.

Ginneken, Jaap van. *Crowds, Psychology, and Politics 1871–1899.* Cambridge, U.K., 1992.

Hunter, Richard, and Ida Macalpine. *Three Hundred Years of Psychiatry 1535–1860.* London, 1963.

Joravsky, David. *Russian Psychology: A Critical History.* Oxford, 1989.

Micale, Mark S., and Roy Porter. *Discovering the History of Psychiatry.* New York, 1994.

Porter, Roy, ed. *Rewriting the Self: Histories from the Renaissance to the Present.* London and New York, 1997.

Rabinbach, Anson. *The Human Motor: Energy, Fatigue, and the Origins of Modernity.* New York, 1990.

Richards, Graham. *Putting Psychology in Its Place: A Critical Historical Overview.* London and New York, 1997.

Rose, Nikolas. *Governing the Soul: The Shaping of the Private Self.* London and New York, 1990.

Rose, Nikolas. *The Psychological Complex: Psychology, Politics, and Society in England, 1869–1939.* London, 1985.

Rousseau, George S., ed. *The Languages of Psyche: Mind and Body in Enlightenment Thought.* Berkeley, Calif., Los Angeles, and London, 1990.

Shorter, Edward. *From Paralysis to Fatigue: A History of Psychosomatic Illness in the Modern Era.* New York, 1992.

Shorter, Edward. *A History of Psychiatry: From the Era of the Asylum to the Age of Prozac.* New York and Chichester, U.K., 1997.

Siraisi, Nancy G. *Medieval and Early Renaissance Medicine: An Introduction to Knowledge and Practice.* Chicago, 1990.

Smith, Roger. *The Norton History of the Human Sciences.* New York, 1997. Published outside the United States as *The Fontana History of the Human Sciences,* London, 1997.

Section 18

WORK

WORK AND THE WORK ETHIC

Peter Shapely

The subject of work and the work ethic in Europe covers an extremely varied number of issues, making generalizations difficult. The term "work" applies to a wide range of human activities. It can describe unpaid activity in the home and with the family or, more readily, a range of paid employment in, for example, manufacturing industries, agricultural work, crafts, or a profession. Each group has numerous subdivisions, such as unskilled, semiskilled, skilled, clerical, management, and entrepreneur. Other divisions are drawn along gender and age lines.

Work is not simply an economic activity. To fully appreciate its significance, work has to be examined and understood as a cultural activity and as a construct of society. Work ethics are a reflection of these social and cultural constructs rather than the economic process. Because it is not simply a physical activity designed to secure material benefits, work and especially ideologies of work have to be seen in the political and social contexts as well as the economic context to be properly understood. This article considers work and work ethics in these contexts and briefly looks at a number of areas. In the preindustrial period the focus was on work in agriculture and, to a lesser extent, the craft industries. The nature of the work performed by men and women was different, though only in the late eighteenth and early nineteenth centuries was the economy of work in Europe perceived as a separate sphere of action for men and women. An inseparable correlation existed between family, home, and work. Industrialization gradually brought a number of changes across Europe. Work slowly moved from the home into factories, and practices and hours of work became more regulated. Industrialization had a significant impact on women and children. Subsequently the state became more involved in providing a regulatory framework that guaranteed hours, pay, and conditions.

Although the European Union brought an increasing sense of homogeneity to work practices through standardizing legislation in western Europe, a singular work experience or set of practices previously did not exist across the Continent. Work was never seen as a sole experience or activity, and work patterns always developed unevenly. This is true of the whole period from the early sixteenth century through the twentieth century. No single model explains the pattern of work in Europe. Even labels, such as the "industrial revolution", are misleading because they suggest that a clear and singular process occurred simultaneously throughout the area and eventually led to the dominance of mechanization and the factory. The process of change was uneven not just between different areas of Europe but also within any particular region. This variety also characterizes attempts to define the work ethic. It is impossible to think about a single monolithic work ethic. During the period a number of ideologies of work were expressed that had existed in Europe since ancient Greece. Central to the work ethic was social status. Society was graded according to each individual's work status. Slaves and poor laborers were at the bottom of the social hierarchy and were employed in low-skilled and hard labor that was generally considered degrading. Above them were the skilled crafts, followed by the arts, including architecture, which all had varying degrees of social value. The large and successful commercial employers achieved greater distinction, but at the top of the social hierarchy in ancient Greece and Rome stood the nobility, whose role was simply that of the warrior.

PREMODERN PATTERNS: THE PEASANTRY

The work ethic evolved as Christianity gradually spread across Europe. The Christian religion had a significant impact in redefining work ideology. However, Christianity did not simply replace the philosophy of ancient Greece. The disciplinarian approach of Aristotle was integrated into the teachings of the Catholic Church. Yet the status given to certain occupations did begin to change. Influenced by Christian philosophers, such as St. Thomas Aquinas, a new hierarchy of occupations developed. Work as a cleric or in other religious careers had the greatest value. Below them were the merchants, shopkeepers, and farmers, followed by artisans and peasants. The church frowned upon those involved in finance, such as money lenders, and in general the populace was suspicious of the profit motive. Work was part of the natural order, and people were born into their positions. All occupations reflected God's will. The medieval work ethic discouraged workers from maximizing their potential income by working longer and harder than necessary. Workers in the medieval period and much of the early modern period had a single notion of what they needed to survive and were not usually encouraged to go any further. Profit and social emulation had limited impact. In the sixteenth century both the Catholic Church and the state promoted meekness, dutifulness, and submissiveness to social superiors. People were taught the virtues of hard work and obedience.

This sense of duty and obedience was reinforced through the structure of early modern rural Europe. Around 90 percent of European workers in the sixteenth and seventeenth centuries were employed in agriculture, and the majority of these belonged to one of the many peasant classes. Peasant workers of Europe had varied experiences and fortunes. In England the yeoman class generally thrived in contrast with the lot of peasants in southern Europe. In parts of Spain and Italy, such as Castile and Naples, the peasant workers struggled under harsh conditions. Landowners and the church kept peasants in their place. The land was poor, and the tax burdens were oppressive. Wide variations existed even among peasant workers in the same country. Of French peasants, the laborers, who were mostly plowmen, had a higher social status than other peasants, though even this narrowly defined class experienced diverse work burdens and levels of prosperity within the country. Their numbers declined throughout the seventeenth century. Some rose into the ranks of the *fermiers,* the small landowners. Others sank to the level of the *manoeuvres,* the unskilled workmen, who used the stock, seed, and land of the local landowner in return for half of the produce. Below them were the *journaliers,* or wage laborers. Many of the French peasants of all ranks were effectively tied to the authority of the seigneurs, the powerful landowners. Some exercised manorial rights, including unpaid labor for a few days each year.

Central Europe exhibited a similar multiformity. In Germany the *Meier,* or free peasants, enjoyed reasonable levels of prosperity in the north, but conditions in the south led to a decline in peasant success during the seventeenth century. In Prussia the free peasant, or *Colmer,* often became a large farmer. Yet even within the German states clear differences developed. In East Elbia in the late eighteenth century serfs could be reduced to a state of virtual slavery, whereas in nearby Westphalia dues were much lighter, movement was far less restricted, and serfs could even inherit their land. In some areas the serfs were simply expected to give up a set number of hours every year to work on the landowner's estate or to pay other dues, including matrimonial taxes and death duties. In England the yeomen were viewed as virtuous freeborn laborers who worked their way up the social ladder.

Most of Europe was dominated by serfdom, which continued in Russia and large parts of eastern and central Europe into the nineteenth century. Serfs worked under poor conditions and severe controls on individual freedom. In Russia, tied to the landowner's territory, serfs were subjected to a number of burdens, including oppressive labor dues. Free peasants lived in Russia also, but even they were usually bound to the landlord by heavy debts. Many sank to the level of the *bobyli,* the landless laborer, or the *kabala,* who had become so bound to the landowners by debts that they were little more than slaves. The ideology of serf work was associated with oppression, servitude, and duty. Peasants could virtually sell themselves into this state of servitude, which freed them from taxation and army service. In the mid-seventeenth century serfs comprised nine-tenths of the working population in Russia. The powers of the landlord increased, and serfs became a status symbol for the landowners, who often held onto their power over serfs not for profit but because of the prestige attached. The precise working conditions were determined by the contract between the serf or the serf's forebears and the landowner. They worked on the land, often barely at a subsistence level. Large areas of eastern Europe, including Poland and parts of the Habsburg Empire, had a similar form of serfdom. In other areas the restrictions on freedom were far greater. Czech peasants, for example, worked in terrible conditions. Serfs in eastern Europe tended to be worse off than those in the west. Serfs could not emigrate without the lord's consent, and they were often allowed to marry only serfs from the same estate. Inheritance taxes were some of the heaviest burdens. In parts of west Germany the relatives of deceased female serfs were expected to give up her best clothes, and the male heir often had to give his largest head of livestock.

The work ethic in rural early modern Europe maintained an essentially reactionary outlook. Many of the European peasants of the sixteenth and seventeenth centuries were conservative in nature. In their "fixed life world," attitudes toward work were based on customs passed on by each generation. Peasants

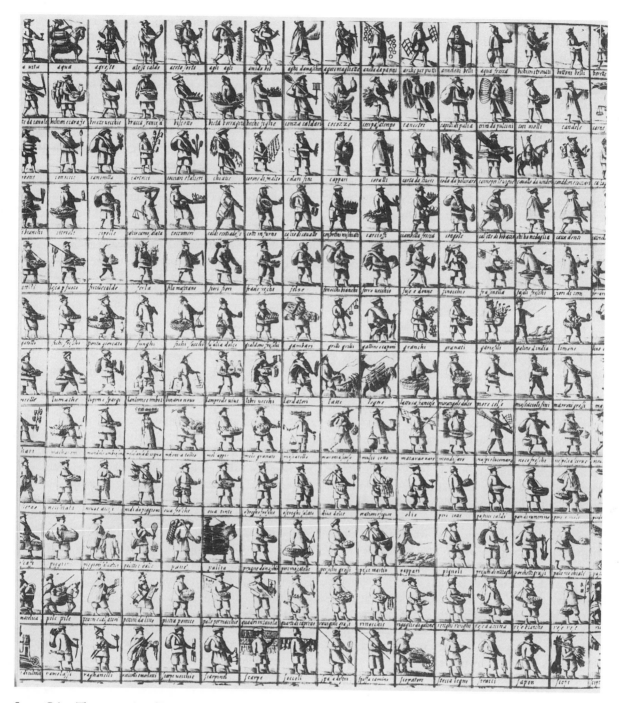

Street Cries. The street cries of Rome. PHOTO: OSCAR SAVIO

worked for the basic necessities of life, at self-sufficiency rather than for profit and economic expansion. They did not compete with fellow peasants, and opportunities for social mobility through work achievements were limited. The Catholic Church did not encourage a different view. Peasants feared that, if they became more competitive and profit-oriented, they would attract the avarice of other peasants, tax collectors, and

landlords. With few incentives, they were slow to adopt new work techniques. Poor laborers regarded themselves as part of a divine order that positioned the landowners at the top.

Even for those who were not serfs, manual labor in the preindustrial period was often physically demanding. The notion of a golden age of satisfying work existing before industrialization is a myth. In the sixteenth and seventeenth centuries work was simply toil, whether the task was paid or unpaid. Work ethics for the laborer or skilled worker did not glorify the virtue of such toil. It was simply a means of survival. The agricultural worker plowed the land as part of the household duties in securing a livelihood, or he or she performed the same task as paid labor. In either case the toil was hard and the conditions poor. Many peasants in the seventeenth century enjoyed only a basic subsistence standard of living. Because their holdings were small, they supplemented their incomes by working as wage labor on big farms or by taking up side occupations, such as weaving. Large Dutch farms employed young servants who worked for board and lodging and who became a part of the family, as many as three generations working and living on the same farm. When sons married, they remained on the family farm.

Not all rural areas were dominated by serfdom. By the early sixteenth century parts of Europe were moving away from traditional feudal structures toward commercialization of agriculture. The status of agricultural workers became more fragmented. In England the traditional yeoman class divided into capitalist farmers on the one hand and wage-earning laborers on the other hand. Agrarian capitalism led to the growth of wage labor, and bonded labor slowly disappeared. The process was quicker in some areas, such as England, where like in the Netherlands, a large section of the working population was employed as farm servants, living and working on big estates. In England they were usually young men and women employed for one-year contracts who became a part of the working family. As such they were expected to perform any of the tasks on the estate, whether in the field or in the house. Day laborers were different. Often married, they were usually older than farm servants. They lived independently of the employer and were employed only when work was available. Theirs was an uncertain position, dependent on the seasons, the weather, and their own health.

While agriculture dominated employment in preindustrial Europe, skilled crafts provided the major source of employment in the towns and cities. From the sixteenth century to the eighteenth century skilled craft workers across much of Europe organized into guilds, which had governed some trades since the Middle Ages. Ethically the guilds stressed quality of workmanship, which they guaranteed by controlling entry into the guild and terms of apprentice training. Moreover they protected workers' rights and offered their members and the towns in which they operated a high status. Independent handicraft production was regulated. In many European countries statutes rein-

forced the rights of artisans to establish wages, rates, and the terms of apprenticeships. Giving artisans an organizational structure, guilds allowed them to wield collective power. Many new guilds originated from older medieval craft associations. They had strict rules and regulations and were highly ritualistic. The size and nature of their memberships differed enormously. Some were wealthy merchants, others were humble craftspeople. Modest tailors, for example, often delivered goods to order, rarely had stock on hand, and usually relied on the client to supply the cloth. Brewers, on the other hand, were often wealthier, owning larger properties and employing workers.

The artisan usually was an independent craftsperson who made and sold a particular product themselves. Some artisans employed one or two journeymen. The term also had wider applications, referring to those who served a lengthy apprenticeship to become skilled in a particular craft. Their apprenticeship and skill gave them the right to exercise work in that particular trade. Most artisans were in reality employed journeymen. They were also socially mobile, and many improved their ranks over a period of time. Some had lower status and wages than others. Indeed, some employed journeymen earned more than independent artisans such as garret masters. Even most skilled artisans were in reality wage earners. In Britain the artisans' skills were seen as male property, a central feature of their ethics that gave them a sense of dignity, status, and respect. They demanded respect from employers and exercised superiority over unskilled laborers. Employers did not interfere with artisans at the workplace and did not expect them to keep fixed hours. Tradespeople controlled knowledge, skills, and practices, restricting entry to their trades. Their status depended upon the possession of proper equipment, tools of the trade, and clothing traditionally associated with their trade. Myths were central to guild ceremonies.

Myths and rituals became more pronounced in the eighteenth century in reaction to increased pressures. Guilds often defended the interests of their members. The Dutch weavers of the late seventeenth century organized in opposition to attempts by local merchants to reduce pay by hiring local and German peasants as cheap labor. The skilled craft workers, artisans, and journeymen attempted to safeguard their positions, but during the eighteenth century the regulations and powers of the guilds diminished. From the mid-sixteenth century to the early nineteenth century French artisans, such as tailors, hatters, and cutlers, organized groups known as the *compagnonnages*, or guilds. The French *compagnonnages* were informal groups shrouded in ritual and mystery whose practices varied according to trade and area. The aura of mystery and myth was important. Some claimed that their rituals actually dated back to the building of Solomon's Temple. Creating a complex system of distinctions, the rituals underpinned hierarchies and the status of graded workers. The *compagnonnages* flourished in the late eighteenth century, due partly to the growth of urban areas and partly to the erosion of the legal rights enjoyed by some journeymen. Those legal provisions had distinguished them from other journeymen, and rituals replaced the legal protection. German workers organized, the *Bruderschaften* with their own ceremonies.

Artisans found their positions increasingly under threat of depreciating in the nineteenth century. In England artisans defended their trade skills, considered their property, against increased mechanization, cheap labor, the repeal of supportive legislation, and the Combination Laws, which were acts passed by Parliament in 1799 and 1800, to prevent formation of trade unions. Their work ethic conflicted with the emerging classic liberal philosophy. Exponents of political economy, including Adam Smith, condemned practices such as apprenticeships, claiming they were too restrictive and a barrier to economic freedom. Artisans, regarding those criticisms as attacks on their legal property established in the sixteenth and seventeenth centuries, were forced to defend themselves against capitalists and the unskilled labor used to produce cheap goods. The eighteenth century through the early nineteenth century was a period of flux for skilled workers with increasing division of labor and differentiation of skills. On one hand skilled artisans were still needed by capitalists, so the workers retained considerable power. Facing frequent strike activity, insubordination, and resistance, capitalists found it difficult to impose regular working habits. On the other hand skilled workers were increasingly separated from ownership of the materials with which they worked and sale of the finished products. New machinery increased productivity, and some machines, such as knitting frames, required less skill. Capitalists produced inexpensive though inferior goods by employing cheap labor.

Artisans attempted to stem the tide of industrialization in different ways. In the late eighteenth century they became increasingly exclusive, prohibiting girls from apprenticeships. The ideology of the skilled artisan maintained a predominantly male hierarchy. Women were barred from many trades in an attempt to protect those trades from cheap labor. Women were even excluded from trade organizations, such as that of hatmaking, in which they were members during the early eighteenth century. Strikes by hatmakers and tailors in the early nineteenth century were aimed at keeping women out of the occupation. While undermining the position of women in the labor market, exclusion ironically led to their becoming a larger body of unskilled labor and further increased the threat to artisans.

WOMEN

Working women experienced lower status during the early modern period, though the clear demarcations that evolved in the nineteenth century did not exist. Women married to independent laborers found it difficult to secure regular employment outside the household, and those who did usually combined agricultural work with washing and cooking for field laborers. Work, paid and unpaid, in much of seventeenth and eighteenth century Europe was organized around the household as the central unit rather than around individuals. For peasants the idea of separate work and domestic spheres lacked any real meaning. Working in the field or working in the kitchen were complementary parts of the same strategy. Marriage was an economic partnership, and women worked alongside their husbands on farms and in workshops. Among the poor, wives usually worked as spinners for the same people who employed their husbands as weavers.

Nevertheless, jobs were divided between men and women. Work ethics connected tasks concerned with the home and garden with the female domain. However, the edges were blurred. In seventeenth-century France, for example, women made the dough, but men kneaded it and heated the oven. Men tended sheep, but either women or men tended cows. The division of work in peasant households varied enormously across Europe. Employment for women varied according to the industry and the area. Women were employed in relatively high-status occupations in the medieval period, but this was not always the case in Britain during the sixteenth and seventeenth centuries. In addition, although they worked in a range of trades, their actual roles were usually restricted. Work ethics subordinated their roles to men. Women dominated certain trades, such as silk, but their guilds lacked the formal status and power of men's guilds in Europe. Apprenticeships were not the same for men and women, involving lower skills and less training for women.

RELIGION, WORK ETHICS, AND THE MIDDLE CLASS

The teachings of the church and the patriarchal structure of society reinforced perceptions of women and

An Eighteenth-Century Manufactory. Interior of the Wetter textile-printing factory at Orange, France. Mural by Joseph Gabriel Marie Rossetti, 1764. PRIVATE COLLECTION/ND-VIOLLET/THE BRIDGEMAN ART LIBRARY

work. The role of the church was important in legitimizing the premodern work ethic; however, it never established across Europe a universal value system based on its ideology. The growth of commercial activity in northern Europe from the early sixteenth century conflicted with the Catholic ideal. Max Weber expounded the notion of the Protestant work ethic in the late nineteenth century and early twentieth century. While Weber's theory has been criticized as overgeneralized and inconclusive, it does highlight important developments in perceptions of work and the work ethic. Weber focused on the fact that the Reformation coincided with economic growth in northern Europe. Loosening the bonds of the Catholic Church allowed greater individual freedom, which was expressed in work. Profit became increasingly acceptable. Commercial growth was characterized by a reinvestment of profits into new business ventures rather than simply achievement of prestige or security. Entrepreneurial activity, the willingness to take risks in business deals, increased markedly, and a new approach to work and the acquisition of wealth evolved. Prudence, sobriety, maximum use of time, and the desire to achieve through individual merit, moral values closely associated with Calvinism, distinguished the emerging entrepreneurial class. Yet this development was not just about the wealthy; it was associated with work at all levels of the social spectrum. The key

was that workers performed to the very best of their abilities, irrespective of the nature of the job.

Weber did not claim that the Protestant work ethic actually caused capitalist growth, but he demonstrated that the values derived from Protestantism clearly favored the establishment and expansion of a capitalist economy. A different cultural approach to work emerged in which the entrepreneur was increasingly successful. Work ethics now stressed the role of the individual working for deferred gratification or concentrating on accumulating virtue and money instead of immediate pleasures. The workers' moral obligations were to perform all tasks to the best of their abilities no matter how small or menial the work, to take orders from an employer willingly, and to value work as a source of meaning and worth for each individual. These values, an oversimplification of the evolving work ethic, did not come entirely from the growth of Protestantism. The transition from the old and largely feudal order to a capitalist system cannot be pinpointed to any particular period. It is impossible to say exactly when one set of relations took over from the other.

However, these values did permeate parts of European culture, beginning in the sixteenth century. The Reformation ultimately if unintentionally encouraged a more secular mentality, which encouraged greater acceptance of the entrepreneur and work discipline. The new work ethic was especially successful in northern Europe, where the Reformation was most influential. In western Europe the Protestant work ethic became manifested in a number of ways, including the nineteenth century "gospel of work" and the notions expressed by Samuel Smiles's best-seller *Self-Help* (1859). Smiles's ideas were not original. His book reiterated the values of hard work, diligence, thrift, sobriety, and deferred gratification in terms of individual moral worth, though with greater emphasis on social mobility as a result. The Protestant work ethic facilitated industrialization, though it was not a major factor in its development. Similar thoughts about work emerged in traditionally Catholic regions, such as France, as the work ethic became middle class more than Protestant. The middle classes used work beliefs to criticize aristocrats, whom they considered idle and unproductive. Deep class identity was involved, as many middle-class people did indeed work very hard.

Industrialization itself had a marked impact on the work ethic, which was affected by the growth of capitalist and market values. Beginning in the late eighteenth century classic liberal economists and philosophers, such as Adam Smith and Jeremy Bentham, stressed the value of limited government interference, especially in economic affairs. They emphasized the role of the individual and self-interest. If individuals were prepared to work hard, they should reap the benefits of their energy and commitment. Those who did not choose to work hard should be left to struggle. Workers should be free to move between jobs according to their own interests and no longer be tied to the land like serfs and many peasant groups. Wages should be set according to the market. Old seigneurial rights were an unjust barrier to natural rights and freedom. Entrepreneurs should be able to operate largely unfettered. Merchants became the eighteenth-century risk takers, forming the driving force behind economic growth and British industrialization. Individuals like Richard Arkwright gradually moved production from the home to the factory.

While many capitalists embraced the classic liberal ideology, it was not universally accepted. The utilitarian view was criticized throughout the nineteenth century both by conservatives, such as Thomas Carlyle, and by the emerging socialists, such as Karl Marx. Marx believed that waged work was essentially a form of capitalist oppression. For him the work ethic was not about profit for the individual but social justice and equality for all workers. Factory owners had widely varied attitudes toward work and their employees. German employers were authoritarian, while the British were paternalistic. The German work ethic viewed labor in terms of time, the British in terms of products. German workers in the woolen industry were paid according to the number of shuttle movements completed in a given time period. British weavers were paid according to the number of threads actually woven. These methods of payment reflected the different cultural assumptions about work resulting from the different conceptions of work. Some nineteenth-century large employers, like Hugh Mason, Titus Salt, and the Cadbury family, built large settlements for their workers to provide homes, libraries, schools, and churches and to promote their own value systems. Still, this group of factory owners formed a minority in Britain. Many employers simply did not have the resources to build such facilities, and others did not share the philosophy. Nevertheless, it was a means of exerting authority outside the factory and was a result of their perception of work as a commodity. German employers in general had a more tyrannical reputation inside the factory. Partly in response to similar employer attitudes across Europe, the working classes formed labor organizations to protect their interests in the face of the capitalist market. In the industrial society workers were defined increasingly along class lines. As the factory became the principal mode of production, modern ideas about class emerged. In Marx's notion of class, workers shared a sense of consciousness based on their relationship to the means of production.

In nineteenth- and twentieth-century Germany the work ethic was also rooted in a sense of dignity and purpose in daily work. Germans, for many of whom work was a serious vocation for life, believed they possessed an attitude toward work that was superior to that of workers in southern Europe. Some nineteenth-century observers, such as Georg Wilhelm Friedrich Hegel and Marx, worried about the decline of traditional skills that resulted from industrialization and the rise of mundane jobs. A movement grew to develop a greater sense of "joy in work." By the end of the nineteenth century some felt that work should be an enriching experience. Wilhelm von Riehl conducted one of the most comprehensive studies into what he believed was the German work ethic. His theory, based on observations of the Protestant urban middle classes, describes an intrinsic value attached to the very experience of working. Work was exalted for its benefits to the community, no matter how mundane, rather than for materialistic reasons. All work serviced the needs of the people. To give workers a stake in the system, capitalists tried to promote a positive attitude and reduce any sense of alienation by offering training for a trade. Industrialists established technical training schools to promote industrial education. However, others saw work as a duty and a burden that should be eased by better pay and conditions. Their ideal was not joy in work but joy after work, and they longed for liberation from work rather than through it.

WORKING-CLASS WORK AND BELIEFS

Social historians have tried to determine what work ethic common laborers maintained in the face of industrialization and the middle-class praise for hard work. Some clearly bought into the idea of work as dignity and even tried to increase their efforts to please employers or to maximize personal gain and advancement. But more workers probably maintained what British laborers called a "lump o' labor" concept. Work was fine, but it should not be frenzied or intensified. A given amount of pay merited a set amount of work. Obviously, given mechanization, this idea was not easily defended, but it entered into considerable labor protest and described some aspects of work in the less-technical sectors, like construction work. When customary work ideas could not be defended, new concepts replaced them, most notably the notion of instrumentalism. In instrumentalism workers admitted they could not defend traditional practices, but they insisted on higher pay in return for concessions so work would be an "instrument" for a better life off the job.

Industrialization in the nineteenth century brought significant changes to work practices, but it was not a universal process. In England the course of industrialization focused on parts of the northwest, West Yorkshire, and small areas of the Midlands and northeast. In Russia serfdom was not abolished until 1861, and even then peasants remained tied to the land through oppressive dues. Large areas of southern and eastern Europe remained untouched into the twentieth century. Those areas affected by industrialization experienced gradual changes in work patterns. Work inside the factory demanded greater discipline, which had a marked impact on the ideology of work. Work habits were restructured so that production was determined by mechanized production rather than by nature. Industrial society demanded the maximum use of time, characterized by systems of bells, timekeepers, time sheets, and clocking in. Work time was distinguished from home time. The emerging emphasis on time discipline was underlined by the decline of St. Monday. Rural workers often avoided work on Monday, called "holy Monday" in France, especially if they had spent the previous day in the local inn. However, industrialization demanded more commitment, and industrialists suppressed St. Monday after the late eighteenth century.

The shift from task-based to product-based notions of time discipline happened by degrees. Traditional practices continued in mining and handicraft work into the nineteenth century. In spite of capitalists' efforts to control time, British workers were renowned for their irregular work habits. Their work ethic was product-based. Many worked for short bursts followed by periods of inactivity. Work experiences also crossed a wide range. Domestic work was not regulated by the clock, and unpaid voluntary work was similarly unconstrained by notions of time. Because industrialization was not uniform in either time or place, craft techniques prospered across Europe alongside factories that employed technology. Cyclical unemployment brought uncertain time disciplines into occupations such as dock work, and periods of high demand had an impact on the time and structure of work in some industries. The seasons continued to dominate work and time practices in agriculture. Capitalists and managers did not always follow a clock-based work structure, even in manufacturing industries. Single industries, such as ceramics in Staffordshire, England, had a variety of work-time practices in the nineteenth and twentieth centuries due to different company sizes, different techniques, and different demands.

TWENTIETH-CENTURY DEVELOPMENTS

Despite the variety in work practices, strict regulation of the workplace increasingly became a marked feature of manufacturing during the twentieth century. In the nineteenth century work dominated people's lives, and most workers had little leisure time. As this started to change in western Europe, the first half of the twentieth century witnessed a mixture of approaches. The expansion of communism challenged capitalist systems. Work in the Soviet Union was transformed under Joseph Stalin's Five-Year Plans and the development of a controlled economy. The industrial workforce doubled to 6 million people by the end of 1932. Peasants moved in large numbers into coal, iron, and steel production in areas like the Ukraine. Work ethics were based on service to the state. The government handed down planned targets, putting enormous pressure on managers to reach hard goals. Collectivization forced many out of the rural areas into the emerging industrial regions, and "shock work" (intensive additional work) was introduced to improve productivity. Younger workers encouraged shock work, but older skilled workers, who had been in industry prior to the Five-Year Plans, often resisted it. The skilled workers even abused the shock workers, including beatings and murders. Older workers also

Saint Monday. Women try to move their men to work. *Wine Shop, Monday,* painting (1858) by Jules Breton (1827–1906). WASHINGTON UNIVERSITY GALLERY OF ART, ST. LOUIS, GIFT OF CHARLES PARSONS, 1905

resisted new practices and attempts to cut rates of pay. The government introduced the continuous working week in 1932, and workers faced penalties if they left their jobs without permission. Managerial authority was asserted with great vigor. These measures were intended to improve productivity as demanded by the state. Beginning in the mid-1930s the state gave increasing publicity and heroic status to dedicated workers, such as the coal miner Aleksey Grigoriyevich Stakhanov, who broke productivity records. In Germany the Nazi government also promoted the virtues of work, and German work ethics centered on the idea of service to the race through the state. Building on the joy through work ideal of the late nineteenth century, the Nazis embarked on a number of propaganda crusades, such as their "beauty of labor" campaign. Joy would be the reward of serving the state.

In the second half of the twentieth century work practices and the hours of work gradually improved across most of Europe, especially in the west. Regulation of time became an asset of the labor movement. Vacation time increased, and a leisure ethic joined the beliefs about work. Overtime was a feature of the time-disciplined work environment, and in postwar Europe full employment and the growth of trade union power led to greater regulation of overtime. Workers demanded rates increase by 50 percent or even 100 percent for working outside the agreed hours. Unions negotiated a series of other strict conditions, including demarcation lines. However, with the decline in manufacturing and union power in the early 1980s, such regulations and agreements faced increasing pressures.

Along with the changes in work structures and practices, the numbers employed in certain sectors shifted significantly. Several classifications gradually replaced the artisan. At the bottom were unskilled laborers, many employed in casual or seasonal work, such as dock workers. For most of the nineteenth century they were the poorest workers, and they were the least organized. In contrast, skilled workers in manufacturing tended to be organized in trade unions. Some historians believe that skilled workers formed an aristocracy of labor. They kept themselves aloof from unskilled workers, and like artisans before them, they jealously guarded their position in the workplace.

On-the-Job Training. A supervisor instructs a worker, Soviet Union, c. 1942. The original caption read "Member of the Supreme Soviet Instructs Worker." HULTON DEUTSCH/CORBIS

Above them stood a wide range of middle-class occupations. Besides the increase in those employed in business and manufacturing, the number of people employed as clerks and in other professions grew notably. The older professional groups, such as lawyers and doctors, multiplied, as did private sector professionals, such as managers and accountants. Throughout the twentieth century the trend toward professions continued across western Europe. Indeed the number employed in manufacturing declined in much of Europe, especially in the late twentieth century. At the same time more workers joined service industries, such as tourism.

LARGER PATTERNS: WORK AND FAMILY

Despite the shifting pattern of employment, work ethics and the underlying changes in work practices and structures from the preindustrial period remained. One of the most fundamental changes was the demise of the family unit as the central work unit. From the mid-eighteenth century the relocation of the workplace away from the family home and into workshops and factories meant a gradual separation of spheres between the economic and the social and between the private and the public. As tasks slowly became divided, women were increasingly associated with the domestic sphere, while men were identified with labor in the workplace. These divisions became a central feature in the ideology of work. The concept of gaining all of the means to live through paid labor emerged in the nineteenth century. Most European households did not rely on income through paid labor in the seventeenth and eighteenth centuries, and in the late eighteenth century most households depended on a variety of work strategies to secure their livelihoods. A single, full-time regular job providing the sole source of income was the exception rather than the norm.

Until the nineteenth century women were likely to be the main money earners because they sold produce at markets or produced textile goods in the home. In the nineteenth century this changed with the emergence of the family wage. Male workers received substantially higher wages than women. Work ethics placed the male worker as the chief earner, the family breadwinner, and his wage was supposed to support all members of the family. Trade unions tried to keep women out of skilled work to keep wages higher. Middle-class morality also decided that the new, heavy machinery was unsuitable for women. Work ethics stressed that physically demanding labor belonged exclusively to men. Traditionally coal miners worked in family units, including wives and children, but this practice ended in England with the 1842 Mines Regulation Act. Until the eighteenth century women were apprenticed in some trades and were employed in heavy labor, but this changed in the late eighteenth century. Women married to upwardly mobile men entered the middle classes and became more idle, while the wives of skilled journeymen lost much of their independence and often entered domestic service.

Much historiographical debate has concerned the impact of industrialization on work opportunities for women. Certainly women remained vital in the workplace. Women and children accounted for substantial numbers of employees in textiles in the late eighteenth century. Lace making was almost exclusively female, and cotton industries employed more women than men. These textile industries were central to the economic explosion in Britain. Women were also significantly involved in the metal industries, such as nail making and hardware manufacturing. In the mid-eighteenth century merchants relied on the cheap and unregulated labor of women. The number of women employed by merchants grew, but it remained low-status work. With mechanization women moved into new industries, but those positions, too, were low-skill, low-wage work. The first developments in new technology were designed for home situations. The spinning jenny, for example, was introduced into domestic production in the late eighteenth century, and the move into factories run by merchant manufacturers followed. That relocation meant that women lost control over their own labor.

However, increased mechanization did not cause a dramatic transition in women's working lives, though it is impossible to make generalizations. On one level it restricted opportunities for women. Certainly as industrialization developed in the nineteenth century opportunities for women in industry declined. The range of available apprenticeships decreased, and less than half of the apprenticeships available to men in nineteenth-century Britain were also available to women. Opportunities for women concentrated in domestic service and textiles, and the status attached to "women's work" was lower than that of "men's work." On another level, industrialization took women out of the home, providing them with a form of liberation from the home. Yet this was not necessarily a positive development. In many ways this transition from the home to the factory led to more rigid subordination of women in the male-governed industrial system.

Women were subservient even in occupations numerically dominated by women. As mechanization in the British cotton industry grew, women accepted a variety of occupations in the mills. Initially in the late eighteenth and early nineteenth centuries they occupied auxiliary positions, including often the most insecure positions. They were paid poor wages, often only half those of men. With the development of the power loom women came to occupy the main positions, such as spinning. Women's wages increased in the mid-Victorian period, in some instances equaling the rates enjoyed by men. However, men held most supervisory and management positions. The majority of women did not enjoy wage equality with men. This was underlined in the sweated labor workshops, where many women were employed. Work there was characterized by low wages, long hours, and poor working conditions. In the late nineteenth century sweatshops attracted attention in Britain, where Parliament conducted investigations between 1888 and 1890. Sweat-

Work at Home. *The Seamstress,* painting (c. 1870) by Illarion M. Pryanishnikov (1840–1894). CHRISTIE'S IMAGES, LTD.

shops were concentrated in the poorest urban districts, such as the East End of London, and they often employed women, children, paupers, and immigrants. Employers often issued outwork, which made it virtually impossible for workers to organize unions or for factory inspectors to investigate their practices. This work was also characterized by subdivision of labor and deskilling, which assured low wages and poor conditions.

Children worked in miserable conditions across much of nineteenth-century Europe. Their smaller physical frames suited them for various jobs in which poor health, mutilation, and deaths were not uncommon. Partly in response to increasing concerns about children's positions, many European nations introduced work legislation. Work ethics eventually viewed children as unsuitable for employment. In the nineteenth century Britain passed numerous acts to provide an extensive protective framework for children. Factory acts in the early Victorian period established hours and conditions of work in textiles and mines. Anthony Ashley Cooper, earl of Shaftesbury, and other leading reformers continued the campaign into the mid-nineteenth century, when legislation addressed a number of other industries. Significantly the 1870 Education Act demanded that all children under ten years of age should attend school full-time. Most legislation was permissive or at least difficult to enforce, but it established important precedents that were improved during the twentieth century. Separating children from work complicated judgments about the nature and utility of childhood.

New work systems also brought attention to older workers, who increasingly were considered less competent to deal with the stresses and learning components of modern labor. Many older workers were demoted or laid off. Pension movements emerged to offer some protection for them, and formal retirement systems took effect during and after the Great Depression. Ability to work and removal from work complicated appraisals of old age by the elderly and by society at large.

Throughout the twentieth century European governments continued to pass laws to protect workers. Women gained rights in the workplace in the second half of the twentieth century. The communist states provided greater equality for women at work than did most other European nations, but beginning in the 1960s the western European democracies passed legislation promoting and supporting women's rights. Most European countries recognized the need to provide maternity leave, preschool child care, and anti-discriminatory legislation. Women entered most traditionally male-dominated work spheres, though in smaller numbers and with lower pay than their male coworkers.

CONCLUSION

Certainly generalizations about the impact of any single work ethic in terms of time or place would be naive. Diverse ethics permeated societies across Europe at different periods and among different classes, and no single ethic dominated. Ethics, ideologies, or meanings developed from social and ideological forces, and precise conditions varied across Europe. Some areas remained untouched after the medieval period, while others, such as Britain, underwent huge changes. Geographical differences and cultural diversity created multiple peasant experiences. No single, all-embracing time-work discipline existed. Ethics centered on freedom or on oppression. They were determined by Catholic and Protestant philosophies, by social structures and cultural traditions, by political and economic ideologies, and by shifting technology. Even in the nineteenth century traditional work values did not disappear. The clock, seasons, life courses, family demands, and mechanization impacted different areas in different periods, underlining the assortment of European work ethics and experiences. Agricultural workers in the early modern period included the oppressed serfs of eastern Europe, the more liberated peasants of Germany, and the free yeoman of Britain. Farm workers in northern and western Europe were not tied by seigneurial dues, but they were subjected to technological changes at a much earlier date than the serfs of Russia, who effectively worked under the same conditions from the medieval period into the twentieth century.

Artisans also had dissimilar experiences and practices. Many were employed as journeymen; some were self-employed and worked from their homes; and a few enjoyed wealth and status, owning large properties and employing other skilled and unskilled workers. Industrialization threatened many groups of artisans; however, its impact on work depended upon the time and place. Workers who moved into the factories felt its effect on work ethics and practices, including stricter discipline and regulations that affected hours, pay, and conditions. The capitalists moved from their merchant houses, where they organized the home-based workers, into the rigid factory system, where they directly employed workers. Yet the factory did not invade all forms of work. Many areas of Europe remained predominantly agricultural. Stalin's Five-Year Plans initiated the shift of Russian workers from rural areas into towns and factories in the twentieth century. Large areas of southern Italy and Castile in Spain remained untouched by modernization.

Industrialization stimulated mixed fortunes for women. Some were liberated from their homes but were still employed and supervised by men. Others, such as middle-class women, had reduced work opportunities. Work ethics subordinated women for most of the period from the Renaissance to the late twentieth century. Industrialization's impact on women continued to attract debate among historians and attention as a subject of studies of work in Europe. Research has continued regarding technological change, the decline of traditional manufacturing industries, and the growth of the service sector. Those challenges have endured with the growing impact of the European Union and globalization of work.

See also **Serfdom: Western Europe; Serfdom: Eastern Europe; Farm Families and Labor Systems** *(volume 2);* **Social Class** *(volume 3);* **Patriarchy; Gender and Work** *(in this volume);* **Protestantism** *(volume 5).*

BIBLIOGRAPHY

Adams, Carole Elizabeth. *Women Clerks in Wilhelmine Germany: Issues of Class and Gender.* Cambridge, U.K., 1988.

Anderson, Gregory, ed. *The White-Blouse Revolution: Female Office Workers since 1870.* Manchester, U.K., 1988.

Andrle, Vladimir. *Workers in Stalin's Russia: Industrialization and Social Change in a Planned Economy.* Sussex, U.K., and New York, 1988.

Anthony, P. D. *The Ideology of Work.* London, 1977.

Berg, Maxine. *The Age of Manufactures.* Oxford, 1985.

Berg, Maxine, Pat Hudson, and Michael Sonenscher, eds. *Manufacture in Town and Country before the Factory.* Cambridge, U.K., 1983.

Biernacki, Richard. *The Fabrication of Labor: Germany and Britain, 1640–1914.* Berkeley, Calif., 1995.

Campbell, Joan. *Joy in Work, German Work: The National Debate, 1800–1945.* Princeton, N.J., 1989.

Clark, Alice. *Working Life of Women in the Seventeenth Century.* London, 1919.

Dambruyne, Johan. "Guilds, Social Mobility, and Status in Sixteenth-Century Ghent." *International Review of Social History* 43 (1998): 31–78.

Deceulaer, Harald. "Guildsmen, Entrepreneurs, and Market Segments: The Case of Garment Trades in Antwerp and Ghent." *International Review of Social History* 43 (1998): 1–29.

Feltes, N. N. "Misery or the Production of Misery: Defining Sweated Labour in 1890." *Social History* 17 (1992): 441–452.

Gray, Robert. *The Aristocracy of Labour in Nineteenth-Century Britain, c. 1850–1900.* London, 1981.

Hammond, J. L., and Barbara Hammond. *The Skilled Labourer.* London, 1979.

Harrison, Royden, and Jonathan Zeitlin, eds. *Divisions of Labour.* Brighton, U.K. 1985.

Hobsbawm, E. J. *The Age of Capital, 1848–1875.* London, 1975.

Hobsbawm, E. J. *The Age of Revolution.* London, 1962.

Hobsbawm, E. J. *Industry and Empire.* London, 1968.

Hobsbawm, E. J. *Labouring Men.* London, 1964.

Hopkins, E. "Working Hours and Conditions during the Industrial Revolution: A Reappraisal." *Economic History Review* 35 (1982): 52–66.

John, Angela V., ed. *Unequal Opportunities: Women's Employment in England 1800–1918.* Oxford, 1986.

Joyce, Patrick. "Work." In *The Cambridge Social History of Great Britain, 1750–1950.* Edited by F. M. L. Thompson. Vol. 2. Cambridge, U.K., 1990. Pages 131–194.

Joyce, Patrick. *Work, Society, and Politics.* Brighton, U.K., 1980.

Kaplan, Steven Laurence, and Cynthia J. Koepp, eds. *Work in France: Representations, Meaning, Organization, and Practice.* Ithaca, N.Y., 1986.

Lee, W. R., and Pat Hudson, eds., *Women's Work and the Family Economy in Historical Perspective.* Manchester, U.K., 1990.

Lindsey, Charles, and Lorna Duffin. *Women and Work in Pre-Industrial England.* London, 1985.

Luebke, D. M. "Serfdom and Honour in Eighteenth-Century Germany." *Social History* 18 (1993): 143–161.

Marshall, Gordon. *In Search of the Spirit of Capitalism: An Essay on Max Weber's Protestant Ethic Thesis.* New York, 1982.

Marx, Karl. *Capital.* London, 1930.

More, Charles. *Skill and the English Working Class, 1870–1914.* New York, 1980.

Morgan, Carol E. "Women, Work, and Consciousness in the Mid-Nineteenth-Century English Cotton Industry." *Social History* 17 (1992): 23–42.

Pahl, R. E. *Divisions of Labour.* Oxford, 1984.

Pahl, R. E., ed. *On Work: Historical, Comparative, and Theoretical Approaches.* Oxford, 1988.

Pennington, Shelley, and Belinda Westover. *A Hidden Workforce: Homeworkers in England, 1850–1985.* Houndmills, Basingstoke, and Hampshire, U.K., 1989.

Pinchbeck, Ivy. *Women Workers and the Industrial Revolution, 1750–1850.* London, 1930.

Prothero, I. J. *Artisans and Politics in Early Nineteenth-Century London.* Folkstone, U.K., 1979.

Reid, D. "The Decline of St. Monday 1766–1876." *Past and Present* 71 (1976): 76–101.

Rose, Michael. *Re-Working the Work Ethic.* London, 1985.

Rule, John. *The Experience of Labour in Eighteenth-Century Industry.* London, 1981.

Scott, J. A., and L. A. Tilly. "Women's Work and the Family in Nineteenth-Century Europe." *Comparative Studies in Society and History* 17, no. 1 (1975): 36–64.

Sewell, William H., Jr. *Work and Revolution in France.* Cambridge, U.K., 1980.

Siegelbaum, Lewis H. *Stakhanovism and the Politics of Productivity in the USSR, 1935–1941.* Cambridge, U.K., 1988.

Smiles, Samuel. *Self-Help.* London, 1859.

Smith, Adam. *An Inquirty into the Causes of the Wealth of Nations.* Dublin, Ireland, 1776.

Sonenscher, Michael. "The Sans-Cullottes of the Year II: Rethinking the Language of Labour in the Revolutionary France." *Social History* 9 (October 1984): 301–328.

Thompson, E. P. *The Making of the English Working Class.* Harmondsworth, U.K., 1968.

Thompson, E. P. "Time, Work Discipline, and Industrial Capitalism." *Past and Present* 38 (December 1967): 56–97.

Thompson, Kenneth, ed. *Work, Employment, and Unemployment.* Milton Keynes, U.K., 1984.

Thompson, Paul. *The Nature of Work.* London, 1983.

Tilgher, Adriano. *Work: What It Has Meant to Men through the Ages.* New York, 1930.

Wallman, Sandra, ed. *Social Anthropology of Work.* London, 1979.

PREINDUSTRIAL MANUFACTURING

Steven A. Epstein

The industrial revolution of the late eighteenth and early nineteenth centuries applied new technologies and sources of power to the traditional handicraft production of earlier centuries. In the period preceding this revolution, from the bubonic plague of 1348 to the 1770s, a sophisticated system of manufacturing had emerged in early modern Europe. This system, called preindustrial for the sake of simplicity, produced products of amazing complexity, from delicate watches and porcelain ware to printed books, pistols, telescopes, silk tapestries, and the great Spanish galleons, Portuguese carracks, and English East Indiamen that sailed across the globe. The quality and diversity of these products are a tribute to the skilled labor force that created them. Whether by 1770 this labor force constituted a true working class anywhere in Europe is one of the most important questions to answer about this phase of labor history. These centuries also witnessed the rise of the first industrial entrepreneurs and inventors who revolutionized manufacturing. How was work organized, what were the social and economic relations between employer and employee, how were specific trades conducted, and why were some parts of Europe more precocious in manufacturing than others? These are other important questions.

Social historians are primarily interested in this phase of labor history because it serves as a bridge between the agrarian and artisanal societies of the Middle Ages and the rise of modern manufacturing in the industrial revolution. These centuries merit attention in their own right because they witnessed a profound transformation in the world of work. The social relations surrounding manufacturing paved the way for rapid technological progress and the acquisition of skills fundamental to subsequent advances. The gulf between the payers and takers of wages widened and hardened long before an industrial proletariat emerged in the nineteenth century. Preindustrial manufacturing transformed European society and introduced many millions of women, men, and children to the discipline of the workplace.

The state of knowledge of this period of labor history remains behind the study of medieval agriculture and modern industry. Research on the social relations deriving from work has yielded a wealth of local studies, primarily on western European cities or specific trades. Broader syntheses of national or regional styles of organizing work remain rare. Given these limitations, this summary of preindustrial manufacturing will begin with a look at the general circumstances of manufacturing at the beginning of the early modern period. Next, a series of case studies on specific trades and issues will illuminate important features of the social history of work and enterprise. Finally, an overview of manufacturing on the eve of the industrial revolution will reveal the major trends of the period.

MANUFACTURING AROUND 1500

The periodization of labor's history remains a vexed issue, and whatever value the term "Renaissance" has in other fields, it does not apply to this subject. Early modern social history, stretching from the calamities of the plague years of the later fourteenth century to the age of revolutions at the end of the eighteenth century, makes a better frame for this field.

Guilds. The most important social institution defining the circumstances of most manufacturing in this period was the guild, or métier, *Zunft, gremio, arte,* or the many other terms by which the institution was known. The guild, a legacy of the Middle Ages, was an organization of employers who banded together to foster the interests of their trade or profession. Guild regulations determined who could work at a trade and often prescribed standards of production that imposed measures of quality and uniformity on objects as diverse as a loaf of bread or a clock. Guilds, primarily urban institutions, controlled large areas of manufacturing, especially in staples like cloth or ironworking.

Guilds existed in nearly every city in Europe, and few trades escaped the principle that employers, and not their workers, determined the customs of the trade. Two important trends were working against the hegemony of guild-based production in the early modern period. First, guild restrictions always prompted some entrepreneurs to find ways to evade the guilds. The best-known instance of this evasion was the putting-out system of wool cloth production refined in early modern England and Germany. Instead of employing weavers in the old-fashioned, intensely regulated atmosphere of urban household production, the organizers of the putting-out system took wool or thread to rural workers who labored outside the reach of the guild system and produced thread or cloth of lesser quality but at a cheaper price. The putting-out system transformed rural society as it brought cash, new skills, and the employer/employee relationship to traditional agrarian society. This system also competed with urban weavers and spinners. Second, by the eighteenth century social and economic theorists, most notably Adam Smith, condemned guilds as medieval relics, conspiracies against the public good, monopolies that benefited only the masters and not the consumers or workers. Guilds were under sustained attack by the late eighteenth century.

The corporations (métiers) were abolished during the French Revolution as a symbol of the corrupt Old Regime, and enlightened absolutists like Leopold of Austria abolished their guilds. Hence the early modern period witnessed the last phase of guild-based manufacturing and began the legend that guilds were a kind of feudal relic—hostile to change and working people. And yet, as the naked exploitation of industrial Europe became more apparent, a certain nostalgia for guilds arose in the nineteenth century, and some of the earliest working-class organizations were proud to call themselves guilds. Hence guilds were viewed in terms of contrary stereotypes: as a grim hierarchy of masters exploiting their apprentices and journeymen and women, or as symbols of a golden age of labor before the horrors of the factory. Like all stereotypes, both of these contain measures of truth and falsehood.

Masters and workers. The masters, the men and occasionally women who were the owners of shops and the full members of the guilds, provided employment and training to the workers who did much or in some cases nearly all the labor. Being a guild master in the early modern period increasingly meant that one had inherited, purchased, or married into the position. Guilds everywhere were increasingly becoming closed cartels hostile to new members. Every city with guilds had a hierarchy of trades, with wealthy masters and merchants lording over the more humble master butchers and candlemakers. The defining principle remained that the master worked for his or her customers, and not for wages. An exception to this rule was the building trades, where master carpenters, masons, and bricklayers often worked for big contractors for wages. In practice, taking wages reduced the status of the trade, for a sharp line separated those who provided employment and paid wages from those who took jobs and wages. In many cities this line also determined who enjoyed full citizenship, with the benefits as expected going to the masters.

The social relationship between master and his or her employees was more complex than simple status might suggest. Even in this relationship among unequals, workers had some rights to bargain over pay and working conditions, and masters were expected to care for their employees, sometimes even in sickness and in health, as the work contracts stipulated. In the skilled trades like weaving, cabinetmaking, printing, and the like, journeymen and women performed most of the basic work. These laborers, having completed terms of apprenticeship, were certified as possessing sufficient skills to practice the craft. They worked for wages, often at rates customary to a particular trade, especially in the years of stable prices in the late seventeenth and eighteenth centuries. Even customary wages allowed some room for bargaining, and while some trades had agreed-upon pay schedules set by the guilds, most allowed masters some flexibility to take into account age and skill.

Wages depended on two basic systems—a fixed rate of pay, usually set by the day or for longer terms of up to several years, or piece rate pay that yielded so many pennies per length of cloth or yards of yarn spun. Workers avoided wherever possible being paid in kind because such payments imposed additional costs on them and really only benefited the employers. Piece rate wages allowed the workers some control over how long and hard they worked, but contemporary observers like Adam Smith knew that they encouraged overwork and exhausted people trying to feed their families. A set daily wage, with time allowed for meals, required employers to keep a closer eye on slackers. The young men and women who worked by contract for a fixed wage had some security of employment because employers were obligated to keep them on, even on slow days when casual laborers found no daily work.

Working conditions, especially the most important one, the length of the working day, were determined by the customs of the trade. (Hourly pay scales

Guilds in Brussels. The senior guilds of Brussels on parade, 31 May 1615. Painting by Denis van Alsloot. VICTORIA & ALBERT MUSEUM, LONDON/ART RESOURCE, NY

awaited the industrial revolution, so the real issue was the length of the day.) Since working by candlelight or oil lamp was expensive and in some trades undesirable because of the possibility of errors, the amount of sunlight generally determined the length of the working day, making it longer in summers. The journeymen and women often worked in shops attached to the master's house, and in such cases meals were usually provided. Craft traditions dictated a large number of holidays in both Protestant and Catholic parts of Europe; everywhere churches frowned on Sunday work, and Saturday was usually a half holiday. Saints' days remained a feature of the work calendar in Catholic countries, where up to eighty days a year, including Sundays, were not workdays and hence not paid working days either. A worker with a weekly or annual salary usually worked in a more prestigious trade than the worker on a daily wage and hence was not so dependent, as casual laborers always were, on a day's pay for a day's work. Saturday, the traditional payday for most artisans, often witnessed bouts of relaxation that carried on into Saint Monday, the customary slack day of the workweek. Clauses in work contracts often required journeymen and women to work in good faith and without fraud, and also usually compelled workers to avoid gambling and other vices, especially under the master's roof.

Regulations hemmed in the market for labor in the early modern system of manufacturing, and traditions dictated that masters did not attempt to steal away another's workers by offering higher wages, though of course some did. Journeymen and women had pride in their skills and sometimes completed a masterpiece or objectively fine product in order to demonstrate their command of their craft, even if they would never themselves become masters. They also had strong opinions about what the just level of wages was in their particular trade. These workers, denied lawful organizations of their own, nevertheless had a strong sense of solidarity that revealed itself in informal associations discussed below. Long before the industrial revolution, a hierarchy of labor existed in which the journeymen and women in the most prestigious and highly paid trades—clockmaking, jewelry, cabinetmaking—ranked higher than their peers in the more common trades. In general workers' status derived from whether or not their trade catered to wealthy customers who purchased carriages or paintings. High-priced raw materials did not necessarily confer high status. Women, active in aspects of the silk trade and in making gold thread, did not enjoy high status or wages because they worked on expensive raw materials. The gender division of labor is a complicated subject best considered in the context of specific trades, but, generally, trades in which women predominated became lower status and poorly paid, and women earned less than men even when they did the same work. The idea of a labor aristocracy—highly paid artisans and mechanics turning out objects requiring great skills to produce—had deep roots in the early modern period. The industrial revolution did not invent a labor aristocracy; it simply upset the older order.

Social and religious aspects of guilds.

The guilds in all parts of Europe retained, as part of the medieval legacy, a strong measure of spiritual and paternalistic features. The guild was usually a religious confraternity with a chapel and common ritual observances. The masters attended one another's funerals and looked out for distressed members. Their employees were often expected to attend an annual service and contribute to the guild's charitable activities. The degree of common spirituality attached to work meant in practice that the workplace, like the wider world, practiced one religion. The goldsmiths of London and Paris had similar institutions, but in the former all the members were Anglicans and in the latter all Catholics. The reliance on oaths and ritual practices generated religious conformity and as a result denied all Jews and various dissenters access to the guild, journeyman status, and often even employment.

These charitable and spiritual aspects of the trade helped to define a specific attitude toward the structure of society as a whole and to the organization of manufacturing—corporatism. According to this social theory of labor, corporatism defines the world of work not in terms of a sharp divide between employer and employee but in terms of divisions along craft or professional lines. Thus a corporatist approach to society views the right groupings as the butchers, the bakers, and the candlestick makers. This emphasis on solidarity according to the type of work—from the richest goldsmith to his or her most humble worker—of course benefited the masters, since it encouraged their workers to identify with the interests of the trade, as defined by the employers. A corporatist vision of social organization imposed on the masters certain obligations defined now as paternalism in its most positive sense—the fatherly duty of superiors toward subordinates—as part of a reciprocal set of obligations that went beyond the simple cash nexus of employment. The preindustrial manufacturing workplace was supposed to be corporatist and paternalistic. In reality it was also intensely patriarchal, as few women ever enjoyed the full powers of a master in their trades. But a sense of reciprocal duties blunted the sharp edges of exploitation, and in some cases the workers in the new factories of the industrial age looked back with justifiable nostalgia on the working conditions of earlier centuries.

Apprenticeship.

The last general aspect of manufacturing across Europe was the near universality of apprenticeship. Again, circumstances varied widely by trade, but a broad picture emerges about the experience of being an apprentice in the early modern period. Apprenticeship was vocational education, and it was by far the most widespread system of teaching and learning in Europe. Boys and girls, typically in their early teens but sometimes younger, were committed by their parents or guardians to long terms of service to a master by contract in exchange for training in a craft or trade. In order to be a full-fledged journeyman or woman, it was required to serve a term of apprenticeship, a length of time usually determined by guild statutes. Masters did not routinely employ anyone who had not been an apprentice for years, learning a craft at a master's side and often living in his or her house. Depending on the trade and city, apprentices sometimes received a small stipend like a training wage. Often in luxury trades the parents had to offer a payment to the master to take on their son or daughter as an apprentice. In these trades the term of service was typically longer, reflecting the value of the training in the years of cheap labor the master received from the apprentice.

Even when parents wanted their children to follow in the family trade, they often thought it better

Glassworks. From a copy of *The Voyages of John Mandeville*, c. 1420. BY PERMISSION OF THE BRITISH LIBRARY

to have another master train the apprentice in a fostering relationship. Training assumed the right of correction, and it was perhaps easier for parents to allow another person to beat one's children into learning a craft. The main obligation of apprenticeship was for the master to teach and the apprentice to learn. By these means technological skills were passed from one generation to the next, and improvements in techniques were not lost because successful masters had pupils. This educational system also encouraged paternalism in the workplace because it was not unusual for a young person to progress from apprentice to journeyman or woman in the same shop. Only for a very few did the story end in the idyllic marriage of the apprentice to the master's daughter. But some workers retained filial attitudes toward their employers because they had been literally raised by them.

Many trades prohibited training women as apprentices, and so they were denied the technical skills necessary to succeed in some trades. Where women were allowed to work at a craft, they too took on apprentices, boys as well as girls. But the patriarchal features of the system denied technical training to women in so much skilled manufacturing like jewelry, almost all aspects of the metal crafts, printing, ship construction—the list goes on and on—that working women found themselves often confined to laborious, repetitive tasks. Of course some women escaped these male-imposed strictures and ran some businesses, but these were exceptions and a tribute to the persistence of strong individuals. These women were not yet perceived as a threat to the mainly paternalistic and patriarchal system of manufacturing.

Household production. Since, with few exceptions, most manufacturing remained small-scale, where the employer closely supervised his or her workers, preindustrial, prefactory manufacturing can be called household production. Yet few family-based operations supplied enough labor from the pool of close relatives, so successful masters were always dipping into the labor market to augment their supply of hands. Hence household production was not static or exclusively family-centered, and it often depended on people who came and went, or childless masters who passed a business on to someone else. Even this labor mobility, which included a fair measure of changing trades altogether as smiths became clockmakers and carpenters became cabinetmakers, fostered the dissemination of new techniques as new ideas from one trade found applications in another.

The guild system of masters, journeymen and women, and apprentices, surrounded by large numbers of casual laborers and those too weak or downtrodden to work, constituted the main features of preindustrial manufacturing. A labor market with an evolving system of wage labor existed. Improving technologies brought forth new trades as the clockmakers and gunsmiths formed new guilds. This system of manufacturing was producing fine silk cloth, ships, muskets, books, watches, and other items that were the most advanced in the world, granting Europeans an advantage over other cultures without steel and guns. Better technologies developed both in the guilds and in the large sector of manufacturing that remained outside their jurisdiction. An ostensibly paternalistic system of labor imposed obligations on both parties to a work contract. A fairly rigid gender division of labor denied women access to many lucrative trades, even when they comprised a substantial percentage of the workforce. These broad social realities varied by time and place, and were changing at different rates in the centuries leading up to the industrial revolution. The best way to understand the variety in the social history of manufacturing in Europe is to examine some specific issues in context.

WORKHOUSES

The attractions of being an apprentice or working as a laborer would not appeal to everyone, and there were always people by temperament not suited to the discipline of the workplace. Cities in particular needed a means to keep a supply of new workers coming to town, for early modern cities were notoriously unhealthy places with low birthrates and high death rates, thus they depended on immigrants from the countryside to maintain their numbers. So the system required a fair degree of socializing new people to the routines of work. The pull of the labor markets benefited from some push to compel people to work, because idleness set a bad example and masters needed hands.

What occurred in the sixteenth and seventeenth centuries across Europe was a number of experiments in forcing the able-bodied to work and not to beg or turn to charity or poor relief. Simon Schama (1987) has noted an example of how compulsion worked in practice, in the case of the Amsterdam Tughuis, a combination of prison and workhouse, which opened in 1595. Eventually, in 1614, when begging by the able-bodied became illegal in Amsterdam, violators were sentenced to the house—for a term of six months for a second offense. The overseers of the Tughuis thought it necessary to discipline and reform the sturdy vagrants and beggars by setting them to work. At first the idle were taught skills like weaving, but in

1599 the house got the monopoly for producing powdered brazilwood. This wood, the fruit of the Dutch colonial trade, yielded a dye essential to the city's cloth industry. Producing the dye required laborers to saw the wood, and the workhouse inmates seemed an ideal labor force. Sawing for fourteen-hour days to make the required number of pounds of dust gained the poor workers a meager wage that no one in a free market would accept for this kind of work. The women inmates were put to work in a similarly grueling system of compulsory spinning.

People refusing to work were put in the water house, where they were given the choice of manning the pumps or drowning in the water they refused to move. The water house of Amsterdam became a tourist attraction as people from across Europe came to witness this stark method of teaching people the value of work. The message to the workers was clear—avoid sloth, beggary, and crime, and work for the wages the market offered, or risk correction. Behind all the wonderful accomplishments of the Dutch economy in its golden age, it must be noted that there was a push as well as a pull into the labor markets. The state was training people in some rudimentary skills that would be useful to them as laborers in the cloth and ship construction trades.

The planners of these workhouses saw themselves as enlightened humanists and reformers combating sloth, a deadly sin. In 1656 the Genoese nobleman Emanuele Brignole proposed the creation of a central institution that would concentrate all the enemies of public order—the syphilitics, the insane, and especially the incorrigible beggars, orphans, criminals, and vagabonds who would not work. The city government agreed, and by 1664 over one thousand people, segregated by sex, age, disease, and crime, were inmates in the Albergo dei Poveri, where the able-bodied passed their time making useful canvas, cheap cloth, and clothing from cotton. The city purchased some slaves who had useful skills to use as instructors for teaching trades to the idle poor. This prison labor competed with some aspects of free-market production of cotton cloth in Genoa (the city whose French word for it—Gênes—became to English speakers "jeans"). The government kept the competition with free workers to the bottom of the trade, where it would serve as a check on wages, and the albergo took up work supplying menial labor and rough products for the private sector.

Some of the best-known experiments in using poor relief to discipline a workforce occurred in England. Elizabethan legislation of 1597 established overseers of the poor, unemployed, and unemployable in every parish. The overseers had the power to raise taxes, the poor rates, in part to purchase raw materials so that children not being maintained by their parents could be set to work. The idle also faced the obligation to work; it became illegal to be unemployed. The overseers also had the authority to put boys and girls into apprenticeships so that they might learn useful trades and become self-supporting. These provisions remained in effect until the late eighteenth century, when even harsher measures were taken against those who would not work. These examples from across western Europe demonstrate that behind the considerable advances in manufacturing and productivity, as well as increases in the general standard of living, lay the threat of compulsion to keep people at work.

SHIPS AND CLOCKS

Preindustrial manufacturing produced many outstanding items that were the marvels of the world—great sailing ships, fine watches, firearms of all types. Individual artisans invented the piano and turned out violins that still are played today. Entrepreneurs like Josiah Wedgwood in England developed pottery works that would soon rival the porcelains of Asia. The surviving examples of this and other crafts demonstrate the high standards and accomplishments. Two distinctive industries, the giant ocean-sailing ships and Mediterranean galleys produced in this period and the much smaller clocks and watches, are useful examples of how manufacturing evolved in the early modern period.

The Venetian Arsenal, with roots deep in the Middle Ages, became in the fifteenth and sixteenth centuries the biggest shipyard in the world (Lane, 1973). By the 1560s the Arsenal employed between two to three thousand men in a variety of trades and was capable of constructing and maintaining a fleet of more than one hundred galleys. These fighting ships, turned out in an assembly-line fashion, were remarkable because they were constructed not as unique vessels but from interchangeable parts. This style of manufacture made it much easier to build and repair galleys. Various guilds of laborers worked on all phases of shipbuilding, but the Arsenal also anticipated modern systems of management because this large work site required vigilant and capable administrators. The Arsenal also became a rare example of a vertically integrated organization. Venice established state forests to secure regular supplies of timber. The need for sails, pulleys, cannon, and other key items involved the Arsenal with a host of suppliers. The success of the Arsenal allowed Venice to remain an international power and stave off the advances of the

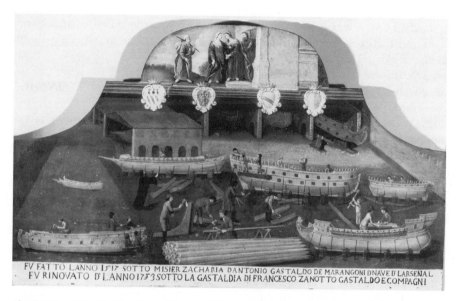

Shipbuilders' Guild. Wooden guild sign of the Marangone, the shipbuilders, of Venice, 1517, restored in 1753. At the top is an image of the Visitation of the Virgin Mary. MUSEO CORRER, VENICE/ERICH LESSING/ART RESOURCE, NY

Ottoman Turks in the eastern Mediterranean, who had large shipyards of their own. But the Arsenal was a unique institution, and its size and fame demonstrated that early modern manufacturing was capable of recruiting a large, skilled workforce, managing large-scale production, and creating a class of artisans with a strong sense of work identity and a willingness to march against the Doge's palace in pay disputes.

Shipyards were plentiful along the Atlantic coasts, and while no maritime power had a centralized yard to rival the Arsenal, the great sailing vessels like the Portuguese carracks, capable of making the long sea voyage to India and carrying large cargoes, were a new style of ship requiring skills from carpenters and caulkers, among many other trades. Peter Linebaugh (1992) has studied the workers in the naval dockyards of England in the eighteenth century. These yards, some of which employed a thousand men, were the largest industrial establishments in the country. A very sophisticated scale of daily wages and overtime regulated the work in the yards. The master craftsmen were in charge of the apprenticeship system and ran it to their benefit. Wages were often in arrears, and the workers were responsible for paying for medical services and the chaplain out of their own pockets. Being in management or a supplier of raw materials to the docks was often the path to riches because of pervasive public corruption.

The yards were certainly no workers' paradise. The dockyard workers struck in 1739 partly because they were paid only twice a year, when they were paid

at all, and they objected to this and the general atmosphere of corruption surrounding public contracting. Worker traditions and management clashed most forcefully on the issue of "chips." By long tradition in the woodworking trades, scrap timber and wood chips belonged to the workers. Their families, especially their wives, had by custom participated in this benefit, which was an important supplement to the stagnant and infrequently paid wages. Over the course of the eighteenth century the government continuously tried to limit the amount of wood the men could carry out of the yards and to exclude altogether the women from scavenging. The workers heated and built their houses with this wood, so they were zealous defenders of their rights. The clash between modern (if corrupt) management and the traditions of the trade shows how a workforce with a strong sense of solidarity was still capable of resisting attempts by employers to control their workplace. In this case the workers were producing warships in a century punctuated by major wars, so the threat of work stoppages was serious, and the workers were even prepared on occasion to fight the Royal Marines to defend their prerogatives. Not all workers enjoyed this self-confidence and leverage over their masters.

Social historians have been interested in the development of mechanical timepieces because these instruments changed the ways people thought about time and the working day. Great tower clocks began to appear on churches and city halls across Europe in the early fourteenth century. These earliest clocks helped to keep a standard time necessary for the cycles of monastic prayer, and their bells fixed the boundaries of the local working day. The story of manufacturing timepieces is the history of miniaturization and increased skill in assembling complicated parts that made up the most intricate machines produced by preindustrial crafts. As David Landes (1983) has described the evolution of the trade, smaller portable clocks first appeared as luxury items in the later 1300s, and jewelers and goldsmiths were active in this trade. Spring-driven clocks first appeared in the early fifteenth century, probably in Italy, and from there it was a small step to making personal watches. Shortly after 1500 very small timepieces appeared, sign of the rapid technological advances in a trade barely two centuries old.

Early modern centers of clock- and watchmaking, northern Italy and southern Germany, soon lost supremacy to English watchmakers, who by the eighteenth century dominated the international trade. By the middle of the century Swiss workers were beginning to turn out high quality timepieces that could compete with English ones. Why the most advanced sector of an industry moves from one place to another remains an important question about manufacturing in any era. The social organization of work usually provides the answer. From one point of view, guilds of clockmakers, which became common only in the sixteenth century, impeded personal ambitions and the development of labor-saving techniques that would allow watches and clocks to be produced more cheaply. The credit guilds receive for educating the next generation in technological skills in this view needs to be balanced against the technological conservatism of guild masters and their desire to divide markets rather than compete over them. Hence in places like England and Holland, where guild rules did not reach beyond the major cities, advances in manufacturing techniques were more rapid than in older centers like Augsburg and Nürnberg. In England, out-work in the unregulated Midlands produced the parts masters assembled and finished in London. Masters benefited from purchasing the cheapest possible parts manufactured by relatively unskilled labor. Soon the entrepreneurs of the Swiss valleys would challenge the English, and in the cantons the trade was completely unregulated.

The rapid advances in this trade, as opposed to preindustrial weaving, may result from the weaker role guilds played in it. This pattern of manufacturing also meant, however, that a larger gulf separated the masters and shop owners from their workers, and gradually fewer people had the chance to rise through the ranks and become self-employed watchmakers. This trade comes the closest to anticipating the effects of the factory system on other areas of manufacturing.

COMPAGNONNAGE

One of the most distinctive and revealing institutions shaping preindustrial manufacturing was the French *compagnonnage*. This association, explored by Cynthia Truant (1994), was a semisecret, illegal group of unmarried journeymen originating in early modern France. More than one *compagnonnage* existed, and it is better to think of them as social brotherhoods. The earliest signs of the *compagnonnage* appeared around Dijon in the fifteenth century, and as Natalie Zemon Davis (1975) has shown for Lyon, journeymen printers there in the sixteenth century were organized enough to strike. By the mid-seventeenth century these associations were common throughout France, strongest in the provinces, less so in Paris, where the powers of the métiers remained strong.

From the point of view of social history, the *compagnonnages* represent a movement of worker solidarity born in a corporate world of work dominated by the employers. The journeymen, though they worked alongside women in many trades, did not allow them to join the *compagnonnages*. Hence these movements against paternalism in work were gendered from the beginning. These journeymen were not primitive rebels or precocious trade unionists, nor were they simply emulating the medieval guild. The *compagnonnages* supported migrant journeymen in searching for jobs and places to stay in new cities. Journeymen took a hand in regulating the circumstances of work against the entrenched but decaying power of the masters.

The members of the *compagnonnages* were bound together by an oath that fostered solidarity. Initiation into the societies involved elaborate rituals, as revealed around 1645 in the customs of the journeymen shoemakers of Toulouse. Denied access to guildhalls and chapels, the journeymen usually met in taverns, so there was always a strong social and convivial component to their associations. A new member swore to obey the rules, and he received a kind of baptism with salt and water that incorporated him into the society. A sponsor, called a godfather, stood at his side as he joined. The use of religious symbols shows how *compagnonnages* grew out of corporate society and drew on the customs of religious confraternities. The most important feature of these rituals was that they attached the loyalty of the ex-apprentice not to his employer but to his fellow journeymen. To the extent that these workers increasingly controlled access to work in the eighteenth century by refusing to work for masters who did not honor their rules, they set the stage for legal associations of workers that developed during the industrial revolution. The secret aspects of the *compagnonnages* made government and guilds suspicious of them. Since the alternative might have been a more direct revolt against the status quo, the *compagnonnages* were usually tolerated. A closer search for these shadowy groups in other European countries may reveal how skilled workers opposed the power of their employers.

NEW TRADES—GUNS AND BOOKS

The increasing use of handheld weapons, muskets and pistols, in early modern warfare—itself a growth business—created oscillating demands for these products. Manufacturing guns was a new trade in this period, and the stages of work represent one of the most sophisticated divisions of labor in preindustrial manufacturing. Carlo M. Belfant (1998) has investigated this trade in the northern Italian city of Brescia, a renowned center of gun manufacture. Brescia had some natural advantages for this trade: iron ore was nearby, as were forests to supply fuel and streams for water power. Why the area should have so many highly skilled gunsmiths as opposed to other types of metalworkers is unclear, but early innovations in techniques probably explain this local specialization.

The stages of production were complex and reveal an advanced division of labor. First, miners had to extract iron ore and turn it over to forgers who produced the first, rough cast iron. Cast iron contains many impurities that weaken the metal, so sophisticated forges heated the cast iron, with mills providing the water power necessary to drive the hammers that literally beat the impurities from the metal. This early use of water power for forging enabled local smiths to turn out high quality sheets of forged iron. Next, the most skilled phase occurred as master gunsmiths produced gun barrels from the sheets. The barrel was the most critical part of the weapon because cheap ones exploded or quickly split, rendering the gun useless. Brescia's weapons enjoyed a high reputation because of the barrels, and the masters who made them presided over the craft. Various other specialized artisans, like borers, finished the basic barrel. The final step was burnishing, a craft dominated by women masters and apprentices.

An allied trade of skilled craftsmen produced the flint gunlocks, the firing mechanism. Other teams of artisans assembled the barrel and gunlock into a musket or pistol. This trade required skill in wood-working as well as metalworking. The early stages of production were out in the countryside, near the forges, while much of the finishing work took place in Brescia. Many allied trades, like the makers of bayonets, powder horns, and bullets, were also located in the region. This complex industrial zone was capable as early as 1562 of turning out 25,000 muskets a year. There was a continuously high level of activity till the end of the eighteenth century, when the industry was still able to make for Spain 150,000 rifles from 1794 to 1797. The market for Brescia's weapons was international and driven largely by the pace of warfare. This unpredictability of demand caused problems for the masters, who along with their workers preferred regular production and profits to bouts of overwork or unemployment.

The Venetian state governing Bresica tried and failed to introduce some regularity into the market for weapons. Hence tensions developed between the masters and artisans making the guns and the merchants who sold them in large lots to customers across Europe. The producers were frequently in debt and turned to new guilds to defend their interests against the merchants. A guild of gunsmiths, run by the barrel makers and including the borers, gunlock makers, and other crafts, emerged in the early seventeenth century, a sign that a guild still struck masters as their most sensible means of mutual assistance. Since the masters had little choice but to sell to middlemen, the social relations of markets and work were changing in ways the guilds found difficult to master. Forge owners were also important to the trade and were not in the guild. The guild masters wanted to force merchants to share big orders among the members, another typical indication that the masters were more interested in surviving in the trade than driving out their competitors. This instinct to form a cartel failed to serve the interests of all the workers and masters in the craft, so the trade in 1717 opted for one central guild including all phases of manufacturing, on a more equal footing, to confront the merchants. By the middle of the century, the masters of the lesser trades, thinking their interests neglected by the barrel makers, asked for and received their own guilds.

All these problems inside the trade led to a decline in quality. The merchants sought to evade the guild rules by engaging in out-work, but cheaper barrels from deep in the countryside hurt the reputation of guns from Brescia. Whether the gradual decline of the industry resulted from anticompetitive guild rules, an inability of the trade to deal with irregular demand, or frustrated desires of workers to rise in the craft remains unclear. Also, international competition had become stiffer as each nation thought it necessary to have a domestic, reliable supply of weaponry and people skilled at the trade. This case study of the trade around Brescia reveals that the advantages of a first mover in this craft did not guarantee a permanent, prominent position in the business of guns. The problem was that the social relations surrounding work could not keep up with the increasingly international economy of Europe.

Ever since Johann Gutenberg of Mainz used movable type around 1450 to print the first books in Europe, the printing trades had evolved and produced millions of books, pamphlets, and prints. As a new trade at the cutting edge of early modern technology, printing still adopted the guild system typical of older industries. Early printed books described new technologies, the diversity of trades, and even occupational illnesses. Printing was an unusual trade because much of its work required literate artisans in societies where overall literacy rates remained low. Also, the printing trade was exceptionally mobile, and skilled masters and workers moved across Europe looking for markets and work. Literate workers and companies left behind records that Robert Darnton (1985) has used to illuminate the craft in Paris and Neuchâtel in Switzerland. In Paris the Crown fixed the number of master printers at thirty-six in 1686, making it difficult for journeymen to rise in the craft. The most skilled workers were threatened by the cheaper work by apprentices and laborers not in the *compagnonnages*. Journeymen in these circumstances often moved quickly from job to job, and a fair amount of violence, drunkenness, and absenteeism characterized the workplace. The journeymen retained some solidarity in the face of all these problems. Printing too suggests that preindustrial manufacturing was no golden age for workers trapped in a rigid guild hierarchy with few prospects for social mobility.

CONDITIONS AT THE END OF THE PERIOD

Printing, a modern trade, experienced some of the first genuine industrial strikes. General strikes among the cloth workers in Leiden in 1644 and 1701 revealed that it was hard to organize against the masters and merchants who dominated the increasingly international scope of work. When the cloth workers of Salisbury revolted in 1738, the government executed the ringleaders, another sign that state authority in this period firmly sided with the employers. As the great European social historian Fernand Braudel (1982) observed about these and other revolts, the putting-out system and the guilds remained the entrenched powers in manufacturing. Where these institutions were weakest, the industrial revolution would first appear. The modern, capitalist employers originated, however, in the social relations surrounding work in the early modern period. So too did a gender division of labor that excluded women from many trades and usually paid them lower wages for the same work. This system put boys and girls to work learning a trade at young ages and forced the able-bodied idle to work. The workers, especially the journeymen and women, faced the start of the factory era in the late eighteenth century with some worker solidarity. But they were in an increasingly weak position as the reciprocity of the older system of paternalistic wage labor gave way to harsher working conditions. A working class was in the making.

CONCLUSION

It is important to remember that the dominant features of preindustrial manufacturing were changing in advance of industrialization. Guilds were under attack, though many survived in strength. Manufacturing in rural areas was gaining ground. In this system, merchants from the cities distributed raw materials and orders to workers who labored in their homes, usually with primitive manual equipment, and then manufacturer representatives picked up the finished products and paid the workers by the piece. An alternative system had workers coming into town to get materials and then later to sell products. Hundreds of thousands of rural (domestic or putting-out-system) workers were involved in textiles, shoes, and metal goods by the eighteenth century, either full-time or part-time. Finally, technological change, though uneven, also affected many branches of preindustrial manufacturing.

See also **Protoindustrialization; The Industrial Revolutions** *(volume 2);* **Artisans** *(volume 3); and other articles in this section.*

BIBLIOGRAPHY

Belfant, Carlo M. "A Chain of Skills: The Production Cycle of Firearms Manufacture in the Brescia Area from the Sixteenth to the Eighteenth Centuries." In *Guilds, Markets, and Work Regulations in Italy, 16th–19th Centuries.* Edited by Alberto Guenzi, Paola Massa, and Fausto Piola Caselli. Aldershot, U.K., 1998.

Biernacki, Richard. *The Fabrication of Labor: Germany and Britain, 1640–1914.* Berkeley, Calif., 1995.

Black, Anthony. *Guilds and Civil Society in European Thought from the Twelfth Century to the Present.* Ithaca, N.Y., 1984.

Braudel, Fernand. *The Wheels of Commerce.* New York, 1982.

Darnton, Robert. *The Great Cat Massacre and Other Episodes in French Cultural History.* New York, 1985.

Davis, Natalie Zemon. *Society and Culture in Early Modern France.* Stanford, Calif., 1975.

Epstein, Steven A. *Wage Labor and Guilds in Medieval Europe.* Chapel Hill, N.C., 1991.

Hanawalt, Barbara A., ed. *Women and Work in Preindustrial Europe.* Bloomington, Ind., 1986.

Landes, David. S. *Revolution in Time: Clocks and the Making of the Modern World.* Cambridge, Mass., 1983.

Lane, Frederic C. *Venice, A Maritime Republic.* Baltimore, 1973.

Linebaugh, Peter. *The London Hanged: Crime and Civil Society in the Eighteenth Century.* Cambridge, U.K., 1992.

Schama, Simon. *The Embarrassment of Riches: An Interpretation of Dutch Culture in the Golden Age.* New York, 1987.

Smith, Adam. *The Wealth of Nations.* New York, 1937.

Thompson, E. P. *The Making of the English Working Class.* New York, 1963.

Truant, Cynthia Maria. *The Rites of Labor: Brotherhoods of Compagnonnage in Old and New Regime France.* Ithaca, N.Y., 1994.

FACTORY WORK

Barbara Bari

Factory work is at the core of industrialization, a process that defined economic change in Europe for more than a century. The factory system was a way to organize work and produce goods that differed from small-scale personal manufacture in homes and workshops. Beginning in Britain around 1750, industrial production eventually became the dominant form of manufacture, though not the dominant sector of the economy, in most European countries by 1914. Whether termed "industrialization" or "industrial revolution," the transformations were neither linear nor uniform. National, regional, industrial, and gender variations existed in the rate and extent of change. While factories gathered more of the manufacturing population, technology, power-driven machines, and large-scale production were a part of the broader process of industrial development. That process experienced variety, unevenness, progress, and regress because many production processes involved a combination of factory work, machines, handicraft workers, and domestic industry. Countless women worked in factories, especially in textiles, yet domestic manufacturing persisted as a critical way for thousands of women to contribute to the family economy. In many areas, especially on the Continent, a symbiotic relationship persisted between old and new techniques, mediating against the notion that industrialization was a startling event. The transformations that altered the economic and social characteristics of Europe were slow, particularistic, and complex. This essay offers insight into the multiple changes and continuities that form the social context for a broader understanding of factory work. It focuses on the major industrial nations of Britain, France, and Germany from the eighteenth century to the twentieth century. For western and central European workers, the role of factories in shaping work experience was especially critical in the nineteenth century. The twentieth-century brought the factory into eastern Europe, and especially after World War II it brought immigrants into the factories of the west. In eastern Europe—however differently communist ideology envisioned industrialization—the So-

viet economic system produced many patterns similar to those observable in earlier industrial revolutions. Factory work has not been a constant, even in countries like Britain that industrialized early. Expansion of factory size and the growth of technical automation conditioned the work experience.

Despite variations with time and place, a number of patterns warrant particular attention. Factories changed the work experience in several important respects. They increased the pace of work, as machines tended to dictate speed. They encouraged work specialization, so ultimately the semiskilled worker, adept at a fairly narrow job, became the classic factory operative. Few workers participated in more than a small stage of the production process, and the separation of work from a clear sense of the end product contributed to what some observers have termed the alienation of factory labor. Factories created new problems with accidents and noise. They also subjected workers to detailed supervision either by other workers or, as time went on and organization became more formal, foremen or efficiency engineers. Finally, factories definitively separated work from home, forcing workers to deal with many strangers as colleagues. For many workers, both in the early days of factories and later amid more complex organization and technology, the quality of the work experience deteriorated. Various protests attempted to address this situation but with little hard-won success. Strikes and unionization often focused more on compensation for work—in the form of pay and benefits—than on the work itself.

BRITAIN, 1750–1914

Mechanization and factories. The strength of Britain's commercial and manufacturing success in the seventeenth and eighteenth centuries formed the base for the first industrial revolution. Important factors facilitated Britain's industrialization. Innovations in agriculture and restrictions on land ownership made farming less viable as a full-time occupation. Domes-

Soviet Industrialization. "With arms we have defeated the enemy; with labor we will get bread; get down to work, comrades!" reads a 1921 Soviet poster. THE DAVID KING COLLECTION

change in the mode of production in Europe. It is symbolic of the factory system in Britain but also in other societies undergoing industrialization. By the 1790s almost all cotton spinning for market was located in factories. Weaving was technically more difficult to mechanize, and increased demand for cotton cloth initially resulted in expansion of hand weaving and home production. Domestic weavers were mostly men, whereas hand spinning was done by women. When power was introduced to weaving in the first years of the nineteenth century, thousands of hand-loom weavers who lived in the countryside were displaced. This disturbance was one of the most visible negative effects of industrialization, and its long-lived lament was expressed by artisans, who were confused and angry, and by labor historians like E. P. Thompson, who wrote *The Making of the English Working Class* (1963), one of the first great social histories of this group.

Among other textiles, industrial development varied according to the types of fiber and the work processes involved. Mechanization of woolens was slower than cottons because spinning and weaving wool fibers was more difficult and more expensive to do by machine. Machines could be used in only certain parts of the production process, such as preparing the raw wool for spinning and finishing the surface. West Riding in Yorkshire became the center of England's wool industry when steam engines were incorporated into various stages of production. The general trend in textiles was mechanization, but factories did not eliminate domestic industry and handwork because some operations resisted a technical solution.

It took most of the nineteenth century for the conversion to factory work to saturate industrial production. The early stages of industrialization were marked by the erosion of old crafts through division of labor and by the development of new skills suitable to mechanized production. New technologies changed the scale of production. Advances in metallurgy were as impressive as those in textiles and perhaps more influential to the expansion of mechanization because machines made from iron could sustain the heavy, repetitive demands of the factory system. Coke was used instead of charcoal for smelting, steam-powered engines increased production, and machines became the platforms for creating other machines. Most of the new equipment required large plants. Iron puddling furnaces, steam and water engines, silk-throwing mills, spinning factories, and weaving machines all needed space.

The goal was to rationally organize production by restructuring the work process and by increasing the productivity of workers. When machinery was ap-

tic manufacturing, usually with whole families working together, established a large protoindustrial base. A considerable rise in population put pressure on existing resources. Large workshops, resembling factories but without mechanization, undergirded the imperial economy, functioning in printmaking, linen and woolen manufacturing, lace and stocking making, ironware production, and the other metal trades. Maxine Berg indicated that the large-scale woolen workshops of West Yorkshire moved into a factory system, incorporating division of labor, standardization, concentration of labor, and the use of unskilled workers, prior to mechanization. Thus factories predated the industrial revolution.

However, technology opened a new path. In 1765 James Watt modified a crude steam engine to make it more versatile, and steam power became available to run a variety of machines that changed the production process in essential ways. Inventions in spinning pushed textiles to the forefront of industrial production. The advent of the spinning mule in 1779 made England "the workshop of the world." Mechanized spinning was identified as the first significant

plied to jobs in which skilled labor performed most operations, a revolutionary change occurred. Standardization and uniformity were achieved by dividing the whole work process into individual tasks that could be mechanized. Adam Smith believed that the division of labor enhanced productivity. With training and experience, worker efficiency increased, and simplified, repetitive work reduced the need for skilled labor, lowering costs. Smith argued,

> The great increase in the quantity of work, which, in consequence of the division of labour, the same number of people are capable of performing, is owing to three different circumstances: first, to the increase of dexterity in every particular workman; secondly, to the saving of time, which is commonly lost in passing from one species of work to another; and, lastly, to the invention of a great number of machines which facilitate and abridge labour, and enable one man to do the work of many. (Berg, 1979, p. 48)

Mass production in factories meant cheaper production. Although numerous studies on specialization were conducted at the turn of the century, the Charles Babbage report entitled "On the Economy of Machinery and Manufactures" was significant in establishing the principles of factory organization. The report sold three thousand copies shortly after its publication in 1833. Babbage concluded that production costs could be substantially reduced by dividing a craft into its constituent parts. He also composed a list of questions for workers. The inquiry form was available to industrialists who wanted a clearer picture of their workforces and work processes. Questions for both employers and workers included: Were various parts of the same article made in one factory or elsewhere? If elsewhere, did the work processes differ? Did the "master" or men provide and repair the tools? What level of waste was tolerated by the "master"? What was the cost of the machinery, and was it made and repaired at the factory? How many persons were necessary to attend each machine? What was the composition of labor—men, women, children? Did age and gender affect job assignments? What wages were earned by each category of workers, and were earnings determined by time or piecework? What was the average daily work time, and did workers have to perform night or shift work? What degree of skill was required, and how were workers trained? Answers to these questions have also assisted social historians in reconstructing the social history of labor.

Structuring factory work: management and regulation.

Large, mechanized establishments created new issues of labor management. Early factories depended on skilled, mature male workers, who made up the "labor aristocracy." In the manner of craft trades, these workers had considerable control over their work and the machines they operated. Robert Owen sought to implement his ideas of work civility in his New Lanark mill in Manchester, which he ran between 1800 and 1829. He advocated organizing his workers into a kind of family, in which community and factory were linked together and the humane treatment of labor would result in "pecuniary profit." Owen's style of paternalism was directed at problems of labor discipline and at transforming persons new to industrial work into a reliable and efficient labor force. Factory discipline was essential to the production process in all mechanized industries. Workers paid substantial economic and psychological costs in regions where machines displaced home industry and separated work from the household. In the early stages of industrialization, these violations caused overt resistance to machines and the mills. One of the most famous episodes of worker violence occurred in the woolen industry in the Midlands and West Riding. In the Luddite "outrages" of 1811 and 1812, workers broke into factories and destroyed the machines, which they identified as the major threat to their economic safety and way of life. Thompson wrote:

> The main disturbances commenced in Nottingham, in March 1811. A large demonstration of stockingers, "clamouring for work and a more liberal price" was dispersed by the military. That night sixty stocking-frames were broken at the large village of Arnold by rioters who took no precautions to disguise themselves and who were cheered on by the crowd. For several weeks disturbances continued, mainly at night, throughout the hosiery villages of north-west Nottinghamshire. Although special constables and troops patrolled the villages, no arrests could be made. (Thompson, 1963, p. 553)

Factory workers left scant records, but inquiries and parliamentary debates over industrialization provide information about conditions on the job and about how workers lived. Housing, food and drink, clothing, and health were all subjects of investigation and evaluation. On the job concerns of factory workers focused on hours and wages. The hours issue was the subject of some of the first attempts to regulate factory work, particularly the use of child labor. Factory work required set hours, punctuality, and productivity rates governed by the machines. In areas of continuous around-the-clock activity, such as the iron and glass industries, laborers usually worked shifts of twelve hours. The glass industry had alternate six-hour shifts. The generally accepted workday for most industries was from 6:00 A.M. to 6:00 P.M. The twelve-hour day was normal in textiles, although with increased mechanization hours were extended, sometimes to 8:00 P.M. Owen addressed the issue in 1815. Consequently the select committee of 1816 formed, and in 1819 legislation restricted child labor to twelve hours daily. The act, however, had little effect. Employers ignored it, and enforcement was difficult. The six-day work week was the norm, with work lasting until 6:00 P.M. on Saturdays. Legislation in 1825 confirmed the twelve-hour day in the cotton industry and limited Saturday work to nine hours, but as with previous legislation, enforcement was practically nonexistent.

By the 1830s regulation of factory work was clearly part of the broader reformist climate in Britain. The parliamentary Sadler commission of 1832 intended to expose the conditions of children in factories, and testimony before the commission came from workers themselves. A twenty-eight-year-old cloth dresser reported that he had started in the flax mills at age ten. Work commenced at 5:00 A.M. and ended at 9:00 P.M. with a dinner break at noon. Boys and girls began working in the woolen mills as young as five or six. As adults they remembered working until 9:00 or 10:00 P.M. in the summer while sufficient light lasted. As youngsters both boys and girls were "strapped" to keep them awake and working. One of the ugliest practices was employing orphans from asylums in cities. The children were shipped to the factories, where they were compelled to work in exchange for food and shelter.

The Sadler hearings and debates led to the Factory Act of 1833. Robert Gray, in *The Factory Question and Industrial England* (1996), explained that provisions stipulated a maximum of eight hours and compulsory schooling for children between nine and twelve years old. For youngsters between thirteen and seventeen, the twelve-hour day was the limit. The act also established a factory inspectorate. With some exceptions, the provisions extended beyond the cotton industry to include all textile production that used power machines.

Once factory work was identified as the cause of debility, disease, and moral danger, the government intervened. This act established the model and structure for subsequent legislation. The Factory Commission's factory inspections legitimated further investigations. Medical opinion was instrumental in forming concern for factory labor and setting the rationale for regulation. Lung diseases, stomach and bowel disorders, varicose veins, leg ulcers, pelvic deformities, and childbirth problems were linked to factory work. In the 1840s, against the background of public and political pressure, the Chartist movement, and worker violence, legislation was expanded. In 1847 the Act to Limit the Hours of Labour of Young Persons and Females in Factories confirmed the ten-hour day in textiles. The precedent for government intervention and regulation of factory work, particularly in textile mills, where large numbers of women and children were employed, was generally accepted by the mid-nineteenth century.

The living standards of workers also came under scrutiny. Thompson described the average worker as living close to the subsistence level, but variations including industry, place of employment, skill level, and gender made the "average worker" somewhat elusive. The standard of living issue integrated questions about family, women's work, child labor, national health, and morality. Inquiries into diet, housing, and sanitation provided information on the living conditions of factory labor, which spurred later debates among social historians about the impact of industrialization on workers' standard of living. Most workers subsisted on a diet of cereal and potatoes. Meat was scarce, available only when someone earned extra money for a proper Sunday meal. Workers' wives bought inferior parts of animals, such as a cow's heel, a sheep's trotters, a pig's ear, and tripe. Beer was considered a necessity by many factory workers. It eased frustrations and encouraged camaraderie in the countless pubs that grew up in factory districts. Despite shop rules, workers liked to drink on the job, explaining that it gave them strength and quenched their thirst.

Change and continuity: 1875–1914. Many of the themes and problems of Britain's early industrialization persisted in the years before World War I, although working and living conditions improved somewhat. Regional industries were still a part of the economic landscape before 1914, with wide variations in the scale and concentration of production, levels of mechanization, wage systems, and workers' earnings. Factory work was almost complete in textiles, engineering, and metal work, but subcontracting had not been eliminated. Expanded and more sophisticated technology was troubling to workers, whose pride was bound up with the job. Although formal apprenticeships declined, skilled labor was required for many operations in the factory, where most workers were trained on the job. Evidence points to generational tension. Older skilled workers were reluctant to accept younger, less-skilled workers as equals. Some skilled workers went to extremes to protect their craft and independence. John Benson reported:

> There used to be a craftsman in this shop who always came to work with a piece of chalk in his pocket. When he arrived each morning he would at once draw a chalk

In the Factory. Cycle factory at Coventry, England, 1890s. MANSELL COLLECTION/TIME PIX

circle on the floor around his machine. If the foreman wanted to speak to him he could do so . . . as long as he stayed outside the circle. But if he put one foot across that line, he was a dead man. (Hinson, 1973, pp. 58–59)

A London engineer said that in 1897 he and his fellow workers used passive resistance and sabotage against new machinery and time monitoring. They deliberately slowed down the pace of work and complained to the "rate-fixer" that the production charts were wrong. The stopwatch was not welcome on the factory floor.

In the 1890s increased supervision became prevalent in most modern industries. New technology flattened the gap between the skilled and the unskilled. A factory inspector reported a policy used in some textile mills to guarantee production and enforce labor discipline requiring that female workers give the foreman a tally when they went to the toilet. The information was collected, and a woman was fined at the end of the month if the reckoning showed she spent more than four minutes for each visit to the facilities. Despite protective legislation, child labor was widespread before World War I. Working-class poverty was a recurrent theme, and children in textile families were expected to earn. Compulsory public education was introduced in 1876, but children continued to work part-time. In the textile mills in Lancashire and Yorkshire, children left school at age twelve to work half-time in the factory and full-time when they reached

thirteen. This practice persisted until 1918, when it was legally abolished.

The British economy underwent structural changes between 1875 to 1914. However, it would be incorrect to assume that all traditional modes of production disappeared. The period of mature industrialization witnessed increased mechanization, wage systems based on speed of productivity, expanded use of piecework, and closer supervision of workers as many firms instituted systematic and "scientific" management. Child and female labor decreased. Trade union membership grew, and associations included more semiskilled and unskilled workers in their ranks. Although aggregate data on worker protests are incomplete, indications are that workers learned to use strikes as effective disruptions to force managements to meet at least some of their demands. Strike activity increased between 1908 and 1910, but in 1911 the number of strikes and the number of workers who struck rose dramatically. They stayed high until the outbreak of war.

THE CONTINENT

Industrialization began on the Continent considerably later than in Britain. Wars, civil disturbances, and political particularism delayed innovation; guild restrictions were tenacious; the agrarian economy remained stable; domestic industry prevailed; and a shortage of raw materials retarded conversion to factory production. Also, deep social attitudes preserved traditional ways of work. By 1830 the only continental country that had introduced mechanization was Belgium, which converted various branches of the textile industry into factory work. France and several of the German states followed, along with southern European states like Italy and Spain, which progressed more slowly and with greater regional variations. For those entrepreneurs who realized the connection between wealth and mechanization, Britain was the source of technology, machines, and skilled labor. British workers installed machinery and trained others to use it efficiently; businesspeople developed factories in Belgium, France, and Germany; and British capital supported many industrial endeavors. W. O. Henderson stated in *Britain and Industrial Europe* (1965) that knowledge, inventions, machines, and personnel were transferred from Britain to the Continent, but conversion to factories also depended on national and regional economic, social, and political considerations.

FRANCE, 1850–1914

The factory worker was not characteristic of French labor in the mid-nineteenth century. Only about 20 percent of workers were employed in factories and mines in 1850. The pattern of development was regional with significant variations. Domestic industry and agriculture engaged most of the population in the first half of the nineteenth century, even while machines and mechanization were adopted in selected industries, such as textiles and metallurgy. However, tradition and relatively good earnings in the countryside made it difficult to entice labor into factories. Robert Magraw offered the following profile in *A History of the French Working Class* (1992). Textiles and clothing were the two largest branches of industrial production, employing about 58 percent of the non-agrarian population in the 1840s. About 10 percent of industrial labor was in metallurgy. Women and children were used extensively in factory work because they worked for lower wages and compensated for reluctant male labor. In 1866 about 30 percent of industrial labor was female. This figure rose to 40 percent by the outbreak of the war in 1914. Children comprised about 12 percent of factory workers in the 1840s, but that number declined gradually as a result of social concerns and the Labor Law of 1841.

Structuring factory work: management, resistance, and regulation. Generally the French were more traditional and less willing to submit to fac-

tory organization than the British. The French held strong ties to the land and to handwork. Industrialists had problems drawing workers, and the resulting labor shortage affected the composition of the workforce, wages, and the way employers treated their workers, especially those whose skills were essential to production. Employers found it easier and cheaper to use domestic industry instead of investing large sums in machines and factory buildings. Employers also faced seasonal interruptions. Factory workers who maintained connections with family and village usually went home for the harvest. In such an industrial environment, skilled workers could command high wages, and many employers offered further inducements to secure a stable core of workers.

It took several years of training and experience for textile workers to reach quality performance, but skill was not the only constraint. French factory workers tended to treat requirements for punctuality and discipline with distaste. They took unauthorized breaks, stole materials, showed up for work drunk, and insisted on observing Holy Monday as a day off to recover from Sunday. If none of these maneuvers relieved the pressure, French male workers often changed jobs and locations, a practice that disturbed production because new people had to be trained and integrated into the factory system. In metallurgy and other kinds of heavy industry, a skilled male labor force was essential. Because of the nature of the work, women and children were not appropriate substitutes. Metal firms paid high wages and raided other plants to keep a full complement on the job. Skilled English workers were used initially to train men in metals, and fifteen years was not an unusual length of time to reach full proficiency.

In textiles women made up half of the factory labor force. More women worked in spinning than in weaving, and more women worked in cotton production than in woolens production. But the composition of the labor force varied from region to region. Several factors mitigated against increasing the use of child labor. Male wages were high enough to limit the need for youngsters to enter the factories. New technology and larger machines eliminated tasks usually performed by children, especially the very young. Indications suggest that employers were aware of the effects of factory work on children's health and morality. Concerns culminated in the Child Labor Law of 1841. The law stipulated that children under eight years of age were prohibited from factory work, it banned night work for children under thirteen, and it required that children receive at least some elementary education. As in Britain, the law was evaded by both employers and families, who needed the meager earnings to get by. Factory inspection was unreliable, and the law applied only to firms with more than twenty workers. At least the issue of child labor was in the public domain, but humanitarian concerns did not override the cost benefits of child labor until the 1870s.

Wages in factory work were higher than in domestic industry, and they rose in the nineteenth century. The level of mechanization affected wage rates in various industries and regions. Notions of a "just wage" were included in pay considerations. What was deemed fair was supposed to be a notch above subsistence and reflective of the worker's skill, strength, and experience. To maximize return on the investment of machines and to keep costs low, manufacturers tried to insure that workers produced to capacity. High wages were one incentive, but piecework contributed to increased production and also to regulation of the work process. Laborers were commonly paid by the day, but skilled workers earned price per piece. Some evidence, however, shows that workers deliberately adjusted their productivity to prevent employers from setting standards of output at higher levels. Fines were imposed for disciplinary violations. It was expected that workers would clean and repair their own machines. To counter absenteeism and job changing, some of the larger manufacturers required that workers sign a contract. Employers often withheld a small part of a worker's pay, which was returned only if the reason for leaving was acceptable. Factory rules also promoted standardization, regularity, and quality work. Too much independence was not tolerated. Peter Stearns wrote in *Paths to Authority* (1978) that workers were prevented from "wandering" about the factory floor, carousing, drinking and smoking around the machines, and even singing. Fines were imposed for such behaviors.

Paternalism was a distinctive feature of large firms. Benefits were seen as a way to insure a disciplined, stable complement of workers, especially skilled adult men. While the approach was more prevalent in heavy industry, large textile plants eventually offered similar benefits. Benevolent policies did more to steady the work force than high wages. Among the benefits were company housing, pension plans, medical care, and on-site company schools, all of which bound workers more closely to their employment. Paternalism was clearly a strategy to promote manufacturers' self-interests and also to transmit middle-class values of family, order, cleanliness, and sobriety. Large textile firms in Nord and Alsace established mutual aid groups that provided a small amount to workers who were out because of illness or accident, and burial funds were popular. Voluntary or compulsory savings banks were also a part of company packages. Firms that established schools not only improved the quality of families and future workers but also complied with the 1841 Child Labor Law. Commonly children went to school for a few hours to learn the basics of reading and writing, then went to the factory. While paternalism provided mutual benefits for industrialists and factory workers, only a minority of France's labor force was eligible. Most workers, especially women, were employed by companies whose approach to labor was cost-effective and exploitative.

Change and continuity, 1870–1914. Between 1871 and 1914 French industrial structure continued to exhibit the characteristics of uneven development. Compared with Britain, small-scale, workshop production persisted in many sectors. The crisis of military defeat in 1870 and a depression that lasted almost until the end of the century slowed industrial advancement.

However, by the turn of the century a "second industrial revolution" was underway. The pressure of foreign competition expanded mechanization and stimulated new industries. Peugeot in eastern France changed from making metal hoops for corsets to producing automobiles. By 1914 France was home to the second largest car industry in the world. Lorraine became one of Europe's major steel areas. Technical knowledge enhanced chemicals, electricals, rubber, and aluminum. In Lyon the number of mechanized looms for silk production rose from five thousand to forty thousand by 1914, and industry diversified to include chemicals, metals, pharmaceuticals, glass, locomotives plants, factory-made clothes, and shoes in 1914.

As with early industrialization, France faced labor shortages prompted by rapid technological change and industrial diversification. The composition of the labor force was marked by certain particulars that were not seen in Britain. The number of women rose due to aggressive recruitment by employers. Women made up 31 percent of the labor force in 1866 and 37 percent in 1906. In Lyonnais half of the chemical workers, two-thirds of the clothing workers, and one-fifth of the metal workers were women. Interestingly, in contrast to England and Germany, married women tended to return to the factory after they had children. Migrant labor also figured largely in French industry. Belgians and Germans were supplemented by thousands of Italian workers brought in for the iron and steel industries. By 1914 about 1 million foreigners worked in France.

The standard of living improved at the turn of the century. Even with variations among industries and economic fluctuations, job security was less uncertain. The severe survival crises of the past subsided, and workers came to think of former extras as necessities. Workers' diets were more varied, often including fruits, butter, and condiments. By the 1900s workers allotted about 30 percent to 40 percent of their budgets to food, whereas at mid-century it hovered around 70 percent. Health and hygiene improved. Clinics for working-class mothers in major industrial areas affected prenatal and maternity care, and child morbidity fell considerably. Contemporaries measured worker health, at least in males, by the increased number of conscripts who qualified for military service. Reducing child factory work ameliorated health generally. Protective legislation of 1874 and 1892 set age restrictions, banned child labor in certain industries, and increased the number of factory inspectors. Parents often subverted the provisions by asking inspectors to ignore the illegal jobs of their children.

As wages improved and work time lessened, more workers had time and energy for leisure. The so-called "English week" of five and a half days allowed workers to think in terms of the weekend. Drinking, of course, was always important, but younger workers also looked to sports for excitement and relaxation. Some factories encouraged workers to organize soccer teams not only for healthy exercise but also to build company loyalty.

GERMANY: RAPID MECHANIZATION, 1870–1914

When Britain's industrialization was described as mature, the German states were just starting to adopt mechanization. Before the mid-nineteenth century mechanized factories were uncommon. Around 1840 German manufacturing was infused with technology from Britain. It is generally accepted that Germany's industrialization took place comparatively quickly and that changes occurred even more rapidly after unification in 1871. Regionalism was a noticeable feature of German industrial development. The centers for textiles were in Silesia and Saxony in the east and the Rhineland and Westphalia in the west. Heavy industry, iron, and metallurgy were located in the Ruhr Valley and Saar. Other areas maintained relatively traditional conditions to the beginning of the twentieth century. The large coal reserves in the western provinces of Prussia were not yet fully exploited. Metalworking establishments were small, scattered, and powered by water. Iron making was usually a supplement to peasant farming. The Solingen metal works employed large numbers of skilled men who worked in the traditional handicraft mode. Following unification, many of the hindrances to industrialization were eased and replaced by government support for economic advancement. The most aggressive period of industrial development was between 1895 and 1914. Huge firms organized in factory production accounted for the greatest increase in labor.

Germany experienced variations in the growth of specific industries and time differences in the process of mechanization and factory concentration. Most obvious were discontinuities between the capital goods and consumer goods industries. Because of the nature of production, an expanding market, and an available supply of skilled and semiskilled male labor, heavy industry could profitably introduce machinery and mechanization. In textiles, clothing, and tobacco a fluctuating market, foreign competition, and a ready pool of unskilled and semiskilled labor, almost 50 percent of which was female, made nonfactory work more flexible and more profitable. In the period of Germany's rapid industrialization, approximately 50 percent of industrial female labor was employed in the clothing industry, which further expanded into domestic industry and the putting-out system with the introduction of the foot-operated sewing machine.

The structure of factory work. Sexual division of labor was a statement about social and economic issues related to factory work. Earning a living was integrated into definitions of masculinity and femininity. When women worked in factories, their employment was often seasonal and intermittent, as industrial demand and personal and family needs guided their work outside the home. Over the course of their work lives, women changed jobs. They combined various kinds of work in factories, domestic industry, and agriculture and stayed at home if male earnings were sufficient for family viability. In the factory gender segregation was integral to questions of wages, skills, turnover, and legal protection. Controlled work assignments segmented industries and operations, as employers, government, religion, and society at large separated men's work and women's work into categories of labor. Sexual division preserved the contours of traditional gender roles by removing women as far as possible from direct competition with men. Protective legislation divided men and women workers by gender and regulated women's participation in the labor force. The same theme was adopted by male-dominated labor unions in an effort to control and even eliminate women from factory work, but that proved impossible.

During Germany's rapid industrial expansion in the 1880s and 1890s, a persistent labor shortage made women the appropriate choice for factory work. Women's factory work is best captured by examining the textile industry, where, as in France and Britain, women made up the core workforce before 1914. Kathleen Canning noted in *Languages of Labor and Gender* (1996) that, in the textile regions of the Rhineland and Westphalia, the lives of both single and married women included work in the factory. Censuses report that the number of women employed in the mills in all of Germany rose by 63 percent between 1882 and 1907, while male employment barely changed. The western provinces were also areas of heavy industry, which drew male workers away from the textile factories. Many factory women came from domestic industry, but the influx of hundreds of young women from the countryside aroused the most attention and worry. The single mill girls symbolized the worst effects of industrialization and factory work. However, employers were concerned not only with filling the line but also with developing a mature, reliable, and productive group of women, many of them married, to "regulate" the younger workers. Most entrants could learn enough in several weeks to do passable work and were considered fully productive within a year. Despite feminization, men continued to earn higher wages in textiles because they had the formal training to execute jobs that required skill, strength, and the know-how to handle the machines. Gender division of work processes and supervision made it difficult for women to improve wages or conditions on the job.

Industrialization brought an entirely new perception of time management and an opportunity to use time to regulate and discipline factory workers. Michael Schneider pointed out in *Streit um Arbeitszeit* (1984) that mechanization increased weekly work hours in textiles from seventy-five in 1825 to ninety in 1850. In the decade from 1860 to 1870 the work week was eighty-one hours. Worker protest was evident by mid-century. In Wuppertal two thousand factory workers went on strike to demand a twelve-hour day with extra pay for overtime. In the metal industries skilled male labor in the huge Krupp and Borsig factories worked a sixty-six-hour week, while male workers in printing and woodworking were in the factory from sixty to seventy hours a week.

Wage structures varied by industry and skill level. Systematic data on wages are not available for Germany for 1871 to 1914, but the existing material is sufficient to convey a sense of earnings by industry and operation. Total wages and wage rates varied according to employers' assessments of the work and the

WAGES IN GERMANY 1871–1914

A survey conducted by the Union of Factory Workers gathered the following information.

Men Workers		Women Workers	
Weekly Wages (in marks)	Percentage of Workers Earning the Wage	Weekly Wages (in marks)	Percentage of Workers Earning the Wage
less than 12	1.12%	less than 8	8.92%
12–15	4.71%	8–10	29.50%
15–18	17.49%	10–12	33.80%
18–21	25.49%	12–15	20.17%
21–25	31.12%	15–	7.61%
25–30	16.40%		
30–35	2.95%		
35–	.72%		

Franzoi, 1985, p. 43

WAGES IN STUTTGART IN 1900

This information was collected by industry.

Occupation	Men's Wages (in marks)	Women's Wages (in marks)	Women's Wages in Percentage of Men's Wages
Painting and Varnishing	20.53	11.28	55%
Shoemaking	18.27	10.89	59%
Upholstering	20.75	10.80	52%
Day Work	16.72	10.59	63%
Printing	27.64	9.82	35.5%
Bookbinding	21.83	9.67	44%
Textiles	20.10	9.13	45%
Tobacco	14.21	8.02	56%

Franzoi, 1985, p. 44

worker, a hierarchical system influenced by custom and social status. Generally workers were considered skilled, semiskilled, or unskilled depending on their training and experience. Many skilled workers in heavy industry had family members in the same trade, and some had apprenticed. But as industrialization progressed, training under the supervision of a skilled worker was carried out in the factory. Skilled workers preferred piecework because it suggested a measure of control over production and gave them the opportunity to increase earnings. Piecework usually sped up production and put extra demands on labor. Many of the workers in the Daimler car factory complained of exhaustion, and textile workers spoke about chronic fatigue from the pace of the machines. Although most indices show that skilled male workers in heavy industry earned good wages, cycles of prosperity, recession, and depression caused underlying insecurity and unpredictablity. Employers also used wages as disciplinary tools. Base wages could be reduced if workers defied regulations. A textile company in Gera docked its workers 25 *pfennigs* if they arrived late or left work five or ten minutes early. The same fine was imposed on any worker caught dirtying the factory or smoking. Disturbing other workers, mutilating cloth, or tampering with machines could cost a worker half a day's pay.

Children were used heavily in the early factories, especially textiles, because they were a source of cheap labor and often were part of a family unit. In the first quarter of the nineteenth century children worked almost as many hours as adults. For example, in Dortmund in Westphalia children were in the factory for ten to fifteen hours daily. In Cologne in the Rhineland work time was eleven to fourteen hours, and in Breslau (present-day Wrocław), an eastern textile center, the workday lasted for ten to fourteen hours. The work was dirty, dangerous, and exhausting. In 1839 a petition from the provincial assembly in the Rhineland to the king of Prussia requested that children under nine be forbidden from working in factories, that daily work time for children nine to sixteen years old not exceed ten hours, and that children not be in the factories on Sundays and holidays. These provisions were adopted by the North German Confederation when it was formed in 1867.

Regulation of factory work.

As in France and Britain, child labor in Germany was one of the first concerns categorized within the social question *(soziale Frage)*, followed quickly by women in factories. The work-time issue was a central theme of the organized labor movement. The socialist trade unions took up the campaign, demanding adoption of the ten-hour day as the normal workday, and that became both the goal and the slogan for improving conditions of the working class. The Hirsch-Duncker Unions called for the protection of child labor and for the ten-hour day. Bishop Wilhelm von Ketteler and other prominent Catholic spokespeople argued for industrial reforms to protect the family and to preserve morality. Owners and industrialists, of course, resisted reforms because to them productivity was directly connected to hours at work. For those who were willing to consider reducing hours, the only trade-off was intensification of the work process by speeding up the machines.

Desires to alleviate workers' suffering and at the same time to curtail their efforts to gain political power led conservatives to support social reform. Otto von Bismarck, who saw the Social Democratic Party and its related trade unions as a threat to the Reich (empire), devised social welfare programs to prevent workers from participating in marxist-based labor organizations. Although only about twenty-five thousand industrial workers out of approximately 5 million were involved with these unions in 1875, the number was growing and labor agitation, including an increased frequency of strikes, was becoming disruptive. In 1878 the Reichstag (parliament) passed antisocialist legislation that dissolved the Socialist Party and its affiliated labor unions. Government anxiety and pleas for social activism by both the Protestant and the Catholic Churches coalesced in the social reform legislation of the 1880s. A national health insurance program formulated in 1883 mandated contributions from both employers and workers. In 1884 national accident insurance became available for workers injured on the job. Lastly, a kind of social security system was introduced that provided workers with a small pension at age sixty-five, but only a minority of workers qualified for the program.

The culmination of the public outcry, agitation by the trade unions, Reichstag debates, and Catholic social reform work was the Labor Law of 1891, the most comprehensive employment law in Germany in the prewar period. The new regulations stipulated general conditions for all workers and mandated specific provisions for children and women. The following conditions pertained to all workers regardless of age or gender. Protections for life and health included prescriptions for workrooms, machinery, light, air space, and ventilation. Preservation of morality and decency required separating the sexes where work processes permitted and providing separate facilities for toilets, washing, and changing. All Sunday and holiday work was prohibited. Children under fourteen years old were forbidden employment, and children had to attend school until age fourteen. Work time for boys and girls between fourteen and sixteen could not exceed ten hours. Daily work time for all women could not go over eleven hours and ten hours on Saturday. Employment in industries with special problems of health, safety, or morality was subject to restrictions. The time-work issue of the 1890s was the struggle for the ten-hour day for all workers, but employers increased machine speeds and used rationalization to prevent any loss in productivity. Between 1890 and 1914 the continued pressure on manufacturers brought down work time, but it was accomplished industry by industry and factory by factory.

WAR WORK

At the beginning of World War I older men in Germany substituted in factories for those called to military service. Quickly, however, women, many of whom had been strangers to factory work, were recruited for industrial jobs. In armaments factories and metallurgical plants the composition of the workforce changed dramatically. Women were actively sought as workers after 1916, when management recognized that the war would be one of attrition. In critical industries the proportion of women rose from 22 percent to 33 percent. The number of women in textiles declined as women sought better-paying work in armaments industries. Sexual division of labor and job segregation diminished in textiles, and women moved into operations that were previously reserved for men. However, men who were essential to the war effort resented the huge infusion of women and fought to preserve occupational exclusivity. The climate was often tense on the factory floor, as men engaged in criticism and ridicule and only reluctantly helped women learn the job. Employers paid lower wages to women, and the male-dominated trade unions were less than supportive of the notion that fair treatment for all should include women. Men interpreted the presence of women in traditional male jobs as future male unemployment and lower male wages. Employers used the labor crisis to further dilute jobs and rationalize the work process. Many tasks were segmented, so operations that formerly required skilled and semiskilled men could be performed by unskilled women.

Reform movements were suspended during the war, but workers responded to increased pressure with sporadic strikes. To maintain the civil truce and to assure a steady supply of labor in armaments industries, the government and employers understood the importance of organized labor in the management of the workforce. Trade unions were recognized, and worker councils and arbitration boards were established. Shop stewards gained tremendous power on the factory floor. Organized protests gradually increased during the war, reaching its highest level in 1917 and 1918. After the 1918 revolution initiated the German Republic and brought the Social Democratic Party into prominence, the eight-hour day was established in all industry branches with the understanding that no reduction in pay would result.

The labor shortage problem that nagged French industry reached crisis proportions during the war, as massive mobilization drained the factories of adult men. Of chemical workers, 58 percent were drafted. The leading engineering and armaments plant, Le Creusot, lost 5,500 workers in the first year of the war, and only around 25 percent of Renault's workforce remained after call-up. The labor deficit was filled by recruiting women, rural migrants, and immigrants and by returning thousands of skilled men from the front to the factories. Women in factories were hardly novel in France, but the war economy deepened existing trends. From 30 percent of the industrial labor force in 1914, women's participation grew to about 40 percent in 1918. Most obvious, however, was the presence of women in previously male industries and jobs. Women were employed extensively in munitions, chemicals, and metals. Women's work in the war sector was usually classified as semiskilled or unskilled, and they were normally under male supervision. They were told that their steadiness and dexterity made them particularly suited to dangerous jobs in munitions factories. Male-female pay differentials narrowed somewhat, but female wages did not reach equality with male wages. As women left the traditional consumer goods industries, wages there increased, too. To retain their female employees, some large companies provided nurseries and infant-feeding rooms. The pressure to produce caused exhaustion and accidents. Reform legislation restricting hours and night work were cast aside, and safety regulations were ignored. Dust, toxic fumes, and dangerous metals caused respiratory ailments, skin diseases, miscarriages, and stillbirths.

Mobilized workers (mobilisés) were those called back from the front to take charge of operations that required skilled labor in the war factories. They were still formally in the military and were subject to military discipline. These "soldiers in the factory" rejected army pay and demanded war wages appropriate to skill level. Their presence in factories and factory towns caused tension and criticism. Many of these workers in heavy industry had been involved in labor protest movements before the war, and their skills gave them privileged status. They were most likely to express hostility to speedups, dilution of work, and company paternalism. However, considerable resentment against them existed. They were accused of shirking and of causing the massive slaughter of men below their station. In the context of the devastating war, all worker complaints appeared trivial and unpatriotic, but a great deal of labor unrest and labor militancy broke out, especially in the spring of 1917. Workers went out on strike to protest falling wages, speedups, long hours, and high accident rates.

In Britain enthusiasm for the war against Germany brought in enough volunteers to deplete the industrial labor force. Thousands of skilled workers enlisted, amounting to a fifth of male engineers and a quarter of the skilled workforce in munitions and explosives. The government recognized the need for formal controls. Cooperation between industry and labor was considered necessary to sustain the increased pressures of the war economy, and British trade unions were encouraged to participate in decisions regarding war production. The government compromised its laissez-faire policies to intervene in areas most troublesome to workers. Food prices doubled, and rents jumped enormously where war industries were located. Industrialists sought justification for demoting skilled jobs to unskilled categories, but certain skilled workers were exempted from military service. To prevent disturbances in production, some employers told male workers that rationalization and technology would be reduced or eliminated after the war to permit the return of "normal" production and work relations. British union workers negotiated written promises that rationalization and women would disappear from the factories when peace returned. The Munitions of War Act of 1915 made strikes illegal, criminalized worker interference with productivity, and suspended safety regulations.

In 1916 six thousand women went on strike at the munitions factory in Newcastle against low wages. To integrate women into the factories, to lessen worker discontent and protest, and to promote productivity, Britain devised the idea of a factory-based welfare system with female supervisors. The welfare principle that women and children needed special treatment was only one part of the objective. As an adjunct to management, the policy seemed a more humane and efficient approach to insuring steady and energetic production. It was argued that the notion of family on the factory floor was more comfortable to women workers and more conducive to worker well-being. Supervisors were not only responsible for canteens, infirmaries, soap, toilet paper, and sanitary napkins, they had control over work, discipline, and interaction with foremen. Their function as supervisors in many ways paralleled that of management, but only regarding women. They were supposed to identify troublemakers, but more importantly, in the spirit of harmony and sometimes of maternalism, they tried to redress grievances over conditions and wages while at the same time minimizing absenteeism and production interruptions. Middle-class values were a part of their mission. Rough women, irregular relations with men, and inappropriate dress all came under the scrutiny of the "welfare lady." Not surprisingly, skilled male workers resented their presence, and foremen viewed them as a silly intrusion.

FACTORY WORK AFTER 1918

The massive dislocations and hardships of Europe's postwar years involved demobilization and reconstruction of the economy. Efforts to handle unemployment and inflation were directed toward rationalization and reclassification of the labor force. Many components of rationalization were intensifications of wartime production methods. Companies increased mechanization by introducing labor-saving machines and standardization of parts. Simple, tiny, and repetitive tasks vastly improved the flow of production with its automated and impersonal assembly-line precision. New forms of work direction, often called Taylorization after the engineer Frederick Taylor, were imported from the United States. New Soviet factories introduced these patterns as well. Dilution of work processes meant the substitution of semiskilled and unskilled labor for skilled workers. Sexual division permitted reclassification of women into a differentiated category of labor that was low skilled and cheap. While this allowed new levels of women's work in industries like chemicals and electrical appliances, it also created a framework in which many women could be structured out of the labor force and reassigned to the housewife role. Indeed, analyses of women in postwar economies have confirmed material and social impulses for restoring gender roles. This approach certainly went a long way to eliminate redundant labor. Old industrial branches were generally slow to recover or actually went into decline. New industries, such as chemicals and electricals, promised recovery and innovation for the future. Automobiles and radios were growing, vibrant, and representative of the new consumer culture, at least for those who could afford them.

CONCLUSION

Historically factory work is not an isolated phenomenon. It is best examined within economic and social contexts related to time and place. Yet recurrent

In the Factory. Sunbeam Rapier automobiles roll off the assembly line in Coventry, England, 1955. ©Hulton-Deutsch Collection/Corbis

themes persist over three centuries. Workers' relationships to machines and the work process influence the sense of self. Factory production evokes images of urgency and depersonalization. Gender and sexual differentiation of labor, with the corollary of anxiety about women's proper role, are evident in the early stages of industrialization and are apparent in schemes to reclassify women in postwar economies. Child labor, the central focus of reformers and protective legislation throughout the nineteenth century, was eliminated from modern societies but continued as an ingredient in developing countries, ironically in those sectors of the economy influenced by globalization. National, regional, and gender factors influence manufacturing in the world economy, while changes in factory production are at the center of labor-management relations. Technology, dilution, and the search for cheap labor are concerns of the modern market.

See also **Technology; Protoindustrialization; The Industrial Revolutions** *(volume 2);* **Working Classes; Labor History: Strikes and Unions; Social Welfare and Insurance** *(volume 3);* **Gender and Work** *(in this volume); and other articles in this section.*

BIBLIOGRAPHY

Babbage, Charles. "On the Economy of Machinery and Manufactures, 1835." In *Technology and Toil in Nineteenth Century Britain.* Edited by Maxine Berg. Atlantic Highlands, N.J., 1979. Pages 41–55.

Bari, Barbara Franzoi. " '. . . With the wolf always at the door . . .': Women's Work in Domestic Industry in Britain and Germany." In *Connecting Spheres: European Women in a Globalizing World, 1500 to the Present.* Edited by Marilyn J. Boxer and Jean H. Quataert. New York, 2000. Pages 164–173.

Benson, John. "Work." In *The Working Class in England, 1875–1914.* Edited by John Benson. London, 1985. Pages 63–88.

Berg, Maxine. "Introduction." In *Technology and Toil in Nineteenth Century Britain.* Edited by Maxine Berg. Atlantic Highlands, N.J., 1979. Pages 4–21.

Berlanstein, Lenard R., ed. *The Industrial Revolution and Work in Nineteenth-Century Europe.* London, 1992.

Bienenfeld, M. A. *Working Hours in British Industry: An Economic History.* London, 1972.

Burnett, John. *Idle Hands: The Experience of Unemployment, 1790–1990.* New York, 1994.

Canning, Kathleen. *Languages of Labor and Gender: Female Factory Work in Germany, 1850–1914.* Ithaca, N.Y., 1996.

Clapham, J. H. *The Economic Development of France and Germany, 1815–1914.* Cambridge, U.K., 1951.

Downs, Laura Lee. *Manufacturing Inequality: Gender Division in the French and British Metalworking Industries, 1914–1939.* Ithaca, N.Y., 1995.

Floud, Roderick, and McCloskey, Donald, eds. *The Economic History of Britain since 1700.* Cambridge, U.K., 1994.

Franzoi, Barbara. *At the Very Least She Pays the Rent: Women and German Industrialization, 1871–1914.* Westport, Conn., 1985.

Gray, Robert. *The Factory Question and Industrial England, 1830–1860.* Cambridge, U.K., 1996.

Haynes, M. J. "Strikes." In *The Working Class in England, 1875–1914.* Edited by John Benson. London, 1985. Pages 89–132.

Henderson, W. O. *Britain and Industrial Europe, 1750–1870.* Leicester, U.K., 1965.

Henderson, W. O. *The Industrial Revolution on the Continent: Germany, France, Russia, 1800–1914.* London, 1961.

Hinton, James. *The First Shop Stewards' Movement.* London, 1973.

Hobsbaum, E. J. *Labouring Men: Studies in the History of Labour.* London, 1964.

Landes, David S. *The Unbound Prometheus: Technological Change and Industrial Development in Western Europe from 1750 to the Present.* London, 1969.

Magraw, Roger. *A History of the French Working Class.* 2 vols. Oxford, 1992.

Mokyr, Joel, ed. *The British Industrial Revolution.* Boulder, Colo., 1999.

Patton, Craig D. *Flammable Material: German Chemical Workers in War, Revolution, and Inflation, 1914–1924.* Berlin, 1998.

Roberts, Elizabeth. "The Family." In *The Working Class in England, 1875–1914.* Edited by John Benson. London, 1985. Pages 1–35.

Schneider, Michael. *Streit um Arbeitszeit: Geschichte des Kampfes um Arbeitszeitverkürzung in Deutschland.* Cologne, Germany, 1984.

Stearns, Peter N. *The Industrial Revolution in World History.* Boulder, Colo., 1998.

Stearns, Peter N. *Paths to Authority: The Middle Class and the Industrial Labor Force in France, 1820–48.* Urbana, Ill., 1978.

Stearns, Peter N., ed. *The Impact of the Industrial Revolution: Protest and Alienation.* Englewood Cliffs, N.J., 1972.

Thompson, E. P. *The Making of the English Working Class,* New York, 1963.

Tilly, Louise A., and Joan W. Scott. *Women, Work, and Family.* New York, 1989.

MIDDLE-CLASS WORK

Peter N. Stearns

Middle-class work is largely a modern topic, and indeed the class itself, as a self-conscious entity, dates back only to the eighteenth century in Europe. The middle class did begin to develop distinctive ideas about work at that point, and in some cases began to follow a distinctive work regimen as well. Gaps between assertion and reality, nevertheless, are an important aspect of the topic. Between the late eighteenth and late nineteenth centuries, the middle-class work ethic had palpable historical impact, not only on the class itself, including its children and the training they received, but also on judgments of other groups viewed as deficient in the work category. By the late nineteenth century, the topic became more diffuse because of growing leisure interests and the development of a lower middle class linked to middle-class standards but not defined by them. Historical analysis of middle-class work in the twentieth century is less well developed.

Regional factors play a role in the timing of more modern commercial and economic structures. A distinctive middle class did not emerge as fully in eastern Europe as in the western areas, and so its work definitions were both less clear and less significant. However, under communism, an implicit middle class linked with the upper echelons of the Communist Party developed some distinctive work and training habits.

Several historical debates are linked to the subject of middle-class work. The German sociologist Max Weber's (1864–1920) ideas about a Protestant ethic related directly to work; his argument has been disputed but remains an important focus for the early modern period. For the nineteenth century, there is inevitable debate about how fully the middle class lived up to its own beliefs, and evidence (and probably reality as well) is varied. Though it is not as clearly addressed, there is a gender issue. Most images associated with middle-class work are male, and mirror images of middle-class women as idly decorative (if repressed) used to be commonplace. This view has shifted, but exactly how women related to class ideas

about work remains somewhat unclear. Finally, the complex issue of the lower middle class, which expanded in the later nineteenth century, significantly involves judgments about its work styles and goals.

THE EARLY MODERN BACKGROUND

As the number of merchants and professionals, such as doctors and lawyers, grew during the Middle Ages, at least two work characteristics distinguished them from the more familiar social groups around them. In contrast to the aristocracy, this new, largely urban bourgeoisie depended on work not only for support but also for identity. It did not carve out a distinctive leisure style, though individuals, once attaining great wealth, might imitate aristocratic opulence. More important was the fact that, in contrast to the masses of urban workers and peasants, this group did not work with its hands. Nonmanual labor could provide real status, and in some corners of Europe, such as the Balkans, clerks even grew their fingernails long to demonstrate their position. More commonly, special clothing, however sober, made distinctions clear. The prestige attached to nonmanual work would linger into contemporary society.

This said, it is not clear that this group shared any particular consciousness about the role of work or that it worked particularly hard. Individuals, eager to amass more wealth, put in long hours with great intensity. But no vividly defined ethic emerged at this point. The bourgeoisie was defined by legal status as well as occupation in many cities, but its self-perception did not necessarily involve work.

Then came the Protestant Reformation. Because Protestant leaders argued that salvation was predestined rather than acquired by holy efforts, they may have encouraged a new sense of the validity and importance of merchant endeavor. In the first place, the old Catholic suspicion of profit-seeking activities, which was declining as western Europe became more commercial, faded in light of the fact that, at least in principle, one's worldly pursuits did not have direct impact on salvation. In the eyes of the Protestant God, it was no better to be celibate than married, or to be poor than rich. Second—in that contradiction so often noted with Protestantism—the very fact that good works did not cause or predict salvation led some Protestants to seek other measures of God's will, prior to death and judgment. So an argument developed that hard work leading to economic success showed God's favor. In sober Protestant communities, leadership was provided by men of means who were assumed, by their worldly attainments, also to reflect God's grace. It was worth working hard to gain the rewards that would show God's favor, even though, technically, there was nothing one could do about salvation itself.

In his work on the Protestant ethic, Weber highlighted these conundrums in Protestantism. He added that the package precluded frivolous spending of the wealth acquired, for that would detract from work and success as demonstrations of holiness. So hardworking merchants piled up profits that they did not fritter away in leisure pursuits or excessive luxury, thus accumulating capital that could be used for further expansion—and Europe's capitalist class was born. Distinctive work devotion is not the only component of this well-known Weber thesis, but it plays a considerable role.

The Weber thesis has, over time, faded noticeably, as it was found to have several flaws. First, European capitalist behavior predated Protestantism. Not only in Renaissance Italy, but in sixteenth- and seventeenth-century France, Catholic merchants could display a work and accumulation devotion not measurably different from their Protestant counterparts. Second, Protestant merchants were not always particularly zealous. A Protestant enclave in southern France, in the Cévennes area, saw a number of businessmen develop small textile firms, but there was no sign that they worked their operations with any noticeable vigor or zeal. Few studies now follow up on Weber directly. It is true, however, that the expansion of commerce and manufacturing in early modern Europe undoubtedly encouraged many businesspeople to step up their efforts. Protestantism for some may have furthered this general movement. No full-blown middle-class work ethic had emerged as yet. Many businessmen, once successful, hoped to emulate an aristocratic lifestyle, complete with buying a landed estate, rather than continue to keep nose to grindstone. But there were signs of change.

It is also important to note that, from the sixteenth century on, judgments of poverty increasingly included concerns that many poor people were to blame for their lot because of inadequate attention to work. A growing distinction between worthy poor—people who because of infirmity or family status literally could not maintain themselves—and the unworthy—defined in terms of failure to work properly—began to enter into poor-law policy and into growing concerns about begging and other manifestations of idleness. Here was another seedbed for middle-class values.

Finally, while the Weber thesis no longer seems to explain either the timing or the reasons for a definitive middle-class work ethic, the Reformation had one further impact that began to affect work values by the late seventeenth century. A host of religious minorities were created. While these may have been influenced by the larger implications of Protestantism, they seem to have been still more affected by minority status. This status left groups like Quakers in England barred from political office, though tolerated sufficiently to operate in the business world. Minority conditions also limited contacts children had with other groups, tightening their relationships with adults in ways that could produce a distinctive work zeal. Whatever the precise mix, it was becoming clear by the eighteenth century that a disproportionate number of some of the most hardworking and successful business families (though by no means the whole set) were emanating from minority segments. Quakers and Nonconformists in England and Protestants in eastern France formed two classic cases. Jews, once legally emancipated, formed a similar component in the business and professional spheres where they concentrated. Later in the nineteenth century, Old Believers played a comparable role among early Russian industrialists. Hard work could be a ticket to success amid discrimination, as well as a personal badge of identity.

A CLEARER TRANSITION:
THE EIGHTEENTH CENTURY

Several factors associated with the emergence of the class in other respects combined to produce a more definitive middle-class work ethic during the eighteenth century. Commercial growth continued in western Europe, augmenting business ranks and their self-confidence alike. An increasing number of manufacturing operations began to separate management from the producing labor force. Woollen production in Yorkshire, England, for example, had seen artisan masters working alongside their journeymen in 1700. With expanded market opportunities, by 1730 a clearer division occurred, which meant that the erstwhile masters moved away from manual labor while also differentiating themselves in other respects from their labor force. Population growth was a factor. Many businessmen were faced with growing numbers of children, mainly because more began surviving than had traditionally been the case. Camille Schlumberger, a manufacturer in Alsace, began to work harder than his own father had, converting his artisanal operation into a full-blown manufacturing enterprise, essentially because he had twelve children to support. If he were to do the right thing by each, in terms of dowries for daughters, schooling and jobs for sons, he needed to expand, and that meant work. (His own sons would then, in the first half of the nineteenth century, move into the ranks of early industrialists, not only in textiles but also in railroads and other areas.) Several developments, in sum, produced situations in which businesspeople probably did begin working harder than had been the case before, to take advantage of new commercial opportunities and to deal with family demands.

The Enlightenment also played a role. Enlightenment theorists praised the value of work, legitimating the pursuit of earthly rewards. They also used work as the basis for virtue and productive citizenship, contrasting it to the idleness of the aristocracy. This line of argument showed up in the early phases of the French Revolution, when classic definitions of the Third Estate insisted that working people (if they were also property owners) manifested the essence of citizenship, and should not be outvoted by parasitic aristocrats.

Then came the industrial revolution, the final factor in creating an articulated middle-class work ethic that became a badge of honor for the class. Industrialization quite simply provided many middle-class people with a growing array of tasks. Early factory owners had to organize appropriate technology, supervise a labor force, and arrange for marketing. Ultimately, of course, bureaucracies would be organized to take care of some of these specialized functions, but in many early factories the practical burdens on individual proprietors could be considerable. Similar pressures could affect people responsible for expanding commercial outlets. Shopkeepers became increasingly adept at a variety of marketing techniques, beyond traditional displays of wares; but these took time and effort. New work demands spilled into the professions a bit more diffusely. But claims of extensive work could be part of professional self-justification in an age in which, increasingly, work was king.

Industrialization also put middle-class people in intimate contact with other groups whose work habits seemed demonstrably unsatisfactory. Many factory owners contended with former peasants or artisans who did not voluntarily adapt themselves to the more intense speed and coordination demands of the new machines. These workers had an ethic of their own, but it did not fully conform to the demands of modern industry, or to the expectations of the managers themselves. A common belief held that workers labored only about 60 percent as hard as they could. And many workers lacked a keen sense of the connection between work and time, which was becoming a vital link in the middle-class view. Bending work to the demands of the clock was not automatic, and this perceived failure or reluctance too could increase a middle-class sense that the lower classes were deficient in work drive. The middle-class home provided another class confrontation—between husbands and wives with strong work expectations and lower-class servants who lacked the motivation to measure up. Industrialization, in other words, created a growing array of situations in which middle-class people could take pride in their distinctive work habits and judge other groups disparagingly on the strength of seemingly different performances.

THE WORK ETHIC

Industrialization thus provided the context in which the full-blown middle-class work ethic was articulated, building on Enlightenment precedent. By the 1820s and 1830s publicists in most Western countries trumpeted the common message. Samuel Smiles (1812–1904) was the most famous spokesperson in England, but he had counterparts in France and elsewhere. Lessons about the value of hard work crept into schoolbooks, for example, in Prussia from about 1780 on.

Hard work was the chief good in life, according to this argument. With work, people were protected from damaging frivolities, from excesses that jeopardized health or morality or both. Work would also allow people to better their station in life: the relationship between work and mobility, and the positive desirability of advancement, were crucial components in the work ethic. Samuel Smiles's stories were filled with the virtuous lives of hardworking ordinary men, but also with stories of people who, through hard work alone, managed to move from humble to exalted station. The rags-to-riches story was a middle-class work-ethic classic.

The praise for work had a harsher flip side, already prepared in some of the earlier attacks both on the aristocracy and on the poor. Commentary on the idleness of the aristocracy diminished in the nineteenth century, as the middle class gained greater power and even, in its upper reaches, merged with the aristocratic group. But novels continued to berate idle aristocrats. Another group was singled out for unjustified idleness and dissolute work habits: the bohemians, taken to represent many artists and intellectuals, some of whom had abandoned respectable middle-class origins. But the clearest brunt of work-ethic judgments fell on the poor. Many cities, under middle-class administrations from the 1820s or 1830s on, attempted to ban begging on the grounds that people who did not work did not merit support. Revisions of the English poor laws (in 1834) also attempted to distinguish between poor people capable of working and thus undeserving of help, and those unable to work and thus deserving, hoping to discipline and reform the former group. Habits like drinking were blasted for their erosion of the capacity to work. Clearly, the new work ethic had some of its greatest impact by undergirding evaluations of and policies toward others, including, in Europe's colonies, "native" peoples viewed as insufficiently industrious. In Europe itself, the nineteenth century witnessed a persistent, if implicit, debate between middle-class and working-class individuals about what work was supposed to be like, and while neither group fully persuaded the other, the middle class disproportionately framed the debate. Factory owners who argued that their workers put forth only two-thirds the effort of which they were capable felt comfortable in limiting wages and conditions accordingly.

As an ideal, the valuation of work served to unify diverse segments of the middle class, who could at least agree on the standard and its applicability in judging social worth. While hard work was pushed particularly by some of the newer, upwardly mobile segments of the middle class, professionals and more traditional commercial sectors could agree at least in principle. Shopkeepers, though usually far less affluent than merchants and many professionals, also subscribed to the ethic, providing among other things an extensive readership for the manuals that praised hard work.

MYTHS AND REALITIES

How much did the middle class itself live up to its own cherished self-image where work was concerned? Inevitably, there was variety, and inevitably there has been some historical debate. During the early decades of industrialization, some factory owners really did seem to live to work. Sixteen-hour days were common—indeed, one of the reasons some factory owners failed to realize the impact of the hours they imposed on their workers was that their own work time matched or exceeded them. They suffered pangs of conscience when they were too ill to work; they shunned vacations and were clearly uncomfortable off the job. Not only work itself, but also the intensity devoted to the process, marked this pattern of behavior.

Still later, in the final decades of the nineteenth century, significant middle-class groups lived lives filled with work intensity. The training process began early. Leading technical schools in France featured heavy demands on time and attention, and diligence counted at least as much as brains. From school, engineers moved into positions where long days with few if any vacations continued to be expected. Many came to work even on Sundays, to keep up the pace. So the work ethic could be very real. Some of the diversions that were most popular in the middle class, such as sports, thrived because they seemed to drive home work habits, not because they diverted from them.

Professional groups often turned to greater work zeal as part of their redefinition in an industrial society. With stricter licensing standards and examinations, preparation in law and medicine required new levels of discipline. But other groups in the middle class, without officially renouncing the new work values, treasured a more balanced life. Some engaged not only in extensive leisure, but also in some of the less respectable forms of leisure, such as drinking, womanizing, and gambling, some of which clearly detracted from the work process. Historians are just uncovering those areas where behavior did not measure up to work-based codes of respectability. For many, students' days, work-related travel, and, even later, age provided periods and occasions when zeal might particularly slacken, even in the mid-nineteenth-century heyday of the proclaimed commitment to work.

Almost certainly as well, work commitments diminished somewhat over time. Once the hardest tasks of establishing an industrial economy and a solid family position were completed, by the later nineteenth century, leisure activities became more openly acknowledged. Work was not rejected, but the single-minded devotion decreased. Revealingly, after about 1870 the sales of works by the most blatant work advocates, like Samuel Smiles, declined precipitously. In later age, increasing numbers of middle-class people also began to seek retirement, which spread first in these ranks. Intense work could be capped by a formal period of nonwork, again a modification of the original vision.

Women's relationship to the work ethic was not always clear. Middle-class standards increasingly urged removal of respectable women from the labor force. Factory owners who began with their wives keeping accounts, in the early nineteenth century, soon pulled back when they won greater success. The growing confinement of women to domestic duties diluted formal commentary about applying the work ethic to women. Expectations that women would be decorative and also accomplished in certain family leisure skills, such as piano playing, also diverted attention from work. In comments on the poor, it was men, not women, who were criticized for unjustified idleness. In practice, however, the demands of the middle-class home might prompt an increase of work pace not totally unlike that experienced by many men. Living up to new standards of health, cleanliness, and child care, assisted on average by a single servant, had its own work requirements. The full intensity of the male pattern might still be missing—among other things, women's work was less constrained or limited by clock time—but women's lives and outlook might shift in similar directions.

THE LOWER MIDDLE CLASS

The rise of the white-collar segment, from the 1870s on, raised additional questions about work. Many clerks, and their employers, were at pains to establish links with middle-class work values. Their occupations were nonmanual; they depended to some degree on education, at least on literacy, they required middle-class attire on the job. And many clerks undoubtedly aspired to upward mobility, based on hard work, for themselves or their children. It was a sense of commitment to work that helped keep most white-collar employees from joining unions, which constituted an admission that work might be sacrificed in favor of protest.

Yet white-collar work was not standard middle-class fare. It was often repetitious. It involved taking directions from others. It did not necessarily generate upward mobility. Employers might talk of middle-class values and assume enough discipline to warrant salaries rather than working-class wages; they were eager to separate white-collar from blue-collar to limit protest, but in fact they regulated and monitored clerical work closely. One German employer in the 1920s even installed steam jets in clerks' toilets, timed to go off after two minutes, to prevent lingering. For female clerks, work was often a temporary status prior to marriage, which further diluted a work-based identity. Many white-collar workers gravitated toward new leisure interests, as a relief from the limitations of their jobs. Here, as in other respects, the relationship of the rising lower middle classes to larger middle-class standards was ambivalent at best. Correspondingly, the growth of the lower middle classes contributed to the implicit loosening of the work ethic around 1900.

THE TWENTIETH CENTURY

Middle-class work in the twentieth century has been less extensively studied than the patterns in evidence during the heyday of industrialization. Several trends deserve note nevertheless. A basic commitment to work as part of self-definition and self-worth remained. Middle-class people were much more likely to profess satisfaction with their jobs than their lower-class counterparts. Pressure on children to perform well in schools maintained socialization toward the work process within the middle class. Condemnations of other groups for inadequate work zeal abated somewhat, but persisted to a degree.

There were signs of increased work interest in some sectors of the middle class. The rise of a managerial middle class, often within the Communist Party, during an active industrialization process in Eastern Europe, involved some echoes of the kind of work devotion that had flourished in Western Europe earlier on. In Mediterranean Europe, including France, from the 1950s on devotion to clock-based work began to cut into traditional long lunches. The movement of married women into the labor force (though hardly confined to the middle class) reduced some of the appearances of gender difference in work values.

But limitations on excessive work zeal gained ground as well, differentiating the European middle classes from their American counterparts in some key respects. Formal retirement spread more widely. While some European countries, as in Scandinavia, delayed retirement until age seventy, others pushed it earlier. The middle classes were characteristically less eager to retire than blue-collar workers, but the sense that a final stage of active life should be free from formal work was widespread.

The most striking change involved the growing commitment to extensive vacations. Again, various social groups participated in the expansion of vacations, which began in part as a response to unemployment but spread much more widely after World War II. The middle classes, however, led the way during the Great Depression, if only because they could afford to make more active use of free time. Vacations of four to six weeks became common in countries like France and Germany, in marked contrast to the United States and Japan in the same decades. This development was not a surrender of the devotion to hard work. Indeed, the alternation of time off with employment was thought to facilitate work intensity. But it did indicate considerable distance from the values and behaviors characteristic of the nineteenth-century middle class.

See also **The Protestant Reformation and the Catholic Reformation; The Enlightenment** *(volume 1);* **Capitalism and Commercialization; The Industrial Revolutions; The Population of Europe: The Demographic Transition and After; Shops and Stores** *(volume 2);* **The Middle Classes; Professionals and Professionalization** *(volume 3);* **Gender and Work** *(in this volume);* **Protestantism** *(volume 5); and other articles in this section.*

BIBLIOGRAPHY

Ardagh, John. *A Tale of Five Cities: Life in Europe Today.* New York, 1979.

Berlanstein, Lenard R., ed. *The Industrial Revolution and Work in Nineteenth-Century Europe.* London, 1992.

Branca, Patricia. *Silent Sisterhood: Middle-Class Women in the Victorian Home.* Pittsburgh, Pa., 1975.

Crossick, Geoffrey, ed. *The Lower Middle Class in Britain, 1870–1914.* New York, 1977.

Davidoff, Leonore. *Worlds Between: Historical Perspectives on Gender and Class.* Cambridge, U.K., 1995.

Lessnoff, Michael H. *The Spirit of Capitalism and the Protestant Ethic: An Enquiry into the Weber Thesis.* Brookfield, Vt., 1994.

Pollard, Sidney. *The Genesis of Modern Management: A Study of the Industrial Revolution in Great Britain.* Cambridge, Mass., 1965.

Stearns, Peter N., and Herrick Chapman. *European Society in Upheaval: Social History Since 1750.* New York, 1992.

Stearns, Peter N. *Paths to Authority: The Middle Class and the Industrial Labor Force in France, 1820–1848.* Urbana, Ill., 1978.

WORK TIME

Gary S. Cross

Time at labor has depended on technological and economic realities but also on political power and cultural values. Work time has decreased with modern industrialization, but that decline did not simply correspond with increased productivity nor has it decreased at the same rate that consumption has risen. Moreover, especially since industrialization, patterns of male work time have diverged from female hours of labor.

PREINDUSTRIAL WORK TIME

The cadence of preindustrial agricultural work was often set by the season and weather. While labor from sunup to sundown was common, the workday varied by the task to be done. It was interrupted by feasts and festivals that mostly coincided with slack periods between fall harvest and spring planting or waiting times within the growing cycle itself. Harvest holidays, followed by a series of festivals between Christmas and Mardi Gras, and then by a festival season from Easter to Pentecost, filled the low point in the activity of rural Europeans. Midseason holidays like Midsummer or, in England, wakes week in August, corresponded to lulls in farm work or to annual fairs during which farm laborers found employment. Lack of reliable timepieces allowed for irregular work habits, and labor was frequently interrupted by play and rest breaks. Long days, often beginning before eating, required three or more meal and drink respites.

In craft occupations, the lack of laborsaving devices meant twelve or more hours of work per day. But long workdays were interrupted by seasonal slowdowns in demand for goods or supplies of raw materials. Capital could not be tied up in inventory, especially when slow transportation already greatly retarded the cycle of production and sale. And the workweek was often characterized by short Mondays because workers had to wait for slow moving supplies or for orders to arrive at the work site. The speed of the oxcart or sailing ship controlled the pace of business for the merchant and producer. Moreover, hours and days of labor varied greatly among crafts: workers in luxury trades, where journeymen were often organized and skills in short supply, were able to restrict work time, especially with traditions of holiday taking. In seventeenth-century Paris, craftspeople enjoyed up to 103 holidays, and in parts of northern Italy in the sixteenth century the figure was about 95 (including Sundays). Many skilled trades celebrated an informal "holiday" at the beginning of the week in what, somewhat mockingly, was called St. Monday. This custom epitomized an often-noted characteristic of preindustrial labor: its preference for leisure over increased income. When prices for their products rose or when costs of living decreased, craft workers sometimes responded with working less and playing more rather than attempting to accumulate wealth.

Still, workers in low-skilled trades or jobs requiring daily effort (like candle making or baking) worked far more hours. Moreover, work time stretched along almost all the course of a life. There was little chance of saving for retirement or allowing the young the luxury of a work-free childhood. In the sixteenth century over 40 percent of the population of Italian towns was under sixteen years old, and as late as 1820 in Britain some 48 percent of the population was under the age of twenty. Small wonder that child's play was sacrificed to work. Even the enlightened John Locke supported "training" children in poor families with work from the age of four, and apprenticeships regularly started at ten. Equally, retirement was only for the rich; with age, workers withdrew from labor gradually or when incapacitated.

In periods of relative prosperity (like the sixteenth or eighteenth centuries), crafts workers reduced the hours of labor sometimes by two hours per day. This was possible because "employers"—often little more than suppliers of raw materials and marketers of finished products—had little direct control over the pace or methods of work. The actual production process was usually controlled by a father in a household of workers, and these laborers were also often mem-

Preindustrial Agricultural Work. *Harvesters,* painting by Pieter Brueghel the Younger (1564–1638). PRIVATE COLLECTION, BRUSSELS/ART RESOURCE, N.Y.

bers of his family. This probably reduced work discipline that might have been imposed if labor and management had been separate. The employer seldom entered this cottage and certainly had no direct means of forcing weavers or spinners to work rapidly or regularly.

Perhaps the greatest influence over preindustrial work time was its common setting—within or near the household dwelling. The so-called domestic economy allowed men to mix wage or piece work time with numerous other forms of employment and tasks that helped to provision and maintain the household (cutting firewood, etc). Of greater significance was the close integration of productive and family-caring work time that fell to women. In the domestic setting they were able to shift quickly from household and child care work to agricultural or craft production according to the needs of the family. The complex

blending of work roles was an economic and biological necessity that often meant a female workday that "never ended."

Attempts to increase output by increasing labor time devoted to the market was a key element in the development of modern capitalism. Repeatedly, governments tried to restrict holidays (for example, to twenty-seven per year in England in 1552) or even to impose a minimum workday (to twelve hours per day in England in 1495). During the Puritan revolution in England authorities attempted to eliminate traditional religious festivals and to impose instead a strict observance of a Sabbath rest. This was supposed not only to increase annual workdays but to create a regular pattern of work and recuperation appropriate for industrial and commercial work. Similarly, during the French Revolution employers were given authority to set work time, and the experiment with the ten-day week was to make a more productive workforce than the traditional Christian week. These efforts had mixed results.

From the sixteenth century, English merchants tried to tap "underutilized" rural labor by putting farmers to work in the winter at spinning yarn or weaving cloth. This so-called putting-out system, however, frequently frustrated merchants because the episodic and slow pace of agricultural work made these part-time peasant artisans undisciplined and unreliable producers. One solution, advocated by early eighteenth-century economists, was to lower pay to cottage workers to force them to extend their weekly working hours (devoted to market tasks). The common view was that domestic workers had a fixed notion of an appropriate standard of living. If pay rates rose above that standard of subsistence, they would work fewer hours. Only the whip of low rates would induce them to lengthen and intensify their work time. A seemingly more effective means of quickening the pace and length of the workday was the mechanization and central management that came with industrialization.

WORK TIME AND EARLY INDUSTRIALIZATION

The centralized workplace is often viewed as the most important development of early industrialization, insofar as it made possible the imposition of work discipline and the lengthening of the working day. Not only did the factory make regular working hours a condition for employment, but new managerial and mechanized techniques enhanced the ability of the employer to intensify work time. Mechanization, especially in steam-driven textile mills, provided employers with incentives to raise working hours to twelve or even fourteen hours by the 1820s (the latter especially in France and Belgium). Efforts to amortize costly equipment over a shorter period, attempts to reduce costs as competition increased and prices dropped, and hopes of taking advantage of new gas lighting all encouraged the lengthening of working hours.

Historians, however, have increasingly questioned the impact of the factory on enforcing time discipline. The sweating system, which imposed on piece-rate workers in the garment and other trades such low prices that they were forced to "voluntarily" extend their working hours to survive, played a major role in the intensification of work. Moreover, many skilled trades outside the factory system (even those with central workplaces) were able to avoid exten-

sion of the workday. In the mid-nineteenth century, male Birmingham metalworkers preserved a three-day workweek. Similarly, skilled workers on the Continent maintained St. Monday traditions deep into the century. The real lengthening of the workday took place mostly among workers in mechanized textile mills and other trades competing against machines and overcrowding. In any case, early industrialization did not mean a reduction of work time, but rather economic growth.

Another impact of the centralized workplace was the gradual removal of wage work from the home. This eventually led to the withdrawal of men from domestic chores and forced women into making difficult compromises between wage and family obligations. Ultimately, the separation of work and domestic life resulting from the removal of materials and machines from the home obliged female workers to embrace a clear separation of wage from family care work. Often this meant that working-class women experienced a new and distinct work life cycle—wage work when young and single followed by home-bound family and household work when married with children—should the husband's income be sufficient to support the family.

Market work time decreased faster than that of home-based work. This was partly a function of different rates of technological change and partly due to the intractable, time-consuming character of domestic work. This put family work on a very different plane than wage work. The "housewife's" work did not disappear, of course, but neither did its value enter the calculus of the money economy. Family work was hidden in the clouds of the private. As a result, work time became sharply gendered. For men, time liberated from wage work became "free" from work obligations in private leisure; for women, family-related chores remained in a privatized realm of work with no segmentation of time into "free" and "obligated" periods.

REDUCING WORK TIME IN THE NINETEENTH AND TWENTIETH CENTURIES

While rising productivity made possible the diminution of work time, the timing and extent of the reduction depended upon international labor and political movements that fought with management over control of the labor market and workplace. This struggle was shaped by the language of industrial efficiency and mass consumption but also by a gender order that rigidly divided wage labor from family work. The reduction of public working hours has been episodic,

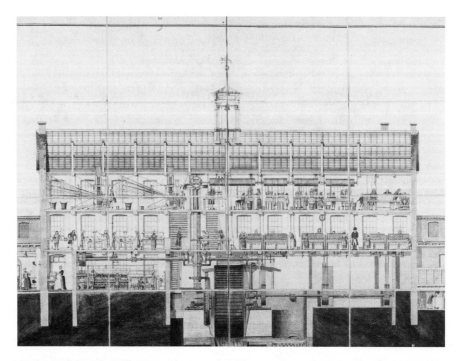

Mechanized Textile Mill. Men, women, and children work together in a mill. The design of the mill allows for more efficient operation of the machinery and longer work hours. Plan of Bedworth worsted mill near Birmingham, England, by L. Lequesne WARWICKSHIRE COUNTY RECORD OFFICE, U.K./COURTESY OF LORD DAVENTRY/VISUAL CONNECTION

usually bitterly resisted by employers and governments, certainly far more so than the other contested fruit of industrial productivity—the increased power to consume.

Efforts to reduce the workday to ten hours spanned the years from the 1840s until about 1900. A generation of agitation for a ten-hour day in the textile mills of Britain resulted in an 1847 law restricting that work time standard to women and children (although men won it also in bargaining and where their work depended upon the protected groups). In France the political upheaval of the midcentury produced a maximum-hour law in 1848, but it was restricted to workers in mechanized factories. Gradually the ten-hour provision was extended in Britain to many trades. Only in 1904, after twenty-three years of legislative struggle, was a ten-hour law passed in France for women.

Movements for an eight-hour day broadly stretched from the mid-1880s until 1919. The "three-eights," the equal distribution of the day between work, rest, and leisure, was a slogan for a generation of May Day labor and socialist parades from 1890. International groups from the socialist Second International to the reformist liberal International Labor Office advocated simultaneous transnational improvements in the labor standard (including a reduction of work time). Despite active movements for a universal eight-hour day in England from 1888 until 1892 and repeated strikes in many European countries in which the eight-hour day was a major issue (for example, the May 1906 general strike in France), employers and legislators stood firm against it. A principle impediment was fear that an hour's reduction in any one company or country would put that entity at a competitive disadvantage with less generous employers or nations.

The eight-hour day became a nearly universal concession only during the labor upsurge that accompanied the closing years of World War I (1917–1919). Eight-hour proclamations, beginning in the Russian Bolshevik Revolution of 1917, spread in 1918 to Finland, Norway, and then to Germany in the wake of collapse and revolution in November. By mid-December the movement passed to Poland, Czechoslovakia, and Austria. From the revolutionary regimes of eastern and central Europe, it spread to Switzerland. In Britain, from December 1918 to March 1919, major industries rapidly conceded reductions in work time. In February the movement reached Italy in a wave of shutdowns that affected, in turn, metals, textiles, chemicals, and even agriculture. And in

France in April 1919, a new parliament approved of an enabling act for an eight-hour/six-day workweek. This insurgency also produced eight-hour laws in Spain, Portugal, and Switzerland by June and in the Netherlands and Sweden by November 1919. Nearly everywhere, workers used this unique opportunity for reform to increase leisure time. International pressure from below was paralleled by hopes that the eight-hour day would become international law, removing the traditional fear that a raised labor standard would put an industry or country at a competitive disadvantage on the international market. Committed to this goal was a transnational network of reformers often rather erroneously labeled "Wilsonians." In 1920 the eight-hour day became a transnational labor standard, protected by an international convention sponsored by the International Labor Organization.

The concept of the forty-hour week with a two-day weekend had its roots in the nineteenth century with the Saturday half-holiday. As a means of granting women workers Saturday afternoon to shop and prepare for Sunday, it was embraced by English textile mills in hopes of improving and stabilizing working-class family life. Skilled male workers also demanded and often won the half-holiday from the 1850s. Only from 1889 did French reformers call for the Saturday half-holiday. The *semaine anglaise* (English week, named after its English origins) alone was a guarantor of the "sanctity" of Sunday rest and family togetherness, they argued. Especially where women worked and where men were well organized, the Saturday half-holiday was won after 1917.

The more radical two-day weekend became a goal of labor movements in France and Britain in the 1930s (in the form of a forty-hour week). This standard became law in France in June 1936 during the strikes that accompanied the beginning of the leftist Popular Front government. However, business bitterly opposed this unilateral disarmament of the French economy, and the work time standard was eliminated in late 1938 as an impediment to preparation for war. Many wage earners in Europe won the weekend/forty-hour week only in the 1960s.

Until World War I a paid annual holiday was rare, except in some white collar and government occupations where paperwork was made up after a break or where a seasonal slowdown in business made a vacation feasible. The movement for the paid annual holiday intensified in the interwar period. Between 1919 and 1925 legislation provided paid vacations in six eastern and central European countries. The movement peaked in the mid-1930s with the widespread support for the two-week paid vacation in France in 1936 and a week's holiday in many British industries

The Five-Day Week. Front page of the first issue of a Soviet worker's newspaper, *The Five-Day Week*, 1930s. THE DAVID KING COLLECTION

in 1938. Ironically, in spite of massive unemployment and deep ideological fissures within Europe, the vacation became a near universal ideal. It responded to deep needs that transcended ideology and economic system. In the generation after World War II, the vacation became the leisure concept of choice for most Europeans: the one- or two-week holiday expanded to three or more weeks in the prosperity of the 1950s and 1960s and commonly was from four to eight weeks by the end of the century. As a result of these changes, average hours worked in France and West Germany dropped from 38 and 44 hours respectively in 1950 to 31 hours by 1989.

IDEOLOGIES AND DILEMMAS OF REDUCING WORK TIME

Popular pressure for reduced work began in reaction to efforts of nineteenth-century employers to impose regular and increased intensity of output on labor. These movements were inspired by a variety of work-based and essentially defensive motivations: to decrease machine use and thus output and layoffs due to "overproduction"; to win a larger share of income from increased productivity by raising wages through greater overtime and making labor more scarce; and to reduce seasonal unemployment by extending batches of work over a longer period.

Arguments for reform. Most historians have seen these short-hour movements as essentially wage driven. A minority, like William Reddy and Neil Smelser, argue that these demands were instead intended indirectly to perpetuate the domestic work unit and patriarchy. Both views, however, underestimate changing attitudes about work and the origins of the demand for blocks of time free from employment. Industrialization not only increased productivity, making a reduction of labor time feasible, but physically separated productive from "reproductive" or family activities. The expulsion of leisure from the workplace and the spatial division of home and work required an equally sharp time demarcation. Thus, interest in regular blocks of daily, weekly, and eventually yearly time free from wage labor increased as the only way for men especially to recover family and leisure time lost to disciplined work. Moreover, many nineteenth-century laborers saw the traditional custom of working at a series of seasonal jobs and tramping from job to job replaced by stationary and regular employment. Wage-earners greeted the passing of the old "porous" workday, idealized by E. P. Thompson and other historians, with ambivalence. Despite the loss of a sociable work culture, in the long run workers demanded a reduction of work time to enhance the opportunity of social relationships off rather than on the job. Working-class men abandoned the pub of their workmates for the neighborhood bar, which they increasingly visited with their wives. Long evenings began to count more than long work breaks. The movement for the Saturday half-holiday and full weekend reflected a similar interest in uninterrupted periods of family and leisure time. For these workers, leisure was to be realized in a new distribution of time—a uniform and compressed workday with longer, more predictable and more continuous periods of personal time.

Reduction of work time was more than an adaptation to industrialization. It was also a practical expression of the demand of wage earners for freedom from the authoritarian relationships of work. For example, shop or office workers sought to limit the employers' access to their time. In seeking to end the "living-in" system that required wage earners to reside at their workplace, these workers attempted to create a clear separation between the masters' time and their own. The intermingling of work and life for many dependent workers—in shops, farms, or domestic service—was not an ideal to be defended but a curse to be overcome.

The eight-hour movement of the early 1890s cut across the trades in England, France, and Germany. It was not confined to long-hour occupations or even to laborers with special workplace rights to defend. Mechanization, reformers argued, should not only provide increased material goods but free workers from "slavery" and introduce them to the "duty" to enjoy life. When the eight-hour day was won for most in 1919, trade unionists argued that a longer day was "unnatural." British trade unionists insisted that differences in intensity, productivity, skill, and danger of work should be reflected in wages, not hours. To deny the eight-hour day was to deprive workers of citizenship and even "manhood."

These arguments clearly challenged laissez-faire orthodoxy by claiming that the workplace and labor contract were subject to public protection and citizenship rights. As important, reduced work time threatened the employers' power in ways that wage increases did not. It could raise wage costs (either in overtime rates or simply because the employer had to hire more labor, which reduced the labor pool and thus raised wages), and it could force employers to buy expensive machinery, accumulate inventories (in anticipation of later sales), and thus tie up capital. By contrast, an unrestricted workday adjusted at will allowed the employer to avoid these costs during expansions. Finally, whereas wage increases could be easily reversed in response to prices (at least in the nineteenth century), employers feared that this would not be possible with hours. A shorter workday, then, threatened to slow the turnover of capital and to choke off profits. At the same time, workers were seldom able to reduce hours through negotiation. During economic downturns—when they had an incentive to share jobs through shorter regular hours—they lacked bargaining power. During economic booms, when they had the advantage of a tight labor market, many individual workers had to replenish income lost during the last recession by working overtime.

Most important, competition, especially as the market extended internationally, dissuaded employers from reducing hours. In the 1830s and 40s competition between English and continental textile mills justified British resistance to the ten-hour day. The same fear blocked the eight-hour day in the 1890s, and economic nationalism in the 1920s similarly threatened the newly won eight-hour day. There were also social and cultural impediments to reduced work time. The idea of the right to free time raised concerns about the use of leisure by the male working class. Elites associated this leisure with disorder, imprudent consumption, and radical politics. This was one rationale for the refusal of the British Parliament to grant the ten-hour day to men in 1847.

Thus major hours reductions were intermittent and very difficult to win. They coincided with the social and political upheavals of 1847/1848, 1919, and 1936–1938, often requiring simultaneous international and cross-class movements, and they often followed long intellectual debate and political struggle. Rarely can they be correlated with economic trends.

This lack of correlation is ironic because the most successful arguments to reduce wage work time were economic rather than political. Repeatedly, reformers argued that shorter hours optimized output and human capital and increased mass consumer spending. Nineteenth-century political elites were relatively open to arguments that linked reduced work time to bodily safety. For example, in France the twelve-hour law of 1848 applied to men working in factories because these workplaces were deemed "dangerous" (as opposed to domestic or open air work sites). Work time agitators were almost obliged to overstress the harmful and involuntary character of mechanized work. This emphasis removed factory workers from the ranks of "free adults" and made them subject to the kind of protection given to minors. Yet the framing of the debate in these terms deflected the argument away from the citizen's right to a shorter workday.

Frustrated hour reformers also embraced industrial efficiency and mechanization as a means of reducing the costs of reduced work time. From the 1890s on the European Left found in the United States "proof" that industrial efficiency made for both less work time and more output. Labor groups found allies among efficiency scientists who sought optimal output over relatively long work periods rather than short-term maximum production at the price of long-term labor fatigue and deterioration. From about 1900 to 1920, various studies found an overly long work period was self-defeating, for it led to absenteeism and reduced efficiency and often was no more productive than shorter work spans. Investigators discovered that early morning work (before the traditional 8:00 A.M. breakfast break) and work on Saturday afternoon hardly justified fixed capital expenditures. This research provided a powerful support for the reduction of work time after World War I.

Wage earners were often slow to embrace the trade-off of increased productivity for shorter hours, fearful that increased efficiency would result in layoffs. By the mid-1920s, however, European unions were beginning to reject the linkage between increased productivity and joblessness. Instead, they embraced mechanization and even the scientific management advocated by Frederick Taylor, as a way to preserve the normal workday of eight hours and to win the forty-hour week.

Work time diminutions were also supposed to stimulate mass consumption. An early form of this argument (from the 1830s) claimed that shorter hours would shift wealth from capital to labor by making labor scarce and thus more costly, and thereby encouraging popular spending. Shorter hours would shift investment away from luxury goods to more profitable mass markets. A different, and in the long run more politically acceptable, argument emerging in the 1880s claimed that shorter hours meant leisure time sufficient to create desire for new consumer goods (without necessarily increasing labor costs).

Work time, family, and gender roles. Finally, given an inhospitable political culture, short-hour advocates did not argue for free time for men (still deemed subversive), but adopted a familial rhetoric in the defense of personal life. In the nineteenth century legal reductions of working hours could be justified only if shorter work time facilitated the fulfillment of family duties. It justified liberation from wage work if it was deemed socially necessary, as was women's "free time." Female time liberated from wage work was not a threat, for it was not "free" but rather necessary family and housework time. Thus legislators were won far earlier to the principle of reduced wage time for women. Nineteenth-century employers attacked St. Monday, the custom of taking part or all of the day following the Sabbath as a holiday, as a threat to work discipline. But gradually they accepted the idea of the Saturday half-holiday (for women especially) because it was necessary to prepare for family life on Sunday. This idea of a protected time for female domesticity had an appeal that crossed the gap between workers and middle-class reformers. Inevitably workers and their allies embraced an ideology of rescuing motherhood, creating at least a "part-time" housewife in the wage-earning married woman. Male-dominated workers' movements thoroughly embraced the ideal of the women's domestic sphere. Even though men often used laws that granted only women shorter hours to gain free time for themselves (because factories often could not function without female labor), this hiding behind women's petticoats fully embraced the primacy of domestic work for women. Indeed, hour reductions for women were conveniently used to drive women out of some jobs. Opposition of women's groups to shift work (especially in the 1920s) shared a similar assumption: factory labor should not be tolerated at "unnatural" hours when women had obligations of child and home care (coordinated with the working hours of men and children). Women's participation in the short hours movement reinforced the expectation that their time was to be organized around "family" needs that stretched across the divide between the private and public. The quest for the "normal workday" of ten and then eight hours was an integral part of an ideology of separate sex spheres.

Familial rhetoric did not exclude the "duties" of men entirely. The short-hours movement embraced the ideology of the "respectable working-class father." Less work time meant more gardening and other quasi-farming rituals for men. By the 1850s in Britain, the Saturday half-holiday had become an important symbol of family life and even of a more "democratic" fatherhood. Reformers argued that Saturday afternoons free from wage work provided fathers with the opportunity to spend time with their children. Early twentieth-century French trade union propaganda painted a picture of the eight-hour father with sufficient job security and time to provide for his family and to "guide" his children. These references to free time for fatherhood, however, were vague and rare. From the 1920s reformers argued that the annual paid vacations would restore the spiritual unity of the family undermined by the modern functional division of family members. Both the Left and Right embraced the extended holiday, for it fitted a common gender and family ideology: vacations would provide family time away from domestic routines. It would enable the father to learn paternal roles while at play with his children.

The family ideology of short-hours movements was not mere opportunism. It was more an appeal to bourgeois obsessions with domestic standards and guilt over denying working-class men housewives. In the details of negotiations over work time in the five years after 1919, family issues were central. Especially important to unions were the elimination of before-breakfast work and an eight-hour day that was stretched out in split shifts. Organized workers resisted two- or three-shift systems, especially in textiles, where women predominated. The ideal was not merely a short but also a compressed workday to free longer blocks of time for private life, especially for meeting the needs of coordinating family schedules.

Still a conflict remained: on one side stood the mostly male model of public obligation and private freedom; on the other, the married female experience of obliged time that made obtaining wage work difficult. For some it meant accommodating a work schedule stretched between wage work, commuting, and private household and family care work. As long as the necessary work of family remained a female responsibility, equity in that work was impossible. And the shorter hours movement systematically avoided this issue, despite talk of improved fatherhood. The predominance of men in the public labor market guaranteed that the ideology of the male provider dominated movements for shorter hours. The language of "free" time implied that men's family work obligations were fulfilled by their wages. The demand for reduced work time reinforced the perception of public time (contested for control, valued as "money" and "productive") as radically split from private time (deemed to be unconstrained and without economic value).

LATE TWENTIETH-CENTURY ATTEMPTS TO REDUCE WORK TIME

This perception of the scheduling of work time has predominated until the late twentieth century. Since the 1980s there have been a number of challenges to this scheduling of work time. Rising unemployment led West German metalworkers to push for a thirty-five-hour workweek, and the French Left, returning to power in the 1980s, favored weekly hour reductions as a work-sharing program.

As important, dramatic increases in married women's employment, especially after 1960, have undermined the prevailing gender division of work time. Implicit in the concept of the eight-hour day/forty-hour week was the assumption that it was worked by men outside the home while family and household care work was done by a wife. The introduction of massive numbers of married women into the workforce (reaching 60 percent or more in most European countries) hardly produced a "symmetrical family" of gender equity in the sharing of wage and domestic work time. In this context feminists, union leaders, and others began to advocate more flexible work schedules. Such adaptability could reduce rigidity in production schedules and staffing services (favored by businesses) but flexible working hours could also facilitate the complex needs of families and individuals. Of special concern were the needs of young families to balance child care and employment time.

As in the past, these efforts have met with strong resistance. The French effort to reduce work to thirty-five hours in the 1980s was frustrated by the anti-regulatory politics of conservative governments in Britain and Germany, which impeded any coordi-

Time Clock. Workers punching in at the Philips electrical works in Mitcham, London, 4 March 1947. ©HULTON GETTY/ARCHIVE PHOTOS

nated hour reduction. Later reformers have been unable to re-create the international coalition that supported the eight-hour day in 1919. In some ways the generation of World War I was a golden age of labor internationalism—when a rough economic equality between industrial states existed. Since the 1920s the opportunities to free time from work on an international basis have been much more difficult to win. Economic nationalism in the 1930s and especially fascism in Germany and Italy frustrated French efforts to institutionalize a forty-hour work week. More recently, the advent of authoritarian third world industrial powers and increased competition between oppressed third world and Western labor has frustrated even those workers who have unions or a foothold in the state, limiting their ability to break with the discipline of the international market and to free time from work.

As important, the goal of reducing the working day may have lost the appeal that attracted so many earlier to the eight-hour day. Time lost in commuting and the marginal usefulness of, for example, an additional half-hour per day may make other allocations of free time much more attractive. Individualized packages of time such as additional vacation, child care leave, earlier retirement, and flextime have replaced the social ideal of a uniform reduced workweek. Yet such personalized schedules have been hard

to win through collective bargaining or law, which generally presume uniform standards and seem to threaten the return of a divisive individual labor contract. Moreover, the older ideal of "family time" has been frustrated by the spread of shift work (first during World War II and then as contract concessions). The efforts of unions and women's groups early in the century to preserve family time by opposing "unnatural" hours has succumbed to the logic of international markets and the drive after 1945 to increase production. Attempts of chain stores to extend hours to Sunday or nights in the 1980s and 1990s generally have failed. Still, the value of family time is increasingly attacked as contrary to American-style consumer convenience.

Underlying these difficulties is the legacy of the short-hours movement itself. On the one hand, that movement addressed the "public" issues of regular employment, work intensity, and job control; on the other, it treated "freedom" as disengagement from public obligation in favor of private time. This dichotomy obscured the sexual dynamics of domestic work time and the fact that "after hours" means very different things for women and men. It also has ostensibly privileged the private life while giving family time no value comparable to waged time and placed its greatest burden on wives and mothers. Meanwhile men (and increasingly women) remain obligated to driven work and segmented lives built around "providing" and the frustrated dreams of private fulfillment. Ironically, the short-hours movement that gloried the private life has contributed to its being undervalued.

The long-term trend of industrial economies toward growth without new jobs may increase pressures for the reduction of work time. And the tendency of economies across the globe to converge toward a similar labor standard may help revive an international desire for short-hours, as in 1919 (at least within the European Community). Moreover, the two-income family with its burden of wage hours is also a likely site for the building of a new quest for time. Inevitably, it will be expressed in terms radically different from the earlier eight-hour struggles because it would not be based on the same gender assumptions.

BIBLIOGRAPHY

Bienefeld, M. A. *Working Hours in British Industry: An Economic History.* London, 1972.

Cross, Gary. *A Quest for Time: The Reduction of Work in Britain and France, 1840–1940.* Berkeley, Calif., 1989.

Cross, Gary. "Vacations for All: The Leisure Question in the Era of the Popular Front." *Journal of Contemporary History* 24 (Autumn 1989): 599–621.

Cross, Gary, ed. *Worktime and Industrialization: An International History.* Philadelphia, 1988.

Deem, Rosemary. *All Work and No Play?: The Sociology of Women and Leisure.* Milton Keynes, U.K., 1986.

Hinrichs, Karl, William Roche, and Carmen Sirianni, eds. *Working Time in Transition.* Philadelphia, 1991.

Hopkins, Eric. "Working Hours and Conditions during the Industrial Revolution, A Re-Appraisal." *Economic History Review* 35 (1982): 52–66.

Horning, Karl H., Anette Gerhardt, and Matthias Michailow. *Time Pioneers: Flexible Working Time and New Lifestyles.* Translated by Anthony Williams. Cambridge, Mass., 1995.

Joyce, Patrick, ed. *Historical Meanings of Work.* Cambridge, U.K., 1987.

Kaplow, Jeffrey. "La Fin de la Saint-Lundi: Étude sur le Paris ouvrier au XIXe siècle." *Le Temps libre* 2 (1981): 107–118.

Landes, David. *Revolution in Time: Clocks and the Making of the Modern World.* Cambridge, Mass, 1983.

Langenfelt, Gosta. *The Historic Origin of the Eight Hours Day.* Stockholm, 1954.

Lapping, Anne. *Working Time in Britain and West Germany: A Summary.* Oxford, 1983.

Le Goff, Jacques. *Time, Work, and Culture in the Middle Ages.* Translated by Arthur Goldheimer. Chicago, 1980.

Leontief, Wassily. "The Distribution of Work and Income." *Scientific American* 247, no. 3 (September 1982): 188–204.

Murphy, W. Emmett. *History of the Eight Hours' Movement.* Melbourne, 1896–1900.

Nyland, Chris. *Reduced Worktime and the Management of Production.* Cambridge, U.K., 1989.

Rabinbach, Anson. *The Human Motor: Energy, Fatigue, and the Origins of Modernity.* New York, 1990.

Reddy, William. *The Rise of Market Culture: The Textile Trade and French Society, 1750–1900.* New York and Cambridge, U.K., 1984.

Scott, Joan W., and Louise A. Tilly. *Women, Work, and Family.* New York, 1978.

Seidman, Michael. "The Birth of the Weekend and the Revolts against Work during the Popular Front (1936–1938)." *French Historical Studies* 12 (Fall 1982): 249–276.

Smelser, Neil. *Social Change in the Industrial Revolution.* Chicago, 1959.

Thompson, E. P. "Time, Work-Discipline, and Industrial Capitalism." *Past and Present* 38 (1967): 56–97.

Weaver, Stewart. *John Fielden and the Politics of Popular Radicalism, 1831–1847.* Oxford, 1987.

Wigley, William. *The Rise and Fall of the Victorian Sunday.* Manchester, U.K., 1980.

Zerubavel, Eviatar. "Private-Time and Public-Time." In *The Sociology of Time.* Edited by John Hassard. New York, 1990. Pages 168–177.

CHILD LABOR

Colin Heywood

Child labor is a subject that stirs the passions. People in present-day Europe react with indignation to reports of those few children still working in "sweatshops" in their own societies, not to mention the millions employed in the poorer countries of the world. They have come to regard the widespread employment of children in the past as shameful. The climbing boy suffocating up a chimney, or the little mill hand working to the relentless pace of a machine, have become stock images of the industrial revolution. Yet such hostility to child labor is a comparatively recent phenomenon. During the early modern period, the majority of families sought work for their children as a matter of routine. Indeed, the authorities worried more about "the sins of sloth and idleness" among the young than about excessive work. It was the nineteenth and early twentieth centuries that brought profound changes to the role of children in modern society. In Europe, as in America, child labor legislation and compulsory education ensured that children would be dependent on their parents and to some extent sheltered from the world of adults. In the much-quoted words of Viviana A. Zelizer, children became economically "worthless" but emotionally "priceless."

The first historians to investigate child labor generally focused on the passing of the Factory Acts in England. They adopted a simple challenge and response model, in which the unprecedented "exploitation" of child labor in the factories and workshops provoked the state to intervene. As Hugh Cunningham has pointed out, their story could be dressed up in the form of a romance, with gallant figures such as Lord Shaftesbury rescuing poor factory children from the clutches of cruel employers. Such a heavy focus on the benevolent influence of the state on child labor was not to everyone's taste, however. There was always a critique from the political right, which emphasized the material and moral progress brought by the factory system and the disadvantages of state intervention for child workers, notably a loss of training and skill. Various historians since the 1960s have argued that rising real wages rather than Factory Acts were the main influence on the long-term decline of child labor. Others have noted that certain groups of employers and workers were more receptive to curbs on child labor than others, thus reinforcing considerable regional disparities in the age structure of the labor force. Others again have charted the changing cultural context in which ideals of childhood were defined and redefined. Finally, Myron Weiner has asserted that it was compulsory school attendance rather than factory legislation that finally eliminated children from the workshops, the former being more readily enforced than the latter. Not surprisingly, perhaps, the historical literature remains skewed toward industrial and urban child labor, and toward Britain and other nations that industrialized early.

When discussing the history of child labor, it is difficult to avoid the influence of contemporary experiences in a modern, bureaucratized society. The temptation is to ask at what age children started work, as if starting work were the same as starting school in the modern era, and whether they were employed or unemployed, categories most adults would apply to themselves. The answers are likely to be misleading, unless one makes considerable allowance for the peculiar nature of children's work in the past. Children's entry into the labor force was staggered over several years, according to personal circumstances and the availability of work in each locality. Some had full-time employment outside the home, but the majority probably worked without wages in a family unit or took on little tasks, such as caring for siblings, that released adults for productive labor. The shift from childhood into youth also proceeded imperceptibly. Definitions of "children" in the labor force varied considerably in different national contexts: most historians have taken fourteen, fifteen, or sixteen to be the upper age limit.

CHILDREN AND FAMILY WORK ROUTINES

Despite the grisly images that loom large in textbooks, much of the work done by children in the past was casual and undemanding. Children gradually drifted into the labor force, mopping up a host of little tasks that were appropriate to their size and experience. They might make themselves useful around the age of six or seven, but were unlikely to train in the more skilled and exacting tasks until around the age of ten, at the very earliest. Censuses of population do not lend themselves particularly well to recording this type of routine working and helping. For what it is worth, the British census of 1851 found that only 3.5 percent of children aged five to nine were occupied. P. E. H. Hair concludes that, even allowing for a high margin of error, "the vast majority of children under ten did not undertake any regular gainful employment." In the next age group, ten to fourteen, the census found no more than 30 percent occupied: 37 percent of boys and 22 percent of girls. Not until the late nineteenth and early twentieth centuries is there evidence of a crisp transition from childhood into the adult world of work, marked by the ritual of leaving school at the minimum age required by the state.

In Europe the majority of children lived in the countryside—at least until urbanization steadily impinged from the mid-nineteenth century onward. Employment in agriculture generally required strength and stamina that were beyond the capacity of children. On the small family farms that were characteristic of many parts of Europe, children of both sexes were confined to such jobs as looking after younger brothers and sisters, fetching water and firewood, picking stones, scaring birds, spreading manure, and "minding" pigs and sheep. Their contribution was also partly seasonal, reaching a peak with the intensive work routines of the harvest period. Younger juveniles took food out to the laborers in the fields, while the older ones bound corn into sheaves behind the harvesters. Some of this work required long, lonely hours out in the fields, but it also left plenty of time for leisure pursuits. Early in the sixteenth century, a native of Segovia described mingling his sheep with other flocks so that he and his fellow shepherds could play games along the lines of hockey and racing.

During their early teens, as they moved from childhood to youth, gender differences among young farm workers became more pronounced. Daughters continued to help their mothers around the house, the garden, and the dairy, while sons began to work more intensively beside their fathers in the fields and stables. At this age, many young people left home for employment in other households. The proportion of the youthful population involved in farm service varied considerably between regions. In Austria, for example, between the seventeenth and early twentieth centuries, a sample of census material from various rural communities reveals that somewhere between a fifth and a half of those in the age-group fifteen to nineteen were servants. An unfortunate minority, drawn largely from the ranks of small peasants and agricultural laborers, had to take this path at an earlier age, perhaps when as young as seven or eight. In general, though, service with another family was associated more with youth than with childhood. Ann Kussmaul calculated from evidence concerning early modern England that thirteen to fourteen was the most common age for moving into service in husbandry. A female farm servant might begin her career helping the farmer's wife with household chores and looking after the children. A female farm servant in Bavaria at the end of the nineteenth century started at the age of thirteen or fourteen, helping the peasant's wife with household chores and looking after the children. She would hope to move up the hierarchy of servants as she grew older. The ultimate aim of such girls was to accumulate enough skills and money for a dowry to secure a husband. In Tuscany during the late eighteenth century, girls preferred to work on larger farms, where they could learn a broader range of skills, and so enhance their marriage prospects. The typical male experience was slightly different. The young Robert Savage started in the kitchen of a big farm in Suffolk as a "back'us boy" (back house boy) at the age of twelve. By his mid teens he had moved on to the more obviously "masculine" work of helping with the horses and assisting a shepherd at lambing season. In isolated cases during the nineteenth century, and indeed creating considerable scandal, children of both sexes joined agricultural gangs, working the arable land of East Anglia and Belgium or the rice fields of Piedmont and Lombardy.

In the towns, particularly the major commercial and administrative centers, paid work for children was not always easy to come by. The traditional apprenticeship system continued to flourish during the early modern period in Europe under the supervision of the guilds. The master undertook to teach all the "rudiments and secrets" of a trade to a boy or a girl. He would feed and lodge them within his own family, so that they could learn all the values and customs associated with their calling. The apprentices for their part agreed to obey the master, in an agreement that might last for up to seven or even ten years. However, apprenticeships did not usually start until young people had reached their early or mid teens, an age when they were considered sufficiently strong or mature to be able to cope with the requirements of the craft. In a few trades that did not need much in the way of strength or skill, such as nail making and ribbon weaving, they might start earlier. In England there were

The Apprentice. *An Old Alchemist and His Assistant in Their Workshop,* painting by Franx van Mieris (1635–1681). CHRISTIE'S IMAGES, LTD.

also the pauper apprentices, who were usually placed with a farmer or a craftsman by the Poor Law authorities around the age of seven or eight. Otherwise apprentices, like servants, were more often youths than children.

Apprenticeships did not usually start until boys, or in some cases girls, had reached their early or mid teens. Again, children lacked the physical strength necessary for many trades, notably those in the construction industry. Where children did go into full-time work, the example of nineteenth-century Lon-

don reveals a minority starting around the age of six or seven, but most delaying until they were closer to twelve. They began with light work such as making clothes or "trimmings" for furniture, street selling, or making deliveries. Even without a full-time job they could help with household chores and perhaps also a domestic trade. Girls in particular looked after younger children for their mothers or, in the words of the social investigator Henry Mayhew (1812–1887), were "lent out to carry about a baby to add to the family income by gaining her sixpence weekly." Their next step, at twelve or thirteen, was often to become a "slavey": a telling indicator of the fate that awaited child servants everywhere in Europe. Domestic service was by far the largest employer of female labor in Europe before World War I. As in the villages, the young girl started at the bottom, as maid of all work in a modest household, or as scullery maid in a large one. At this stage her life became one of constant drudgery: cooking, cleaning, running errands, and lugging the laundry to and from the wash place.

In sum, children were perhaps the most flexible workers within the family economy, ranging from full-time employment outside the home to helping their parents with a wide range of light jobs. As such, although it is difficult to measure their precise contribution, they were valued members of a team. Young people were also likely to accumulate a varied experience of work by their late teens. Edward Barlow, to take an example from mid-seventeenth-century England, began his working life in Lancashire as a casual laborer at harvest time and in a colliery. He went on to apprentice in the Manchester textile trade, and then tried his hand in London as successively an errand boy, a post boy, and a vintner's apprentice. He finally settled on a seven-year apprenticeship as a seaman. In late-nineteenth-century Germany, the anonymous female author of *Im Kampf ums Dasein!* moved from gluing bags at home to domestic service, later found jobs in a series of factories, and ended up as a waitress. For the most part, the work performed by children in agriculture, the handicraft trades, and the service sector remained uncontroversial. However, indignation aroused in the late eighteenth century by the fate of the climbing boys employed by chimney sweeps, or *petits savoyards* as they were known in France, gave a hint of battles to come.

CHILD LABOR AND INDUSTRIALIZATION

During the eighteenth and early nineteenth centuries, the authorities in many regions were keen to promote industry precisely because they hoped it would provide a reliable source of employment for women and children living in poverty. Whether industrialization did in the end bring an increase in the proportion of young people who were gainfully occupied is a matter of dispute, particularly among British historians. Some of them assert that since most children in the preindustrial era had been expected to make a contribution to the family economy, there was little scope for a general increase in child labor during the industrial revolution. A more common assumption would

be that industrialization did draw in more young children to the labor force—although it is not clear whether the peak was during the "protoindustrial" phase of the eighteenth and early nineteenth centuries, or the later factory-based phase of the 1830s and 1840s. Most historians would also accept that industrialization brought a more intensive use of child labor in certain occupations. Children working in, say, cotton mills and urban "sweatshops" were everywhere a minority, but they faced more regular employment through the year, longer hours, and a more sustained level of effort than their peers.

The first signs of change appeared in the countryside during the seventeenth and eighteenth centuries, when merchants decided to profit from the supply of relatively cheap and docile labor for their manufacturing operations. Families in these "protoindustrial" workshops were goaded by the pressures of poverty and the seemingly endless round of agricultural and industrial work into erasing the customary division of labor by age and gender. The historian Hans Medick has drawn attention to child labor among rural weavers, spinners, and knitters, "which both in its intensity and duration went far beyond that of the corresponding labor of farm peasant householders." During the early nineteenth century, among the handloom weaving families of the Saxon Oberlausitz, young children wound bobbins and prepared spools, while both adolescent boys and girls learned to weave. Similarly in England a royal commission on the employment of children in 1843 reported that the children of knitters in the Leicestershire hosiery industry began work around the age of six, seven, or eight. The boys worked up to twelve hours a day as winders, the girls as seamers. Boys as young as ten years of age worked on the stocking frames, and allegedly were soon able to earn nearly as much as their fathers. Other trades that employed countless numbers of children in the countryside included lace making and embroidery, straw plaiting, nail making, and other forms of metal working.

Pressure on child workers in the smaller workshops also increased in the towns during the eighteenth and nineteenth centuries, as guilds and apprenticeship regulations crumbled in the face of free markets. Take the example of children employed in the silk industry of Lyon. The development of *grande tire* looms for the production of fancy brocades involved numerous *tireuses* (drawgirls) pulling their heavy cords for up to fourteen hours a day—until the invention of the Jacquard loom in 1807 eventually made them redundant. Silk reelers fared little better. In 1866 the legal authorities of the city investigated the case of ten-year-old Marie Péchard, a so-called ap-

Factory Workers. *The Factory Children from the Costume of Yorkshire,* painting (1814) by George Walker. THEARTARCHIVE

prentice reeler, after she ended up in the hospital with a serious eye disease. They found that a certain Dame Bernard was employing Marie and two other girls in their early teens for sixteen hours a day, from five or six in the morning until ten or eleven o'clock at night.

The climax to the story came, of course, with the massive "exploitation" of child labor in the cotton mills, coal mines, and factories of the industrial revolution. Steam power and machinery, it is commonly assumed, allowed women and children to take over work that had previously required the strength and skill of an adult male. Certainly the earliest spinning machinery of the late eighteenth century was designed to be operated by children (strictly, in this case, ousting adult females), in a bid to reduce labor costs. By a fortunate coincidence, from the point of view of employers, large numbers of pauper children were available for industrial work on long-term contracts. Robert Owen (1771–1858) estimated that he employed five hundred parish apprentices in his cotton mill at New Lanark, in Scotland, in 1799. Overall, children under thirteen accounted for 40 percent of the workforce in this mill. As a rule, though, children continued their customary role of acting as assistants to adults, taking on ancillary tasks and at the same time learning the skills and general culture of their trade. Examples are legion: the little piecer who tied broken threads for a mule spinner; the winder who prepared bobbins for a weaver; the trapper who op-

erated ventilation doors for miners at the coal face; and the carriers of bottles for glassblowers.

Children of both sexes often did the same work, though there were variations between trades and regions. Young girls sometimes worked underground in the coal mines, as the 1842 children's employment commission found in Yorkshire, Lancashire, South Wales, and East Scotland, but the pits increasingly became male territory in most parts of Europe. The temptation is always to emphasize that children might start work in the mills "as young as seven or eight." Most, however, probably waited until they were ten or twelve in the textile trades and into their teens in a heavy industry such as iron and steel making. At the Heilmann spinning mill, for example, in the Alsatian town of Ribeauvillé, an industrial census of 1822–1823 listed twenty-seven children aged eight to eleven but eighty-one aged twelve to fifteen. Employers liked to argue that the new machinery had taken over the physical effort of work, so that children only had to bestir themselves intermittently. A less partial view would surely stress the long hours and sustained concentration required in the early mills. A piecer in a cotton mill during the 1830s was likely to have to work for thirteen and a half hours a day, and be prepared to rush forward and mend any of up to five hundred threads.

There is evidence, then, that the early *industrialisation sauvage* of the eighteenth and nineteenth cen-

Children in a Coal Mine. Bradley coal mine, near Bilston, Staffordshire, in the nineteenth century. NORTH WIND PICTURE ARCHIVE

turies brought an increased reliance on child labor. How far this varied between the countries of Europe is difficult to estimate, given the lack of reliable statistics. The safest conclusion must be that child labor in the manufacturing sector was particularly important for the early starters on the path to industrialization, notably Britain, Belgium, France and the western parts of Prussia. An industrial enquiry of 1839 to 1843 in France found 143,665 child workers under the age of sixteen, equivalent to 12.1 percent of the labor force. Another, but not necessarily comparable one, for Belgium in 1843, counted 10,514 child workers, or 19.5 percent of the total. Much of this was concentrated in a small number of industries, particularly textiles, as can be seen in table 1. The often distressing experiences of factory children were therefore far from typical, yet it was their plight that loomed large in the debates over child labor launched by social reformers.

CHILD LABOR AND CHILD WELFARE

Lurid accounts of harsh working conditions for children in the factories and workshops were grist for the mill for all those who feared that industrialization and urbanization would cause massive social dislocation. The public health movement that emerged in France during the 1820s and 1830s reflected such concerns, notably with the investigations by Dr. Louis Villermé into the "physical and moral condition" of textile workers. There was talk of a "bastardization of the

race" in the wake of industrial expansion. The new manufacturing centers were allegedly producing children described by Villermé as "pale, enervated, slow in their movements, tranquil in their games" who would later be incapable of defending their country. The heightened economic and imperial rivalry between nations of the late nineteenth century, combined with threats to the established order from the labor movement, only served to reinforce the obsession with "degeneration" in certain circles throughout Europe. A British doctor, Margaret Alden, warned in 1908 that "the nation that first recognizes the importance of scientifically rearing and training the children of the commonwealth will be the nation that will survive."

The first observers to ring the alarm bells were doctors in the industrial towns of Britain who were disturbed by the physical condition of child workers. As early as 1784 a report on conditions in the Lancashire cotton mills by one Dr. Percival, following an outbreak of typhus, noted "the injury done to young persons through confinement and too long-continued labor." The case against child labor on health grounds was not as straightforward as might be thought. In the first place, the costs of working at a tender age had to be set against the benefits of earning a wage and contributing to a higher standard of living. Employers even liked to emphasize the cleanliness of their factories in comparison to the slums, and the "moderate degree of healthy exercise" that work involved. Hence reformers generally argued against the dangers of excessive work for children rather than against work per se. In the second place, providing statistical proof that child labor in industry undermined health was not always easy. Apologists for the factory system asserted that the health of children was undermined more by the poverty of their families than by their working conditions. Villermé was surely right to note the cluster of influences that lay behind the poor physical condition of so many workers in the towns:

> I do not seek to establish whether the poor succumb most readily to their lack of nourishment; to the poor quality of their food; to their excessive work; to the bad air; to illness brought on by their trades, humidity, unhealthy lodgings, squalor or overcrowding; to the anxiety of being unable to raise a family; or even to the intemperate habits common amongst them.

As for the specific influences of child labor on health, reformers first highlighted the strain of a long working day on a small and partially formed body. During the 1840s, for example, children in the cotton mills of Ghent worked from dawn till 10 P.M. in winter, and from 5 or 5:30 A.M. till 8 P.M. in summer. Such long hours produced twisted limbs and curved spines among the poor "factory cripples," as they were known in Lancashire, and weakened the eyes of thousands of girls engaged in close work such as lace making and embroidery. A second set of problems noted by doctors and other observers was the unhealthy environment created in the workshops by dust, noxious fumes, humidity, and high temperatures. Adelheid Popp recalled being poisoned by her job with a bronze manufacturer in Vienna during the 1880s; Alice Foley in her turn described a spell working in the basement of a Bolton weaving shed where "the frames stood on damp, cracked floors and I recall that the captive clouds of dust and lint could never escape." The young operatives were vulnerable to a sad catalog of afflictions such as typhus epidemics, "spinners' phthisis" and other forms of tuberculosis, anemia, eye infections, and white phosphorous poisoning (in the matchstick factories).

Industrial accidents were another hazard for child workers. These were a particularly unwelcome feature of the industrial age. Before the nineteenth century a child might suffer a mishap such as being run over by a cart, but this paled into insignificance before the dangers associated with power-driven machinery. The early factories were a menacing concentration of fast-moving shafts, drive belts, flywheels, and gearings that could seize the hair or loose clothing of a passing operative. Piecers were all too often crushed by self-acting mules; "tenters" on the power looms might be hit in the eye by their shuttles; drawers in the mines fell under their wagons; and children

TABLE 1
MAIN OCCUPATIONS OF BOYS AND GIRLS UNDER FIFTEEN YEARS IN BRITAIN (1851) (Thousands)

Boys

		%
Agriculture	120	28.4
Textiles	82	19.4
Navigation and Docks	46	10.9
Mines	37	8.7
Metal Workers and Manufacture of Machinery and Tools	26	6.1
Dress	23	5.4
General Labor	15	3.5
Dealing (various) incl. lodging and coffee houses	12	2.8
Building	11	2.6
Domestic Service	9	2.1
Earthenware	6	1.4
Total Employed	423	

Girls

		%
Textiles	98	41.3
Domestic Service	71	30.0
Dress	32	13.5
Agriculture	17	7.2
Metal Workers and Manufacture of Machinery and Tools	4	1.7
Navigation and Docks	4	1.7
Earthenware	3	1.3
Dealing (various) incl. lodging and coffee houses	2	0.8
Total Employed	237	

Source: Booth, Journal of the Royal Statistical Society, *49 (1886); From E. H. Hunt,* British Labour History, 1815–1914 *(London: Weidenfeld and Nicolson, 1981), page 14.*

cleaning machinery had fingers and hands mutilated by the moving parts.

Contemporaries were probably even more perturbed by the threats to the moral and educational development of child workers. They disliked the idea of the young being snatched from the bosom of their families and launched into the rough-and-tumble of life on the shop floor with its coarse language, licentious horseplay, and sometimes outright brutality. Of course, employers' representatives countered that the tight discipline of a well-run factory ruled out such pernicious influences, and some of the larger factories arranged separate workshops for males and females. At the extreme, silk mill owners in southern France brought in nuns to supervise the girls and young women they employed. All the same, many children must have found entry into the world of work a trying experience. The pauper apprentices of the early industrial revolution were doubtless more vulnerable than most to abuse. How representative the experiences of Robert Blincoe were is open to question, but his alleged sufferings at Litton Mill in Derbyshire certainly make grim reading. Older "stretchers" in the mill regularly kicked and beat him, threw rollers at his head, and played sadistic games such as tying him by the wrists to a cross beam so that he had to draw up his legs every time the machinery moved under him. Other children suffered at the hands of adults impatient with their pace of work. Lea Baravalle, who worked as a *shattitrice* in an Italian silk mill immediately after World War I, recorded how the throwsters hit her and splashed boiling water in her face if she was slow in supplying them with thread.

Finally, the tension between work and school aroused a series of impassioned debates throughout the nineteenth and early twentieth centuries. During the medieval period, according to Philippe Ariès, "all education was carried out by means of apprenticeship," meaning that boys learned their trade and their "human worth" living and working with adults. This type of apprenticeship was gradually replaced by an academic training, but this was a slow process, particularly in the "mechanical arts." Young people, particularly the males, continued to follow apprenticeships during the eighteenth and nineteenth centuries, yet it was generally agreed that the whole institution had become seriously debased. An extensive division of labor in the "sweated" trades and the mechanization of production in the factories permitted so-called "apprentices" to be exploited as a cheap source of labor. There remained a residual feeling that starting work as early as possible had its benefits, notably acquiring arcane skills and learning the disciplines of the workshop. It was also plausible for employers to assert

during the early nineteenth century that children excluded from the workshops would merely idle away their time on the streets, given the absence of school places for them. Certainly, peasant and working-class families had to weigh the costs and benefits of investing in the schooling of their offspring. The novelist Jules Reboul highlighted their dilemma by staging an argument during the 1870s, in the Vivarais province, between father and mother over the future of their son, Jacques Baudet. The father was willing to make sacrifices for him to continue to attend school, even after he had acquired a basic literacy, in the hope that he might secure a better job. The mother would have none of it, asserting that a school certificate would never be enough to land someone from their background a white-collar occupation: better by far for him to start earning in the hope of building up a landholding. The young Jacques duly started work as a shepherd.

If the need to earn a living sometimes ruled out any schooling at all, in other cases it confined time in class to the winter months, allowing children to work on the land during the harvest season, or undermined schooling's effectiveness by requiring them to work before and after class. Heinrich Holeck, born in Bohemia in 1885, had to help his stepmother with her brick-making job by getting up at four in the morning to prepare the clay and resuming work after school making bricks. As a broad generalization, the schooling of girls was sacrificed to work more readily than that of boys, and country children attended class less regularly than those in the towns. By the late nineteenth century, however, such disparities were fast disappearing as school triumphed over work.

CHILD LABOR IN DECLINE

The obvious starting point for analyzing the causes of the withdrawal of children from the labor force would be to pinpoint when the process started. If, as Clark Nardinelli claims for the British case, the long-term decline set in before the passing of effective Factory Acts, then one would have to look farther afield than state intervention for explanations. Unfortunately, such evidence is hard to come by, not least since many of the statistics on child labor first appeared when states attempted to justify and implement factory legislation. Nardinelli uses data from the textile industry to show that child labor was decreasing relative to adult labor before inspectors began to enforce the 1833 Factory Act, the first such act to have any teeth. In 1816, he estimates, children under thirteen accounted for 20 percent of the labor force in the cotton

Children outside a Coal Mine. Crew waiting to go to work at the Sirland & Alfreton coal mine in Derbyshire, England, c. 1905. CORBIS-BETTMANN

industry, but by 1835 the proportion had fallen to 13.1 percent. He also notes the relative decline of child labor in the silk industry during the 1840s and 1850s, even though its mills were not covered by factory legislation in this period.

The broader picture of a gradual elimination of children from the economically active population cannot be documented before 1851, when the British census began to record the occupations of young people. At that point, as noted above, 96.5 percent of children aged five to nine were without a "specified occupation," and from 1881 the census no longer considered it worthwhile counting them. The next

group, aged ten to fourteen, experienced an uneven decline in the proportion occupied from decade to decade, but the long-term trend was clear: if 30 percent were occupied in 1851, only 17 percent were in 1901. Other countries in Europe were less preoccupied with this issue. The French census, for example, did not publish information on the active population by age group until 1896. In that year only one-fifth of those aged ten to fourteen were occupied, and as in Britain, most of these would have been aged thirteen or fourteen.

Social reformers in all countries certainly attempted to use state intervention to curb the abuse of child labor. Their motives were largely humanitarian, though other parties might support them for more mercenary reasons. Howard Marvel argued that the 1833 Factory Act in Britain was designed to favor the interests of the large urban manufacturers in the textile industry. He reasoned that they employed relatively fewer young children than their rural counterparts, and that with steam rather than water power they rarely needed exceptionally long working hours to compensate for interruptions to production. British factory operatives and weavers in the Ten Hours Movement also agitated during the 1830s and 1840s for shorter working hours for children, making it clear that this was part of a wider campaign to lighten the burden of labor on all workers. Everywhere the state proceeded by a process of trial and error, gradually extending the scope of factory legislation and tightening the systems of inspection. The British paved the way in 1802 with an act that limited itself to protecting apprentices in the cotton mills, moved on to a broader but still ineffective one in 1819, and had to await Althorp's Act of 1833 for the first workable system of inspection. Among later landmarks, the 1842 Mines Act attempted to ban all females and boys under the age of ten from underground work; the 1844 Factory Act pioneered the half-time system, permitting children to divide their time between work and school; and the 1867 Factories Extension Act finally branched out beyond the textile industries. Prussia and France in their turn began tentatively around 1840 with child labor laws that were hamstrung by feeble means of enforcement, and went no further until 1853 in the former case, 1874 in the latter.

All such legislation aimed to regulate rather than abolish child labor. To begin with, it tended to set minimum ages, such as eight or nine, which made little difference to employers, and concentrated on grading hours according to age, banning night work, insisting on sanitary measures in the workshops, and enforcing a limited amount of schooling. The impact of these laws on child welfare is open to question. On the one hand, they undoubtedly drove some child labor "underground," into the small workshops that were either exempt from legislation or difficult to inspect. They may even have deprived some needy families of income. On the other hand, they curbed some of the worst abuses of children in the workshops and encouraged the shift from the workshops to the school benches. Even Nardinelli concedes that the 1833 Act in Britain caused what he sees as a short-term boost to the secular decline in child labor by placing a "tax" on it, in the form of the costs incurred by employers in taking responsibility for the education of the children. The fact remains that the clear-cut demands of

compulsory schooling until the age of thirteen or so did more to keep young children out of the workshops than child labor legislation.

Before concluding that state intervention provides the key to removing children from the workplace, however, one should ask why the climate became favorable to legislation during the early nineteenth century, and also why the initial opposition to it from many quarters eventually weakened. Historians have sought answers in both the cultural and the socioeconomic spheres.

In the first place, eighteenth-century thinkers began to formulate new ideals for childhood, which ultimately made it unthinkable for young people to work. Out went the existing orthodoxy that children were essentially idle creatures who needed to be put to work as soon as possible. In its place, Jean-Jacques Rousseau proposed that people "love childhood, indulge its sports, its pleasures, its delightful instincts." Doubtless the sentimental approach to childhood championed by Rousseau and by the romantic poets initially reached only a narrow, middle-class audience, and their ideas were always contested by those espousing less sentimental viewpoints. Nonetheless, by the late nineteenth and early twentieth centuries, something of a consensus emerged portraying children, in the words of the historian Harry Hendrick, as "innocent, ignorant, dependent, vulnerable, generally incompetent and in need of protection and discipline." Such a construction of childhood went against the grain of earlier peasant and working-class experience, though it did complement demands for a "family wage": a wage high enough to allow a male breadwinner to support his wife and children without their having to work. It also meshed neatly with the growing interest in formal education among the "popular" classes. By this period opposition to shorter working hours and at least part-time schooling was often associated with "rougher" elements among the laboring population. Glassworkers provided an egregious example: in 1875 a French divisional inspector described them as "the most appalling collection of undisciplined good-for-nothings, drunks and idlers that it is possible to imagine." The upshot was an increasing acceptance at all levels of society that children should spend an extended period in school.

In the second place, changes in the labor market arguably tended to push children away from the world of work. On the one hand, the rising real wages, which sooner or later trickled down to workers during the course of economic development, made families increasingly reluctant to supply their children to employers. Sections of the working-classes remained anxious over the loss of earnings from their children implied by child labor legislation, but they did gradually shift the balance from work to school. On the other, technical progress in industry reduced the demand for juvenile workers. Cotton spinners, for example, allegedly found that they needed to employ fewer piecers once the self-actor had replaced the hand mule. Let it be added that there was nothing inevitable about these forms of change on the shop floor. Per Bolin-Hort highlighted the stubborn persistence of operatives in the Lancashire cotton industry continuing to put their own children in the mills as "half-timers," even though they were a relatively affluent group of workers. He also documented the diversity of strategies open to employers in deploying different types of labor on the same technology.

Finally, it should be noted in passing, historians of education have revealed the growing demand for education among the "popular classes" well before it was made compulsory. The French scholar Roger Thabault showed how in his village of Mazières-en-Gatine the peasants were won over to primary schooling from the middle of the nineteenth century onward when improved transport, commercialized agriculture, and elections ended their isolation from the rest of the nation.

In sum, the virtual extinction of child labor in the developed economies of Europe was a protracted process, linked to a broad range of changes in society. The implication for "third world" countries today is that campaigns to improve conditions for child workers will face a long haul, in the context of tight family budgets, labor-intensive methods of production, poor communications, and established conceptions of childhood. At the same time, there is no denying that from an early stage of industrialization efforts at reform made a difference to the welfare of the young. A very mixed bunch of philanthropists, politicians, working-class radicals, journalists, civil servants, industrialists, factory inspectors, and schoolteachers contributed in their various ways to imposing a "modern" conception of childhood.

See also **Youth and Adolescence** *(in this volume); and other articles in this section.*

BIBLIOGRAPHY

Ben Amos, Ilana Krausman. *Adolescence and Youth in Early Modern England.* New Haven, Conn., and London, 1994. Conveys the varied experiences of young people in a "pre-industrial" society.

Bolin-Hort, Per. *Work, Family, and the State: Child Labour and the Organization of Production in the British Cotton Industry, 1780–1820.* Lund, Sweden, 1989. Concentrates on the Lancashire cotton industry, though adds some interesting comparisons with the Scottish and the American experiences.

Coninck-Smith, Ning de, Bengt Sandin, and Ellen Schrumpf, eds. *Industrious Children: Work and Childhood in the Nordic Countries 1850–1990.* Odense, Denmark, 1997. Informative on child labor in agriculture as well as industry, and on the impact of compulsory schooling.

Cruickshank, Marjorie. *Children and Industry: Child Health and Welfare in North-West Textile Towns during the Nineteenth Century.* Manchester, U.K., 1981.

Cunningham, Hugh. *The Children of the Poor: Representations of Childhood since the Seventeenth Century.* Oxford, 1991.

Cunningham, Hugh. *Children and Childhood in Western Society since 1500.* London, 1995. The best general introduction, which includes sections on child labor.

Cunningham, Hugh, and Pier Paolo Viazzo, eds. *Child Labour in Historical Perspective, 1800–1985.* Florence, 1996. Includes studies of the Belgian, British, and Catalan historical experiences of child labor.

Davin, Anna. *Growing Up Poor: Home, School, and Street in London, 1870–1914.* London, 1996. A fine local study of childhood experiences.

Hair, P. E. H. "Children in Society, 1850–1980." In *Population and Society in Britain, 1850–1980*. Edited by Theo Barker and Michael Drake. London, 1982. Helpful on the demographic data available.

Hendrick, Harry. *Child Welfare: England, 1872–1989*. London and New York, 1994. Interesting material on changes in the social construction of childhood during the nineteenth century.

Heywood, Colin. *Childhood in Nineteenth-Century France: Work, Health and Education among the "Classes Populaires."* Cambridge, U.K., 1988.

Hopkins, Eric. *Childhood Transformed: Working-Class Children in Nineteenth-Century England*. Manchester, U.K., 1994. Excellent survey of various dimensions to childhood.

Horn, Pamela. *Children's Work and Welfare, 1780–1890*. Cambridge, U.K., 1995. A concise survey of recent British historiography.

Horn, Pamela. *The Victorian Country Child*. Kineton, U.K., 1974.

Lane, Joan. *Apprenticeship in England, 1600–1914*. London, 1996.

Maynes, Mary Jo. *Taking the Hard Road: Life Course in French and German Workers' Autobiographies in the Era of Industrialization*. Chapel Hill, N.C., and London, 1995. Provides interesting material on the experience of child labor

Nardinelli, Clark. *Child Labor and the Industrial Revolution*. Bloomington, Ind., 1990. A highly polemical work that focuses on the economics of child labor, making some comparisons between Britain and other European countries.

Smelser, Neil J. *Social Change in the Industrial Revolution: An Application of Theory to the Lancashire Cotton Industry, 1770–1840*. London, 1959. A controversial work, but one with interesting material on parent-child relations in the factories.

Stearns, Peter N. *Paths to Authority: The Middle Class and the Industrial Labor Force in France, 1820–1848*. Urbana, Ill., 1978. Includes a full account of the campaign to reform child labor.

Thompson, E. P. *The Making of the English Working Class*. Harmondsworth, U.K., 1968. Includes a powerful assertion of the radical critique of "child labor under industrial capitalism" from the marxist camp.

Ward, J. T. *The Factory Movement, 1830–1855*. London, 1962. Standard account of the campaign for factory legislation in Britain.

Weiner, Myron. *The Child and the State in India: Child Labor and Education Policy in Comparative Perspective*. Princeton, N.J., 1991. Draws on the European perspective to argue for compulsory primary education as the most effective means to end the practice of child labor.

Weissbach, Lee Shai. *Child Labor Reform in Nineteenth-Century France*. Baton Rouge, La., 1989.

ISBN 0-684-80580-4